Love And Terror

in the

Middle East

4th Edition

Frank Romano, PhD

PUBLISHED BY AB FILM PUBLISHING
New York USA

Published by AB Film Publishing
290 W. 12th Street, Suite A
New York, NY 10014

ISBN: 978-0-9897068-6-5

Design of this Fourth Edition by Thomas Romano, USA.

Rev. date: 03/20/2014

To my Mother (Always with me, my soul) and my Kids (My life)

and to the following friends:

Lance Wolf (Jewish peace activist, soul brother – murdered in Jerusalem)

Dr. David Leighton (Christian peace activist – my interfaith freedom co-conspirator)

Ibrahim Ahmad Abu El-Hawa (Muslim peace activist – my sustenance and spiritual man)

Juliano Mer-Khamis (Jewish/Palestinian peace activist – my inspiration-murdered in Jenin, West Bank)

Contents

Book III: The Epicenter

Book IV: Death and Rebirth

Introduction

"Dr. Romano has written an insightful and soul-searching book in describing his and others' efforts to try to bring diverse peoples together in a region long known for conflict."

—Craig Paul, Esq., Sacramento, California

This book recounts the fulfillment of a 30-year-old vision that I would someday work for peace in the Middle East.

To pursue that goal and the quest for spiritual meaning and passionate purpose to my life, I set out on a long journey from Paris that led me to an Islamist mosque in Morocco. There I was held captive by members of a militant cult. After my escape, I fled Morocco and returned to France, thus abandoning my quest....

Until five years ago! Friends dared me to pursue my voyage to determine whether it was a true vision or an illusion. I took them up on it and traveled to the Middle East to find the answer.

I could never have foreseen what I would find there! Not only did I discover it was a true vision, but my life became quickly intertwined with many people of all faiths in the intense struggle to bring Muslims, Jews and Christians together under the roof of peace and understanding.

In sum, it was not an empty calling....

My search led me to the most contested areas in the West Bank, such as the Jenin Refugee Camp and the Old City in Hebron, to especially work with extremists. My life became quickly tangled with the people there, some still living in the shadow of the Intifada, others motivated by hate, fear and illusions.

To arrive there, I often traversed a gauntlet of checkpoints, walls and was subject to countless interrogations, arrests and even...attacks.

Those challenges, however, reinforced my vision and the importance of continuing my work as I found that the interfaith peace movement—working with individuals, in particular—is one of the keys to peace in the Middle East. During my journey, I had to make some necessary sacrifices, sometimes compromising my own safety. But I could never have predicted the impact that it would have on my own personal relationships, intimacies and even some close friendships, lost in the battle to remain faithful to my vision...But the greatest sacrifice was made by two

1

friends and fellow peace activists, Lance Wolf and Juliano Mer-Khamis, murdered in Jerusalem and the West bank, respectively. This book is dedicated to them.

Their dauntless, loving spirit lives on in me and now, my friends...in you.

With love,
Frank Romano, Paris, March, 2014

P.S. This Fourth Edition includes a new chapter, Chapter 82: "In the Midst of a Riot." It recounts a recent harrowing experience in Jenin, West Bank, when I was trapped in the midst of rioting Palestinians following the killing of a Palestinian youth by Israeli soldiers.

Acknowledgements

So much love and thanks go to Ethel and Frank Romano, Sr., my parents, who were my first examples of unconditional love and who believed in me when nobody else did.

Special thanks to Lance Wolf for his steadfast dedication to truth while pursuing his work as a peace activist and his unconditional support of even my craziest projects. I miss him!

Thanks to Juliano Mer-Khamis, who originally gave me the idea to announce my interfaith events as "Freedom Marches" instead of "Peace Marches." He and his mother, Arna, were right; there can be "no peace without freedom." May they rest in peace!

I thank my sister, Lorna Romano, who has turned into a real pro, as my number one editor/proofreader. I acknowledge her work in this fourth edition, and her suggestions for improving the first, second and third editions.

A big thanks to my brother and incredible artist: Thomas Romano, for the extraordinary front cover, whose excellent illustration of me reaching for the sky has become a cornerstone of this book.

I'm greatly indebted to many others for their support and in particular, my children—Frankie, Victoria, Regina and Juliana—for their perseverance and patience throughout the years of nonstop work, travels and meditations that sometimes took me far away from them.

Prologue[1]

S treams of Arabic flowed from the speaker's mouth. He raised his hand from the podium from time to time, ejaculating strong words while provoking loud clapping or yelling from the crowd. I cringed....

This Kafkaesque moment seemed so unreal as just nine hours ago, I had been on a hill in Jerusalem rolling up my sleeping bag, surrounded by Jewish peaceniks as a cool breeze gently stirred the leaves littering the ground. Everything suddenly shifted into slow motion as I watched the girls talking to each other, sitting next to two men. The older man contemplated the date between his thumb and forefinger before sliding it into his mouth, a cavern of yellow teeth. The line of men off to the left seemed to stream onto the stage from oblivion, walking through the bold lights of a black tower, which were illuminating us. The speaker, who stood nearby, turned his arms around as if they were the blades of a windmill, moved by the waves of energy emanating from the audience.

Then somehow breaking through the barrier, one of the girls came over and introduced me to the older man who had been sitting next to me all this time: "This is Abdullah; he is the oldest Palestinian prisoner of the Israelis, who was liberated a couple of years ago. He was in prison for 28 years."

Overcome by fear, my body began to involuntarily tremble.

"What had he done to be condemned for 28 years?" I muttered under my breath and nervously looked around, hoping no one had heard me.

Abdullah's smile faded into his wizened body. He was clothed in a drab grey prison uniform. Twenty-eight years in prison...twenty-eight years in prison echoed repeatedly in my ear. The apparition now standing in front of me asked why he had been in Prison all those years. He didn't know...but he kept smiling, smiling as his grey body receded from view.

My spirit soared in some strange dimension as it followed his strange, crooked smile, the tawny teeth reflecting a blurred image. On the left, next to the man still speaking at the podium, a group of about 15 men of all shapes and sizes sat in a row facing a crowd of about 300 people. Some were wearing green bands over their heads

---

1 The proper names of many people in this memoir have been changed to protect their privacy.

5

with white Arabic words inscribed on them,[2] while others wore red and white or black and white keffiyehs. A few men proudly displayed long, flowing beards hanging from their drawn, ashen faces. Their eyes moved rapidly from side to side like those of pent up goats in a corral, waiting to be released to pasture.

I could have remained in this ethereal state awhile longer but Abdullah, probably seeing that I was floating in some unknown space, brought me partially back by whispering in my ear, "Those men are long-term prisoners of the Israeli government and have been recently liberated. We are celebrating it."

His smile widened to reveal silver in the back of his mouth, in a shadowy cavern, that seemed to close in around me. A hollow feeling of helplessness took over and I felt a tingling down my spinal cord, casting me into a panicky frenzy. Taking a deep breath, I quickly scanned the room for an escape route; but I was surrounded. My eyes shifted from face to face, to Abdullah, to the speaker then back to Abdullah, whose eyes met mine under a furrowed brow. Oh God! I exhaled and forced air back into my lungs as I purposefully shifted my gaze to a bowl of dates in the middle of the table, to avoid detection.

I would have excused myself for fear my nerves would soon betray me if Abdullah had not jolted me from my dismal musing by his urgent whispers, "Furthermore, the speaker is the head of the West Bank Hamas party who is welcoming them back and speaking to the people in this hotel."

The words, "…this hotel, this hotel…." kept repeating over and over again as my old enemy, pure, unabashed fear, surged down my sides and froze me to the chair.

Could this be the infamous radical group having a conference in the hotel my friends had selected for me?

The same group that had allegedly been involved in several suicide bomb attacks in Israel? I can't be here…I…The ethereal cloud completely burst, along with the balloon I was hanging from as I plummeted to earth. I muttered and then muffled a cough….

Later, alone in my hotel room, I phased into a semi-dreamlike state as I reflected on the beginning of this trip in Jerusalem. I had spoken with a Jewish man wearing his kippah so that it covered his bald spot, which was surrounded by a few grey hairs. I told him I wanted to go to Ramallah and then he took a deep breath: He looked straight ahead, appearing as if a stiff, ashen specter. Without looking at me, he said, "I take you to checkpoint, it's ok, you can maybe take…." Then the same head turned toward me, but the face had a darker hue, that of an Arab wearing a larger Muslim skull cap. He smiled a broad, inscrutable smile under a trimmed moustache. "Cheap, cheap…." he repeated over and over again.

My thoughts drifted to The Lion, the Witch and the Wardrobe,[3] except the entry sequence was in reverse as I came from the other side into the wardrobe, then into the mysterious room…and into this enigmatic Palestine.

---

2   The Shahada: "La 'ilaha 'illallah, Muhammad rasulu-llah," in Arabic meaning: "There is no God but God, and Muhammad is his messenger." It is the Muslim profession of faith.

3   C.S. Lewis, The Lion, the Witch and the Wardrobe (London: Geoffrey Bles, 1950). The first published book of The Chronicles of Narnia.

Suddenly a voice echoed from somewhere: "Beware, beware, fool...." so loud it woke me. I sat up rigidly with my back flat against the wall and tried to focus, but everything seemed to fade into fuzziness, maybe to soften the reality of this destitute place. I flicked on the remote control of the television perched on a metal tray overhead and watched with glazed eyes as several people wearing red and white keffiyehs spoke, madly gesticulating. I looked at my watch—it was 2 am.

I had heard enough angry speeches for one day so I abruptly clicked the TV off, got up and went to the window.

I looked over this desolate city, startled that most of it was in total darkness, yet it was not that late.

Sepulchral buildings all around me pierced through the veiled, black night. I couldn't call anyone as my cell phone had gone dead long ago and I'd forgotten to recharge it. There was no land line in the room. I was cut off...In spite of the warm welcome today by the sisters and the old man, I was so alone, vulnerable and surrounded by Hamas militant extremists....

There was a morbid silence in the streets, in the corridor. I was sure no clerk was at the front desk as there was no one there when I had returned late last night; so strange for a hotel! A cold wave rolled down my back; my hands shook as I heard a creaking noise outside my door and turned my head, immediately imagining a group of black-masked gunmen dragging me out the door. No one would know.

A piercing cry in the night curdled my soul, turning my head back to the window; I looked out and could only see the reflection of the lamp on some dark windows of an abandoned building, appearing like a dingy phantom.

I wondered if I'd live to see the sun again....

Book I

Busted

… flirting with emotional, mental disaster upon every breath that I
shall ever take
I will ——— cross over
To your love[4]

4   Frank Romano, from the poem, "Over the Line," p.11. Crossing Over (New York: World
Audience, 2008).

Chapter 1: Illusions

My life was a paradox, which shuffled between the fight for love and the illusion of love. I thought I was successfully re-doing my life which had become tormented and guilt-ridden. Living alone in a big city with lost intimacy, I lost touch. I thought I had gotten over losing my second wife, who had left me in Paris a few years earlier and headed for San Francisco with our three kids. I tried to cast aside all thoughts of Sylvia as I desperately held onto the paternal strings with my children through phone calls and eventually emails.

I thought I could turn the page, at least, ease the pain and replenish the empty nights. I was wrong. The phantom of that moribund relationship hung over me for years, intervening in everything I did, condemning to failure any serious relationships that tried to claw their way to fruition. The love pathos was always manifesting in the inflections of my thoughts. The fact was, it wasn't dead, and I was gone, lost to another world and quickly becoming a specter of myself. The hurt feeling was plunging me into a void, bringing me down. I later wondered if I would ever return to the world of the living or if I even wanted to....

As I trudged from room to room, my thoughts were invaded by blurred memories as I passed toys strewn over the floors and the graffiti scribbled on the walls in the girls' room. I kept everything the way it was the day they left me.

But it was sadly true; my reclusive life often consisted of trudging in and crashing on the couch in the living room. Feverish images infested my dreams— bodies moved in slow motion, my mouth opened and moved, but no words flowed.

During occasional bouts of lucidity, I snickered as I reminded myself of Miss Havisham's pathos in Great Expectations[5], a character I used to ruminate over from time to time. This time it was real and it was happening to me.

During an agitated midnight telephone conversion, and swept up in nostalgic love rhythms and the possibility of reviewing our relationship, Sylvia and I even set a date for her and the kids to return to Paris. At least that was the plan and I was desperate...My hopes soared as I followed up with calls, several times weekly. Her

---

5 In Great Expectations by Charles Dickens, one of the main characters in the book, Miss Havisham—who was dressing for her wedding when she received notice that her fiancé had abandoned her—thereafter lived her life as a recluse, with her wedding dress on and the decaying, uneaten wedding cake remaining unserved on the wedding table.

voice vibrated with emotion as she contemplated returning to the city of love…that our love was renewed. But it was perhaps more our love and hate….

The date grew more and more elusive: once within our grasp, slithering again through our fingers. We would set a date; then a few weeks hence she would postpone the trip for one reason or another. Hope glowed so brightly it blinded me; the light transformed the usual winter gloom into an emotional furnace.

Our last communication about reconciliation took place about two weeks after we had set another date, two days before Christmas. All night I dreamed about the first time my eyes had met Sylvia's; it took me back eight years.

Chapter 2: Italiano Latino

I met Sylvia by chance, at a rendezvous originally set up for a group of Italian friends and it eventually led us from San Francisco to the streets of Paris

It was the spring of 1988, the year after I had graduated from law school; the scenario was North Beach Restaurant, in the middle of the Italian district. I was the head bartender that night as the bar manager had quit the night before. I guess he had hired me a week earlier so he could train me before his orchestrated departure.

I had the early evening dinner shift downstairs behind an unusually long service bar in back of the room…40 feet of pure blue and white marble. It was juxtaposed to the banquet room in which Italian prosciutto hung from strings in neat rows, made by Lorenzo and Bruno, the owners. I did not know for sure, but I thought it served to furnish the restaurant in order to avoid difficulties in importing it from Italy. I called it the "Prosciutto Room."

The bar was close enough to the "Prosciutto Room" from which wafted the pungent, hammy odor directly from the Mediterranean, every time its door opened. The scent hung in the air, quickening my pulse and making my mouth salivate while I poured gin and tonics, martinis, margaritas and handed out bottles of Italy's finest Chianti.

When I walked underneath the prosciutto on the way to the storeroom, a drop of pork fat would sometimes fall into my hair. Then the smell of my hair blended in perfectly with the omnipresent odors of North Beach, especially those of Molinari's delicatessen on Columbus Avenue. I'd sometimes walk in front on purpose and linger there even after the deli had closed while deeply inhaling a mixture of Romano cheese and prosciutto; it would be my Italian fix for the night.

From 7 to 10 pm, I poured drinks "fast and furiously"; after that, the downstairs room started emptying and eventually closed. After the last order for drinks was placed, I added up sales on the receipts left by the waiters after every sale, and compared it to the cash register read-out. I then placed the receipts plus the read-out roll into a canvas pouch and submitted it to the night manager before heading to the door. The manager was a tough Sicilian and nodded with a gruff snort when his massive hands folded over the pouch.

On the way to my rooming house, to relax my mind, I'd stroll down Grant Street towards Broadway; the former was narrow and full of cafés and odd boutiques, including one selling masques, multi-colored purses with hippy tassels flowing down over them and strange bohemian clothes with feathers poking out from the collars and pockets. My eyes gazed at Caffé Tivoli, like they did every night as I passed by, scanning for a friend. Most of the people I met in North Beach were Italians working in the restaurants and cafés. They would hang out in the cafés and bars after hours, to wind down after a long day before going home.

On the terrace were seated two of my Italian friends: Marcello, a Perugino with golden, curly locks fresh off the plane from Perugia, Italy, looking to work in the Silicon Valley; in contrast was Pino, a short-haired, slightly jaded Milanese from Milano, a permanent big-city smirk bending the corners of his mouth, over which were faint sproutings of a moustache. Sitting across from them were three girls, straight, dark hair flowing down, except one wore a discrete pony tail fixed with a tight bow in back, restraining her shiny black hair, so shiny looking…so fertile, full of Latina-smooth lushness, flowing like the Rio Grande…into my heart. She held her nose slightly but not too high, traces of Andalusia in her seeming Mediterranean features, actually baked in her blood from south of the border.

The Italians waved me to them with exuberant Italian gestures, entreating me to join them. The girls looked either Mediterranean or perhaps South American, with olive to dark skin, and long, jet-black hair. The girl with her hair in a tightly-drawn bun on top of her head introduced herself as Sylvia and the other girls as Rosa Alba and Theresa. Sylvia seemed the most feminine and least talkative, so I was automatically drawn to her; my pounding heart shook my body so to avoid discovery, I shrank from touching her as she was sitting so close to me.

It was clear that Pino was attracted to the same girl, Sylvia, and since he met her first, I tried to avert my eyes from her and focus on the black-haired girl with straight hair sitting next to me. She looked a bit like Sylvia, but a bit heavier, her face a bit harder, with heavier makeup, a deep blue around the eyes and a bit too much blush on her full cheeks. Marcello, in the meantime, had turned to the curly- haired one. She was the lightest-skinned of all the girls and even though her face was slightly pock-marked, probably from a bout with adolescent pimples, her bright red mouth opened in a wide, inviting smile.

Our desultory conversation became anarchic, running from the depths of Calabria, Italia, to Puerta Vallarta, Mexico, and everything in between; then our conversation turned to similarities between the Mexican and Italian cultures. I was flipping from speaking Italian, rolling my r's and singing, back to Spanish, fervently rolling the r's again then back to Italian. Sylvia and the others spoke a beautiful, fluid Spanish, the Italians stuck to Italian. The conversation then turned to music, from Lucio Dalla, the Italian pop singer, to Vincente Fernandez, the king of the ranchera song, from Mexico.

At the end of the evening, we exchanged numbers and then the girls, after saying "Adios" almost in unison, walked down Grant Street toward Café Trieste, another Italian hangout where artists, poets and writers met. We walked parallel to the girls, on the other side of the street. They passed Caffé Trieste, then turned around and waved to us. Pino, walking next to me, expressed that he was interested in Sylvia and wanted to take her out. I kept silent but intended to respect his wishes and not contact Sylvia. He was my friend.

I did not expect a call from her, a few days later. She invited me to dinner at her parents' house. I figured that she would also invite Pino and Marcello.

I arrived in the Mission district, the Latino section of San Francisco, with a bottle of Chianti from the wine store in North Beach and a loaf of panettone bread from a bakery on Stockton Street. I knocked and Rosa Alba greeted me at the door. Her bright smile was mitigated; something was stirring in those black eyes. I looked again and she looked away. Her olive skin glowed with the familiar Latina hue, and emanated a scent of sweet apples soaked in honey.

Her long, black hair flowed over her dark shoulders, and a white blouse she had paired with white pants. She wore red lipstick that highlighted her beautiful Latina spirit. In spite of that, I recoiled slightly as I had expected Sylvia to answer the door. I assumed Pino would already be occupied by her somewhere in the house.

She led me into a living room, in which we were surrounded by pictures of kids sitting in a half-circle around the parents, a slender man with a long moustache, tight jeans and cowboy boots sitting next to a woman with sweeping, black hair tied to one side, affixed with a rose. Her smile was loose, one of contentment that her kids were all near her. I surmised that the pictures featured members of her family.

The warmth of the Latino smiles filled the room, as well as still life photography, including a picture with a basket featuring a mixture of yellow, orange and green fruit. Juicy mangos, grapes and bananas spilled over the sides of the bowl. In the photos, I made out a father and a mother; the father, I learned later, a gardener and florist shop employee, was wizened by the sun's rays, his glistening eyes receding into the grooves of his skeletal face. There was an aura of comfort and love permeating the walls of the house.

I was drawn to this family aura....

There was an adolescent boy waiting there, sitting on a couch. He introduced himself as Miguel, a broad grin on his face. He reached out and grasped my hand as Rosa Alba stood next to him. She gave him a peck on the cheek, mumbling something like she'd be right back, then escaped down the hall in the direction of the strong smell of corn tortillas.

I wondered where Pino and Marcello were, assuming they had been invited, as well; maybe they were already in the kitchen talking to Sylvia. I expected to run into them any second.

The aroma of corn tortillas mixed with meat wafted throughout the living room as we sat on the couch looking out the window. The toasted corn smell permeated the entire house, adding to the quaintness of the place. I spoke with Miguel in English, he responded in Spanish, so I continued in Spanish.

I suspected the dining table conversation would eventually be in Spanish and I was desperate to review my spoken Spanish, so I insisted on speaking their language. He did not refuse.

I had to dare ask, "You and Rosa Alba been together long?"

He laughed, "You know, I don't even know where I stand. Yo la quiero mucho." He stopped cold as sounds of shuffling feet approached from the kitchen.

Rosa Alba brought a tray in with two, big shot glasses filled with a golden substance and a plate of limes and salt. It was tequila. She placed the tray on an end table in front of us and left the room.

The Latino grabbed a wedge of lime between his index finger and thumb, licked the area between the two fingers while holding the lime and sprinkled salt there from a salt shaker. He then, with his other hand, grasped the shot of tequila, licked the salt in between his fingers, opened his small mouth and slammed it down the hatch. He then bit into the lime wedge, sucked the lime juice and put the used wedge on the tray, followed by the empty shot glass.

I tried copying him, but as I licked the salt in between my fingers I spilled most of the tequila on the floor. Miguel couldn't help it as he doubled over laughing and then, of all people, Sylvia pranced into the living room as if she were entering a stage scene. Embarrassed, I put the shot glass to my lips and slammed down the drop that remained. Miguel was almost rolling on the floor by this time.

She was dressed in a short white dress, her hair was neatly tied in a ponytail and her eyes were slightly darkened. Her smooth, light-brown legs spilled out from the dress, down to her brown sandals; she was a natural beauty. I trembled a bit: her smooth olive forehead sloped down towards her black Mexican eyes, and her skin shone with a natural gleam.

She smiled and reached out her hand; I rose to take it, wobbling a bit, and bit my tongue, straining not to show it. As I finally grasped her hand, she pulled me towards the back, where the wonderful odors were coming from, at the same time calling to Miguel to join us. He followed me. In the kitchen, Rosa Alba was already seated and Miguel sat across from her. Sylvia sat across from me.

I was still a bit slow to catch on. I thought to myself, This is strange—where's Pino? Maybe he couldn't make it.

I felt awkward sitting in front of Sylvia, because she was supposed to be reserved for Pino and Rosa Alba for me. I just didn't get it! Sipping more tequila from a shot glass that was constantly being filled by Rosa Alba, I wasn't focusing on anything but the smooth corn taste, mixed with cheese and a tomato sauce, momentarily resting on my tongue and then making its way down my throat. I finally washed it down with another shot of tequila.

My plans that evening were to have dinner at Sylvia's, then excuse myself early to attend a party organized by my first wife, Rosalia, who had just returned to the Bay Area from Spain. She had left San Francisco in September, 1987, and it was now July, 1988; we had been separated for almost a year. The "fiesta" was being held in our old apartment, where we had lived during my last year of law school. We had moved out when we separated, but friends still lived there. I was simultaneously excited and worried about my reunion with her. When the hour for my departure for the party arrived, I hesitated....

The hot, steaming posolé, the king of soups, with hominy grits and pork meat, was then served. It was topped by a layer of chopped union, a squeeze of lime and homemade Mexican hot sauce. We drank Dos XX beer. The desert was a soft, creamy flan, so smooth it melted as it slithered down my throat, gently nudged by another stream of tequila.

At the end of the meal, I noticed that everyone had left the table except for Sylvia and me. She cautiously rose to take my desert plate away.

"Would you like coffee?" She asked so sweetly, like it was a natural thing. "Si, gracias."

She carried the steaming cups on the tray and asked me to follow her to the living room. I slid onto a sofa surrounded by pillows; this was, no doubt, the center of the household place of comfort. She sat in a straight-backed chair next to me, smiling in the direction of her sister who was engaged with Miguel in semi- intimate conversation on the corner of the couch—their faces grew closer and their lips met. Semi-intimate since Rosa Alba would from time to time flash a dancing eye at her sister, appearing to say to her, "It's not serious!" Yet it didn't seem the same with Miguel who was totally absorbed with Rosa Alba....

"I'm invited to a party only about two blocks away; there'll be music and dancing...." My voice trailed off as I phased out; the tequila had gotten a hold of me. She didn't respond, so I kept going. "So I have to leave in about 10 minutes as I told the people I'll show up...it would be rude."

"Ok," was her response.

An hour later Sylvia and I were walking up a street I had known very well during the last two years of law school. Living in the Mission, the Latino district had been my therapy while going to law school in the financial district, in the center of San Francisco. As I would leave the 24th Street subway station on my way back from law school, an opalescent haze would surround me, a multitude of reds, blues, yellows, violets, while the Spanish language, salsa, cumbia, merengue and samba music filled the air. Every once in a while the melodic Caribbean air was disturbed by a shot of African-American soul or Latin jazz blowing out the window of a passing low rider, the lowering and raising of the car through an elaborate hydraulic system seeming to synchronize with the pounding beat.

I had lived in a miniscule room with my Spanish wife in the middle of the Latino district. It was almost too much...too much emotion as I had so loved her, with such irrational passion. And now, we had grown apart; it seemed impossible.

As Sylvia and I walked up the street, I remembered having breakfast every morning with Rosalia, in our tiny room situated above a Latino sports bar. Sometimes the bottoms of my stocking feet would feel the drums bludgeoning the floor through the thin ceiling, in the early morning hours. We would heat the instant Italian espresso on the hotplate placed on the small strip of floor between the bedand the wall, and eat little breakfast cakes purchased below in the Salvadorian bakery, soaked in hot coffee. Her lips would open and close, moving in rhythm as she tasted the coffee and savored her breakfast. She would dress quickly as I shifted behind the curtains to start my infernal study routine. An eerie silence would sometimes engulf me as I poured over the book. I'd turn around to see Rosalia, her hand pulling back the sheet, red lipstick mouth gleaming, watching me study while her face jiggled like a Russian doll on its axis before she kissed my lips. I would remember her face moving like that, her fiery red lips and round cheeks accentuated by a shadow of rouge, whenever I thought of her. It was the familiar beginning of a new day, the advent of a new morning, together, in the Mission.

Apart from our modest coffee klatches, the mornings were gloomy, as the cold, misty light from the street swept over us, illuminating the shadows, announcing the beginning of another fight to prevent expulsion from law school. For her, it was another day working in a Spanish-owned café restaurant—serving mainly Latinos, some Spanish people and a scattering of white Americans, an eclectic collage of European and Latino cultures—imbedded deep within a working class neighborhood. After leaving her job to return home late at night, she would be on her guard as a block away was the installation of infamous projects, the pink elephants, where drugs were the main sustenance of its residents.

Quivers of emotion streamed through me as we climbed the familiar stairs leading to the apartment where I had spent the last two years of law school, a room barely large enough to fit a bed, desk and closet. That was the exact place I used to share with Rosalia....

I knocked as Sylvia stood behind me. Out of the corner of my eye, a slight frown marred her smooth olive forehead; for the first time, she seemed wary. Then I followed her eyes to the paint peeling from the door as the melodious pounding of live Conga music flowed through the small window above the door, where my little room....

The door opened and José poked his head through the opening. He was a wiry, sharp-nosed Mexican who had rented me the room about three years ago. He was the apartment manager and collected the rent from the various occupants of the rooms situated around a large communal kitchen. He occupied the large bedroom at the end. The usual combination of paraphernalia—miniature Mexican sombreros and Mexican flags—adorned his coffee-stained door. His thin, brown left hand slapped open the door and his right hand grasped for mine. The Conga drum beat plunged into our hearts and made our feet move involuntarily.

"Hola bro, nice to see you, and what may you have there?"

He peered in back of me and Sylvia looked away a bit embarrassed; then he pulled on my hand and we climbed more stairs. At the top of the stairs, we were greeted by more people including Rogelio and others who had been fellow members of a Latino street theatre group called "Tupac Amaru." Rogelio, a taciturn Mexican writer, stood in the corner, watching, as usual; he was tall with proud, tight jowls prominent on his dark face, shadowed in long, scraggly black hair.

"Romano, venga...hey."

I must have hugged about ten people and shook twenty hands stuck in my face in about one minute. I looked back sheepishly to find Sylvia scrunched in a corner, her eyes glaring at an unfamiliar world. As I was hugging people, I felt a heavy, inscrutable look beaming from an unknown source, casting down on me at every turn. I could not escape it. Then I spied a shadow standing in back of José, who was dancing with a blond girl. I knew that frame.

At the same time I looked up, the dark face drew into the light. It was Rosalia;

her indelible Spanish smile filled up the room. We drew closer, hugged and I gave her a peck on her cheek.

"Is that it, esposo (husband)?" Her voice petered out, as her mouth flickered with a humorless grin.

That somehow echoed the time we were together, in this very building, in that very room just a few feet away. I remembered her looking out the window as I caressed her, with her eyes half-open, beckoning me…during one San Francisco night in the Mission, lulled by the murmur of the sweet Latino waves of the salsa/cumbia district, I remember the smell of salsa picante and burritos wafting from the taqueria…and the huge side of the building featuring a fading mural, a scene from Woodstock: Santana pressing on lead, Chapito on drums….

"No but, ah…." I stammered, not knowing what to say, "It's been a…long…."

Then I was whisked away from her eyes by Rogelio, into the kitchen, where a huge glass bowl was providing spirits of sangria to the party goers. Over the sink, the same print of Che Guevera hung, one of its corners bent. His long, dark hair enveloped a dark Latino face, embellished by a full moustache. Rogelio poured a glass for me and handed me a chicken empanada. I took a glass and an empanada to Sylvia who was standing in the same corner.

"Sorry," I said apologetically, handing her the glass and snack on a paper plate. "No, it's fine," she smiled. I felt relieved. "These are your friends?" she asked, unbelieving.

Her eyes squinted, probably trying to minimize the bizarre scenario around her. Even though she had been partially raised in this district, she led me to believe that she had not gone to parties like this. She had earlier told me in passing that she spent a lot of time traipsing around with the jet setters in the upscale downtown bars and discotheques. Maybe she just wanted to get away from her world, the Latina world—a seeming attempt to move up when she just wanted to go beyond the limits of her life.

I was ironically, at least in my own mind, bringing her to taste, for the first time, some of the spice in her own neighborhood. My pride was however tempered as I suspected she had already tasted it, but didn't, for some reason, want me to know.

Finally the Latin soul music of Santana was blaring over the loud speakers "Samba Pa Ti," the slow romantic one; its powerful resonance cut through cultural barriers and brought hearts together. Her face moved slightly from side to side in rhythm with the music. A warm wave moved down my loins. Her family knew Carlos Santana's family, especially one of his sisters. This place, the Mission, was not only his old hangout—where he allegedly got his start—it was family, a big, rhythmic, unpretentious family with friends hovering around.

"Let's dance." Before I got an answer, I took her hand and led her to the dance floor.

As soon as we reached it, the music switched to the loud salsa of Sonora Ponce-a.

"Moreno soy porque nací de la rumba y el sabor yo le heredé del guaguanc—" ["I am black because I was born of the rumba and taste I inherited it from guaguanc—." (Cuban Rumba, a rhythmic dance and music style)]

That drove us to dance, so I grabbed her hand and pulled her to the middle of the

19

dance floor, dancing the only salsa I knew, street salsa, which I picked up in late-night Latino parties. My feet started moving to the beat without following the usual steps, but following heartbeats of the sensuous Latino music. The street salsa style was completely unorthodox compared to what some people called "studio salsa."

A Latino couple next to us was following the steps, and they danced with smooth rhythm, without a hitch. When I danced there were nothing but hitches but, I mused, with more spontaneity in the moves and, I was convinced, with more enjoyment as I forced myself out of a dancing comfort zone. I even surprised myself as I jumbled together all the past moves I'd learned here and there, mixing American swing moves with French rock, twirling her as my left knee hit the ground. Then the Tango, cha cha cha, even a little waltz, also throwing in a little studio salsa as I refused to learn but the basic steps to avoid corrupting spontaneity. I eventually returned to French rock, which didn't prescribe any particular moves for the feet, unlike American swing. I wildly kicked and jumped out of the studio salsa moves which were getting too predictable.

I rationalized that the apparent dancing anarchy can always be overcome by a strong lead and an inventive and sometimes fearless partner…in spite of putting deep grooves in Sylvia's otherwise smooth olive-skinned brow, after making another wild move. I tried not to judge that street salsa was better than studio salsa—I was certain I felt freer than the couple next to me, free from conforming to the standard moves and more fluid, at least until Sylvia tripped over my feet as I grabbed her to do a little tango with the salsa beat. But my embarrassed laugh tried to cover up for my failure to telegraph to her the unorthodox move that I had just made for the first time ever. I reminded myself that if I danced with emotion, flaunting the rules, going with the feeling at the time, my dance partner was not going to follow unless my lead was super strong.

I tightened the lead, pressing my hand into the middle of her back to flag the next move, and we began swinging together, albeit tenuously; but I preferred it that way. She seemed to like it too and caught on fast; then she caught on fire as we began soaring in the middle of the dance floor. It was an exceptional moment as I allowed myself a respite from my previous thoughts. Part of the problem getting into the groove was the tequila I had drunk that night; but we soon got into it, frenziedly jumping across the dance floor until I felt a strong elbow piercing my ribs.

"Ouch." I winced as I turned.

It was Rosalia, dancing with Mario, the street artist, a dark circle permanently splashed around his left eye, his yellow teeth revealed in a cracked smile as he twirled her. She planted her foot, stopping in the middle of it and twisted her head towards me.

"Well I thought you were going to dance with me. I guess you don't care anymore!"

Her head raised, as did her brown eyebrows, her eyes casting a familiar evanescent look across the room while her lips formed a stern, straight line. No words needed to be spoken: I understood as I followed her glaring eyes—swiveling my hips to the beat of the hard salsa beat—to the closed door of the small room we had shared for two years. A familiar padlock, connected to a drooping chain, clamped it shut. I winced again…and my eyes shut.

Then I crossed over and danced in front of Rosalia, taking her hands as our eyes fixed on each other momentarily, but intensely, like two Flamenco dancers. The same look had flashed from her Andalusian eyes light years ago, high above "Las Ramblas," during our weekend storm in Barcelona. I flashbacked to the time we danced Sevillanas in the apartment of her eccentric Barcelona artista friends.

Mario did the same with Sylvia as we changed partners to the beat of Sonora Ponce–a "Moreno soy porque nací de la rumba…." that had returned over the loud speakers. I imagined I was black like the singer as I twirled Rosalia around, and that we were still together as a time warp closed in around us, shifting my thoughts to a nightclub in San Francisco where we had danced salsa all night until we dropped, a couple of years ago, deep in the city. It had been our first date. The Caribbean jungle beat sizzled our blood, somehow enhancing inchoate yearnings, on the eve of a misty, strobe-lit night until we returned later to the Mission's cool morning breeze, the only place that could temper my raw, unbridled emotions sometimes running amuck…in those days.

I returned to Sylvia. As she looked up into my eyes, a vague smile formed on her dark lips, as if she began to understand the molten emotions gushing from one of my wounds deep within, sweeping me away from her, so very far away, as I saw Rosalia nod rapidly. It seemed like she followed the molten trail as she watched me burn inside, flashing her wide-toothed Mediterranean smile while her red lipstick formed a red tunnel for my eyes, like a bulls-eye.

I just knew that my life with Rosalia was over. A dark sadness cloaked me as I saw her turn her back when Mario twirled her. Her half-turned face accentuated her smooth, red lips, tantalizing me as my mind contorted them into a tight smile. Could it be true? I had to turn away. My eyes then returned to Sylvia who I caught observing me before turning away…this time without emotion. My hand slipped over the spot in my side where Rosalia had almost punctured the skin with her elbow.

Rosalia quickly returned, dancing in my face. "So your amor…!" I needed to balance the scales with her.

"Heard you've been going out with someone."

She recoiled as she danced; I turned and drew closer as I fished for a direct line into her vivid Spanish eyes which always revealed what she was thinking.

"How did you find out?" The corners of her red lips curled upwards, more contented than surprised.

I never answered because I didn't really know—I had just guessed, but my words seemed to have set her back a bit. Someone in the back suddenly opened a door and light streamed in as Rosalia danced, twirling, wearing a flowery dress from her "traje de gitana" (gypsy outfit) from Andalusia, with ruffles erotically layering out from the bottom; the top was cloaked with a red scarf. She danced while clenching her fists… like a muzzled dancer who could bite through at any time. It was my turn to recoil….

My heart thumped under my shirt, pumping the whole scene out of control; then it dissipated into nothingness and whirled behind a protective emotional barrier. The resulting void pushed my desperate, pained soul to searching. My eyes settled on Sylvia. Her dark lips lifted to a secretive Mona Lisa smile against the backdrop of smooth olive skin; her shiny brown eyes looking up at mine brought me back from desperation and eased the pain.

She then came closer and reached over, touching her palm to my shoulder whispering into my ear, "I have to go...." I mumbled something unintelligible.

She added, resigned, "You can stay...I can walk home, it's only two blocks." That snapped me out of soaring emotional limbo and brought me back down to earth. It was late and the dark Mission District—though full of Congas, bongos,classical Latino music, as well as Latin jazz, including the omnipresent Santana and Gato Barbieri, Willie Colon, Hector Lavoie, "fiestas," the smells of meat tacos mixed with onions and tomatoes—could also be treacherous territory. It was the cruising ground of attacking low riders, the hunting grounds of lonesome cowboy crazies, gangs, thieves, and sometimes killers. No, I would take her home, but maybe I'd return....

"But I couldn't return, could I?" I mumbled to my troubled self.

If I did, my insides trembled with the thought that Rosalia and I may start all over again...and this would be the catalyst: a piquant mixture of hot salsa and flaming jealousy.

Too hot to handle, I tried to ease out, by rationalizing that we had already made a clean break, kind of; Oh, I don't know, phhhhhhhh...My dilemma returned with a vengeance.

I feared a new union would spiral me upwards only to spin me out of control again and crash land. I swore to myself in the middle of this place, the last bastion of our intimacy, that it would be fatal, the next time.

Shifting to the periphery of the dance floor, gently pulling the willing Sylvia, I raised my hand and loudly yelled, "Adios" to the bodies flailing in semi-darkness on imaginary Brazilian beaches, dancing the lambada. Then I spotted Rosalia in the corner—she refused to turn her head as she dipped out of sight, grasping a shadow closely to her.

I reached around Sylvia and took her hand as I slid to the door; I knew we had to leave quickly or soon, or I feared, I wouldn't be able to.

Finally, we reached the door as José ran up to us while the beat of live congas spilled out of an open bedroom door, overpowering the canned music over the loudspeakers and then abruptly stopped as the bedroom was shut by an invisible hand.

"Leaving so soon?" he cried. I nodded.

"It's ok." Like a true scandal contriver, he looked away, perhaps seeking Rosalia as his curious eyes shifted to the dance floor. He knew our story as he had lived in the same apartment with us during our life together. Without turning to us, he uttered fatalistically, "I understand...." as his marijuana-drugged voice faded away. "Come by anytime, amigo, for a beer and we'll talk. This is always your casa. Nice meeting you," he said, as he looked after Sylvia, who had opened the door and was already half-way out.

She didn't look back as we inched down the first flight of stairs to the door at the bottom. I turned and waved blindly at the group of people hovering at the top of the stairs; at the same time, my eyes met Rosalia's omnipresent, dark-brown Mediterranean eyes flashing at me before she turned away, repulsed and at the same time, perhaps strangely inviting....

The door was stuck so I pried it open and out slid Sylvia. I was almost out when I looked again upwards and glimpsed Rosalia's eyes, inscrutably peering down again from the top of the stairs.

Our bond came back in a bright flashback, once so tight, formed in this very place during the turmoil of law school, until the end. The Sword of Damocles was constantly over my head at the end of every semester. Only one bad grade would bring me below average, resulting in unceremonious, permanent expulsion because I already had been kicked out once at the end of the second year.

Rosalia held me up through all that; the image of her drinking coffee in the room just above my head came back again...dipping Spanish cookies into her coffee in the morning shadows and then biting off the moistened corners. When the cookie was down to her fingers, she'd just pop it into the cup then fish for it with her spoon and then slide the moist bits into her mouth. The steam from the cups was circling up, cinching around my throat, suffocating me with memories of the many mornings shared before she went to work...and then I would turn to my books unscrupulously waiting for me behind the closed, coffee-stained curtain. I repeated to myself again, "She stayed by my side through it all, through it all, through it all." Words cascaded through me like a love mantra.

And those years came back again in torrents, flooding me with inexorable heat as I saw myself pounding the heavy law books piled on my desk next to me. Somehow, she never left me echoed through me as Sylvia and I walked away.

The warmth was overwhelming, sweeping from my thoughts into the heartache I was able to repress after my breakup with Rosalia. I had managed to ignore the feelings that could have pulled me down to emotional bedrock when she departed for Spain; but I couldn't do it anymore. I could feel Rosalia's footsteps mercilessly on my spinal cord, dancing and giggling. She was in control and suffocating me. My feet moved down the steps in one motion as the music snuffed out temporarily when the apartment door shut; then the congas revived their warm tropical beat behind me as I caught up to Sylvia.

I followed her out the street level door, closing it behind us almost in one action, before we headed down the sidewalk in silence. No words came and I thought I'll take her home and I won't see her again. So what's there to say? I'll return to the party.

After walking her the two blocks to her house, I climbed back down the steps to the ground level after scribbling her phone number on the back of my quaking hand. I was totally lost in confused, conflicting thoughts, wondering what to do. I began to contrive feelings for Sylvia but that only added to my confusion.

Then it hit me! Rosalia had been the one who told me about the party and somehow there must have been an expectation of getting back together after a year's absence from my life. So she just blows in from Spain and expects everything to be the same with the same magnetic passion as the first night together?

In retrospect, we had left the Mission and moved to the Italian District before she left town. The last scene in our North Beach room when she gave me the final ultimatum—I remember it because her shrill voice still echoed, grating on me then like it did before: "Either you return to Spain with me, as you love me and my country—you said so, and we could have a good life there—or it's over. You said so yourself…you'd love to live in Spain; come now or we're through. You know my family loves you, imbecile!!"

She curled a sardonic smile and then sat on the bed, her head bent downwards, the tears sliding down over her Grecian nose and onto the cold floor below.

I looked out the window, trying not to show her I had reached the emotional end. I was on the brink, back on the razor's edge, and could not control the surge heaving through my lungs to my quivering lips. I bit down on them to restrain myself from flying to her side to dry her tears, embracing her with infinite, sensual passion. Instead, I let my mind take over, for once, telling myself, I've always hated ultimatums and tended to do the opposite….

I took a deep breath as I opened the window on the Italian streets below. Somehow the vibrant sea air blew strength in my veins to contrive excuses I wasn't sure of at that time, such as, "I need to go as far as I can from here, take the bar exam and practice for a while, in my country, then I can go…."

But she had already left the room, dragging her heavy suitcase with her; she turned her head, flashing a look of mocking irony, and let out a deep, exasperated gasp, her face contorting as the tears streamed down her face. She looked even more like a fragile doll. I turned, the tears rolling down my cheeks…Two days later she was on a plane for Spain. That was about a year ago and I didn't see or hear from her the whole time until I got the call about the party.

Only a week ago I had found out she was in town and the invitation to the party left on my answering machine by Rosalia was about our rendezvous: maybe she wanted to see me, then move back, or try to convince me to return to Spain with her….

All I knew was I didn't know anything about these possible machinations—my emotions were like a cyclone, swirling endlessly, as my feet involuntarily walked me back to the party. It was one block more and I could already hear the congas; as I approached, my tongue scraped over a sangria taste still lightly caked in my mouth.

My feet kept carrying me there and then, I stopped for some reason, turned around and somehow found my pick-up truck parked nearby and crawled inside.

I sat there as I couldn't drive and I had no designated driver. I fell asleep.

A deep veil of darkness closed in on the Mission as I slumbered in the truck. Voices woke me up from a deep sleep. I shook myself and looked at my watch, an old rusty wind-up with no band that I had slipped in my pocket. It was 4 am. An uncontrollable urge hit me, to find Rosalia, to ask her to forgive me, to see her again.

I quickly started the engine and drove the two blocks to the party. I stopped and parked the car in the middle of the street across from the door that I had walked through with Sylvia a few hours earlier. No music was seeping out the windows, not even the congas, as I stood there in the stillness of the San Francisco night. I knocked on the door—it was shut, cold like a vault. There were no signs that a party had been going on hours before.

No chance now for reconciliation; I tried to salvage something as I reminded myself that at least she was still my wife. But now I could not even salvage that; it was all over. My heart rained tears as my head slumped to my chest standing there alone, in the dark…It can't be those years in the room right above my head are gone …barely getting by with wheat tortillas, bread, sometimes Salvadorian cakes and butter, a little coffee and an occasional burrito…with nothing else, nothing, but we loved each other. That's all we had to fill the room with!

I moped down the stairs and then stopped, hoping for some sound, any sound. Nothing. I looked ahead and saw the fog rolling in over the hills before me, the hills on the other side of Noe Valley.

I got back into the truck and took the brake off while turning the key. I then gunned the engine, burning rubber as I headed for Noe Valley, driving down the avenues toward the ocean. I parked the car a ways from the Cliff House in a turnout along the highway that skirted the ocean, where I could find the sky hanging over it. I turned the knob, opening the window. The fog horns were resonating sounds of profound loneliness, way out on the deep, empty seas.

As I sat looking over the scintillating crests of midnight ocean, I ruminated over the five-year law school hell that all came back, blowing past my inner gatekeepers that had managed to suppress for so long those memories, until that moment…to no avail as it uncontrollably flowed out….

Chapter 3: Sandra

During the first year of law school, in 1981, I lived in Nob Hill, in a small, funky studio apartment on Pine Street; it came with one of those famous bay windows in front of which Sandra, my first law school girlfriend, would sit for hours, forlorn, looking out as I studied behind a curtain nearby. Looking for a city adventure, she had gladly followed me down from the Oregon mountains, where I had been staying with my folks before entering law school.

She was an attractive Northwestern-bred blond, with blue-green eyes and a slightly upturned nose; her body vibrated with that enthusiastic strut of a mountain-grown girl alive with energy. Her mouth was small and her lips full but stretching out at the corners. She was very feminine, gliding from one room to the other with her swaying hips and soft step, wearing blouses with violet flowers and frills around the cuffs and collar, which contrasted with her ruddy cheeks and the brown hiking boots she wore to work at a nearby health food store on Geary Street. There, she was considered an original "Earth Mother." After work, she would slip on her jogging shoes to walk the few blocks to the apartment. She loved working there as she was very much intertwined with the world of organic food and meditation. But the key phrase was "stress avoidance" at all costs, which unfortunately did not coincide with my law school life.

To compensate for her "mellow" organic lifestyle during the weekdays, weekends we spent moving from discotheque to discotheque under the phosphorescent San Francisco lights. We often danced until we dropped, usually around five o'clock in the morning, in a glitzy world of fast music and fast people. She loved discotheques and the life surrounding them. I was less enthusiastic about that lifestyle, except for the dancing, which I hungered for after a week of sweating between the covers of the heavy law books and anxiously responding to tricky questions posed by law professors. I tried to sound like a lawyer while avoiding humiliation before a class of a hundred ambitious students, listening and sometimes snickering at my answers.

Seemingly soft-spoken, Sandra was fastidious in her lifestyle, carefully selecting what she ate—making sure it was strictly organic—and making sure she meditated daily. But Sandra metamorphosed into another when flying across the dance floor, bumping and grinding, twirling, her legs moving so fast she appeared to be jogging in place at a horrendous pace. Some spectators would surely tire just watching her. I

26

was one of them but I tried to keep up while wiping sweat from my brow to focus on her next move and respond with my own version of disco dancing, mixed with tango, swing, French rock and whatever I could throw in; but she was in control on the dance floor, dancing circles around me and giggling the entire time. She turned her body as her braided hair flopped on the sides of her face and her eyebrows lifted, her hands rhythmically skimming down her sleek body to her hips.

The disco music sent her to another place, to a place she dared not go during the day. The night would fall around us as she sensuously bit her top lip when she was twirling her smooth hips, making love to an imaginary dancer gliding across the floor.

My goal as a future lawyer was to represent victims of any kind—I had true compassion for them as I had been one during my youth[6] —in particular, of racism, ethnic discrimination, social deprivation and injustice and victims of stalkers. I had written many unpublished poems, especially while studying in Europe a few years earlier and publicly recited them, as well as works of others. But my creative spirit was constantly butting up against the demands of law school. I felt an increasing conflict between the pressure to push my creative yearnings to the back burner and my need for creative expression.

My mid-semester grades were low so I consulted Professor Goldhirsch, who analyzed one of my test answers. She seemed to have compassion for students and a remarkable understanding of the philosophy of teaching which gave me faith in her ability to assess my potential. She observed that I had unusual reasoning abilities and explosive creativity. The former was good for law school, as long as I showed my work, which I was not doing; hence the poor grades. My explosive creativity, she said, although it should be stifled as much as possible for law school survival, would greatly contribute to my being a great lawyer, provided I survived law school and passed the bar. According to her, survival would be a challenge for anyone like me with raw creative talent. She thus encouraged me to prevent it from being destroyed permanently by the law school killing machine, while tempering it until I could uncork it as a trial lawyer. She somehow had me figured out and that was by far better than I could do! I tried following her advice, with mixed results.

My fight was, however, not shared by Sandra who, during study breaks in the apartment, would hold my hand and say, "Law school is stressful; it's unhealthy, so drop out. You'll be better."

But I needed motivation more than someone opening a back door escape route whenever I shook my head. As such, I began to screen her away from my work and draw inside myself, rarely speaking to her about school. We meditated together, shared metaphysical thoughts and dreams, ate sparingly and slept in each other's arms. Law school didn't exist between us anymore. My appetite subsided under the stress so I lost weight.

The beginning of exams was marked by catastrophe. The night before the first exam, I drank a glass of brandy to relax me. But nerves, poor nutrition and the brandy

---

6   Editorial Review of Frank Romano's Storm Over Morocco, 3rd Edition. Amazon.com. "—after fighting his sometimes violent father and struggling as a counselor for some of Northern California's most dangerous young criminals —he turned to fighting for victims of world conflict by organizing interfaith peace projects in the Holy Land."

sent me to the bathroom, where I vomited so hard that Sandra came running thinking I was having a heart attack. I was weak afterwards and didn't get much sleep. I awoke in a daze and my stomach ached. I was so angry at myself for being in such despicable shape for the first exam that I punched a hole in the wall. Sandra's petulant squint followed a frown and she shook her head as I stumbled out the door, headed for the first testing gauntlet.

At the end of the semester, the exam results were posted on the bulletin board.

I had failed to completely follow Professor Goldhirsch's advice as I received a lamentable collection of D's and F's, thus flunking every course except one: criminal law. Professor Moskovitz was the only one who saw any redeeming value in my work. He was perhaps prophetic, as we'll find out later.

I did not blame Sandra for the poor test scores but her constant suggestions to drop out became added pressure and contradicted my need to continue the fight. My motivation to be a lawyer was the only thing keeping me from dropping out; but she obviously did not accept that as justification for continuing the fight. To keep focused, I secretly derived a motto that I often repeated daily: "Fighting for myself without giving up would be the supreme test of my will to fight fervently for the rights of others."

As the first semester grades only accounted for 15% of the final grades, the second semester would be decisive. I needed to explode out of the starting gate after January to counteract the almost total failure of the previous semester. As such, I needed to ignore Sandra's comments that law school was too stressful and thus was bad "karma" because I was afraid I might start listening to her as I was definitely on the edge.

After we split up at the end of December, I moved into a one-room studio apartment in the same building and she moved into an old hotel-turned-rooming house closer to her job a few blocks away. My studio apartment included a bay window as it was located on the same side of the building as the one previously shared with Sandra. I had to walk down the hill daily to the financial district to attend school, about fifteen minutes away. When we were still together, Sandra would sometimes walk part of the way with me, until she would turn back up the hill, which would give me courage to tackle it. No more...it was over between us.

Chapter 4: The Mission

The second semester started and I had an early morning class. As I walked the early San Francisco streets, the stench of disinfectant burned my nostrils. I imagined that it was spilled onto the sidewalks to clean up the inner city street slime which had accumulated the night before. A pellucid morning light illuminated the city as the Pacific Ocean blew through its corridors, colder and more forlorn than before, because now, I walked alone.

I barely held on, alone now to fight the hell of law professors looking at me, demanding a response to their questions posed in the middle of an artificial Socratic dialogue, which I began to loath as it interrupted my inner musings. I was writing less and less poetry as my brain began to slide into the mold. I feared an artistic lobotomy as I grasped at some of the ideas I had pondered, such as the meaning of existence, while I was a philosophy student at the Sorbonne two years before I became a law student.

I did not remain distracted for long as a professor, miraculously reading my thoughts, would send a disdainful glance at my long hair (I had the longest hair of my classmates, even though it barely touched the top of my neck), with red, hateful eyes, admonishing me to pay attention and start looking and thinking like a lawyer. That triggered lugubrious thoughts about a couple of professors—notably my property professor, Levine—who would stand in front of us with a stuffy white shirt and red tie, demeaning us at every turn, insulting us, even ordering us to stand when addressing him. (I hated him then but commended him later when I realized that in spite of his ranting and raving, he had effectively prepared me for the California Bar exam, arguably the most difficult one in the US). Half-way through the year I vowed that the last thing I wanted to do was look like or think like him!

During the week, I attended classes and spent the rest of my time in the law library. I'd return from class to an empty apartment, quickly open the windows and look out over the skyline sitting listlessly, staring out the bay windows. The dense fog would roll in over the brow of the skyline as I sat there, deeply breathing in the crisp, salty San Francisco air before attacking the books…again.

The second year, I had to enroll in night school as I was flat broke and needed to work full-time. I signed up to work at the law library and started that morning, as well as continuing to work at Pillsbury, Madison & Sutro, a corporate law firm, afternoons.

My job was "roadman" (later changed to "road person"), which sent me daily to the courts to file documents. Classes were from 6:30 pm to 9:30, Monday through Friday nights. After that, I'd return to the apartment for a two-hour nap and then hit the law books again until 4 or 5 am. I'd be up again by 9 am and out the door at 9:30 am for work at the law library. I would catch up on sleep on weekends when I would sleep for twelve to fifteen hours at a stretch. It was a nonstop grind!

I would return nightly to a cold apartment, sometimes damp from the coastal humidity and heat up hot chocolate while resisting a telephone call to Sandra as I was adamant to go it alone, to keep the ambiance positive. Whenever I was tempted to call her, I would imagine her brow-beating me regarding my decision to stay in school, and that I could not bear again. Dropping out was simply NOT an option. Since it would be too tempting to quit, I had to insulate myself, as much as possible, from any thoughts of quitting, hence of her.

In spite of my obstinate attempts to stay in law school, I got kicked out at the end of the second year because I failed one course. It was a remedies class that was almost exclusively taken by students in their last year. I knew I shouldn't have taken the course as I wasn't ready to compete with students who had survived all the years of trimming down the student population through drop-outs and expulsions. But I was carried away by hubris after I passed all my first-year courses, except for one, so I thought I was untouchable. Overconfidence eliminated me...a lesson I learned the hard way.

In the fall of the year following that disaster, I petitioned for re-admittance, along with some 25 other expelled students. Failure to be reinstated meant, I was told, that it would be very difficult to be accepted at another ABA law school (first rate law school) and would have to be content to seek enrollment at a second rate school. After a two-month proceeding, including an oral interview with the academic dean, only two students out of the twenty-five were reinstated, and I was one of them. I worked the rest of the fall semester as I was only allowed to enroll again in the spring quarter. After being kicked out once, I was adamant not to let it happen again; if so, I swore, they would have to drag me out kicking and screaming.

I now had several months to work and save money. I worked during the week and locked myself in my apartment on weekends to read, study Spanish and meditate. My new project was to learn Spanish, which helped me resist calling Sandra, but loneliness was breaking me down. I was desperate to change the scenery, even for a couple of hours on a Friday night.

After a late shift working at the law library, I took a bus in front of the law school on Mission Street, instead of routinely locking myself in my apartment, and ventured toward the "Barrio Latino" (Latino district), where I eventually found solace. I wanted to hear "live" Spanish and sought to immerse myself in a different culture. As the bus rumbled down Mission Street, I fantasized that I was traveling to a foreign country. For some reason, I needed to feel the excitement and intrigue of being a stranger, a foreigner again, as I had been a few years before in Paris and during my travels to Northern Africa. I was not disappointed.

On the bus, two short Latinos were sharing headphones, listening to music full of drums and percussion instruments as their heads bobbed up and down like river castors; their bodies swayed like African tribal dancers whose pulse jumped involuntarily to the beat of bush congas. I followed them out when the bus stopped on 24th and Mission Street, into the streets filled with more music, pouring out of bistros and the open windows of passing cars. Entire families walked the sidewalks, returning from an evening service at a local church or a nearby restaurant. I walked and walked, traveling down Mission Street, the main street, until I reached a place marked by a sign, "El Zocalo."

Several rickety wooden chairs formed a half-circle at the counter where several men were munching on thick crepes. A waitress, her dark hair tied in a bun highlighted by a red ribbon, spoke several incomprehensible words to me in rapid Spanish. I shook my head, "No comprendo."

"Here, menu...."

Her lips curled into a smile and she bent over, slightly biting her lower lip in an almost motherly way, reaching out. I took it. A dark man wearing a cowboy hat was sitting a couple of seats to my left in the corner and spooning large mouthfuls of soup into his wide mouth. From time to time, his gold teeth flashed as he opened wide for another spoonful. He looked up, a menacing scowl appearing over his soup bowl. I pretended I did not notice as I turned the page of the menu. Peeking over the top of the menu I noticed dark-haired ladies, wearing white aprons splattered by brown and reds, their hair tied in a series of tight braids flowing down. They were lined up in front of a long table in back of the service counter patting the dough into a pancake-like shape, like the Mexican women patting rounds of dough into tortillas all afternoon on 24th Street. But there was a major difference between the two rounds of dough: these were thicker as these Salvadorian crepes were either filled with cheese, meat or both.

The waitress came by and I pointed to the plate of a husky, short-haired man with pudgy cheeks eating the crepe.

"Pupusas? Meat, queso, ah cheese?" "Si"

She nodded and went to the kitchen. In a few minutes a plate of thick meat and cheese pupusas was slipped in front of me alongside a dish of "ensalada de col" (cabbage salad). It tasted a bit like coleslaw.

In the meantime, the man in the corner sat down beside me, wiping his mouth with his shirt sleeve. His moustache was moist, drooping over the corners of his mouth. He leaned over me as I cut the cheese pupusa in two parts. I tried to nonchalantly pop one piece into my mouth, but part of it dropped to my plate; I could see his brow furrowing. His eyes followed my every move. "You know something, Gringo, people here serious. People above," he motioned wildly, pointing towards the street, "have knives. The people below," he pointed in the opposite direction, "have guns."

Even though his words sent electrical charges down my spinal column, making me tap my foot on the linoleum, I tried to cover it up by keeping time to the beat of the mariachi music in the background as I focused on my newly found "délice" (bliss). I succeeded in flashing a naive smile, although nerves began causing my lips to twitch at the corners. Fortunately he didn't notice it. His words having no palpable affect, he shifted back to his corner and began nursing a bottle of Dos XX beer. He looked away, totally ignoring me. I breathed out slowly as I poked at the cabbage salad with my fork.

This new and foreign world piqued my interest and I began looking forward to weekends, especially since I had finally found a way to avoid thinking about Sandra. I continued walking the streets on Fridays and Saturdays, listening to this musical Spanish language which emanated from buildings, cars, and the mouths of Latino families scurrying about, carrying bags full of fruit, corn and tortillas. Signs in Spanish were scattered everywhere, in windows, roosting on top of doors: "tortillas baratas" (cheap tortillas), "Pollo Loco" (crazy chicken) and "Joyería" (jewelry store).

A large white sign "sopa des rez" (beef soup) was taped to a window, behind which was a mural splashed with violets, reds and blues in the forms of yawning tropical flowers, with green stems stretching across the wall. I walked in and sat down. In a few minutes, I was dipping my spoon into a large bowl with huge chunks of beef, slices of yucca and chayote.

I later ducked into a Latino bistro and sat next to a group of mariachi musicians at the bar, wearing grey or black tight pants with two rows of parallel silver buttons linked by silver strands running down the sides of both pant legs and swirling white designs; their guitars were suspended from colorful neck bands and silver trumpets lay on the bar. Their black jackets were adorned with parallel silver buttons on the sleeves, and linked by silver threads like the ones on their pants. The musicians were turned to the front of the bar, busy wolfing down enchiladas and tacos before the next gig. Their black sombreros—the edges twisted with bright silver sequins, silver tassels suspended by silver meshing from the top and adorned with lines of finely designed silver at the edges—lay across their laps or strewn over the bar.

Even though I was still an outsider, especially since my Spanish hadn't evolved much, I began immersing myself into the "barrio." One night I walked into a local bistro where two men with loose, white shirts and red bandanas around their necks wearing wide-brimmed, grey sombreros sang folk songs in Spanish. Their smiles radiated through the waves of the music, bringing pedestrians within hearing distance to a full stop to listen, as the night was full of rhythmic strumming, bringing old tunes from the hills into the light. The warmth of the culture and the people here began creeping under my skin, slowly replacing my lonely Nob Hill existence and the bleak coldness of the financial district.

I hung out for periods of time at the Mission Cultural Center on Mission Street, where a Latino theater group would perform. One day when I arrived at about 12 midnight in front, there was a group of dark-hued people leaving through the main door and grouping into a circle on the sidewalk. I moved toward the circle which opened for me to join in. They did not recoil. I asked a young, bright-eyed man holding a bow what they had been doing. He responded in almost perfect English that they had been playing music for a Brazilian capoeira group. He said his name was Jorge R.

"I'm Frank, Francesco."

"Italiano?"

"Italo-Americano. And you?"

"Salvadoreño."

Jorge R. and I became friends. In fact, after that moment, we met once weekly in a local café; I usually bought him a beer in exchange for an hour of Spanish conversation.

He told me that he was a refugee from El Salvador and that he had to leave his country with his family due to the relentless violence there. One night he invited me to a Latino party where I met many Chileans, Salvadorians, Mexicans, Nicaraguans, Argentinians, Chicanos, Puerto Ricans and "Brasileiros." (Brazilians)

The week after that, I noticed in the law school newspaper an ad placed by an adjunct law professor asking for candidates to work as law clerks in a political asylum clinic connected to the law school. Because I could speak a little Spanish, I was hired by the lawyer/teacher at the Political Asylum Law Project for Salvadorians in the Mission District. It was sponsored by the Catholic Church and located in back of one of its branches in the Latino District. I remember my first job, which was to interview a Salvadorian refugee seeking political asylum to determine if we could represent him. I entered a room in the clinic expecting to work with the lead attorney in the case. Only one person was waiting for me, a slender Latino male, the potential client. His name was Alfredo Rodriquez. My Spanish had improved, but that day I was put to the ultimate test as I was the only person there to understand his story.

From that day forward, I worked as a law clerk at the clinic and even assisted the managing attorney during the hearings. At Alfredo's initial asylum hearing, I was accepted by the judge to work with the lead attorney and appointed a "certified law student" by the judge, which meant I could represent our client at the hearing. I did the direct examination of Alfredo with the lead attorney next to me, helping me with objections and other procedures. It was the most meaningful and enlightening part of the law school experience, not to mention my first trial lawyer experience. I learned best under fire, anyway....

I sometimes worked the Friday late night shift at the law library when I didn't have any classes that night. As I got off work, the entire week would fall on me with a heavy thud; but I just couldn't go home and go to sleep. After my shift ended around 9 pm one night, the void of being alone rocked my tired frame. Before taking the bus, I picked up a fifth of brandy at a local liquor store on Mission Street and then ran to grab the Mission bus which was gliding away from the bus stop. I slapped the side of the bus, which stopped in its tracks. The black bus driver shook his head and his white teeth spread across his face as I opened the door.

"Thanks," I said. He nodded and as I reached in my pocket for change, the brandy slipped out of the brown paper bag and hit the rubber floor with a thump.

His chuckle followed me down the aisle after I dropped the fare in the box.

I got off the bus at 24th and Mission, to the familiar smells of fried meat and corn tortillas permeating the air; excited Spanish sounds were everywhere, taking me on a cultural carpet ride. I walked into the corner of a closed barber shop and took out the bottle. I unscrewed it, keeping it hidden within the confines of the brown paper bag and took a long swig.

People were walking in groups; a cute Mexican girl, her long hair tied in pig tails secured with yellow ribbons, swayed back and forth as she skipped behind her parents. They were carrying Bibles so I assumed they would soon be proselytizing, setting up behind a microphone on the street corner and handing out brochures, praising the Lord in Spanish, over and over again. My body automatically zeroed in and turned in the direction of the corner taqueria where I found the best burritos in town, huge and dripping with guacamole, queso, rice and "carne de cabeza" (meat from cow jowls). Ahhhh, another "délice"! It nourished my hungry soul and at least temporarily filled me with exotic tastes, along with the refried beans.

On my way out of the taqueria, I noticed that, sure enough, the family had set out a table with bibles on it. The father was reciting verses in Spanish over a taped microphone connected to a small loudspeaker that buzzed. He should have worn a t-shirt saying "Made in the Mission"; it was all part of it and I loved it. My lingering financial district trepidation began to slowly dissipate as I stepped lively down the street.

I walked into Café de la Bohème where I hoped to meet some of my friends from Central, South America, Mexico and Europe—all from other worlds. I needed the warmth of a smile, poetic words from my Mexican troubadour, songs from another Salvadorian, Jorge A., and philosophy from my Gualtemalteco conspirator, Victor Hugo. I crossed my fingers that one would be hanging out. As I slipped through the wooden passageway, my face was slapped with the warmth of the coffee machine, the rich scent of Brazilian coffee and brown sugar-rimmed cups. That would be my medicine for the night as I slipped the bag and brandy into my book bag.

My head did not desperately swivel around for long looking for a soul partner; surrounding a table in the middle of the café were several of my friends. A couple of carafes of wine were in the middle of the table.

I joined in as Jorge A. was singing folk songs by Silvio Rodríguez Domínguez, sensitive romantic melodies from the streets of Havana that "déchire le coeur et qui me déchire aussi" (are heartrending and also tear me apart); frozen, I was forced to sit on the nearest stool. My Mexican soul man, Isaac from Jalisco, put his hand on my shoulder and observing my inward withdrawal, withdrew it, nodding while leaving me in my contemplative space. He then backed up to sit by a couple of new girls dancing together next to the table. One was a young girl with dark-brown hair wearing black boots and jeans. Her red cheeks and fair skin hinted at a Nordic extraction while the young lady she was dancing with was beaming, shining as bright as her smile which revealed bright white teeth contrasting with her black lipstick. Her body moved with the sad tunes. But for some reason, she seemed different than the others.

Then the nightmarish evenings with Sandra—discotheque hopping to the crescendo of the music, revving up the music madness until I couldn't stand it blasting in my ears—invaded my thoughts. "This is such a mellower scene," I whispered to myself, almost out of breath.

Those surrounding the guitarist were a mixture of Latinos and Spaniards; Jorge R, as usual, was in the midst of it all, with a couple of girls at each side. He was busy talking to them and putting out his cigarettes in the ashtrays. The music seemed to have everyone mesmerized, on a Caribbean wavelength, as the other patrons were peering over their books and even interrupting their conversations.

There was omnipresent Isaac, again, with his beaming smile, his dark but strangely freckled face turning to someone. As I got closer, his dark, shiny hair loosely falling down his neck stood out like a sign post. He spotted me weaving through the tables and let out a long siren sound, vibrating his tongue at the end.

He stood up, knocking over a chair, let out a hoarse yelp, grabbed my two hands in his and pulled me to his table.

"Hey hermano, brrrrrrrrrrro, que paso? Good to see you, meeeeeeeeeeeeeeen!"

Next to him was seated Rogelio, who was next to José and Jorge R. Some were drinking Dos XX; others held a coffee mug with coffee splattering down the sides. Isaac was reciting poetry written in Jalisco, hitting me hard as he portrayed a sunny afternoon in his homeland, in the country, bringing back memories of the northern California countryside where I was raised. I spent years working on chicken farms building chicken coops, preparing the vineyards for the grape harvest by breaking down the grooves left by the tractors with a heavy metal mattock, waking up to the cock crowing and to homemade pancakes at five am and starting work as the sun came up, looking over the fields in the naked, crisp morning air. Even though my hands were often blue with cold, the smell of the earth, with a backdrop of the orange-yellow sun creeping up over the hills, settled in me like a slow-moving river. This would always represent a better world somewhere deep in my heart, where the country boy was always to be found. It was something I could depend on as I would return often to this place imbedded deep in the grooves of my mind's terrain.

Isaac picked up his paper and reached out to grab up my hand as he was leading me out of the café, following Rogelio and company. We walked towards the outer Mission. Every time we passed a bar, the ambient cumbia or merengue music would blare out of the speakers and we'd walk to the beat of it: "Bomp pa ta tom, ta tom, bomp pa ta tom"…It carried me into a new world…a new planet.

"Please take me away," I whispered to myself.

We walked side by side, two by two, the bodies becoming blurred, walking in the night on Mission Street. I was hitched to a healing wagon—I could feel my ethereal being heal its parts, my mind becoming whole and my body regaining its feeling.

My rebirthing continued until we turned up a street a couple of blocks after passing the huge salsa nightclub called Cesar's Palace. Salsa caliente was blaring over the loudspeakers and spilling into the streets; but no one in this group turned his head. As if in a trance, we headed uphill away from the nightclub until Rogelio stopped in front of an unassuming white house, in shadows. He walked down a narrow path bordered by short tufts of grass crowned with violet wildflowers on the left side of the house and then turned and waved for us to join him.

We followed single file down the pathway, our black shoes making muffled clomping as we sauntered toward an open door; the sound of cumbia music became increasingly louder as we approached. Then the door opened wide and a short, dark-haired girl, waved to us. She was attractive; her alluring dark, sleek skin deflected my eyes from a slightly darkened tooth peering from slightly drawn lips.

The door then flung open and two girls danced through the doorway, one slender with tawny hair and the other hefty as she bounced across the floor, thrashing her long, black hair. The tawny-haired one reached out and grabbed my hand, dragging me inside.

"Venga!" she said, with a slight accent.

I entered a small dance floor; at the head of it was a short, stocky man pouring glasses of wine from a two-gallon carton. It was red rot-gut but it helped slide down tampanadas offered at the bar for a couple of dollars. The short, dark-haired girl served me. After I had taken a swig, she said,

"Soy Teresa, Colombiana y seas bienvenido." (I am Columbian and I welcome you.)

How I got to the dance floor I'll never know, and even less how I found myself twirling around a short-haired American girl, the one who had said "Venga!" at the door. But there we were, in the middle of the dance floor, dancing to a sumptuous cumbia turned salsa. I was in heavy street salsa mode, but the music took me far away, making it more difficult to follow my street salsa as all the rules would give way to a fluid stream of wildly creative dancing. That did not seem to bother her as she seemed at ease and incredibly flexible with my chaotic street style and my sometimes futile attempts to be a strong lead as the music took me away.

It seemed that the more I made up new dance steps, the weirder they were, the more she stepped up and added her own, while flowing with mine as we glided over the dance floor. I bent her head back over my arm in a tango move until her hair almost swept the floor; then she let herself go in my arms and was strangely unafraid of falling, even though she didn't know me.

So strange, so incredible! Who is this woman?

The music gripped me and made my feet move spontaneously, mixing steps to the American swing, French rock, sometimes tango, with salsa. Each time she moved with it and even added her own twirl, while even twirling me a couple of times. We kept going like that until I noticed we were the only couple dancing as the music had stopped. But the powerful vibes were still in our heads. We sat down, sweat pouring down and dripping onto the wood floor as Samantha, my dance partner, introduced me to the bubbly Jewish-American, Rina, the husky one sitting next to her Guatemalan friend, Antonio.

Then Jorge R. interrupted, and nodded toward the bar. We shifted towards the line of wine glasses filled with the red liquid. I ordered two glasses and paid for them, one of his perks for being my Spanish language coach. He took a swig and then went back and grabbed Samantha who jumped to her feet and followed the Salvadorian, who made it a point to show me his more refined, or perhaps more orthodox, dancing moves.

Next to me was Concepción, a plump and lively Latina with golden-brown hair flowing down over her bare shoulders. She smiled coquettishly as I put down my wine glass. She then covered my hand with hers, gently tugging me to the dance floor where she broke out into a Columbian folk dance, bending down so far that her hair almost touched the floor as she swayed back and forth. I melted into intoxicating passion as the wine, I was convinced, helped me to glide, to soar, to remain there, returning to earth another time, hopefully in a day or so.

I needed to soar, to glide, to feel free, as if I needed to escape something…I could hear the violent San Francisco wind beat the walls even though the music was several decibels.

Being swept into the sea of music, smiles and wine was the mélange on the dance floor. Then the singer, in the middle of a strong salsa, blurted out "Viva Columbia, El Salvador, Argentina, Guatemala, Mexico, Italia…." after every country named, yells and clapping. When Italia was yelled out, everyone turned to me and I yelled out "Bravo!" They considered me more "Italiano" than Americano sometimes, and I was proud of my Italian roots, but I'm also proud of my British background on my mother's side; this crowd seemed only interested in my Italian side.

After about an hour, the music stopped and I looked around to meet new people. They came from all over the world, from South and Central America, as well as Europe. I was lost in my own country, recuperating from the bohemian but meaningful lifestyle that I had lived in Paris. They also seemed lost here, but somehow we meshed and they accepted me, for whatever, whoever I was.

The next moment, I was headed out the door, with Rogelio in the lead, followed by me, then José. Somehow we lost Isaac and I hadn't spotted Jorge R. in a while and had no idea where he had gone. This place was in constant motion, with people coming and going.

We headed down the road back to the center, to Mission Street. I was feeling a bit weary and hungry. As we returned, I noticed the tables on one side of the street that were behind glass walls looked familiar. The same long table where the Latinas were patting the flour rounds into pupusas jarred my thoughts of the past, taking me back to my first visit to the Mission. It was "El Zocalo," which I hadn't visited since that baptismal day…seemingly light years away.

We arranged ourselves around a table and ate pupusas. Rogelio ate Salvadorian nachos, a mixture of dark beans mixed with melted cheese. He dug his chips in and pulled out a clump of beans that he quickly closed his mouth around. Rogelio, smacking his lips, spoke first as José and I buried ourselves in the pupusas and "ensalada de col."

"I've been thinking a long time about forming a street theatre group; would you be interested?"

José looked up as he sliced open a cheese pupusa and spooned in a layer of "ensalada de col." We formed that night a street theater group called Tupac Amaru[7], directed by Rogelio.

My first performance was at the El Salvador Cultural Center; its members were active in the Salvadorian civil war fighting the U.S.-sponsored military-led government.

I recited poetry by Mario Benedetti, a Uruguayan writer/activist whose work I had memorized in Spanish. By the time I rose to recite the poem, a crowd had

---

7   Tupac Amaru was a leader of the Incan Empire in Peru that fought against Spain in the 16th century.

gathered in support of the Salvadorian people in their struggles against oppression during the war. Samantha showed up and her blue eyes blinked with the fear I would flub up, as she would tell me afterwards, especially since I was reciting a poem in Spanish. But I immersed myself fully in the work, about love and revolution; by the time I reached the last stanza I had worked up to a frenzy and the sweat poured off my face as if from a wound sustained during the atrocities committed in El Salvador.

In the end, the people clapped and I sat down. Rogelio put his arm over my shoulder on one side and José did the same on the other side. I was also flattered by a handshake and a hug from Amilka C., an important member of a family profoundly active in the liberation of El Salvador from the grips of the cruel military government.

Afterwards, other people recited poetry and a group from Mexico sang a folk song to close out the event.

After that day, I was indelibly connected with the world in the heart of the Latino community. It was total therapy being in the Mission away from the financial district, away from the blinding, crunching stress of the clanking of doors, bank vaults, computer trays, where the money runs and delivery boys ride erratically, weaving in and out of traffic and its infernal honking. Downtown San Francisco was where the white collars mingled with panhandlers, their hands aggressively jutting into your face, disguised entrepreneurs, but I felt compassion; at least they needed to eat...it wasn't about out-consuming their neighbor. I was out of place hanging out among the early morning cable car bells, resounding among the empty streets at 6:00 am, through the dismal alleyways and up and over the bounding hills.

I took a Greyhound to visit my parents in the Southern Oregon mountains for the weekend, far away from the relentless shine of city lights. After an all-night bus ride returning from the visit, I pulled my suitcase up Powell Street. The last of Saturday night party goers were munching on pizza wedges at an all-night store; others who had nowhere to go, shifted up and down the sidewalks, trying to show to themselves that anywhere is not nowhere, but somewhere. It was the cusp of the Tenderloin, well-named as girls catcalled from the shadows of the indented doorways while I strolled upwards toward my studio at the foot of Nob Hill.

As I reached the top of the first block, I approached the second level of ravenous prostitutes, now standing on the corners and focusing mainly on Johns driving by. Pimps also drove by in their slick Cadillacs, some wearing white suits, others subdued silver and black, sometimes stopping and chatting with their prostitutes. It was the ugly downtown emptiness scraping at my insides, pleading for something to "hang my hat on" when I found no hat rack. Nowhere in this empty jungle. The only thing sustaining me was my low whistling of a song, and my obstinate head determined to see, to focus on the sky somewhere hidden above, enveloped in the mournful morning haze. I kept plugging along in this lonely morning air, just kept going....

Another block went by and I started to cross the intersection when a sleek, black Cadillac stopped and parked in front of me, in the middle of the intersection. I looked around for police cars; nary a one, as usual, in this district. A long, black, violet-rimmed pimp hat was poking out the window, its owner engaged in an argument with a plump, blond working girl. She ended up approaching his vehicle, opening her purse and giving the man something, after which the idling engine slammed into gear, grinding up Powell Street.

I didn't want to see that...I denied seeing it as I focused on the white sheaves of seagulls flying overhead, calling on their way to the Bay while mangy pigeons dropped down from their perches onto the pavement, pushing dried pizza crusts with their crooked beaks. Their deformed, often stubby instead of fully-formed feet, trembled as they curled inwards and were dragged along the heartless streets at three a.m.

It was now so quiet that I could hear them pushing their prizes, grating over the cement with their beaks sometimes hitting the pavement. They moved in rhythm with the sound of my shoes carrying me up the hill to my awaiting cold apartment, to get a few hours sleep before heading back down the same stretch to my first class.

I passed by the hotel where Sandra was sleeping, maybe rising in few hours, drinking her organic tea, before walking to the health food store a block away. A nostalgic shiver jostled my soul as I climbed the street, remembering that not long ago our lives were so closely entangled, the sweat pouring down our bodies a couple of blocks away, not long ago, but so long ago...I walked into the blue sky, up and up to the top of Nob Hill as the morning sun presented its golden face, sending shafts that bounced off buildings, finally reaching me—unmoved and removed as my only focus was to throw my body down on the bed.

I couldn't sleep right away and scribbled down these words:

> What did it feel like? To be in love
> Us two
> In the city
> Running from building to building
> Searching for tenderness
> Caring
> Trying not to play the games
> But playing them anyway
> I stopped to think How lucky I was You were here
> To share the masked face of the city
> quick minds and fast tempers
> Where the money flowed
> Where the street people scratched, looking for scraps of food in the
>   garbage leaning over, busily rummaging
> You chased the lonely spirit from me lurking—bouncing from one
>   side of the street to the other
> We weathered it but our time had come to flee and refresh the
>   wayward heart palpitated again—
> Breaking from the clotted rut that we were getting into
> Yet the warmth of your being is missed

> So missed—that I imagine you are here
> Sometimes next to me just to make me feel secure again
>
> Are you there?
> Next to me holding my hand telling me…it's OK.[8]

That was the elixir as I curled up with moist eyes and somehow fell into a deep, confused sleep.

---

8 Frank Romano, from the poem, "City," p.24. Crossing Over, supra.

Chapter 5: Rosalia

It was late when I arrived at Café de la Bohème on 24th Street which had become our usual hangout. As I crossed the threshold into the hold of the café, I searched for a familiar smile. Being so late, and in the middle of the week, none of my friends were there. As I sat looking out the window nursing my café, looking out over the increasingly vacant street, a scrawny Salvadorian slipped in next to me. Ricardo C's broad smile flashed at me.

"Que pasa, man?" "Nada, y tu?" "Vamanos!"

He took my hand in his usual subtle way and we walked out the door; as he accelerated, he dropped my hand while we walked up 22nd Street; I had no idea where we were going. Suddenly, he stopped in front of a door from which smoke poured out; he opened it and blue smoke billowed out, thicker as he stepped inside. He looked back at me...my cue to enter.

I followed him into a large room with tables on both sides; I didn't have to walk far to feel the warmth. Isaac was there and reached out, strongly clasping my hand, "Hey maan, good to see you," he greeted me, then imitated a siren and noises like those of a pinball machine, in a bar.

It was his way to make sarcastic imitations of the glitzy, modern, impersonal world turned into a technology swamp. Spontaneous poetry!

I continued to walk towards a bar straight ahead, passing another table where Rogelio was sitting by himself, emitting a curl of smoke. His eyes met mine, he nodded, then looked toward the smoke. I didn't interrupt his inner musing.

I continued walking and a huge-jawed man smiled, his thick lips stretched across his face, bridging his two plump cheeks. I had never met him. His hands moved in long, sweeping gestures, like he was cleaning a window. His bloated, bibulous face squeezed his eyes into their sockets as he looked up and spoke to an adolescent with light-brown hair sitting next to him: "Hhhhhhhhhhhhhhhhey, cabrón!"

Then he reached out to shake my hand. "Hola, I'm Robinson, Chileno."

(Chilean)

"Hi, nice to meet you," I responded, before I could continue the formalities.

But Robinson helped me dispense with them by grabbing my hand and putting his arm around me. His red cheeks screamed to the world that he was very drunk.

His smile widened as saliva formed at the corners of his mouth. "You know, I heard about you in theatre group, and you American." He nodded at Rogelio sitting opposite the table. Rogelio nodded back.

I didn't know what was happening in this place. I detached myself from his tourniquet grip and headed to the bar where Teresa, the Columbian, waited.

She must have seen my scowl.

"Hi, Francesco. After Bernal Heights, thought we'd open our own place here." José stood next to me listening, whistling approval through his teeth.

"Hey we got our own place, own, Bbbrrrrrrrrrroo!"

I looked around at the many familiar faces, all amassed together under one roof. That explained why no one was hanging out at Café de la Bohème; the entire gang was camping out here. I had to get used to new things sprouting up and realized that I would only find out about them, like this new place, if I hung around. No one was going to call me or wait for me to show up after work late on Fridays to lead me to this new, hush hush place. The buzz word here was total spontaneity— overly-planned events or orchestrated happenings would stifle creativity. This was a purposefully, spontaneously generated world that people preserved to counterbalance the linear clanking of the mechanized world, where even emotions ran "on schedule." It turned out that the owners of this business were the same ones who owned the house where we had met for dancing and drinking the other night.

It was called "Café Macondo."[9]

"Bienvenido, Francesco. Adelante!" the bartender exclaimed, as she moved the lever over a glass, filling it with wine.

Next to the bar a group of girls, their long brown hair streaming down their sides, were dancing to an African beat blasting out of the loudspeakers positioned behind the bar.

I put down two dollars and turned to walk down the aisle between the tables; everyone seemed to be too consumed in their discussions to notice me so I kept walking, enjoying a moment of being incognito. Then I shuffled over to where the girls had been dancing and sat down at their table. They were still smiling and gesticulating in circles, like southern Italians. The girl with dark-brown hair introduced herself as Rosalia, from Andalusia, the south of Spain, and Gloria, from somewhere in the north, near Bilbao, the Basque country.

I sat down next to Rosalia. It turned out we had at least one thing in common: a desire to explore another part of town, North Beach, the Italian district. A couple of nights later, I took her out of the Mission to a salsa dancing place on the other side of town, between Nob Hill and North Beach.

That night marked the moment we became inseparable for the next two years.

During the week, I trudged through the swamps of law school, stumbling, sputtering, falling, getting up and hacking the underbrush—that is, the cans and other rubbish collecting in the streets of the lower Mission—on my way to pick up Rosalia at her job at Café Picaro on 16th Street, catering to Bohemians, Latinos and others.

Late on Friday nights, I would walk down Mission Street towards Café Picaro from the room I had recently rented on 22nd and Capp Streets. On my way, I passed

---

9   Named after a town in One Hundred Years of Solitude, by Gabriel Garcia Marquez.

the usual lower Mission street scene: prostitutes slinking in the corners, drug dealers rushing to make deals, Latino immigrants trying to get by selling tacos and popsicles on the streets, pulling around their portable ovens and freezers. I admired their industrious spirit, selling their wares as they roamed the streets with their heads up and bells jingling to announce their presence. They probably only made pennies, but every penny was used to feed the mouths of their hungry children, one penny at a time. One night as I turned up 16th Street, I saw three police officers interrogating a fallen man, one of his pants legs ripped opened, revealing a line of three gunshot wounds, as confirmed by a local bystander.

When I finally reached the café, Rosalia's smile was there always to greet me, her worn lipstick peeling but courageously, like her, hanging on. From the moment I saw her, everything became real, allowing me to blur the cruel street scenes. If we weren't too tired, sometimes we'd get together with a group of Latinos, Spaniards and other Europeans for poetry readings or music concerts in one of the local cafés. Other times we'd take a bus across town to a Spanish café at Fisherman's Wharf and spend an evening clapping to the gypsy tunes of invited Flamenco musicians. After that, we'd always end the evening hanging out in an Italian café to sip a cappuccino before closing, then back to the Mission on the late-night bus to our room.

The next day I'd return to the law school gauntlet, the law firm and law library jobs during the week. Rosalia made it survivable, especially since she was now sharing my room with me. Sometimes I overheard her conversations with Spanish friends who'd visit us and sit on the bed drinking coffee with her while I studied, as usual, behind the faded white curtains next to the bed.

"How can you stand living in this little dump?" they'd ask.

After they left, I'd take a break and we'd drink coffee and cuddle for a while until I slid behind the curtains again. Sometimes we'd take a nap together. One time I awoke and saw Rosalia's eyes sadly regarding the cracks on the ceiling: "You know, it's a small place, but if we fill it with love, it's already more than most cold castles have, with no love."

And she put her fingers over my lips and kissed my cheek before we fell asleep. She'd heard many times before the derogatory comments of others, but she never complained that we lived in a hole. We'd fall asleep in each other's arms, in peaceful transition from the negative vibes brought by her friends. But more challenges were around the corner. One night we were talking at Café Macondo, and across from me, I could feel two hateful red eyes staring at me. I looked up and saw a dark, young man, staring full face at me, a red bandana tied around his neck. His lips curled up in derision. "Hey Gringo, you speak Spanish, huh? You think you know something about us—you know nothing. I'm Nicaraguense and I'm proud!" (Nicaraguan)

He turned and smiled at Rosalia, who turned to me, her brow creased as she was confused by his hostility. All of a sudden, loud cumbia music filled the room and the angry man stood up but before he reached Rosalia, I turned my back on him, pivoted and stood in front of her, grabbing both of her hands as I pulled her to the dance floor. "Cabrón...." I could hear the words trail off, interrupted by the entrance of my

Spanish language tutor, Jorge R. "Hey, amigo." Jorge R. was also Central American, arriving at the right moment to distract the angry man.

"Está loco." (He's crazy) Rosalia watched me, shaking her dark-brown curls as we clasped our hands in cumbia rhythm, which transitioned into a slow dance. She responded to Jorge, "Está raro. Gracias!" (He's weird. Thanks!) and continued but her voice fell off.

As I danced slowly with Rosalia, the corner of my eye noted the man who was pointing at me, yelling epithets as Jorge R. tried to talk to him, to calm him down. Finally, Jorge pulled him toward the door, opened it and dragged him out.

But that was not the last of him.

The next weekend on Saturday night, Rosalia and I were seated in Café Macondo, this time with a group of Spanish friends. The angry man with the red bandana, a cigarette dangling from his lips, walked up to the bar. He then approached us with his glass of wine and sat in an empty seat on the other side of the table. Beads of sweat showed on his smooth forehead sloping down from strands of his black hair drawn back into a short pony tail.

My eyes flashed in the direction of the man but Rosalia brushed it off as she handed the blue package of Dulcados to me. They were Spanish cigarettes and although I was not a smoker, I had told her I wanted to try one. I lit one up and could barely inhale it as the smoke made my throat feel like sandpaper on fire. I rested the cigarette in the ashtray.

The insidious man reached over and put out his cigarette in the ashtray, knocking my half-smoked cigarette to the floor; then he stood up and moved toward Rosalia. The smoke made me cough uncontrollably which made me slow to react. He was suddenly standing in front of her, speaking to her in rapid Spanish and I saw her shake her head. He grabbed her hands, pulling her up and to the dance floor.

Blood rushed to my head as I stood up and started to follow. Out of the blue, Jorge R. was in front of me, holding up his hands trying to stop me. As I crashed into the palms of his hands they did not give way. "Hey amigo, déja-lo bailar una vez con ella. Está peligroso, este Nicaraguense: Revolutionario. Déja-lo." (Hey friend, let him dance with her one time. This Nicaraguan is dangerous: revolutionary. Let it go.) He screwed his face up in a typical expression, with lips down-turned and his palms turned upwards, as if pleading me to let go, that it was unimportant or harmless.

I approached the dance floor and saw him twirling Rosalia, in tropical fast movements, but his rhythm was impeccable and Rosalia was flowing with it. My cheeks enflamed with jealous anger. He returned her to where I was sitting and went to the bar for another drink. I didn't see him again that night.

That summer, we decided to visit Rosalia's Spain. We woke up early to take the shuttle to the airport. The streets were full of masked people, painted in yellows, greens and reds; the air was full of the enchilada picante smells of revolution. The Cinco de Mayo celebration had brought a huge crowd of people but our intrepid shuttle wove in and out to get to Cézar Chavez Street and then to the freeway.

From our very first arrival in Madrid, a contingent was there to greet us. As soon as we exited the plane, three sets of handkerchiefs waved in front of us, accompanied by smiles as wide as the Mediterranean, stretched over a myriad of signs saying "Rosalia and Francisco". Her white-haired, dark-skinned father was the first to reach Rosalia, and her heavy-set mother panted as she followed close behind, one hand holding a gypsy fan, frantically fanning herself and her husband, soon in Rosalia's arms. Then came her tall, lean, short-haired brother, a law student, and the only one flashing a tight smile. The father, while hugging her daughter, held me close with his left hand. The mother then stepped towards me, her warm, dark eyes following mine as she held my hand.

We were whisked away into the streets of Madrid, dodging in and out of the typical fast-flowing, crazy European traffic and across to the highway, which took us across Spain to Murcia, where the family had its homestead. It was heaven for three weeks, surrounded by tapas bars, music and the constant flow of smiling faces and gypsy influences. The family apartment was overlooking a huge square in the middle of the city, not far from open-air markets. We'd descend the stairs around lunchtime, do our shopping in the markets before they closed and then did what I called "the tapas stomp." We'd head first for the tapas bar displaying bowls placed one alongside the other, heaped with paella, rice and bits of fish, crab meat and chicken. Then we'd run to my favorite place for "patatas alioli," Spain's amazing potatoes smothered with garlic mayonnaise, then move to "gambas al ajillo," grilled gigantic prawns with garlic, parsley and olive oil.

We would cap lunch off with a strong Spanish carajillo (espresso coffee mixed with brandy). The first night we went to a wedding and danced the classic Flamenco and the newer Sevillanas in the town square. Rosalia's family, its roots from Andalusia, in the heat of southern Spain, spread across the dance floor. First, her mother jumped to the middle of the dance floor, twirling around as if she were possessed by the gyrating spirit of an old Spanish gypsy. Then her father swung her around, both of them emitting sparks as hot as Mediterranean red peppers across the floor, as a Spanish flamenco guitarist pounded blood-pulsing rhythms on the strings.

But my trip was destined to end abruptly. The third week, I called my mother, who told me that my Father, afflicted by deadly cirrhosis of the liver,[10] had taken a turn for the worse and was going downhill. I made out from her trembling voice that Dad refused to continue taking his life-saving medicine, a sickly-sweet syrup called Lactulose, since the sugary substance made him sick and lose his appetite. But, between intermittent sobs, I understood that the medicine was the only thing that could rid him of toxins, thus helping to somewhat restore the function of the liver and if he didn't drink it, he would surely die. Her voice trailed away and I could hear faint sobbing. Mom never complained, never lamented like that; but it was

10 As my Dad only drank one glass of wine per day and only with dinner, and never was drunk nor was an alcoholic, the doctors surmised that he contracted cirrhosis in an extraordinary way: During war II, while serving as a US Army officer near the Philippine Islands, he contracted malaria. The doctors speculated that part of his treatment was regular injections; however, due to lack of proper sanitation during wartime, the syringes were not always sterilized and contaminated my father with hepatitis B. My Dad almost died from malaria, so because the symptoms for hepatitis B were masked, it was never treated and it destroyed a good part of his liver before somehow receding from his body. That manifested later as cirrhosis of the liver... when he was about 65 years old.

clear she was desperate and wanted me home. I had to cut my visit short. Rosalia's father, a well-known journalist, pulled some strings and I was on a flight to San Francisco that night. In spite of my precipitated trip to the Madrid airport, half the family accompanied me there; the last thing I saw before the doors closed behind me was a series of handkerchief waving in the cool Castilian air. I swore I'd return....

At the San Francisco airport, I had to run to my connecting flight to Medford that left the airport 35 minutes after I landed. I arrived there at six pm and was at my Dad's bedside in 30 minutes. He was out of whack; his pale skin was an indication he was becoming more and more contaminated with toxins.

My dad was a fighter but I guess he was tired of fighting, and was resigned. I couldn't believe that he may even...want to die.

I left the room and met my mother as she was climbing up the stairs. She looked up through her red, swollen eyes...the light-blue luster that was always there, was gone.

I remembered that before law school one day, to give me a wake-up jolt before an exam, I had prepared a lemon drink with real lemon juice mixed with honey and the fresh lemon was so piquant, like acid, it would eat through and break down the honey until it ran like water. "I've got an idea, Mom. If you could get Dad to take his medicine, I've got something that will probably break down the sweet syrupy stuff so he won't get sick and maybe it would help bring his appetite back."

My mother was usually cool, not panicky, but her eyes were flickering panic. She nodded, her white face pale from lack of sleep. She was trying so hard to keep him going and was desperate to give him his will back...to live.

"It's ok, Ma, I'll tell dad about it." I hopped up the stairs. "Dad," I began. He could barely turn his head." I think I've got a drink for you that will break up that thick medicine, so it won't make you sick."

He shrugged and turned toward the wall. His skin was pasty yellow, extremely jaundiced with the poison spreading throughout his body. I met mom at the door, told her I'd prepare the drink and would be right back. "It'll be OK, Ma," I tried to reassure her.

She reached out and grabbed my shoulder, and her usually robust voice, now frail and listless, uttered, "So glad you're here, Frankie. Love you."

"Love you, too, and glad to be here, Ma," I gulped as I headed downstairs.

I prepared the drink, without mixing honey with the lemon, just a half a teaspoon of sugar to help it go down easier. Then I called Mom into the kitchen to help me with his medication. We headed upstairs, Mom first with the tray of medicine, and I followed holding the glass with the lemon juice, even stronger medicine. We were on a mission.

And it worked! After Dad took his medication, his mouth screwing into almost a silent growl, he washed it down with the strong lemon drink. He frowned with the pungently acid lemon taste burning down his throat, but his reaction was immediate. A good sign followed: for the first time after taking his medication, he asked for lunch. Mom and I celebrated as we clomped down the stairs to prepare his lunch. She took him a huge plate of spaghetti and he ate it all before our unbelieving eyes.

Trying to be light, I came up with, "Sorry Dad, no wine."

He gladly cut me off; "Thank you, son; I feel better" before sinking into the covers for a well-deserved nap.

Tears started flowing so I had to get out of there. We silently, but this time with more alacrity, walked down the stairs. We didn't know how long it would last, but Dad was willing to take his medicine, chased with strong lemon juice…and we were elated when the dangerously pale, jaundiced look began leaving his jowls.

* * *

An opalescent flash shot through me like an arrow as my eyes slowly opened to a ball of fire against an almost clear blue, Mediterranean-like sky. I was still parked near the Cliff House in San Francisco, but blinded by the sun beating down on my face as I jolted up, hitting my head against the steering wheel. I had fallen asleep after spending several hours ruminating over the law school nightmare that I had held inside me for so long, in my repressed memory.

Seeing Rosalia, for the last time in our old apartment, and the chagrin of our break-up against the backdrop of the diverse Mission culture, must have triggered it. I fumbled in my pocket and pulled out my watch. It was 10 am and I had spent the entire night in the front seat of my pick-up truck.

The Latino music, tequila and salsa dancing with Sylvia amidst the rhythmic pounding of the African congas seemed such a long time ago.…

Chapter 6: Sylvia

The next Friday, soul music was blasting on the radio, as my camper pick-up rumbled along the interweaving roads above Fisherman's Wharf on the way to the Mission district. Earth, Wind & Fire was blasting over the speakers as the wind streaming in through the opened windows blew my hair everywhere. But it didn't matter as I was on my way to pick up Sylvia at her house for our first official date.

I drove the truck up her driveway, got out and climbed the stairs, two at a time. I needed to see her and felt elated but a bit guilty that I was taking her out, as this was my first date with anyone since my separation from Rosalia. I felt guilt that I did not try to rekindle the flame with Rosalia at the party even though I now believed our time together had ended. But the guilt remained and I couldn't shake it, at least that night....

As I stood before Sylvia's door, memories of the last year of law school with Rosalia came back, searing through my anxious body:

My Dad had passed away two months before graduation and a black veil of death descended over my entire being; but Rosalia stayed with me to the end and I graduated with a JD (Juris Doctorate). She was present at the graduation ceremony and the graduation party with my family and all the graduates reunited at the Mark Hopkins Hotel, ironically a block away from the original Nob Hill apartment I had shared with Sandra.

As we walked across the threshold of the entrance to the hotel that day, my eyes couldn't stop glancing down a block to view the top of the drab green apartment complex that was my home for the first two years of law school. At the party, I even saw Professor Moskovitz[11], my first-year Criminal Law professor who had given me the only passing grade the first semester—he nodded as I walked by. He was the only

---

11 Professor Myron Moskovitz is a noted professor, writer, lawyer and appeals court expert, among other things, who later, after I became a lawyer, gave me good lawyering advice on criminal appeals. A couple years after I was admitted to the California Bar, I won a criminal appeal before an excellent California State Court of Appeals that set a legal precedent for the State (People v. Fenton, 1993). Years later, I became a tenured associate professor at the University of Paris and we formed a friendship when I invited him to teach one of my mock trial courses there.

professor who had believed in me; maybe he figured something out that the others, except Professors Goldhirsch and Minkus, had missed.

Professor Minkus, my Professional Responsibility teacher, was standing on the sidelines as I danced with my mother, first. He was observing us, and vicariously sharing our joy. I knew it and felt it; I looked at him from the dance floor and he looked at me, without nodding. His brow was creased as his beady eyes focused on something, while the corners of his mouth were turned slightly up, in an inscrutable half smile. He was sharing our joy...in his way.

Professor Minkus was the one I had gone to after my father died; I cried in his office and threatened to drop out of law school as I couldn't attend classes, or do anything. I could feel he truly understood my pain but gently and skillfully advised that I stay in law school and graduate that year. Fortunately I followed his advice.

After the graduation party, I drove my mother and sister, Lorna, to our room and proceeded with Rosalia, this time to North Beach, where we ended the evening as we usually did, talking with Italian and Spanish friends at Caffé Italia.

Those memories weighed on me still, as I crossed the Golden Gate Bridge with Sylvia. The early evening mist had floated over the bridge; the hands of an unseen giant cradled the bay, with lights of ships piercing through the mysterious fog bank. Off in the distance, the lights of Alcatraz blinked a reminder....

We took the second exit to get away from the highway, and drove under it, following the road which rose up and wound around, taking us parallel to the bridge which we viewed from above, as if we were flying over it. It was lit up and appeared as if a soaring passageway to the mystical lights of San Francisco. My stomach dropped at the enchanting sight. The texture of the lights winding around the city came into view as we continued our ascent upwards. Then the road turned into a hilly area, where shadows of trees brushed the tops of the truck with their spindly hands. We didn't meet any other sets of headlights on the road. It was as if the only cars were ghostly vehicles shimmering through the mist, creeping out over the road, blowing into us through the shivering-cold salty sea breeze. It was dark and foreboding. Then we turned left and the blinking light magic of San Francisco sprang out again, entreating us, enshrouding us with its passionate support and love, without conditions. It was there to remind us how to live....

I reduced my speed as the road began to skirt the beach and I opened the window. The motor masked the sound of the waves but the salt air whisking in through the window, bringing in the distant crashing, reminded us they were there, out there somewhere, at the edge of a low drone of a monstrous sea...in the blackness. I stopped the car in a parking lot overlooking the breakers and turned off the ignition. The waves rolled and rambled, whispered, thundered and crashed endlessly. The frothing foam could be seen from the window, against the tenebrous waters, as we looked out, in silence. Reaching for her hand which was cold, but wistfully trembling, I wrapped it around mine. I scooted closer and at the same time pulled her gently closer to me. Our first kiss was against this backdrop, in the middle of the ocean, alone, the rhythm of the waves soothing our love, undulating with tenderness, crescendoing during the symphony as our lips touched.

Every Friday for the next three months, I picked her up and we traveled to another part of the City or extended our trip to a small town lost among the hills on the way to Bodega Bay from Santa Rosa, where I had spent youthful years. We drove to Occidental, near Santa Rosa. There we drove by the famous corner of Italian restaurants and stopped to make a to-go order of spaghetti Bolognese and buy a bottle of Chianti for our picnic.

As the truck stopped at a red light, a warm flurry passed through me as I looked over in the distance to where a drab, brick building stood. It was the hotel where Rosalia and I had stayed after a series of law school exams. We had slept in each other's arms for at least two days straight, getting up to walk to a local café and eat a late Sunday brunch. I remember the wind fanning our faces on the way, but it didn't matter as it was a cool mountain summer breeze that had glided across the humid soil and fir trees, carrying with it a redolent odor of oak wood and ferns.

I stopped the car in a turnout somewhere up in the high hills outside of Occidental. Opening my window, the crisp mountain winter air blew across my burning forehead as we ate spaghetti and drank glasses of Chianti in silence, listening to the mountain wind ruffling the trees with its relentless, smooth breaths.

Then we drove to Doran Park, which was a peninsula jutting out into Bodega Bay, forming a barrier between the bay and the raging seas beyond. We parked again; the luscious waves crashed more violently than at Cronkite Beach, perhaps a presentiment of our crescendoing fervor, at that moment: would we soar or ultimately crash? It would be the mist rising from the undulating waves, spraying our wistful faces with sheer, raw ocean that would draw our intimacy into carnal tenderness.

It had been three months since we had begun going out every weekend, and our bodies had not interwoven, yet. But this night was different; something was happening. We gently rocked each other in the front seat of the pick-up truck until the morning rays came over the hills surrounding Bodega Bay. Such love, so warm, so intense, so strange, as it was the first time in several years I had been with someone other than my estranged wife. As I drove over the road and down into town, I marveled at the contrast between the yearnings in my heart and Sylvia asleep beside me, and the little town of Bodega where Alfred Hitchcock, so many years ago, had directed The Birds.

We drove in the morning light up the coast, and just kept going—we couldn't stop. I was awake but in a semi-trance, from the feverish night spent in the grip of the crashing waves. I just kept going and didn't want it to stop, as if I didn't want the night or day to end or another day to begin. The road twisted around and somewhere I drove onto a side road and got on the main road. We ended up in the town of Bodega again. I parked my car near a bar where I went inside for a cup of coffee leaving Sylvia, still slumbering in the car.

As I left the bar with my Styrofoam cup, I looked over to the other side of the road and an old school loomed up over the hill. It looked just like the original school where people hid from the vicious attacks of flying birds in Hitchcock's movie. I looked around for threatening birds; apart from a few crows cawing overhead and a seagull flapping its wings, everything seemed uneventful, even a bit blasé, but peaceful....

I shivered as I got into the car. I opened the door and two black eyes looked into mine.

"Where are we?" "In Bodega."

"You're kidding! Oh no, it's late! I mean early," she giggled. "Better take me home. My parents are going to be very, very worried. Oh no!" she exclaimed, bending the rearview mirror to reflect her face. "I'm a mess! Let's go."

We arrived back in San Francisco after about an hour and driving over the Golden Gate Bridge, found life in full swing on that late Sunday morning.

Chapter 7: Whirlwind

On my way to pick up Sylvia, my truck edged by a myriad of Mission street scenes: A Latino low-rider driving up beside me, his slicked-down black hair contrasting with the shiny white car he was driving; the accordion and bajo sexto collage of Norteno music from Northern Mexico filling the streets with campesino Latino culture. His hand hit the top of the steering wheel as he revved the motor. He grumbled when the green light flashed, followed by a shrill shriek of wheels turning in place as his car jumped ahead.

She would invite me to dinner at the house, especially when her mother would make special dishes like "posolé," a combination of hominy grits and pork meat, with a layer of fresh unions on top. It was the king of soups. Even though I was, to the family, still the "gringo," my Spanish was better, allowing me to understand some of the jokes and the subtleties of the culture. As such, I felt more and more accepted. About once a month, after eating brunch at a long table in the kitchen underneath a small television sitting on a metal television stand, we retired to the living room where some members of the family would sing. Sylvia's sister would do a comedy routine before the family, taking off her black low-heeled shoe and speaking into it, pretending it was a telephone.

I sang Riccardo Cocciante love songs in the living room before the family that congregated there before dinner; soft and melodious, the songs sent us into a dream world, where we were in love, and each time I sang, my eyes would spill over with moist tears I was adept at hiding, by bending down and looking at the words. I had started singing those love songs alone every day after I separated from Rosalia, to try to bring her back, but to no avail. The emotions would arise so strongly within I couldn't sing and would have to stop and let the convulsive whimpering settle down before singing again for the awaiting audience: the twitching, sleek cockroaches running along the walls of my North Beach apartment. Now I was no longer alone and thus exulted in singing those beautiful songs before Sylvia and her family; it was strange singing the same songs, but I did, with tears of joy.

We would sit down at the kitchen table and eat together, Sylvia, Rosa Alba, their mother, Susanna, and father, Rudolfo, and myself. Her parents were immigrants from Mexico and had worked hard all their lives; the result, they were able to own their own house in San Francisco and raise the children, always able to provide food on the table. No small feat, especially for Latinos who experienced great hardships in the US, from cultural differences to rampant racism.

Then tension started three months later when Sylvia, as we were parked way above the San Francisco Bay in Pacific heights, overlooking the lights on the water, made the announcement, "I think I'm pregnant."

My heart pumped in my throat and my breath was short and staccatoed. I took her the following week to the doctor who not only said she was pregnant, but also could hear two distinct heartbeats. That meant twins.

After the doctor's visit, without thinking, I drove to the exact same spot in Pacific Heights where she had made the initial announcement and parked the car.

I had not a clue why, other than maybe I was subconsciously trying to return to the moment where we had left off our discussion…about keeping the babies, starting a family.

I had orchestrated a bit what I planned to tell her, that I thought it was premature for us to have a family. That even though I had left the bartending job and had a better job, this time working as an agent for an electronic legal research business dedicated to training lawyers and judges how to engage in computerized legal research, it was minimal pay. I had not yet taken the bar exam after law school so I hadn't become a lawyer yet. I rationalized that it would be better to wait for children until I became a lawyer and was making better money.

She sighed, profoundly; I opened the windows to let out the steam. We separated that night on a note that we'd both think about it.

At first, we considered an abortion, but I quickly changed when she told me that she had tried different old fashion Mexican methods to abort the babies. But the kids held on and that was a sign…and I castigated myself for ignoring such an obvious one.

The entire week I thought about it and Friday came, the day we were supposed to decide. It was a life or death situation, and I trembled to think that the decision was ours. My will began subconsciously lobbying to have the kids, to stop procrastinating. Were couples ever ready for children? It seemed I could put up roadblocks forever.

A part of me wanted to say, "Let's do it, we can, we will and we surely want to raise these kids." One decisive moment was when she let me touch the outside of her womb one night and I felt I already loved them and couldn't do anything to hurt them.

We needed to get out of the city, to make a new life somewhere on the seashore, maybe in Tiburon or Sausalito, so our thoughts could gently mesh together. We kept driving until we came to a small town nestled among the Northern California hills, Mill Valley, about 20 minutes north of San Francisco. We had dinner in a small restaurant there; it was magical. I threw my ready-made solutions out the window, and went with my feelings. During dinner, I reached in my pocket and pulled out a ruby ring, what I called a friendship ring, and handed it to her. It brought a smile to her face and a sparkle to her eyes, but it meant more than that. It was really a pre-engagement ring, unbeknownst to us.

It led us into a mood that would meld us together. I looked at her lovely olive-colored skin; I couldn't help myself, so I reached over and followed my fingers down the side of her face, with eyes looking at me. She did not look away. So I told her I loved her and I wanted her to have our kids, in one of the most emotional moments of my life. The circle of life had soaked into me and somehow gave me courage to cast aside the comfort zone-motivated road blocks. There was no tomorrow, no need for tomorrow as it was all today. And then the lyrics of a song came over the radio on our way back to the City: "Because you and I've been in love too long to worry 'bout tomorrow".[12] Like a warm blast, it shoved us into an emotional whirlpool. My mind and soul were flying and I was looking for hers, desperately.

"Crossing over to your love, there's no return...."

Now I wondered if this was for real, forever, but I did not really know how she felt, and hoped we could grow together.

The lyrics reverberated in my head again: "Because you and I've been in love too long to worry 'bout tomorrow"[13] over and over again....

We planned on marriage so there was no turning back; however, there was one major problem: I had been separated a year earlier from Rosalia—we'd never divorced. I filed a petition for a divorce from Rosalia the next week. Pending the legality, Sylvia and I moved into a large apartment in North Beach. Time went by and Sylvia got bigger and bigger....

It was a sweet life living together; I would come home from work, have dinner and then the all-night caresses. One day I saw a 1/4 carat diamond engagement ring displayed in a shop window near work, but even that I couldn't afford and had to borrow to buy it.

That night, Sylvia was so tired that she fell asleep on top of the bed wearing her hand-woven, off-white Mexican nightgown. The seams were joined with ornamental stitching, and it was embroidered, with gathering at the sleeves and wrists and frills on the shoulders. Her smooth, brown face nuzzled snugly in the lines of embroidery on her chest and her dark hair flowed outside like silk sheets.

I got out the ring and put it on her finger. That's how she woke up. Her eyes first blinked as they cast over the round object placed on her left ring finger. She reached over and placed the ring to her purplish, sleepy lips, almost subconsciously. She gasped.

"What's this?"

She placed the back of her left hand up to her eyes and turned her finger over and over again, looking at the lone diamond in the setting. It wasn't much of a ring as you almost needed a microscope to see the diamond, but she smiled....

It was just a few days before term when the divorce with Rosalia came through. It was urgent now that we marry immediately as she was due any day and we wanted to marry before the twins were born. It was 1989 and even though we were living in a liberal San Francisco where there would be no problem having babies out of wedlock, we weren't sure if some members of the ultra-traditional side of her family would accept that.

---

12 "You're the Only Woman," sung by the group, Ambrosia. Songwriter, David Pack (Publisher: Rubicon Music Co., 1980).

13 Ibid.

We had several options: getting married at City Hall or having a church wedding. It was too late for the latter, and the former, we could hardly imagine waiting in line at the Courthouse, a huge hump jutting out in front of her…with occasional sniggers….

I had fortunately met an Italian-American who worked with a family court commissioner; she came to the house and married us at home. My mother, who was living with us to help care for the twins when they arrived, was the only witness to the wedding. Four days later, the twins were born at Children's Hospital. I was there the entire time, helping Sylvia during labor, halted by the doctors who decided to deliver the twins by Caesarian section. It was a success and two plump babies were gently pulled from the small womb of the most relieved lady in San Francisco. I had to take a double look as I looked at their size, hardly able to imagine where such large frames fit in my wife's small torso.

It was time for rejoicing, bringing the little ones into the world and creating a more profound bonding between Sylvia and me. No one was prepared for the shock waves that would vibrate through our relationship after we relocated our happy family to Paris, the "City of Love," several years later.

Chapter 8: Jewish Paris

For about three years, we bonded, especially with the coming of the little ones. I passed the California Bar and, after working with a series of businesses and law firms, opened my own firm in downtown San Francisco while Sylvia worked as an assistant buyer for Levi Strauss. From our apartment, we could both easily walk to our jobs. It was the "dolce vita," but a disguise.

Three years later, in 1993, I wanted to extend my practice to the international sphere and was accepted to do a graduate fellowship in one of the stellar international law masters programs at the University of Paris in France. I had to close my law firm and extend my professional horizons to the international law world. This would be my chance to meet potential clients and international lawyers by stepping over the European threshold of Paris, before returning to San Francisco a year or two later to establish a new—this time more international—law firm.

Fortunately, Sylvia was adventuresome, and was very much in favor of the move to Paris. So we took the kids and traveled there after I was able to sell my law firm. The twins had just turned four years old.

We stayed in a modest hotel, Hotel Baudin near the Bastille, a block away from a Sephardic Jewish district that became a very active part of our lives. Little did we know that we would become intimately intertwined with the people there for the next three years.

During the first two weeks we stayed in the hotel, owned by an Algerian family. I became friends with the owner, Mustafa. He was a tall, laconic, strong-jawed man with a confident smile; his thin upper lip tightened as he spoke of his homeland. We had been at the hotel for a week when I sat down with him for our daily dose of strong espresso coffee at a bistro next door. Before speaking, we both sipped our coffee, sitting across each other; without staring, we sized each other up. He was a retired military officer and his approach to everything was methodical. Our conversation was almost always about how his country was moving forward and that it was ripe for investment, as exemplified by the many visits of foreign investors. An impediment to this was problems with attacks by militant rebel groups.

But his imperious demeanor was a mask, betrayed by the warm brown eyes of a father who had lived many moments of intimacy with his woman and with his kids. He paused and stared at me, his brown eyes trying to penetrate my thoughts, but they were not as nuanced as his. I had a pressing need and I needed his help. As I started sipping my second cup, the steam of the strong Lavazza coffee opened my nostrils and seized my palate while the aromatic liquid headed down my throat. I thought to myself that coffee drinking could be an exquisite drug.

I finally asked Mustafa if he knew where we could find an apartment without leaving the 11th district. He responded affirmatively and would introduce me to a friend on the way back to the hotel.

We walked back to our temporary home. I was about to open the door to the hotel when Mustafa tugged on my shoulder and motioned me to follow him as he entered a small jewelry store I had passed a hundred times without even looking in. Jewelry was not on my list of priorities as I barely had enough money for hotel rent and to feed my family.

Before us, a short man with dirty-blond hair was stooped over a workbench and didn't look up. He appeared to be toiling over a silver object. He finally acknowledged Mustafa with a smile and quickly flicked his eyes in my direction.

He looked back and cocked his head, as if to ask, "Why did you bring this man here?"

Mustafa nudged my arm which I guessed was my cue. I told him that I was presently staying in the hotel, that I paid on time and was a good, clean customer.

The Algerian added that I was looking for an apartment for myself, my wife and two young kids. Without looking up, the man nervously uttered, "I'm Eric," reaching out for a quick handshake. "Un instant et je suis avec vous." (Give me a moment and I'll be right with you.)

I was to find out later that these two, one a Muslim Algerian and the other a Jew from an Algerian-Jewish family, had a close friendship, one of many friendships between Arabs and Jews in this community. That was the beginning of the road to permanently abandoning my misconceptions about Jews and Arabs, one by one, as I lived in this community, as I awakened....

The next day after returning from the university, I followed the short man as he briskly walked. A block later, he led me down a small street lined with rows of apartments and a café.

He stopped abruptly and his right hand pushed several buttons on an external keypad. A metal-on-metal click opened the door and we walked inside a courtyard. The click kept resonating in my ears, the signal for a new chapter in the book of our lives. The door creaked open, unbridled....

As soon as we entered the courtyard, Eric reached over and touched a vertical[14] object attached to a green door, and then kissed the fingers that touched it. The ambiance had radically changed: the lines of apartments, honking cars and aggressive pedestrians outside had transformed into a narrow courtyard surrounded by potted plants, over which an arbor had grown, covering a part of the path that led to the entrance of a narrow flight of wooden steps, on the left. We walked straight up the dark stairs. I walked close behind him; he emanated tension.

---

14   That was a mezuzah, often attached to the doorpost of traditional Jewish homes, containing a tiny scroll on which, among other items, Jewish prayers are written.

On the second floor, we turned to the left and Eric knocked on a small door over which dark green paint was caked, seemingly covering over something. The same object that I had seen on a green door in the courtyard was attached to the door frame. Eric touched it as well and then kissed his fingers again. Voices echoed from the other side, mixed with the sound of sliding chairs and other clatter. The jeweler/landlord let out a long breath and shook his head; I suspected that it meant we would wait. After a full minute, the door was opened by a rather large-jawed woman who smiled and motioned us in. She turned, revealing a head scarf neatly wrapped around her head; an orthodox Jew, I wondered?

The sofa in front of us was crowded. Another rather large woman, with equally full jowls, smiled and stood at the same time. A short, stout man with red, gleaming cheeks and short, dark hair wore a kippah with a silver yarmulke clip weaving through his sparse hair, to hold the cap in place. He stood up proudly and waved us through. They all gesticulated, motioning us to park on the sofa, which we did.

The woman, who was now standing, came and shook my hand. Then she spoke: "Welcome. Where are you from?"

"I'm from the US."

She beamed and nodded, her head jerking with quick up and down movements, upon hearing that—not like, I thought to myself, the usual strained smile of most French Parisians upon hearing the same.

"I'm Leah and I'll be your neighbor. These are my cousins," she said, pointing to the other large woman and the man with the kippah. "You'll love this place…we're family."

She seemed to be already reaching out like a friendly neighbor, anticipating that I'd take the place. Well, she was right, as I wanted it from the start. On the right was a long chest of drawers with a slab of sleek marble on top, in an intermittent black and white design. I thought right away it must have been imitation antique marble, as it seemed so out of place compared to the drab, well-used sofa and the wooden living room table in front of it, its finish worn off, revealing streaks of tired wood. While Leah chatted with the short, stout man, Eric took my hand and pulled me gently to the left, away from the living room, away from the excited voices and entreaties of the present lodgers.

As we proceeded through a narrow passageway, he quickly indicated a small kitchen, which passed in a blur. Wedged in between the living room and bedroom, serving as a narrow corridor between the two rooms, it seemed more like an afterthought. It consisted of a sink, a hot plate to the left and a cupboard on the right. I thought to myself that Sylvia wasn't going to like that much. As we slowly walked through, I had to slightly turn my body or I couldn't get through to the next room where he was leading me. We entered a small room which had recently been wall-papered, but the wall paper was already peeling in some of the corners.

He followed my eyes, and quickly interjected, "The wall-papering has not been completed. It will be done in a couple weeks. If you move in before then, I'll send the workers to set up a schedule with you so they can come and finish the job."

His flushed face showed great effort as he spoke through his teeth. He shook his head, as he had failed to hide that unfinished project from me, and feigned disappointment in the workers.

As I followed Eric down the wooden stairs and into the patio area, the warmth and the unassuming welcome of the place hit me. But something mysterious was happening here: I felt the inner stirrings of imminent change. This connection with the Sephardic Jewish community would offer a bridge from my past—unfolding over many hundreds of years—to the present, the possibility of Sephardic Jewish roots, that I would discover later during one of my trips to the Holy Land.

I brought my wife and twin daughters the next evening to meet the neighbors and introduce them to Eric, who I had met in his jewelry store, before walking the couple of blocks to the apartment. We moved in that night.

That place turned out to be one of the most incredible, magical places I had ever known.

After returning from classes at the university, I would walk into the courtyard, shut the door, and immediately was immersed in an unusually peaceful oasis; it was almost unreal. Men and boys with kippahs either on top of their heads or dangling from their fingers, in preparation, would all wish me a fast "Shalom" (Peace) while rushing to the synagogue at the entrance of this haven; it was truly a community of love imbedded in one of the most dynamic cities in the world. It was an unreal bastion of peace for my family and even more, as I was to discover later, for myself.

Then, words of a strange language known as Judeo-Arabic, spoken by the residents of this place ["Juif-Arab" (Judeo-Arabic)[15]], floated through the air and greeted me like a warm breeze from afar. It came somewhere from above sliding down a smooth spiritual path on its way to this place, to this peaceful place, where we were raising our kids with guiltless love, joy and unity with our generous, loving neighbors. My eyes followed the modest but sturdy windows bordering one side of this place; the other side was a stone wall to which the grape arbor blanketing the courtyard was attached. The windows were bordered by old wooden, typically Parisian sashes, crumbling in disrepair, the paint half seared off by the sun's summer rays. A lady was talking to someone behind her while looking out the window. It was

---

15 Officially, Tunisian Jews spoke Judeo-Arabic, a mixture of Hebrew, Arabic and Aramaic. I found out later that Leah's family had migrated from Tunisia to Europe, shortly after it had obtained its independence from France in 1956. After 1956, all non-Muslims in Tunisia were unofficially considered aliens. In 1958, the Jewish cemetery was transformed into a public park and the Old Great Synagogue was destroyed in Hara. The French maintained, however, a naval base in Bizerte that Tunisia wanted to close in the crisis of 1961. Also, another important event was the Israeli-Arab Six-Day War of 1967. Those events triggered a sudden wave of Muslim-Arab nationalism, anti-Semitism and discrimination, such as the arbitrary arrests and interrogation of Jewish merchants, plundering and destruction of their stores. The exodus of thousands of Jews who had been living in the region for over 2000 years became inevitable and necessary. Ultimately, anti- Semitism, French colonization, the creation of the Muslim-Arab state of Tunisia, among other conditions, led most Jews to abandon Tunisia. Shaked, Edith Haddad. 19th Int'l Congress of Historical Sciences, Norway. "On the State of Being (Jewish) Between 'Orient and Occident'". 6-13 August 2000. In Jewish Locations: Traversing Racialized Landscapes, Lisa Tessman and Bat-Ami Bar On, eds., Rowman & Littlefield, pp. 185-199. <http://www.u.arizona.edu/~shaked/Tunisia/Jews.html>.

Leah, the same rather boisterous, large-jawed lady who had been in the apartment the day the landlord showed it to us.

She motioned me to join them. I climbed the stairs, one flight past the entrance to our apartment.

At the top, I peered around the corner and saw her face poking out of her apartment while her hand waved me in. She stepped into the corridor and walked toward me; when we got within about a yard of each other, her arms reached out and she pulled me into her for a hug. Then she turned and headed to her apartment; she reached the entrance and reverently touched the Mezuzah in the doorstop before entering. I followed the low-ceilinged corridor until I arrived before her. I looked where she had touched. She bent her head through the door opening and pointed to a little rectangular box apparently fastened to the doorstop. "That is a Mezuzah, inside of which are sacred writings of the Torah. Come in, my friend."

I reverently proceeded inside, into her sanctuary, and she led me past a spotless kitchen into a dining area, surrounded by a few pictures of grey-haired men with long, white beards over long, flowing robes. A slim, dark-haired man with a ruddy, wind-blown face sat at the head of the table. His smile was warm, his small lips spreading over stained teeth. A cigarette was propped between his fingers and a half-empty pack of Gitanes lay on the table. The pungent smell of strong, black tobacco fortunately only half-filled the room as several windows were wide open; but still the odor stung my nose until my head spun and my legs turned a bit rubbery. He pulled out a chair next to him and motioned me to sit down, which I gladly did, all the while smiling a warm, Mediterranean smile. I was able to quickly recover as he extended his hand and I took it.

"I'm Yosef. Coffee?"

"Frank. Um, sure. Thanks."

He placed three cups on the table as he spoke a few incomprehensible Arabic-sounding words to Leah that she later explained was "Juif-Arabe."

I sat down while she went to the kitchen to prepare the coffee. A few minutes later, Leah returned with a steaming saucepan, and poured its contents directly into the awaiting cups.

It was strong, Turkish-like coffee and I drank it down to the coffee-ground sludge in the bottom. Yosef lit another cigarette with the stub he was rubbing between his forefinger and thumb; the smoke wafted towards me when the wind seeped through the open window. The thick smoke stung the inside of my nose again. I was still not used to the heavy smoke of this rich, black tobacco. Leah, after sitting down and cradling her cup as if she was heating her hands, lit up a filtered cigarette in front of us and placed it more femininely between her first and third fingers, after she took a drag.

Silence reigned as the wide rings of smoke, one lighter than the other, rose and sailed toward the ceiling, creating a haze which blurred the pictures of the old, bearded men.

Leah spoke first. "Je m'appelle Leah Elhakim and this is my husband, Yosef Elhakim." He nodded and let his wife speak.

"My name is Frank Romano." They both nodded.

Leah got up and walked slowly to the window. "Come over here, Romano; my daughter and her family live over there," she announced, pointing out the window.

"My cousins were our neighbors but they just bought an apartment and you've got their old one."

"We're Sephardic Jews from Tunisia. You know where that is?" I nodded, she went on.

"We know a lot of Romanos, Moranos, and they're all Jews. You're Jewish?" I wasn't sure that was a statement or a question.

"I was raised Christian but I've been around Jews all my life and my closest friends are reform Jews from San Francisco. I've always felt a closeness to the Jewish culture and to Judaism."

Their brows furrowed a little, and I didn't know what that meant.

Yosef told me they were orthodox Jews and did not recognize the reform Jewish movement. They were orthodox, at least to the extent they followed all the rules, celebrated Shabbat religiously, not to mention all the holidays. They were originally poor and worked in the outdoor markets in Tunisia until they had to leave to find work in France, about 40 years ago.

"Since then, I've been working in markets, lately in one only a few blocks away called Marché d'aligre." He paused.

"Pour nous, tu es juif. Ta figure, ton nom sont juifs." (For us, you're Jewish. You have a Jewish face.) He looked at Leah and she nodded.

It was no coincidence we were accepted and cradled by this community. The strange aura of this place contributed to the revelation of secrets later when my travels lead me to the West Bank, to Hebron, to the Cave of the Patriarchs, where Abraham and Sarah and others were buried…and where I found a connection from my family to the ghosts of Sephardim and this community.

We celebrated Jewish holidays with our neighbors, including Hanukah, Rosh Hashanah, Purim and Sukkah. I felt Jewish especially during those times and very much a part of the community. I was invited into the synagogue at the entrance to our community several times to pray, especially during the holidays. Either I accessed the synagogue through the small door with the omnipresent mezuzah in the courtyard, or through the door leading directly to the street.

When I entered that door during holidays, like Yom Kippur, I felt more part of the community than ever, especially since the metal barriers were secure outside the entrance to the synagogue/apartment complex, in front of which stood two police agents with automatic weapons. Leah told me later, as we sipped coffee in her living room overlooking the grape arbor below, that the policemen were there to protect us as the Rabbi of the synagogue, in particular, had received death threats and threats of violence. The metal barriers stretched across the sidewalk, from the edge of the synagogue all the way to the end of the entrance, about 10 feet away from the entrance of our apartment complex; this was to prevent cars with bombs from parking there.

I watched the steam rise slowly above my cup as it tangled with the steam rising from Leah's, in silence. She added, "Every time they finish repainting the door to the apartment complex green, somebody paints over it again," she began stuttering nervously, "in black, the following word:" She wrote it on a piece of paper and showed it to me: "Mascr."

"Massacre?"

"Massacre." She added, "Somebody paints it over the new paint job every time, some twisted people, I don't know…." She raised her arms in despair. She was on a roll. The next thing she shared with me was that someone threw a bomb into a synagogue down the street which went off and destroyed part of it. She added, her eyes rolling, that it was never reported in the press. "What?"

"I know. The only explanation, strangely, was that it was during another tense period between the Jewish and Arab communities in Paris and they didn't want to make a big deal out of it—maybe they were afraid of more copycat bombers…I don't know!" She ended by throwing her arms up in the air.

I walked down one flight of steps to our apartment, a cold fear washing through me as if it was pushing the marrow from my bones. I secretly knew I wanted to endure everything with this community, even the threats from unknowns, but I'd never forgive myself if I exposed my wife and kids to danger. But I felt Jewish and that their struggle was our struggle, not as an outsider looking in but as a real part of it. I hoped Sylvia felt the same way because I wanted to stay, but I had to tell her about my conversation with Leah.

I wondered if this was what the Jews felt when being persecuted, during the many pogroms, as in Germany and Russia. I felt Jewish, and the police were outside, the door was locked, but….

Sylvia and I had a late-night coffee klatch, sitting on the sofa when the kids were fast asleep. Their breathing could be faintly heard behind the bedroom door.

I thought she might freak out over hearing about the bomb in the synagogue, the death threats to the local rabbi, but she was surprisingly calm.

"I'm not surprised, the way Jews are treated. Anyway, I feel secure here and so do the kids."

I was so proud of her and her principles, and her obstinate courage. I felt relieved that she felt as much as I did that we were with family here, and we'd endure and fight alongside everyone in this community, if need be.

After Sylvia went to bed, I sat on the couch, relieved and sighing; our homecoming was assured, we were home…but it was with her, not here with Leah and Yosef and the other members of the family, that a false security prevailed.

Chapter 9: Stillborn

A few days later, I visited Yosef at the market, at his invitation; it was only about four blocks away. The entrance was blocked with people talking to the vendors in the outlying booths and the vendors situated directly in the entrance. There were several blocks of vegetable and fruit stands, and some where household utensils were sold.

Oranges, apples, rows of tomatoes, heads of lettuce were displayed in carefully-trimmed boxes, the ones they were probably delivered in. This was a Mediterranean-type place for bartering, as everyone was gesticulating, squabbling over prices, nodding or shaking their heads. In the background was an ongoing din of footsteps, the sounds of women pulling their children from stall to stall where they touched the fruit, until the vendors placed their hands over those of the youngsters to stop them from squeezing it, followed by a few choice and sometimes inflamed words. Then he would grab a sack and start filling it up, aggressively swinging it over to a woman who would feign surprise, but grab the sack out of the hands of the vendor.

Sacks of potatoes were thrown in a basket on one side of a crude wrought iron balance scale, weighed against flat pieces of iron on the other side. The vendor barked the price to a Muslim lady wearing a brown headscarf, and then dumped the basket into the bag again after it reached the weight desired by the nodding customer, while she foraged in her coin purse for the francs requested.

I then walked down the line of stalls, some laden with kitchen knives, glasses, tiny pots, plates, silver, couscous pans and cezves or Arabic coffee pots. A neatly-clothed French woman, her dark dress covering her knees and a red purse matching her red lipstick, foraged through a box full of kitchen utensils, from spatulas to knife sharpeners.

As I was weaving in and out of throngs of mothers pulling their children along the sidewalk, I heard a gruff, "Bonjour."

It was Yosef; he was bending over a counter laden with garlic and plump grapefruit spread out on leaves carefully laid down. A grape vine or some other vine was draped on a line held up by a series of small wooden poles standing upright on the counter. Around the poles were draped strings of heads of garlic.

His eyes twinkled as they settled on his outstretched hands, in which a plump clove of garlic rested.

"Romano, take it and put it in the soup; it's fresh."

I took it and thanked him. He opened his mouth to say something but a customer interrupted us, asking him a question. He raised his finger to me, half saying that he'd get back to me, half saying "au revoir." I knew we'd have other moments to speak so I took my clove of garlic and returned to the apartment.

Our relationship with our neighbors was tested early, when catastrophe struck hard. Sylvia had been pregnant for about four months when she suffered pain in the uterine area. I dropped our daughters off with Leah who gladly agreed to look after them; then I rushed Sylvia to the hospital. The doctor diagnosed her with an infection but he failed to prescribe anti-miscarriage medication. Even though he was able to treat the infection, Sylvia began to open, first two centimeters, then three. I rushed her again to the hospital after calling a taxi at about midnight one evening. The attending doctor required that she stay in the hospital but wouldn't confirm if we would lose the baby. The next day, I was getting ready to go to work when I received a phone call from the hospital. The doctor explained in a linear, unemotional voice that it looked bad for the baby.

The hospital was about four blocks away; in a couple of minutes I flew out the door and tried to flag a cab. There were none in sight so I decided to run to the hospital. I was praying and crying the whole way, looking up at the sky, pleading.

To no avail...the fetus died. Sylvia had a miscarriage about two hours after my arrival on that fateful, dreadful afternoon, so far away from our home in a now strange, gloomy, land. The doctor told me that the baby had already begun to descend and died en route. Then I was asked to help my wife deliver a normal- sized, five-month-old fetus...but stone cold dead. I cringed but tried to hide it from Sylvia as I applied what we had learned in one of the childbirth classes we had taken before the birth of our twins. The instructor, however, hadn't prepared us for birthing, with all her energy and enthusiasm, a "cadaver." It was worse than the worst nightmare; inside I dreaded this with all the resistance in the world, yet I still had to help her breathe, keep positive and smile for her without overdoing it. I had to be strong for both of us after she was laid out helpless on the table....

Then a crazy thought crossed my mind: If it were too much for me, I could walk away from it all; she couldn't. I didn't, I couldn't...walk.

It was almost as intense as the delivery of a live baby, only labor was artificially shortened, with medication. Sylvia had a few painful contractions and while she was delivering the dead fetus, she pushed so hard that after delivery—when the doctor took the body of the fetus to another room, followed by the nurses—she emptied her bowels on the delivery table.

Her face was crimson with embarrassment so I quickly cleaned up the large stool before the doctor returned. She was so thankful and so extremely apologetic that I had to explain to her several times that it didn't bother me in the slightest and that I was fortunate to be able to be there when she needed me. Her creased brow and her eyes glued to mine hinted that she maybe didn't believe me; but I didn't care as I loved her so much, nothing else mattered. I loved everything about her, even her stools....

It was traumatic because in the back of my mind, I was aware that the next strenuous moments would be focused on sending a dead fetus into darkness before his first breath. Afterwards, I fell into deep mourning for our lost child. It was exacerbated by a test that was performed a day later that declared he was a healthy, good-sized male fetus. An intense loathing of the negligent doctor, in my mind the killer of our only son, perhaps temporarily calmed the fervor of bereavement…but nothing could stop me from falling into a deep depression.

I stayed to comfort Sylvia and the kids for the first three days after her return from the hospital; then I had to get back to work or I'd lose my job, our only source of income. I wondered, though, if it was more her and the kids comforting me. One thing was for certain: our neighbors were there daily to comfort us and Leah would often descend the one flight of stairs and invite Sylvia to tea during her convalescence.

To her credit, Sylvia seemed to overcome this disaster much quicker than I did. She sprightly bounded across the house, laughing into her new life, no longer hampered by a delicate pregnancy. She was cheerful and every time she saw my gloomy face she'd pull me close to plant a wet kiss on my cheek. One night lying in bed, I was in another somber mood but was relieved to see her peacefully sleeping. The fetal position she was in made me return to my dreary thoughts which, to avoid total insanity, required me to write, write, write:

You were born there
In that place
You were in my arms there Fighting for your breath Your head—angular Gleams
of hope
Empuja a la vida (push to life) You did it
We did it
We revived….
My dead son
Fetus without a chance
A doctor's fleeting choice
Your life leaking out
With the doctor's distracted voice
But I held you
My stillborn
And I love you,
But from me you're torn.[16]

My bereavement continued unabated until Sylvia made another announcement a few months later:

"Guess what? I'm pregnant!"

I would find no more time to mourn our loss from that moment onwards, especially since one night she complained of the same pains that had given rise to the previous miscarriage disaster. Even though she was beyond tired and wanted to sleep, I convinced her we should not wait and immediately go the emergency room. She was

---

16 Frank Romano, from the poem, "Held You," p.26, Crossing Over, supra.

so cool while she dressed, but I wasn't as I jerked on my shoes. I was deathly afraid we wouldn't survive another loss of a baby; but I wondered if I was mainly worried about myself. We wanted this one badly, to make up for our recent loss.

Before taking off to the hospital, I grabbed the sleeping kids and put one over each shoulder, heading upstairs for Leah's apartment. A sleepy lady opened the door and took them in her strong maternal arms without hesitation. We arrived at St. Antoine Hospital at one a.m. and walked down an empty corridor to get to the emergency room, after being let off by the cab. I had to bite down on the finger I shoved between my teeth a couple of times to calm myself during our wait of almost four minutes. I went to the nurses and asked why the wait, as there was no one in the waiting room. They just shrugged. I was about ready to hit high gear when they called out "Romano," and we followed the nurse into a long corridor and then into a room shrouded in the usual whiteness—the walls, the paper towels over the sink, and the white paper spread over the patient's chair where Sylvia would sit.

It was a chair with two metal footstools next to it, where Sylvia would put her feet when the doctor examined her. After about five minutes, an older doctor peered through the door and stepped in. He hesitated, probably feeling the dissonant waves emanating from me. His long, white hair was combed back and his face was drawn under his horned-rimmed glasses. He ambled toward us; I scrutinized every gesture, as I followed his slow, lazy pace. I wondered what his slothful approach meant. I was soon to find out. He asked Sylvia to sit up on the chair and to pull off her panties. He quickly glanced at her file and immediately went to work, checking, probing.

I had to stop him. Something was wrong; his jerky movements made it almost seem as if he were unaware of what the file had highlighted in red print. I could peruse it from where I was sitting; the part highlighted in red referred to her recent miscarriage.

I asked him, "Dr., I'm concerned." He ignored me and kept palpating. A hot tempest pounded my face and my heart thumped.

Through clenched teeth, I said firmly, "I wonder if you've read the file. She's just had a miscarriage after being open for several months and she's pregnant again."

He grudgingly got up slowly as if I'd disturbed him from a deep slumber while he was calmly, perfunctorily examining my wife. My blood rose and I swore I would not let him go further, whether he woke up and read the file or not; my fists clenched. But I wondered if that was for the present situation or for my dead son, even though he wasn't the doctor responsible for killing him. I was burning with hate, trembling and trying to bite my lip to quell the forces inside me that had been welling up since the miscarriage.

I couldn't hide it from Sylvia: "Are you OK?" I asked.

I was worried that if she responded to my question, saying anything like she was hurting, I would explode…so I focused on his movements as he reached for the file sitting on the examining room counter and reread it.

"OK!" his eyes flashed contemptuously at me; he then slowly set the file down, more like a coroner than a regular doctor.

I clenched and unclenched my hands several times but I was afraid I would lose control and haul off and smash him hard, at any time, for Sylvia, for our new baby (Frankie II), for Frankie I (we had already named him), our dead son, and last but not least…for me.

"You've got another infection and you are open two centimeters. Which means you've got to take it easy. No strenuous activity, OK? Also, your last lab tests show you're low in iron so I'm prescribing pills for you to take."

He refused to look at me again and I gutturally growled, "Ha hum!"

I surmised from his reaction he must have felt my heat, and was now paying attention. Super!

"Does that mean doctor, she should be bed ridden like a couple of months before the delivery?"

He interrupted me, "No, it's not necessary. She should be ok this time as we're treating the infection much earlier than last time."

He turned to leave and I helped my wife out of the chair.

Before he got to the door, I asked the doctor, "Oh doctor…." He turned with a strained smile, "Yes?" he answered as he looked to the other side of the room without looking at us.

"Since she is open, shouldn't you prescribe anti-miscarriage medicine so we nip it in the bud, and start it early? Last time…."

"Yes, yes, yes…right, right!"

In a minute he handed the prescription to me then added some quick scribbles and mumbled, "She'll also need some iron tablets as she's probably low in iron as she's already lost some blood."

I looked at Sylvia, and she looked back. We shook our heads at the same time—he had probably already forgotten about the lab report. At any rate, it was evident that our path was going to be another rocky road, and we'd have to work closely with the doctors and monitor everything they did. Everything!

Our trepidations were enhanced after visiting the local pharmacy and purchasing the two bottles of pills, one the miscarriage prevention medicine, the other the iron pills. I brought the pills home and took them out of the bag and gave Sylvia a miscarriage prevention pill right away. I opened the iron pill box and dug out a pill and handed it to her. But before she could take it, I closed my hands around the pill.

"What?"

"Wait a minute, honey. Let me just check something out."

She shook her head as I read the label and the paper in the bottom of the box with instructions and warnings.

"Bravo, thumbs up; at least they are iron pills and not something else, but."

She tried grabbing my closed hand as I whipped it back out of reach.

"But the incompetent _____ doesn't even know the medicine he prescribes! Look what it says." I handed her the piece of paper and pointed to the fine print which specified: "Pregnant women should be aware this medication can provoke miscarriages."

She shook her head and turned away to separate Regina and Juliana, who were wrestling on the cold floor.

I was livid at the doctor's negligent inattention, again.

"Unbelievable!" I mumbled through my teeth as I cast the pills in the garbage. The glass shattered as it hit bottom. That was the turning point, the moment when I knew I had to completely take over my wife's pregnancy, to make sure there would be no miscarriage repeat. That would be devastating as we were already pushed to the physical and emotional brink; that would kill us, beyond devastate us....

I jumped on a subway that day and visited a bookstore where I purchased books on pregnancy, child birth and you name it—everything I could get my hands on about nutrition, medication, to the delivery itself. I was determined we wouldn't lose this baby.

Later the next day, Sylvia and I sat on the couch after putting our twin girls to bed. We held hands. I knew I had to share something with her.

"You know I'll be there with you; you can count on me. I made a mistake on totally trusting doctors. Never again!"

She nodded, her eyes glazing over the TV screen.

"But I feel the doctor either doesn't know what he's doing, or is distracted... again."

Then I paused before I spoke, knowing she didn't want to hear the rest. But I had to push forward:

"I've read some books on this and I've learned a few things. One thing is you've got to stay in bed because you're open a couple centimeters and probably opening more, which could end up in a miscarriage; I'm sure of it." Her forlorn eyes swept the floor.

"I don't want to scare you but I don't care what that doctor said, that it's ok to walk around; you've got to stay in bed. It's just until you give birth."

She frowned and then bent down covering her face with her hands.

The next seven months were probably the worst, the best and definitely the most challenging of our lives: keeping her happy and in bed, while taking care of the kids. I had to do all the cooking and cleaning...and juggling that with a full-time job in a law firm.

But we did it! She took the anti-miscarriage medicine that fortunately made her sleepy and she stayed in bed, for seven months.

Leah's daughter, Ester, indirectly motivated her to stay in bed by telling us her story, at the appropriate time. About three months into staying in bed, Sylvia got very restless and starting getting up, even doing light housework. She wasn't supposed to even do that! Ester lived in the apartment next to us with her husband, Amiel. She visited us one day. I met her at the door, her black, curly hair framing her oval red face. It was Sunday afternoon and Regina and Juliana were taking a nap. As we sat on the sofa drinking our afternoon tea, Ester told us her story:

"I was working in the markets even when I was seven months pregnant. I noticed I had not gained much weight so I visited the doctor who did an echography. It revealed that the placenta was wrapped around the neck of the fetus which was not getting enough to eat, especially when I was stooped over. He prescribed that I stay in bed the rest of my pregnancy. However, I insisted on working, at least part-time. My baby was born a bit prematurely but that wasn't the problem: it was so dehydrated from not being able to absorb enough from the placenta that it died a week later."

She dabbed the tears streaming down the sides of her full red cheeks, as I dabbed mine, thinking about her baby and my son…my son….

The fear of another miscarriage, coupled with Ester's story, reinforced Sylvia's treatment: bed, bed and more bed. After hearing the story, Sylvia's upper lip clamped down on the lower one, and I knew she'd fight to keep the baby in. She was courageous, especially since she had to put up with my meals and my cleaning, for months…no small feat!

But it was our beautiful neighbors who saved us, especially on Friday nights, Shabbat. The last day of the week was especially challenging at my law firm job. All the accumulated work had to be done. Even though I got home from work late almost every night, Friday night was the latest and sometimes it turned into an all- nighter. I would often have to stay until two or three am and take a cab back to the apartment, as the subways would be closed at that time.

We were always invited to attend Shabbat dinner at our neighbors' upstairs, shortly after sundown. While I was a student, we often climbed the flight of stairs to the family apartment and partook of Shabbat dinner with them. I would always bring a bottle of kosher red wine. Leah and Yosef would prepare a typical Tunisian dish, couscous, a delicious mixture of semolina wheat with ground wheat flour, served covered with meat and/or a vegetable stew, with a Jewish flair. They called it kosher couscous, since it contained kosher ingredients, purchased mainly in the Belleville district where they used to do most of their shopping.

But after I began the law firm job, and during her pregnancy, I could never make it for dinner during the week with Sylvia and the kids. She had to keep away from the kitchen so I prepared food in advance each weekend to last all week; she only had to heat it up at dinner time and serve it, when warm. I used to make a big pot of spaghetti sauce and a huge salad; we ate the same thing every day. Except Leah and Yosef changed that, at least on Shabbat evening. She would put a heaping serving of couscous in a huge bowl and Yosef would descend one flight of stairs to our apartment and deliver it.

Life in the community was God-sent. Saturday afternoons, our girls would play in the courtyard with the local kids. Their excited voices, the tramping of little feet, the bouncing of balls, and constant giggling touched us above, as we watched through the opened window. Once in a while, the tinkling of broken windows hit by the balls sounded on the cement below, but even that didn't bother us much.

During the week, if I happened to leave for the law firm a little later, I experienced the "Levy" parade. Mrs. Levy, an incredible Jewish lady, small and spindly with frazzled brown hair and glasses propped up by a long, slender Jewish nose, would lead a group of kids, including our two girls, down the courtyard and to the nearby school. First, she would walk in front of her boy triplets. One was handicapped and walked with an arm brace and cane. Or sometimes his slender legs rested as he sat in his wheel chair; his short, dark hair exactly matched the hair of the two who followed.

They were followed by my daughters, walking hand in hand. It was a sight, the parade led by the female pied piper, who kept order all the way to the school a couple blocks away.

One night, I walked up the stairs to Leah and Yosef 's place. She opened the door and led me into the living room where a couple of elderly Arab men were seated around a table, eating kosher couscous. Their eyes were so focused on the victuals that they did not see me go to the kitchen with Leah, who was grinning.

"You know we're close to the Arabs," she informed me, bending down to whisper in my ear. "It's Ramadan and the poor elderly, they have problems fasting so they come here to eat, en cachette!" (secretly) Her eyes twinkled.

That was probably the first true interfaith gathering I had seen, Jews and Muslims sharing, helping each other, without conditions. Leah and Yosef didn't do that hoping to secretly eat at the house of the two Arabs during Yom Kippur, their day of fasting. They did it unconditionally to help their friends, because she knew the elderly Arabs sometimes suffered when fasting due to health problems, but still could not be seen by especially traditional Muslims eating during the fasting hours of Ramadan. The Jewish community was, without a doubt, the best place in the world to eat and hide from fellow Muslims during Ramadan.

Such was a connection between Jews and Muslims I would never forget in the heat of dialogues and marches that I would eventually organize in Israel and the West Bank.

Chapter 10: Abandoned

One Saturday night, there was a muffled thumping at the door. I looked through the peephole into the eye of a young man wearing the typical black hat of Hasidic origin. I opened the door, and his warm smile greeted me as he reached out with a box of candles and a small metal menorah. He wanted to make sure we had everything for Hanukkah.

I thanked him and brought them into the apartment to my beaming wife and kids, looking at it curiously. I briefly shared the story of Hanukkah with the kids, and then went upstairs with the menorah and the candles to contribute to the Hanukkah preparations that were to take place that night, chez Yosef and Leah.

I knocked on the door and Leah answered, happy to receive candles, but we decided to use her beautiful silver menorah already set up on the carved wood chest at the end of the living room. After reciting several blessings, we lit a candle that night with the shammus candle, the one that kindles the other candles, commencing with the one on the far right of the Menorah.

That night, Regina cried out in the night. I flew to her side.

"Papa, I'm dreaming, it's awful…."

"It's Ok, honey."

But she often had nightmares. One day I was having coffee with Leah and Amiel, Ester's husband. He asked what had been wrong the other night. His kindly face squinted.

"Did you hear that?" I asked.

"Did we! She kept us up, as our bed is just on the other side of the same wall."

But his smile disarmed the potential bite of his remarks.

"This is what you do: you put a knife under the mattress for a few nights. Then… no more nightmares…it's simple."

I reluctantly put the kitchen knife under her mattress that night, without telling Sylvia. I nervously dreamed up scenarios, such as she could drag the knife out in the middle of the night. She did sleepwalk but I would hear her. I left the knife where I had put it.

No more nightmares! When I informed Amiel and then quickly thanked him as I walked through the courtyard on the way to work, he winked as if he expected it.

Seven months later, our son, Frankie, was born. Sylvia got us to term, the full nine months, bless her—it was a daily struggle, but she made it. With a new baby, we became the highlight of the community. Frankie was adopted by all the Jewish mothers who lined up outside to get a look at the fat little baby snuggled up against the full breasts of Sylvia.

One night we sat on the sofa, the baby sound asleep next to us under a warm Mexican blanket with designs of indigenous Indians of Mexico bent over a fire cooking tortillas. Little Frankie looked so warm and content inside the blankets. Fortunately, he was not concerned about the disastrous news I had received the day before from the immigration authorities, denying my request to change status from student to employee, since I needed to officially be able to work full-time in the law firm. That had a perverse effect on my job status since I was required to leave my job while my appeal was pending. As such, we had no income. I informed the landlord that I had no money to pay the rent.

The landlord had already been pressuring me to rescind the lease before the three-year period since he wanted to sell the apartment. Since I had no money to pay the rent, I had to agree, this time.

But I wasn't going to leave the apartment until I had a safe place to live with my wife and kids. The only possibility was to move to the projects, the "pink elephants" I used to call them in the States, where we would have to stay until my job problem was resolved.

Within one week, we moved from the Sephardic Jewish community. I'll never forget when the truck—supplied willingly by the landlord, happy to get us out—came and I loaded our meager possessions onto it with the help of Jacob, the son of Leah and Yosef. As we piled into the truck, Leah and Yosef were standing in the courtyard, "waving…waving."

We drove to the projects on the outskirts of Paris, in a raw suburb named Suresnes. After moving in, we all flopped in our beds, utterly exhausted.

That night it snowed. In the early morning, the windowsill was almost framed with sheets of snowflakes. The image of that morning would remain with me years afterwards. I woke up in the middle of the night, cold; Sylvia was not lying next to me. I got up and went to the rectangular-shaped kitchen. She was sitting at the far corner looking out the window to the square, covered with a white carpet. I inched up closer, to share this intimate moment, watching over the white square. The image of Sylvia in the kitchen, with a forlorn, lost expression drawn over her smooth face will forever be engraved in my memory.

"I can't believe that we regressed to such a place, from San Francisco, a large apartment, my job, your law firm, to this squalor, these…these ugly…." tears crept down her olive cheeks, "projects."

I marveled at the difference in perspective between us. Here I was, sitting in a warm apartment with my little family, out of the snow, with not a cent to my name, food in the fridge and we were out of harm's way, elated. All I had was a credit card with thousands of francs overdrawn. But I knew this was only a temporary setback and that I would get my job back and we could move back to Paris. I knew we could…we would overcome this with prayer and faith, and if we stuck together.

And we did. A few months later I was offered a professor chair at the University of Paris, which required me to leave the law firm and focus on academia. It even paid better than the law firm and provided all the benefits, allowing us to start looking for a place in Paris.

We found a small apartment in the Marais, near the "Hotel de Ville," the Parisian mayor's office. It was on the Rue de Pecquay, a small, quaint street, only wide enough for one car to get through. When one looked down the narrow street, it looked as if the buildings were bowed, like the legs of a cowboy walking after a long stint on a horse. The landlord had told me that most of the buildings here were about 300 years old. To access our apartment, we had to pass through a metal gate and then we trudged up narrow, wooden stairs to the fifth, the top floor.

Beyond the "porte blindée" (reinforced door), installed by the landlord who was a retired policeman, was an old-style Parisian apartment, with old sashes at the windows that we had to keep locked during the day for fear the kids could fall out. The lattice work around the windows curled down the sashes, edging into places where parts had fallen off. To air out a stale room, I opened the aged sash that could easily have been held together with bailing wire, but it wasn't, and it creaked open; one side stuck and the other reluctantly opened into a courtyard several stories down.

Part of the wood on the bottom was dislodged and fell, end over end, before breaking into several pieces on a ledge below. The lower edge of the window was only a foot up from the floor which worried me. I thought about my kids stepping out the window and nervously closed them. That prompted me to keep the sashes closed during the day so the only light from the outside peeped through the small openings in the sashes which turned out to be jagged holes carved over time by the vicissitudes of the harsh winter weather.

The pale green paint covered every corner; even part of the floor was covered with green drops left by the painter. It was a rustic place. It had two rooms, a medium-sized bedroom that served as a living room and bedroom for the kids, and a small back room which was Sylvia's and my bedroom. It was the playroom during the day, as well as my study which consisted of a small desk, a chair and a white sheet drooping down from the ceiling, separating it from the rest of the room.

To keep my job and achieve tenure, I had to successfully defend my thesis and obtain my PhD in International law at the Sorbonne University within one year. Tenure would bring us permanent security and we could start making plans, even visit our home across the Atlantic.

But the last year before I defended my thesis, I was working almost full-time at the law firm, as well as teaching 3-4 classes (4-6 hours) a week, and it seriously compromised my relationship with Sylvia. I would get home night after night when everyone was in bed and the house was quiet, cold, shut. Only the soft breathing of its inmates could be heard.

When the big moment arrived, my professor at the Sorbonne gave me the green light to defend my thesis before a jury of four professors, experts in my field. I returned home with the announcement and Sylvia and the kids were long in bed. I walked into the bedroom, too anxious to save it for tomorrow, and whispered the news in Sylvia's ear. She sighed and turned over. That was almost the same reaction I received when I told her the next day over dinner.

Two days later, she had news of her own. She was taking the kids for an overdue vacation to the states a week before I defended my thesis. I was shocked as I wanted so much for her to be there with the kids and then to celebrate with me afterwards. But she was making a statement...that wasn't the last one....

I successfully defended my thesis at the Sorbonne in her absence and waited to celebrate with Sylvia and the kids when I joined them in San Francisco. But we were never able to heal our relationship together. Even after her return to Paris it was never the same. It was over.

A few months later, she ended up leaving Paris permanently with the kids. I was deeply depressed by her departure, and the separation from my kids cast me into the gloomy purgatory of crying nightly, reaching for them and then realizing in the eerie quiet of the night they were gone, long gone away from me. The apartment, although small when it was full with my three kids and wife, was an empty tomb with me inhabiting only one room. I'd fall asleep cloistered in my sleeping bag next to my desk, closed off from the window. Then I'd wake up suffocating, gasping for air, my heart pumping fiercely like it was trying to overcompensate for something, in the middle of the night. It seemed that unsettled emotions attacked my very bones, stifling breathing, and my life. Was I to die here, I wondered? If I did, no one would know for weeks, maybe months. But I felt like it....

I lived and tried to survive in the ruins of our existence. Sometimes, late at night when I could not sleep, which was often, I'd stroll around the apartment. That was a mistake! The walls slid by me as I walked: they had earlier been stripped by Sylvia with the help of the kids, preparing to paint them. So the walls were rough and un-sanded in places and several strips of faded wallpaper still hung lifelessly from the ceiling, some so old they had partially rotted away. And since we planned to paint the walls, we had let the kids write on them at will, which they did—everywhere. Reminders of their fun marking up the walls galore had turned into graffiti streaking by as I continue my ghostly inspection. In fact, there were reminders of my kids everywhere, on the walls and in the toys strewn on the floor. It looked like they had been playing in front of their bunk beds up until the moment they left for the airport: a half-dressed doll with one arm lay among a pile of other toys, dropped upon the arrival of the airport shuttle, rooting them away from Paris...away from me.

As I walked the four corners of their room, I came across their etchings, hearts punctured by hearts, monkeys, cars, houses with the family sitting at the table as well as pictures of classmates, of a mother and father watching over their kids. It was over, so final, yet it was not so long ago that my two daughters had inhabited this room. A bunk bed was wedged in the corner. I pictured them playing with their toys in front of me, before lights out. I'd run my fingers over the illustrations on the wall, retracing their writings, as if my hand was in theirs; I was desperate to hold their hands, hug them. It was too late to make up for all those missed hugs now that they were 6,000 miles away. I turned to the darkened room.

I then traveled to my son's room, the bed he lay in, still half covered with model cars, dinosaurs—toys that couldn't fit in the suitcase. I sat on it and pretended I was telling him a story. The walls wept copiously.

Now the only sounds were an occasional mouse looking for food, foraging in the kitchen, with a little pitter-patter of feet across the floor. This was a strange and gloomy replacement of the pitter-patter of my little ones. And yet I was oddly comforted....

My fate was loneliness, working many hours at the university, staying late to make me exhausted so when I arrived to a somber, cold house, I'd be too tired to feel, to weep, even to eat. But suffused with emotions, I wept the cruel punishment I felt.

Sometimes I'd listen to songs and sing myself into oblivion. The Earth, Wind and Fire song "After the Love Has Gone," about love gone sour, just hit me to my core; I never could get to the end of the song without breaking down. I was a serious mess and somehow had to get myself together...I was desperate.

Sitting alone on the couch, my head buried in my hands for hours until I just couldn't sit up, I'd slouch over the armrest, its cover half on as it drooped toward the floor. I wasn't going to last long like this, alone.

After sleeping on the floor next to my desk, I awoke from the dream, suffocating again and could not breathe. I was claustrophobic, for the first time ever, and I was afraid of dying alone, because nobody would know, nobody cared...I now had to stand up or my soul would snuff out, a remnant of the dust accumulating on the floor....

I opened the door to the abandoned living room, my heart sunk deep into my bosom. I had to go to the kitchen. The mouse scurried, the little feet reminding me at least I wasn't alone, temporarily a respite from stark abandon. I grabbed a saucepan, filled it with water and putting it on the electric stove, turned the knob all the way. One day I fantasized that it was gas and I would forget to light the burner...The steam from my cup curled upwards as I gripped the handles on each side. The Earl Grey tea with extra bergamot burned my lips slightly. As the tea traveled down my throat, the honey I had used supplied a whisper of sweetness....

Chapter 11: Latifa

My faith in my reunion with Sylvia and the kids in Paris waned and I lost complete hope several times, after several cancellations of plans for her to move back. I became completely defensive, deciding I couldn't continue hoping: the ups associated with knowing she was coming with the kids could not cancel out the downs when our reunion was cancelled. I finally sent her an email calling it all off; I had to conclude that it was no use—we were destined to fantasize about what could have been. Before reading the email, the tears welled up in my eyes as I knew that was the end of the fantasy.

After sending the last email I felt sepulchral chills, so cold and so alone as if a coffin lid had clamped down over me, forever holding me inside the four wooden parameters of a failed life, marriage and fatherhood. I couldn't stand her retreating from the plan again, yet this time I had thought she might really come, but I was afraid of hoping, followed by lonely despair.

There would still be more talks of a joyous reunion in Paris later, but maybe those would be the final gasps....

Our exchange of emails continued to flow hot and cold, for months.

In the meantime, I decided to prepare to take the French bar exam, to eventually become a French lawyer. The preparatory class taking place in the evening for an entire year provided me with an elixir for the abysmal lonely nights. Even though to date, I was satisfied with some of the international law cases I had worked on with the lawyers in the law firm—notably antitrust—and the contracts that I'd drafted, I wanted to get out of the corporate world and get back to my working class roots: to litigate, to wrap myself in the lives of victims and go to court on their behalf, as I'd done in the US before coming to this place.

It had been a long-time goal as I needed to get back into the gritty trenches of life and ease out of the ivory tower of my safe professorship. I was also desperate to get away from the carrot-on-a-stick greed of the world in corporate law firms (where I was employed as a law clerk previous to the professor position), of shifty corporate types skulking around in a superficial business world, oblivious to the world's suffering and sometimes the heartless cause of it.

I met an Arab girl, Latifa. Her short, dark Cleopatra hair hung on either side of her round face, like two satin curtains. She wanted to establish a relationship but I

76

warned her that I was trying desperately to rebound from a 12-year marriage, and the separation a year earlier had destroyed me. In sum, I was damaged goods and no gift for my enthusiastic Algerian-Egyptian friend. But she hung in there, even though she surely felt this would be a dead-end for her.

One day she cleaned my kitchen, much to the chagrin of the mice and cockroaches; there was an accumulation of a year of serious neglect. Arming herself with brushes, chemicals and extending her elbow grease to the limit, she took on all the rodent and insect life there with serious growls.

After the kitchen was spotless beyond recognition, she put a CD on and we listened. They were beautiful, sad tunes sung in Arabic by an Egyptian singer, Abdel Halim Hafez, especially the songs "Fi Youm, Fi Shahr, Fi Sana" (In a Day, a Month, a Year) and "Qariat el-Fingan" (The Fortune-teller). We sat on the couch listening to his distant melodies reaching into our hearts, misting us with somber words of love. Somehow, I often understood the meaning of the songs, i.e. odes to loved ones, to his lost lover, without understanding Arabic. Even though her Arabic was shaky, she spoke some to me, explaining the sad words as I sat there sometimes lifeless, listless and thousands of miles removed.

One day we were sitting in my kitchen after breakfast and I told her about my vision, revolving around interfaith peace in the Middle East. Learning from my experiences in Morocco[17] I believed that fanatic beliefs were not the answer, that true understanding would be the precursor to peace.

We wrapped our arms around each other in caresses and forlorn, desperate grasping as our lips slowly melted together on the couch, until sleep ebbed into us, and all was silent again...and the graffiti from my children's hands faded into the shadows.

Latifa told me later that I woke up yelling, "No, no, no Sylvia!"

But my feelings could not lie: I woke up thinking Sylvia never, never loved me, and that was why she had so abruptly abandoned me to this paltry, empty, childless life in this foreign country; I still felt very much alone. I cried, trembling like a newborn, in Latifa's arms. She looked away, probably disgusted, but she caressed my hair just the same.

She was also probably disappointed to hear my heart was still beating, at least partially, for another but held me in her arms until I fell into a dream world, thinking of Sylvia. In the morning, I heard faint clinking in the kitchen as I turned over to face the light over the stove.

Latifa had prepared a sumptuous repast of scrambled eggs, coffee and toast. I didn't have a toaster, so she had skillfully fried the bread in a lightly buttered frying pan. At the table, my smile was a bit restrained and she looked at me inquisitively, a bit puzzled.

"Great breakfast!"

Her half-smile indicated she may have been thinking about what I had screamed in the night.

---

17 Storm Over Morocco, 4th Edition, Frank Romano, (New York: AB Film Publishing, 2013). Experiences in Morocco discussed later.

"I guess I just exploded. Haven't yet overcome the separation. Don't feel you have to…."

"I'm with you for right now and that's what matters."

But I knew her response meant we would not be together for long as it was clear she did not want to compete with a ghost. But we were close, and she had at least temporarily saved me from descending further into blackness, to a lonelier, self- contrived world; she succeeded, at least the times she shared with me at my apartment, in preventing me from passing out with fatigue in the fetal position on the couch, as I had done many times before.

My university colleagues, of course, all blamed my wife for the rupture, but grew disenchanted with my half-hearted efforts to shove thoughts of her behind me, for not immediately seeking her replacement, or not striving to become a "bon vivant" (jet set partier) like them. I was separated from my wife and had been totally faithful during our marriage. When I told Étienne, a fellow professor at the law school, his nose wrinkled and he looked down on me as if I were a member of an alien species.

"Even some of the married ones, men and women, have lovers on the side. No big deal; this is Paris!"

I was marked as "square" and thus no fun. Their calls dwindled; if they did call, it was only to ask for a professional favor, like sending them a US Supreme Court judgment or replacing them, teaching their course for a week. To them, I'd become a moping stick-in-the-mud….

Latifa and I predictably slipped away from each other. I don't even recall how it happened. When it did, I feigned confusion before nodding off on the couch in the fetal position, no energy to walk the few steps, undress and slip into the sleeping bag laid out over the bedroom floor.

To pass the time, I started taking "bon vivant" Parisians girls out for dinner and sometimes dancing or a movie, very much to the surprise of my colleagues. But I dreaded the end, when I would say goodbye, and they expected a "hello roll in the hay." But the ghost of Sylvia would be leaning over us. The result was predictable. A confused look inevitably spread over the girl's face or inquiries ensued as to whether "something was wrong with me" until I just raised my hand with a short "Bye" and receded into the night like a lonely midnight tide.

That scenario played out over and over and the result would always be the same. At the moment of truth, at the end of the evening, when I went into my monologue about having difficult withdrawal symptoms from my marriage, I finally realized that the women didn't want to hear that. A "bon vivant" just couldn't or wouldn't understand that. I castigated myself in the morning for always going out with that type of woman, but it seemed I was attracted to them probably because there would be no "Attaches amoureuses" (Bonds of Love[18]) with a bon vivant!

I remembered one of my last dates with a "bon vivant," after the warm expected kiss on her doorstep, and the inevitable pull into her apartment. I followed her to the living room where I sat on the huge, cold leather couch dominating the other

---

18 Whenever "Bonds of Love" is mentioned, it is inspired by: "Touch not the nettle, for the bonds of love are ill to loose." D.H. Lawrence, Lady Chatterley's Lover (Cambridge: Lawrence Edition, Penguin Twentieth-Century Classics Series, 1994) Chapter 7, p.83.

fixtures in the room. A painting of a café in Bordeaux was prominently displayed in the middle of the wall in back of her TV. I imagined they were just props for the anticipated theatrics to be acted out between her sheets....

She hastily served me a cup of espresso coffee and laid a small bowl of sugar cubes next to it before withdrawing to her boudoir; she returned in a few minutes with a see-through nightgown. When I got up to go, she offered a glass of brandy to cap the delicious cup of coffee. I was calmly direct as I refused and headed for the door. I opened it and glanced back. She hadn't moved from her position near the coffee table. A hurt look passed over her face, visible under strands of dark- brown hair. As I shut the door, my footsteps resounded down the stairs and I swung out the street-level door to the dripping Paris night. Curtain closed!

That night, I swore I would no longer go out with "bon vivants" and promised to occupy myself in other ways on Friday and Saturday evenings, like transforming my dissertation into a book and studying for the bar exam to be held at the end of the year. I took a deep breath and headed for the subway. I got there just in time to take the last train from the 18th district to the 4th district, the "Marais."

Chapter 12: Concetta

I experienced a short-lived reprieve when I met an Italian girl, Concetta, who was introduced to me by a couple of well-intentioned Italian friends. They had visited my dismal apartment, an obscure monument to the last two years of living with my wife and kids.

My Italian friends had started inviting me to all their parties, trying to drag my bereaving self into the light of a new relationship. The impossible came to fruition when I met Concetta.

One Friday in March, I was returning from the bar school when I got a call from my Italian friend, Gargiulo. He said he needed to introduce to me a nice Italian girl who recently was divorced and that maybe….

"It's been a year since my wife left and I've really no time…." He insisted.

"She is having a birthday party and will make dinner for about 14 people in a town called St. Gratien."

"Where's that?"

"No che problema, come trenta minute di Pariggi." (No problem, about 30 minutes outside of Paris)

He explained that I had to go through the usual subway and RER (subway under the subway) routine to get to her place and then gave me the address.

The party had started at seven pm and I arrived around nine on purpose, towards the end, so it would be over quickly and I could go home. I wasn't into this! I pushed the button and a squeaky voice in French sounded over the intercom. I couldn't understand it but the outside door buzzed and soon I was taking an elevator to the fifth floor.

I knocked and the door was opened by Gargiulo and his Italian girlfriend, Graziella. Being welcomed by my Italian friends brought a warm glow into my abandoned heart, and in particular, because I knew that whoever they would be introducing me to would not be offering me brandy to coax me into her bedroom. I was relieved—the ghost of my wife followed me in, almost strutting across my heart.

Gargiulo pointed her out, a short, dark-haired girl, her slick legs pumping in a short dress, as she went from person to person, like a bee from flower to flower, making sure her guests were happy. She looked, at least on the outside, maternal.

My turn came and she bent over to serve me, spooning a mound of pasta bathed in tomato sauce into my plate. She then held a bottle of what looked like parmesan cheese over my plate and I nodded before she shook the shavings of cheese over the pasta. Her head swung back to regain her stance. As I caught her eyes, a sad expression returned my lonely, empty look. I recognized that look....

"By the way, I'm Concetta...."

My friends had forgotten to introduce us, probably figuring it would happen naturally. Back in the kitchen, I asked Gargiulo if the girl were free; he told me yes, that she had gone through a hellish divorce about six years earlier and had not found someone new.

I glanced over to her as she was engaged in a half-smile, somewhat mysterious but very attractive, the corners of her wistful lips turned slightly upwards; I was astonished that someone as appealing could be alone for six years. Gargiulo knew me and what I was thinking, and interjected, "Raising her son. By herself." His Italian gesture followed, palms rising to the sky; it didn't need to be followed with words.

"But her eyes...."

Gargiulo cut me off: "Cha triste, vero?" (Sad, right?) He was unbelievable in his ability to discern my thoughts. Maybe somehow his Italian family roots across the Gulfo di Sorrento were bonded with mine, in Napoli.

My head bent down and I mumbled, "Si." I could have been talking about myself.

Gargiulo looked at me, in silence; he knew.

Years later, after Gargiulo lost his mother, I finally visited him in Sorrento, to spend some time with my friend still in mourning and suffering through or enduring his first Sorrento summer without her; she had lived in the apartment directly beneath his. During that visit, I found out more about why the bond between us was so strong. From Sorrento, we looked out across the Gulfo di Sorrento, and I was so moved as I viewed Napoli, the birthplace of my Italian family roots, that I wrote down this poem:

> Across the Gulf of Sorrento
> A wind plays to the heart
>
> Of a lonely beach lonely beach.
>
> Like the grapes you held out to me,
> as you dreamed in Napoli
>
> With deep chocolate espresso eyes,
> Gazing over the sugared edges of the brioché[19]
> You gawk at open truths

---

19 Referring to my Grandparents on my Father's side, both born and raised in Napoli.

Crossed the ocean
You brought me there
Touch of a baker man[20]
Painting from long brushes you never saw

On the beach, Caruso's breath whispered
Of a lonely beach,
lonely beach

But when the mist rose
There was Napoli,
That you gave an open breath

Crossed the ocean
You brought me there
Touch of a baker man
Painting from long brushes you never saw

With makeup powder pervading the air about you
with every bounce, Caruso y mio Nono,[21]
dancing, over the Amalfitano cliffs,
I could not reach you
as you dreamed of America

With deep chocolate espresso eyes,
Gazing over the sugared edges of the brioche
You gawk at open truths

In your womb, mia Nona,
Your eyes blinked
Only in those creamy brown Mediterranean eyes
They dropped so . . . that night

On a Lonely beach,
lonely beach
And then rose to fly across the Atlantico,

---

20 My Grandfather, Francesco Romano, a Napolitano, (born in Napoli) was a baker after he was released from Ellis Island, New York. He then lived in New York City—I believe in the Bronx—and probably Brooklyn and at some time, apparently lived in Chicago. Then, part of the family moved to Providence, Rhode Island, and to Walpole, Massachusetts, near Boston.

21 Caruso again, with makeup during a performance, this time dancing with my Grandfather. Enrico Caruso, born in Naples, was one of the greatest opera singers.

And in the end,
Your chocolate espresso eyes closed, just closed[22]
Bringing everyone blinking into your womb[23]
Blinking for you, Nona Blinking for you, Nona

Crossed the ocean
You brought me there
Touch of a baker man
Painting from long brushes....
you never saw

I invited Concetta to the only place I knew that was 100% Italian in Paris, Caruso's restaurant near the Place des Vosges. We walked in and to the left, was a typical array of fresh antipasto, Italian "hors d'eouvres," namely milanzano (eggplant), pepperoni, olives, slices of mozzarella cheese garnished with pieces of pomodori (tomatoes) and more...we were in "la bella Italia."

The owner knew me and came right up to us; he was robust, with a white moustache, and strands of wavy white hair supporting his white chef 's hat. He greeted us with a boisterous "Come stai?" (How's it going?)

He personally led us to a table with two wooden chairs, next to the window. We stayed until closing. After the owner closed and locked the door, he came over with a mandolin and began singing a song from his native Calabria. He was accompanied by all the waiters as they all came from the same part of Italy. Before the meal was served, we traded stories about the bella Italia and I was surprised that Concetta spoke Italian so well.

We got up to leave as it was getting late and the owner led us to the door. After we closed it behind us, the melodic sounds of Italian being spoken were heard over the street cleaning, over the incessant thrumming of car motors as we moved down the "Rue de Rivoli." We continued talking in Italian as the "ambiance" was set for the night.

We strolled along the Seine, the "Isle Saint Louis" of the "bella Pariggi"; although we were in the middle of a bustling city, it didn't seem like it. We passed the artist studio of Camille Claudel, the sculptor and Rodin's lover, who ended her days in an insane asylum after the split with Rodin. She lost her mind for love? I didn't know, but I could feel it so as the empathy was flowing through me like the Seine flowed below, while we read the plaque about her outside the building where she had crafted such beautiful sculptures; her story was sad but prophetic...I began to feel the emptiness of lost love, maybe as she had, so long ago.

"Crossing over to your love, there's no return...."

The small waves of the Seine lapped up against the edges of the quay below us,

---

22 Referring to my Grandmother's death; she was Napolitana, (born in Napoli). Her maiden name was Fatima Gallucci.

23 My grandmother had complications after giving birth to my father, and I think she had other health issues. I believe she died either giving birth to my father or not long afterwards.

more violently than yesterday; under muffled breath, I couldn't stop myself: "Maybe because we were standing next to the plaque commemorating you, your beauty."

The lamp reflected the setting sun on the crest of the undulating current spilling over as we walked along the quay. I couldn't resist continuing my murmuring: "You were taken from us by a fearful, most hypocritical family, not helped much by them, some professing to be so close to God. As your brother's writings foretold, your family's actions reflected a single-minded focus on chasing after prestige, careers, while protecting the mediocre and throwing out the truly brilliant spirit—yours. You shone so brightly until you were snuffed out in an asylum, placed there by your family, finally rid of you, and, apart from a few visits…forgotten."

I had fallen into a slight trance but I felt Concetta's gentle hand on my shoulder and snapped out of it. At this point, I didn't care if Concetta thought I was weird;

I began talking about my love of truth and need for sincerity after our walk along the Seine that night, which was surely inspired by Camille Claudel. She helped me be true to myself at that very moment, walking along the river banks where she had collected clay for her works so many years ago.

Concetta looked at me with vague, distant eyes. That outburst was probably too much coming from me, a complete stranger; but she didn't shrink away, at least physically, as she walked with me step for step, even when I sometimes gently put my arm around her.

From that moment, we were inseparable and things moved at lightning speed. I even convinced myself that I had finally come home to roost and that she would be my life's pursuit. If one were to look at me through a window, one would imagine that I was the happiest man on earth. Things started looking up as I hummed lyrics from the song "Wishing on a Star," sung by Will Downing, all day long, repeating over and over "…and I wish on all the rainbows that I see." I started seeing incandescent colors again, instead of the cloak of gray that had veiled my mind for so long.

I moved in with her temporarily until we found an apartment in Paris a few months later. We moved into an apartment in the 20th district in Paris and soon Concetta was pregnant. I suggested marriage but she explained that she had been traumatized by her divorce from the father of Alexander, her 12-year-old son, and swore never to marry again. She was adamant so I didn't insist. But I think she knew something that I refused to accept, that our love was already doomed.

Concetta intuited that my heart was still in the grip of Sylvia, something I was not willing to consciously admit. I thought I loved Concetta, but memories shared with Sylvia refused to dislodge from my heart, and reminiscing about our moments together from time to time caused pain to shoot through it, a warning sign.

"Crossing over to your love, there's no return…."

Were they haunting me? A distinct sign of this persistent love flashed in my head one day while Concetta and I listened to music in our Paris apartment. My eyes, still veiled with sleep, began to focus slowly, like a camera automatically adjusting from a blurred to a sharper image as the shutter speed changed, while letting the light in. Concetta had fallen asleep next to me on the couch as my eyes wandered from pictures to paintings hanging on the wall.

I was still semi-conscious as I listened to the dissonant music; at the end, the clashing of the timbales simulated the imminent end of the world. My eyes opened, with the jarring crashes and screams. The first thing I thought about was my mother—I must save her. Then my thoughts turned to the image of Sylvia and my children, her hands pleading for me to save her. But her face became distorted as she was cruelly sucked into the depths of a whirlpool. I tried pulling her out, one last grasp…then I awoke from my half-sleep. I phased into the room while the music was still playing. The first thing that flashed in my mind was to see if Sylvia was alright.

"Attaches amoureuses" (Bonds of Love)

In a muffled voice, I cried, "I so, so miss you! We had lived through so much, only for you to be uprooted from me…the roots sinuously moving and clinging, still growing in me, weaving through my body and bones, and interlacing around my heart and through it…and now the roots are drinking my blood."

My feverish dream was still with me as my semi-awakened body arose; I realized the end of the world had been postponed, to culminate another time in an internal crashing session like the one that had just occurred. I still needed to talk to Sylvia, as if the music had planted something in me, stemming from the roots of our love. I had to excuse myself early to go on my nightly jogging run in the streets below and, after jogging a couple of blocks away from the apartment building, I called her on my cell phone. Her voice answered almost immediately, even though she was six thousand miles away; it was as if she had been waiting for my call. Had she somehow already divined the nature of my dream about the end of the world?

I recounted my dream for a minute then stopped, listening for her reaction. Silence, except for her deep inhalation and exhalation, rhythmically filling the phone.

Her voice quavered, "A few minutes ago, I guess about the time you had your dream, I felt fear. Some unknown element invaded me, then nothing."

The sun pierced through the dark clouds of my thoughts, heating the very essence of my being with inspiring feelings that what had transpired between us proved we were still connected, at least subliminally…but maybe only temporarily.

She then related her nostalgia for Europe and that she missed me. The phone melted while plastered against my ear as I would not miss a word, even a syllable. She added that if I ever were to take sick, she would come and take care of me. As she spoke, a faint glimmer of hope glittered in the distance, but then the solemn face of reality appeared, telling me that she would never live in Europe again. I thought to myself that she had no notion of how sick I was of being alone, without her, and how mentally and physically exhausted I was since they had left Paris. I almost pitied myself, but self-pity would be a dead end.

Her voice was soft, entreating, and my heart spun to the tune of shadow dances and our remembered whispers in the night, sometimes desperate, which kept echoing in me. She then swore again that if I were sick, she'd come and take care of me. Sweet lies, but so sweet anyway—I wanted her to continue lying to me as they replaced the lonely, cold-blooded sensation streaming through me with the heat of hope. Such was my thirst for re-establishing.

But the mourning over the death of our relationship was suspended again by the birth of another beautiful daughter, Victoria, on Bastille Day, July 14th, 2003, to Concetta and me. But after the ecstasy over her birth, which helped us meld together as a family, no one could have predicted that it was the high point of our relationship. Little did I know that through it all, a dark veil shadowed us....

But the fallout of the separation from Sylvia had the greatest impact on my relationship with Concetta. Every once in a while, she overheard my telephone calls with Sylvia, and she felt the tone of my voice was overly cordial, sometimes seductive. I had no objective clue and disagreed. But her intuition was powerful, and prophetic. For months after Sylvia's departure from Paris, we hardly spoke. Now we were calling each other several times a week, which was a prelude to my visit to San Francisco a month later, to visit my kids and Sylvia. Then I planned to head to Oregon to spend time with my mother, brothers and sister.

The calls were building up to the moment I would see Sylvia again, whom I met with our son Frankie for Valentine's Day dinner in an Italian restaurant. There was "déja vu" written all over the outside of the place as we were greeted by Italian waiters I had known when I lived in the district. It was dangerous to be here at this same place, when we had been so, so close, sharing our every breath, not so long ago. It was so dangerous that I worried I'd cross over to her and it would cause an irreparable rupture in my relationship with Concetta. But love bonds were still so strong that I could not resist, in spite of inner warnings.

We had lived in North Beach for about four years before leaving for Europe, and had often walked into cafés where Italian was sometimes spoken, to show my kids the evidence of a strong, cultural city and the Italian side of their roots. Memories of our courting, mixing with the Italian community, doing the "giro italiano,"[24] crowned with gasping embraces in the car parked overlooking the crashing waves along the Great Highway near Cliff House surged through my mind.

During one precious moment, we were family, during our dinner, as I tried to freeze time, in the middle of it. Then it switched to slow motion; I looked across the table at Sylvia's black eyes and her lips slowly moving, saying something to Frankie who smiled often. He was beaming, happy to see his father and mother together, finally. I drove Frankie and Sylvia home after dinner, then I parked a half a block from the house. In a few minutes Sylvia opened the door and sat next to me.

It was a modest, non-star hotel. My friends fondly called it the Ritz or the minus 5-star hotel in the middle of North Beach. That evening, the rhythm of our nostalgic embraces was inflamed by the echoes of the distant fog horns in the Bay and the occasional clanging of a cable car bell. The next day, I traveled to Oregon to visit my mother then to Paris, where I returned to the apartment shared with Concetta and our daughter, Victoria. But my relationship with Concetta had temporarily dwindled to a cordial recognition of each other's presence, at the reigniting of my relationship with Sylvia.

We separated. Our deep love for Victoria was the only survivor of my relationship with Concetta for the next few months; but the little one never gave up trying to

---

24 "Giro italiano" means Italian circuit, voyage or tour. What some Italians in North Beach referred to when playing pool in Café d'Italia, then proceeding to Franco's Café to talk with some friends, afterwards going to Café Puccini for a cappuccino, and returning to Café d'Italia.

get us all back together again. Words flowed through me like a tidal wave after our devastating separation, which inspired me to write the following:

> L'arbre silencieux
> Like a shadow Love,
> You lobby for love
> To bring us hence into one
>
> Your mother and I
> But, programmed passion? How can it be?
> Once radiant...embrace
> Turned cold
>
> Like the ashes of
> Yesterday's campfire....
> Not your fault
> Ma fille
> Ma fille
> No more hope
> But you
> And me.[25]

Telephone conversations between Sylvia and I then became a daily tradition and we, as so many times before, began fantasizing about her and the kids' return to Paris. We even spent flaming, delirious evenings together during my visit to San Francisco, hanging onto the threads of the past. But our plans, just like the ones we made after she left Paris years ago, turned out to be unrealistic outpourings of pure emotion. After I returned to Paris, our calls became more and more infrequent and our plans for our reunion were inevitably abandoned. Consequently, we grew farther and farther apart.

Concetta and I, on the contrary, with the help of Victoria as the catalyst, grew closer and closer together. We were finally able to patch up our differences and rekindle the passion. Our lives became more and more entwined as we spent more time together and our relationship soared. We eventually moved in together, as a family.

But strong winds of a new challenge tested the joy of our renewed passion, threatening to change everything....

---

25 Frank Romano, from the poem, "Ma Fille," p. 35, Crossing Over, supra.

Chapter 13: Mediterranean Lawyer

At the same time Concetta was living her passion, raising a baby daughter, I was nurturing a passion carried over from practicing law in the US: arguing cases in court as a trial lawyer. My renaissance was made possible the moment I passed the Paris bar exam and was thereafter sworn in as a member of the Paris Bar. While I continued teaching at the university and working as an associate lawyer in Paris, Rolland, a Paris Bar School classmate, who had become a member of the Marseille Bar, invited me to visit him in Marseille and check out the growing opportunities for lawyers on the shores of the Mediterranean.

My body rocketed through the middle of France on my first trip on the TGV, the French fast train. As I looked out the window, trees blended with the skyline and both seemed to pass in a quick blur. On arrival, the gloomy haze that seemed to perpetually hover over the city of love had been replaced by the blue sky of the Mediterranean... as far as I could see, a deep, dark-blue sky lying over the sharp blade of the horizon, illuminated by a glowing sun.

I left the train and the soft Mediterranean breeze caressed the Italian part of my soul, detaching it from the heavy Northern cloudbanks preventing the anxious sun from popping through and dissipating the yellow haze blanketing the Seine. Parisians trudging through overcast streets sometimes didn't know what season it was as they desperately needed a breakthrough reminder that it was summer. Nothing ambiguous in Marseille about a Mediterranean summer....

I had only walked a few paces down the quay after leaving the train, when a poem I had written flew into my thoughts. I recalled it from memory:

> Mediterranean
> Dreaming about the cool breeze wafting foam riding abreast the
>   wave
> upon my face in the impassioned grasp of the Mediterranean—
> caressing with voluptuous Italian waves holding me close to my
>   ancestor's bosom The Mediterranean—spontaneous laughter
>   inward warmth rising to the surface
> in the shape of a smile—
> this is where I belong

this is my home—thousands of miles from the cradle of my birth
I still have the warm water flowing through my veins
I salute you, Mediterranean, from the coast of Spain to the flaming
    shores of Italy,
the white sands of Israel to the Egyptian beaches, to the rolling
    dunes of Morocco
the cool, caressing waves
deep-blue eyes mystifying the desire.
to passionately grasp the tips of the smooth waves
hurl hearts of lovers
floating on the crest of the old world
and renewing its strength as the new world embraces nurtured
    traditions
red-blue explosive adrenalin popping
mystical blue
vibrating from the inner womb of the Mediterranean.[26]

After spending time applying for positions in Marseille, I received an offer of Civil Law Litigator for a law firm. It was owned by the one of the most famous lawyers in France, Mr. Gilbert Collard, who was best known for his criminal defense work, albeit of sometimes infamous clients.

I was offered the management of his family law department for a couple of months, since the previous lawyer had left on a two-month maternity leave. Even though I had sworn after leaving the practice of law in California a few years before that I would never again represent parties in a divorce action, I accepted the position. I quickly rented an apartment which I would stay in during the week, and then I would shoot back up to Paris at the end of the week to teach my courses at the University of Paris and spend time with Concetta and Victoria. I'd return late Sunday night or early Monday morning to the law firm. A month into the job, I was promoted to be in charge of the labor law, as well as the family law departments. To keep up I was working around the clock and traveling by rail, plane, bus and by chauffeur all over France to argue cases, even during strikes.

Mr. Collard, best known for his criminal defense work, had collected a famous and infamous client list. The French press interviewed him almost every week at the law firm or at court and sure enough, he would show up on prime time almost weekly. Every time he'd appear on TV, new files and new clients would rain on the firm. Even though all the lawyers working for him had a specialty, because of the deluge of clients each one, if available, was required to represent clients outside of his or her specialty. There were only about 11 lawyers, besides the senior partner, and we all worked overtime.

I won an important case in the Lyon Labor Court of Appeals that, according to a lawyer friend in Paris, was a major victory. He told me he couldn't remember another case like that in France, where the judge in the court of appeals allowed a

---

26 Frank Romano, from the poem, "Mediterranean," p.97, Crossing Over, supra.

party (my client) to return to the Conseil de Prud'hommes, the lower labor law court, even though he had previously lost the case there. To compensate me for my victory, and this was typical, Mr. Collard would give me new files, new clients to work with. That's all—no promotion, no bonus, just new cases to work on.

That evening, Michel, who I assumed had heard about my recent victory in the labor law matter, came to my office about seven o'clock in the evening with a file under his arm. He was in the entrance, his meaty jowls accentuated by a slight smile and short-cropped, gray-brown hair, matted on top. His blue eyes drooped with fatigue, but there was still fire deep inside. For some reason, an unlikely friendship existed between us. He was Mr. Collard's right-hand man and the lawyer who had been with him the longest. I was a recent recruit whose expertise lay more in labor and family law and he was a criminal law expert. He'd given me great last- minute advice in a criminal matter that had saved my client and me, once. That you don't forget, ever....

I waved him in and couldn't help but smile; it probably was weak as I'd put in about 20 straight hours with about two hours sleep, trying to get caught up with cases I was preparing for trial.

He slapped a file on my desk; as I reached for it, he put his hand out to stop me. Somehow he knew how to motivate me, in spite of my listlessness, by recounting how he was able to overcome a horrible scenario in a recent murder trial in a courtroom stacked against him, with even a hostile client. His client was the biggest problem as he had expected to be represented by Mr. Collard, and was disappointed with the last-minute substitution of Michel.

"But I saw the folly of the prosecutor's case who was working to finagle, by hook or crook, my client into jail. I went to the middle of the floor, and first remarked that the judge's podium was the highest, next highest was the prosecutor's then my lowly desk, below. Got the jury to focus on the unfairness of the whole set-up. But it got their attention."

He paused and looked at me, his blue eyes penetrating mine, and he knew he had me, as well! I didn't question why he was telling me this; he was shaping (or manipulating) me, and I was lapping it up, all of it!

"Then I hit hard at the inequities of the proceeding—forged against the defendant from the get-go—and his childhood, living isolated from all other kids, at the mercy of cruel parents. Then I laid it out. Against all odds, he became a gifted painter, and now...."

He raised his voice, "Then I went to the jury and looked at each one in the eyes, and said, 'The prosecutor is trying to force a conviction, only interested in putting another notch on his gun handle. But he knows he's wrong—look at his face! He trembles at the inequity. This is a despicable charade, flying in the face of a principle that goes to the heart of our entire legal system, the presumption of innocence!'"

He sat down to catch his breath, as it was late, and I'm sure Michel had already put in long hours, as I had.

"I looked around and even the prosecutor was on the edge of his seat. I ended by stating, 'In light of that, just imagine you won't be able to fool your conscience, echoing your decision months later if you rule against my client—clearly no choir boy—but here he is definitely not guilty."

He stood up again and walked to the door, "When I summoned my client to the office and read the verdict, not guilty, he tried to hide his joy with a badly-disguised knitted brow as he looked at me, hostility still projected by his teeth grinding in his square jaw, in spite of the verdict."

"But you know, Romano, I didn't care what my client thought; it was exalting. I...I put everything into it...I couldn't have done better than that!"

I can't describe the intensity of his eyes, something almost from another land, another planet. All I remember is I totally connected with him that night, and imagined that we both were charging into battle, together....

He walked back and sat down in front of my desk, crossing his legs, his pant legs riding up to reveal long, black socks, falling down from use.

"I'm called into court—another murder case in Bordeaux—tomorrow."

His big, blue eyes flashed toward me but he didn't have to do it again to get my attention. I had forgotten I was tired a long time ago....

"I also have a client, who was almost brutally murdered by his ex-wife and barely escaped with serious injuries after she attacked him with a knife and a pickaxe when he was sleeping in bed. Well...."

He stopped and his eyes fixed on me to see if I was still listening. My face was drawn to him like radar. He continued, clearly trying to draw me into this; but he already had me....

"Well, the lower court decision rendered a suspended sentence, so no jail time for the witch, and paid him little damages[27] so he and the prosecutor filed an appeal. They want her to pay damages, then get her off the streets and locked up for having committed this grisly crime."

He scanned the wall, "Our client has since lost his job, was divorced by his wife and has no income and has to see a series of shrinks ..."

His voice lowered and he cupped his hand next to his mouth, to add emphasis,

"This kind of macho man from Marseille is now afraid of women, like he was castrated...and is seriously depressed and has no money to pay the shrink."

His lips curled and his beady blue eyes turned a bit crimson; he was pleading his case.

It was evident that the intention of my busy colleague was neither to make a social call, nor to tell war stories. I had anticipated his next move, which was to ask me to do something.

"I feel this case, but I can't make it to court. The trial is in the Massif Central, in the middle of France, tomorrow afternoon and I'm due in court in Bordeaux for opening arguments in the murder case I told you about, the same day. I need a good lawyer to replace me, Frank."

I saw it coming and it hit me hard but I couldn't resist nor let him down; besides I owed him. I also felt like I was already in it too deep, but I felt apprehensive as I

---

27 French criminal procedure allows victims of crimes to a claim for damages during the criminal proceedings.

envisaged my first experience in French criminal court would be an attempted murder case!

"I'd like to help you as you've saved me before, but I had a relatively minor criminal case before and I've never argued in the criminal courts yet in France, and to break the ice in an attempted murder...."

He laughed, shaking his head, as if he obviously knew something I didn't. "You'll do fine. I've got a lot of faith in you." He paused and reloaded; I knew what was coming...."The file's on your desk. Just redo the brief and submit it tomorrow to the court. Also prepare the 'dossier de plaidoirie' (pleadings) to submit to the judges after the arguments, as usual. Any questions-you've got my cell? I've got to get out of here...."

I felt frozen as he inched out the door, but before he disappeared, he turned around brusquely. I was still staring at him and hadn't moved.

"Here's Sammy's cell." He handed me a scribbled post-it. "Just call him and he'll chauffeur you there tomorrow, as there's no other way to get there in time and... thanks!" He was gone before I could even open my mouth, which means he moved like lightning!

I leafed through the file, my head in a daze, without reading as the pages turned over and over and I was mesmerized. I don't know how long that continued but suddenly I snapped out of it and closed the file, pulling my watch out of my pocket where I hid it to hide time. It was already about nine pm. I opened the file again, this time determined to focus my eyes; the first page slapped me in the face:

"The trial is scheduled for Wednesday, XXXX, at 2 pm, Cour d'appel, Chambre Correctional." (Criminal Court of Appeals).

A sobering blow! The city of XXXX would be in Auvergne, in the Massif Central region of France, about five to six hours away by car. A deep sigh involuntarily released from my lungs as a lawyer colleague walked by and just giggled, without stopping. Everybody in the firm, already working double-time, knew I now had twice the number of files than any of them, since my "promotion."

But the lawyer coldly continued walking by and the main door creaked before it slammed shut. I mumbled, disgruntled, to myself as I shifted my chair in front of the desk, seized my coffee cup and gulped down a mouthful of bitter cold coffee, to give me strength.

"Another all-nighter," I inwardly groaned, as my body slid down in the chair. But then it straightened, as I almost shouted, "Get a grip, poor baby! Isn't this what you've been preparing for all your life, to fight for victims who depend on you, anywhere, anytime? You're lucky you can do this so...move it!"

I grabbed the scribbled post-it as it was about to flutter to the ground. I called the number and a pleasant voice answered immediately. Sammy was waiting for my call, as Michel had obviously given him a heads up. He told me the trip would take five hours, maybe a little more, depending on traffic, and he'd pick me up in front of the firm at 6:30 am.

I left the office at 5:30 am, a cross between a homing pigeon and a zombie. I walked the seven blocks to my apartment, took a quick shower, wolfed down a peanut butter and jelly sandwich, and changed clothes. I headed back to the firm in forty minutes. Sammy was already waiting in the firm's brand new SUV in front of the building on Rue de Paradise. I pulled up next to the car and froze. My feet became numb with the vibration of the motor, and chills raced up and down my spinal column and legs as it all came down on me, at once: I was preparing for war, to argue before the French criminal court on an important case—ATTEMPTED MURDER, no less—in a city I didn't know, in the mountains of central France.

I motioned to the driver, who watched me impassively as the window slowly descended.

"Bonjour," he nodded. I told him I'd return in five minutes with the file then I turned toward the door of the building leading to the firm a couple of floors above.

Upon my return, the door latch was down and opening the back door, I hoisted up the file and my fold-over garment bag containing my lawyer's robe (French lawyers wear long, black robes in court) and flopped them on the far seat. I sat down as the door automatically closed.

I had practiced drafting my arguments and repeated my lines several times earlier and all I needed now was to sleep. "By the way, Sammy, could you wake me about 15 minutes before arrival so I could review my arguments...."

He cut me off, "We'll have an hour when we reach the courthouse, so you can do it during lunch."

The car sped onward toward the Massif Central region. The faint voice coming from the GSM was the only sound in the car as I fell fast asleep. The next thing I was aware of, the car jumped and jerked me awake as a blur of figures and buildings flew by.

"We've arrived. I'll take you to a nice little place...old style cuisine."

"I just want to see the courthouse first...."

"There it is on the left." The high walls, like those of a fortress, made it seem impenetrable. I hoped that wasn't a bad omen.

"Bon!" (Ok)

I wasn't good company during lunch but he seemed to relax and slowly masticate his veal steak, looking around contentedly as I spent the entire time with my face in a file, coming up for air to stab the food on my plate and stuff it in my mouth. I don't even remember what I ate as my head was in the file, thinking about my lines, gestures...He seemed used to chauffeuring lawyers around all over France, probably watching them pore over files during lunch. Not surprising as lawyers in this firm traveled at least twice a week to the four corners of France and sometimes across the borders into other European countries. His round face, black hair and oval eyes made me think of the Orient. He told me he was Filipino and had worked for Mr. Collard for about ten years.

All I remember was Sammy said it was time to go. I closed the file, paid the bill, and then followed him to the car.

We arrived within minutes and the high, vault-like walls seemed so closed, even more impenetrable than before. We went in one entrance to find the way to the courtroom and quickly butted up against a closed and locked door. We finally found the main entrance and after walking through a maze of corridors, through alcoves opening up into a labyrinth of long and short corridors, we saw a group of people crowding around an entrance to a room. A sign "Criminal Court of Appeals" confirmed we were in the right place. It was 30 minutes before trial. A dark-haired man approached me, his quick steps rhythmically clicking across the polished courthouse floors.

"You Mr. Romano?" I nodded, putting my garment bag on the floor. "Thank God!"

"Jean XXX?"

"Yes, that's me," he responded nervously as he grabbed my garment bag. "We have time, Jean—let's go around the corner." I looked behind me and Sammy had retreated back into the hallway somewhere.

After informing him of the procedure, that I would be called to argue first, etc., his hand twitched nervously; sweat glistened on his receding hairline as he reached for his handkerchief. I reached out and gently grasped his hand to show him I was steady. "We're here and we're going to fight. We need to calm down and enter the courtroom like we own it, ok?"

I tried to have compassion for him, thinking that he was probably more nervous than I was; after all, in a few minutes he would be facing his would-be killer wife, and his life depended on the decision.

So I tried a smile. It came out purposely a little tight: I was trying not to make it seem like it came from a screw-loose complacency, but to show confidence and courage and give him courage in the face of imminent danger. We both needed it as the lawyer for the wife, his adversary, was a criminal law specialist who had many years experience in the courtroom trenches. My nerves were grinding and jumping inside and I could feel my heart literally thumping against my rib cage—my mouth was dryer than the Sahara. I had to fight for my client, keep my head up, avoid the flack and meet the attack head on. Fortunately I had been able to sleep in the car at least four good hours....

We entered the courtroom in the middle of another trial. I sat next to my client and saw Sammy join us, then walk briskly to the back of the room, a newspaper clutched in his trembling hand. Even he seemed nervous...The name of the case was soon called, "People v. YYYY, with Jean XXXX, claiming damages. Mr. Collard, representing Jean XXXX, Mr. WWWW, representing the respondent YYYY."

I got up and looked across the room. The courtroom was set up old style. Several judges, their sleek black robes with long strips of red fabric flowing down on both sides, sat in a semi-circle in front, about 50 feet from two podiums about 15 feet apart, from which the lawyers spoke, their clients seated in back of them. The set-up was extremely intimidating, formal and institutional, and the judges in front, stoically sitting in judgment, peered across the room as if they had descended from heaven with just enough time to judge the poor, lowly plebeians before ascending.

The lawyers in the case made their introductions, including the prosecution on behalf of the state. I informed the court that I was replacing Mr. Collard on behalf of our client, Mr. Jean XXXX. The presiding judge nodded like she expected the absence of the great star celebrity of the firm. The prosecutor went first.

The prosecutor on behalf of the people argued briefly, but fervently, against the lower court decision n o t to put the attempted murderer of my client behind bars. He did not mention that my client was seriously harmed and requested compensation; that was my job. "Counselor for Mr. Jean XXXX, you have the floor." My client hid among the crowd in the benches in back. I curled my finger, trying to get him to sit nearer. He wouldn't budge....

I walked to the podium and then stepped up the stairs. It was a commanding view of the courtroom; then my eyes cast over the attempted murderer—the respondent (defendant on appeal) sitting in front and to the right of the podium— and her lawyer, my adversary, already standing at the opposite podium. Her truculent spirit was disguised by a feminine appearance, her hair neatly tied in the back...I thought, More like a pit bull with lip stick.

An internal red warning flag was already at full mast, cautioning me that the set up here would take me away from my game plan. I hoped to get close to the judges as French lawyers normally argue within about ten feet of them in most civil proceedings. I needed my whole body to get the attention of the judges, to appeal to them with my orchestrated arguments, gestures and distract them away from my accent.

I stepped down from the podium a few feet and stopped. I asked,

"Madame la présidente (your honor), vous me permettez...." (Will you allow me...)

She nodded, granting an exception and allowing me to argue my case in front of them, eye to eye, not more than eight feet away from the respondent. I began, "Madame la Présidente, les conseillers, members of the audience, vous me permettez, there has been a serious travesty in the lower court." I argued, "It is unfair that my client is not compensated for the brutal attack while sleeping, his life almost yanked from him, taking doctors a while to stabilize him in the emergency room and subsequently suffering serious physical and mental trauma."

I watched closely the judges and saw eyebrows raise, probably trying to figure out what accent they were hearing. That was the first step, getting them to focus on my words through my accent, then punching my arguments through with impeccable French. So far, so good...."He subsequently lost his job in spite of regular visits to psychiatrists, and was relegated to damage control after the cruel divorce: visiting rights, losing his house, being without any income. He squats at his brother's house at present in Marseille."

Then I went into the murderous attack by his ex-wife, "With a pick ax and a knife, she attacked him during his sleep. No hard evidence was submitted showing she was provoked in any way, just rumor and innuendo. Was it not expedient for her to get rid of her husband so she could have total custody of the kids, and make it look like she was driven to kill him?"

"That may have worked, but there was not a stitch of evidence...a shameful travesty...."

My planned pause, during which I intended to refer to my notes, turned out to be cataclysmic and decisive as I realized I had left them at the podium. But the judges—

who I only took my eyes off of to glare at the respondent and when I gesticulated in the direction of the audience when talking about Jean XXXX—were watching every move I made, hanging onto my every syllable. We connected.

I quickly assessed that if had I walked back to get my notes, even if it took just a few seconds, I would break the momentum, break the spell, and would lose them completely; and that would be it, the lost margin I was grasping onto through the force of my eyes. So I did the only thing I could do—I kept arguing. My preparation had fortunately left me with an outline of my arguments engraved in my brain. The rest I filled in, with gestures, lowering and raising my voice, seldom taking my eyes off the judges, shifting my gaze back and forth to all three sets of eyes, but focusing on appealing to the presiding judge's feelings.

Then I did something that wasn't in the script as I saw the murderer turn up her nose in an ugly frown, putting wrinkles in her otherwise perfect face. I turned to face her as her eyes were bearing down on me, scathing, as if she wanted to tear a bite out of me:

"You are a dangerous woman." I pointed to her and her eyes lowered.

I ended my sometimes emotional appeal to the judges: "I respectfully request, judges, that my victimized client be able to afford help to pull his destroyed life together, and request that the respondent pay him the amount of 50,000 Euros (I don't remember the exact sum) in damages, and that the people be protected from this dangerous woman who (and I slightly raised my voice, pointing my finger downwards) is free to walk the streets with impunity…."

My nerves were now jumping out of my shirt; but I tried to remain calm and returned to the podium to gather my notes and step down to join my client.

I had consumed about 12-13 minutes maximum and finished before the maximum allotted time which was about 15 minutes.

"Mrs. WWWW." My opponent was called to the podium, and standing there, projected a deadly calm, ready to take my client down….

I breathed a silent, inward sigh and faced her.

The first five minutes of her arguments, as expected, stung my client, as she made it look like my client sadistically abused his poor wife, the victim according to Mrs. WWWW. I shifted my eyes over to her client, who was hunched over, trying her best to look as small and abused as possible. I shook my head objecting, hoping the judges would see I objected to those theatrics, totally contrived and not supported by the record other than respondent's self-serving testimony. I began to object, but I shoved my index finger in my mouth before I could do it. In French court, verbal objections are not accepted, especially in the court of appeals (even US appeals court judges rarely allow objections). As a French litigator, it was a never-ending challenge to temper my conditioned reflexes formed in American trial courts as an American trial litigator.

I caught a look of anguish on my client's face popping out of the crowd; it was contorted and red, as if he were holding in a desperate scream. My heart dropped into my shoes as she spoke beautifully and the judges were zeroed in on her every syllable…she had them.

She should have stopped there, and if she had, I mused, we were dead—my client and I both felt it.

But she kept going on and on, and at some point, lost touch with the judges. After about 20 minutes, I noticed the judges began to look at each other, brows furrowed, pens starting to tap…I then became my opponent's cheerleader, cheering her on to self-destruction.

She continued for about 40 minutes and during that time, she managed to neutralize the impact of her earlier arguments by obstinately stretching them out, sometimes even repeating herself. She had gotten carried away on her soap box and just couldn't step down. She was too full of herself and her speech was too intent on trying to show the judges that my succinct arguments, according to her, ignored important points she would cover in detail, to annihilate my client. This instead of paying close attention to those who had the life of her client in their hands. In spite of her experience, she fell into the trap and got caught up in the resonance of her own arguments.

After we handed the judges our written pleadings at the end of the trial, I walked toward my client who was cowering in the back; before I could reach the podium, the presiding judge spoke:

"Mr. Romano, you requested 80,000 euros in damages, right?"

As I turned around, the epitoge (vertical strip of black material hanging from the left shoulder of my robe) wind-milled. Surprised, I struggled to keep my composure and balance as I stood for a few seconds, collecting my thoughts.

"Excuse me your honor, but I recall requesting 50,000 euros for my client."

"Are you sure it wasn't 80,000?

"Your honor, if you insist, yes, I respectfully request 80,000 euros in compensation for my client!"

"I'll send you both my decision in about three weeks."

The gavel came down on the hard wooden bench, and that was it.

I left out the back door with my client, followed by Sammy. We went to a local café. I took a sip of my espresso and inhaled a deep breath; my client did the same.

"She was good, real good!"

"Yes, but I think she took it too far, and maybe upset the judges."

"I don't know."

"Anyway at the end, the presiding judge was insisting on me asking for more compensation for you than I had asked originally. Judges rarely do that…that's a good sign! Oh well, I think we put our best foot forward. We'll see."

"Thanks counselor, for being there. I feel more relieved now." He meekly reached his hand out and I shook it, holding my eyes on his for a second. He blinked but his expression told me he had renewed confidence and was happy someone was fighting for him. That feeling was the only compensation I sought.

Sammy drove through town as I sat in back on the reclining seat, my mouth already beginning to open. Before falling back into a deep sleep, I couldn't help thinking that this broad-shouldered young man, probably at one time full of confidence in his Mediterranean youthfulness growing up in Marseille, was reduced to a fragile shadow.

We returned to Marseille late. Sammy left me off at the firm; it was empty and the floor boards creaked as I walked down the corridor to my office. I dropped off my robe and the file and grabbed a couple of other files to take home to prepare for the upcoming trials in Nice and Lyon.

Three weeks later, I met Michel in the hallway while we were both rushing by, he with his robe slung over his arm headed for court, and me with several books under my arm headed for my office. He smiled and shouted that the judgment was rendered in the Jean XXXX case and the client was very happy. Before I could ask any of the details he was out the door. It was his way of saying we won!

I left the firm early that evening for the first time in months and strolled down "Rue de Paradise" to the cold fanning of the Mediterranean breeze on my face. The mistral's early warning didn't affect me, not that evening, as the blood had risen to my face imagining Jean XXXX eating "bouillabaisse"[28] with his brother, contented and now able to start his new life. My brimming eyes looked up toward the blue, velvety Mediterranean sky and I thanked God I could do something to help, thanked the sky, the wind, the earth, that in this sometimes cruel and unfair world, a voice is heard....

---

28 Bouillabaisse is a famous Marseillais traditional dish consisting of 1) fish soup containing vegetables, chunks of fish and shell fish flavored with garlic, bay leaf and other herbs and spices, served with croutons and "rouille"—spicy provincial mayonnaise with garlic and olive oil—2) potatoes and 3) whole fish.

Chapter 14: The End

After returning to Paris a few days later to teach my classes, something extraordinary waited for me one day at the University of Paris, where I was still employed as a full-time professor. I was scheduled that day to teach a course in comparative law. The director of the English department invited me to attend a lecture by an Israeli professor concerning the relationship of the writings of the Kabbalah with the works of Isaac Newton.

I didn't know much about the Kabbalah, other than it was the mystical teachings in Judaism; but I couldn't imagine its connection with Isaac Newton. After the conference, we were all invited to a kosher lunch set up in the teachers' lounge. By chance, the speaker sat next to me.

The host introduced her as Ayval Ramati, an Israeli Jew and expert in the Kabbalah and its connection to science. She had taught at Tel Aviv University. Her reddish-brown hair was neatly tied in a bun behind her head, and she held her nose up proudly.

We were served an array of kosher dishes and dipped pita bread into hummus, shakshuka (tomato and egg mix), fava bean spread, fried eggplant, red pepper salad and other specialties. I waited patiently while Ayval spoke to the director of the program seated on her other side. Then my turn came after the tea was served on a nearby table. She got up and placed a cube of sugar in one cup and returned to our table, slyly looking towards me. I introduced myself and she did the same; there was great warmth in her voice.

As soon as I mentioned the subject of interfaith work for peace in the Holy Land, her soft blue eyes lit up. Her spiritual beauty radiated from every pore of her body as she made it clear to me that there was a lot of interfaith activity going on where she came from. She started relating that her sister was working for the UN and engaged in discussions between Israeli Jews and Bedouins living in Israel.

As we discussed the interfaith activities taking place in Israel, an inner force hibernating inside woke up, hungry and in need of immediate nourishment. The vision of many years ago came back, piercing through the crusty layers of yesteryear, as if it had been birthed at this very moment.[29]

---

29 Storm Over Morocco, 4th Edition, supra, p.134.

She indicated to me that for the last few years, more groups had come together to organize dialogues among Jews, Muslims, Christians and people of all faiths. That started me salivating…I shared with her my story, that I'd traveled about 30 years ago from Paris headed to the Holy Land and had been impassioned by a vision I had while living there that someday I'd participate in the non-violent interfaith peace movement in Israel and the West Bank.[30] I explained that I got as far as Casablanca where I entered a mosque to learn about Islam, which had been inhabited by a fanatic Muslim cult. I was held prisoner, which prevented me from continuing my voyage to the Holy Land as I needed to muster all my energy to escape from the grip of that cult and return to Paris.[31]

She was silent, her blue eyes trying to size me up. She then spoke, encouraging me to plan a trip to the Holy Land to experience what was happening first hand. Then we exchanged emails. That was an epiphany….

In the subway returning home, it seemed I had ascended from a dark hole where cobwebs had thickly spread over my dreams, until today. There was no doubt now that I had to travel to the Holy Land as soon as possible, at least to determine whether what I had experienced long ago was a true vision or just another one of my meaningless fantasies.

Concetta, who was employed organizing conferences in an international organization, had spent hours discussing the Middle East with co-workers from Israel and the West Bank. She was far more enlightened on the details of the conflict than I was. She, in fact, had recently explained to me in detail what the situation was like in Israel and the West Bank. I was sure she would be an enthusiastic supporter of my following through with my envisaged interfaith projects in that troubled land.

I was wrong.

Even though she recognized that the Middle East was a powder keg and the great need for people to visit, in particular, Israel and the West Bank and work on peace projects, she didn't see why it had to be me. She lectured me that the only people who had the right to do that were single adventurers who didn't have a woman and dependent kids. She then reminded me of my responsibilities to spend time with her and Victoria…and to stay alive.

"I don't see what staying alive has anything to do with it!"

Her stone-cold eyes measured me and she frowned as if she was looking through the lens of a camera pointed to an inchoate, blurred image. I refused to let her focus me in the image she wanted as I needed to share my vision with her. She shook her head and turned abruptly and walked to the kitchen, banging pots and pans as she pretended to be busy.

She would never share my vision; to her, the Middle East remained a topic to be analyzed and dissected on a screen, but she would not cross over into the field, to the trenches. To her, they were for others to fight in.

But that's what most people were already saying to me: "That's for them to do—why you?" I could never understand who they meant by "them." Besides, I

---

30 Ibid.

31 Ibid., p. 323.

sincerely believed that if we all had that attitude, the trenches would be empty and nothing would get done. I only knew I longed to participate in the actual field work, to go to the Middle East and do something, even in my own little way, for peace. This cold war between Concetta and I pushed our relationship into the red zone, and became a catalyst for endless conflicts between us. But the more we fought, the more determined I was to visit the Holy Land and do what I felt I was destined to do. That would mark a new beginning...and another sad end. After several months of thinking about what Ayval said, and reflecting on a heavy meditation session during which I had had my initial vision that I would go to the Holy Land [experienced while sitting in a "Chambre de Bonne" (servants quarters) in Paris looking across the river Seine, about 30 years ago][32], it was time to make a move.

Events in the Holy Land helped expedite my plans: On February 8, 2005, Ariel Sharon and Mahmoud Abbas, in a joint agreement, decided to end years of violence during the infamous Second Intifada, which had started on September 28, 2000, and had claimed many victims.[33] Many people were killed by Israeli soldiers and Palestinian suicide bombers as the region erupted into a gushing bloodbath. That wasn't a good time to visit the region; but times had changed...and I was ready.

Thanks to the TGV, the fast train, between Paris and Marseille, it only took about three and a half hours to travel, as opposed to the standard trains that took seven to eight hours. My life consisted of shuttling back and forth to see Concetta and our daughter, Victoria, and teach my courses at the University of Paris, then back on the train to the law firm, back to fighting in the courts.

The hard work, faith and a little luck helped me win most of my court cases. As compensation, I was given more and more challenging cases at the law firm; however other opportunities were arising as well, such as teaching a comparative law course at my alma mater in San Francisco coming up in March, all expenses paid. In addition, the trip to the Holy Land was imminent. I requested a month off in March and Mr. Collard refused, saying it would be too hard to find a replacement and that was a big month; I was indispensable. My response to him was the following typical French expression and Arab proverb, but it fell on deaf ears: "Les cimetières sont remplis de gens qui se croyaient indispensables" (The cemeteries are full of people who believed they were indispensable).

Three days after that, I gave the firm two month's notice and left at the end of that time. I purchased a round-trip ticket to Israel and planned to visit the Holy Land for about 2 weeks. Upon my return to Paris, Concetta's reception was cold and distant. As she sat in a chair next to the bed on which my suitcase lay, she continued: "Well, remember how blockheaded you were about defending the State of Israel in its treatment of Palestinians: you spoke as a typical indoctrinated American...."

She was right about my initial misconceptions concerning the Middle East and thanks to her I had awakened to what was happening. I also referred to my 30-year old

---

32 Storm Over Morocco, 4th Edition, supra, p.134.

33 'Intifada' is an Arabic term literally meaning "shaking off" and used to mean "uprising or insurrection." "La Résistance se poursuit" (The Resistance Continues). Le Figaro.fr. 9/28/2010.

vision to inspire me to proceed with plans to participate in interfaith dialogue there. Only by visiting would I discover the shocking truths about the Holy Land.

"Now you understand why I must go, then."

Silence. She didn't need to say anything as it marked the end of us. The reflection of the plaque of Camille Claudel, near the River Seine in Paris where we walked during our first date, grew dimmer, dimmer....

The expectations of meeting my dormant fate filled me with ecstatic rhythms undulating down my spine as I contemplated that I would finally arrive at my destination, the Holy Land, after setting out and failing 30 years before.

Then the fear dampened my expectations as I contemplated something happening that would again stop my forward motion into the Holy Land. I had this vision burning inside begging for confirmation, to be proven it was not illusory. The only way to find out was to test it....

Book II

Holy Land, Finally!

"Touch not the nettle,
for the bonds of love are ill to loose."[34]

---

34 D.H. Lawrence, Lady Chatterley's Lover (Cambridge: Lawrence Edition, Penguin Twentieth-Century Classics Series, 1994) Chapter 7, p.83.

Chapter 15: Ayval

It was the end of the beginning or the beginning of the end of my long search for something to take me from my comfortable "chambre de bonne" (servant's quarters) in Paris to the streets of Morocco in 1978, where I had planned to proceed across Africa, destination, the Holy Land. My plans had been drastically changed, but I was back on track, 27 years later, and doubly determined not to let anything deviate me from my path. The soft humming of jet engines sent me into a hypnotic, meditative trance as my head rested on the window.

It was now July, 2005, and from the moment the plane touched down at Ben Gurion Airport in Tel Aviv, something inside that had been blocked broke loose…my path had looped around to complete the circle. Flying over the crashing beasts shored by ocean gales storming the coast of Casablanca 27 years hither, I finally made it to the tender but contested shores of the Holy Land.

Everything I had ever learned would soon be tested. I had been warned that my gestures towards interfaith peace would be ill-received, that I would be suspected a spy the moment I touched down on such disputed ground. Ayval would lead me to the people involved, maybe even to the desert to meet with the Bedouins, but my vision would be tested on the spot; then I'd discover whether my sacrifices would be justified or not.

I disembarked onto the ramp and was immediately welcomed by the warm, heavy mantle of an Israeli summer. The rainy, Parisian summer dampness was far behind me as I stepped from the ramp onto a long corridor lined with paintings hanging under rows of windows, through which penetrated the scorching Mediterranean sun.

Lines formed before several exit interview booths and moved very slowly. Each passport was carefully checked, researched on a computer screen and sometimes the passengers were asked questions. Finally my turn arrived. I approached the booth. A young girl sitting comfortably inside watched me as I approached. I handed her my passport. She looked up to check if the photo fit my face. Then she asked me why I was visiting Israel. I told her I was there to visit a friend and to participate in the interfaith peace projects. Her brow creased as she appeared to look into a computer or on some list.

After at least five minutes, she stamped my passport and waved me through. I passed through another long corridor until I arrived at the baggage claim where

I found my suitcase resting on a round conveyor belt which had stopped turning probably a long time ago: the exit interviews had held us up for at least 45 minutes. I claimed my suitcase and rolled it toward an arched passageway through which I proceeded to a fountain where people were waiting for the passengers, some carrying signs, others shouting and pointing. It was like entering into a huge room of people preparing for a birthday celebration, with balloons rising to the ceiling and people hugging each other. It was like a continuous homecoming, to the promised land....

No one was there to greet me but it didn't matter, as I was swept into a party mood by others. As I boarded the train, my perception of things would forever be changed. For the first time, I saw youngsters, men and adolescents alike in khaki uniforms, carrying rifles on shoulder straps. I had to remind myself that Israel was constantly in a state of alert. I'd never lived in a country where so many soldiers were going to and fro.

The train interior was dotted with drab green clothing as at least 60% of the passengers were soldiers. I asked a young man looking out the window in front of me, his kippah slanting to the side of his head, where the Central Train Station would be. He looked about 18 years old—his hair was closely cropped around the neck of the drooping kippah—as he smiled, pointing out the window. "Three more stops." His accent was surprisingly heavy. I had to remind myself that I was in Israel talking to Israeli, and not American, Jews.

The cultural shock had whisked me through a time warp, as I was an American coming to this place at the speed of sound. It took a while to be sure I had crossed into the Middle East and was no longer speaking to my Jewish friends in San Francisco at a wedding or some other function. The dark, horned-rimmed glasses perched on the nose under the withdrawn eyes of the Israeli soldier made him look like he was in deep in thought. Maybe he was thinking about whether he'd survive the next tour of duty in Hebron, a hotly contested part of the occupied West Bank.

It was tragic to wrench these youths from their families, schools, their loved ones to go off and fight someone else's war on some obscure, arid plain, or in a desert where water and survival were a luxury. The boy could find himself at some lonely checkpoint in the West Bank, not knowing why he was there and why he was so exposed in such a hostile, occupied land, his youth not able to come to the rescue when the machine gun starts rattling and his youthful body becomes lifeless before hitting the ground. But it's for a good cause, the survival of the State of Israel, for better or for worse, is it not?

I left the train at the designated stop and faced the heat swooping down on my pale, city frame as I walked through the train station annex corridor. I called my friend, Ayval, on my cell phone then headed out the exit door where she was to pick me up.

As I left the train station, the intense, humid heat closed in, surrounding me with a stifling stillness. All seemed to be in slow motion compared to the streets of Paris as the unbearable humidity imposed its suffocating heaviness. Panhandlers sat on the sides of the sidewalk, their dark, hairy arms rising to the passersby, their parched lips pleading for small change.

An aged man with short, white hair and a multi-colored kippah raised his pallid hands, conspicuous among the dark hands of the younger men—poverty doesn't discriminate. As I was focused on my reception from the local beggars, I felt eyes burning into me. I looked up and beheld Ayval, that same inquisitive smile laughing with me as her reddish-golden hair swirled around her neck and fell backwards. The same slow, meticulous voice welcomed me to her country as her slender hands groped for my luggage.

She led me to an old hatchback car. Without hesitation, she opened it and flung my suitcase in the back. I followed with my computer bag. As I took my place next to her in the front seat, she took out a pen and wrote some inscriptions on a piece of paper. I couldn't recognize them at first and after squinting for several minutes, finally realized she was writing in Hebrew. She wrote slowly and deliberately and at first I thought she was practicing her Hebrew to impress me. As she continued, her writing accelerated and I finally was awakened to the fact that Hebrew was probably her mother tongue and so writing it was normal.

An excited chill satisfied my need to be jolted from my cushioned existence; I was ready to discover something new, experience exotic desires, as life in Paris had become overly linear, routine. Underneath the surface, I was shaking with welled-up passion as I was moving toward realizing the unforgotten vision held fast inside me for many, many years.

The car passed signs in Hebrew, Arabic and some in English, reminding me I had entered into a new world. They instantly drew my thoughts to the semester at the Université Libre de Brussels (Free University of Brussels) where bilingual signs written in Flemish and French were everywhere. The Middle Eastern sun mercilessly beat down on the car reminding me that I was far away from Europe. Ayval had stopped and parking the car on the corner, saying she had to call someone for directions. She spoke Hebrew, a smooth but sometimes guttural language. While on the phone, she took out a pen that had been wedged in the overhead visor, and began writing in strange hieroglyphics on a tablet. My knee-jerk reaction was just as off-the-mark as the first time: It cannot be real she's writing Hebrew!

Then I had to slap my blocked mind into realizing that this was Israel, that Jews had brought Hebrew out of mothballs and made it the official language. So even though she spoke fluent English like many Israeli Jews—some who spoke with an American accent—I had to accept that Hebrew was the first language in this place and Ayval was writing notes on a tablet, logically in her first language, not English or French. Oy vey!

First, she drove to her apartment where we languished in her kitchen, drinking tea and talking peace and love. At first, she was convinced that in spite of our conversation in Paris, I must be there to visit the tourist spots in Israel. I had to convince her I was not on a classical pilgrimage to the holy land.

"Besides, if I were to join a tourist group heading to the Old City in Jerusalem, where Jesus had carried the cross to the Church of the Sepulcher—and where the tourists would be hunting for the Wailing Wall, the Temple Mount and other religious sites that would be too powerful, too emotional for me to experience—I wouldn't do that. I predict that it would be better for me to discover those places preferably one at a time, while working to bring people together during interfaith events, marches and dialogues."

Her blue eyes transformed into those of a startled pigeon, scrambling in front of a person who had abruptly reached out with a handful of bread.

"There's something else in this place. For some strange reason, it seems to be the epicenter of the world and holds the key for world peace or perpetual world conflict. I think it has nothing to do with that it is the land of the prophets and all the events that happened in the past."

Her look was more understanding and less startled this time. I expressed to her that the present situation in the Holy Land showed that little progress towards peace, understanding and unconditional love of our brothers and sisters had been made since the time of the prophets.

"In fact, it seems that similarities abound between Jesus' time and now. When Jesus was about, the Holy land was occupied and people were persecuted by the Romans. The Jews were sometimes dominated and persecuted by other Jews, notably the Sadducees and the Pharisees. Jesus claimed to have been sent to save the people, to free them from ideological and physical slavery. What is happening now is similar, except the persecutors have changed: the State of Israel is occupying Judea, Samaria, the West Bank, instead of the Romans and the persecuted are mainly Palestinians."

"My vision was clear: that several people, not just one person will be sent to work with Palestinians and Israelis to set this region free, and I would like to help out in my own little way."

She nodded as if she somehow understood, then she got up, collected the cups and walked to the sink. I mused; a strong magnetic-like force was pulling me to this place. Something had drawn me, so many years ago. It was all about feeling that all the woes, triumphs, loves of this life were set on a spinning world turning around and around, knowing they would come out a fine fiber, interwoven with all the peoples of the world, creating an everlasting peace. And somehow, I felt I would be part of it.

In the car, she told me she was taking me to the house of a person, Miriam, who was involved in the interfaith movement in Israel and lived near the beach on the outskirts of Tel Aviv near Jaffa. Ayval told me that she had just met her at an interfaith event in Galilee at a kibbutz. The car slowed and stopped in front of a fence. On the other side was a combination of trees, including a palm tree, plants and flowers, growing in anarchy all over the property.

The gate opened to a garden area surrounded by modest, off-white apartments with doors barely hanging on their hinges. Off to the side was a table and several chairs on which a couple of cats, one white the other a paltry orange color slept, their tails wrapped around their warmed bodies. The buzz of insects filled the air as we followed the walk-way to an opening in the side of a building. Through this passageway vigorously walked a stocky lady, her hair trailing behind her plump face, covered with a beaming, toothy smile. As she descended the pathway towards us, I could make her out better, including the bright-colored sweeping designs splashed on her granny dress. Was she a hippy "wannabee" or maybe an anachronism from the past, from my past?

I reached down to hug her drooping shoulders and her perfumed body sent a sweet smell of violets wafting upwards, filling me with a soothing sensation: It felt as if we were kindred souls, joining hands and life purposes after a lapse of lifetimes. The perfume seemed to slide from my nose, continuing its path through the plants in the garden. Then the pungent sea air filled my nostrils again, turning my mind to the spray rising from the pounding waves that our car had just slowly skirted. I had opened my window, as the car inched along, and eyed the seaweed and algae dancing in sea salt "snowdrifts." I imagined fish gliding by, their scales flashing opalescent images in the cool water, swishing their tails weaving in and out of the tentacles of Medusa-like jelly fish, long and flowing like satin evening gowns.

She spoke in a strong, East European-sounding accent. She explained to me later that she was part of a Shoah survivor group which included members of her family. I surmised that her accent may have come from her many conversations with Holocaust survivors and other escapees from the furnaces who had migrated to Israel.

"Hi, I'm Miriam," she announced, her cheeks reddening with sincere pleasure. "Hi, I'm Frank and I guess you know each other," I responded, not knowing what to do except wink at Ayval, whose stone smile didn't flinch.

Ayval, even though reserved, approached and embraced Miriam with a soft hug. They held each other for a few moments exchanging contented smiles, as if they had been friends for life. Yet they had only met once before; such an exchange was so different from the often mechanical big-city hugging and kissing—two times at first, four times at departure—in Paris, sometimes done quickly to get it over with.

Miriam led us up the pathway to a door of her corner flat; it was painted with several psychedelic-type designs, with yellow and purple flowers intertwining in the center of it. She reached into a corner of the door and whipped out a key. She opened the door and we stepped into a modest kitchen surrounded by small windows.

As we sipped herbal tea brewed from leaves of a plant found in the garden, we shared ideas on interfaith peace, on our hopes for a peaceful Holy Land, peaceful world. One thing for sure: I didn't realize so many Jews were working on interfaith projects with Muslims, Christians and people of other faiths. You don't hear about them in the news; lately the press seemed to only allude to Israeli Jews and their State's brutal occupation of the West Bank. Ayval left an hour later and Miriam gave me the tour of her apartment, first showing me the living room that I'd soon call my bedroom for the next week. It was organized like an Arab home, with cushions lining the wall all the way around, and a rug languishing in the middle of the floor. She told me she was married to Samuel, who was visiting friends and family in the US.

A bronze meditation gong stood on a wooden corner table under a shelf from which strands of incense reeds extended out like peacock feathers, some burned down to the stem, others half-way, others not burned at all as their red and amber tips reached out to greet me. Incense essence still permeated the air with the soft, contemplative aroma of cinnamon. This place was like the magical curio shop I had stumbled into in the middle of San Francisco, years ago.

My eyes flipped over to an eerie corner of the room where a lattice-like structure hung with several marionettes, their beady eyes watching me. Some were wearing stocking caps, others kippahs, and yet several had no hats; one hatless marionette's bushy red hair sprang out from the sides of his otherwise bald head, his glasses magnifying his eyes shining like polished marbles. The phone rang and Miriam returned to the kitchen. I sat down on one of the large cushions; after a few minutes, the heavy heat had oozed into me and my eyes began to slowly close. I was left alone to rest, to meditate among several sets of watchful eyes, but I was too tired to be bothered about the little people who surrounded me. This marked the first stage of my trip. The soft night air seemed to caress me, the breeze as soft as rose petals against my cheek. It seemed to be telling me that the Holy Land may have accepted me, for now.

The real test was ahead....

Chapter 16: Anti-war

The next day, Miriam drove me to Jerusalem to participate in an overnight interfaith event. We arrived on Friday night at a beautiful wooded area on the top of some hill in the outskirts of the Old City. Carrying our tent and sleeping bags up a dirt pathway, we saw Jews wearing white, black or multi-colored kippahs and Muslim women with their hijabs draped over their heads, walking among the groups. The cool Jerusalem air was blowing through the trees, softly rustling their leaves.

Smiles abounded as we reached the top of the hill. Our heads were stroked by long tree branches. Dotting the hills were tents, sleeping bags and people crouching down or sitting cross-legged, listening, watching….

Long-haired hippy Jews draped in loose, sheet-like togas played guitars while others showed their talent playing the didgeridoo (long cylindrical wind instrument) as we entered the square area that turned out to be the center of the activity. The longhairs seemed a bit oblivious to everyone and more interested in posturing as individuals sent to show others the way—maybe Moses wannabees— or just hanging out. But they seemed to be more into each other, into hippie chicks, like the ones sprawled out over the commons at San Francisco State in the 60's, hugging only each other and mostly ignoring the others. It was all an anachronism from decades past, my generation.

Bored with the theatrics before me, my mind wandered to the year at San Francisco State University, during which I opted to participate in the anti-war movement as opposed to hanging out on the lawn smoking grass, playing music with the "beautiful people," the long-haired freaks who I sometimes called "pretenders."

There were among them, however, very beautiful, real believers, non-pretender freaks with whom I got along well. I even jammed with them at communes near Guerneville. I played a weak harmonica but they didn't seem to mind. I was close to these truly beautiful hippy freaks, who sincerely endeavored to do something to change the world instead of spewing forth bland statements about peace and love, vegetating on the lawn in the center of the campus, high as kites. I just got fed up with so many bandwagon hippies who seemed to live their lives imagining being cool dudes in B movies. My rebellion against that brought me to the threshold of the anti-Vietnam war movement. There, I was motivated.

110

In the spring of 1970, I helped organize an anti-war protest on campus following the announcement by the US Government that it would extend the ruthless bombing and perhaps napalming of Cambodia. All day I had trouble concentrating during lectures at the University as I was nervous, intuiting that something was going to happen.

Early evening, I was walking with about 100 protesters in a circle in front of the campus, carrying anti-war, anti-imperialism signs and chanting anti-war slogans. It was a beautifully orchestrated demonstration against the establishment, against the accepted order and its involvement in an unwarranted, barbarous and unpopular conflict, which ended many youthful lives before their time, on both sides. Students of all ethnic backgrounds, faiths, from long-haired hippies to crew- cut athletes, lined the streets protesting this nonsensical war funded by the military industrial complex, disguised as our savior from communism.

All of a sudden, the police yanked an African-American protester out of the line and threw him to the ground. I recognize him as Ted who lived on the same floor as I did in the campus dorms. One policeman held him down with his knee, mashing one side of his head; the other side was flattened against the stone-cold cement, while another policeman was rifling through Ted's backpack. I was on the other side of the circle so I had to plow through several protesters to reach him. When I arrived at his side, he had already been released and had rejoined the march. His black, frizzy hair was matted and he walked wistfully carrying a cardboard sign, something about "No more slaughtering, no more napalm." I walked alongside him in silence. His eyes were wider than usual and bloodshot with fear, contrasting with the standard colors of his army surplus khaki shirt and paratrooper army fatigues, the thigh pockets bulging with leaflets.

"What's happen'in, Ted?"

"The police yelled at me, saying some people had been throwing rocks from the surrounding buildings. Maybe people doin' it, but not us. We peaceful!"

He stopped, shifting his poster and looking sheepishly behind him.

"I repeated, WE PEACEFUL, to the cops. They didn't care and grabbed me, looked through my stuff."

"Well, we know why they grabbed you."

Ted seemed too afraid to respond, pretending not to hear, but he answered by his silence and then raised his sign and yelled, "Down with the War...."

But my blood had risen—it was irreparable! The hate rose in my veins, hate of the racist establishment, the racist cops here...most cops I had met were not like that. But something was seriously wrong with this squad. Then my thoughts shifted to before Ted's attack; the beginning of this peaceful march came back to me as cops surrounded us, catcalling us, egging us on to strike them so they could bust us for felony assault and battery against a police officer, or resisting arrest.

"Come on you wimps, fight like a man...You're a bunch...commy pigs!"

I could hear the cops yelling out, trying to incite violence by their taunts, "Look at them niggers, here! What they doing raisin' trouble? We're goin' to bust 'em all!" and then they'd belch a loud ha, ha, ha from their bloated bellies.

My simmering insides turned to boiling, and I couldn't turn the heat down. Ted was obviously targeted for his blackness and the alleged rocks in his backpack had nothing to do with it. The catcalls by the reactionary police echoed…How could this group of racists be the "protectors" of one of the most liberal communities in America? It was pushing me over the top. Like a volcano, it was uncontrollable.

That was it; the heat had risen in me and something exploded. I walked to the policeman at the fringes of our circle and stood in front of him.

"Move along, pinko dog."

"I'm not moving. You had no right to take the black…."

He cut me off, "That's my business. Get out of my face!" the tall, white policeman barked, his long whiskerless face puffy under the blue visor pulled over his eyes. He sneered, his sharp, yellow teeth flashing like they were hungry to bite.

"Don't talk to me like that! Who do you think you are? You're disgusting…."

Busted! He grabbed me and yelled for an another policeman, who came running to help him pull me out of the march and toward a group of squad cars parked in the middle of Holloway Ave, completely blocking traffic. The two cops on both sides yanked my arms. Then the one I had words with suddenly stuck out his foot to trip me, probably hoping to drag me the rest of the way to the waiting squad car; I managed to stay on my feet in spite of both their efforts. I gained my footing each time and each time the cop growled and punched the arm that he fastened in his strong grasp. That didn't work either so the first cop grabbed me around my neck with one arm, locking the hold with the other in a headlock, maybe to trip me more easily; but I quickly broke through that too.

"What are trying to prove? I'm not going anywhere," I spat out coldly, starting to lose patience but holding myself from striking the brutish man.

We finally arrived at the squad car. Frustrated at not being able to victoriously drag me to the car, he opened the door with one hand and shoved me so violently into the back seat that my head hit the opposite door. He slammed the door and I was trapped inside, since there were no door handles within reach.

The first policeman opened the front door and slipped into the front seat, his billy club drawn. He turned, holding it over his head and yelled, "Got you, commy pig! Give me your name, now."

"You don't talk me like that. No, you get nothing…."

Before I could finish, he swung the end of the club over his head and pounded down on my head. I thrust my arm up in the nick of time to deflect the hit; pain exploded in my arm. Then he used the club like a pool stick, targeting my vital parts; I closed my legs just in time to thwart the attack. He then rammed my stomach, knocking the wind out of me. He was trying to get me to hit him, to commit a felony—I was sure of it. Then he could beat me wantonly. His wild, black eyes danced sadistically, holding the club as his mouth salivated, white drops gathering like foam at the corners of his wide mouth, like a rabid beast.

"Sue you for brutality…." I coughed out barely.

"Ha, ha, ha, you got witnesses, chump? Your name and I'll stop."

He raised the billy club to hit me again but the door on the passenger side swung open and he immediately lowered the club on the seat and twisted his head toward the door. A young, crew-cut policeman sat down in the front seat; his face was long with beefy, red cheeks. He twisted around, sneering at me.

Without saying another word, the marauder cop turned around, slid into the driver's seat and revved up the motor.

"We're goin' to haul your ass downtown, communist slut, and you're going to jail for a long time. Your name?" He held the billy club over my head."

I covered my head with both hands. "Ha!"

He signaled to the other policeman to get in the back seat next to me, as he revved the motor again. As soon as the other policeman was next to me, the driver floored it, burning rubber about ten feet as we flew down abandoned Holloway Avenue. We passed through a roadblock set up by three patrol cars, which explained the empty street in front of the University.

They took me to a holding cell not far from the campus. A kindly old policeman at the counter smiled. I still didn't give him my name and was quickly finger-printed under the name of "John Doe." This must have been the home office of the "marauder," as he had changed into his street clothes and was sitting with a scowl on his face in front of me as the older officer did the prints. The complaining officer signed a document and left; looking back, the veins in his high forehead bulged out as he shook his finger at me.

I was handcuffed and escorted by two officers to a holding cell. It was adjacent to an empty cell, not empty for long. In a few minutes, the door to the holding cell clanged open and in clomped five officers surrounding, pushing and shoving a black adolescent wearing a massive Afro. They shoved him hard until his back was flat against the cold bars of the cell door. They then pulled him away and opened the door. The opening of the cell was so narrow, only one could enter through it at a time. The man in front had a cracked lip with red splotches on his chin; he was wearing a large, metal badge on a dark blue shirt. He pushed the boy through with such a force that he stumbled and hit the floor with a thud as another policeman stepped through the opening.

While the one with the blood stains ferociously kicked the boy's ribs, another one held his shoulders to the cement floor. The boy, weak with pain as he was being pummeled, was only able to feebly raise his arm to try to soften some of the kicks.

Three other blue shirts managed to enter the small holding cell and took turns kicking the downed boy. I banged the sides of the cell, yelling, "What're you doing? You're going to kill him! Stop it, cowards!"

I was afraid they would get carried away and kill the poor, defenseless boy squirming below their blows.Then, the white-haired policeman with a long scar on one side of his face—who was bent over the struggling boy—looked up, his icy blue eyes transfused with hate, and yelled,

"Shut up or you're next!"

I continued banging the bars with the palm of my hands, but the police ignored me as they continued kicking the now lifeless body lying on the floor, blood running profusely down the corners of his mouth.

Then almost as quickly as they entered, the policemen left, completely ignoring me. Some left with eyes red with hate, others with panic, their heads turned in the direction of the lifeless boy. One of the cops who had left looked back and his hateful eyes turned to panic as they widened. He returned in a minute with a bucket of water, spilling it all the way from the door. Kicking the door of the cell open, he doused the kid still lifelessly sprawled on the cement floor. He began to stir. As soon as the officer saw him move, he whipped the empty bucket through the door and felt for the keys in his pocket. Pulling them out he turned the key while watching the youth who had since risen on his elbow. I then noticed it was the cop with the split lip, the blood lightly caked on his chin.

He slammed the door, turning the keys around several times and then left through a series of doors. Their clangor shook our cells, magnifying the cold isolation that had closed in around us.

It was one of the most cowardly acts I'd ever witnessed. I couldn't believe that San Francisco police officers had done that as I had met many great ones in the past; some had even given me rides out of dangerous areas when I was lost, given me directions, etc., and I loved this city. But my nauseated body could barely grasp hold of the bars and just watch the boy. I had felt so useless just watching him getting savagely beaten and not able to help him in any way. The boy stumbled to his feet and almost fell over, holding the bars of the cell as his chin dropped to his body; he managed to pull himself up. He walked to the cracked mirror, fingering his bruises on his face, feeling his loosened teeth and touching his cut lips. His hands were bloody and he dried them on his pants.

"Man, I'm goin' to lose some...." he said, stretching back his lips to look more closely at his teeth. His raspy laugh sent chills through my body.

He then turned the water on filling the plugged basin. Shoving his entire face into it, he pulled it out, grabbing a drab yellow towel hanging on a rusty, metal ledge next to the sink.

After drying his face, he turned and walked toward the front of the cell to an overturned wooden chair. He righted it and plopped down on it. At the same time his reddish-black eyes caught mine.

He nodded and sighed, his courageous smile somehow giving me life. "Are you ok?"

He nodded and even smiled again a little, shaking his head. Water from his brow sprinkled over the cold floor.

"What were they beating on you for?"

"They was hassling me," he stopped cold, crinkling his eyes, perhaps holding back tears, "calling me coon. Some racist pigs, they is, and I hauled off and hit one of 'em."

That must have been the one with the cracked lip and red stains on his chin. "But wow, they came back to mess me up with five of them."

"I can't believe it!" I said, not knowing what else to say.

He reached out and grabbed the towel draped over the sink to wipe his bleeding nose, the drops of blood pooling on the floor. His nose seemed to have ruptured.

"Y-yeeah, that was cold, man!" He put the towel down and sniffed, blood bubbling from his nose.

"Look, I saw it all. They can't get away with that." He raised his hand halfway, like he'd heard that one before. He spoke again.

"Hey man, what's your name? "Frank. Yours?"

"Leroy."

"Look, you said you want to help me, right?"

"Yeah. What? You want me to talk to a lawyer?" His face screwed up, like he'd heard a bad tune.

"Go see my mama. I love my mama. She worried. Tell her I'm ok, man, please do that."

"That's it?"

He nodded, shoving the palms of his hands outward, indicating he didn't want to talk about anything else—no lawyers, no witnesses…nothing like that!

He then patted the outside of his front pockets and pulled out a crumpled piece of paper.

"I got a pen hidden in my shoes," I said as I bent down, taking my shoe off. I wondered how I knew that I would need the hidden pen today.

He started ambling to the bars separating us and I inched toward him.

He approached me, reaching out his hand. At that moment, a crew cut, large-jawed policeman opened the door to the holding cell room. Seeing the black man move closer to the bars that separated us, he yelled, "Hey, get back, niggah!"

The black youth scowled, and looked away.

After the policemen shut the door, I waited a few minutes to see if he would be looking through the little stained window above the door. After a couple of minutes, no face appeared at the window so I threw the pen between the bars to Leroy who crouched down to pick it up. He quickly glanced at the door, smoothed the crumpled paper on the floor and began writing.

He handed me the paper through the bars. I snatched it as my eyes skimmed the words "Hunter's Point projects." Before I could think about what I'd just read, two policemen came into the room. Fortunately, they were focused on turning the key to his cell. I bent down pretending to scratch my foot and stuffed the paper in my shoes. I cringed, expecting a new confrontation. Leroy waited, suspended in the back of the cell. Two officers who I hadn't seen before opened the door and one of them crooked his finger at Leroy, who turned around so they could handcuff him. He turned and winked as they led him away in silence.

I remembered the piece of paper was marked "Hunters Point projects" and Iremembered it was considered one of San Francisco's most dangerous districts.

Two hours later, around midnight, two policemen came into my cell. I don't know why but I was sitting on the floor. One walked in and held out his hand, which I took. He helped me up and gently turned me around to put the handcuffs on. He clamped them on me as another waited. Then they walked me to a garage area and put me in a white paddy wagon with "POLICE" inscribed in big black and white letters. It hit me hard that I was going to have a police record, for the first time.

That evening, however, marked one of the highlights of my first year as a university student: being taken down Market Street on a Friday night at midnight, about the time the nightlife traffic snarled on San Francisco's main street...IN A PADDY WAGON! I was en route to the infamous downtown Bryant Street County Jail. The paddy wagon pulled into a driveway. The security gate opened and closed behind us—we drove up to an unloading area. I was escorted in by police on either side, who led me to a processing counter. After they introduced me as "John Doe," the clerk sardonically said, raising her eyebrows as she spoke through taut lips, "Mr. Doe, take your seat."

The policeman who had brought me in the room gently seated me next to several other handcuffed prisoners and whispered, "Young man, go up when they call out 'John Doe,' ok?" He smiled. I was in no mood to smile but I remembered His.

When "John Doe" was called, out I went to the counter. The husky lady looked down at me through dark-rimmed glasses. Her blue shirt was rolled up at the sleeves.

"Look, kid, you'd better give me your name if you know what's good for you.

If people want to see you from the outside, they won't ever find you so you'll just rot inside here...."

"I still don't know what the charges are!"

She leaned over, her merciless face seeming to quiver with excitement, "Mr. Doe, you're in trouble, and there are several charges against you: unlawful assembly and refusal to disperse, among others."

"What do you mean 'others'?"

She chuckled mockingly but didn't respond.

The threat of rotting inside that cold dump calmed me down fast so I gave her my complete name.

When the door clanked shut this time, I turned around to a large holding cell surrounded by bars and in the middle of it, I swore, it looked like I had just stepped into a circus tent. There were about 50 men and youths strolling around the room, with several bunk beds in the back against the barred wall. There were midgets, giants, half-dressed men, men with beards, with shaved heads, with long, flowing hair, men wearing flowery pants, with hair dyed pink, others wearing multi-colored jeans or just faded jeans, some with distant looks, others belligerent expressions— they were all there. I was led by the jail monitor through the circus to my bunk, where I sat down to look around.

My eyes fixed on the toilet in front of my bunk. A young man was using it to wash his clothes in; he'd dunk them in the toilet bowl, then pull them out, wring them out then drape them over a small stool to dry. I could smell the toilet bowl from where I sat. My nose burned.

I was so exhausted a ring-side seat didn't stop my eyelids from slowly closing. I must have slept as I almost jumped out of the bunk when someone touched my arm. I looked up and a bald man barked in my face, "Got a visitor."

"What? What?" My eyes couldn't focus and I was panicking as I forced them to open wider. I thought I had a quick glimpse of hell and I shook with fear, visualizing the frown of the last cop I had seen.

Somehow I sat up, put my shoes on, stood up and started walking. I didn't know who I was following, maybe another jail crazy, and I had no idea what time it was. The man was already at the other end of the room with the iron door open, his shiny, shaved head reflecting a light hanging from a wire overhead. I walked through an obstacle course of men sprawled everywhere: on the benches, floors, even on the toilet, their hands and arms cradling their heads as they slept. I guess these guys didn't like the dismal gray bunks lining the wall….

The man led me through the opening but this time there were no handcuffs—the door slammed shut behind me. I wondered what that meant.

We walked down a long, barren corridor toward a huge man waiting at the end, underneath a large clock prominently featured on the wall. He must have weighed at least 400 pounds underneath a bulging gray trench coat. The clock clicked on 7:30 am as we stopped in front of him.

"Follow me" is all he could say as he turned around, pushed some buttons and stepped into an elevator. I started picturing myself in a strange, haunted house movie, where the guests follow the butler…if I hadn't jumped in at the last moment, the doors would have shut in my face and he would not have stopped them.

The elevator descended in silence as we stood next to each other. His body took up almost the entire elevator, except for the corner I was hunkered into. I was still half asleep, in a daze. I was so tightly squeezed into the corner I couldn't even find the room to move my frozen hands to pinch myself.

"Could you tell me what's…."

"Don't say nothin' now." I shut up as I wasn't going to quarrel with this monstrous human barn breathing down on me. "You might be gettin' out."

"What do you mean…me?"

The elevator jolted and stopped, then the door slid open. The man squeezed out first and I followed; I was still crumpled up but at least I could start breathing again. I walked alongside him down quiet, melancholy corridors. Watching him from the corner of my eyes, we shuffled along in silence. He looked sinister and gruff, his bushy moustache covering his mouth; so no clues, there.

Then we came upon the same counter I had been at with the gruff female clerk hours before. This time, a kindly, slender man with a receding hairline was sitting behind it. He looked up and his straight lips looked like they held the hint of a smile. Without a word, he shoved some papers to the end of the counter that the big man began filling out.

"Come here…sign!" "What's this…?"

He cut me off, "You want to stay inside this dump?"

I quickly skimmed the piece of paper that said something about bail, bail bonds service—I didn't know—but my trembling hands eked out a signature.

The big man slid the paper to the man behind the counter who perfunctorily slid a plastic bag containing my wallet and some change towards me. I thanked him and he looked up, his beady eyes staring at something above my head.

"Better get out when you got the chance." The big man pointed to a large door in front and I veered away from him as he kept walking down the corridor.

I felt light-headed as I took an exit different from the way I had come in; this time I left through the main door. Market Street was just a few blocks away and when I arrived, the translucent morning light hurt my eyes and was almost blinding as my mind whirled back to the midnight paddy wagon rolling down the street, slowly, like a funeral hearse inching to the morgue. This place, with all the hustling of people— running, screaming to catch the bus, to go to work, to school, or whatever—clashed in my head like an iron door clanging shut, dissonant metal on metal, painfully jarring my body. My head hurt as I took a muni bus and headed straight for the campus, for the dorms. When I found my room I plopped down on the bed and slept like death.

Other than my participation in the anti-war protest, I still wasn't absolutely sure what had transpired, neither the day nor the night before, until I saw my friends at dinner that night in the dorm cafeteria. They told me that the moment I was busted, they had passed the hat and got enough money to pay a bail bondsman for my release, except they couldn't find me. I was embarrassed to tell them I was so upset, I refused to give the police my name for the first few hours in the holding cell, until they took me downtown. They shook their heads. The albino student, active in all the protest activities and probably the one in charge of my release, piped up and exclaimed, "We could have gotten your release a lot earlier if you had given them your name!" I bit my lip with embarrassment. "That's ok, man, we're glad you're ok because we were worried that since you weren't listed in any of the jails, we were sure you were injured. We saw them pulling you away, trying to trip you and everything, but as soon as they took you, about 20 of them showed up like a protective wall and we couldn't get to you. It was like the mass bust on campus last year; except this time, you were the only one." He shook his head and slightly exhaled as he curved another spoonful of jello into his smiling mouth.

A week later, I took a bus to the infamous projects in Hunters Point. The bus weaved and turned and finally arrived at the lower San Francisco area; I was the only white passenger. But the passengers hadn't looked at me like I was some kind of freak; they had seemed to accept me in silence as the bus hummed to its destination.

After going through a labyrinth of buildings, abandoned cars and fields used as garbage dumps, with empty packages of cereal, Kleenex tissues and coke bottles littered everywhere, I knocked on a ground floor door. Half of the apartment number was chopped off and the indentation made on the door where the numbers would have been looked like the slash an axe had made. A voice on the other side could be faintly heard.

"What chu wont?"

"I came about Leroy—I met him in jail." "Hold on...."

The bumping of furniture and feet dragging went on for about five minutes until the door slowly creaked open and a smiling black face poked through the door.

"I'll be darn, you come here...come on in."

She held out her hand and I took it. She led me into a modest living room, with only one long sofa in front of the wall; she motioned me to sit down in front of a black and white TV broadcasting an American soap opera. The actors in the show were droning on and on in the background, as I turned to speak to the woman.

"You're Leroy's Ma?"

"Yeah. My son—what they do to him? He was too quiet on the phone the other day. He told me he met a nice white boy...."

"Well, I'm the white boy. Don't know how nice I am."

She smiled which made me smile. Hadn't smiled in a while and it felt good, like pure warmth stealing through my body.

Her head was wrapped in black fabric and her loose dress hinted at a slight pudginess, hints of another on the way. I hadn't even noticed but a young girl of about fifteen was sitting next to her. I spared them the gory details of how their kin was badly beaten by the police.

"Leroy got in a fight with the police...." I stopped and tried to pick my words. "Go on...."

"Well, he's fine but the cops kinda...you know, overdid it."

Her brow wrinkled and the girl next to her began fighting with a piece of plastic. "What...?"

"Well," I had to finesse this without hurting the mother or the sister, whose eyes were already moist, "he hit a cop for calling him a coon, and the cops kind of ganged up on him and...."

She interrupted, "I told my son over and over again, just take it, don't say nothin', don't do nothin', and there he go again!"

She reached over and took a tissue, covering her face with it—she was sobbing.

Tears formed in my eyes and I wiped them on my sleeve. She dried her eyes and looked out the window listlessly, while her daughter went to the kitchen. "Tell me about my baby; he ok?"

"Yeah, he made it through it, no broken bones. He was even laughing a little bit. He's got guts...."

"That my son: he's too brave, not afraid of nothin'." She blew her nose in the tissue, balled it up and put it in an orange waste paper basket next to her.

"You want coffee, cookies?"

I nodded. I was thirsty but I didn't know how to ask.

Her voice called out in a higher-pitched African-American drawl to the girl who had left the room, "Pamela, baby, make some coffee and bring out some cookies."

"Ok, mama, right now...." a squeaky voice came from the kitchen.

Then her head turned and her eyes focused on me.

"You ain't scared comin' out here?" Before I could answer, she continued, "White folk wouldn't be caught dead around here."

"Why?"

"They don't come here never 'cuz we colored folks, they thinkin' we bad, but really we just in this ghetto—no other thing we can do, but hold on, defend ourselves... survive. They don't know us!"

"Yeh, I hear ya!"

I didn't know what to say as I looked into her shining, dark-moon eyes. She had succeeded in pushing my buttons, which started a long discussion about the ghetto, racism, the Vietnam War and freedom. The daughter returned with a tray, three cups of steaming coffee and a dish heaping with Oreo cookies. I muffled a low, coughing laugh, as I mused to myself that in some ways I felt black: black on the inside and white on the outside, like a reverse Oreo cookie. And the white on the outside was a cocktail of Italian and English.

So why would I be afraid of coming to the ghetto to be with some of "my" people? I thanked her, taking my cup as I grabbed a few cookies. I dunked one in the hot, instant coffee and quickly devoured it; the acid had been churning in my stomach, as I hadn't eaten since the night before and it was already long past lunch. Forget breakfast....

As the door shut behind me, I let out my breath: I had almost held it during our conversations about her son, so I would resist telling her any of the gory details of his brutal beating. That would have been too cruel and unnecessary. I still could not understand why his mother had acted surprised and somewhat honored by my visit, as it seemed a natural thing to do, especially since I had promised Leroy. I guess some things I wouldn't understand until much later, until I saw it written before my eyes... like during the writing of my book. Then something would click....

I fell asleep on the bus, its engine slowly propelling me toward the dorms, until I felt a gentle nudge on my shoulder....

Chapter 17: Peaceniks

Miriam was bending over me, nudging my shoulder as I had fallen asleep during my reverie. I awoke almost in a trance, still thinking I was rumbling along in a bus headed for the San Francisco State University dorms.

"Shalom, Frank. Still buzzing away?"

"Ah…oh, Miriam. Yeah, I'm awake, I'm awake. Sorry!" "No problem, Frank. I want you to meet someone."

I followed her to a circle of people holding hands and chanting or praying. A stocky, energetic man with the side curls of Hasidic Jews looked towards us and quickly stood up.

"This is Benjamin, the leader of this interfaith event!" Miriam spoke to him in Hebrew and he turned to me.

"Shalom; you're welcome here. I heard a little of your story."

He had a day's growth on his fleshy face and his eyes flashed, perhaps with a touch of wonder as to why he was speaking to the likes of me, with such a busy schedule. He did not have the hippy, hazy daze in his eyes; they were fiery and active. I silently voiced, "Here is a leader."

He led us down a path where people were encircled above a lower area. He then descended into a small gorge and was greeted by a group of youths who seemed to be waiting for him. Benjamin then began shifting from right to left, verbalizing the words "Shalom, Salaam (peace)," moving his body from side to side. The crowd quickly began imitating his movements, repeating the same words, "Shalom, Salaam." (Peace in Hebrew and Arabic)

It was an attempt to connect people by encouraging them to voice the same words, like a mantra, together. I joined in a bit, repeating "Shalom, Salaam" but I was reluctant to mechanically voice the words that everyone else was articulating and to bend my body left and right, in rhythm with all others. I was loath just to follow gestures and I was not sure of the reason why we were doing it…group bonding? I wanted to feel what I was saying.

I had to be true to my quest which was for enlightenment, a quest for universal reality. I had come a long way and gone through a lot to get to this place and wanted to contribute something, in my own little way, for peace. I just didn't have time for frivolous, senseless, spiritless motions. I resisted subjecting myself to the body

121

rhythms imposed by others, that I thought might just be "going through the motions." This seemed to be a kind of group therapy probably aimed at encouraging people to feel as one: one with the Muslim women wearing hijabs as well as with the Jews, some wearing kippahs, and one with Christians and members of all faiths. But it seemed so phony, like a theater prop, just to repeat peace in Arabic and Hebrew in order to feel united with all, to feel one. All I could ask myself was: Is it necessary to jump through hoops, using props for unity? I was here to spread love through heart connections and soft words, not through mechanical body movements coupled with a mantra.

I wondered if I was being too harsh with my hosts. But no; I perceived this as an orchestrated group activity, almost like a club event. Group bonding activities seemed superficial and were often overly orchestrated, like some TV game shows. Or maybe this project was the overly-structured offspring of a group of control freaks. I preferred to meet people in an informal, spiritually-charged setting and then just let it happen.

It was Shabbat and mainly Hebrew songs and prayers were being sung and repeated, but nothing in Arabic, at least at first. When the speaker, who was standing on top of a hill, took the microphone and officially announced in Hebrew and English the beginning of the overnight interfaith event, his voice rose to an emotional pitch when he informed us that a group of about four Palestinians had joined us. He pointed to a group sitting in a circle at the foot of the grassy slope before him and introduced them. I looked down the slope and saw three girls in hijabs and an adolescent—four faces beaming at the speaker. But then it seemed they were forgotten. In fact, that was the last I heard of them until I sought them out later.

I noticed that no efforts were made to integrate them into the group mainly consisting of the star-studded cast of robed, long-haired, bearded Jews, apparently profiling for peace and unity. The Palestinians sat alone in the corner throughout the songs and prayers in Hebrew, as if they had served their purpose as the "token group from Palestine." They were there to show it was truly an ecumenical event. That's all!

The leaders surely confronted great difficulty in obtaining the papers for the group from the West Bank to attend the event. But the Palestinians were the ones who braved hours of checkpoints, passing through cement walls, checks on their papers, maybe even searches before they made it into Jerusalem. And yet Ramallah, the capital of the West Bank, is about 15 minutes away, as the crow flies.

Even though I totally was in sync with the theme of this event, I began to feel that some people there were more concerned with assuaging their guilt over the cruel occupation by the State of Israel in the West Bank, than sincerely working for a durable peace with different groups and members of different faiths, from Israel and Palestine. I was sure—or at least hoped—there were some people there who truly wanted to find peaceful solutions, allowing the Israelis and Palestinians to live together as God's children, with equal rights and equal freedoms. But we have a long way to go....

The group led by Benjamin seemed to have its agenda and was bound to it. He was a scrupulous man, but perhaps insecure, as he was constantly trying to prove his credibility as an interfaith leader by often recounting the interfaith events he had participated in. That need would be confirmed a few months later, during an interfaith event at his apartment in Jerusalem, when he showed me a picture of himself and several other world interfaith leaders during a famous interfaith encounter in Sevilla, Spain. He emphasized over and over again that all the world interfaith leaders were invited, including him. I tried to show I was impressed, as he needed me to show him that; but I was not. Profiling interfaith love, for me, had so little to do with real love. The song "Real Love"[35] played over and over in my mind.

The principle of bringing people together for an interfaith happening was good, except I had strong feelings that there were too many agendas among many of the mainstream Jewish peaceniks. It seemed that they were trivializing the problems in the Holy Land and making them seem easily resolved by organizing interfaith events in Israel where Jews, Muslims, Christians and members of other faiths would share a moment, hug, sing together, eat together, have a happening together; but there would be no serious follow-up or progress toward real peace. They seemed to be ignoring problems caused by the myriad checkpoints, walls and growing settlements implanted in the West Bank. Anyway, that subject was off the table. Several of the peaceniks shared their reasons privately with me, that they were concerned such talk would trigger too much emotion, too much hate against the State of Israel.

But I kept asking myself, "Why were the Israeli Jews so protective of their state, right or wrong?"

Hugs and mantras and words of love...what was the use if we didn't put those beautiful words into real actions, such as those against the Israeli government's repression in the West Bank or into building hospitals, homes, schools and other buildings destroyed during the Intifada, on both sides of the walls? There were interfaith groups doing that but far too few, in my mind, were making a real impact on bringing about a durable peace.

There were already many tangible efforts to bring interfaith peace groups together to rebuild buildings, replant destroyed or uprooted olive trees due to the buildings of walls and the taking of Palestinian land, etc. There were also many demonstrations against the occupation by many Israeli-Palestinian groups, but still not enough acts compared to the words expressed about them, and in particular, it seemed, not enough concrete actions from the interfaith peace groups.

I was speaking in a small group with Miriam about bringing more people together and the importance of integrating interfaith efforts with helping to resolve the conflict in the Holy Land. I saw Benjamin's stocky frame as he visited with each group. I timed my comments to coincide with the time he approached. As soon as I saw his eyes targeting our group and walking toward us, I began speaking, "What about peace with the West Bank? Do the Palestinians share basic freedoms, allowing them to really participate in these groups heart to heart? What about the occupation of the West Bank? Is there a way to temper that, eliminate some of the checkpoints, withdraw from most of the settlements and bring down the walls? That would allow Palestinians to breathe easier."

Upon hearing that, Benjamin abruptly turned, shaking his head, his lips tightening as he stalked away.

---

35 "Real Love," sung by Michael McDonald of the Doobie Brothers. Songwriters: Michael McDonald and Patrick Henderson, 1980.

Chapter 18: Taste of Palestine

Miriam went to bed as the faint echoes of the muezzins calling Muslims to prayers rolled over the clouds hugging the cool hills. I couldn't sleep; it was too early and so many songs, prayers and ideas were swimming in my head.

I crawled out of the tent and threw the flap back. There were still a few bearded peaceniks walking around in the eerie silence. I stood up, putting my jacket on in the crisp air of Jerusalem and started walking down the hill. A road led towards a wooded area, so I took it. I had walked about five minutes when I heard a low banter. The wind had picked up and the trees swayed; the whispers seemed human, but not seeing the bodies attached to the voices, I wondered...At the end of the road ahead, I could see several head scarves, green and white, grouped together. Then I saw that the scarves were completely covering several heads, tied under dusky chins. It was the group from the West Bank.

They turned together and four smiles emerged from the silky hijabs. In the middle of the group was the profile of a young man, his dark, shiny hair gleaming in the dusky night.

I broke the silence that had befallen the group:

"As-salamu alaykum." (Peace be upon you.)

"Wa alaykum assalam." (and upon you peace.)

"Kayfa Haal-ak?" (How are you? Literally: How is your condition?) "Al-Hamdu-lil-laah." (Praise be to God)

"Ahlan wa-sahlan." (Welcome.)

"Sorry to interrupt your conversation...."

A young girl with glasses smiled, her blue hijab shining almost as brightly as her eyes, and said, "Ahlan wa sahlan."

She moved to open the circle wider to let me in.

Not knowing what to say, I observed, "Well, here we are...."

A stocky lady who seemed the leader laughed, "Yes, you are right. Kind of here!"

"I haven't seen much of you after you were introduced. Do you like it?"

Another girl, probably the spokesman for the group because she spoke the best

English, replied, "It's OK. It's nice to meet new people...." "But you're meeting them?"

"Not really...."

"You speak Hebrew?"

Several hands gestured, which I understood as a unanimous "No."

"I'm having a hard time following it; if you don't speak Hebrew...."

The younger girl spoke up, "It's difficult and we feel isolated, a bit ignored. Where you from?"

"I'm American but I live in France...."Ahlan wa-sahlan."

"And you?"

The girl with the glasses responded,

"We are Filistineena: me, Ramallah, this boy, Jericho. You know it?" (Palestinian)

"Sure—heard of it in the Bible. Never been there."

"You come to Filisteen, no?"

"Yes, I want to come, but some people tell me...."

She interrupted, "It's not dangerous." She smiled. Her smile was warm, welcoming, not nuanced.

"What your name?" "Frank. And yours?"

"I'm Hafa and these are my two sisters, Asma and Kalila, and this boy is Gilad, our cousin."

"Nice...." I stumbled and didn't complete the phrase. Everybody laughed with me. Laughing at a klutzy American broke the ice...and somehow bonded us! Oh, well—I'll take it.

I handed her my card, as she was still "hee hee-ing"; she took out a card and wrote an email on the back of it. As I started to walk away, she said once I get to Ramallah to call her and they would meet me there. I didn't know who "they" were but I assumed "they" meant her sisters. I left the group as night surrounded me with its dark arms, but I felt the luminous heat and saw the glow of my first connection with Palestinians. My original vision taking me to the Holy Land included the West Bank.

That was the beginning of my search for a way into Palestine, to Ramallah, the threshold of the Holy Land.

Chapter 19: Warning!

As soon as my head hit my makeshift pillow, a folded pull-over, I was out... gone to reverie, dancing with the vision I had experienced thirty years ago. Something had clicked! Miriam and I slept in a tent on the side of a hill near a group of tents. It was late morning when I opened my eyes and stuck my head out the tent flaps. The dry heat laced the air, wafted about by the wind gusting up the hill, propelled, I imagined, by the voices of centuries past...the voices of peace long drowned out by the battle cries of war.

I rolled the flap up and crawled out. Miriam joined me for a walk over the hills and through other campsites. Other participants were sitting up, stretching, smiling as they recapped songs sung during the night. We approached a couple sitting on a log drinking coffee. The man, bald with a bushy salt and pepper beard, had shiny stones for eyes which reflected a smile as he straddled the log. The woman wore a head scarf on which green Egyptian cat figurines played; her black hair was neatly parted in the middle. Miriam knew them and approached, hugging them both at the same time. She introduced Tal and Baruch. They invited us to join them for breakfast.

As we sat on the smooth stones chomping on hummus and flat bread, falafel bread, these warm, loving people made me feel one with them. Miriam introduced me to the others and within a short time summarized my experiences in Morocco; I was then asked to tell my story.

For one of the first times ever, I recounted the story of my spiritual voyage from Paris, France, in 1978, headed to the Holy Land and how I was imprisoned in a mosque, held by an extremist Muslim group in the outskirts of Casablanca.[36] I guess I was saving it for this occasion: I had been on my way to Jerusalem in 1978 to participate in the interfaith movement for peace. I was on my way to this same place, but about 27 years ago. I hadn't made it, then; a cold shudder shook me.

The wind shifted and blew in my face. I wondered if even the wind in this magical place was trying to tell me something...maybe I had said too much? In the middle of the monologue, I stopped; birds chirped in the distance and swooped down on our breakfast party, flapping their wings as they flew over our campsite and into the sky high above. My words flowed all around me, over the rocks and bounced among the

---

36 Storm Over Morocco, 4th Edition, supra.

branches and leaves above as the people around me listened; no one attempted to interrupt me.

When I finished, eight sets of eyes were blinking with disbelief at my experience there. Then Baruch, his salt and pepper beard framing his cheeks, asked,

"Where are you now, spiritually? Aren't you bitter against Islam?"

I had anticipated that question but I had no answer, yet. I told him that I would be glad to address that question once I had finished my story. He winked with enthusiasm as I continued....

At the end of my discourse, I expected enraged and suspicious Jewish smiles, at my having lived with extremists. But no, just understanding smiles. My apprehension withdrew to the depths of my inner soul, where remnants of fear and paranoia still survived. Then silence; I could even hear the wind rustling the dry leaves of the trees.

Miriam was shaking her reddish-brown full head of hair. Her glistening eyes seemed to match the sheen of the morning dew clinging to the leaves overhead.

"Wow! Wow! Wow!!" she typically said in times like these.

Baruch leaned over his plate of hummus and greens: "Thank you for sharing that experience with me. It's amazing that your path has crossed ours, at this time, as we celebrate brotherly love. You've got much to share with us, my friend." He reached out and shook my hand.

I had come full circle. About 27 years ago, I headed out from Paris to this Holy Land, where I now sat on a rock in the outskirts of Jerusalem, to find my spiritual truth and thereafter engage in the interfaith movement. Now I was recounting my experiences in Morocco, my imprisonment by an extremist Islamic group which halted my progress and forced me to abandon one of my goals: to visit the Holy Land.

"So," he reminded me I hadn't answered his previous question, "what did you learn...spiritually?"

I shared with them my views on Islam which I considered a loving, peaceful religion, and that the extremists distorted the true meaning of it. I continued by focusing on my faith, which was to pray and study, as well as live according to the common denominators among religions. I sought to be unattached to a specific church and/or the rituals of one religion and not confuse them with truth, the light. I then, remembering the teachings of Ramakrishna, shared the idea that one should not confuse the physical church and rituals with the truth, that they were just vehicles and paths to the true light; and, most importantly, there were different paths leading to it.[37]

On the way back to Tel Aviv, I asked Miriam how to get to the West Bank to visit my Palestinian friends. She was surprised, then grew silent; the only sound for the next few minutes was the humming of the motor.

"You have certain powers and you will persevere, over many obstacles—I feel it—but this challenge you can't overcome, at least for now."

I didn't know what she meant by certain powers. My furrowed brow must have expressed my confusion. She explained, "Let's say you get as far as the gates of the

---

37 This thought is inspired by the Hindu teacher Sri Ramakrishna (1836-1886), Marcus Braybrooke, Learn to Pray, (San Francisco: Chronicle Books, 2001, p.54).

West Bank; you can't get in as you're American and not authorized, like Israelis. Anyway, if they allow you to enter the West Bank, the Arabs will take you hostage. They might even hurt or kill you."

I'd soon find out, I thought to myself! Either she was wrong or the Palestinians I had just met in Jerusalem were lying, trying to entice me into the West Bank....

Chapter 20: Breakaway!

My brain told me to listen to Miriam, but my innards screamed for me to trust the Palestinians. Remembering what they had told me, that it was safe in the West Bank, I grabbed my garment-tote bag which was already packed from our trip to Jerusalem, including the sleeping bag, and left everything else in Miriam's apartment. As I walked by her I whispered, "Shalom" and headed out the door so fast I couldn't hear what she was saying.

I grabbed a cab to the Tel Aviv bus station and easily found a bus headed for Jerusalem. At the Jerusalem Central Bus Station, my past caught up with me; it hit me profoundly as I walked through the long corridors of the station. The pain of my last separation with my wife came back and jolted me so hard I had to flop down at one of the metal tables in a café.

Then I knew: I needed to ask myself why I was so intent to go into the West Bank. It seemed as though I was blindly ignoring the risk but I needed to find out, once and for all, what my motives were. I sat and drank a strong espresso and looked out the window of the bus station, watching the myriad of people walking by. I wondered if they ever stopped to question things. Sometimes I wish I'd just run around with a million things to do so I wouldn't have time to think. But I was tired of doing the hustle and bustle dance, making myself too tired, too busy to think, to feel, while others did the thinking, the feeling. It was my turn.

So I had to ask myself, Are you following your vision or are you looking for a quick fix for the pain you still feel for the breakup with your wife back in Paris? Looking for an elixir, or….

I questioned whether this trip was planned because I harbored vestiges of a "Messiah complex," or was the pain of losing my ex-wife so great inside, that I still occasionally felt the jagged edges after all these years? Was it simply a "death wish" disguised as a desire to help bring people together?

But I don't want to die, I thought to myself, burning inside, and I'm an idiot for even thinking of it!

Sitting in front of a square metal table with chairs strewn around it, I fell into a deep meditation even though people were everywhere, shuffling here and there, running to catch a bus, running, chattering….

Before I proceeded on this voyage to the West Bank, which would be a turning point in everything I'd done so far, I needed answers…now. I sat stretched out against the back of the chair. In a few minutes, I heard no sounds, other than my breathing. Then a strong image came to me of *Storm Over Morocco*, my first book about my vision, in which I traveled from Paris to the Holy Land, via Morocco. It occurred to me my escape from the extremist group had been motivated by my initial vision, to travel to the Holy Land and organize interfaith groups….

I came back from my meditation, my face and body wet and streaming. My hair even felt hot. I must have looked like a disheveled scarecrow, but my ideas and vision were clear: I had organized my thoughts. I have come this far and my destiny is to organize interfaith dialogues and marches…that is my purpose in life, my passion. Whatever else is driving me, it will have to take second place to my vision. So let's go!

Traveling to Israel was one thing, but even though I had definitely envisaged traveling to the West Bank, as it is also a very important part of the Holy Land, now that it was time for my incursion into those unstable, unknown lands…I hesitated.

A heavy sigh of relief seeped through my lips, prying them open as I realized that I would continue my voyage to Palestine, the West Bank. I was convinced it was the vision that was pushing me.

Emotions shook me. I still felt lost, but my vision returned, crystal clear, giving me brain manna as I focused on my main "raison d'être." As for my pain, I decided that even though I could still feel it, I must continue on and let time heal me, if ever that would happen.

In Ramallah, the threshold of the Holy Land, I didn't know what awaited me and sometimes this crazy "not knowing" jolted me into mentally recoiling. I had called a couple of Palestinians, the two sisters I had met at the interfaith event, and they said to call them as soon as the cab pulled into Ramallah. That was the only plan I had.

I stood up and started grabbing my things. My thoughts were invaded by some black memories as I took a final sip of the strong espresso coffee I had purchased before setting my cup down. That sat me back down again in the chair; doubts were pulling me back.

Flashbacks assailed my mind, of a TV program I had seen in Paris a few years back, in 2000, which showed that many Palestinians—including several children— had been killed during the Palestinian uprising, the 2nd Intifada, (discussed earlier) against the Israeli occupation. In particular, a young Palestinian boy caught in the cross-fire between Israeli and Palestinian forces—even though his father had tried to shield him—was allegedly shot and killed by Israeli soldiers in the Gaza Strip. The footage of the killing was broadcast worldwide. Although several subsequent reports were unclear and some inconclusive as to whether the boy was killed by Israeli soldiers or by Palestinian National Security forces, its broadcast created furious, massive rumblings, especially throughout the Gaza Strip and the West Bank.[38]

The simmering hate felt by Palestinians had apparently exploded during a subsequent lynching a couple of weeks later of two Israeli soldiers, reservists

---

38 "2000: Shocking images of boy shot in Gaza." BBC News Online: On This Day. 30 September 2000. <http://news.bbc.co.uk/onthisday/hi./dates/stories/september/30/news-sid_4295000/4295024.stm>.

according to Israeli authorities, who had taken a wrong turn on their way to their Army base in the West Bank, and found themselves lost in Ramallah, under the control of the Palestinian Police.[39] The Israeli soldiers were apprehended and taken to the police station. A rumor circulated around town that the Palestinian police had apprehended two members of the hated undercover units of the Israeli army who dress like Arabs and attack Palestinians in the middle of Palestinian towns. An angry mob stormed the police station and got a hold of the soldiers, savagely beating and killing them.

I could not blame either side for this tragedy, neither Israelis for the horrible repression of Palestine during the uprising against the bitter occupation in the West Bank nor the frenzied Palestinians involved in the mob reaction committing the atrocities that day. It was a perverse consequence of a chain of events that had given rise to the 2nd Intifada and the subsequent violence which erupted before and after the lynching of the soldiers.

The image on TV, however, of a young Palestinian looking out the window of the Police Station in Ramallah and showing bloody hands to the angry crowd that day sent waves of shock down my spinal column, all the way down my back and legs. I guess I shouldn't have been totally surprised that human beings could be so vicious, pushed to commit atrocities by so much pent up hate and emotions, exacerbated by the cruel occupation of the Palestinian territories and the killings committed in the current uprising. Hence, the urgent need for interfaith unity to spearhead the non-violent movement to liberate the Holy Land, in the name of all Muslims, Jews, Christians and people of all faiths…a movement of love and understanding, fueled by the sincere desire to bring people together to work for peaceful coexistence in the Holy Land.

My body began to shake outwardly but deep down, I felt nothing bad would happen, that I'd somehow be protected if I went into the West Bank…in any case, the vision I had almost 30 years ago specified I was to go through all the Holy Land and not just to Israel.

That thought sent incandescent streams of energy through my body, making it almost involuntarily rise, stand and start walking down the long corridors of the bus station. In my mind, I was going to Ramallah, to the West Bank, even though I still had no idea how to get there!

I descended the stairs and headed out the doors which were patrolled by Israeli police; but since I was leaving, they just waved me through until I found myself in the clamor of the streets, walking toward a couple of buses parked on the curb. As I approached one of them, its door swung open, like a reflex action. I walked up the steps and an elderly bus driver was seated up top, his black kippah shading the top of his head.

"Shalom. Could you take me to Ramallah?"

His furrowed brow raised: "Impossible: prohibited, but I can take you close to the Qalandia checkpoint…you can walk."

"If I were to walk to the check point from here, how long would it take?"

---

39 Asser, Martin. "Lynch Mob's Brutal Attack." BBC News Online: Education. 13 October 2000. <http://news.bbc.co.uk/2.hi/middle_east/969778.stm>.

He frowned, deepening the sunbaked creases at the corners of his eyes. Smirking, he tried to muffle a sardonic chuckle:

"That may take you a couple of hours. Forget it."

Qalandia was a new word and I learned later it was the name of the main checkpoint between Jerusalem and Ramallah. But I was determined to get into the West Bank and it didn't matter what they called it.

After climbing down the steps, I continued walking desultorily down the sidewalk. I had inadvertently almost crossed the street when I heard two rapid beeps. I looked to the left, and a man was shrugging his shoulders as if to say, "Where are you going?"

Then I saw a taxicab parked on the curb in front of me and walking over to it, I poked my head in the window. The thin, balding driver wore a white kippah neatly placed in the middle of his bald patch.

"Can you take me to Ramallah?"

He shook his head but spoke in a low, gruff voice: "Illegal for me. I, Jew. Come—I take you to check point."

His hands jutted out with the palms facing upwards, as if he were pleading. He shrugged his shoulders and seemed so unsure, I kept walking.

Another taxi driver accosted me on the sidewalk, placing his hand on my shoulder, forcing me to face his fierce, gray eyes and straggly beard. A group of taxi drivers were seated, drinking coffee on a bench. "What you doing? Where go?" he asked.

I spoke to him in a low voice, "Ramallah."

He laughed, shaking his head, and looked at the other drivers who were all jeering, laughing and pointing.

He turned to walk back to the bench and after he had taken a couple of steps, abruptly turned, saying "You crazy. You can't go there: prohibited," as he reached for a coffee cup being extended to him.

He blurted out, "I take you checkpoint for 200 shekels" before sitting down in his comfort zone; knowing smiles surrounded him.

I couldn't remember what the exchange rate was but it sounded like a lot of money. Now it was my turn to shake my head and continue walking. I tried to keep calm, but the reaction of the taxi drivers coupled with the uproar in the streets was starting to jangle my nerves. I walked around the block and leaned against the bus station building. I took a mental accounting of what I had, so far:

I knew I could at least walk to the checkpoint which would, according to the bus driver, take me about two hours. As for the buses or taxicabs taking me close to the checkpoint, I had no clue what all that meant or how close they could get me to the checkpoint separating Israel from the West Bank. I didn't feel I could trust any of them. Would they just drop me off on some lonely road far from my destination? Even if they could get me there, there was no guarantee I could get through the checkpoint.

I kept walking not knowing what to do. I figured I'd just listen to my heart; I didn't doubt for a minute that I was going to find a way to get in somehow, in spite of my reception thus far and what Miriam had said.

As I was walking on the sidewalk in front of the money exchange store, I heard a horn toot on my left. It was coming from a taxicab parked at the curb. Through the window, a dark-skinned man wearing a large skull cap motioned me to the window on the passenger's side.

"Hi!"

"Welcome. Where you go?"

"Can you take me to Ramallah?"

His response was almost too fast, too easy. "Sure, no problem. Hop in, my friend!"

By this time I was almost convinced there was no direct way to the West Bank, and that I'd have to take my chances at the checkpoint. And the words, "my friend".

I approached the window. "I've been asking around for the last hour, and no."

He waved like a windmill, "Come in, come in, come in."

"Oh well, here we go," I blurted out as I opened the back door, shoving my garment-tote bag in the back seat and hopping in after it. He started his car and slid the stick shift into gear—the car jumped forward.

"Wait a minute, a minute," I said, holding my hand up. He looked through his rear-view mirror and stopped the car, letting out a frustrated oath.

"Wait—you agree to take me to the West Bank, all the way to Ramallah. If so, how come the other...."

He started the engine again.

He emitted a low chuckle which chilled me. "I'm Arab," he said, pointing to his white, Muslim skull cap. "I ok to go to Ramallah and Jerusalem, both. Ok, let's go!" and he began to switch gears again.

Since everyone there seemed to be saying something different, I didn't know if I could rely on the taxi driver.

"Wait! Wait, please!"

His back to me, I could see it heave as he took a big breath then waited, tapping his fingers on the steering wheel.

"OK, how much?"

He hesitated, "For you, 100 shekels. Cheap! OK!

I made a quick calculation: 100 shekels...the exchange rate was three or four shekels per dollar—I couldn't remember—so about $25 maximum.

I nodded. He interpreted that as ok and put the taxi in gear, burning rubber as it zoomed forward. We passed the parked bus, the line of taxis and swerving to the right to follow the boundary of the bus station, careened around a curb and onto a crowded avenue.

"Why go Ramallah?" he asked tersely.

I explained to him my mission, and he nodded saying, over and over again, "Insha'Allah!" (God willing!)

The odyssey to the West Bank had changed the course of my travels as the taxi bounded forward like an Arabian steed. Then he descended into a quagmire of slow-moving traffic, swerving left and right then easing into tight spots.

After I opened the window and shoved my head out, I could finally ascertain what the hold-up was. In the distance was a mass of people under a smoky haze, a mixture of smoke from the kabob meat grills and dust kicked up by the passersby. Through the haze, I could see a long line of people waiting to pass inspection and a couple of Israeli soldiers stationed at the head of the line.

The car had been stopped for five minutes when the driver jammed the gear in neutral, pulled up on the parking brake and then turned to me.

"I'm going to have to leave you here. There's no telling...."

I had anticipated his saying that so I cut him off: "The deal was 100 shekels to take me to Palestine." I clenched my teeth in his face. He understood that there would be no payment until the car got to the West Bank.

He turned around and sighed, shaking his head as he looked at me through the rear-view mirror. "You mean you want me to get in line with the cars? It could take... hours...."

I stared back at the image in the rear-view mirror.

"Yes, yes, yes...that's it; there's no discussion. You get me in—that's the deal, or you don't get paid...not one shekel!"

He lifted his hands from the steering wheel and slapped them down in frustration. As soon as the car in front moved a couple of feet, he jammed into low gear and sluggishly followed it.

To the left was the traffic quagmire, at least seventy-five cars waiting to pass. It was a sprawling, slithering procession full of angry faces, spinning wheels...but no one dared honk a horn.

The drivers were too afraid to show their profound discontent. Silent frustration radiated from them as sweat streamed down their faces.

I stretched my neck out the window. I could barely make out a tower in the distance, looming ahead of the cars inching towards it. I wondered why there was an inspection of cars leaving Israel since I thought Israeli soldiers would be more concerned with incoming cars from the West Bank, the territories occupied by Israeli soldiers. It was an asphyxiating place, where people often could not move about on their own land without running into walls and checkpoints, where masses of cars traveled on the single lane road on the opposite side of the road we traveled on, trying to get through to Jerusalem.

I supposed that although the second Intifada had just been deemed over, the tight controls over traffic going either way were still being enforced. The car slithered forward, its belly seeming to barely scrape through the piles of dirt littering the road. As our turn came, the tension mounted that had accumulated over the past few hours, starting with my conversation with Miriam. I couldn't help but reflect on her warnings that I would not, under any circumstances, be allowed in: I had no authorization, I am American and would probably be treated like an Israeli Jew and turned back. But if I did succeed in getting through to Ramallah....

I wasn't able to continue the thought as I held my breath while the driver crawled forward and stopped at the control tower. He opened his window and passed his ID card to the soldier. I looked up and incredulously beheld a young man, age of around 20 or younger, wearing a battle helmet and holding an M-15. Thus, a boy not much older than an adolescent would decide my fate. The peach fuzz sprouting from his chin belied the firm set of his jaw, which made him seem like a jaded, battle-weary soldier of advanced years.

But I suddenly mused that I wouldn't want to be the soldier standing in the tower; he was probably there only to fulfill the required military service. Two unfriendly lines of cars on either side of him, he would be completely defenseless in the event of an attack. All these things came to mind as the soldier gave the card back to the driver, and then reached for mine through the opened back door window. He inspected the photo, raised his face to look at me, then returned his gaze back to the passport. This was repeated several times. He then returned the passport to me, looking at me with curious brown eyes. His brows furrowed as he turned to consult a piece of paper crumbled in his hand. A minute passed and I had still not taken a breath. His eyes were lowered over the list. I was sure, for some reason, I would be detained, hassled, or who knows what! I imagined myself being dragged out of the car and apprehended by the guards, or at the least, the taxi driver being ordered to turn around.

The guard's eyes met mine; he seemed to completely ignore the driver. It seemed as if only the soldier and I existed for a split second. His eyes glanced down, then into my eyes, then down again. His lips tightened as he raised his hand and then… he waved us on.

The driver pushed the gear stick into first and the car rocketed forward, as if to avoid any possibility the guard could change his mind. I looked back and noted that another car quickly scooted into our place at the front of the line. It was clear to me now why the driver had tried to let me out before the gauntlet at the checkpoint; his promise to deliver me to the West Bank was unrealistically dependent on one very young Israeli soldier, as the life of a gladiator was determined by a thumb and the whim of an emperor. My shoulders relaxed; I could breathe easy.

"My God, I'm in…the West Bank!" I mused that my intuition had served me better than my friend's in Tel Aviv. But maybe Miriam had been trying to persuade me not to go into the West Bank, an unstable place, just to protect me. I wondered to myself what was waiting for me here in this mysterious place. What were my Jewish friends trying to warn me about?

Chapter 21: Ramallah

I wasn't sure exactly when it happened, but the features of my surroundings had dramatically changed. The paved roads leading out of Jerusalem, with the exception of the sparsely paved road leading up to the checkpoint, turned into a mixture of dirt and gravel pot-holes, interspersed with mud puddles. The sides of the road were piled with rubble and stones and wooden hovels, some partially completed or partially destroyed. Rectangular and square cement structures with chopped off corners, seemingly filed down by a huge grater, were part of the terrain. Heaps of refuse, soggy cardboard boxes, pieces of red material, torn mattresses with springs poking out and a nauseating mixture of gunk appeared along the road, with pools of water oozing black substances looking like tar. I was so absorbed by my surroundings that if it weren't for an aching nose, I wouldn't have noticed the stench wafting through the open window.

Men with dark, white and salt-and-pepper beards and some with a two-day growth wearing keffiyehs draped over their heads walked on the side of the road alongside women wearing multi-colored hijabs, replacing the headscarves worn by many Jewish women on the other side of the wall.

The surrounding buildings were teeming with loose boards and ragged shingles, as well as doors hanging off their hinges or completely missing. The car easing over the pot-holed road allowed me to view everything, including the crude wooden boxes lining the streets with vendors selling prickly pears, huge medjool dates, dried apricots and other fruit.

A skeletal barefoot boy approached the driver and offered to sell him a newspaper through the window, which the driver purchased by giving the boy a coin, without stopping the vehicle. How he was able to grab the paper, reach into his pocket for a coin and steer the vehicle with his chest was beyond me.

As the crude dirt road turned into a paved street, hovels were replaced by stores and even some semi-modern apartment buildings with the famous Arab balconies extending over the road. I suddenly remembered that the Palestinian sisters, whom I called from Jerusalem, told me to call them as soon as the taxi entered Ramallah and approached the famous "Mukata'a," the location of offices and administrative centers of the Palestinian government. I asked the taxi driver if we were near it and he responded that we were just a couple of blocks away.

I called my friends and handed the cell phone to the driver for instructions on where to leave me. He quickly put it to his ear. After a few words in Arabic, he passed the phone to me.

"Hello," I said, but she'd already hung up.

As the taxi approached a street bordered by a circular off-white wall, it slowed down and the driver turned right and stopped. It was about four pm on Friday afternoon; an eerie feeling seemed to envelop the tall wall. No one, not even a cat was lurking about in the middle of this city, near the wall. The taxi driver turned to me and then pointed to the left:

"That's the Mukata'a, where Arafat[40] buried."

I reached into my top pocket, pulled out the 100 shekel bill and handed it to the driver, thanking him and apologizing that I didn't have a tip for him.

"That's ok, my friend. I see you want do good things...no need tip."

"Insha'Allah," I responded as I opened the door.

"Wait," and his long brown arm reached over, shutting the door. "I wait for you until your friends come. There's no one and this place is dangerous."

"Thanks—appreciate it."

I looked out the window down the lonely road. Not a car was in sight and no one was walking. I realized later it was a Friday afternoon, the Muslim Sabbath.

"Here, take my card. When you want ride back, call me when ready and I come."

I looked at the card: on one side was Arabic and on the flip side was English. I opened my mouth to ask a question.

He was astutely watching me through the rear view mirror.

"Same price...." and he started to smile when a face covered by a hijab popped into the rear view mirror next to his face, startling me, until I saw the huge smile in the middle of it.

Following her were two other hijabs. I expected to be welcomed by the two sisters I had met at the recent overnight interfaith event; it seemed so long ago!

I dragged my garment tote-bag out of the cab and waved to the driver. The three hijabs surrounded me. I kissed each cheek but I refrained from a full-blown French greeting as I felt a bit of hesitation over a peck on the cheek. And then I realized that a Muslim woman wasn't supposed to greet a man with a kiss on the cheek. Oh, well, it was done and the girls smiled before recoiling a step. They nervously giggled as we strolled down the street.

I asked them if they could recommend a hotel.

Hafa, the consistent spokesperson for the group replied, "Yes, there is a 4-star hotel on the outskirts of Ramallah—good for foreigners."

I had to interrupt, "I mean, I'd like to stay in a local, cheap kind of folksy place."

Also I needed to dispel their probable expectations that I was the token rich American.

---

40 Yasser Arafat was the former Chairman of the PLO (Palestinian Liberation Organization) and President of the PA (Palestinian National Authority), the present Palestinian government.

"And I don't have much money," which was true! I was always in the red at the end of the month.

This time Asma spoke, testing her shaky English. "It's just...." she lost her words.

Hafa to the rescue, while Kalila kept mum. "Over the hill there, see? We walk you."

But I was unaware of a new odyssey waiting for me there.

Chapter 22: Curdled My Soul

The façade of the building they were leading me into was gray and marked by billboards with pictures of women shrouded by hijabs, wearing milk carton smiles while advertising fruit juice; captions were in Arabic. The signs were in different round and rectangular shapes; some were so old they were leaning to one side and the sides were curling. Letters had torn off or were peeling. We entered an area surrounded by gray cement walls and turned into a courtyard leading to a couple of booths in front of which were hung long women's robes, more hijabs and baby clothes.

We entered an elevator that seemed to be a dubious form of transportation. But it ascended, bumping and sometimes turning a little. The girls looked up at the ceiling with worried eyes shifting back and forth. It stopped on the third floor, but the door didn't open; after a few tense seconds, it slightly opened, but seemed to be stuck. Immediately the girls pushed it and filed out with me on their heels.

They led me into a hallway then into a room where several men with keffiyehs greeted the three girls with handshakes; there were no kisses. The toothy grins of my companions stood out on their full, radiant faces, surrounded by their hijabs. They sat down in chairs provided by male attendants. I was given a special chair by an older man who had crossed the room and placed it next to me. I mechanically sat down across from the girls. He was lean, his dry hair curling at the razor's edge into a mossy bush framing the sides of his head.

The waiter was a young man with greased down, short, black hair and a pointed nose, wearing a black and white lattice-designed keffiyeh, tied in a knot around his neck. He served us coffee and dates. I was to learn later that a black and white keffiyeh[41] represented Palestinian heritage. Asma, still smiling, reached over and reverently shook the older man's hand. She leaned over as the other girls smiled, saying, her cheeks flushed as if embarrassed, "This is Muhammad."

I shook his hand and pronounced my name as his smile encircled the room, his white teeth flashing. On the left, next to a man speaking from a podium, a group of about fifteen men of all shapes and sizes sat in a row facing a crowd of about 300

---

41 Black and white keffiyehs symbolize Palestinian pride in their heritage. Palestinians also wear red and white keffiyehs and other colors. The colors sometimes conform to a political affinity.

people. Some were wearing green bands over their heads with white letters,[42] others red and white or black and white keffiyehs. Long, flowing beards hung from a few drawn, ashen faces. Their eyes moved rapidly from side to side like pent up goats in a corral, waiting to be released to pasture.

Streams and streams of Arabic were flowing from the speaker's mouth. He raised his hand from time to time, ejaculating strong words while provoking loud clapping or yelling from the crowd. I cringed....

When he paused, clapping forced back his Arabic streams and incited him to further waving of his hands and more streams of Arabic. Strange visions phased into my mind of masses of people on the other side of the wall that separated us— like the ominous gray monstrosity I had faced before arriving here—pounding the stone slabs to get in. That nourished my fervent desire to be instrumental, through non-violent interfaith work, in bringing the labyrinth of walls down and removing the myriad checkpoints slicing up the land into festering parts. That would hopefully give rise to unity of the Holy Land, freeing it for all Muslims, Jews, Christians, and all people. These thoughts effused me as I swallowed the sweet dates washed down by strong, Palestinian coffee.

This Kafkaesque moment seemed so unreal as just nine hours earlier, I had been on a hill rolling up my sleeping bag in Jerusalem, surrounded by Jewish peaceniks.

Then everything changed to slow motion as I watched the girls talking to each other, sitting next to two men. The older man contemplated the date between his forefinger and thumb, rolling it softly before sliding it into his mouth, a cavern of yellow teeth.

The line of men seated to the left of us seemed to stream onto a platform from oblivion, walking through the bold lights targeting us, beamed from a towering, tarantula-black structure. The speaker, who stood nearby, turned his arms as if they were the blades of a windmill, moved by the waves of energy emanating from the audience.

Then somehow breaking through the invisible barrier between the men and the girls, one of the girls came over and introduced me to the older man who had been sitting next to me all this time, "This is Abdullah; he is the oldest prisoner of the Israelis, who was liberated a couple of years ago. He was in prison for 28 years."

"What had he done to be condemned for 28 years?" I muttered under my breath and nervously looked around, hoping no one had heard me.

Overcome by fear, my body began to involuntarily tremble; I had to move, do something, so I shifted my legs to the other side of the chair to disguise my reaction, desperately trying to contain myself. My mouth must have dropped open as the girls' dark eyes, which had shifted to me, widened and then returned to the old man, their expressions exuding profound admiration, perhaps adoration. Abdullah rolled another date before gently placing it into his mouth. He turned and smiled, his silver teeth glistening. He seemed a man at peace, ready to embrace his freedom. That smile injected me with a calming elixir.

---

42 The white letters represented the Shahada: la 'ilaha 'illallah, Muhammad rasulu-llah (in Arabic) meaning: "There is no God but God, and Muhammad is his messenger."

Even though he was certainly aware of the admiration and adoration of the girls, and probably of all Palestinian people, his gestures were modest, not arrogant.

The ridges on his face deepened when he smiled; but his welcome manifested as a soft film spreading over his sensitive but distant eyes. I consciously tried to focus my thoughts to calm my intense trepidation at being in this place, by zeroing my eyes in on the old man, thinking silently, Didn't prison jade him, break him, make him a bitter old wretched man?

He just sat there smiling in his unassuming, marine-blue suit, a striped green and white tie knotted under his chin dotted with the white sprinkling of a day-old beard. As I drifted into semi-consciousness, I envisioned Abdullah's smile fade into his wizened body. He was clothed in a drab grey prison uniform. Twenty-eight years in prison...twenty-eight years in prison...echoed repeatedly in my ear. The apparition standing in front of me asked why he had been in prison all those years. He didn't know...but he kept smiling, smiling as his grey body receded from view...My spirit soared in some strange dimension as it followed his strange, crooked smile, the tawny teeth reflecting something I couldn't make out.

I could have remained in this ethereal state awhile longer but Abdullah, probably seeing that I was floating in some foreign space, brought me back partially by whispering in my ear, "Those men are long-term prisoners of the Israeli government and have been recently liberated.[43] We are celebrating it."

His smile widened to reveal silver in the back of his mouth, in a shadowy cavern, that seemed to close in around me. A hollow feeling of helplessness took over and I felt a tingling down my spinal cord, casting me into a panicky frenzy.

Taking a deep breath, I quickly scanned the room for an escape route; but I was surrounded. My eyes shifted from face to face, to Abdullah, to the speaker then back to Abdullah, whose eyes met mine under a furrowed brow. Oh God! I exhaled and forced air back into my lungs as I purposefully shifted my gaze to a bowl of dates in the middle of the table, to avoid detection.

I would have excused myself for fear my nerves would soon betray me if Abdullah had not jolted me from my dismal musing by his urgent whispers, "Furthermore, the speaker is the head of the West Bank Hamas party who is welcoming them back and speaking to the people in this hotel."

Could this be a radical group having a conference in the hotel my friends had selected for me? The same group that had allegedly been involved in several suicide bomb attacks in Israel? I can't be here...I...The words, this hotel, this hotel...kept repeating over and over again as my old enemy, fear, jolted down my sides and froze me to the chair.

The ethereal cloud completely burst, along with the balloon I was hanging from as I plummeted to earth. I muttered and then muffled a cough....

Intifada uprising was considered officially over.

The Arabic coffee was strong and rushed through me like a tidal wave...I asked

___

43 Many Palestinian prisoners were released by the Israeli government in 2005 after the Intifada uprising was considered officially over.

Abdullah where the bathroom was. He waved his arm in a half-circle. I imagined following his instructions, but the only way to the toilets was to walk by the speaker and then, as I found out, cut down a narrow corridor right in front of the audience of three hundred people. I got up and slowly pushed my chair under the table, needing to immediately heed my intestinal calls. I then walked toward the speaker and, following the imaginary arm, I veered left. As I turned the corner I was facing about three hundred heads, some covered with black and white or red and white keffiyehs, others with Muslim skull caps. Many hijabs adorned the crowd while others were wearing green bands like some of the released prisoners on stage. A few sat there with their arms folded, their long beards surging downwards.

They were all fortunately more intently listening to the speaker than paying attention to this strange-looking member of the audience skittering toward the bathroom. My tired, rubbery legs took me to the back of the room; the myriad faces still pointed toward the podium when I walked by. Only a few turned in my direction, vaguely distracted, then back to the podium. As I moved, my eyes nervously flitted to the back then the side walls, until they rested on a lone, unmarked door cracked slightly open. That must be it, I whispered to myself, as I lunged for it.

I returned to my seat after passing through the same gauntlet. As I approached the table, the white-haired ex-prisoner smiled and held out another date to me as I sat down. Then the three sisters stood up and Abdullah leaned over and told me we'd go see the hotel clerk about the room.

While the speaker was still wildly gesticulating and the former prisoners and audience boisterously clapping, I picked up my garment-tote bag, slipped the strap over my shoulder and shook hands with Abdullah; the three girls slightly, but respectfully, bowed as we drifted out of the room. The dark hallways flanked by long, ghostly drapes led into a small corner office. There alone, a man with a dark complexion was sitting behind the glass window of a small wooden booth. His toothless smile curled over his lips as he stood up and put his hands on the rough, wooden counter. He waited for us patiently, as if he hadn't anything else to do. I flashed back quickly to the crowd in the adjoining room and figured many of them would be checked into the hotel; I knew I didn't have a chance.

The man nodded and flashed a crooked smile. I wondered if there was miraculously a room available as I began to feel the sludge of deep fatigue manifest the slow motion of my limbs. Arriving at the counter, one of the girls spoke in Arabic. The clerk turned to me and said in very broken English, his lean face tightly wrapped around thin jaws, that it would cost about 80 shekels a night. I couldn't believe that in this big, downtown hotel it would cost about $20 a night, maximum. I dug into my wallet and produced four bills of 20 shekels each. The man took the money and laid a key in my hand.

I turned to the three sisters who seemed to say almost in unison, "Ahlan wa-sahlan," as Kalila pushed the button for the elevator.

I asked them if they'd join me for dinner tomorrow and they all smiled as they piled into the elevator. Before the door closed on them, Hafa asked me to call the next day around 4 o'clock, then the door closed and I was on my own.

The clerk had moved around the counter and was now standing next to me. I stood in front of the elevator thinking that my room was on another floor. Instead of entering the elevator, he motioned me to follow him down a corridor, covered by an aging, rust-red carpet, its worn edges a dirty white.

We walked down the hallway bordered by drab-green wallpaper, crumbling where the corners met. I followed him all the way to the end where he stopped. I joined him as he inserted the key in a corner door and turned it. The door opened into a comfortable room with two beds and long curtains covering the back window. He quickly walked across the room and opened the curtains. The bottoms swept the floor and sent a cloud of dust curling upwards. I could still see the cloud of dust particles as the man bowed and backed out the door, after placing the keys on the table next to one of the beds.

I draped my jacket over an open door and sat on the thick bed cover, woven with reds, blues and swirling desert scenes. They were compatible with the collage of thoughts swimming in my brain, from the Hamas conference to the three sisters, their eyes peering over their hijabs that turned into veils during my musing, hiding all but their shiny brown eyes. My eyes refocused and stared at the huge closet with two doors that were drifting open.

I felt alone, physically, but the warmth of the welcome, the sweet dates and coffee running in my veins, ironically brought me to the edge of sleep. My heavy eyelids closed. I was alone, surrounded by Hamas—chills engulfed me like a tidal wave...I sat there silently, my head buzzing with all that had happened that day, in a semi-trance: It had all started at the bus station in Jerusalem, the challenge and frustration of not knowing how to get to Palestine, and at first, getting help from no one. My mind retraced my steps, starting with asking the bus ticket clerk, a dark-haired lady who wore a blue head scarf, like some traditional married Jews. When I asked how to get to Ramallah, the furrow in her brow almost rose to meet the edge of the scarf sliding down her forehead.

Without answering my question, she had retorted, "I don't know. Say, why do you want to go there?"

"To visit friends," was my answer as I drifted away from the booth and more scowling. I guess she doesn't receive many requests like that, I had thought to myself. Anyway, what gave her the right to question my destination, to play "police"?

Since the ticket agent didn't know, it was obvious that no buses went to Ramallah from the Central Bus Station. So I left and began walking along the sidewalk that surrounded it. A line of taxis was parked along the curb. I bent over one as the passenger side window began to open.

A man scooted over to the window, his kippah covering his bald spot, surrounded by a few grey hairs. I told him I wanted to go to Ramallah and then he took a deep breath: He looked straight ahead appearing as if a stiff, ashen specter. Without looking at me, he said, "I take you to checkpoint, it's ok, you can maybe take...." Then the same head turned toward me, but the face had a darker hue, that of an Arab wearing a larger Muslim skull cap. He smiled a broad, inscrutable smile under a trimmed moustache. "Cheap, cheap...." he repeated over and over again.

My thoughts drifted to The Lion, the Witch and the Wardrobe[44], except the sequence was in reverse as I came from the other side into the wardrobe, then into the mysterious room, and into this enigmatic…Palestine. And then a voice echoed from somewhere, "Beware, beware, fool…." so loud it woke me. I sat up rigidly with my back flat against the wall and tried to focus, but everything seemed to fade into fuzziness, maybe subconsciously to soften the reality of this destitute place. I flicked on the remote control of the television perched on a metal tray overhead and watched with glazed eyes as several people wearing red and white keffiyehs spoke, madly gesticulating. I looked at my watch—it was 2 am. I had heard enough angry speeches for one day so I abruptly clicked the TV off and got up and went to the window.

I looked over this desolate city, startled that most of it was in total darkness, yet it was not that late. Sepulchral buildings all around me pierced through the veiled, black night. I couldn't call anyone as my cell phone had gone dead long ago and I'd forgotten to recharge it. There was no land line in the room. I was cut off….

In spite of the warm welcome today by the sisters and the old man, I was so alone, vulnerable and surrounded by militant extremists….

There was a morbid silence in the streets, in the corridor. I was sure no clerk was at the front desk as there was no one there when I had returned late the night before; so strange for a hotel! A cold wave rolled down my back; my hands quaked as I heard a creaking noise outside my door and turned my head, immediately imagining a group of black-masked gunmen dragging me out the door. No one would know….

A piercing cry in the night curdled my soul, turning my head back to the window as I looked out and could only see the reflection of the lamp on some dark windows of an abandoned building appearing like a dingy phantom.

I wondered if I'd live to see the sun again….

---

44 C.S. Lewis, The Lion, the Witch and the Wardrobe (London: Geoffrey Bles, 1950). The first published book of The Chronicles of Narnia.

Chapter 23: Searchlights

I slipped into a deep sleep and didn't even hear the early morning echoes of the Muezzin reverberating from the mosque's minaret a couple of blocks away. A warm blanket enveloped me as my eye opened into the rays of the sun baking the room. My tongue stuck to the roof of my mouth—I bent over feeling for the bottle of water I had set on the night table next to the bed. I grabbed it, and after two long gulps it was empty. I dizzily flung it across the room and turned over, throwing the heavy blankets off me; drops of perspiration rolled down my cheeks.

My body was still aching with fatigue; I sat up and looked around me. The drab green walls contrasted with the towering wooden closet on my left. A door had swung open and on it rested my jacket that I had draped over it the night before.

I reluctantly rose to my feet as I knew I'd need to go downstairs at least for water and some food. I remembered that I had vaguely agreed with the sisters to meet them for dinner, sometime after five. I looked at my cell phone which was lying on a small table beside the bed. The time was 3:20 pm. I had slept for at least 13 straight hours; I hadn't done that in years. No wonder I was barely able to pull myself up.

I got up and looked out the water-streaked window to a sight below, a hodgepodge of streets, cement buildings, and swarming people. I opened the window, stirring up the dust that had accumulated on the sides, as if patted out from a camel's hide.

An hour or so later, the air filled with the voice of the muezzin bellowing forth, entreating all to prayer. It seemed to be coming from the right of my window but I could not see the minaret. I looked at the sky, the West Bank sky, with its churning gray clouds, and tried to discover something different about them compared to other skies. I found nothing....

I walked into the bathroom and turned the cold water on full, placing my hands underneath and liberally splashing it onto my face. That chilled me, shaking my body down to its core. I ventured to look at my red, distorted face in the mirror and a smile crept across my lips. I had defied my friends to come here, to discover Palestine for myself, with my own eyes. I desperately wanted to share with the Palestinians, bring them together with Christians and Jews for peaceful coexistence—I wanted to help free the Palestinians held behind the walls, prevented from traveling into Israel to some of their holy places and even beyond, as they once were freely allowed to do. But the wall also meant two sets of prisoners: bringing it down would free Israelis

145

to travel to the West Bank so they could visit many of their Holy sites they'd been excluded from.

I picked up my recharged cell phone still lying on the table; it was after five pm. I called and Hafa answered.

"Marhaba." (Hi) "Hi, this is Frank."

"Hi. How are you liking Ramallah?"

"Great, what I've seen of it!" I didn't have the heart to tell her I'd seen Ramallah through a hotel window, so far. "So when and where do we meet?"

"I come to the hotel. You wait there."

"I'll wait in my room, downstairs. When?"

She had hung up. I assumed they'd show up soon because they all had to get up early the next day and go to work.

I had calculated right. I had just put my right shoe on and sat on the bed to look out the window when a light tapping sounded on the door.

I opened it to a pink-cheeked face surrounded by a hijab. Kalila, the most beautiful emissary of the bunch walked into the room. I felt a bit uneasy as I was sure that a single Muslim lady wasn't supposed to enter the hotel room of a man. But she didn't seem nervous.

To add to my concern, she sat on the bed and acted as if she was quite comfortable there. She looked up at me naively, her clear, white chin supporting an unadulterated smile.

"Well, my friend, are you ready?" Her eyes gleamed at me as she stood up and gingerly took both my hands in hers, leading me to the door.

In the streets, she squeezed her arm under mine as we passed a group of children with their binders under their arms, their hijabs neatly in place, some green, some blue with glitter on them. Even though the sun beat down on us mercilessly, they seemed to be unaffected by the warmth of the hijabs surrounding their spry faces. It was amazing!

The sweet mixture of Palestinian scents filled the air: the scents of sumac, allspice, pimento, dioica, paprika, oregano, garlic, union, cumin seeds, mint, parsley, coffee beans and powdered cardamom (used in making Arabic coffee). We walked by vendors of medjool dates, apricots, spices, their trays full of their wares, behind which they sometimes called out in spirited Arabic. I assumed they were giving us a great deal!! Kalila looked in their direction and she smiled; the vendors smiled back, their white teeth flashing and their eyes widening, as if they'd never seen a foreigner before.

"This is Manara Square," she said in a squeaky voice as she held her cell phone close to her face and pushed some numbers. At the same time, she pointed to the middle of the busy square; small cars buzzed around as members of the Palestinian police, wearing black berets and camouflage uniforms, directed traffic. In the center there was a round, cement square encircled by several statues of white lions, sitting—perhaps waiting—with their proud white manes flowing down. The square was surrounded by white buildings covered with advertisements in all shapes and colors: red and green, yellow lettering in Arabic, pictures of cars, even a big Western

Union sign adorned the square. Cars were slowly circling around the square while pedestrians wove through the vehicles, as if they didn't exist.

"By the way, what type of place you want to eat?"

"I wanted to invite you girls to dinner, but I don't have much money...." I watched her facial reaction, but she didn't frown, and just said, "OK, I know a good, cheap place."

Arabic then flowed from her mouth which bent in a half-smile, as she looked up. She waved as her two sisters crossed the street to join us.

We were soon three women in hijabs and a Yankee walking the twilight-infused streets of Ramallah.

As we almost strutted down the sidewalk without any cares, it seemed, I reflected on what Marko, my Jewish-American friend, had advised me when I called him from my room about an hour ago. First, he couldn't hear me very well and thought I spoke with a tremulous voice. Second, he couldn't believe I was in the West Bank, as he had also thought I wouldn't get in when I called him from Jerusalem. Then, half-jokingly, he warned me,

"Don't forget to duck." We both laughed. I needed that!

We had turned down a main street walking away from the city center when a radiant light beamed down from a spot above us, temporarily obscuring my vision and forcing me to look away. When I looked back into the light, it was so bright it made me see double.

I turned to Hafa and asked her what it was. Her lips tightened and she spoke through semi-clenched teeth, explaining, without turning her head or even looking at them, that they were spotlights from a Jewish settlement, nightly sweeping over them.

"Like a searchlight?" I guessed.

"Yes, yeah, that's it...the Jews are coming in on us." She put her hands protectively over the hood of her dark hijab. "You know, reminding us they are there, watching," but her hijab did not hide the anger seeping from her skin, transforming its hue to flaming auburn.

We continued to walk along as the light appeared to follow us; surely this was an optical illusion. Finally, Hafa and her sisters entered a door that looked like it led to a bistro, with tables outside and men smoking hookahs, their red eyes flicking up at us as they took a long drag. Inside were tables with people seated at them, eating rice, hummus, unions, creamed eggplant, falafel, kabob, pieces of liver, and chickens skewered with thin skewers arranged on dishes in the middle of the table.

The girls found a table to the side, next to a fan blasting air like desert winds through our hair. The girls squirmed to the back of the table and sat on a cushioned bench while I sat in the chair. Menus were distributed. As I couldn't read Arabic, I told the ladies to choose dishes and some pita bread, and we'd share.

Asma ordered the food. While we waited, I gave each girl a gift I had stashed in my book bag. I handed them bottles of perfume that I had specially selected in Paris to give as presents to young ladies. A friend in Paris said I should bring gifts for men and women, in the event I found myself in a difficult situation and needed to bribe my way out of it. Their smiley giggles told me they were well-pleased. Hafa blushed a little as she sprayed a little on the back of her hand.

About 10 minutes later, a waiter began bringing the dishes, heaped with potatoes, hummus, chicken, shawarma and falafel. Then the waiter brought a plate with several layers of taboon bread that we all took pieces of, dipping them in za'atar and olive oil. The girls would then dip pieces of red bell pepper and carrots into the za'atar.

Hafa pointed out that "This is mansaf." She forked pieces of lamb on top of a plate of yellow rice with taboon bread, and handed it to me. For a while after the mansaf was served, silence reigned over the table as brown-to-darker hands passed the various dishes, spooning the fragrant delicacies onto bigger plates; bread was broken and sometimes dipped into hummus.

After dinner, we walked back to Manara Square. The night traffic was sparser as a trickle of cars circled around, compared to earlier. While we stood on the sidewalk looking at the lions in silence, a taxi slowed down and stopped next to us. One of the girls must have flagged him as Kalila opened the door and said a few words in Arabic; then she and the other girls turned to me and almost in unison said, "Sucran, assalym walaykum." (Peace be upon you.) before climbing in.

I had barely uttered, "Walaykum assalym" before the taxi joined the cars in the square and was quickly hidden behind them.

Chapter 24: The Wind Howled

My eyes opened into darkness; I must have slept for hours, again, as the heavy buzz from the streets was gone. I got up and went to the window. Four flights down, the streets were almost empty, except for an occasional Palestinian sandwich vendor; the lights were off.

The remote TV channel changer lay on the table. I pressed on the start button, but this time nothing happened. I stood up and walked across the room to the outline of a television, its screen covered with dust. I fingered the buttons below and began pressing some of them. I heard a click, then a voice. A man with a red and white keffiyeh was speaking Arabic. I changed the channel and the screen flashed a woman wearing a hijab who was serving food to a man sitting solemnly at a table, the camera focused on the tears gliding down her cheeks. I switched channels to a soccer game and then turned it off.

I needed to get out of the room for a while; looking down I didn't know where to go as darkness engulfed the streets…I opened the door and stepped out to an empty corridor. Walking down, I arrived at the hotel front desk which was locked tight, with nobody looking out the counter window. The elevator took me to an abandoned courtyard below. The clothing shops were all closed and the windows covered by green boards, makeshift shutters transforming the court into a green tomb, with a light bulb attached to an electric cord swaying in the breeze above my head. In the middle was an eerie stairway, its gray, peeling paint making it look like it was strangely abandoned, leading nowhere. I looked up to the top and saw signs written in Arabic. One slanted downwards and off kilter, with the word "Close" written on it, missing the letter "d."

A chill came over me—I felt like I was entering the "twilight zone." All was closed; not a sound was made as a chilling silence breathed its cold emptiness into my bones. The only thing moving was the light bulb above and Kleenex floating in the turbulent air, along with dust and other particles blowing in my face as I walked slowly.

And then it happened: I saw it or thought I saw it—a hooded man, shrinking into the corner of the building. I kept walking toward the light, the open door, which I hoped would remain open. But I told myself I hadn't seen it, that I only felt it, since

I had escaped from the Muslim cult that held me prisoner in Morocco 30 years ago.[45] Had he been following me ever since? Was this a man or an imaginary man? Was this evil stalking me or a saint protecting me? I am going nuts! I thought.

Images of Miriam warning me invaded my mind. Maybe she was right; I don't belong here. I need to stay with the Jewish 'beautiful people' at the interfaith events and at least pretend to do something for peace, love. My mind drifted gloomily. Thoughts came and went in a confused collage of words: But it all seemed so artificial there, didn't feel like a true interfaith...didn't seem anything constructive would come of it. Except...I met my first Palestinians, the sisters living here, but I don't even know where they live...in Ramallah? I had to come here. But I'm an outsider in this strange....

Barren loneliness and paranoia shook me to the core. Would it happen again tonight? Would I see the hooded man? Was I just hallucinating or was it real? Miriam's warning came back. But then, my Jewish friend's words after hearing I was in the West Bank—Don't forget to duck—echoed in my ear, loudly. I smiled....and that snapped me out of it.

The opening to the street was wide; no doors blocked it as it was always open, day and night. Such a strange world compared to Israel, where there were no doormen, no security guards with pistols protruding from black holders strapped to their belts. Just the moon lingered, dangling over the tops of the squat buildings.

Along the sidewalk, a couple of taxis were parked, without drivers. I assumed they had called it a day and were sleeping soundly somewhere in the Medina. I marched back to Manara Square. A couple of taxis were there and their drivers were still at the wheel, stiffly looking straight ahead like zombies ready to take me...The omnipresent lions hadn't left as they were still encircling the center area, their presence known to the lights flooding down from the buildings.

On the opposite side of the square there were two Palestinian policemen leaning against their cars marked "POLICE." It seemed that their black eyes looked right through me, searching for something. Cigarette smoke curled up from their brown fingers; they repeatedly flicked ash from the butts. So it was clear they were police, but why were they there? There was no one around.

The wind had swept up some papers and sent them flailing through the air, to land on the back of one of the lions. They slid down its side and alighted on the road.

I shivered—it was cold. I had been so warm in the arid breeze coming from Jerusalem during the day. Now it was cold and windy but I hadn't brought any jacket as I assumed the weather would remain the same. I continued my walk down the deserted street in the direction of a light flashing at the end. As I drew near, I saw some gray djellabahs hanging from a string overhead, as well as hijabs and several book bags. I walked into the well-lit store and noticed a man putting things in boxes on the counter.

He looked up as I was upon him, and smiled. "Assalym walaykum," I announced.

"Walaykum assalym," he responded, not taking his eyes off me.

I began to shiver again and asked him if he sold jackets. He shook his head and

---

45 Storm Over Morocco, 4th Edition, supra, Chapter XL, 313-315.

shrugged his shoulders at the same time. Then he pointed across the street. I thanked him and backed out of the store.

It was strange as most of our communicating was through gestures. At that moment, I truly regretted not knowing much Arabic, but I was amazed we could get by with body language. As I reached the shop across the street, I noticed two young men carrying boxes back and forth, from the front to the back of the store; they were closing down the outside outlet.

I approached and asked one of them for a jacket; he shrugged his shoulders like the other vendor, but he saw me shiver again and raising his finger, he said a few words in Arabic and strode to the back of the store. In a couple of minutes, he returned with a black jacket lined in white. From my limited experiences in the markets, I remembered that my next move must be to offer a low price. So, thinking it was worth about forty shekels I offered 10. He wrote down his price on a piece of paper: thirty shekels. I took the pen and countered by writing down fifteen. He countered with twenty-five. I then wrote down my price, twenty shekels, and then waved my hand to show him that was my final offer.

He responded,

"Ok!"

The wind blew the jacket above my head as I struggled to place my arms in the sleeves, while I walked. I faced the abandoned entrance to the hotel once again, this time with a jacket, but even it did not completely insulate me from the frigid cold.

I pushed the elevator button; it did not work. The wind howled through the corridors, warning me I should have stayed in my warm room. "Too late, too late," I breathed out as I looked for another way to get to my room. Steps were reflected by the light from the front of the elevator shining through an opening around the corner of the cement wall. I entered the opening and began climbing the steps, now in total darkness. I had to feel my way up, following the smooth wall. I realized I had reached the second floor only because there was a lone door overlooking a small landing. There were no markings on the door and it was closed and sealed. I had two more to go as the wind howled in the stairwell like a banshee, whipping up rubbish collecting in corners: papers, old cartons, a cup with dried coffee in the bottom and olives pits. A strange, tapping noise came from above, forcing me to creep along the stairs. The third floor arrived and again there were no markings on the ghostly door. All was still, in total darkness. The tapping noise seemed to be coming directly overhead as I crept up the remaining stairs, sheepishly turning the corner and heading up the final flight. I looked over the top of the last stairs and could vaguely make out a door flapping open and closed, to the rhythm of the violent wind current in the stairwell. Just as I pushed past the door, a light went on in the hallway and a man I recognized as the clerk walked toward me. His parched smile and lips indicated he'd been sleeping.

"I'm sorry…forget tell you elevators not working and you need call cell to let in. No work after eleven."

He took my hand and pulled me inside the stairwell. He then turned me around and pointed to a note taped to the wall next to the door, with the words "cell," then Arabic letters and a number next to it. I had missed it earlier, in the shadows.

The next day I met with Hafa for coffee to discuss my visit to the West Bank. We sat in a local café where old men were smoking hookahs, drinking coffee and playing cards. She looked up at me over her cup of Arabic coffee in silence but was watching me closely, as if she was sizing me up. She took another sip of her steaming coffee and the vapor climbed and twisted and swirled right between her eyes. She told me that her youngest sister, Barika, whom I hadn't met yet, was returning to Jenin to school where her family lived. I nodded in silence, thinking I'd like to visit the town, as she stopped and took another sip of her coffee. Her eyes never left mine and the soft brownness sent me dreaming of an Arabian princess waiting for my arms in a hidden cave....

My villainous memories sent the beautiful dream into purgatory, casting a sullen cloud over our conversation as I remembered talking with friends in Paris about Jenin. They had warned me not to visit there because it was the center of the conflict between the IDF (Israel Defense Forces) and Palestinians during the Second Intifada. They explained that many Palestinians were killed and houses were bulldozed in the refugee camps, not long ago, emotions were running high and the people were still full of hate for the State of Israel, Jewish Israelis and citizens of any country helping Israel—namely Americans. I had also read somewhere that most of the suicide bombing attacks in Israel derived from the Northern West Bank cities of Jenin and Nablus, and from the southern city of Hebron. All those cities were on my list to visit, for interfaith marches/dialogues. The idea that the interfaith work had to succeed there or nowhere kept circling in my mind and I didn't know where I got the idea... only that I had to go to Jenin!

Hafa lowered her cup and reached out and touched my hand, grasping my cup, then suddenly retracted her hand as if she had caught herself.

"I think you'd enjoy visiting my home. You'd be welcome...."

Those few words made me forget everything my friends had said in Paris about Jenin and anything else I ever knew, for that matter. I nodded again, dumbly but not numbly. Her eyes looked down and her lips turned under as she spoke.

"But, you could get caught for hours in the checkpoint between Ramallah and Jenin."

"Well, could I visit the refugee...."

She continued, "It usually takes about an hour to drive there from Ramallah, but you could take from three to five hours because of those checkpoints. One time it took me ten hours and I barely got home...problem!"

I finished my sentence: "Could I visit the refugee camp as I've heard so much about it, about how most of it was destroyed and how the people survived...."

She interrupted, "Na'am, of course." (Yes)

One of my goals was to visit some of the refugee camps before I left the West Bank to hear the Palestinians' stories and test the theory that progress through interfaith peace projects will never be made unless the people participated— especially those from the most contested places, including members of the fanatic religious groups in the West Bank, the Gaza Strip and Israel. I was going to the exact place where some of those groups were known to be active...without knowing exactly why.

152

Chapter 25: Jenin

I was to meet Hafa and Barika at Manara Square in about two hours, where I'd join them in a special shuttle bus, with a driver hired by her family. Hafa explained to me, as she winked, that it was better to know the drivers, when they take someone to a place like Jenin. I didn't understand her meaning until later.

I walked down one of the streets that lead into Manara square; passing the familiar stalls and sniffing the sweet scents of the East, I proceeded, as if I were being magically led me down the street by a pied piper. I walked next to men, some wearing keffiyehs, some not, passing others outside a café drinking tea and smoking a hookah.

One spry young man got up and came to me, "Where you from?"

"I'm American...."

"Ahlan wa-sahlan. Sit down with my friends."

He told me his name was Fawwaz; his short, graying hair lay atop a long face with pale olive, closely shaved skin. His smile was a bit crooked, but his brown eyes were clear. A man I sat next to was short and stocky with a well-trimmed moustache.

He was eating some kind of nuts and he furtively passed me a few on a napkin saying, "These are good for...shhhhh...." he put his finger on his lips as if he was about to tell a secret, "you know...." his eyebrows rose. I got the idea what the nuts were good for!

It turned out that he and the others were high school English teachers. Being a university law professor, as well as a professor of Anglo-American literature, we had something in common. We exchanged teaching stories. The two hours went by quickly. I told them I was going to Jenin and my shuttle would be waiting for me at Manara Square in a few minutes so I got up to shake hands and wished them all well. I then grabbed my tote bag and started for the door.

Fawwaz followed me and explained, "I'll go with you...I'll wait until your friends come. It's...better."

"Oh, it's not necessary...."

"You know, sometimes dangerous. All someone has to do is yell out, 'Jew! Jew!' and they can attack you, just like that. It's a...strange place, sometimes."

I flashed on the incident in Ramallah a few years ago and the photo of the adolescent showing his bloody hands out the window to an enraged crowd below.

"Yes, ok. Thanks, Fawwaz."

He waited at the corner of Manara Square and one of the side streets until a yellow van pulled up.

I thanked him as he walked away. I looked into the face of a young girl sticking her head out the window:

"You Frank?" "Na'am."

"I'm Barika. Come in."

She opened the door, slid to the other side and I slid in next to a long-haired adolescent who smiled as she extended her hand. I shook it. In a few minutes, we were going around Manara Square in a shuttle driven by a long-faced Arab with bushy eyebrows; a gray shadow seemed to hang over his face. Two women wearing hijabs were sitting in the front seat next to a bearded man. We had the back seat to ourselves. The driver nervously tapped his hands when the traffic stopped and then charged ahead, burning rubber until he slammed on his breaks, butting up to the next traffic jam.

On the outskirts of Ramallah, the car careened off the road, the driver trying to break all records to arrive at our destination. The shuttle barely made it around several turns. I looked around but his driving didn't seem to affect the passengers as it did me; they just went on talking while my finger was held tightly between my upper and lower incisors. It seemed as though everyone accepted the necessity of always driving fast down roads that could be closed for hours at the check points, or sometimes for days after a violent confrontation between Palestinians and Israeli soldiers and/or Israeli settlers.

I got my first glimpse of vast stretches of the arid, rocky terrain between Ramallah and Jenin; it seemed to go for hours and hours. A welcome break in the monotonous landscape came every thirty minutes or so when the shuttle would drive by Bedouin camps, with the men sometimes leading camels by long leather reins down the side of a barren hill. My eyes popped out as nothing seemed to have changed in these hills inhabited by Bedouins, driving their camels since Biblical times.

We arrived in a town and the driver announced "Jenin"; but he drove right through without stopping. In the outskirts, he let out all the passengers, except Barika and me. She, sensing we were near her home, lifted her waxen face from the corner of the seat. Her face slowly regained color as the mild breeze ruffled her long, black hair while the shuttle barreled down a series of country roads. Even though I trusted Barika who continued surveying, no doubt, familiar landscape as the color returned to her cheeks, I had only just met her and her family and wondered why I trusted her and her driver...especially since the shuttle had not let us off in Jenin, our destination. The shuttle drove by acres and acres of farms and mules pulling carts along the side of the road, as in Biblical times. The only difference seemed that today the roads were paved. I looked at Barika who didn't look worried and without saying anything, smiled and lifted her chin, nodding as if to say, "It's a bit further."

The shuttle finally turned into a small town, Arraba, with posters attached to a post elevated above. Even though I couldn't read Arabic, since the faces on them were very young and this region was a well-known center of conflict between Israeli soldiers and Palestinians, I wondered if the photos on the posters were of the "martyrs." That being a delicate subject to all people in the region, I didn't ask Barika about them. The driver stopped the shuttle in front of a two-story farm house. Barika and I were greeted by her father, mother and a young brother she introduced as Amoudi, who opened the door of the shuttle to let us out. I breathed easily now as we were chaperoned up a couple flights of stairs to the entrance of the house. After leaving our shoes outside, we were led into a room lined with cushions and corpulent, tall-backed sofas, where we sat. Food was brought out consisting of eggs, za'atar and other goodies.

As we were eating, I could feel my cell phone buzzing in my pocket. I got up and went to the door to answer it without bothering my hosts. The father, wearing his red-checkered keffiyeh followed me with his beady eyes.

"Hi Frank, it's Miriam. Where are you?"

"I'm in Jenin." I allowed a little time for her reaction. I could hear her violently expel air.

"Wow, amazing! Ok, you can tell me the rest…when you return…but . ." There was silence at the other end then another sigh, and then her voice continued, "I have news! Before you return to Paris, you got go to Galilee to visit woman in a Kibbutz. I told her about you and she thinks you—don't know how say—maybe one of the five she thinks sent from Jehovah to the Holy Land to work with her and help lead it to peace."

"I…don't understand…how would she…?"

"No worry, she explain. Can you go now because she meet with other leaders in about two hours and you meet them? She needs to see you…today, must my friend, please."

"I'll try but I'm in Jenin…West Bank…right…." there was a silence.

"But Jenin is not far from Galilee, it's the north, but…."

"What's that?"

"You may have checkpoint in North or you have to go back south to Jerusalem, then back through North Israel. Ask people…." then the phone went dead.

My phone buzzed and an SMS text message flashed on the screen: "Sarah, Hukuk Kibbutz, tell driver toward Tiberius plus give cell."

The name, Tiberius, rang a bell in my head, somewhere deep within the hidden recesses of my past…or maybe a past life. In this Holy Land, more magical than I expected, things—feelings of déja vu—were surfacing perhaps from events a thousand years old.

The phone buzzed and it was Miriam again. Her voice had toned down a decibel or two, was calmer.

"I'm not surprised you made it into the West Bank! You magician, I can feel it. If you return to Jerusalem at Qalandia checkpoint, call the following number and give the cell phone to the cab driver. He'll take you there. Try to arrive within two hours as they are having a meeting there, organizing the next interfaith conference and you can meet the organizers."

My head was spinning with all this new information. She gave me the number, said a quick, "Shalom" and hung up.

I returned to lunch and announced that I needed to return to Jerusalem, and pronto; the cab driver was invited to lunch and he heard me.

"I take you, 100 shekels."

"Ok, but first, I want to see the refugee camp in Jenin. Can you get me through it?"

His dark, bushy eyebrows knitted and his head moved just a bit for me to interpret it as a nod. After lunch, the entire family waited at the foot of the stairs to wave good-bye to me. As the taxi driver and I walked toward the cab, I turned my eyes to rest upon such a warm nest in the middle of all places, where many people had allegedly died, with a smile on their face. I imagined my own death and hoped that no matter what I had lived through or died for, I'd die with a smile on my face to show others there was no reason to fear death: the smile would be a send-off to the afterlife. I hoped if I died, it would be for a good cause and, with courage....

The figure of the father, with his red-checkered keffiyeh, the mother with her white hijab, and Amoudi, his mischievous crooked smile, and Barika, her hair blowing about her like a medusa, were now an afterthought as the shuttle plowed forward, with me sitting next to the driver, this time.

The driver hit the gas once out of the center of the village, a stream of particles and dust spewing behind us in our wake, until we reached the Qalandia checkpoint. I could see the long line of people standing and waiting that I'd have to join several blocks ahead. I paid the driver, and shook his hand. His dark moustache hid his lips as he turned away and, without emotion, grabbed the wheel while I shut the door.

I joined a long line of Palestinians, some wearing hijabs, some large white skull caps, waiting to get through the checkpoint: the metal corridors, then the reinforced window through which I was observed by a young Israeli woman soldier, who looked at my passport deposited in the metal tray that was immediately swallowed up on the conveyer, then the metal turnstiles and metal detector machines. An Israeli soldier, after inspecting the machines, had to buzz each person through the next door, then the next....

Progress was as slow as it had been entering the West Bank, by taxi. Even though worried mothers carefully wrapped their babies, rifling through their bags for baby bottles and food, there was no pushing or shoving. Toward the end, I noticed a couple of frustrated men, both wearing dark, marine-blue suits and day-old beards, flashing worried, black eyes looking nervously at their watches while clicking their tongues as if to say, "Get going! We're late for work." But they had no control whatsoever over this. If they began shouting and carrying on, they would surely be in danger of being turned back by the all-powerful Israeli police. They resigned themselves to their helpless, unfair situation. It took about an hour and a half to get through to the other side.

On the Israeli side, I scanned the sinister cement wall looming over us and the shuttles and taxis lined up to take those that got through to Jerusalem. The ones turned away, for whatever reasons—their papers, their looks—had to walk to the other side of the gauntlet I had just gone through, to take a shuttle back to the occupied land, back behind the myriad checkpoints and walls. There was no end. I hailed a thin taxi driver with a multi-colored skull cap and a straight, flowing beard. He motioned me inside.

I opened the door and sat down on a cushioned seat, a thin layer of foam rubber trying to disguise some rusty springs poking out of the upholstery. He started the taxi and it began to move even before I could tell the driver where I was headed.

"Wait! You don't know where I'm going." He stopped the car, turned off the ignition and pulled out the key, letting out a well-orchestrated sigh, like the one I'd heard before.

"Sign him up for Hollywood; here we go again!" I whispered. "You have to get out of here first, to Jerusalem."

"I'm going to the Galilee. Can you take me?" "Yes, for only 500 shekels. Cheap!"

"Too much...I don't have it," I protested and pulled the latch to open the door.

"Wait, wait, what you want?" "I can pay only 150 shekels."

"Not possible, not even pay petrol. You kid me?"

He looked at me and let out a low chuckle. My steadfast look told him there was little leeway here.

"OK, 400 shekels—that's it!"

"No, I don't have it. I really have 200 maximum to spend. It's OK, don't worry."

I pulled the latch and opened the door. He put his hand on my shoulder and stared coldly into my eyes, as if I were the devil himself: "350...."

"250."

He looked at me and had to bark a laugh, half dog, half man. His chuckle turned into a course growl in his throat, either as a warning or indicating that he smoked too much.

"Very last, no...forget it...300...." I cut him off, "Deal...let's go!"

He let out another planned sigh, this time longer and more dramatic. His top lip vibrated when he exhaled.

He shoved the key in, turned the engine over and gunned the car, making the door bang shut on its own. "Ok, Ok!" After another measured sigh we were on our way. Theatrics over...for now!

"I have to get there in about two hours."

"Alright, I get you, no problem. Just sit back; you sleep."

I couldn't sleep as I was amazed at his skill in weaving in and out of traffic, and getting us quickly to the highway linking Jerusalem to the Galilee.

As the miles and miles of highway sped by and an hour elapsed, I began to slip away. Somewhere I noticed an expanse of water.

"This is the Kineret, you see?" (Sea of Galilee)

I sat up to view the vast water, a blue, floating sheath, the place where Jesus had walked...and often the middle of the strife among the countries of Israel, Lebanon, Syria and Jordan.

Mixed emotions suffused my body as the blueness faded and a blue-grey replaced it. The taxi sped on. A mist barely touched the top of the vast, clear blue lake. It seemed to be the embodiment of the magical, historical events that have shaped humanity for eons, this big lake called the Sea of Galilee.

I remembered Miriam telling me to call a number when we reached the Galilee. I called it.

A soft woman's voice responded, "Yes, Frank?" She was expecting my call. "Shalom, Sarah; here's the taxi driver."

Words in Hebrew were spoken and the taxi driver gave me back my phone. I hoped that she'd still be on the line but the buzzing indicated she had hung up.

Chapter 26: Hukuk Kibbutz

The taxi started its ascent along the green fields of the Kineret, driving inland until I could no longer see the "Galilee." A rumbling in my stomach continued until the taxi pulled up to an iron gate. The driver got out and walked to the gate. He returned with his hands reaching up, palms out, indicating he did not know what to do.

I called Sarah; her excited voice said, "You've arrived! I'll open the door. Take the first right and you are here." That was strange as she could see me, but I couldn't see her....

The iron grate door opened and we were welcomed into the Hukuk Kibbutz. The driver pushed the whining taxi onwards and had to brake hard as a peacock with fully-displayed feathers crossed in front of the car. He took the first right and a white-haired lady with bright pink cheeks was there to greet us. The driver stopped the car and she opened my door. I got out and the lady reached out; we hugged.

"Sarah?"

"Yes Frank. Welcome...shalom."

She was a tall, statuesque lady, with deep blue eyes and small lips that slightly curved upwards. She was wearing a multi-colored necklace around her neck, a loose, silky white blouse with ruffled sleeves billowing out slightly, and loose, white slacks. Her sandals flapped on the pavement as she walked.

The taxi driver got out to stretch his legs and walked to the curb, looking out over the fields, then turning back to me. He was waiting to be paid. The mystical Sea of Galilee spied on us from the distance. It loomed larger than ever over the rolling hills, in the cradle of mankind, portrayed in so many stories...so many lives rising with the mist curling upwards toward the heavens. I paid the driver and he was all smiles as he backed out, waving and then looking over his shoulder. Sarah took my arm and led me to a garden where several people were seated, mostly women.

"We just did a reading from the Kabbalah," she informed me as we walked toward the group. She said that the event was over and unfortunately many people had to leave, but some of the Jewish members remained to welcome me.

I looked over to the group, their bright cheeriness reaching out to me under the warm sun of the Galilee. An elderly woman wearing a white shawl with her curly hair brushed back nodded, her curls jiggling; she held out her hand and I took it.

"You are welcome among us—we are here for peace. We just had our meeting with leaders of our group from Jewish, Christian and Muslim communities in Israel."

She smiled and gave me another look beneath her curly white hair and head scarf. "You'll be one of our leaders—I feel it."

Sarah announced to the group that it was predestined that five people would be sent to lead our peace movement, and I could be one of them.

I asked, "Were there Christians and Arabs in the conference?"

"Yes, but they left early."

The peacock let out a screech resounding through the trees and across the kibbutz. I looked out over the Sea of Galilee and envisioned all of our souls bathing in the holy waters, embracing centuries past, a sweet clasping of hands across time in the spiritual ecstasy of this magical place.

They were all Israeli Jews and they spoke of peace, love and understanding, that we were all roots leading to the same trunk. A short, bleached-blond woman held my hand in hers as we spoke. The black roots showing through blond strands did not distract me from her blue eyes entreating me to connect with her deep desire for peace. She said she lived in the Golan Heights and invited me to visit her family. It was surprising how nonchalantly she spoke of the Golan Heights, that it was natural she should live there with her husband and her daughter. Yet, it wasn't long ago that there were many raging battles in the Golan Heights between Israeli and Syrian forces in the Six-Day War of 1967 and the Yom Kippur War of 1973.

In spite of the mystical aura of this Kibbutz, I thought to myself that it was going to take a while to get used to this place, not far from where the Zohar was written—the foundations of the Kabbalah and mystical Judaism—yet it was also the center of heated conflict for years. I imagined the tears of grief washing into and nourishing this sea, the lake, this now grayish reminder of a volatile past. And I was visiting the place I had only read about, whereas these people lived it, felt it and breathed it every day.

Sarah was the leader of the group, and would make sure we were reminded of that by her subtle and not so subtle words and actions: sometimes she would stop the discussion and focus our attention on the highlights of what was just discussed. Then she would arbitrarily select someone to comment by saying, "Deborah, or Tal, we haven't heard from you yet."

She announced to the group that I had been sent to help organize the next peace reunion, and I would return many times to this holy place.

That night she let me sleep in a cozy guest bedroom next to the kitchen. The next day, we drove to a restaurant which was built at the end of a pier jutting out into the Sea of Galilee, maybe even over the spot where Jesus walked. As we sat there in silence listening to the waves lapping against the sides of the pier, a magical presence cloaked us in warm velvet on this warm afternoon. A growing fervor fed by being in this place infused me in silence, with the wind blowing gently through my hair and the waves rolling in and out. I could feel it, feel it....

Sarah was partially prophetic as I would return to Hukuk three times, once as the main organizer and leader of the main meditation session during a major interfaith event of a hundred people. But I could never have predicted that this group, this interfaith peace group from Hukuk full of loving vibes, would turn against me one day....

Chapter 27: Houston

Upon my return to Paris, I was so infinitely inspired by what went on in Hukuk and the interfaith group that I needed to tell the world, to share with people what was happening in the Holy Land. I fervently desired that more and more people visit the region and see for themselves the many Jews, Muslims, Christians and people of other faiths that are working for peace. There was so much to live and so much to do in helping to bring about peace in the epicenter of world conflict, which became my goal, my passion...or had it always been?

I was convinced that the first major step in this "interfaith" non-violent peace process was to bring the whole world to the Holy Land, to see what was happening with its own eyes.

In the meantime, a dynamic New York City publisher, World Audience, decided to publish my first book, *Storm Over Morocco*. In the aftermath of an extensive promotional campaign for the book, I was invited by several churches, synagogues, schools, universities and bookstores in the United States and England to participate in conferences, talks and author signing events. Bingo; I was all of a sudden scheduled to visit several US cities in about 13 states, including New York, California, Texas and others, as well as London. Even though I wasn't looking forward to the hectic traveling, the airport hopping, I embraced the opportunity to share my spiritual path during my trip to Morocco, almost 30 years ago, and even more importantly, share with people my plans to engage in interfaith peace activities in Israel and the West Bank.

I envisaged it being a great way to get feedback for the book and my activities in the Holy Land, to hopefully inspire people to join me in Israel and Palestine as well as encourage people to organize interfaith events in their local communities.

I was also receiving invitations to participate in some TV interviews, as well as the conferences, author events and talks mentioned above. I had already coordinated with my publicist to send out promotional blurbs to several bookstores, libraries and community centers. The first visit was scheduled for three bookstores in Houston, Texas; so I purchased tickets to Houston from Paris. At the end of a week, I was scheduled to hop over to the Silicon Valley in California for a series of events, and then to visit other cities. But I had no idea I'd soon be meeting, during a book signing event in Houston, an Evangelical Christian African- American, Dedra, an energetic preacher of the gospel.

As I deplaned at Houston International Airport, the summer heat hit me like a hot towel across the face while I walked down the steps to board the bus to take us to the terminal; I was caught off-guard by the humidity which inflicted an uppercut to my senses. I didn't wait for the KO as I ducked into the air- conditioned airport, only to return to the humid furnace before jumping on another bus that would take me to the inner city. I asked a man with a closely-shaved beard and a cowboy hat where I could find a cheap hotel. He advised that I get off downtown as there would be places to stay there, though a bit trashy; he added that they'd be no different than your typical heart-break hotels. I wasn't sure what he meant by that.

The bus left me off at the downtown bus stop. I waved at the man and he waved through the streaked windows of the top-heavy bus, as it thundered by.

Walking with my portable suitcase, I noticed homeless people and their blankets, backpacks, tins and things were strewn over the grass strips along the sidewalk. An African-American man was walking ahead of me, his hair frizzing straight up while the side of his afro was held down by a large wooden fork clamp. I rolled my suitcase faster and caught up to him.

Without looking at me, as if I was part of the scenery, he spoke, "What's happen'in, bro?"

"Nothin' much. Alright!" He turned his head as if I'd spoken the magic words and smiled.

"Looks like you either comin' or goin'."

I followed the rap, "Sometimes I don't know whether I'm comin' or goin'."

"Ok, how can I help?"

"First, why are there so many homeless people around? I feel bad."

"What do you care? Looks like you got it made!"

I looked sternly at him and he got the message.

"Alright, alright, don't feel bad about me or other street people; we done come to Houston after the Hurricane Katrina disaster put a lot of people from Mississippi and Louisiana in the streets."

I passed him and my eyes swept right and left but I couldn't find any cheapo hotels. The same man I had spoken to was following a few steps behind. I turned and signaled him.

"Can you help me find a cheap hotel? I mean the cheapest."

"Sure man. Can you drop me a five and I'll look into it...find you a bus to take you to one if need be, ok?"

I dug into my pocket and pulled out exactly a five and that was all I had except coins jingling in my pocket. I hoped my credit card worked, this time....

He was like a small time hustler that I had met in San Francisco when I was living in the ghetto while going to school; he even carried the same size brown paper bag. He told me to sit down with my luggage and he'd be back with all the info I needed and disappeared into a building. I thought maybe that was the last I'd see of him, but no. In about 10 minutes, he ran back through the same doors and passed me a piece of paper.

"Got the bus number; you see where those sidewalks are on the other side of the street? You take number 85 and then stay on it for about nine blocks; the bus will go under an overpass and after that there are several hotels bunched together and they're all cheap. You get off there."

"Thank you so much! Knew I could believe in you."

"Whoa, whoa—back up, dude. You paid me, man, and when I promise, I deliver. You need anything else; you know where to find me."

His wide grin displayed cracks at the corners of his mouth, probably due to malnutrition, and he had no upper teeth. This was a soul man, keeping on keeping on, in the streets. I admired him for his never-give-up spirit, as he hustled the streets to survive while holding onto his principles. He could have held onto my five and done nothing but he was a man of his word. I had met a good man.

The bus was waiting on the corner and I dragged my suitcase up the steps before I collapsed on one of the hard seats. In exactly nine blocks, the bus went under an underpass and, as the man had instructed, there was a group of hotels huddled together on the other side of the highway.

I found the cheapest room. I only remember sinking low into the bed, clothes and all and then I was out, cold. I desperately needed to sleep as the next day I had an author signature event at a Barnes & Noble store in a huge shopping center outside of Houston.

Being originally from the North, specifically Northern California and Oregon, and not knowing the South, I expected a lot of nice, down home people wearing cowboy hats and speaking with a thick accent. However, a crowd showed for the book signing, including people wearing cowboy hats as well as people from all over the world: Europeans, South Americans, Mexicans, and many others. I was shocked!

While I was speaking to a South American writer, I felt a strong sensation in back of me, like someone was scrutinizing my every move. I quickly looked up—no one was there. Then around 9 pm, I noticed an African-American woman pretending to look at best sellers arranged on a table obviously staring at me: her face turned in my direction and away again, when I glanced towards her.

The tall, black stranger with red, strappy shoes started walking towards me and without looking up, I felt something pulling at me. She drew close to me and stopped. Our eyes met. Her sparkling demeanor grabbed my jet-lagged frame and woke me to her presence.

"What's your book about? Looks spiritual and that's what I'm looking for."

I recounted my experiences in Morocco, and she smiled, stating, "Praise the lord, you' free."

Her eyes glistened like midnight stars and her shiny, voluminous hair framed her soft, dark-brown face. She had the most voluptuous lips, brown, tender and open like a springtime archegonium. I felt something electric between us, a strong undercurrent as she took the book from my hands and said she wanted to buy a signed copy for a friend. I signed it for her. She turned to leave, then turned her head.

"I have been stalking you; did you feel it?" So it was her….

"I felt something strange…."

"I'm not strange, just appreciating your aura!"

I stood there and for once, didn't know what to say…just smiled inanely.

"Yeah! I'm Dedra, host of a Christian show. It's a Time Warner TV station, and I'd like you to be a guest on my live show. It's on spirituality and this week, talking about mega churches and hip hop music in churches. Here's my card—call me!"

Her smile was the wave of energy that made my jet lag go away…and the warm feeling rise in my loins. I called her the next day and she gave me directions on how to get to the TV studio.

Following her instructions, I arrived by taxi about an hour before the live broadcast. I was shown into a busy room, where camera crews were setting up the myriad mics, platforms and other props. People were running around with earphones, followed by announcers; some had guitars and others wore bright gold saxophones strapped to their torsos.

Dedra sat in front; a middle-aged man with headphones was attaching a microphone to her shirt. She saw me and motioned me over, disturbing the man who frowned as he tried to clamp the microphone to the long collar of her purple blouse.

I stood in front of her and she beamed, flashing like black lightening.

"Mr. Frank, you made it." She pointed to one of the seats next to her and told me to sit and someone would come and fix me up with a mic. Two other invited guests were escorted up to us and Dedra set them up in chairs next to me as a man came to set us up with microphones to be clamped onto our suit lapels.

In front, an audience of about 20 people sat waiting for the program. In a few minutes, a cameraman shouted, "Roll 'em!"

Dedra just ignited the guests with her bubbly demeanor, her curly, frizzy hair and red lipstick: her aura was so bright it beamed its own colors that no prism could have outdone.

"Welcome, yah'all. Just wanted to say Praise the Lord, we've got a loaded group today talking about mega churches, good or bad. Our next topic is Christian hip- hop music in the church."

Dedra then introduced me to the audience as someone who organizes dialogues and peace marches in the Holy Land. She knew that my reason to participate in the program was to reach as many people as possible and to encourage them come to the Holy land, maybe someday with me.

"He come all the way from Paris, France, to be wit us today."

I couldn't help it; "It's my honor," I responded, and the crowd clapped.

She introduced the other members of the panel who were mainly African-American pastors. Her first question asked what we thought of mega churches, which were defined as congregations having a membership of 2,000 or more at a weekly service.

I fortunately knew something about them as I had attended one with my brother, John, in Wyoming. A member of the panel was a pastor of a mega church and he did most of the talking.

The next question Dedra asked us was, "What are your views of Christian music taking on hip hop form in church?"

She looked at me first. I knew a little about the origins of hip hop as my daughter, Regina, helped me understand them. I responded, "If that's going to bring the teachings of Jesus to the youth, then hip hop is a great, loving vehicle because the words of Jesus were about love." The crowd applauded again.

That surprised me, but taught me something; from that moment on, I decided I was never going to be afraid to "speak from the heart."

On the air, I felt a catharsis coming on: I was proud to be with these African-Americans full of love, caring and bringing the word to the people. Proud to be with these religious leaders expressing their love and care for the people, and sharing it with the viewers and the audience. Dedra had served to catalyze such loving warmth among us, linking us to the viewers and the audience. I wanted to learn to do that, to capture what Dedra did and put it in a box and then let it out during dialogues/marches in the Holy Land.

The broadcast was over in about 30 minutes. As Dedra signed off, she thanked her guests.

I now had to find a ride to another author event at another bookstore near the airport; Dedra asked one of the Christian hip hop performers who was headed near the airport to give me a ride.

I hugged Dedra, who had been such an incredible host, who had brought the show off with questions inspiring impassioned answers from the panel members, as well as answering on-the-air callers from the community. It was an overwhelming success. After the final cut and the panel members began detaching their microphones, her beautiful lips were still spread with a juicy smile and her eyes shimmered, projecting light all over the place. She was an all-embracing, warm magnet and her sincere "Praise the Lord" that she often repeated took her essence out of the mundane and into a truly spiritual realm. Something happened between us.

"Let me take you to dinner my next visit," I suggested. She nodded and smiled as I walked out the door following the energetic African-American hip hop singer with curly hair and sleek legs, wearing blue and gold shorts and brown leather sandals.

Before I left, I turned and told Dedra, "I'll definitely see you soon!"

After the last event in Houston, I took a plane back to the Holy Land as I was called to participate in an impromptu interfaith event in the Galilee region. I was thus forced to reschedule the events in the Silicon Valley and elsewhere: I'd have to put off sharing my story in the US and looked forward to returning to the cradle, to the source, which was still pulling me persistently....

Chapter 28: The Fig Dropped

The kibbutz was a raucous mix of Muslims, Jews, Christians and Sufis milling about, some sitting on the grass, others crossing over the garden to shake hands with friends and newcomers. When I arrived, Miriam was singing, the tremolo of her high voice reaching the sky. She stood next to a man, Samuel, who she would introduce to me later. He was her husband and had returned from his trip from the United States. His sun-dried skin was dark and profoundly lined; deep grooves slanted downward from the corners of his mouth, in a permanent frown.

When Sarah arrived, her handshakes, hugs and warm, gentle smiles spread from her hands into the hearts of the guests, bringing a feeling of tranquility and meditation to the place. About 50 people, inspired by Sarah's guiding leadership, began arranging themselves in a large circle. Some of the Jews were from the Golan Heights, there were Christians from Nazareth, and Muslims came from as far away as the intensely militant Palestinian City (in Israel) of Um el Fahm. But here under the embrace of a large fig tree, even though their politics were all across the spectrum, it was not important. Their chairs touched, elbows grazed each other while seated around this circle...as one.

While I was sitting, listening to the words of Muslims praising Jews and Christians—also a discourse by a Jew who considered Muslims and Christians his brothers and sisters—a dried fig fell into my lap. I got up and spoke to all, making a mad allusion to its falling as an omen, representing first the unity of all of us in the magical "Galilee." Sarah interrupted me briefly to put words in my mouth by saying, "You mean Rose of Galilee," which was the name of the interfaith peace group she had founded.[46] I repeated "Rose of Galilee" but her need to orchestrate things and even reword my comments indicated that she needed to pull strings behind the scenes. It seemed that at all times, she needed to be in control of the energy flow of the group.

Then once in a while, she would flail her hands as she sat in the circle, as if she were brushing away evil spirits, a strange esoteric mannerism; I could not understand that. But some, obviously her followers, apparently understood as they strangely imitated her exact gestures, the strange flailing of arms. My body shivered slightly as that implied a type of cult worship, as if they were sharing some subliminal signs. It

---

46 The Rose of Galilee interfaith movement glorifies the rose as a holistic symbol of love.

was weird that other members sitting in the circle seemed to ignore those flailing their arms, or perhaps they didn't see them.

Sarah's need to orchestrate and the imitation of some of her gestures by her followers made me feel suspicious that there was some manipulation behind the scenes.

I wondered if she expected me to fall into the mold and say things, like "Rose Galilee" on cue, like she had just wanted me to do. I didn't see why we needed to be controlled in order to transcend our being and work together for interfaith peace. Or perhaps she was doing it to prevent total chaos? Still orchestrating the meeting, Sarah asked a golden-haired lady with a guitar resting at her side to play a song. Another girl sat next to me to translate the song into English.

She sang in Hebrew a love song, a song that made my body tingle and nerve endings stream warmth down to my loins, helping me throw out some of the wretched impurities that still inhabited my being; it embraced my entire focus and took me over, immersing me in universal love. Something seized my heart—it felt like a spell. The melody rose above the trees encircling us and, in my imagination, drifted out across the Sea of Galilee, reviving the sacred waters, bringing them gushing forth to dry, thirsty mouths. It was not just an everyday song chiding us for not being able to live together: it was seducing us into the love stream, to float down to the cosmic sea, hand in hand. It was beyond beautiful. No song had ever before captured my inner whirling, twisting and turning than hers.

After the event was over, a boy wearing a blue kippah, his brown bangs hanging down over his forehead, stood in front of me holding a black and white soccer ball. He seemed about 9 years old, little younger than my son, and my eyes got blurry as I recalled last summer playing soccer with my son, Frankie, in the mountains of Oregon...he held out the ball. I took it and without thinking, dropped it on a waiting foot and sent it across the grass where we had just finished our interfaith session. He ran, screaming after the ball and was chased by another boy. Before a smile could form on my face, the boy was back with his friend—his dark hair pushed back into Jewish side curls—tugging at his friend's shirt, trying to get his attention. The first boy asked, "Your name?"

"Frank—and yours?"

"Tovi. You play!" That was it; I ran across the grass as he kicked the ball to me. The participants, Jews with their kippahs and Muslims, some wearing the larger skull caps, busied themselves leaving; their hugs and handshakes interwove with kicks of the soccer ball or forehead headers, knocking the ball to my little friend. After kicking the ball, I heard a soft question, "You like playing soccer?"

I turned to match the voice with the person who had just spoken. It was the singer; standing next to her was the young boy with brown bangs, my soccer partner. Her eyes were red, and imbedded deep in their sockets, as if she'd been weeping....

Chapter 29: Freida

Ibarely had time to respond, "Yes" and then "Shalom," waving as Miriam and her husband put their arms around me on each side, telling me that we had to head for the van as they were due back in Tel Aviv.

I never thought I'd see her again, the singer of songs that had melted me to my core. But the next day I returned to Miriam's apartment after jogging on the beach. After setting down on the kitchen table a large bag of medjool dates I'd bought at the outdoor market, I saw a long, red dress spilling off of the couch, attached to a familiar face—it was the singer. Her face was slightly turned as she was speaking to Samuel in Hebrew. Her long, red dress hugged her slim, curvy, inviting body. Something had changed: her eyes were clear, glistening, and the ridge of her nose aquiline, smooth, curving. Her voice was soft, trembling, entreating.

Samuel got up, walked by and nodded. His crooked smile flashed mischievously as he reached into the sack, took out a date and walked out. The girl came forward where I was standing, her moist, Mediterranean lips almost touching me through the air.

"Shalom."

"Shabbat Shalom," I responded, as it was late Friday afternoon.

"Yes, you're right. My name is Freida and you're Frank. They told me."

I was desperate for words: the dress, her dancing curves, her moist lips had temporarily stunned me.

"How about a date?" As I said it, I tried to retract the Freudian slip, but it was too late so I groped for the sack of huge dates on the table to hand to her, but several dates fell to the floor with soft thuds.

She giggled, fortunately, and her red cheeks glowed. She was so close to me I could feel her breath on my neck. I turned to tell her something and she must have known. Our lips met and I couldn't withdraw. They remained attached in this warm place until I heard stirring at the kitchen door.

I took the bus with her to her place that evening. It traversed the entire city of Tel Aviv, starting in Jaffa, and headed to her town, Ramat Aviv, a suburb on the other side of Tel Aviv. It turned down Ben Yehuda Street, a long street that stretches across Tel Aviv and runs parallel with the beach, at some point. The bus came to an abrupt stop, where it stood for at least one hour. Frieda's golden eyebrows rose as she looked out the window at a group of policemen wearing the omnipresent yellow vest, and turned her head to listen; she raised her finger as I opened my mouth. Then she turned to me.

"They say they have found a bomb someone left on the sidewalk and are dismantling it."

She sighed then shrugged as if it were a daily experience.

"This happens sometimes but you don't always read about it in the news the next day!"

We arrived at her apartment. It was midnight. We sat on the sofa, our embrace interlaced with soft caresses; I kissed those eyes I'd seen red with tears in Hukuk .. . kissed them again and again. The night mist rose over Tel Aviv from the warm laps of the Mediterranean on the near shores and enveloped us for a night. . a night that had risen and was slowly receding, a union of gentle embraces, lips searching, finding warmth and joining almost instinctively, as they had in Miriam's kitchen for the first time.

Sometime in the night, unconsciously, I must have gotten up and found the diamond ring I had carried on me since the breakup with a Lebanese girl in Paris a couple of years earlier. I kept it in my wallet and now I slipped it on her finger. Everything was going so crazy fast, but I let this mystical Holy Land take hold of me. I was defenseless to stop it....

The warmth skimmed across my face. My eyes opened to the ray of Mediterranean sunshine poking through a hole in the curtains. In the soft crest of morning's rays something was glistening and projecting opalescent colors onto the wall next to us. Was it merely the sun hitting the multicolored scarf partially covering my naked side as my palm slid under the side of her soft cheek resting on the white pillow? The sun's rays were hitting rather a bright object resting on her finger. It was the ring.

We were engaged! It happened ultra-fast, like a warm, salty Mediterranean wave pushing me, rolling over me, then flattening...and while ebbing, pulling me over the crest of another wave. But was I ready to be thrown back into the swirling waters of matrimony?

Freida reached her hand over and raised the diamond slowly to her pale morning lips, without the red, sensual sheen she had over them the night before. I touched it gently.

"We'll make a happy husband and wife," she said, as her eyes met mine. Our lips met in the promise of unconditioned love. I swore nothing could change that.

I awoke from my love swoon, sprawled alone on the bed. The luscious aroma of meat and onions in the air stirred my taste buds, causing them to emit a hint of anticipatory moisture. I got up and the voice of a young boy reminded me of her son, my soccer partner. I grabbed a towel and headed to the bathroom around the corner. After a long shower, I walked briskly back to the bedroom, put my shorts on and a shirt, and walked barefoot into the kitchen where Freida was preparing food. The boy, his short, brown hair combed under a neat, white kippah looked up from his plate a bit solemnly and tersely said, "Shalom."

Freida waved me to a chair.

"I've made a breakfast for you, eggs and meat."

"Toda," I remarked as I sat down next to the boy. (Thank you)

"Today is Shabbat and we were all going to the orthodox synagogue next door. Can you come?" She asked, with a slight hesitation.

"Of course—I'd like that!" She beamed, revealing small spaces between her ivory teeth, as her lips parted and stretched to the corners of the universe. I was getting high from this place.

After breakfast, we went to the bedroom to prepare for Shabbat. As she looked at her reflection in the mirror, her eyes gleamed with mesmerized interest. She viewed her figure with intensity, which made me wonder if she really did see other reflections when she left the mirror.

I began to wonder if my being there was a fulfillment of a need for a father figure for her son, and not for true companionship. She had her mirror…which she often looked into from that moment on.

"Ok, no," I silently responded to my question but I couldn't keep myself from wondering whether I had met another narcissist whose focus was her career, her reflection, with me, just an afterthought. My sentiments could not have been totally contrived as I really felt them strongly; I had learned to listen to my intuition.[47]

These thoughts still plagued me as we kissed before I caught the shuttle that was to take me to the airport. But as our lips met again in tender warmth, the glow was still with us…we were engaged! I wondered if it was going to last.

---

47 My trepidations were at least partially confirmed as I found out later she was a known singer in Israel and moving up!

Chapter 30: Victoria

I returned to Paris. At the Charles de Gaulle Airport, while picking up my luggage, emptiness hit me as I walked to the subway. I had been so mesmerized during my stay with Freida and her son that I had not thought a lot about my children the last couple of days.

I sorely missed my daughter Victoria in Paris, my kids, Frankie, Regina and Juliana and my mom, so far away over the Atlantic. The forlornness echoed inside as I returned to my empty apartment, suffering the yearnings of a long-distance father and son. I was so sad and sentimental, that I walked out on the subway platform and continued on until I could look across the Seine to Isle St. Louis, the only place of compassion to greet me, it seemed, since my wife and kids had left. My heart sank into my heels, but at least, I reckoned, I could still feel something. I was still alive even though the memories of my children and mother engulfed me daily. Even though I was busy working in a law firm and teaching at the University of Paris, just living under the same roof with my kids had provided me with a deeper connection to myself, to my kids, to my ex partners than I experienced now…something real. And Victoria, my youngest, only four years old when I separated from her mother and returned to live in my lonely apartment, about 10 minutes walking distance from her…how should I contact her? I had to call her, but would have to talk to her mother, first. I wanted a direct line to Victoria, right now, without a curious mother sometimes looking to squabble.

As the subway rumbled along toward the center of the city, I thought of the part of the poem I had written about her mother, Concetta:

> … How can it be?
> Once radiant…embrace
> Turned cold
> Like the ashes…of
> Yesterday's campfire …[48]

I turned to the window as tears poured down; I couldn't let anyone see me. I

---

48 Frank Romano, from the poem, "Ma Fille," p. 35, Crossing Over, supra.

arrived at my apartment I had moved into after separating from Concetta. It was only ten minutes away from my "petite fillette" but we might as well have been separated by an ocean, like the vast Atlantic that separated me from my other three kids.

My message machine was blinking; I didn't cringe this time. Oh, well, that was something on that dreary day, as not long ago, I would have shunned the blinking.

My ex's voice was distinctly heard above the scratchy sound of my old machine. She was concerned that our daughter, Victoria, was becoming depressed. She explained that Victoria's teacher was concerned because Victoria had transformed from a great student at elementary school to a distracted, confused and often distant one.

"Whenever the teacher would ask her to stop daydreaming and pay attention, she starts crying...." She ended, "She misses you...." Then the phone went dead.

"Poor, sweet darling," I whispered as a long sigh escaped me.

The ardent moments beneath the Mediterranean sun with Freida were already eons away. The old emptiness re-emerged that I thought was forever in my past; that same bitter feeling stung me, thinking about my last serious talk with Concetta that had concluded with a "mutual end" to our suffering. Immediate relief was quickly replaced by loneliness and the emptiness of having lost a family, again. It was Saturday morning and I immediately called. I thought I would visit my loving daughter. My ex answered with a faintly recognizable, sleepy voice, that struck my memory chord, somewhere deep inside. I asked if I could come over and spend some time with "la petite."

"Yes. In fact, we were just getting up. If you get here in time, there will even be a cup of Italian coffee for you."

Well, something congenial in her voice, for a change. My heart pumped and blood began to warm my cold body. I'd already thrown my clothes on and needed no more inspiration than to see my little one, give her plenty of kisses and drink that cup of sumptuous Italian coffee, only my Italian ex could make. Those thoughts breathed life into my bleak heart.

I grabbed the movie I had bought for her in an airport somewhere, and stumbling over my suitcase, reached the door, slamming it behind me.

I ran, and in five minutes, I was pounding on their door.

My little sweet Victoria answered it, rubbing her eyes, smiling widely:

"Papa, papa...."

I grabbed her and we hugged and kissed for such a long time, until I heard her mother's voice behind her: "You'll catch cold out there. Come in, come in. You're always...."

The door slammed so I couldn't hear her last words. "Ma petite" held my hand as we walked side by side to her bedroom. A male doll was resting, half of his torso sticking out of her covers. His head was a bit twisted with long hair and a half smile. She reverently approached it, and put the covers around his shoulders. She turned to me, her little head with brown curls shaking a little, "Papa where were you?"

"Oh, I was in a lot of places, in America, Israel, Palestine, but I'm always thinking of you," and I was not exaggerating.

She came to me with hands out for a big hug. She then sat on the bed looking over the doll and began stroking him, talking to him in a low voice. I couldn't understand a word. I heard a creak in the floor and looked at my ex, her finger over her mouth, motioning me to follow her into the living room.

We sat down. "You know, I've had to take her to a child psychiatrist." I was in shock.

"Why? I've been away before and this...."

"But this time, you were away over a month and a half and you didn't call her very often, less than you usually do."

I just sat there stiff, glacial.

"Listen, listen—did you see the doll she has in the covers?"

"You mean that scraggly man with the weird smile and half-nude body?"

"Yes." She looked toward the door of the living room to see if the little one was watching.

"That's you!"

"Me?" my loud voice resonated.

"Sh, sh." She put her finger to her lips. "She won't let anyone touch the doll, or even go near it!"

Her lips formed into a tight line as she looked at me; I'd seen that face before. I had to sit down; my eyes filled with tears. My poor little one...all this because I was no longer part of the family nest—I was an outsider. Oh, I missed our mornings together, especially weekends when we'd eat breakfast together, so, so much. I missed my "petit souris," (little mouse) I'd call her. Life was so cold, impersonal now. Freida was a distant whisper....

"Ok, I'll try coming more often," I promised, my head drooping. "I don't want her to suffer. After all, if we...forget it!"

I got up, and went to her bedroom. She was asleep, gently cuddling the strange, dark man in her little, pink arms. I put the covers around her shoulders and left the room. I went directly to the door, opened it and went out, leaving it half open. I headed back and opened the door all the way. Concetta was standing in front of it.

"Thanks. I'll call soon; I'll call more often!"

I went home and couldn't stop the tears. I dried them with my sleeve as I opened the apartment door and immediately went to bed, burrowing into the covers. I woke up the next day at five pm.

I wanted to spend a week with my baby, my little girl, who I had raised with my ex for the first four years of her life. I had changed her diapers many times. I realized at least someone in France needed me and that alone filled me, made it worthwhile... even though the days were long under the gray skies of the city of love.

The next day, I moved out of my apartment in the 20th district and into a small studio apartment in my old stomping grounds, the Sephardic Jewish district, near Place Voltaire in the 11th district. I was farther away from my baby, but surrounded by friends in the Jewish community. I needed that badly!

That night, I received from Sarah an email requesting that I help organize an interfaith event to take place in a small town, Peki'in, in Northern Israel where Jews,

Druze, Muslims and Christians had lived in true interfaith harmony. She stated that the people there had heard about our last event and wanted us to join them in a couple of days.

She also invited me to be the co-director of the next huge interfaith event in Hukuk to take place in a couple of weeks. I agreed and we started working on it, albeit through email messages, right away!

My chance had come to play a greater part in the interfaith movement in Israel so it was back to Charles de Gaulle....

Chapter 31: Zohar

I was called to help lead an interfaith encounter group in the town of Peki'in (Hebrew) or Brunei (Arabic), a mysterious place in Northern Israel, where Druze, Jews, Muslims and Christians had lived for hundreds of years in peace and harmony.[49] I arrived early in the morning at Ben Gurion Airport in Tel Aviv and took a shuttle bus directly to Northern Israel. I met the interfaith group from Hukuk in Peki'in, a magical town located in upper Galilee.

We descended the side of a steep hill toward the famous town square where there were many houses of worship, and where people mingled peacefully in the cafés. Palm and olive trees surrounded buildings including mosques, synagogues and houses, which extended down through the valley and up the mild slopes of a distant hill. The birds seemed to be singing in a distant dream. A cool wind gently brushed the tree tops as we stepped out of the shuttle and made our way to the designated meeting place. A group from the Hukuk Kibbutz was there, including Sarah. We hugged and then descended the stone steps to the cave where Rabbi Bar Yochai hid from the Romans while he wrote the famous Zohar, the heart of the Kabbalah.[50] Even though the blistering sun beamed crimson rays on us, in this sacred place, we were under a protective shield that nothing, not even the sun, could break through. I'd shored up so much spiritual energy from this place that, as I descended the stairway, I secretly swore that I'd try to extend that love shield even into the most contested places, into Hebron, Jenin and East Jerusalem. Even though the path was shaded by long, hanging trees and bushes, the effect of the sun's inexorable rays was a dryness that fried my thoughts. The blistered rocks were covered with a white, caked powder, baked into them by the merciless sun. A drooping but stalwart palm tree stood on the side, its branches fanning downwards, gently swayed by whispers of air as we

---

49 "Peki'in Village in Israel." Travel Israel Online. 12 September 2010. <http://www.trav-elisraelonline.com/miscellaneous-sites/peki%E2%80%99in-village-in-israel-%E2%80%93-druze-village-in-the-galilee/>. & "Peki'in." Jewish Virtual Library. 2008. Source: "The Gale Group." Encyclopedia Judaica. 2008.
<http://www.jewishvirtuallibrary.org/jsource/judaica/ejud_0002_0015_0_15533.html>.

50 This is considered the foundation of Kabbalah, mystical Jewish thought. Its origins are derived from a legend that the Zohar was written by Rabbi Shimon Bar Yochai in a cave near Peki'in during the Roman occupation of the 2nd Century AD.

kept walking downwards, looking for the cave. As each step was taken, we came closer to the famous town square, the main attraction, as well as the cave of the Zohar. I reflected on how I had finally been able to overcome intense hate in my own life, the hatred of my father, after years of silence—how our bitter fights had left me injured and physically beaten, when I was a small boy. I was able to overcome years of abuse and finally forgave him, opening the door for my father to say he was sorry. That allowed us to turn the page and seek our individual paths, unencumbered by unresolved issues; my search for a universal peace, which had been shackled by hate, had now expanded to the other ends of the earth, to this place. As we walked toward the sacred cave, I asked Spirit to give me strength to overcome suffering and weaknesses, and spread the unconditional, united love feeling that I felt with this multi-origin group. I vowed to uproot myself from this comfort zone, when the time came to spread this beautiful energy around.

My spirit embraced this group and I felt comfortable here, but my personal feelings had to take a back seat to my pursuing interfaith peace. In my heart, I was aware that my real contribution would not be here, as these were already the "beautiful people" and they didn't need me. My real mission was to help beautify "hell holes," help bring interfaith peace to those people, where it is needed the most. Ironically, it's in those "hell holes" where roots will grow and world peace will flourish. I needed to bring my unswerving interfaith spirit to those places—often abandoned, forlorn places—like the refugee camps in Jenin, and in particular, zone H-2 in Hebron where Palestinians live with Jews under draconian Israeli control. Those places show great hope through working with some Israeli settlers and Palestinian inhabitants, sometimes under the auspices of the understanding of Israeli soldiers.

We were at the entrance of the cave, standing there in a half-circle. In spite of the hardships, one thing was sure: the Rabbi Bar Yochai did not get all wound up in self-pity during tempestuous times when he wrote the Zohar while living in the cave and continued unabashed, making his inspired contribution while focusing on the revelations of Elijah and divine inspiration.[51] Thinking about Rabbi Bar Yochai made me think about the Bhagavad-Gita of Hinduism, come to life again: "Even as the unwise work selfishly in the bondage of selfish works, let the wise man work unselfishly for the good of the entire world."[52]

While he hid for thirteen years, Rabbi Shimon Yochai purportedly survived by drinking spring water and eating the fruit of a miraculous carob tree. The Kabbalah, so profound, was a part of our interfaith group. Standing in front of the cave in silence, a vibrant wave permeated us all. The Jews had inhabited the area since the 2nd temple was destroyed in AD 70 and the exile of Jews from Israel.[53]

The Arabs arrived in the 11th C. AD, the Christians in the 12th C. and the Druze had arrived in the 18th C.[54] We descended to the famous town square called

---

51 "The Key to Kabbalah- The Zohar." Chabad.org. 2001-2012, Chabad-Lubavitch Media Center. <http://www.chabad.org/library/article_cdo/aid/361877/jewish/The-Zohar.htm>.

52 The Bhagavad-Gita, trans. from Sanskrit Juan Mascaro. Penguin Books, 1962. 17-19.

53 "The Key to Kabbalah- The Zohar," Supra.

54 "Peki'in Village in Israel," Supra.

HaMa'ayan Square,[55] where we expected a new phenomenon to welcome us and entreat us to further harbor ideas of the possibility of peaceful coexistence among Jews, Muslims, Druze and Christians.

We were not disappointed. Upon our arrival, we were pleasantly surprised that restaurants and cafés surrounded a natural spring flowing through town, over which a large green-leafed tree spread its branches, like protective wings over its young. I was told that there was a synagogue, a Druze hilwah (Druze praying house), and two churches.

Among its Christian, Jewish, Druze and Muslim inhabitants[56] who were milling about, some men wore brown pants and shirts; some of the women wore long, white head scarves, tied in the back. I sat in a café with a group of Muslims, Druze, Christians and Jews. We were served by a Druze. A short, dark man next to us wore a kippah and was dipping pita bread in a small plate of hummus. The kippah appeared to be centered on a place where his dark hair was thinning. I asked what he thought of this area. He responded by informing us that he had recently moved to this town and he and his family were warmly received. At another table, a group of Arabs from the village were also having lunch. The gurgling spring could be heard in the background, as we absorbed our surroundings. I sipped my coffee and casually looked over the town square, imagining that this would be a great place to live, a living manifestation of interfaith cohabitation and real-life understanding. The waiter, a stocky man with long, graying hair tied in the back in a short pony tail—his pudgy cheeks shining and his smile like a crescent—told us that even though each group conserved its own relations and customs, it was hard to distinguish one group from the other because of similar dress, food and language. He said he was Druze but some of the Jews spoke Arabic as well as the Druze did, dressed like them, even celebrated some of their religious holidays, like Eid al-Adha[57].

After thousands of years of almost total peace, riots erupted a year later in this unbelievable place. Sarah sent me the outrageous news....

---

55 Vered, Ronit."8 Hours in Peki'in." Haaretz.com. 26 April 2007. <http://www.haaretz.com/travel-in-israel/8-hours-in-peki-in-1.219035>. & "Yom, Michael. "Coexistence and Conflict in the Village of the Four Religions." Yalla Journal. 29 January 2010. <http://yallajournal.com/2010/01/29/coexistence-and-conflict-in-the-village-of-the-four-religions/>.

56 "Druze Villages – Peki'in." Kfarim. 2008. <http://www.jabel.org.il/Kfarim/Templates/showpage.asp?DBID=1&LNGID=1&TMID=84&FID=323>.

57 Eid al-Adha (when the traditional Muslim families commemorate the faith of Abraham, who obeyed God by preparing to sacrifice his son who, after God intervened, was spared and a ram was sacrificed instead).

Chapter 32: The Bubble Burst

I returned to Paris to teach at the University of Paris. At the end of the school year, I received a shocking email from Sarah citing the headlines: "Arab Druze are rioting in Peki'in." I was standing when I read the message; my legs went numb and I flopped in the chair in front of the computer. I was in total shock; this could not happen—not there! It was my model place, for world peace. And now it was unraveling as much as the rest of the world! The bubble burst....

I read on; she explained to me that it had all started when several young Druze set fire to a chicken coop owned by a Jew after a cell phone tower was installed there. Members of the community were convinced that the antenna transmitted radiation and was the cause of some cancer cases in the outlying neighborhoods.

The Israeli Government sent a small contingency of police to investigate and arrest the perpetrators. It was apparently rebuffed, so the Israeli police massed together a force of 200 policemen and border guards to arrest the seventeen young men who had set fire to the coop and thrown hand grenades. They were met with force. Most of the Jewish homes were burned and looted.[58] Twenty-seven police officers and ten locals were injured, as well as two paramedics. Sarah in her email related that she could not understand why the police reacted so violently since the village is normally tranquil and, as we had joyfully discovered, enjoyed an excellent inter-ethnic climate.[59] In fact, Druze consider themselves loyal Israelis and law abiding citizens, manifested by the fact many villagers were members of Israeli security forces.[60] She feared this would provoke tension and turn this peaceful place—where different peoples of different ethnic backgrounds had traditionally lived in harmony—into a center of conflict and tension. I looked on my favorite travel website and found a cheap round-trip ticket to Israel. I was on the plane the next morning. I met Sarah and Freida in Hukuk; from

58 "Police Chief: We Must Make Sure Peki'in Events Don't Recur." Arutz Sheva. isreal-nationalnews.com. 27 February 2008. <http://www.israelnationalnews.com/News/News aspx/125399>.

59 Rebinowitz, Dan. "The Police Don't Get It!" Haaretz.com. 31 October 2007. <http://www.haaretz.com/print-edition/opinion/the-police-don-t-get-it-1.232223>.

60 Raved, Ahiya. "Dozens Injured in Galilee Clashes." Ynetnews.com. 30 October 2007.<http://www.ynetnews.com/articles/0,7340,L-3465602,00.html>.

there we were to travel in cars to Peki'in, in view of helping bring peace back to this spiritual paradise...but I wasn't sure what we could do.

We were greeted by a Druze artist and musician, Harubi, who I had earlier met in Hukuk. He welcomed us to his home/artist studio. It was more like a museum: works of pottery and other artifacts lined the wall, along with colorful headbands and musical instruments; a rebab (bowed instrument) and violin hung on the wall. He gave us first the grand tour around his place. It was filled with sculptures, including the sensual, moving figures of a man and woman, in clay. Then he led us to a room which was his artist's studio. Various instruments were lying about, and blocks of clay, stone and wood were strewn all over, half formed. Artistic energy radiated from this welcoming place. The words "Ahlan wa-sahlan" came to my mind, as his home and studio truly embodied the meaning of "Welcome."

He led us back to the main room where there was a kind of wooden podium surrounded by earthen benches, soothing and comfortable to sit in as we faced him; he was preparing to play music with a local female musician. He played the rebab while she serenaded us by singing a ballad in Arabic and Hebrew. Freida, sitting closely next to me, explained that it was an intense song interweaving love and mysticism. After the girl stopped singing, Harubi came to us, reached out his hand and Frieda took it. She accompanied him to the podium, stopping off to grab her guitar propped against a chair. Freida started out singing her Hebrew melodies acapella, then accompanied herself on the guitar, filling the room with distant yearnings from indescribable places, like the breathtaking Nagev desert or the ghostly Mediterrancan brume in Tel Aviv. I had heard her sing it at her apartment in Tel Aviv and I remembered the word "Adonai" (Lord). She often hummed meditatively her songs, which evoked the sound and feeling of water, as her voice was reminiscent of Edith Piaf's singing, melodious, seductive, transporting me far away, so far it was like falling into a deep, meditative trance.

After a few songs to rouse us, we sat in a circle to discuss the latest shocking events in Peki'in. Harubi explained in Hebrew while I listened, Freida, my trusty interpreter at my side. He explained that talks had been successful between local Jews and Druze, and soon everything would be back to normal.

During the discussion, I asked him how we could help calm things down, that some of us had come a long way to lend a hand to mediate between Druze and Jews. Since members of both groups attended our interfaith events, we had great relations with them. I suggested that our united group of Jews, Christians and Muslims could help show the way toward interfaith understanding.

He responded by suggesting that our presence there was already felt as we were among the first outsiders to dare visit Peki'in since the riots. He expected the news to be circulated that people could return to their homes, including the Jews, and tourists would be encouraged to come as they had stayed away recently. Part of the town, especially the famous soap business, depended on tourists. Harubi was sure that our visit would restore confidence and help temper the fear and hate that had suddenly developed between the two groups. We meditated on that and prayed for peace, understanding...for the residents of Peki'in—Druze, Jews,

Christians and Muslims—to talk, reconcile their differences and then turn the page and move on.[61]

There, I saw Freida in action and my ardent physical desire moved toward my heart. However, when Harubi came to her after her performance, she was beaming while one eye, I could see, was on me. Other people came to crowd around Harubi and her; like a Diva, her voice was a bit condescending, and she did everything but give autographs. Even though I stood next to her, I was quickly relegated to fixture status and went almost completely unnoticed. Somehow, I felt it pleased her.

To add to the ambiance, it seemed like she was overly gushing and thus feigned interest in the Druze man and his works. Even though they were consumed in conversation that I couldn't understand because it was in Hebrew, she was constantly glancing my way, it seemed, to glean my reaction. I tried to look nonchalant but I didn't fool her. I left her side to look at a few of the sculptures placed in another room, and to try and diffuse my mounting jealousy. I couldn't believe I was being childish and that she knew it and nourished it gladly. I returned fifteen minutes later and they were still standing close to each other, talking. In the meantime, the others had left the building and climbed up the incline to the awaiting shuttles. I walked up and sat down with the others and now everyone was present, waiting for Freida to arrive. She, like a diva, made us wait…I was seething. I had to climb back down the stairs only to see she hadn't moved an inch toward the door, knowing we were waiting for her. In spite of the fact my interruption, I intuited, would please her, I reminded her that everyone was waiting for her in the shuttle to take us back to Hukuk. Pangs of jealousy rose in me—she looked at me, knew it and although I tried to push it down, it was to no avail. She was the master of the situation!

But something incredible was developing that helped me take my mind off that: one of the most important interfaith gatherings ever in Hukuk, in the Galilee, and I was the co-organizer.

The meditation session that I would lead was to reveal something extraordinary, strikingly profound…but it got dangerously out of control.

---

61 Raved, Ahiya. "Dozens Injured in Galilee Clashes," supra.

Chapter 33: Beyond

We returned to Hukuk the same day so Sarah and I could prepare for the huge interfaith event in the Kibbutz to take place that weekend. We had been working on it together for the last month, and now all the hard work was coming to fruition.

I must have been out for at least an hour as the next time my eyes looked up we were driving through the iron gates of Hukuk Kibbutz that enclosed this magical world where peacocks roamed freely, emitting their shrill sounds often at some cathartic moment in a meeting, during a conversation, a meditation or while singing a song.

Sarah accepted my suggested theme as the one to use for the event, "Unconditional Love Celebration," and I was scheduled to lead the main meditation session that was the main focus of the interfaith event.

I had selected several artists to perform songs and dance routines, including Frieda, but for some reason, Sarah chose other artists. Even before the trip to Peki'in, I had sent an email to inform Frieda that she would not be performing.

As soon as I informed her of that, even though she had told me she was free that weekend, she emailed me a message that she was not available anyway as she had a "singing gig" in Tel Aviv. I think she made that up!

I was sure she was hurt that Sarah didn't want her to perform and there was nothing I could do to convince her to come to the event as a spectator. I sent her an email saying that I wanted her to share the incredible moments with us, however I feared she was more interested in being the diva than spending time with me.

That was confirmed as, somewhere on the way to Hukuk, she got off the shuttle bus we were riding in and took a bus headed for Tel Aviv. I agreed to visit her there soon, but would our romance continue?

I didn't have time to be disappointed at Freida as I was busy with Sarah and the interfaith event as soon as we arrived in Hukuk. I was surprised Sarah allowed me to be the co-director of the event as I thought she liked to be in control and could never share management of the events with anyone.

I had suggested to Sarah that much of the conflict between Israelis and Palestinians derived from ignorance about each other's culture, traditions, etc. She agreed to, in the very beginning of the interfaith event, allow each group to discuss the tenets of its religion. I felt a lot of the misunderstanding among Christians, Muslims and Jews was caused by not understanding, in particular, the common denominators among them.

My main job, however, would be the key to the event: to lead a group meditation centered on the voice of God through unconditioned love. Then the group of about 100 people would be divided up into 10 different groups to discuss messages they had received during meditation on that theme. The leaders of each group would then report back to the general assembly.

Preparing for this event summoned all the interfaith energy and love stream connections I could muster. I suggested that it be opened up to the world, and so invitations were sent all over the world, giving rise to the participation of Americans, as well as Israeli Jews, Muslims and Christians.

Usually during our meetings, we gathered around a lady who put herself in a semi-trance and became the medium through which the spirit of God communicated with us. They called it channeling. I remember the first time it happened about a year ago: I looked over at the Muslims who showed disapproval, as they believe no one can be the mediator between Allah and his servants. However, they explained to me, not wanting to obstruct the peaceful interfaith meeting, they begrudgingly bowed their heads and listened to the woman channel.

Not wanting to alienate anyone during this event, I explained to Sarah why the event should not include channeling. Since it was almost a tradition to have a medium channel at each interfaith event, I did not expect her to agree. But she did.

That night, I slept in the same room next to the kitchen I had slept in before. Hearing a commotion outside, I got up and opened the door. It was 9:30 am but already I felt the heat of the sun broiling my skin as I walked toward a large group of people in the back yard. They were clustered like bees on honeycomb, around the queen: Sarah.

I returned to her little white house to freshen up and upon leaving through the back door that led to the garden, I saw Sarah sitting in a garden chair with her back to me; the people were hovering. She turned her eyes which swept over the bushes and lawn into mine, like a homing pigeon. Quickly standing up, she glided over to me, embracing me like long-lost family, even though we had spent a lot of time together during our trip to Peki'in and last night during dinner. I stepped back a bit then rendered myself to her hugs, expecting a big show. This hug was sincere, as she looked at me with unrestrained emotion: "Welcome to your interfaith meeting," She whispered. Before she could finish I had to interrupt: "Ours, Sarah; without you, it could not have happened." My emotions overcame my true thoughts as I knew that was not entirely true but it seemed she needed to hear it as her fervent need to control often needed to be massaged.

"I have someone I want to introduce you to," she responded, taking my arm.

"This is Hamal, a noted writer from a Palestinian city, Um el Fahm."

A man was standing next to her, his face featured large jowls and his dark, oily Mediterranean skin, contrasted with his pure white cloud of hair. He extended his big work-roughened hand and I clasped it, worker to worker—I had spent many years laboring on farms. We had something else in common: we were both writers.

We had a connection that would get stronger, especially when I visited his city later on. Judy, an American, whom I had met at an author event in Ashland, Oregon, my first hometown (my second one is Santa Rosa, California and my third is Paris, France), was standing in front of me, holding her arms out in an air hug. I fell into them and we hugged. Before words could flow, Sarah was holding my hand and leading me away from Judy to the front of the group. This was the biggest turnout of all with about 100 people present, mostly Israeli Jews, Muslims and Christians, Judy from Oregon and me from France.

Sarah passed me the microphone after calling the group together and saying a few introductory words. I was to announce the three speakers who were to briefly discuss Judaism, Islam and Christianity.

My first guest speaker was Hamal, a Muslim Arab, who spoke about Islam, then a Christian Arab, Fawwaz, from Nazareth, who spoke on Christianity and finally Moshe, an Israeli Jew, spoke on the major tenets of Judaism. Each speaker also talked about the common denominators mainly among Christianity, Judaism and Islam. They did not, however, ignore differences, such as Christians believe Jesus Christ was the son of God whereas Muslims believe he was a prophet, but not the son of God.

In the glow of this event, the speakers compared similarities and differences among the main three religions in order to explain the nuances. Some of the common denominators mentioned by the speakers were the belief in one God, the obligation to help the poor, the interdiction of killing and treating neighbors as thyself, with respect and dignity.

Sarah led a brief morning meditation session. Then she announced that the afternoon program would include my leading an unconditional love meditation session that would take place after lunch.

We broke for lunch. A table was brought out in the middle of the lawn, filled with hummus, pita bread, salads, rice wrappings with olive leaves, dates, and different bottles of soda and water. It was a sumptuous feast where everyone came up and filled their plates: Jews served Muslims, Muslims served Christians, and Christians served Jews. We all served each other while smiles abounded. Pieces of pita bread fell onto the lawn where birds swooped down, scooped them up and flew away with the tasty morsels. Every once in a while, a distant peacock would emit its shrill sound that petrified some of the group members at first, then loosened them up.

The afternoon session began. I announced the theme of the event, "Unconditional Love Celebration" and that I'd lead the meditation session.

My eyes glanced over the smiles and eyes willing to be a part of this heart-warming event, an event without precedent in this kibbutz in the Galilee. Sarah summoned Moshe to interpret for me.

I began by discussing the theme of the event: "I believe in unconditional love—let our Love for God and our love for others be unconditional. As such, loving is the extension of our pure loving of God and if sincerely done, we connect with the universal love stream. To love in order to be loved in return, to give and to receive, in return, are not examples of "unconditional love." To love and to give without expecting anything, unconditionally, is the love water we can bathe in and that flows, and is joined by different small streams, forming one big cosmic love stream."

I breathed deeply and looked up towards the towering trees as the peacock sounded its distant wails and ended at the perfect moment—the beginning of our group meditation.

My meditation/hypnosis session began with me entreating everyone to close their eyes and concentrate on the light and colors as if they were filtering through a prism that would take us out of our physical form and into the pure, loving, ageless light. Then I imagined we were walking on a road leading to the beach where we took our shoes off and walked barefoot on the sand alongside the rolling waves, at the edge of the water, with each step creating footprints in the sand. With each footprint, I invited everyone to go deeper into a deep, deep meditative state. One, two, three, four, five, six, seven, eight, with each step leaving a footprint, each participant going deeper, deeper, letting it flow, letting it go, just being....

Sometimes I spoke too fast and Moshe would whisper "Slow down—you're getting too far ahead of me."

When we had reached the tenth footprint, I looked up and noticed that everyone, all 100 people, had their eyes closed and were following me. It was time to ask the people to do the key thing: "I want you to take a moment to think about a moment in your life where you were the happiest, the most loved. Remember that moment, bask in the light of the love, the exact strong, warm emotions you felt for that loved one; you were so, so happy, free and loved."

I paused for an instant. Then I continued, "Now I want you to put your middle finger and thumb together on your right hand. Just remember, whenever you feel stressed, worried, tired, alienated from your principles, hate, prejudice, just put that middle finger and touch it with your thumb and remember that pure unconditional love feeling and your love for all people."

"Now I'd like you to transfer that pure love feeling—that intense, unconditional love—let it flow and let it be pure, unbridled love of a loved one and let it flush through your mind and bodies, spreading like a love stream throughout the entire body, healing it from any bad thoughts and fear. Then finally transfer that profound feeling, that profound, unconditional love to all people...friends and enemies alike."

Now a delicate moment arose. It was time for me to bring people out of this trancelike meditation session. I opened my eyes and saw that everyone, with eyes firmly closed, were still far, far away. Had the words, the ambiance, the place working together hypnotized them? I had to be careful here and bring them slowly back to the present.

"Now I want you to visualize walking back the same way, placing your feet in your same footprints, and with each time your foot covers your footprint in the sand, you are becoming more and more awake. Then finally, we walk back from the beach, with every step more conscious—10, 9, 8, 7, 6, 5, 4, 3, 2, 1. Now you're awake, totally awake and aware of your surroundings, the trees overhead, the chair you are sitting in, your neighbor sitting next to you."

I looked up and expected to see 100 pairs of brown, black and some blue eyes shimmering back at me. Some eyes flickered but most of them were closed, still in trance-like meditation, some sitting cross-legged, some lying prone, some standing with palms up reaching upwards toward the trees. No one stirred and I felt only a few pairs of eyes on me. A strange, empty feeling swamped my senses, to be quickly replaced by awareness as my thoughts began to focus, like the lens of a telescope. I hadn't properly awakened them and they were still on the beach, transcending.

I started counting down from 10 to 1, slower this time, and each number I would emphasize: "With each number, you are more awake, you hear louder and louder your own breathing. Now you have left the beach and are walking down the same road. " I reached the number "one" and said, clapping my hands, "You are now totally awake; open your eyes and see me in front of you, then see your neighbor."

That did it! Their heads faced me and their eyes flickered and started to focus. "Welcome back! You are on this unconditional love path, with me. And I love you all, every one of you."

What had happened was a kind of group catharsis; we did a kind of group Channeling through meditation. Everyone had meditated and transcended individually as opposed to allowing one person to be the medium, the channeler, through which the cosmic spirit would speak, which the Muslims and I, in particular, did not appreciate.

After the meditation, after giving the group some time to stretch and go to the bathroom, we divided everyone into groups of ten people. That allowed everyone, including those who did not feel comfortable speaking in front of the entire group, to discuss what happened during the individual channeling/meditation session.

About eight groups spread out over the lawn and the other two or three groups went inside Sarah's house to be away from the other groups.

I was part of the group for English speakers that was headed by Moshe. He remarkably posed the right questions which were unobtrusive and ultimately motivated individuals to share what they had learned or what they felt during the meditation session.

Abigail, a slender girl from Sfat, was emotional; her red-streaked, tender blue-gray eyes flashed as she shared her vision with us. During the meditation, she had entered a dreamlike state envisaging the world coming together under one peace channel, under a great warm light.

Others shared that they felt stillness, calm, a smooth, loving energy force among us and that something new was happening. We had communed with each other, our souls touching one another without the body getting in the way; we were pure spirit, unconditionally loving. Moshe was the generator of the discussion during which only our deepest, most impassioned emotions were expressed. Hence no controls shrouded our impressions as the channel was opened among our hearts to the love stream, pure impassioned feeling of love and unity within ourselves, with each other and the creator, letting go of all doubts and fears....

Judy then spoke; she was not moved by the meditation session but she admitted that she never has become very motivated during group meditation. Also, she said that the group transcendence or channeling did not inspire her. But all of a sudden, she opened up her heart and spoke about something mind-boggling that had happened through meditation: "With us here sharing today, it makes it seem like the center of the world, that through tolerance and understanding, we will feel unified through Frank's passion for interfaith peace."

My turn came to recount my impressions of group channeling. I didn't know what to say—as I was still in the afterglow, still in a transcendent state—other than I felt strong, positive energy and although our coming together into individual groups was a bit distracting at first, it now seemed an integral part of our intimate communing with each other.

After about an hour the small groups came together as one large group which met again on the grass; representatives of each small group shared the highlights of each group's discussion.

At some point, I couldn't help but comment before the entire group that I appreciated hearing everyone's comments, but to me it was clear that something new was opening up through this meeting, that the group power synthesizing a heartfelt wave seemed to bring us to the threshold of a new and durable solution to peace and understanding in Israel and Palestine.

What was it? Why? Who knows? But all agreed something was almost subliminally happening, except no one could articulate it. All we could do was to feel the embodiment of some spirit we tapped into...the universal love stream. No one could really come up with what was happening and I was short on words as this had never happened during any group meditation sessions I'd experienced or heard of. Everyone agreed that the new vibration was electrifying and somehow bringing us together.

I was spellbound, frozen as I sat on the grass, hot waves effusing through my body. At some point, I opened my mouth and expressed, to anyone near enough to hear, the need for us now to do the walk as well as the talk, with respect to making this new thing come alive and be shared with others. People around me hesitated to articulate it, maybe due to fear that something new would take them out of their intellectual/spiritual comfort zone, and confront them with a new grassroots solution to help establish a durable peace in Israel and Palestine.

The solution for a durable peace was upon us; it's what had happened that day: Meditating together in the light, communing, connecting like the roots of a cosmic tree. In any case, I sensed I was part of something new that would raise the bar of efforts already made in Israel and Palestine...something universal, something beyond anyone's imagination. But was it the same thing to me as to Sarah? Was this "something new" conforming to her vision of a united world in the Galilee, a new shift in human awareness and peace, in which all religions would be welcomed?

In my mind, a collective force was created to bring peace to the region by bridging the conflict between Israel and Palestine, and Sarah's and my vision where interweaving, I hoped. After a short coffee break, the gong sounded to announce the final short goodbye meditation, as people sat in chairs set in a circle. Muslims wearing keffiyehs sat in chairs beside Jews wearing kippahs. The circle was complete with Christians interweaving throughout the group.

The cool breeze blowing over the Galilee and rising to the knoll on which the kibbutz was built stroked the trees overhead and then stopped, bringing stillness to the group. That day, it seemed as though the ethnic differences had melted into the swirling waters of the Sea of Galilee far below, and no longer divided us into separate, warring ghettos.

Chapter 34: Paranoia

Several of us sat around in a circle after most of the participants had left. We had experienced an epiphany and few words could explain what had happened that day. At the same time I was profoundly inspired, I was bothered by thoughts that my Palestinian brothers and sisters, on the other side of the wall, could not participate in today's oneness.

As we sat lapping up the boundless beauty permeating this kibbutz and extending out into the waters of the Sea of Galilee, my feeling of oneness was not totally fulfilled. I had to speak.

"Brothers and sisters, we need to share this cathartic experience with the brother and sister Palestinians who could not join us today. They couldn't get authorization and couldn't get through the checkpoints."

Sarah responded in a voice hoarse from the goings on: "What do you mean, my love?"

"I mean, someone has to physically go into the West Bank to share what we did today."

My words spread a cover of silence over the group and the only sound was a Galilean breeze fanning the branches overhead. Not even a peacock cried out.

Miriam looked around the group and then at me as my eyes surveyed the ground.

"You could send them an email and photos. Here—I have made an entire roll of pictures I could send you...."

"But someone needs to share with them directly what we have done today."

Now Sarah intervened: "But Frank, dear, if you try to go there, you'll be treated like a Jew: they'll shun you, maybe even take you hostage, or worse. You have plenty of work to do with us." And her omnipresent smile flashed, unabashed, stalwart... and relentless.

"I've already visited the West Bank, Ramallah and even Jenin...I'm still alive."

"You're lucky...Jehovah's protecting you, but maybe not forever...."

I looked to Hamal and the Arab contingency from the Arab city in Israel near Tel Aviv, Um el Fahm. They stood in the background, shaking their heads. I went to them. Hamal spoke first.

"I no want speak disrespectfully of Sarah, the leader, but she does not understand. My people in Palestine will, if you go for peace, accept you like brother." He smiled, his lips spreading over his yellow smoker's teeth; his eyes said more that the words. The others nodded their heads as Hamal reached in his pocket.

"Look, my friend." He handed me a paper. "I wrote my phone number on it for you. Come visit us—you will always be welcome in my home, anytime."

Then he smiled again, motioned to his Arab friends and they walked together towards the parking lot. Hamal turned and waved saying, "Assalymu alaikum."

"Wa alaikum assalam," I responded, waving.

At that moment, Miriam put her hand on my shoulder.

"Frank, you have a message from my friends in Nahariya, in the North, who invite you to spend time with them, maybe to share with them what we have done at Hukuk." She gave me the phone number.

The ambiance reflected the same feelings that I had felt a year before during the Peki'in riots, when Arabs and Jews were, in a way, vying for my presence. The decision later became clear as to how I was to spend the next two weeks. If I had chosen Nahariya, I would have been forced underground with the family, trying to escape Hezbollah rockets.

Chapter 35: Underground?

The breeze that had blown in off the Sea of Galilee gave me strength, courage. It shored up my faith, helping me to follow my vision.

That last event in Hukuk helped to hone my vision: It was to work in Israel and Palestine, go back and forth helping to bring peace and understanding. If I fell short of that, then I would not be carrying out my initial vision that led me to Morocco years ago. Hukuk confirmed that vision and provided a spring board for me to launch into the next stage, to help bring peace through the interfaith movement.

To do so, I needed to go beyond talking with the beautiful people coming together in these human paradises like Hukuk, and take my heart energy to the trenches. My calling was leading me to the contested areas like the refugee camps in the West Bank, especially Jenin, to Hebron, to Damascus Gate, an entrance to the old city in Jerusalem, near the Wailing Wall and the entrance to the Al-Aqsa Mosque. Those were the places calling the loudest....

Sarah and the Rose of Galilee Jews in Hukuk clearly did not approve of my travels to the West Bank; that would become a simmering point of contention between us. But the final wedge that was driven between us was caused more by my volatile relationship with Freida, who was very close to Sarah and her Rose of Galilee group, than by my visits to the West Bank.

After getting a ride from Miriam and Samuel to Tel Aviv, I went immediately to Ramat Aviv, to spend some time with Freida. We went to a restaurant with her son near her house, in the middle of the park. She sat across from me, smiling, reaching over and grabbing my hands, her wide lips entreating me, seducing me with her bright-eyed charms, while her son Tovi jumped up and kicked the soccer ball to me. Waiting for the dessert to be served, I got up and kicked the ball back to his gleaming eyes.

The bed was a collage of arms and legs, with the Mediterranean morning sun glistening on the side of Freida's golden head. After breakfast, we sat on the sofa, looking out the window at the array of herb shrubs—basil, sage, mint and other plants—a soft herbal scent wafting in with the late morning breeze.

It was the perfect moment to announce that, as a follow-up of our interfaith meeting in Hukuk, I needed to travel to the Arab city, Um el Fahm, before returning to Paris, to share with them and possibly organize an interfaith dialogue there. I also wanted them to help me with organizing interfaith dialogues in Palestine.

She sat there, stunned, "First, there is no Palestine. Those are the 'Occupied Territories.' Second, I thought you were going to spend the next three days with us before returning to Paris."

Her smile reduced to a bitter frown; she compressed her lips in disapproval.

I was on the bus that afternoon, wondering how I was going to make good on my promise to Freida that, if I could visit Umm al-Fahm for a couple of days, I would spend a couple of weeks with her and Tovi over spring break. Oh, well—I decided to worry about that later as I needed to focus on the next challenge, visiting that militant Arab town near Tel Aviv.

My decision to go to the Arab city instead of Nahariya was a lucky break, as a war with the Hezbollah was looming and if I'd gone to Nahariya, I would have spent weeks underground in a bomb shelter.

Chapter 36: Umm al-Fahm

I arrived at the main bus terminal in Jerusalem in the late afternoon, went straight to the ticket office and asked for a round-trip ticket. The ticket agent's brow rose as she glared at me.

"Why you go there?" I couldn't understand why the interrogation but I found out later.[62]

"Visit friends."

"You have friends, there?" her face contorted and she shook her head. "Thirty shekels."

I paid and asked her when the bus left.

"Fifteen minutes, over there." She pointed to the left to an empty bus stop. "Good luck," she sighed, and turned away.

I took an Israeli bus and arrived late that afternoon. The bus driver left me off at a bus stop along the highway. I walked to a café on the corner where several roads met and ordered an Arabic coffee. While the coffee was brewing in the copper cezves on the stove, I called my friend, Hamal. In a few minutes, a white pick-up truck pulled up next to the café. A man and a boy walked toward me, waving. The young man was in his thirties and the boy was no more than ten years old. The man wore jeans and he had short, black hair with a closely-shaved face. His toothy smile spread over his face as he approached, but it was warm, and his teeth glistened against the backdrop of opalescent ebony skin. His son was a shorter and a bit stockier version of his father.

Hamal must have described me to them because they knew who I was immediately upon entering the café, even though there were several men sitting at the counter next to me. Of course, I stood out with my long hair and luggage!

"Ahlan wa-sahlan," came a voice. "Marhaba," I responded The man reached for my garment-tote bag and his son shook my hand as we walked to the car.

Hamal was at the door; his hand reached out, grabbed my shoulder and we hugged. His white hair contrasted with his full, tanned cheeks, tanned over the many years in the Israeli sun working as a building contractor.

At the entrance, he squared himself in front of me and said, "You made it! I knew

---

62 Umm al-Fahm had been a known center of demonstrations supporting Palestinians and claims of Israeli-Arab rights versus land expropriation by the Israeli Government, and other issues.

you come. Many not come; you do what you say, my friend—I love you for that. Come into my home. My home is your home."

We entered a spacious living room with some Egyptian figurines on a wall ledge that held a tray with small, gold coffee cups. To the left was a long sofa on which was comfortably installed a lady with a long, flat smile, a tooth protruding from her tight lips. She was tightly packed into a blue hijab. Her pale face shone, highlighted by the sheen of the satin-smooth garment encircling her full cheeks.

He pointed to an arm chair placed next to the sofa and I sat down, my tired legs feeling spry under the spell of the welcoming vibes in this house. But I knew in advance from the way Hamal had greeted me in Hukuk that his home would be just as welcoming, and even more so as I would meet his family. I was not disappointed. Thinking about the Israeli cashier interrogating me on my plans to visit this town almost made me laugh.

His dazzling, irresistible smile, coupled with his effervescent face full of cheeks and teeth…it was a smile that put a spell on everyone, irradiating the room. A young girl carrying a baby wrapped in several blankets later walked into the apartment; her white hijab was wound around her face in such a way, I couldn't see it. She sat next to her parents on the couch.

Hamal introduced his daughter, who partially opened up her white hijab. Her fine aquiline nose and white skin resembled her mother's more than her father's, indicating a cleavage in the family: the whiter skin color was genetically linked to the mother's side, the darker skin color to the father's side.

Then the son arrived, with long dark hair and a full beard. He was like his father in that his smile filled the room, a silver tooth glistening as he approached me with long strides to shake my hand.

"Ahlan wa-sahlan," he exclaimed as he extended his hand. "Ismi Muhammad Abdul-Samee, maaism-ak?" (My name is Muhammad Abdul-Samee, and yours?)

"Ismi Muhammad Abdul-Azeez el arabiyya." (My name is Muhammad Abdul-Azeez, in Arabic)

He was a most fervent practitioner of Islam, but his style was more enthusiastic than fanatic. He invited me to join him in the mosque the next day.

It was early afternoon, about ten minutes before prayers. I walked downstairs from his father's apartment to the apartment below. Knocking, the wife answered, this time wearing a light green hijab, and ushered me into a small room. Abdul-Samee was wearing a pearl-white skull cap over strands of long, black hair, sitting with three others, one wearing a keffiyeh, and the other two wearing white skull caps. It seemed as though I had interrupted something as a tense silence reigned as soon as I entered. Then Muhammad Adbul-Samee announced to the group, "Huwa Ameriki." (He's American) More silence! I couldn't stand it so I had to break it: "Looks like a bunch of terrorists. I'm supposed to be afraid, right?"

For some reason, that broke the ice and they all laughed and I with them. Abdul-Samee motioned me to join them and we drank coffee and ate sugar cookies.

"Go masjid, na'am?" I nodded.

Then he looked down and saw I was wearing my usual khaki shorts.

"La ilaha illallah!" (There is one God) he pronounced with a sigh and ran to the next room, bringing back dark-blue jogging sweats.

"Put on and we go!" His wide-grinned smile filled the room again as I slipped the jogging pants over my shorts. We were off!

We drove in his truck until it could no longer get through the crowd; then he parked. We walked the final block and passed through a door that a couple of young men were scurrying through, leaving their shoes off in the entrance. We did the same and followed them into a large prayer room, full of men and boys, all lined up. Some were waiting for the main prayer session to begin, others were in different stages of preliminary prayer. A few worshippers were bowing with their hands above their knees, while others were already on the mat, prostrated, touching their forehead, returning to the sitting position, then bending forward, again.

Then the muezzin called us to prayer: "Allahu Akbar, Allahu Akbar." (Allah is the Greatest, Allah is the Greatest) "Allahu Akbar, Allahu Akbar." (Allah is the Greatest, Allah is the Greatest) Ash-hadu alla ilaha illa-llah. (I bear witness that there is none worthy of worship but Allah)

We lined up, standing, with the right hand over the left, waiting for prayer to commence.

Chapter 37: Two-Front War

The next evening, while munching on a lamb kabob in the kitchen, Hamal was teaching me Arabic while I was teaching him English. It was a tandem language session.

His wife then burst in and began speaking a stream of Arabic. Hamal frowned and shook his head.

"My friend, Hezbollah and Israel are at war. They are attacking and many people will be killed." His tremulous voice faded as he walked through the archway to the living room where the TV blared.

"What happened?"

"Don't know exactly. I think Hezbollah attacked Israeli soldiers in the North and captured and killed some of them. The "Yahoudiyy" (Jews) bombed Southern Lebanon after."

He stopped after the television announcer spoke something in Arabic I didn't understand. Then his wife began talking and Hamal responded; he looked at me and smiled. His smile beamed across the room, his lips exposing his partially yellow teeth. Glowing with amiability, his brown eyes shone. Even his teeth could not detract from the mesmerizing smile, a smile that radiated unconditional friendship, humility and deep understanding.

He informed me that a conflict had escalated between the IDF and Hamas in the Gaza Strip, a month earlier. I had already heard about it while I was still in Paris. He explained that there was a shelling of a Gaza beach, allegedly by the IDF, according to some Palestinians. In retaliation, an armed group of Palestinians infiltrated Israel, attacking an Israeli military post, killing a couple IDF soldiers and taking a prisoner, Corporal Gilad Shalit. After that, the IDF engaged in a massive attack of the Gaza Strip, targeting Hamas military forces and attempting to free the Israeli soldier.

Israel was engaged in a two-front conflict.

The next day, late morning, we watched the news in Arabic, sometimes with English subtitles, with Israeli soldiers firing missiles on the airports and Israeli warplanes attacking several targets in Southern Lebanon, dramatically enhancing the death toll among civilians. Pictures of the bloodied bodies of children were aired. The Al Jazeera interviewed people accusing Israel of targeting civilians, as many homes had been destroyed. I had to turn away from watching mothers wearing hijabs yelling and crying at the loss of their loved ones.

We spent most of the day in front of the TV; a steady stream of family members funneled into the house all day long. Hamal shook his head and his eyes moistened, his mouth curved as if on the verge of crying.

"My friend, so sad, so sad..."

Then rockets were launched from Southern Lebanon into Northern Israel; hits were made in Tiberius and Nahariya, where I could have been. Guilt overcame me as I pondered my decision to come here instead of visiting Nahariya; it was just by chance I was not spending the next few weeks in a bomb shelter in Northern Israel; but my heart hurt at the reports of many rockets destroying buildings in Nahariya .

I called the number in Nahariya that Miriam had given me; there was no answer. Then I called Miriam in Tel Aviv to get the news of our friends but Miriam didn't respond, either. My body shook with worry and a feeling of despair filled me as I felt so helpless against this unbridled violence...so helpless that I could do nothing for my friends.

I wanted to grab a bus and head for the North to be with them but it was announced that no buses were running either way. Hardly any automobiles were on the roads in the North and I was certain no taxi would take me there. I had to share my worries with Hamal.

"You are lucky, Frank. If you had visited them, you would have been with them in the shelters under siege. It's terrible: the bombs are dropping everywhere and have hit some houses and killed people...."

I wondered if I'd get a different story viewing the same events on Israeli TV. I would soon find out.

A couple of days later, I arrived in Tel Aviv and went straight to Miriam's house, as Freida was traveling with a group of singers. In the meantime, I had called her and she told me our friends in Nahariya were safe in the bomb shelters. In fact, the family was used to having to descend into the shelters and had them fortified with several months of food. She also said that they had all the conveniences in the shelters, telephone, TV, etc. and whenever they had to occupy them, they would just carry on with their daily routines, albeit without the sun. I was amazed at how they could adapt to adversity without hesitation.

Watching the crisis on Israeli television in Miriam's living room provided a different experience. It showed the destroying of several homes and people being rushed to the hospital after a Hezbollah bomb attack.

Watching the constant rain of bombs over Northern Israel and the retaliatory bombing and destruction in Southern Lebanon, I had reached the real gates of hell, far more blood-curdling and real than the Gates of Hades, Rodin's sculpture I had seen in Paris.

Is there no end, I agonized?

War, so terrible, so unnecessary, so cruel; it was often just a blowing off of steam or like retaliatory actions countered by more retaliatory actions. The end result was often the many innocent victims paying for the short-sighted and ruthless excesses of others, only to be shoved to the side in importance, losers in the struggle for power. This was the value of a human life?

I could hardly think of it...those children...thankful my own kids were out of the line of fire, in France and the United States. But that didn't make it better as I empathized with all parents at the loss of children, those who lost loved ones so unfairly...senseless killing brought about by unbridled emotions ruled by hate and ignorance. When would this stop?

Then on TV, a program came on in Hebrew, with English subtitles. Government officials were interviewed; they claimed that warplanes that had bombed civilian homes were justified because certain individuals were paid a hefty sum by Hezbollah to allow rocket launchers to be installed in their homes and gardens; thus, according to the officials, they assumed the risk. These Israelis accused the Hezbollah of the despicable practice of using humans as shields, hiding behind the civilian population to avoid detection or to pressure the Israeli military to avoid targeting the homes they used to house the rockets, soldiers and other arms.

I didn't know who to believe; when watching TV in Umm el fahm, Al Jazeera journalists reported that there were no traces of rocket launchers, other arms or Hezbollah soldiers in many homes targeted and destroyed by the Israeli Air Force. They also televised interviews of people accusing the Israeli government of targeting the population and killing many civilians.

Were they all spinning the reality to suit their propaganda goals?

Freida was scheduled to return from her performance tour in three days but I was going to miss her as I had my ticket to the United States and my family—three of my children and my mother, in particular—waiting for me to spend part of the summer vacation with them in Oregon. When I called Freida to tell her I would have to leave Tel Aviv before her return, she hung up on me. I tried calling her back but the phone kept ringing and ringing....

A day later, I received a call from Abigail and her girlfriend, Maya; I had met them both at Hukuk during the last incredible interfaith event and they wanted to see me before I left Israel. They were at the beach and invited me for drinks that evening.

It was a warm, sultry evening as I took off walking through the dark, abandoned market in Jaffa that had been so full of life just a few hours earlier. Only an occasional cat crossed my path, its tail stretched behind it, slinking from corner to corner looking for leftover tidbits. My thoughts were on Freida, still my fiancée, I supposed, and hoped I wouldn't lose her over this. I wasn't in the best spirits to meet people but maybe speaking with the girls would take my mind—at least for an hour or so—off Freida, off the wars.

I called her on my cell phone as I crossed over to where the abandoned market street spilled into the main street, where cars circulated among kabob cafés and souvenir shops, including a hookah shop adorned to attract customers. She still wouldn't answer....

I headed down the cement steps to the beach. I walked on the sand dodging theripple of white water after a wave had pounded the turf. Only a few people were strolling on this part of the beach, which was not lit up, as the trendy beach cafés were about a half a mile closer to the center of Tel Aviv. I could see the lights hanging on wires surrounding the cafés down the beach.

I arrived at the café where I was supposed to meet the two girls. About three rows of chaise lounges were spread out and people were lounging about, drinking, playing cards, singing…I called Abigail on my cell phone.

"Shalom. I see you; can you see us waving?"

I scanned the chaise lounges until I saw Abigail and Maya frantically trying to get my attention. They were in the row closest to the waves. I strolled over the sand to them. Abigail was a bit stocky but her soft, white cheeks peeked through her long, silky strands of black hair. Maya was thin, with sleek, dark-brown hair impeccably combed back and ending in a short pony tail. Her attractive blue-grey eyes surveyed me….

We sat on the beach and reminisced about the incredibly intense and profound interfaith event in Hukuk. It was ironic that our conversation was about interfaith peace, love and working together with people of all faiths, when overhead Israeli Air Force helicopters were traveling in opposite directions, North & South, passing each other in the sky. Abigail told me that those going North were headed to Southern Lebanon to fight the Hezbollah, and those going South were headed to fight the Hamas in the Gaza Strip. Definitely it was another Kafkaesque moment, added to the growing list since I had arrived in this strange and enchanted Holy Land.

Chapter 38: Gaza

It was surrealistic for me to be sitting there, drinking a gin and tonic, with two beautiful Jewish girls, discussing peace and love, understanding, while soldiers flew overhead to two fronts...confusion, guns, bullets and killing on both sides.

Then Abigail, who I called Princessa,[63] had her own story to tell about Palestinians and Gaza, which brought us back into the churning conflict: "I had hired Nazim, a Palestinian from Gaza—a sub-contractor—to restore my house near Tel Aviv and to add onto the bedrooms. A great relationship between us gave rise to a regular work schedule and immediate progress on extending the house. Within a couple of weeks, already one bedroom was beautifully extended a few feet; the work proceeded.

Then the 2nd Intifada erupted. One day Nazim called me into the temporary workshop he had set up in my cellar. I arrived and he was standing in front of his desk. He asked me to sit down in front of him but I intuited foul play as his normally smooth forehead and dancing eyes were replaced by deep furrows and a gray sheen over sullen, cryptic eyes.

He was holding something at the side of the chair and I couldn't make it out. A tremor rose up from within...and a cold chill felt like a waterfall down my back. Something was up. He slightly lunged forward and started to pull the object from the side of the chair. I backed up and held my hand in my shirt pretending I was holding my gun. I was a lieutenant in the Israeli army and he saw me take it out from under my shirt one day as I returned from work. He sunk back down in the chair and looked away. Then he said, 'You know certain people in Gaza pay a lot of money if we kill Jews, but I won't hurt you, you know that!'

I had to report what happened to the police and one day they came and took him away. I had no choice but," she choked with emotion, then cleared her throat, "to fire him."

"What happened to him?" I tried to prompt the end of the story.

"I don't know, exactly; there was an investigation and Nazim was deported to Gaza! I've never seen him since."

I arrived at Ben Gurion Airport nervous, as I heard that Hezbollah had recently purchased long-range rockets that could reach as far as Tel Aviv. I was so paranoid

---

63 Because she had refused to sleep in a sleeping bag in a tent with us in Hukuk and needed a bed with all the comforts.

after all that had happened over the last few days that I wanted to write Freida while I could; I missed her beaming eyes and warm embrace, her voice, her everything. I was so distraught with worry about everything, about whether we had broken up without breaking up and whether I'd see her again.

It took me a while to find a hotspot so I could use my Wi-Fi to send her a message. I finally found it, in the corner across from the fast foods stands, and quickly sent an email to her. I hoped to ease the tension and open up communication by reminding her of my promise:

"Two weeks with you and your son...."—I had to add, as things were moving so quickly in the Middle East—"provided that I'm not called anywhere for an emergency in Israel, or elsewhere and that it be after January because I have to return to teach in Paris from September to December and I have a series of author events in the US until the end of January."

I knew I shouldn't repeat the word, "Palestine," which had already caused a rift between us.

I boarded the plane and as it soared over Tel Aviv and over the waves, I nervously waited until it was beyond the reach of the wars, beyond the range of missiles...After an hour, I figured we'd be flying somewhere over Sicily and I fell into a deep sleep, still not having heard from my Freida. Her kiss was still warm on my lips....

Chapter 39: Purim

At Charles de Gaulle Airport, a special shuttle waited for me. David, a French Jew, provided low cost shuttle services to anyone going to or coming from Israel. All the people in the shuttle were Jews, excitedly sharing with each other and the driver the magic of Israel, the magic of the Holy Land. David nodded and often cursed the drivers circling, cutting him off, typical of the cutthroat streets of Paris.

I arrived at my apartment near Place Voltaire and the Sephardic Jewish district where I had returned, alone, after having previously lived there for three years with Sylvia and our three children. I lugged my suitcase up the wooden steps to the second floor, turned the key, opened it, shoved my suitcase in, locked the door and walked the few steps to my bed; I immediately sank into it and fell asleep, without undressing.

When I woke up, I opened my computer and had a gift from Freida. Forgetting what had recently transpired between us, her message was short: "It's a long way away and I will miss you, my love, but let's spend Purim together in March. Shalom, ahava, Your Freida." (ahava, love) I yelled and cried, "She loves me, forgives me, everything!" I was totally in her clutches. I quickly responded, "Ken, ken, ken, my love. Frank." (Yes, yes, yes)

For the next few months, I was busy teaching in Paris, representing clients in various courts, spending time with my daughter, Victoria, in Paris, and then absenting myself for two weeks to participate in more author events in the United States, mainly in New York and California. In San Francisco, I picked up my kids, like every Christmas, and took them to Ashland, Oregon, for about 10 days to visit Mom. My son, Frankie, always came with me to Oregon to visit his grandmother. Regina and Juliana, young teenage rebels, went with us rarely over the Christmas holidays.

Being so busy didn't take my mind off Freida; I missed her and was counting the days until our reunion. Such a long time passed, it seemed, until March rolled around, and Purim was announced. It is one of the most joyous holidays on the Jewish calendar. It revolves around the biblical story of a beautiful Jewish woman, Esther, who became queen of Persia. Haman, the king's advisor, plotted to kill all Jews in the kingdom because Mordecai, Esther's cousin, refused to bow down to Haman. Mordecai persuaded Esther to speak to the king to save the Jewish people. Esther, at great risk to her own personal safety, revealed she was a Jew to the king for the first time and also the plot to kill her people. The Jews were saved and Haman and his conspirators were executed!

I arrived in Tel Aviv to a truly festive atmosphere beginning, as usual, at the airport, as many Jews were arriving for Purim. After the entrance inspection gauntlet, where we were individually interrogated by an immigration officer at a booth, we walked down a long ramp again into a huge room, surrounded by the usual water fountains. There, masses of people congregated to welcome their friends and their family to the Holy Land. It was a huge party!

That night, Freida and I celebrated Purim together in the orthodox synagogue and we went in costume. Tovi celebrated it with friends in another village and would spend the night there. I wore an orthodox Jew outfit with the hat, black suit and tzitzit (fringes) and Freida wore a gypsy outfit, a multi-colored scarf draped over her hair and tied in a knot in back of her head.

We arrived late as food was being served to break the one-day fast. We ate kosher sandwiches, dipped bread in hummus and drank wine. The Talmud[64] says that "a person is required to drink until he cannot tell the difference between 'cursed be Haman' and 'blessed be Mordecai'.[65] It is the only night where, theoretically, an orthodox Jew can be justifiably drunk and many of the men dancing in the circle seemed very tipsy—mainly the men and the boys would dance in a circle as the women and girls looked on.

Finally, I joined the dancers and noticed some women had joined in, too. Finally, Freida joined me. Her hips swiveled in the middle of the group. It seemed she was only intent on her own dancing, on watching herself from the inside out. She twirled and whirled more and more toward the center, her legs taking big steps and her torso following with jerking motions, erotic, tempting, but it didn't matter even in this orthodox Jewish group as everyone was dancing and drinking, according to the book.

By the end of the evening everyone was dancing with everyone else; it was a blast! I did, however, feel distance from Freida as she seemed to be making her moves while totally oblivious to everything else. That would be merely a starter for what waited for us in the Galilee.

The next day, we were joined by Tovi as we hopped on a bus to head back to Hukuk, for a second Purim celebration. We arrived at Sarah's, where we were led by members of the kibbutz to a community center in the middle of the compound.

There, we met for dinner the members of Sarah's Rose of Galilee group in a large dinner hall with about six long rows of tables. The Rose of Galilee reserved one row of about 30 places and the five other rows were for other people from the Kibbutz. This was how I imagined Kibbutzim were run: while working the land together, they shared costs and profits and sometimes ate together in one big eating hall, like that one.

It was also Shabbat and Freida grabbed her son right beside the table to repeat Shabbat prayers with him, since the table seemed more secular and Shabbat prayers

---

64 Judaism's oral laws.

65 Rich, Tracey R. "Purim." Judaism 101. 1995-2011. <http://www.jewfaq.org/holiday9. htm>.

were done individually. It was strange that I was left out of the prayers that normally I would have been a part of when celebrating Shabbat together in her apartment.

Then we rose and followed Sarah into a special room next to the dining room for our Purim celebration. I looked around and everyone was Jewish except for one Arab. Everyone was in costume. I wore the same orthodox Jew outfit that I had at the party in Tel Aviv and I would have guessed that Sarah would be dressed like a queen. And she was....

Another couple sitting next to us was dressed like court jesters, with the three-cornered multi-colored hats. They sat laughing at the other costumes, especially the bunny and the monkey outfits; they seemed to be the inveterate criticizers of costumes. At each person that walked by in costume, they'd snicker. Just watching them made me shake with inner laughter.

A couple of men under the supervision of Sarah set up a computer linked to speakers. As soon as the music began, against the backdrop of the slow jazz beat, something struck me like lightening; my warm, loving companion turned into a Mr. Hyde. She pointed to a chair near her and told me that was where I should sit. I started to speak but she turned away, not looking at me.

I ambled over to the chair and sat in it, confused by her sudden mood change. This curious metamorphosis took me by complete surprise. I had no idea that her dancing in her own world at the Purim celebration in Tel Aviv, almost ignoring me completely, was just a warm-up for Hukuk. She was in full rebellion, or full manifestation of independence, and in heat to provoke my Italian side...jealousy.

As she danced with one man after another, I sat and watched. From time to time, she flashed a furtive glance in my direction that I pretended not to see. I thought to myself, "Here we go again!"

Then an "Earth, Wind and Fire" song was played and I had to dance. I asked an attractive, robust lady dressed like a school girl, wearing jeans, with a lunch box and rouge spread on her plump, red cheeks; we hit the dance floor. Her moon-shaped blue eyes flashed fearfully so I knew she didn't dance much. I danced the swing with her, holding her close and guiding her gently with my right hand in the middle of her back. Then we separated as the rhythm accelerated; she tried to pull closer even though it was a fast dance, but my eyes and mind were on Freida. The man she was dancing with swung her around and her hair almost swept across my face, but her eyes were sweeping over me and she unfortunately saw my slight frown. She had triumphed!

I was slow to realize it, but the truth of her confusing mood swings—when I felt rejection from her—finally hit me: the circus she was promoting was the classic "jealousy game." Even though she was an amateur, she surely deemed herself a master. She was dancing with passion, while all the time looking out of the corners of her eyes, watching me. I tried not to look at her, as I danced my game with the big, busty blue-eyed girl.

I stuck to my game plan and it paid off. She flew to my side for the last dance. We embraced like long lost friends and our mutual theatrics converged as we moved with the music. It was a salsa dance, which I loved, and felt a surge of emotional power. But that was pathetically diluted, decaffeinated, as it turned into another "performance opportunity" for Freida: she flung her head back, her lips tightening like a serious Flamenco dancer. In full "femme fatale" performance mode, she tried to detach and do a solo number; but salsa was more a together dance so I held on tight, refusing to let her do her number as I bent her slightly down at the end of a beat. She quickly adapted and bent over my arm almost to the floor, and then twirled around, grabbing my hands. I had to admit, she adapted fast. I was learning a lot about my "fiancé," this time as my dance partner.

No slouch at salsa as my Latino friends had taught me well when I lived in the Latino district in San Francisco, I followed with a twirl of my own, and decided to make it a mutual performance. But I loathed such showings because if dancing did not come from the heart, it meant nothing to me. Freida, smirking as she flew in my arms, showed her continued desire to perform, to be seen, and seen some more…all show, no heart.

It turned out that we were the only couple left on the dance floor and the 50 or 60 people quickly transformed from costumed dancers into a boisterous audience at the edge of the dance floor, egging us on. They clapped vigorously until the final drum beat, after which Freida, right on cue, bent down and swept the floor with her hair, sending her multi-colored headband flying, as I held her tight. The end….

The place resounded with applause and Sarah came up and blessed us, dear heart, as she interpreted our impassioned dancing as a sign of our consummated, strong love. Freida glowed in all her glory. But, in spite of my hypocritical smile, I was secretly disgusted, feeling nothing inside after the performance. Empty….

In the bus back to Tel Aviv, Freida and I argued over the legitimacy of some Jews who interpret the Torah as giving unrestricted rights of Jewish settlers to stake claim to the West Bank and settle there. Perhaps to change the subject, she grabbed a drum and began drumming with a group of party goers in the back of the bus singing folkloric and popular songs in Hebrew. I felt she was pounding the drums like she would have liked to pound my head since I hadn't reacted to her jealousy game as she would have liked. She was expecting a morose, depressed man, flaccidly following her every move, I presumed.

In spite of the constant drumming, I fell asleep as I began envisioning work left to do organizing interfaith dialogues and marches in the West Bank in the next few days. I just couldn't deal with any more of her games. Exhausted by them, by her, I fell into a disturbed sleep and even slept through the drum pounding next to my ear.

When we arrived at her apartment at 12 midnight, we slept in separate beds, she in her bed, and me on the couch. She didn't say anything as she slid into the covers of her bed while I read lying on the couch, so I stayed there all night, I was so turned off. I could have been wrong about her, but I was sure my intuition was talking to me, this time with strong words…get out!

The next day early, amidst her sleepy mumbling next door, I began collecting my belongings and packed my suitcase for my trip to the West Bank where I would stay for several days, organizing an interfaith dialogue. I had waited until the last moment, as I hadn't found an appropriate moment, a moment of calm and tenderness during this trip, to give her the bad news that I had to cut short our scheduled time together.

I was originally going to leave the big suitcase with her and then return after my visit for a couple of days, before heading to the Tel Aviv airport on my way back to Paris. But after what we had lived through these past few days, I felt seriously disappointed, that the love I thought we shared seemed to have been more a fleeting infatuation. If our relationship was just at act two of a play entitled "Masquerade of a Couple," I needed some time away from her. I decided to take all my belongings with me....

As I bent over my suitcase, I heard a rustling behind me and turned to see her long hair hanging over her forehead as she dropped in the chair behind me.

She sighed loudly, perhaps her way of expressing her disapproval of my sleeping on the couch the past night. Finally she spoke, her gravelly morning voice rising to a squawky shriek, "So you're going to leave me...and your promise to stay with us for two weeks? You've only been with us one week and my son will be disappointed."

Of course, she didn't mention she would be disappointed, as well. She was still triumphing from last night, at least in her own mind. I looked up into her morning face and for the first time noticed her nostrils were inflated like a bull's and clearly visible under a hooked nose. Sadness spread over me as it seemed such a long time ago I was, albeit blindly, focused on her aquiline nose, her red-streaked impassioned eyes and inviting lips. "I need to go away for four days...to Palestine. I suppose you don't remember my promise was conditioned on whether I had to continue my...."

"Come on: first, it's not Palestine, it's 'occupied territories'. And second, you're going for four days, and that's four fewer days of being together as a family."

I cringed guiltily at the word "family"; but those other words matched her distorted face, her mouth crumpled into a ball, her bulging eyes projecting an exasperated, hateful gleam. I knew this was going to end badly—it was on a roller coaster to disaster and I didn't know how to stop it. I wasn't yet sure I wanted to.

"Don't think of it like that, Freida, as time away from our little nest. It is an equal part of my vision to work in the West Bank with Palestinians, for peace...."

She interrupted me, showing me the side of her I didn't want to see:

"What's the point of trying to work with them? Look, when we get Palestinian neighbors, they stick to themselves. We had Palestinians neighbors the first year; they only seemed interested in stealing from us and not at all in becoming friends."

It was so shocking coming from someone so supposedly involved in the peace process, at least with a group dedicated to peace like the Rose of Galilee which brings together Muslims, Jews and Christians. Or maybe her attitude was symptomatic of some so-called peace-loving groups—like many mainstream Israeli Jews—in denial over what was happening in the West Bank...in Gaza.

"What about the Arabs, Israeli Christians and Muslims alike, who often join us during the interfaith events in Hukuk?"

She turned in a huff and went into the bedroom as I continued to prepare my luggage. I felt nauseous listening to her, a peace worker and a singer of love and spiritual songs, talk like that.

She reminded me of another Israeli peace activist, Chana, who I had met before I met Freida.

Chapter 40: Bedouins

Chana and I used to do healing together: she would use a tuning fork vibration method and I would use meditative healing, notably with one of her patients who had kidney cancer. She was a love soul and an incredible healer!

The cancer victim would lie flat on the examination table. Chana would make the preliminary connection, relaxing the body with her tuning fork technique. Then she'd focus her therapy on the kidneys, vibrating the tuning force in that area of the patient's body. Then, she would call me; I would gently place my hands over the spot and concentrate, letting flow a pure meditative healing energy of love through my fingers.

The room would be silent for the fifteen minutes we did tandem therapy. When the patient sat up, she would comment that she had felt a strong, hot healing feeling when we both worked with her.

Chana also did healing work using her tuning forks with members of a nearby Bedouin family; they loved her. One night she was invited for dinner in their tent/ restaurant in a Bedouin village. She spoke to them about me and told me later they welcomed me, as well.

Her car strained and sputtered as it hurled over the narrow roads leading to the village. I expected to see tents, goats, camels and a campsite with Bedouins and their families sitting around it, draped in red and white keffiyehs. As we drove in silence I was amazed as I saw rows of neatly kept houses, with gardens. There were no signs of goats, camels or tents. Chana was giggling at the wheel, her short, dark hair creeping over her forehead to her long nose, swinging as her head bobbed up and down.

She read my mind: "Surprised, huh? I suppose you were expecting small herds of sheep, shepherds with long staffs, climbing rocks and hills after them." She couldn't help erupting in a full-blown belly laugh.

"You watch too much TV!" She choked a bit, wheezing and turning red with laughter.

"You got me!"

I exhaled as she parked the car in front of a building that was built to look like a huge tent.

"Ah," I said to myself. "At least something recognizable...."

She looked at me and snickered as if she read my mind. This urban Bedouin environment seemed the antithesis to the nomadic lifestyle they were known to lead. A young, dark man and a girl greeted us at the door; hugging Chana, they shook my hand. We were led into a huge room with long, draping muslin curtains converging at the center. A sumptuous repast was served. "This mesaf—take," said the girl. Long, brown hair dangled over her eyes, and her round, plump cheeks brightened to a light-red hue, dwarfing her small mouth.

She placed a dish of steaming rice over lamb in front of us, and then gave us plates and silverware to eat on. Other dishes were prepared and sent to our table. I thanked Chana for suggesting I not eat anything before coming to this place; no way could I have enjoyed this incredible spread if I had.

After dinner, we were served mint tea in multi-colored glasses. As we sat back, contented, the young man brought in several hookahs, handing one to the young girl who had waited on us. They both sat across from us smoking hookah as we sipped our tea. He puffed contentedly, his mouth covering the nozzle, his thin mustache barely visible.

He spoke in broken English and from time to time looked at the girl next to him, who nodded. When he opened his mouth to speak, I noticed two teeth on top, one on each side of his incisors, were missing. He was so young that I could imagine he had lost his baby teeth and was still growing permanent teeth.

And yet, he recounted that he was an officer in the Israeli army and was to be deployed to the Gazan front in a couple of days. He told me many of his Bedouin family were soldiers and considered themselves loyal Israelis.

I was learning so much.

There was a strong bond between Chana and the Bedouins; every time the young boy or girl addressed her, they would beam with warmth, with love. I turned to Chana, to speak to her about this incredible, obvious bond tying her to a Jewish lady, to a Muslim Bedouin family.

"So you said you did some healing with the family?"

Chana responded, smiling at the two hookah smokers across from us, "Yes, their mother had severe pain in her back and arms and the doctors couldn't figure out why or how to treat it. I was called to their home one night and used the tuning forks treatment. I was able to...."

The boy said something to her in Hebrew, and she smiled and responded, "Ken, ken."

She continued, "I was able to stop the pain. In fact, they've called me back several times and each time, I was able to help when doctors couldn't. You can see they are so, so thankful. In fact, I'm a permanent guest here and can come whenever and eat with them. I love them...."

No doubt, a sincere smile of love on her mouth connected with the two. It was another rare, warm, spiritual moment, one I'll never forget.

It was on the way back to her house in the car, however, that her shocking views on Palestinian Arabs came out. That changed the ambiance and sent me from drifting among the clouds, falling to earth . . "I'm preparing to visit Palestine...again."

She quickly responded, "There is no Palestine—those are occupied territories."

I interrupted, "Well, the Palestinians consider themselves having a country. They have elected politicians, a government...."

It was her turn to interrupt me, "Oh, well, it's meaningless, just as the Palestinian claim on the West Bank is spurious, as they all came from other places, like Syria, Saudi Arabia, Iraq, Jordan—they are not originally from there...don't see why they are making claims to the land...." I shrugged not knowing where to begin my response...She didn't wait, "You are wasting your time going there."

Wow, I thought to myself, words reflecting the exact same thoughts as those of many mainstream Jews. She continued, "Anyway, all the Palestinians want to do is kill us, wipe us out and sweep us into Mediterranean!"

"I don't agree: many recognize the State of Israel and most Palestinians do not believe in killing Jews or Christians, nor pushing Israel into the sea...Also, many historians believe that the ancestors of the Arabs and Jews arrived in Judea and Samaria about the same time, approximately two thousand years before the birth of Jesus Christ."

She shook her head. I was so surprised that she, another liberal working with Hukuk and the interfaith movement, and Muslims living in Israel, would believe something like that. I guessed her closeness with Bedouins was enhanced by the fact Bedouins considered themselves faithful Israelis, but she opposed Palestinians since they fought against the occupation. I was confused.

* * *

From thinking about Chana, I switched my attention back to my luggage which had been placed in front of the sofa. I headed for the door and looked behind me, hoping Freida would follow but feared her pride would stop her. I opened the door and before pushing my luggage on rollers out onto the porch, she shuffled near me. I managed to push my luggage and place my garment-tote bag on the porch and stepped out. As I started to walk down the steps, I looked back and she had poked her head out, her long hair trailing down the side of her face. Her mouth trembled as she struggled with something on her finger...the diamond ring. She was trying to take it off. She succeeded and handed it to me. I reached out and she placed it into the palm of my hand. She then looked me square in the eyes; her blue-gray eyes met mine. "I guess we're not ready...."

A heavy iron door clanged between us, sending me into a funk that would last for months.

Sarah, after hearing about our breakup, certainly blamed it on me. That, coupled with my using the word "occupation" in my fliers, and constant visits to the West Bank led to my being black listed by many mainstream Israeli Jews, including Sarah. I was no longer invited either to organize or participate in Hukuk interfaith events. To them, I was a radical....

Chapter 41: Fight Training

I almost felt like returning to Oregon, to my home, to the mountains to be with my kids and my mother, to hide from my misery, to regenerate my devastated emotional batteries. But I had committed to this trip to the West Bank, which was a litmus test to find out—this time from the Palestinians themselves, from Ramallah to Jenin—how I should organize the interfaith dialogues/marches with Muslims, Jews, Christians, Druze, Sufis, Bah'ai's and people of other faiths, for peace.

I was desperate, lonely, lost, having lost the anchor—albeit imperfect—which I had thought would redeem me, make my life feel whole…being with the woman I loved and her son, who I loved and missed. All that had slipped from my grip, like the rope of a life raft in the middle of raging seas.

I prayed on the bus from Tel Aviv to Jerusalem, and as usual, when I was down, I picked up my book, *Storm Over Morocco*. It automatically opened to the page I wanted, as I had read it so many times:

"A cool wind blew, ruffling the curtains to the tune of some invisible, heavenly organ. I meditated to the Supreme Being, to God, to truth, to love and a light was cast in the room, reflected from the dense fog outside. In spite of the intense moments of the day and my utterly exhausted body, my mind felt rejuvenated, uplifted to a light which had shone through the crusty ceiling of closed mindedness. The path visualized through the opening was not necessarily that of one ideology—Islam— but was a path on which Muhammad guided me. Then, like a spiritual tag team, the guide changed to Jesus, and as I ascended, I was met by Muhammad, who continued leading me up to the steady, warm hand of the Buddha, there to embrace me as I continued my ascent. My hand was then grasped by Moses; with strong arms, he held me before him, becoming the many-faceted, omnipresent spirit of Krishna. Proceeding towards the heavens, I was received by all of the prophets and handed by Krishna to [Ramakrishna] then to Jesus, Muhammad, Buddha, [Abraham] and Moses, who received me with spontaneous joy and humility. With their arms around me, I basked in their love shared by the Supreme Consciousness, who was neither man nor woman, but transcending all things, reigned within and without, melding pure love together into one good, pure force. This energy linked me to the love of all creatures, to the peace deep within me, to the tolerance and understanding that armed me against the threat of ignorance, fear and allegiance to material things. I felt finally free of the confining embrace of the superficial, neon world, where pure, innocent love and passions are inhibited in the name of progress."[66]

That passage brought me back to focus on my "raison d'être," to the important purpose for this trip. I pledged that whatever happened, I'd stay with it.

Once in Jerusalem, I headed to the Damascus Gate and proceeded with my plan to go to Ramallah and meet with Abdullah, whom I had met with the three sisters during my first visit. I called him on his cell phone; he gave me a rendezvous at Manara Square, in the center of town.

As soon as I got off the bus, I walked to the designated meeting place. I arrived and stood in back of the hand rails near the vendor that sold dates and apricots in cartons, next to Manara Square. A man with a two-day growth leaned over and pointed to his dates. They were beautiful, big medjool dates—my weakness. I bought a half a kilo, just as I saw a white-haired man in a suit walk down the middle of the street. He walked by the rail in the streets, as cars zoomed around him, honking, drivers yelling out. He was completely oblivious...no fear!

"Abdullah!" I yelled out.

He turned his head, his smile revealing a couple of gold teeth.

I thought as I held his hand, for a man who spent 28 years in Israeli prisons, he certainly had not let bitterness take hold of him. I prayed for his strength.

He took me to an upstairs hookah bar. Adolescents were drinking a kind of strawberry/chocolate cocktail. When the waiter came, I invited Abdullah to drink a cocktail; he surprised me by ordering a soda. I ordered café, strong Arabic café. I needed revival, and immediately.

He asked me how I had liked my first visit to Ramallah. "Loved it, but it's strange: no tourists around."

He smiled courteously, but beneath it, he really meant: heard that before...you should know that's one of the perverse consequences of the occupation...so let's move on.

He was right, that was trite!

"You know my goal is to start organizing interfaith dialogues and marches all over the West Bank, to bring more people into the area to understand what's happening here, and to encourage the peace movement. What else can I do?"

My voice probably sounded desperate and I was, desperate to overcome my ill-fated personal life, to shove it aside and focus on my vision, to help bring peace, understanding and freedom to the Holy Land. It was, besides my kids, my mother, siblings and a couple of friends thousands of miles away, the only thing meaningful and enduring left in my life. Everything else was in shambles! He somehow seemed to know that.He smiled: "Ahlan wa-sahlan! Wonderful—how can I help you?"

I was concerned that his years of suffering in prisons had cooled his activism; I was wrong. His energetic, perky but raspy voice indicated he hadn't given up, that he'd fight to the last breath, unafraid.

"And God, he had a good excuse for giving up," I whispered under my breath.

I loved this man, a truly amazing human being. I hoped I could share his passion

---

66 Storm Over Morocco, 4th Edition, supra, p.171.

and patience, waiting years and years to be free to see his loved ones. Yet he was not broken—not bent on just damage control, protective measures—no, not him! I wanted to be like him, without, of course, the prison time.

Surrounding us were groups of students smoking hookahs, joking and drinking cocktails, adolescents wearing tight jeans and striped shirts.

Abdullah seemed to be in a hurry; he drank his soda quickly and stood up. He was announcing that it was time to go.

"Oh Abdullah, could you give me names of people who could help me?"

He sat down with pen in hand and produced a piece of paper, spreading it on the table.

"Ok, where you go?"

"I wanted especially to visit Jenin, Hebron and Bethlehem." His lip curled up in a toothy smile.

"Fantastic! Don't forget Jericho and Nablus. I'll give you a list of names and people you could contact."

In about five minutes, he handed me a list of names and phone numbers underneath several West Bank cities. Then he stood up again and this time the meeting was over.

As we returned to Manara Square, I thanked him and he flicked me that toothy, fearless smile, raising his hand for a cab.

He was surely on his way home as I was on my way to my first complete tour of the West Bank, full of hope and a list of phone numbers. First stop, Jenin. I had no idea that soon I'd be in the heart of a refugee camp which just a few years ago, had made world headlines during the greatest resistance to IDF forces, resulting in fierce fighting and massive destruction of dwellings. That would be my first stop…into the jaws of the beast!

Book III

The Epicenter

Don't ever leave
Can't forget

Burns inside

At remembering
Each time

I can't forget

If I do
Then I'm numb
Until death
Frees me

to feel again.[67]

---

67 Frank Romano, from the poem, "Cronkite Beach," p.22, Crossing Over, supra.

Chapter 42: The Test

Surrounded by dark, mustachioed Arabs smoking a hookah, I sat waiting for my turn to speak. I sat in the dimly-lit patio of a somber house, just outside the Jenin Refugee Camp. The moment of truth had come, many years later; I was to test my vision of peace in Palestine and in Israel—at the heart of the conflict. There was no way I could fumble my way through this situation, as each one sitting around the patio had spent an average of seven years in Israeli prisons.

One look in their eyes and a "thumbs down" death call for the gladiator could result; but I was sure this 30-year old vision embodied truth and the time had come to share it, live it...or bury it. I had to remind myself that they had been through the war, as their distrustful eyes raked over me. They spoke about their suffering, the conditions in the refugee camp. Even when intense emotions gave rise to frantic gestures and their hands shook with frustration, their dark eyes remained fixed on me—there was no turning back now. In a few minutes, it would be my turn to let my heart speak.

During that brief interval, I could almost hear my Israeli friends warning me: "Whatever you do, don't go to Jenin; it's a hotbed of terrorists and they would love to get their hands on a Jew or an American that they could torture, perhaps kill or take hostage."

My thoughts shifted to earlier that morning when I was jogging on a country road in Arraba, a Palestinian village near the town of Jenin, where I was staying with a family. The Middle-Eastern sun baked the crumbling soil. As I jogged up a slightly inclined dirt and gravel road, I heard the low rumbling of a motor. I stopped and turned toward the sound; a pale-green car coming towards me stopped simultaneously. I turned and began jogging again and heard the crunching of the tires on the gravel, inching up to me so slowly, slowly edging forward, on my right.

No doubt, the car was following me. My eyes frantically searched ahead as far as they could see, but spotted more dirt roads and fields of dried grass reminiscent of a Van Gogh painting. The brittle plumes swayed erratically, joining the dance of grass on distant, golden hills. I saw a remote farmhouse surrounded by tiny sheep and smaller livestock I couldn't identify. I was alone and seemingly at the mercy of the occupants of the vehicle, with no possible escape. I envisioned jumping over the nearby fence and heading across the field, when the car crept up almost even with me.

I had to stop but my eyes didn't leave the open field. When the car caught up to me, I had no choice but to turn and face the driver. He was a young man who appeared to be in his twenties, with short, black hair combed back, glistening with hair cream, and a cropped beard bristling at the sides. His eyes were black and angry, glaring at me with suspicion. I imagined his profound distress at seeing me in his town, a refuge from the endless, cruel conflict.

Inside the car there were two young men sitting beside the driver. One youth, with a shaved head, wore a skull cap. His head slanted to the right and his arm extended downward, as if weighted down by some hidden object. I could see the silhouette of a third young boy, very thin, plastered against the far door; he was looking out the window, as if keeping watch.

As my eyes met the hateful glare head-on, my legs began to shake and buckle. Finally, he spoke through clenched teeth what sounded like Hebrew. I inclined my head from side to side, showing I was trying to understand. He spoke a few words in Arabic, and I interrupted him.

"English?"

His tense lips barely moving, he eventually uttered the question, "What do...you do?" he asked as he leaned out the window, his dark, spider-like hands still clenching the wheel.

A wrath that had accumulated over the ages seemed to flow from his every pore. My insides vibrated; I was shaken and panicky, not knowing what to do or say. Then a ray of light: what was the name of the family I was staying with? And what was the Arabic word for friend? I wondered what else I could say—I hadn't prepared for this. I was shaking as my thoughts collided, becoming confused.

The hateful eyes blinked, and turned to the others; his lips drew tighter. "Zahout," I blurted, the name of the family. And the name for friend, what was it? Oh, yes... ."Anna sadiq." (I am a friend)

At first, his whiteless eyes beamed a coldness into mine, reflecting years of the cruel suffering of a captive people, living in an occupied country and a war zone. Some fight, daily striving for the upper hand; others struggle to find a piece of bread or a drink of water, where water rights are often rationed. In his eyes I saw a reflection of the faces posted on flyers of fallen young fighters, many too young to show the slightest stubble. This was one of many reminders of the brutal past experienced by small Palestinian towns like Arraba, Jenin. A truce hangs from a very thin fiber. A full-scale war could erupt anytime, especially here and in Jenin.

The driver repeated the name, "Zahout...ahhhhh, Zahout, na'am." (Zahout, ah yes) He looked at the other youths, repeating the name, and the corners of his mouth twisted into a tight smile, cracking at the edges. He turned to me, repeating the name of the family; I nodded, he looked at the other two adolescents again, and their frowns turned into smiles. The tension faded as they nodded their heads.

Then the driver detached his hand from the steering wheel, turned it over and, after repeating the name "Zahout" again, kissed the back of it. Glancing back at me he nodded again; then with the same hand, he clasped the gear knob and shifted it in reverse. He spun around and gunning the engine, churned up dust from the dirt and gravel as he careened around a turn and down the hill.

I took a deep breath, my body frozen and eyes focused on where the car had disappeared. After a few minutes, I turned uphill and began jogging again, even though my body wasn't quite ready to move. I thanked God, with all my heart, that I had remembered the name of the family and the Arabic word for friend. I could have easily forgotten my own name under the stares of such hateful, vengeful eyes.

Earlier that day, I had traveled from Ramallah to visit a farmer and his family in Arraba, Jenin, about twenty minutes from Jenin. A short-haired, athletic-looking young man with an aquiline nose and pearly white smile greeted me as the taxi door swung open in the middle of this farming village. He introduced himself as Taysir and took my hand, pulling me as we walked toward a two-story white house. At the entrance, I was greeted by an old, gray-haired man shrouded in a black and white checkered Palestinian keffiyeh and a hooked-nosed woman wearing a white hijab and a long chocolate-colored robe. She was followed by two daughters: one had wavy golden hair falling down over a light-brown, pudgy face, with a huge, toothy smile; behind her stood a more timid creature, a young girl with long, dark hair restrained by a head scarf, her small, plain mouth curved upwards in a shy smile. In her warm, dark eyes I observed an inner, quiet beauty.

Then, from behind the father, out sprang a short-haired young boy, flashing a huge smile featuring teeth so crooked, his lips were unable to contain them. He almost jumped in my arms and hugged me. I felt like a brother coming back from the wars. That night after my jog, I was scheduled to travel to the nearby Jenin refugee camp to speak to a man named Ra'ed who could introduce me to people who could help me plan an interfaith peace march in Israel and Palestine. Abdullah from Ramallah had given me the name and the phone number of his friend, Ra'ed, who lived near the camp. I had called him from Ramallah and he invited me to join him.

When I returned from jogging, my legs were still shaking from the confrontation with the group of angry young men. I decided to tell no one as I did not want to be restricted to the house or have someone accompany me on walks. I retired to my room to be alone with my thoughts.

Taysir arranged for a taxi to take us to Jenin after dinner. We left the house and walked down the stairs; his ten-year-old brother and two sisters waved from the windows. We passed the rusty tractor and headed down the dirt driveway to the main road.

We were greeted by a dusty orange taxi already parked in front of the driveway. Taysir climbed into the front seat and motioned me into the back. He shook hands with the taxi driver and turned to me.

"This is Kamel, my friend. He give you good price."

I wondered what he meant by that because it only cost six shekels (about $1.50) for a day taxi.

"Hi, Kamel. How much will it cost me?"

He twisted his head towards me, "Only fifty shekels."

I was shocked at the price difference and told Taysir, "That's too much, as I only pay six shekels during the day."

Taysir explained that the day service taxis charged like buses because they were a regular run, but Kamel had made a special trip to take us to Jenin that evening.

"Besides," he further explained, "the service taxis don't run at night."

I finally paid and was thankful later that this driver had accompanied us to the refugee camp. As the taxi left the lights of the small town, it plunged into darkness, passing several farms on the outskirts, consisting of wooden shacks around which livestock, sheep or mules were often tied. Some scrawny goats, their little ears twitching, wandered around nibbling on dried tufts of grass. Lights beamed over low trees as we approached an intersection. I asked Taysir if those were the lights of Jenin. He nodded and a hard lump lodged in my throat. This would be the first real test of the validity of the vision I had had in the arid plains of Morocco: I would actually be involved in helping bring peace and brotherly love to the Holy Land. But I couldn't forget the car of angry men and hoped I was not headed to yet another hostile confrontation.

Taysir turned to me and announced that we were now entering the refugee camp. I got my first glimpse of the place I had heard so much about, a place that had been the center of so many problems for Israeli soldiers. What I saw were hastily-constructed buildings, one stacked on top of the other, one drab building after another, adjacent to an occasional café or "Ma and Pa" corner store. I could not fathom that this small, obscure pocket of a third-world country challenged an entire industrialized nation. My eyes were dry from constantly gaping in disbelief. It must have been David versus Goliath all over again; but here, at the end of the day, Goliath had won...at least for now.

Winding into the Jenin refugee camp, the taxi slowed as it passed groups of men sitting in cafés, wearing the typical white keffiyeh, a black cord snaking around it. People shifted aimlessly about or walked slowly down the alleys between the small, modest off-white houses huddled together, their dilapidated roofs like broken sawhorses.

A dark loneliness settled inside me; I felt estranged from this life where time seemed...frozen. Then I became a part of it as I imagined sitting in a cart drawn by mules, my feet flopping over the sides, in this forgotten part of the world, its rugged, parched terrain endlessly scorched by the sun. I wondered if being lost in a time warp resulted in the fervent attachment to traditions, in spite of the encroachment of other cultures. Or perhaps this part of the world was so isolated and restricted by the Israeli occupation—in the midst of constant destruction followed by hasty reconstruction—that it could never evolve, never give rise to change. But what change? And why change?

No answer came as I thought of the paradox of change: did Western civilization, with its version of "progress," offer a better way of life to a people steeped in ancient traditions? I gravitated towards the latter so fervently, that I refused to recognize change as progress, as something better. I often wondered if I were living on a cloud, thinking life was better here than in Paris or New York. There, no camels walked, no mules bellowed forth into the arid plains. Yet in those "civilized" areas, many civilians were steeped in their own wars…of drugs, gangs or other forms of violence. I felt the contrast between the two societies and was strangely drawn to the one I was experiencing.

Women, wearing Muslim hijabs covering all but their noses, carried babies— there were no baby carriages in sight. Maybe the babies would be safer in a carriage but not as close to the warmth of their mothers' bosoms. I had instructed Taysir to take me into the depths of the camp to meet a man called Ra'ed. There, the greatest resistance to Israeli soldiers had taken place a few years ago, during which time many "freedom fighters" and "kamikaze" bombers were born. A brutal response by Israeli soldiers had resulted in many casualties and gave rise to the bulldozing of the houses of suspected members of terrorist groups. I wondered if I soon would be meeting men on whom the ravages of this war were stamped so profoundly that nothing could be said to them, nothing could be felt by them, and worse, nothing more could be done for them.

I felt, however, that if I could succeed in convincing these people of the sincerity of my aims, my vision, the doors would be opened throughout the West Bank to spread the word. This place would be the hardest sell; that is why I was there, and then would come Hebron, my next visit, beset with violence among Palestinians, Israeli settlers and Israeli soldiers.

I called Ra'ed on my cell phone. A loud "Allo!" greeted me at the other end. I responded with a quick, "Assalym walaykum" and handed the phone to Taysir, who let out a stream of incomprehensible, guttural-sounding words. He then turned to the taxi driver to give him instructions.

"Are we stopping soon, near this refugee camp?" I asked.

Taysir responded, "We'll go a bit beyond it and stop at house in the outskirts where your friends are waiting."

Friends? I hadn't met them, yet. Would I find my way, as I entered this unknown place? Fear began to creep back in, filling a dark, impenetrable place in my mind. I felt claustrophobic; a suffocating panic engulfed me as I squirmed in the back seat, holding my breath and hoping my eyes were hidden.

Thankfully, I was jarred out of my thoughts by the thumping of the car wheels on the uneven, pocked roads. We jolted our way into the village on the outskirts of Jenin where the taxi turned down a dirt road. The car hobbled and shook as the tires slammed into more pot-holes and bounced over stones. Up ahead, a dark- skinned boy wearing sandals and khaki pants walked toward us as the car slowed.

Arabic words flowed again from Taysir and the boy pointed up a dirt path to where a man wearing a long, white djellabah was walking. In a minute, he was standing next to the car, his eyes glistening like black pearls and short-cropped, matted black hair protruding below a white skull cap. The engine whined and sputtered as the car crept up a steep hill before arriving at the summit, where another young boy appeared wearing a baseball hat over his long, black hair. I noticed his atypical features, including a pointed nose and ears, as he motioned us down an alley, on the right. Standing in the middle of the road waving us on was a red-faced man, with a wide, black moustache wrapped around his face like a ribbon; his white-and-black striped shirt flagged the way. Straight, black hair was slicked back and hair wax shone on the top of his oval-shaped head.

Our car followed him as he walked down a gulley towards a cluster of modest, two-story wooden houses, in the shadows below. He motioned us to park by placing his two massive worker's hands in a parallel position and moving them up and down. After parking, we followed the path toward the houses and the red-faced man came towards us, his O-shaped smile revealing teeth through his moustache, like those of an octopus. He extended his hand and I was the first to shake it. His handshake was gentler than his smile.

"Ra'ed?

"Yes," he replied.

"Thanks for inviting us here."

He led us through an archway, down to a patio around which seven to eight men were seated, huddled together; the hum of hushed conversations drew us on. The voices stilled; a dim light bulb hanging from an overhead wire revealed faces with black, bushy beards, a couple of moustaches and pairs of wide, penetrating brown eyes as the men turned to greet us. From somewhere beneath the mesh of hair and beards, their upturned mouths displayed yellow-toothed smiles...the first spontaneous sign of welcome.

Some of the men stood up to make room for us to sit together. Two of them left through a side passage and returned with plastic chairs. Eventually we were all seated and staring at each other in silence; the only sound was the bubbling of the hookahs and dogs barking somewhere, in the night.

Three or four of the dark mouths were busy sucking on silver hookah nozzles. They all looked up at the same time, like members of a startled herd. Above the patio was a layer of hookah smoke, reflecting gray-blue in the light, enshrouding the patio like gentle, smoky hands. The smell of roasting cherries emanated from the pipes and I marveled at my presence in the midst of this ancient culture.

As I quietly sat, there was no doubt I was sitting in the heart of Palestine, the West Bank. A slow chill crept up my spine as I was reminded that only a few years ago, the silence of the night—maybe even while sitting and smoking in a group, as we were—would have been horribly disrupted with the blasts of rifles, machineguns and tank fire, punctuated by the sound of screams, children running and helicopters swooping overhead.

The deep, dark silence spawned fearful thoughts and once again, I felt trapped in a time warp I couldn't escape. My heart thumped against my chest as I imagined this area transformed into a killing field if another Intifada were announced.

Somehow I felt I had been here before, or perhaps I was experiencing someone else's memory of times past. I could hear the incessant roar of jet fighters overhead, the machine gun bullets pelting the ground at my feet...I've got to leave—run— no, I'm ok; it's a dream...It's madness!...people screaming, people crying, calling for water...I'm dying!...tears welling up...stop...stop...got to take a deep breath . .

I looked around at the anxious, but calm, faces and wondered if they had heard the machine guns. No one stirred. The silence, the calm...impassioned thoughts formed in my mind: We've got to have peace! This is total insanity, in the eyes of God. What? Why?

Choppy breathing almost gave me away. I wanted to announce right then, I can't stand it because I only love you—I love everyone! What has war got to do with it? All it does is take my people away from me.

"As-Salamu alaykum," I proclaimed, in a raspy voice.

"Walaikum assalam," chorused the group, and there was silence. Their dark, war-weary eyes rested on me, waiting. They were more resigned than hateful or vengeful, unlike the adolescents in the car. Somehow I'd seen those eyes before, but where? One man, his long jaw resting on his right hand, placed the tip of his hookah on the table before him, clearing his throat. Somehow I knew it was coming…THE QUESTION.

He extended his hand to me, saying, "Welcome. I'm Jawad. Why have you come to this place, so far from your home? What are you doing here?"

Many heads bobbed around the circle. In spite of the question, I decided to hold my tongue as long as I could, while observing him and the men surrounding him; then, at the appropriate moment, I would speak. I needed more time to quiet my thoughts and carefully choose my words.

God help me—let me calm down, let them trust me, let my heart…reach them! was my desperate, silent plea. I felt alone again. I knew this would be the "moment of truth," where I had to convince them that I was there for a legitimate purpose, and not as a CIA agent. Nor was I from the feared Mossad, the Israeli Secret Service, pretending to be their friend while taking pictures secretly, quietly.

How many spies had they caught, or not caught infiltrating and why should they even trust me? I was alone with my thoughts, trepidation…it seemed like questions were only answered by more questions—nothing seemed clear. I looked up and instinctively searched for an escape route. I had been warned that Palestine was rife with spies, especially in Jenin, that I might be suspected and that, God willing, I would be not subjected to mass hysteria and lynched. I didn't want to think about what could happen if I were suspected.

Fear was mounting in me, in spite of my efforts to push it out. I tried giving it the bum's rush, whispering to myself, Got to risk it, something's got to be done; results are measured in proportion to the risk taken. The words calmed my mind temporarily, focusing me…chasing away panic.

Jawad slowly extended his hand toward me. Holding a hookah tip, he motioned with his hand for me to take it, which I did, placing it in my mouth. The blood rose to my face as I remembered accepting a gesture, a peace pipe handed to me by my American Indian friend at a party at the University of California, Davis, where we had both been students. He had handed me the hand-carved pipe as we sat around a fire eating fish cooked in leaves. Even though I was not a smoker, I had to smoke, as a gesture of peace and unity, even if it made me dizzy.

This sweet stuff is so light, soothing and here, we are brothers, I thought silently. The warm rush began to loosen my tongue. The moment had arrived to speak. I took a deep, smoke-filled breath—without coughing, this time—and let the words flow:

"I had a vision during meditation and prayer thirty years ago in Morocco." I looked around the circle; they were all leaning forward, listening.

"I was called to Israel and Palestine to help find a peaceful solution to interfaith discord and world conflicts, and maybe find a universal religion."

A young man of about 25, with a slight stubble about his lips and bright, curious eyes, interrupted, asking "Did you find the universal religion?"

"No, I realized that creating or spreading a particular religion is not the solution and...." He interrupted "Islam is the universal religion. La ilaha illa Allah, Wa Muhammad rasul Allah" [There is one God, Allah, Muhammad is his Prophet (in Arabic)]. His voice was accompanied by other voices, whispering, "La ilaha illa Allah...."

I planned to raise the bar by saying something very controversial, but necessary, to show faithfulness to my vision of promoting an interfaith—not just a Muslim— approach to peace. I had to rally any courage lingering within me by repeating under my breath, I've come this far and taken many chances—got to continue....

I began reciting some words to Muslim, Jewish and Christian prayers: in Islam, 'La ilaha illa Allah'; in Judaism, 'Sch'ma, Yisrael, Adonai, Elohaynu Adonai Echad' [Hear, Israel, the Lord is our God, the Lord is One (in Hebrew)] and in Christianity, 'God the Father, God the Son, God the Holy Ghost.'

Their eyes clouded with confusion, but they did not draw away from me; they even seemed to lean closer to me. That surprised me, as I had expected a hostile reaction. I continued, "That's just it: the major principle is the same in Islam, Judaism and Christianity. They all teach that there is one God: 'La ilaha illa Allah.' There are other important common denominators among these three religions, such as 'Thou shall not kill', give alms to the poor, etc. And, if we share the same God, it doesn't make sense to kill in the name of God, right?"

I looked around and again I was amazed. Even though I had recited part of Sch'ma, Israel, a fundamental Jewish prayer, and part of a Christian prayer, there was no outward hostility. I knew some of them understood Hebrew and the line I recited in the Jewish prayer. The others seemed to at least feign understanding of what I had just said. In spite of that, no one rose to silence me.

Instead, Jawad stood up and turned around; his eyes shot up toward the second floor of the house, after hearing the windows slamming overhead. He motioned with his finger to anyone hiding behind the windows, as if to say "Don't worry— everything is alright." He then spoke a few incomprehensible Arabic words before sitting down and grabbing a hookah nozzle.

"What's wrong?" I asked.

Jawad smiled and then a deep chuckle emanated from him. "My family—my wife and children in their bedrooms above—heard Hebrew and English, and were afraid."

I could not fathom that fear, a fear that could be felt by merely hearing words, but my heart understood this profoundly sad reality. I tried to place myself in their shoes, that only hearing Hebrew or English words, the language of "the enemy," could evoke panic, making them want to run and hide.

I stumbled over a few words and stopped. I could not continue. I couldn't even remember where I was. I wondered if this was another symptom of jetlag, which afflicted me frequently, due to constant international travel.

Dogs barked, followed by silence among the men, as though collective thoughts were centered on the cause of the barking. Waves of sad memories engulfed me as I frantically grasped for the words that refused to come.

The tide of sadness ebbed, leaving pools of despair at the very roots of my being. I stumbled:

"I'd like...share...."

The words again refused to spill out, perhaps inhibited by my inability to pull myself out of a dark hole. I tried to organize my thoughts and push troubling thoughts aside, at least for a while. I had to persist: "Four years ago, I...I...I finally made it to Israel," I closed my eyes, continuing, "where I have been involved in organizing—and participating in—interfaith events there and in Palestine, especially in a kibbutz named Hukuk in northern Israel, near the Sea of Galilee."

The words started to flow again; I opened my eyes. "During the events, people of different religions come together and talk. We even meditate but we don't really pray together; each person's religion, rituals and prayers...respected by all. At each meeting Jews, Muslims, Christians, Cabbalists, Sufis and Druze attend, mainly from Israel, some from the US; however, the Palestinians invited to join us can no longer get through the checkpoints."

Many faces contorted into frowns, probably upon hearing the word "checkpoints."

"So that's why I'm here: to organize interfaith events in Palestine; to find an interfaith solution to the conflict by taking religion out of it; to involve the Palestinians and to invite the press to join us. My vision predicted a durable peace in Palestine, but warned that people—especially outside of Palestine—need to do the walk as well as the talk and too many people are just talking and talking, including French and American politicians, doing nothing to work towards a durable peace. A lot of profiling, counting on Palestinians and Israelis to find the solutions themselves, with help from people coming from the outside, like me."

Jawad interrupted, "I have no more hope. Since our grandparents were forced to leave their lands around Haifa, we have lived, until recently, in Palestinian refugee camps. We were able to get jobs and pull ourselves out of the ghetto and build our own houses; otherwise we'd still be living there, with no hope, with nothing to do and barely surviving...."

I interrupted, "I feel your suffering is beyond words."

Jawad nodded. I stopped because my words were muted by tremors of excitement, as I realized that somehow I was starting to connect with him.

The impossible seemed almost possible. The words kept coming: "To help find a durable peace in Israel and Palestine; that's why I'm here today, why I've come to Jenin, the heart of the conflict."

The dogs were barking somewhere again, as the furious puffing of the hookahs churned the water, filling the air with a sweet fragrance. The continuous barking and the sound of the hookahs seemed to warn me; terror shot through me, and the thought that I should pull back. Again, I had to fight back—again and then again. Courage... courage, I thought silently.

Say it, say it...they need to know. You've come this far...."And about the Israelis...."

I felt a loud buzzing through me, as if warning me that the subject was extremely sensitive and what I had to say could enrage the group, alienate them from me forever. But I knew I had to say it; otherwise, my being there just to tell them what they wanted to hear would be a lie. "My Israeli brothers and sisters have suffered, too, for hundreds of years in the Holy Land. I know an Israeli Rabbi who lost over a hundred friends and family members during the 2nd Intifada. Most Israelis sincerely want peace. But politicians and religious leaders often get in the way."

Their eyes still raked over me but no one interrupted, so I continued: "Because of this, I've come to work with the people, with individuals like you, directly, and with Israelis. That's the key to finding a durable peaceful, non-violent solution, and it will happen. It must happen—soon. I've been told there are at least sixty groups in Israel fighting, including many Jews, dedicated to liberating Palestine and freeing Israel from this terrible bondage." I looked up and eight pairs of eyes widened in disbelief, as if to collectively say "Jews? Fighting for us?"

A man with a reddish-brown tuft of hair in the middle of his scalp spoke for the first time: "They want war, not peace; they are making money on the occupation."

I sighed within, thinking Now I've lost them; it's over. "But many do love you and want peace, and like the extremist groups in Ireland, even extremist Jews and Palestinians are sick and tired of the needless spilling of innocent blood—the blood of children—and are now willing to listen, and to start ending the occupation."

The same man smiled sardonically, while light-brown eyes fixed on me, in disbelief. They seemed to be saying I was just another naive idiot, a mere American tourist, only lacking the ever-present camera, splashy shirt and Bermuda shorts.

My chest heaved. I felt nothing inside. I was drained. The only thing left was the little voice inside telling me, You've got to go for broke. It's too late, now. Then the argument, Stop, you can't go on. Finally, I heard, Just say it; say it because you believe it. Face the fear, head on...your worst enemy. Fight it, fight it....

Somehow the words came back again, and suddenly, I was no longer worried about tomorrow. I said, with all the passion I felt, "I love everybody and I want peace! I believe God wants peace and I'm just a conduit, nothing else. I'm acting on a vision I had thirty years ago and I want to make it happen—you can count on me to do the walk. I'm sick of the talk! Bear with me; you've got to believe me. I'm not here as a tourist...believe me."

I gave it all I could. I was sure that if I looked up, I'd see the hate that I had seen in the driver's eyes that morning in Arraba. After a minute went by, I finally looked up and instead of looking into treacherous, hateful eyes, I saw them sparkling with curious interest, reflecting the image of the lone bulb handing overhead. For some reason they seemed to believe or wanted to believe me.

The taxi driver who had driven us to the meeting interjected, "But how do you do it? Many people have come and gone in Palestine, promising many things, but do nothing. Still, there is occupation, walls, checkpoints—our people can't breathe!" His voice trembled with emotion and then despair, as he added softly, "Nobody cares about us."

His words spurred me on: "One thing is for sure: something new is happening. I led a meditation session of an interfaith peace group of a hundred people in the Hukuk Kibbutz a few months ago; afterwards, we broke into groups of ten people. At the end of the day, all the groups reported back to the main group that something new was happening, something real, and that permanent peace was around the corner. But no one could describe exactly what was happening. There was a strong wind blowing over the Sea of Galilee, which echoed, 'Peace is near, brothers and Sisters.'"

"But only if we roll up our sleeves and do it. It's God's will, I feel it. I don't intend to lead one event, like a peace march, and then stop, return to the Champs Elysées in Paris, sit contentedly drinking a cappuccino in a corner café and say to myself, 'Well, I've made my contribution to the Middle East. I've done my Middle East thing," then puff on a cigar and say, "That's that. What's next?"

I stopped and looked around. Weary eyes were still on me; the men were waiting, waiting for something to happen, maybe for a miracle....

"I plan to organize more events with Palestinians and Israelis, invite the press to come visit Palestine and Israel and write articles revealing the truth, that close cooperation is greatly needed between Israelis and Palestinians working together to pressure the Israeli government to withdraw from the settlements and end the occupation."

I looked around again. Taysir passed around a tray full of glasses containing fruit juice; everyone took one. The silence throbbed with an increasing tenseness.

I leaned towards the taxi driver and asked him, "Did I answer your question?" He did not seem convinced, his brow furrowing the gray dust on his forehead.

I turned to Jawad, who, as apparent spokesman for the group, nodded, saying "Insha' Allah. (God willing) I feel you're sincere and I wish you all the success. Our people have suffered long enough. Maybe there is hope...if you do something from the heart. Peace here means world peace. The Israelis are our brothers, even spiritual brothers. There is no reason...."

He didn't finish; bending forward, his lips closed over a hookah nozzle and his words became the smoke he exhaled. I couldn't help noticing that in spite of perhaps losing many people dear to him, he had not lost faith; he was still capable of forgiving.

I silently said a prayer: God forgive me for giving up. Help us...please give us strength to overcome the hate and embrace each other, forever. It is our only hope and our destiny. My vision, my vision...can't be a lie, can't be a selfish dream, designed to only help me forget my own pain, the hurting from past loves, the birth of a stillborn child, suffering...I can't believe that's all there is behind it. If I were completely insane, God, at least let my vision be true. Amen.

But hadn't Jawad said the word "hope" and hadn't he been the first to say all was "hopeless"? I wanted to help them see hope. My thoughts were interrupted when they all seemed to be talking at the same time, some gesticulating in my direction and others amongst themselves.

I asked Taysir what they were saying, and he replied, "Their hopes are with you, my friend, and they would like to know how they can help."

I could have fallen out of my chair. Wow! They're with me, they're with me, they're with me! I thought to myself, in amazement.

My voice cracked with emotion. "For now, I'm visiting certain West Bank cities, learning from Palestinians about a plan of action. When I return to Ramallah and eventually to Jerusalem, after discussing it with Jewish friends, I'll draft it and send it to you for your comments and corrections."

But the momentum for building a strong connection between the men and me was suddenly interrupted when a round-faced man with small, flinty eyes stood up across the patio and directly challenged me: "But, who are you working for?"

Don't go to Jenin, don't go to Jenin...echoed in my head.

I had anticipated the question but couldn't remember the answer I had rehearsed. I looked him directly in the eyes, without blinking, and wondered whether I should say what I truly believed. Could I risk being thought a madman or a pretentious westerner, with all the answers?

"I'm working for Allah; I have no other boss. With Him, let's work together and make peace happen."

More thoughts raced through me, now that I had let it all out. Would I lose them, now? Maybe they would think I was just another blasphemous fool, an arrogant would-be mystic or someone who deemed himself superior to others.

The only movement was nodding heads, the only sound, the gurgling of the hookahs. An older man with a long, stringy gray beard flowing over a black shirt handed me a hookah nozzle. All eyes were on me, again. Perhaps they wondered whether smoke would flow from my lips or would they emit lies. After a short cough, I held the cherry-flavored smoke in my mouth. It rolled off my tongue and mixed with the smoke emitted from the others; the blue haze was like a visible bond.

One man with dark, blood-shot eyes asked me how I felt after talking with them.

I surprised myself by spontaneously answering, "I won't feel good until Palestine is free. Both Israel and Palestine are imprisoned by the conflict. The Israelis are held captive by their profound paranoia and fear of attacks, largely brought on by themselves."

He smiled and nodded, looking around the circle for approval of my words. I don't know whether it was the smoke or the ambiance or the need to let it all out that loosened my tongue....

"For example, after arriving in the Holy Land, I stayed with Jewish friends in Jaffa, near the big furniture souk. I jogged through the souk to the beach which helps me get a jumpstart on my day of organizing interfaith groups and meeting people working in the peace process. My jogging outfit includes a heavy green and black jacket to help me sweat. But when jogging on the beach, I don't fit in with the "beachgoers" since I'm not wearing a wet bathing suit, not throwing a frisbee or playing in the sand like them."

I looked up and all eyes were following every word. I continued, "When they look up from their play to watch me jog by, their eyes reflect intense fear and they draw away from me. I guess they think I'm carrying a bomb under my jacket."

"What are you getting at?" Jawad asked aggressively, his hand grasping his chin. "I believe that this tremendous fear that seems to well up inside them is inspired by guilt from their government's actions in Palestine, even if they are in denial and even try to justify the occupation of Palestine. But their hearts don't lie as they are constantly afraid of new attacks. That is their prison. They need to be freed, as well."

"Are you referring only to the Jews and their guilt feelings about their soldiers' activities in Jenin?" Jawad asked.

"Not just Jenin. Also due to a settlement of about 500 Jews along with many Israeli soldiers stationed there to protect them, found in the middle of Hebron, a city of about 120,000 Palestinians, and the tension that creates. As such, many Israelis cannot visit one of their holiest sites, the tomb of Abraham,[68] shared by a mosque and a synagogue. That is what I call a self-imposed prison."

In spite of some grumbling in the group, most smiled and nodded. At that point, I think they accepted me and believed in the vision, as I did. I'm sure these ex-prisoners of war had their visions. In spite of all their suffering, I was convinced that they still had hope.

Then, suddenly, Jawad threw back his head and cried, "Ahlan wasahlan!" (Welcome) and they all chorused "Ahlan wa-sahlan!" putting down their hookah nozzles as eight sets of lips formed wide grins.

They pointed towards me, to their neighbors, then back to me. I could not help but return their smiles.

My lips quivered, while responding to the warm voices,

"Ahlan bik!" (Welcome to you, too.)

Apprehension of what I would find in the Jenin Refugee Camp had welled up in me long before arriving in this small, obscure Palestinian village, but for the first time, it began to ease. The hot tension seemed to drain upwards and out the top of my skull into the night air, with the words, "Ahlan wa-sahlan." And in spite of the adrenaline pumping through me while sitting among them, a heavy blanket of fatigue began to envelope me in the hookah smoke. A nozzle was passed to me and I puffed on it as my eyes met the owner of the hand; our smiles widened.

I turned to Taysir next to me, who must have intuited there was something I was not ready to accept—his head nodded in the direction of the taxi. A stream of Arabic flowed between him and Jawad. The latter turned to me and, speaking English, invited me to stay with them that night.

"I will teach you more about our people and our suffering," he promised.

My eyes turned to Taysir, again, who saw I was tired and answered for me, in Arabic. "I told them you come back tomorrow, but you sleep Arraba tonight."

My qualms eased and flowed out of me, with the hookah smoke. I did welcome the break. I don't think I could have stayed there that night as I needed a respite, to recuperate from this incredibly emotional meeting and catharsis. Even though I

---

68 The tomb of the prophet Abraham, as well as that of Isaac, Jacob, Sarah, Rebekah and Leah.

didn't like Taysir making decisions for me, I had to admit he was right. I needed to sequester myself away for a night of prayer, meditation and much-needed sleep. So it was decided I would return to Arraba that night and reconnect with Jawad, his friends and family the next day.

Everyone stood up at the same time. We shook hands, some stooping over so they could hold onto the Hookah nozzle with the other hand. As the taxi pulled out, I was warmed by the number of friendly hands waving at us.

Distancing ourselves from the late-night shadows of the village, I knew the events of that evening would become one of the cornerstones of instilling hope in the hearts of all who despaired, of bridging the vision of peace and brotherhood with the reality. I thanked God I had experienced this, that in this place of so much suffering, after sharing a couple of hours with several long-term, former prisoners of the state of Israel, hope shone in their eyes. My 30 year-old-vision was not an illusion—it was real.

Chapter 43: Jihad

That night, we returned to Arraba. Amoudi met me at the door of the two-story farm house. I hugged him and shook Taysir's hand. He led me into the living room, the place his family and I had shared a meal during my last visit. This was now my bedroom. They wished me good night and I rolled out my sleeping bag on a huge, high-backed couch, typical for Arab households.

The next day after breakfast, Taysir suggested, instead of going back to the refugee camp, that a relaxing walk would be perfect after yesterday's ordeal and my long ride from Ramallah before that.

He and Amoudi led me back toward the front door. After passing through it, instead of stepping down the stairs toward the front yard where we had come in yesterday, we walked upwards and upwards until we arrived at a small alcove; the sky peered through a half-opened door at the end. Taysir pushed and it creaked open; sunlight poured through a crack in the door. It seemed like it was an opening into someone's secret hideaway. We walked onto the roof past an old green sofa, which sat in one corner—the stuffing was seeping from its tears. Next to the sofa were end tables with plastic coffee cups, remnants of dried coffee caked in the bottoms. It looked like the place had been used as a clandestine meeting area or a place for a family hideaway, where members of the family could relax on warm summer nights while looking at the stars.

At the end of the roof were stairs leading down, almost dropping into nowhere. Taysir started walking down, but I hesitated following him because I didn't see where they were leading. Amoudi smiled and held my hand, leading me down the stairs that seemed to drop off in the middle. He was about nine years old, and the shining eyes showed me he was active, a little mischievous...very alive!

After touching ground, Taysir led us on a circuitous route, around and through archways and small buildings. We passed several workmen with long beards, some sitting on ladders, a few standing next to a building while others were hammering. Two of them seemed to be examining the construction.

Taysir led us around another building, then up stone steps until we were standing on the roof of a different building and looking down. Several fold-up chairs were strewn over the roof-top which appeared to be a meeting area. Looming in front was a bold minaret attached to a rectangular mosque of white stones. Below was the door

228

opening into the mosque and if we crouched, we could barely see the carpets laid down for worshippers. Both sides of the door were adorned with long, colored fabric draped along the sides. I had never seen long pieces of fabric next to a mosque door so I asked Taysir what they were. He responded, "They flags: one is for 'Islamic Jihad,' and the other for 'Al-Aqsa Martyrs' Brigade.'"

I was appalled; as my legs crumpled, I quickly slid down on one of the fold-up chairs to keep from falling over. I had heard that both "Islamic Jihad" and "Al-Aqsa Martyrs' Brigade" were involved in many of the attacks against Israeli soldiers, settlers and even suicide bombings.[69] It was unsettling that the flags of these militant groups would be displayed at a place of worship.

I would have trembled to the core if I had known that soon I would confront the head of the Jenin Al-Aqsa Martyrs' Brigade.

---

69 The "Islamic Jihad" is a militant Palestinian network of cells which reflects the non- secular Jihadist ideological stance, including the idea that only armed confrontation can resolve the Arab-Israeli conflict. It has grown closer to Hamas over the past few years. Because of its in-volvement in a series of attacks, including suicide bombings mainly against Israeli soldiers and settlers, it has succeeded in winning some popular support in Palestine. The "Al-Aqsa Martyrs' Brigade," a largely secular militant Palestinian group, also consists of a network of cells that have carried out the same type of attacks. It is associated with the Fatah organization: "Who Are the Islamic jihad?" BBC news. 9 June 2003. <http://news.bbc.co.uk/2/hi/1658443.stm>. "Profile: Al-Aqsa Martyr's Brigades." BBC news. 1 July 2003. <http://news.bbc.co.uk/2/hi/ middle_east/1760492.stm>.

Chapter 44: Relief International

The next day, Taysir walked down with me to a shuttle bus which stopped in front of the house. It took me back to the Jenin refugee camp where I would meet Abdullah's friend, Rafi, who I had called earlier from the farm house. A stocky man with olive skin and red cheeks opened the shuttle door as soon as it stopped. It was Rafi. His English was very rough but I was able to understand that he had moved from the refugee camp into a house that he shared with his brothers.

He told me that he had arranged an appointment with a humanitarian organization that would help me with my peace projects. We walked a couple of blocks and he dropped me off in front of an aging white building, its corner posts crumbling and the paint peeling. A small overhead sign read, "Relief International," with several Arabic words underneath.

I walked forward and saw arrows pointing up a stairway. A sign read RI, 3rd Floor. I walked up the stairs and through an open door on the third floor into a reception room. There was a typically high-backed sofa in one corner and chairs placed around an end table in the other. I headed for the sofa.

People were using the room as a thoroughfare as a constant flow of people, especially adolescents, walked in a door on one side of the room and out the door on the far side. Kids entered with natural smiles, so wide they crinkled their little brown noses. Some wore tight jeans and tee shirts, others keffiyehs, skull caps or no hats; the girls almost all wore different colored hijabs. Boys had typically short, black hair, cropped on the sides and allowed to grow a half an inch on top; the top hairs were often slicked down with hair oil. Then a young, stocky boy entered the room smiling, a black and white keffiyeh flung over his shoulders; his dark, slender hand beckoned me to follow him, as if he knew who I was:

"Dr. Romano, this way please."

I got up and followed him; I could hear the patter of shoes as the boy led the way. We entered a large office space. A dark-skinned man with full cheeks smiled, standing in front of a large desk piled with papers, pamphlets, books and other office paraphernalia. He came closer, his brown eyes twinkling. His swarthy face wore an expression of pride, perhaps in the beauty of his Palestinian heritage. His dark, full eyebrows formed ledges over his dark, moon eyes and his face was crowned by shiny, black hair, with the typical trim at the sides. His entire being was the epitome of the dark, alluring Mediterranean male. His smile, in spite of his stunning physique, was modest as the corners of his mouth turned up like a school boy's, mirroring a blend of childish curiosity and even perhaps naivety! But such a countenance displayed openness and sensitivity as he reached out to shake my hand. There was no doubt in my mind that we would work well together.

I explained my intentions to him as he listened patiently. He agreed to help me. I first asked him to translate from English to Arabic the following blurb that I was going to hand out during the dialogue/marches:

INTERFAITH PEACE MARCH

You are welcome to participate in The Interfaith Peace March on [Date]. The group will set out at [Time and Address of event].

The people in the Holy Land, Muslims, Jews and Christians alike, are enshrouded by deep suffering, terrible restrictions on freedoms, limitation of circulation, restricted access, unfair confiscation of land, etc. Whenever that happenss in the World, we all suffer because I truly believe, my friends, we are all connected.

When they are free (of suffering, etc.), only then can we be free! It's time we all do something about it, in an effective, non-violent way.

Let this march be a precursor to freedom through love and understanding by bringing all people together, as brothers and sisters and as children of the creator, showing the world that all people want peace in Israel and Palestine.

—Dr. Frank Romano[70]

He worked quickly on his computer translating it into Arabic and handed me a printed copy. He then called someone on his phone, briefly speaking in Arabic. Standing up, he told me I was to meet with several volunteers who could help me. He led me into a large room, with benches lined up in front of a solitary chair. He motioned me to the chair and I walked over and sat down. In a couple of minutes, several young adolescents and girls with hijabs filed in and sat on the bench. After I made a short presentation of my intentions and a short question and answer period, they agreed to help with the freedom dialogue/march.

One of the interns, Nasser, volunteered to be my interpreter during the remainder of my visit to Jenin and stayed with me the entire day to help me during my visits to other organizations; the next one was scheduled for the famous Freedom Theater, located in the middle of the refugee camp. It was run by Juliano Mer-Khamis, a former Israeli actor, whose mother, Arna Mer-Khamis, is Jewish, and his father, Saliva Mer-Khamis, an Arab Christian. They are all Israeli citizens. Juliano considered himself 100% Jewish and 100% Palestinian.

Naseem had called ahead of time and made an appointment for us to see the director, Juliano himself, a prince of peace.[71]

---

70 A copy of the entire flier is held by author.

71 "Kessler, Oren & Abu Toameh, Khaled. "Actor Juliano Mer-Khamis was gunned down and killed in Jenin," The Jerusalem Post. 4 April 2011. <http://www.jpost.com/NationalNews/Article.aspx?id=215116>.

Chapter 45: Juliano Mer-Khamis

It was shocking and strangely symbolic that after about two hours into the writing of this chapter about Juliano Mer-Khamis, about five years later, I took a break and then accessed the news on my computer. A news release flashed across the screen announcing the murder of a peace activist in Jenin. I held my breath as I clicked on it. My searing scream echoed off the walls of my isolated room in the outskirts of Paris, as I read the shocking and depressing blurb about my friend:

"Juliano Mer-Khamis was brutally murdered by masked gunmen."

He was murdered near the place where I had interviewed[72] him in 2006, in the Jenin refugee camp in the West Bank, the same year he had established the "Freedom Theater" there. Naseem had brought me to the refugee camp after my visit with Relief international. I was searching for assistance, in particular, suggestions on how to plan and carry out my envisaged interfaith marches and dialogues. Juliano was a peace activist, a former actor and director of the "Freedom Theater," a children's theatre in the middle of the refugee camp. It was a continuation and an enhancement of his mother's dreams.

The idea originated with his mother: Arna Mer-Khamis' project was called "Care and Learning," implemented for children in the Jenin Refugee Camp, during the First Intifada. Her goal was to provide a theatre through which children could express their fears, depression and traumas during that violent occupation. It was a way for the children to sublimate their hate and aggression, give them a chance to express themselves, live the childhood that the constant battles had robbed from them and give them a reason to live other than for revenge, for killing, for becoming suicide bombers. It was a place where children could seek refuge from the fierce fighting and loss of life around them. As a part of that original project, the Stone Theater was built, but was destroyed by Israeli soldiers during the invasion of the camp in 2002.

Juliano directed and produced a film called "Arna's Children-Children of Palestine," about his mother's incredible work and about the lives of the actors; most of them died during the battle for Jenin.

---

72 There must be a reason why Juliano's murder happened at the exact moment I was writing about him in this memoir. But what? Perhaps it means I should write more about him, about the "Freedom Theater" and about his—our—struggle. May you rest in peace, Juliano, and be assured that YOUR SPIRIT is still with us and your beautiful works will never be forgotten!

One actor, Yousef, was always the joker and made everyone laugh. During the Intifada, an Israeli tank fired a shell into a school. Everyone ran, including the teachers and Yousef was the only one who went inside. He found a little girl who was bleeding on the floor and carried her to the hospital. On the way, she died in his arms. He was apparently seriously traumatized by that experience and couldn't stop talking about her. According to friends, he became hardened and no longer laughed or made jokes.[73] He, with a friend, subsequently carried out a suicide attack in Israel and was killed.[74]

Naseem and I stood in front of the theater, below a sign in Arabic. We walked down the gravely path to the entrance. A tall man, anxiously rubbing his hands, waited for us, there.

I was taken to a 2nd floor office and told to wait for a man called Juliano. The door opened and noises sifted through the hubbub of talking, rustling of paper and other office sounds, until Juliano, himself, appeared at the door. He walked to where I was standing. We shook hands; his grasp was strong. He was a tall, muscular man, with long, wavy black hair and fiery brown eyes. The bright glint in his eyes reflected a serious, unabashed, almost raw determination that I hadn't seen in anyone else. Before he said one word, I knew standing before me was a remarkable man!

"Hi. You're Frank?"

"Yes. Juliano?"

"In person, my friend. Heard you were in town to set up some dialogues, peace marches?" His English was impeccable!

"Right—trying to get ideas."

"Most people that show up here throw ideas around, and then they take off, without doing anything. Just profiling...smiles, pictures, then...nothing." His head bowed in disgust.

"That would be a waste of time for me."

"What do you mean?" he asked, as he headed for the desk in front.

Walking around it, he sat in the wooden chair, his eyes never leaving mine.

"I mean, my vision started about 30 years ago, and I've been faithful to it all these years. Finally I'm...."

"What do you mean, vision?"

I continued where I left off: "I'm carrying it out now, that is, a vision I had in Paris about being a part of the interfaith peace process, like organizing dialogues and peace marches."

"There is no effective model, nothing I can spoon feed you; you have to make it yourself."

I surmised that he was a bit jaded by beautiful people using beautiful words of intentions, but with no follow up, no acts to back them up, nothing. He seemed a bit frustrated at the indifference of visitors and their unfulfilled promises.

"I'm aware of that...."

"And the idea of peace without freedom is meaningless—so many have died.

---

73 Producer: Juliano Mer-Khamis, "Arna's Children," 6 April 2011. <http://www.youtube. com/watch?v=cQZiHgbBBcI>.

74 Ibid.

Two actors of our theatre group were killed in this place by Israeli bullets in 2002. Look at the refugee camp; almost all the buildings around us were destroyed." He continued, looking at me fiercely, trying to detect something in my eyes—maybe weakness, lack of sincerity—or maybe that I was a spy. He examined me closely, watching my every move.

"Peace marches have come and gone; everyone wants to do one and then just take off and consider it done. Waste of time! But you, you look serious…so I've decided to help you. First, you should call them 'Freedom Marches' and not the clichéd 'Peace March' as there can be no peace without freedom!"

"Thanks! That sounds right. I'll call them from now on 'Freedom Marches.'"[75]

"But do you know, do you really feel what freedom means? Freedom means the possibility to travel around your own land and not be totally stopped by a myriad of checkpoints, walls. Freedom means to cultivate your land without having to share most of your water with the nearby settlers. Freedom means you have the right to not be thrown off your land to make way for a new settlement by Israeli Jews, seeking to confiscate your property." He continued, working into a frenzy, his deep, dark voice vibrating off the walls: "And I am 100% Jewish, because my mother is Jewish. My father is an Arab and I'm 100% Palestinian, because this is my home and these are also my people; I know what I'm saying! But because I fight for freedom, some Israeli Jews call me a traitor. And I used to be a paratrooper in the Israeli army…."

He stopped; his eyes left me, fixating on the wall as if he was struck by something powerful and needed to regain his composure. He shifted his fierce gaze back to me. I recoiled a bit, then leaned forward to meet it: "I encourage girls and boys to participate in this theatre together—the equality of girls and boys—and the Islamists condemn me for that."

He sat, shaking his head as he glanced over the stacks of mail in front of him. But his thoughts were not about letters…." I have studied the awful situation in the West Bank, and I think I have insight on…."

"Oh, yeah, you just show up and you think you have insight…."

"I haven't just shown up out of the blue: this step, coming here to the Holy Land, to organize dialogues and participate in the peace process, I've been working on, praying on it for years. I'm ready to do it…now."

I looked at him with one of my own fierce looks, and he recoiled a bit, his eyes fluttering as if he had lost focus and then they were fully trained on mine, which hadn't left his, not even for a heartbeat. At that moment, I think he knew I was for real and I wasn't planning on turning back—doing a quick profile for Palestinian rights then leaving quickly in the night, like most of the "liberal peaceniks" who had come before me.

His eyes narrowed: it seemed he was trying to read me, testing me again, trying

---

75 From that moment on, I called all interfaith activity, i.e., dialogues and marches, "Freedom Marches." The above fliers were changed from "Interfaith Peace March" to "Interfaith Freedom March." After viewing the film Juliano produced, "Arna's Children— Children of Palestine," I learned that the words, "There cannot be peace without freedom" were originally the exact words of his mother; Arna Mer-Khamis. Her legacy lives on, in Juliano, and now in . . . me.

to be sure I was sincere, and not just full of "jive talk." Just then, a young adolescent came into the room; the interruption changed the direction of our conversation. When the boy left, Juliano turned to me. "I've got someone who you should talk to; he is well respected by all Palestinians and he founded this theater with me. His name is Zakaria Zubeidi."

His dark brows rose, as he waited for my response. My stern expression did not change, which surprised him.

"Haven't you heard of him?"

The tone of his voice made the question sound more like a threat, as if I wasn't supposed to know who he was. It was another test...."He is the present leader of the Al-Aqsa Martyr's Brigade in Jenin and he was a freedom fighter during the Intifada here." He gesticulated wildly in a circle to indicate in this area. "And he is still hiding from the IDF. His mother and brother were killed during an invasion of Israelis into the refugee camp. He could have been a suicide bomber—God, he had a good reason—but he instead picked up an arm and he's been fighting ever since. Israeli police and the secret service have tried to kill him four times; he has always escaped."

A tense silence followed as he sat looking at me. I didn't know what to say. A chill ran down my spine and I felt a rising panic. In the silence, curiosity and fascination with the possibility of talking to a member of a known terrorist group began to slowly sink in and tempered my growing trepidation. A slight warmth effused my body, which felt jittery as I contemplated the meeting...I never expected this!

He looked at me inscrutably, cloaking me in the veil of his intense deliberation. I thought That must have been his Arab side scrutinizing me.

And then he stood up, his decision made. "Come, he will be here any minute. Let's go to the conference room downstairs."

I emitted a raspy, meek "OK...."

I desperately hoped he didn't interpret my tremulous response as a sign of hesitation...a silent anguish unmasked by my weak reply. In fact, I wanted to take that feeble "OK" back, but it was out. A Jewish-Arab peace activist—who often receives death threats, works in the middle of the Refugee Camp in the midst of hostile forces, is followed by Islamists, watched closely by Israeli intelligence officers and spies and is under the control of the sometimes uncooperative Palestinian Police—would not understand that. I groped for my courage and confidence....

Chapter 46: Zakaria Zubeidi's Martyrs

I followed him down the steps to a room that had pictures of actors in plays and other photos. Juliano asked me to wait there and left through a side door. In a few minutes he entered again. A tall, very dark, short-haired man followed him. Juliano passed by me and went to the main door where he spoke in Arabic to someone. The dark man stretched out his hand and I took it, unabashed. He pointed to an easy chair where I was to sit; he would sit in the sofa next to me. Two young Arab adolescents brought in a tray of hot, steaming Arabic coffee, much needed to rev up energy for the interview. He brought the cup slowly to his lips, tight and decisive; above his eyebrow and below his eyes were blotches of black that I found out later were gunpowder wounds from the explosion of a bomb he had been preparing.[76] He put down his cup, his large black eyes looking into mine. He was searching. Something in his eyes seemed to move, as if reflecting terror, profound sadness and laughter, all at the same time. What his eyes had seen—what this young man had lived through during his limited time on this earth—was unfathomable, to my limited vision. I needed to learn and learn fast.

"You mind if smoke? You?" He passed me a pack of L&M cigarettes. "No, go ahead. No problem."

He lit the cigarette and placed the lighter on the end table. His eyes followed the smoke rising upwards and forming a haze below the ceiling. I wondered what he was thinking. Silence reigned in the usually boisterous refugee camp, in this room of one of the vital Palestinian art centers, offering a place for youngsters to act out their emotions, through theatre.

He looked up, silently waiting. This was a patient man, perhaps necessary for his survival during these barbarous and remorseless times....

My nerves gave out and I had to break the silence.

"What do you think about my plan to organize peace…ah…freedom arches and dialogues in your home, the West Bank?"

I cringed at his viewing me as a naïve, stupid Westerner who had never fought or anything.

---

76 "Zakaria Zubeidi: The Marked Man," The Independent. 28 May 2004. <http://www.independent.co.uk/news/ world/middle-east/zacharia-zubeidi-the-marked- man-564957.html>.

"I support any help we can get—we are desperate, we have no power, and the Israelis keep taking our land."

He slowly inhaled, deeply, contemplatively and gradually exhaled a thin line of smoke that settled in a deep, violet haze over the furniture in the room. He then continued, "Of course, I cannot physically participate in marches or dialogues.

They are still looking to capture me," and his wide grin flattened his dark eyebrows, "but so far, I've slipped away...they try many times. Al hamdu lila!" (Thanks to God) "I show you bullet wounds!"

He chuckled deeply as he proudly rolled back his sleeves and showed me several large scars on his arm, almost in a row. Then he took his shirt off; all across his back were several dark scars.

I could almost hear the violent hammering of the machine guns spraying his hiding place, the smoke rising as he pointed his AK-47 (Kalashnikov) at the Israeli soldiers, some very young ones already writhing on the ground. Some men and young boys in back of Zakaria were perhaps wounded and lying in their blood around him, crying and praying. Some would have been silent as the blood crusted at the corners of their mouths, victims of an unjust war, of the rounds fired in the sultry afternoon of the Jenin Refugee camp. Many—even kids—would be silenced forever, many survivors, homeless.

He put his shirt back on then sat down and took a long drag from his cigarette, as if it was his last, and looked around the room searching, turning in different directions like a periscope; then his eyes returned to me.

"But why do you care about us, my friend? It's a big world. You know by even talking to me you are taking a big risk. What about that?" His bold smile stretched the corners of his ebony mouth.

"I don't care about that. I do feel that we are all connected! When an injustice occurs in the world, where people are persecuted, imprisoned unfairly, as here, and where people are subjected to walls, checkpoints...all of us share that suffering. So we don't have the right to sit back and do nothing. Part of us is hurting so we have to do something...and not tomorrow. "

"But...."

I interrupted. "Especially this, the Holy Land, this is all our Holy Land, and for us to appreciate it, for peace to come, I agree with Juliano: we must be free, first."

He smiled, his large black eyes reflecting experiences that made me inwardly tremble, without knowing what they were—maybe I wouldn't want to. He nodded. I interpreted that as a sign that my story, in spite of my quavering voice, seemed credible to him.

Without warning, a door flew open and a loud drumming preceded the entrance of a man wearing a red and white keffiyeh, speaking Arabic. Zakaria nodded and stood up, carefully smashing his cigarette butt into the ashtray. "There's a famous Palestinian rap group called DAM[77] doing a concert here now. You come?"

I rose and followed him out the door into the courtyard, at the entrance to the building. He walked ahead of me and every time he passed a group of kids, their eyes

---

77 DAM means eternity in Hebrew, blood in Arabic.

lit up: they struggled, pushing aside others, to get close to him, fighting to reach out and touch his shirt and shake his hand; he was a true local hero.

"Here go in—I cannot stay!"

Zakaria looked around distrustfully then up to the sky, his worried look a flash of dark pupils against the glittering white of his eyes. Satisfied he was not being watched or followed, he turned to me, shook my hand and smiled. His strong lips tightened before he turned and walked up the incline to the street, his loose khaki jacket swaying as he moved, until he turned a corner and was out of sight.[78]

---

78 A year later, in 2007, Zakaria Zubeidi and many other members of Al-Aqsa Martyrs Brigade and other Palestinian militant groups agreed to lay down arms, cease attacks against Israel and join the Palestinian Authority in consideration for amnesty. Lebhour, Karim. "Un chef de guerre dépose les armes." (A Warlord lays down arms) RFI. 15 July 2007. <http://www.rfi.fr/actufr/articles/091/article_54084.asp>. However, representatives of the Al-Aqsa Martyrs Brigade withdrew from the amnesty agreement in August, 2007, allegedly due to the arrest by the IDF of two Palestinian men who were supposedly on the amnesty list. Helevi, Ezra. "Fatah Claims Shooting Attack Terrorists Break Amnesty Deal." Arutz Sheva. israelnationalnews.com. 23 August 2007. <http://www.israelnationalnews.com/News/News.aspx/123470>.

Chapter 47: DAM

I opened the door and the music poured out. Juliano was at the entrance and he stretched out his hand. I grabbed it; he pulled me inside and reached over to shut the door. The room was full of children and adolescents of all shapes and sizes, some chanting and some even screaming. Several girls, their white and black hijabs tied tightly around their heads, were wailing in the back.

Juliano took me by the hand and led me to the front of the mass of people, his hands wildly gesticulating while speaking Arabic. All of a sudden, several youths got up and cleared a space for me on the bench right in front of the platform, where a group of three young men were moving their hands like American rappers, but singing in Arabic. It was wild and I couldn't sit as everyone else was standing....

A group of girls in hijabs were twisting and turning and pointing their fingers to the beat of the music, articulating all the words. They all seemed to know the words and sang proudly, totally uninhibited, letting themselves completely go... something they probably would not do so freely in the streets. But here, it was OK, even encouraged, as the girls screamed and laughed, turning their hijabs left and right to the beat of the deafening music. On stage, Tamer Nafar, leader of the group, wore baggy rapper pants and a striped shirt. The other three rappers looked to Tamer to set the beat; he would then walk down off the stage and do his Arabic rap over the microphone. The crowd went wild, applauded and stood up; I did the same.

Naseem, my interpreter, smiled and applauded too. He reached over to me and started interpreting DAM's lyrics: "He was talking about our struggle, stop ignorance, ethnic cleansing knocks at the door." Here, there was no difference between men, boys, girls, women...they were all letting it out, screaming it out, a stream of molten lava hardening in bitterness, then melting again in the passionate release of pent-up emotions.[79]

Powerful words and vibes; it was also magical. A mass musical catharsis shook the place. The group got us all rolling to the music.

My interpreter was going crazy at my asking for an immediate translation for

---

[79] If you look closely enough, you'll see me at this very concert at Juliano's "Freedom Theater" in 2006. I'm the one with the glasses, wearing the blue shirt and the dark blazer: <http://www.youtube.com/watch?v=MG-bTU4axPw>. In the video, DAM is performing their song entitled "Meen Erhabe," which is phonetic Arabic translated as "Who's the Terrorist?"

every every syllable sung by the rappers. He belted it out as my ears echoed and rang: "They are singing 'of a dove trapped under a hawk's regime' and 'you will not sever me from my roots' and 'ethnic cleansing knocks on the door' and then 'the separation wall mutes her hope, like a bird that breaks out of its cage, she'll spread her wings and fly.' Then they all were singing the words, and everyone, even the little boy over there [he points to a six-year-old in the corner standing, singing, swaying to the beat] are singing and then yelling 'No Fear.' Then they do a new song singing 'you're the terrorist, you've taken everything I own while I'm living in my homeland.'"

I could thankfully see the light had not yet extinguished in this group, deep within the Jenin Refugee Camp, where vicious fighting and destruction had been experienced not so long ago…that in spite of the destruction, the walls, the checkpoints, they were dancing, singing, under the light of God.

"They will…overcome. It's unbelievable that they keep going in the face of the ruthless occupation. Such faith…." I spoke out unabashed in the middle of the concert.

The only person exhausted here was my interpreter. Then Naseem leaned over to say something to me, but I waved him away as somehow I uncannily understood the words.

This was a musical, cultural, love-magical and powerful catharsis. It stayed with me for weeks afterward. With such positive vibes in the midst of incessant suffering and despair, in the middle of the Jenin Refugee Camp where many people had recently died to protect homes, family and pride, there was still hope…hope through singing as well as acting out the pain, in this "Freedom Theater." It even survived a fire bomb attack in 2009, three years after my visit.[80]

For the next three weeks, during my tour of the West Bank and Israel, I prepared for the Interfaith "Freedom March." I then headed back to Paris, overflowing with emotions, with renewed hope for peace and spiritual unity among my brothers and sisters of the Holy Land. But how to live it, feel it, think it, share it and find a way to return…and return again.[81]

---

80 Kessler, Oren & Abu Toameh, Khaled. "Actor Juliano Mer-Khamis was gunned down and killed in Jenin," supra.

81 Storm Over Morocco, 4th Edition, supra at 348.

Chapter 48: Blind Faith?

I found a way to return two years later to Jenin to visit a homeopathic doctor named Hadad, whom I had met during my first visit. He invited me to stay at his house for a couple of days.

After dinner the second night, he invited me upstairs to take tea on the rooftop overlooking Jenin. As I sat there opposite his son and him, we looked over the magic carpet of city lights and beyond, lulled by a warm summer breeze. We drank mint tea and reflected on the true path to peace. I needed to discover the Palestinians view on the words for my flier as my friend Moshe's words echoed in my mind. After I had sent a copy of my flier for his comments, he warned me against using the word "occupation" in my fliers as it would trigger an emotional reaction of hatred of the "State of Israel." He also implied that I would compromise our friendship if I insisted on using the word.

I wanted to ask Hadad, because he was a voice of moderation, and was not a radical or an extremist, whether I should leave in the flier that the State of Israel must withdraw from the occupation. "If I don't leave the part about the occupation in the flier, will the march have much meaning for Palestinians?"

His eyes revealed a glimpse of suffering, but also a glint of patience, of understanding despite living a precarious life in this place, surrounded by Palestinian police and with the ominous shadow of Israel looming overhead. "No, it probably wouldn't make sense." The lights glistened as his daughter looked over the roofs; I thought I saw enduring hope in her gentle smile. How could it be? Were these people of blind faith?

It then was clear to me that my Jewish friends, Moshe and Benjamin, so closely intermeshed with the Holy Land peace movement, were focusing on peace through "beautiful words" and "beautiful people" dialogues, with endless hugs and promises, and keeping any talk of politics out or at a minimum. Ironically, many members of those peacenik groups were seriously engaged in politics, in profiling their causes or themselves, their businesses and NGOs (Non-Governmental Organizations), and their motives were not, I believe, always humanitarian. In any case, they seemed to think that their peace activities made them immune, for example, from face to face confrontations with the treacherous reality of the occupation in the West Bank. I knew that we would eventually distance ourselves.

At first, the night was so clear we could see the lights of Haifa, Israel, according to

Hadad. So close and yet…but now dark shadows rolled over the distant hills, a secret hand creeping into the light, bringing sad tidings of more suffering. I had to push that hand away and think about getting some rest.

I took my leave, and headed for my bedroom. The dusk of the night would hopefully shine its diffuse light into my doubting, questioning mind…to reveal viable approaches to peace. But I desperately cried inside, But what is this peace? Why here? Why now? Why me?

I stifled a wail and forced myself not to dwell on thinking I was stuck in this oversized concentration camp with these Palestinians, somehow getting by from day to day, like them. But why did I, for God's sake, feel like that, a feeling I could not get rid of?

I imagined I could never leave this place, as most Palestinians cannot leave Palestine. I craved the sensations accompanying a walk down the quay of the Seine in Paris to my favorite spot hidden beneath the trees in the Isle de St. Louis, near Camille Claudel's former artist studio. In Paris, I could speak my mind, I could freely come and go, and not worry about control labyrinths, walls…spider webs of repression trapping me in one place. Ironically, this was the exact same place where Camille's freedom was definitively uprooted from her and her artistic expression ultimately silenced. In fact, near her studio was where this vision to come to the Holy Land started thirty years ago.

Now look where that's got me! I thought. I felt a brief madness: Shaytani…was Shaytani (the devil) inside me, or trying to get inside? I silently cried, Freedom is a universal concept that cannot be totally felt unless the place is FREE. This place! Now! Why?…I don't know…but because I'm going crazy here, surrounded by a strong power holding me in, without breaking, no matter how much I push against it, wherever I go… How do the Palestinians do this, every day? I'd explode!

I jettisoned Shaytani out the window. Then I fell back on the bed and, without taking my clothes off, fell into a deep, dreamless sleep.

The next day, I was surprisingly untroubled. An epiphany had happened since I had finally begun to listen to a voice inside telling me I must go further for peace, without hesitation, without politicking. As such, I became determined that the "Freedom March," the "Freedom Dialogue," would never be gutted of all substance and never fall into the rubbish heap with all the other aborted peace movements. I surmised that throwing the Shaytani of self-doubt out had opened up passages that had been obstructed by his dark presence and now I could hear the voice of truth much clearer. At the risk of losing Moshe's friendship and maybe that of other peacenik Jews, I would call the marches "Freedom Marches" and "Freedom Dialogues," from then on as well as condemn the occupation in my fliers. The renewed vision—that of planting seeds that someday would grow, even after I was gone—had somehow appeased my misgivings.

That night, in the refuge of Hadad's house, I planned my next trip, this time to one of the oldest cities in the world: Jericho. It had, from time to time, been a center for conflict between Israeli soldiers and Palestinians. To prepare the way, I sent emails to people to announce an upcoming visit to Jericho to discuss a future freedom dialogue/ march with local peace activists.

Chapter 49: Road to Jericho

The next morning, as the echoes of the muezzin filled the air, I focused on Jericho and thought of Joshua in the Bible, hoping I would have even an ounce of his courage. I walked down the hill lined by twisted cement rubble held together by rusty metal rods, on my way to the taxi/shuttle station. As in many other towns, there was no real bus station in Jenin.

It was a central station loaded with yellow vans (shuttles) and taxis that would take passengers all over the West Bank. I arrived at a busy center, where men crowded around a small tawny van, gesticulating, shouting in Arabic. Weaving through the crowd were young boys carrying trays of coffee and packs of cigarettes for sale.

I passed cafés already filling with customers, some wearing the red and white, white and black or white keffiyehs crowned by "agals," black bands encircling the head, keeping them in place. Others were wearing signs of the western world: jeans and a T-shirt.

I began zigzagging through the crowd. I was amazed that no matter how busy the people were—talking, gesticulating, hustling, carrying plastic bags full of mint tea leaves and bread—they all found a moment to turn to me and gawk. Some smiled, some frowned as if to say, "You dare show your Western face here!" but most smiled and said, "Ahlan wa sahlan" as I passed by.

A man poked his face in front of me, his lean features highlighted by a dark, black moustache. I asked him, in my shaky Arabic, "Ana youridou taxi, service Jericho?" (I want a service taxi to Jericho?)

I was looking for a long service taxi, which was the cheapest transportation in the West Bank. It was usually a long, yellow sedan with one wide, black stripe painted across the back fender. It often held three rows of seats and had a crown- like structure on the roof, bordered by a low metal railing to hold suitcases, which were sometimes tied down by ropes.

After questioning several persons, I was finally directed to a long service taxi where several men were seated, already; a group of men were placing something in the trunk. I asked the group, "Jericho?" A pudgy man with a trimmed beard carrying a cup of coffee poked his head out from the crowd and responded, "Na'am." (Yes)

He grabbed my garment-tote bag and added it and two other items to the luggage in the trunk. Pointing ahead, he directed my attention to the back door where I entered, squeezing in between two bearded men.

Two more young men piled in, one wearing western jeans, the other a djellabah; the doors were shut. The driver, the man who had originally motioned me to the back seat, flew into his seat and the taxi started moving forward, even before the driver closed his door.

The car began weaving between other taxis, men wearing djellabahs, women dressed in hijabs, even a man in a carriage yelling something at the mule pulling him. These unusual blends of the present and the past always caused a warm feeling to flow through me; it felt like a return to Biblical times, when the prophets had walked here or nearby. I wondered if it was because I couldn't completely accept the modern world over the old, or that I was simply a dreamer, romanticizing the past and shying away from the reality of the present.

Before long, the taxi was speeding down a desolate country road, tires screeching as it careened around turns, sending stones flying over the embankments. The surrounding hills became more and more arid as the car proceeded to gain momentum. They were steep, devoid of any plants, almost like gigantic sand dunes in the middle of the desert.

The car veered to the left and in the distance, I saw an oasis of houses appearing as if they were growing out of the tops of a huge conglomeration of parched hills.

I asked the driver what it was and a mustachioed gentleman in the back seat leaned into the front seat saying, "Colony...the Jewish...."

"What do you mean a 'colony'?"

He explained that it was a colony of Jews who had built a settlement on top of the arid hills. "They always choose the choicest land, sitting above the rest, for their homes. Sometimes throw us off. Israeli soldiers do nothing."

I had heard of the settlements but not that they existed on the road to Jericho. As the road wound closer and closer to it, the large apartment structures towered increasingly over the barren valleys and comparatively small shacks of the Bedouins below. The taxi sped down the curved roads leading around one barren hill after another, distancing itself from the settlement, which became just a spec in the distance.

We passed many small, broken-down farm hovels and arrived at the foot of an immense, dry, sandy hill. Spotting a small grove off to the right, I couldn't believe my eyes: a camel was half-crouched waiting for its owner to mount it. By the time I could drag my camera out of its case, the camel was gone. From that moment on, I held the camera in my hands.

Then the unassuming, dirty sign overhead marked the entrance to Jericho...such an ignominious entrance into this Biblical city! I was visiting a group of Palestinians but had no idea where they lived. Abdullah had recommended that I visit this Nigerian-Palestinian community which had been active in interfaith peace movements. I had called a lady named Adesina from Jenin but the connection was fuzzy and all I heard at the other end was "Ahlan wa sahlan." So here I was and I had no idea who was waiting for me. "La Ilaha ilahla, Adonai Elohaynu Adonai Echad, God the Father, the Son and the Holy Ghost," I whispered under my breath.

I called the number again and, as usual, handed the phone to the taxi driver. After a short conversation, he handed back the phone, veered off into a dusty driveway and stopped.

In front of us, a speeding small European car skidded to a stop. Out popped two African men, their profound blackness contrasting with the light brown, barren hills surrounding us. One of them opened the taxi door. He held out his hand and shook mine, easing me out of the taxi. The other spoke to the driver and then went to the trunk to take out my suitcase.

Now I was in the hands of the Nigerian-Palestinian community as the small car we were in sped down the dusty, narrow road to a house looming up at the end. It was a two-story house built on the side of a hill; several black faces backlit by the scorching sun stared down at us.

They got bigger as the car careened off the sides of the road, twisting and turning, sending a long cloud of dust shooting back like rocket exhaust. We sped toward the white house with its dark-skinned occupants.

The car almost touched the corner of the house, then descended down a narrow dirt road and circled around. Two women were waiting at the front door; one was sure to be Adesina, the lady I had been calling.

The driver stopped—the ladies approached with smiles stretched across their faces and flowery robes flowing down over pointed shoes.

The man sitting on the passenger side opened his door and spoke to the ladies in a foreign tongue; it was definitely not Arabic. It sounded African but I didn't recognize its origins. What was certain was the tone was welcoming. The two women almost simultaneously turned their heads and greeted me with their broad smiles and creased foreheads.

Right away I knew the smiles were tinged by something seriously bothering them. I would soon find out that a man was murdered and I had arrived in the middle of a family feud....

Chapter 50: Black African Palestine

The men struggled with my garment-tote bag which was heavily laden with books and things I had begun collecting on my trip. As usual, I kept a small travel case and my computer with me.

I met the two ladies with warm handshakes and smiles. "Adesina...?"

The most attractive one nodded; her beautiful thick lips drew together and a dark sheen of hair flowed down over her slim body. She was gorgeous. "Haah," I sighed!

"And you're Frank...this is Dayo...."

I nodded and grabbed my bag as I watched Dayo. Her wide grin and pearl- white teeth radiated out from her pink and gold hijab. Her large frame ambled slowly as we walked together. They immediately turned and led us through the fly-repelling, beaded curtains at the entrance of the door, much like the ones I had seen in front of southern Spanish homes, when traveling in Spain years ago. A cozy living room greeted us; it was lined with comfortable high-backed sofas and easy chairs, in which two young men were already sitting. A strange atmosphere pervaded the place that I could not fathom. Something welcoming but at the same time...threatening. Something murky was hanging in the air.

I would soon find out. The ladies' tempered smiles flashed as they took their places in the chairs standing next to the sofas. I immediately thanked them for receiving me, even without having met me. The younger girl, Adesina, smiled and said, "You're welcome. You had no idea, but you came at a bad time."

Their frankness confirmed my initial suspicions that something heavy was pervading the atmosphere. My curiosity was piqued—I needed to know.

"What's going on?" I asked. "First, let's drink tea."

I sat there while the ladies stood up, went to the door and looked out across the desolate fields. They waved to another group of Africans on the porch of the house across the fields. I was left on the sofa to wonder as the suspense mounted...Adesina sat next to me, her beautiful curves and luscious smile, her black eyes entreating, beckoning me to...I decided just to drink my tea and bite my tongue at the same time. No small feat, for me!

"My friend, I have to tell you something sad, so sad! My best girlfriend's fiancé was murdered yesterday by a rival lover. We're trying to stop a war between the fiancé's family and the family of his murderer."

She sighed deeply and turned to hide her face, but the tears in the corner of the eye half-turned to me could not lie. She dabbed her eyes with a silky white handkerchief, its white fluff partially hidden in the contours of her ebony hands.

I was totally floored! I had come from the middle of a refugee camp, where some of fiercest fighting had taken place between Palestinians and the IDF, and was now in the middle of a deadly family feud. Her eyes were filled with glistening tears against the backdrop of her dark eyes.

"We were just talking about her wedding dress the other day; oh, I'd never seen her happier, and now…oh, my God!"

She buried her face in the palms of her small, black hands. She was pleading for something. An older, rather stocky lady—perhaps her mother— wrapped her arm around Adesina as she sat there wanting to cry, but not able to, perhaps due to my presence. The old lady was wearing a multi-colored dashiki, with squiggly designs running up her sleeves: the colors of red, green and black. The patterns extended down to her breasts, v shapes in red and gold, descending all the way down the long, elegant robe.

I let a long, long silence go by. She broke the spell.

"Well I guess you didn't come this far to listen to all our woes…our crying."

She muffled a nasal chuckle. Then she reached for a Kleenex which the older lady handed to her out of a tissue-covered box.

"Please," I tried to look unabashed, calm, understanding, supportive of this beautiful creature, "I'm sorry…."

She put her hand on my arm, gently relieving me: "But you will tell me about the peace march you plan for Bethlehem…."

"We can talk about it later, or another time."

"I'm afraid this is going to go on for a while. Right now, we're trying to calm the two families down, to avoid any fighting…more killing."

"You mean between the killer's and the victim's families?" Her nose wrinkled in a grimace at hearing that.

I wished with every bone in my body I could have taken that back, but it was too late. Then I begged for help to keep my mouth shut sometimes.

"I mean…."

"Yeah…that's right. A war can break out at any time between the two families." She stopped and the only thing that could be heard was the flapping of the outside door after the two young men walked out.

"I'm friends with people from both families; it just can't happen. Anyway, tell me about your…peace march." Her voice drifted off.

"Well, that's why…like I tried to explain by phone, I've come to get your support and suggestions for an Interfaith Peace March—I mean Freedom March— to take place in about a month in Bethlehem, followed by a march in Jericho." She seemed to be listening in spite of the crises revolving around her and the people outside… serving as guards?

"I just don't know what else I can do…."

"That's already a lot...." She said deliciously, calmly...honeyed words flowing from her lips.

"Really? How so? I've just begun!"

"You're coming from a foreign country to organize dialogues and march for peace. Wow! I'm going to try to be there."

She smiled an angel's smile, making me almost fall in love with her right there, in spite of everything. "And about you...you work here in Jericho? And didn't your family emigrate here from a foreign country?"

She giggled, and I loved it as the little girl in her was still peering out into this harsh world...through these harsh circumstances. "Yes you can see we're from Africa, Nigeria originally. We migrated here a couple of generations ago. But we consider that we're first, Palestinians, Nigerians second."

"Do you still have family in Nigeria? Are you still connected?"

"My immediate family left; only distant cousins remain, but we never go back there. We've kept the language that we speak amongst ourselves—and the food!"

The moist corners of her chocolate mouth convinced me that Nigerian cuisine, having nourished this specimen of sheer beauty and grace, must be incredible!

She also told me she worked as a social worker and loved her job. She shared, saving me from asking, that she was presently married to her job and no suitors were on the horizon. I don't know why I was so relieved. I surely felt that I may have found the gem I'd been looking for the last few years, since my wife had left me in Paris. I had no idea that we subliminally had just agreed to a short-term, long-distance courtship, at least in my mind. I was attracted to this unforgettable African beauty, and the beauty seemed so deep inside her. Feelings of total surprise and amazement changed into a warm anticipation. I hoped it wasn't just a hormonal reaction, as I'd been trying so hard to be led by my heart and not my hormones.

"If I go to Bethlehem," she told me, "I'll go with another lady, Hazika. She's in Jordan today but she is very active in peace marches and I'm sure she'd go with me."

"Well, if you come to Bethlehem, I could probably find a cheap hotel room for both of you and work out a deal with the owner."

She nodded and said she'd try to make it and then her eyes turned to the front door as the two young black men returned. "I'm expected in Bethlehem tomorrow, but I could stay over if you know a place I could stay."

She seemed to have anticipated my saying that. "You know," she spoke looking out the far window like she was searching for something, "I'd like to arrange housing for you but at this time, it's too complicated."

I got the message so I stood up and informed my host that I must push onto Bethlehem that night and that I was grateful for her hospitality. I added, "Could you please call me a service taxi that will take me to Bethlehem?" I asked, a bit put off, but trying to calm my nerves. I put my finger in my mouth and clamped down on it between my teeth, pleading with myself to be sensitive to her situation, her family crisis. Sweat poured down my forehead as molten waves of pure emotion oozed from my pores, compromising reason. I was sliding out of control in the middle of this desert, seeing the oasis before me...She needed no more encouragement and quickly picked up the phone to make a call. After waiting a few minutes, the phone was answered and she emitted a fluid stream of Arabic. Before hanging up, she leaned over to me and said, "The local taxi can take you to the town center that has special service taxis that will take you to Bethlehem."

I got up and her cool dark hand held me back, as she said, "Take it easy; the taxi won't be here for another thirty minutes."

I could have dropped down on my knees right there and begged to stay another day, but it was obvious her thoughts were on the family crisis and worries about the possibility of it breaking out into a full-scale battle between the two families. I was starting to come up for air. After 30 minutes I heard the familiar crunching over dry rocks and soil, warning me a car was approaching. She took my computer bag and I grabbed the rest.

She smirked, "After all this traveling, you still travel…."

I had to cut her off, "You mean I should learn to travel lightly!"

I dragged the garment-tote bag out the door and down the steps to the awaiting cab; the trunk was already flipped open. After the taxi was loaded, I gave the two-cheek French kiss goodbye—I had to and Adesina let me. I waved to Dayo, who remained in the doorway above us, as I sat in the cab and Adesina closed the door with a jolt. The older lady was nowhere to be seen. The taxi took off, spewing forth a mixture of dust and gravel, forming a cloud for a mile behind us, covering everything in a dusty haze.

Chapter 51: Christian Palestinians

The taxi took me to a town square where several yellow taxis and shuttles congregated. I paid the driver 35 shekels and got out.

I found the long, sleek yellow cab I assumed would be my service taxi to Bethlehem. I walked to the driver's side where the driver was engaged in a conversation with another man. I asked him, "Bethlehem?"

"Na'am," (yes) he replied. So I showed him my luggage and he pointed to the trunk. I put my garment-tote bag in and climbed in back with the rest.

The taxi spun through a seeming never-ending web of small streets, thoroughfares, and bumpy country roads. It felt so odd to think that two major biblical cities should be linked by such a primitive roadway system.

Hélas! I mused, What should I expect in an occupied country where much of the construction, according to Palestinians, is stifled?

Every 20 minutes or so, I asked my neighbors if we had arrived in Bethlehem. The response was always, "Up ahead" or "Insha'Allah." Nobody seemed to know exactly as I slowly became resigned to the slow, unsettling pace. We were, after all, approaching the birthplace of one of the all-time great prophets and enlightened human beings, but I did not detect any surge of emotion around me. The passengers must have traveled this road for years; and anyway, even though Jesus was important to the Muslims, he was clearly more important to the Christians.

Just as I was beginning to settle my emotions, one of my gray-bearded neighbors pointed with a bony, sun-scorched finger that Bethlehem was ahead. My heart palpitated as I strained my eyes but all I could see was a foreboding wall off in the distance and a line of Israeli soldiers to greet us at a typical checkpoint—no clarion calls, no fanfare....

I swore that I would never be indifferent to the importance of this place, no matter what I saw or what I suffered.

The car stopped and the passports were all collected by the driver. One young Israeli soldier with a helmet covered by a net approached. The driver handed him the passports, which the soldier quickly examined. He stopped at a blue passport: mine. He said something in Hebrew and the driver turned to me.

"He wants to know who is the owner of that passport."

The soldier stared for a while at the passport, looked at me, stared again at the picture and then abruptly returned the passport to the driver. Motioning the latter to drive ahead, the Israeli soldier held on to the other passports.

It was clear that an American passport was privileged. I was glad to have touched my passport again but I felt an awkward silence around me, that I was being favored over the other passengers. Something was so wrong about that but I didn't know exactly what it was. After about 20 minutes, an Israeli soldier handed the rest of the passports through the open window; twisting his lips with a petulant smirk, he raised his hand to waive us on.

As the taxi rolled toward Bethlehem, I called Mr. Abid, the name Abdullah had given me as a contact in Bethlehem. A heavily accented voice answered. The man apologized that he could not accommodate me in his home but that he would put me up in a local hotel, as his guest. He asked me to hand over my cell phone to the driver.

The driver spoke Arabic to the man and then gave me back the cell. A few minutes later, we drove up next to a foreboding gray structure, with splashes of angry graffiti. It was another Israeli-built wall, this time the Wall of Jericho, in all its looming bleakness. I paid the driver 20 shekels and he helped me drag my tote bag up the steps into the comfortable western-styled lobby. I was greeted by a very kind smile.

"Welcome to the hotel. You have been invited by Abid and you can stay as long as you want. How many days do you intend to stay?"

"I don't know, two maybe three."

"Here is your key. The room is on the 2nd floor. Tomorrow at noon, Mr. Abid will come and have a coffee with you."

I was grateful for him putting me up in the hotel as I would not be able to afford it and may have had to sleep in the streets for at least one night. Such hospitality was unheard of, especially extended by someone who had not even met me.

In a few minutes, I had laid my things on the bed and then walked to the window to look at the lights of this magical city; it was unbelievable that I was standing there. As I stood there slightly trembling, the tense and heartfelt moments in Jericho replayed in my thoughts. But something was tormenting me: maybe the attraction to the African goddess in Jericho that I had to leave.

I lay down, but couldn't sleep. So I rose about one in the morning, made my way downstairs and out the main door. The sky was dark, cloudy and looming; the isolating cover of blackness settled heavily over me, one lone star twinkling, so far away....

The prodigious wall, spreading out to my right and left, blocked my forward motion as I left the front door. The light from that lonely star seemed to cast ominous shadows over the grotesque drawings plastered over the wall, distorted faces with bulging eyes and twisted, toothless smiles. This must be the famous wall I had heard so much about, dividing Bethlehem and the surrounding areas, cloistering people, screening them away from their own lands and impeding circulation.

Then my eyes caught a huge hand drawn on the wall; in the middle of it was a large red heart, palpitating before my eyes, with five fingers. Under each finger was written a word: Buddhist, Hindu, Muslim, Jewish, Christian. My heart beat hotly, almost stopping, as my legs crumpled from the intense emotion flowing through me.

It hit me profoundly down inside, deep into the recesses of my heart, my mind, my being....

But I had had enough and needed to walk away from that wall, a vivid reminder of strife, suffering, unhealed wounds...pain.

Something strange happened that night. I walked along this huge, gray wall, a monument to the occupation of the West Bank by Israel. I followed the wall in the dark. All I could see in the distance was a shadow of a tower, imbedded in the wall. A light was inside and I imagined Israeli soldiers were watching me, with binoculars....

A man wearing a Palestinian djellabah walked by and I asked him where I could find the nativity church. He said, "Gate over there," and pointed down the road in back of him, without slowing down.

I continued walking away from the wall, trying to follow the instructions; another huge wall emerged ahead. I approached—it stretched to the left and to the right, for miles.

I saw a long pathway to the right skirting the wall and bordered by metal railings. I walked up it and halfway up the path, I saw a dark figure walking on the path going in the opposite direction. The dark figure was long and sleek and when it came level with me, its eyes met mine. In the pale light, its eyes mysteriously lit up like something was inside. It was a mule walking freely down the path away from the wall, as if it had passed through the wall, but that was impossible as above the path from where it came were turnstiles—the checkpoint—which was closed.

I felt the heat of strife flowing through me, coming from the checkpoint above, the hours of frustration endured by the Palestinians trying to get through to feed their families. And the young Israeli soldiers, stuck in their roles as guards, often sharing the Palestinian frustrations, wanting to go home, tear down the walls, end the strife and conflicts. They desired, as did the Palestinians, an end to the turmoil, hate, desperation, rash actions, and violence.

I followed the wall down the hill until it blended into the shadows below. I continued on the path which turned into another gray prison wall up ahead and stopped at a turnstile next to a type of booth, or guard tower. But it was not manned and the turnstile was closed.

I wondered what the mule was doing up here, all by itself. This was surely not the church of the nativity where Jesus was born. This was part of the wall that divides Bethlehem, so that the Christians and the Muslims live together in relative harmony and the Jews on the other side of the wall in nearby settlements and in Jerusalem, just over the hill. What would happen, I asked myself, if someone wanted to go to the other side even though the turnstile was closed and the tower wasn't manned, in the case of an emergency?

It appeared to me that no one was getting in or out, like being imprisoned in a concentration camp. I looked above and to the left and right of the turnstile and saw that carefully placed rolls of treacherous barbed wire would prevent anyone from trying to scale the turnstile or the guard tower.

It also occurred to me why the man I had crossed paths with sent me here. He probably thought I was a Jew trying to get back through the wall to the Jewish settlements or to Jerusalem and knowing all was closed, he wanted me to share the Palestinians' daily experiences of being stranded and frustrated.

Such an artificial way to divide the land! In addition, I'd heard many stories that the wall was built to protect the Israeli settlements, often at the risk of dividing Palestinian land, often preventing Palestinians from accessing their property and sometime preventing them from going to school or even going to work on the other side. And if the wall doesn't prevent them from doing those things, I heard that a fifteen minute drive to work becomes a two-, sometimes three-hour drive, each way.

I walked down the endless gray wall, the images and writings becoming more and more blurred as I hastened forward, until I decided to totally ignore them. I needed to get out of the dreaded politics of the conflict and into a spiritual frame of mine as I was headed for the Church of the Nativity.

I desperately needed to see it before I left, to pray to Jesus to help me focus on peace, love and understanding instead of the evidence of war. Another conflict, even another Intifada—perhaps even a religious war—threatened to erupt farther away and throughout the West Bank. I felt this in my veins, unless peace activists— Jews, Muslims, Christians and others—could reach out, share, and mobilize people here and in the world to unite and pressure the world powers, notably Israel and the United States, to free this country.

The words of the mainstream Jews came back to me as I trudged on and on toward the Church of the Nativity, repeating to myself that I must be true to my vision to unite people through interfaith dialogue, marches and not dwell on politics or "the occupation." My words echoed within as I flew toward the Church of Nativity, to quench my thirsty soul.

When I reached the immense structure, it was hard to fathom that the little Jesus was born there. An immense church had been built over the manger, covering it with institutional trappings. I wanted so desperately to walk into the original shelter, sit in the hay, smell its freshly cut scent, and imagine the overflowing manger as the bed for the sweet soul to rest his little head.

But oddly enough, even though I tried to visualize Jesus inside, I did not feel the presence of Jesus in this place, as I had earlier in the Galilee! The undercurrent of struggle, the myriad walls and checkpoints seemed to pull me away from profound spiritual feelings…and I wanted to feel them so badly, especially there.

I walked around the outside of the church, desperately searching for an opening. It was tightly closed. Bordering on despair, I suddenly felt the presence of Jesus, like a brother to me, and I thought They can't deprive me of visiting his birthplace, even at three in the morning. As I returned to the entrance, a short opening in the high wall of the church, a Palestinian guard approached, wearing a beret and carrying a typical wood stock AK-47.

"What want?"

"I want to get in. I have a right…."

A raspy cigarette laugh sounded in his throat. "Come tomorrow—closed."

I was incensed; I needed to feel the presence of my brother, the man of love, the one who gave so much, to recharge my batteries. I didn't realize how depleted they were getting until I gazed into the kindly eyes of the guard, who somehow understood.

"My friend, come back tomorrow."

He shifted his head to the side and held out his hand, touched my shoulder and smiled warmly, his stained teeth hidden in the blackness of the night.

I nodded repeatedly, feeling as if I was waking from a light, mystical trance although I could feel the hardness of the cement under my footsteps. The guard didn't waver but stayed with me as his kindly smile penetrated the obscure night.

I raised my hand in salute to the guard and walked away from the entrance, arriving soon at a square overlooking the church. The steeple was lit up with small pillars rising up. A golden cross crowned the steeple, its light a lantern in the dark sky. And then the awakening; I wouldn't be able to detect the spirit of Jesus anywhere in this institutionalized place, even in the structure around the simple manger that was there to cradle Jesus in the arms of Mary, under the watchful eyes of Joseph. Jesus and his spirit were in my heart, and that was more important to me than fanfare and structures.

But I wanted desperately now to feel his presence, the passion that had mounted in me as I surveyed the Sea of Galilee, not long ago. What was more important, anyway, than to instill unconditional love in our hearts and minds, to fill them so there would be no room for hate or jealousy?

Upon my return to the hotel, I passed by the front desk. The same man who had been there before motioned me to stop. He turned his back briefly and took a piece of paper that had been deposited in one of the cubby holes above the counter. He handed it to me; I thanked him and slipped it into my pocket.

In the elevator I took the note out. On it was written the following message:

"Mr. Frank, welcome to Bethlehem. Let's meet tomorrow for coffee at the hotel around 12 noon. Signed, Abid.

I sank into my bed and was asleep before the covers were pulled up over my head by some invisible force. All I know was that covers were over my head in the morning and I could have sworn I had not touched them from the moment I lowered my head and fell into a deep sleep the night before.

The next morning I arrived at the lobby about 11:45 am and was surprised to find a man conversing with a different clerk.

I introduced myself to the clerk who pointed to the man sitting in the lobby. I approached his table. He was a small, dark man wearing an impeccably-ironed short-sleeved white shirt. He was certainly my benefactor, the one who had welcomed me to Bethlehem by paying my hotel room.

I sat opposite him. His bushy mustache swept his pock-marked face. It was a kind, discerning, wrinkled face, its lines showing a road map of fighting, protecting his family, his land.

"I'm Abid. Would you like a beer?" I nodded and thanked him.

"No, no, it's great to meet you in person, Frank, you, who are making many sacrifices to help my people."

"I haven't done anything yet!"

"But you intend to and that's all that matters. Many people who were enthusiastic about peace in the West Bank have abandoned us. You know, it seems as though many people have come here from the West thinking that an easy, peaceful solution is at hand. They discover that when they came over here there would be great difficulty in bringing peace; one my one, they move on to other things; they abandon us."

The clerk served the sudsy brew in a clear glass about the size of a dinner glass at home that I used for milk or water. "I'm Christian and a chicken farmer. I have hundreds of acres of land that the wall has cut me off from. There's no way I nor my people can get to it, cultivate it or use it. It's like they stole it from me."

In his gleaming eyes, I imagined a reflection of his far-off, unkempt lands. But his lips tightened and he nodded; there was no giving up by this man. I thought to myself, This man's a fighter and probably had the means to make his fortune elsewhere. But he'd rather stay and fight with his people. We sat there contemplating each other in complete silence. I mused that this amazing chicken farmer, who had reason to lose hope, was still trying to free his country by inviting a complete stranger to meet with him—me—and paying for 2-3 days of my hotel. The spark of love for his people, his willingness to struggle on their behalf, were stamped on his determined face.

Outside, the wind shifted and I heard the outside awning slapping the sides of the hotel. My thoughts shifted to the enigmatic lonely mule walking down the path away from the Israeli checkpoint near the wall the past night; I experienced another surrealistic moment, talking to this man who, according to Abdullah, had spent at least 15 years in Israeli prisons. So much for the theory that all the fervent anti-occupation activists were Palestinian Muslims!

I asked Abid where I should visit next in Bethlehem. He suggested I visit the Ibd'aa Refugee Camp to talk to the people there. We hugged and he turned and walked out the front door.

The next morning I got a service taxi to the famous refugee camp. I paid the driver 10 shekels and he pointed to the entrance. A minute later I was walking in front of three huge, overflowing refuse bins marked UN, crawling with feral cats looking for a meal. Meat, squashed, half-eaten oranges and other items were all fermenting beneath the sizzling afternoon sun. I walked quickly, hoping the wind would not shift....

Off to the side, women in hijabs were sifting through the garbage, looking for scraps, maybe furniture? I could hardly imagine what they could salvage from this squalid heap on which masses of flies flocked for an afternoon meal. But before I could clear the bins, the putrid odor assailed my nostrils as the wind changed.

I entered a tall, narrow building with paintings of human rights activists like Martin Luther King, Nelson Mandela and others hanging on the walls and mounted the stairs. Mr. Abid had given me the name of Areej to contact about events at the refugee camp.

As soon as I pushed the door open, a young man sitting behind an open window motioned me forward. I articulated the name "Areej" and he pointed upwards, saying "Top." I headed upstairs.

I passed a collection of brightly colored paintings of activists and some quotes from radical poets encouraging the people to fight for their rights. Bob Marley's words "Get up, stand up: don't give up the fight" were plastered on the wall.

A young man hopping up the stairs, two or three at a time, saw I was fumbling along and stopped to ask me if I needed help. I said I came to see Areej. He motioned me to follow him.

At the top of the stairs we were met by another young, dark-haired man who motioned me to keep walking through the doors. I was led into a large room with tables and covered alcoves in the back—separated by brown, red and green splashes of curtains—in which people were sitting and drinking tea and coffee.

The young man told me to sit at one of the tables in front of the alcoves and Areej would be joining me soon. The recorded voice of the muezzin suddenly bellowed from the speakers in a minaret outside the open window next to my table so I couldn't hear what other words the man was telling me before he backed into a room. In a few minutes, he served me a cup of hot Arabic coffee, its grounds settling to the bottom as my lips touched the rim of the cup. The strong, vibrant coffee stirred my soul as it flowed through my body.

The TV was blaring about the recent release of Hezbollah prisoners by the Israeli government. I asked the young boy who had led me into the room what was going on.

He recounted the story of the release of prisoners on July 16th, 2008, including a long-term prisoner, Samir Kantar.[82] The story goes that on April 22, 1979, he and three others, acting on behalf of the Palestinian Liberation Front[83] arrived in the Israeli town of Nahariya in a small boat. He and the other three stormed into an apartment of a family and took a man and his four-year-old daughter to a beach nearby, as hostages and for protection. On the beach, Kantar was alleged to have shot the father in front of his child, then smashed the child's head with the rifle butt. He denied having done this and claimed that the child was killed in the crossfire between him and the Israeli police. The Israeli government portrayed him as a terrorist and child killer.

However, some Palestinians I spoke with believed it was not true and that Kantar, who was 16-years-old at the time, was framed. Some stated they did not believe he could have killed the child and believed Kantar's version. They claimed that when the Israeli soldiers discovered that the four-year-old was dead, they smashed her head with a rifle butt to make it look like she died that way, at the hands of Kantar. Upon his release, the Hezbollah treated the latter as a hero.

Whatever the truth may be, children on both sides of the wall have been killed and the ugly face of vengeance continues to froth at the mouth.

---

82 Witt, Griff & Ibrahim, Alia. "Israel Mourns, Hezbollah Exults." The Washington Post. 17 July 2008. <http://www.washingtonpost.com/wp-dyn/content/article/2008/07/16/AR2008071600282.html?sid=ST2008071600771>.

83 A militant Palestinian group considered a terrorist organization by different countries.

Chapter 52: In the Shadow of Al-Aqsa Mosque

Areej had an emergency so I set up a meeting with her during my upcoming visit to Bethlehem. I headed back to Jerusalem and walked on the other side of the wall to the main gate that links Bethlehem with Jerusalem; a complex of revolving metal doors, metal detectors, and a maze of metal corridors greeted me. It was a gauntlet that I had to get through to get to the other side and then take a shuttle bus to Jerusalem.

After about 40 minutes of waiting in lines, being screened by metal detectors and showing my passport, I got through the final metal turnstile. On the other side, below the checkpoint, a group of shuttles and buses were parked. I walked toward them.

I looked inside one shuttle of about 20 seats and saw a couple of empty ones.

Paying the driver and heading to the back, I sat next to a dark man covered by a white djellabah, with a red keffiyeh draped over his head.

"Where you from?"

"I'm American and I'm visiting people here that can help me organize interfaith dialogues." I stopped as the wrinkles on his forehead indicated he understood nothing of it. "I bring together...." and I gesticulated with my hands, "coming together, Mouslim, Yahoudiyy, Masiyiyy." (Muslims, Jews, Christians)

"Takallama...koullouhoum." (to talk, everyone).

I was met by more confusion. I then imitated someone talking by tapping my fingers together.

"Oh, yes, cuellos, cuellos." (good, good) "Where go now?"

"I'm returning to Jerusalem."

The shuttle bounced and turned as it glided through the streets of Jerusalem. When it drove by the high walls of the Old City, behind which was the Temple Mount, I felt relieved that the bus stop was near.

The man leaned over to me and gave me a piece of paper with a number and the name "Mohammad" on it. "I have friend—you call him in Jerusalem; he talk you. Tell him my name is Ala."

The bus parked in the lot designated for buses with destinations in the West Bank. We piled out; I thanked the man who smiled broadly, maybe too broadly. My hands closed over the piece of paper that seemed to burn in my palms. I confronted the usual masses of people walking the sidewalks: women wearing hijabs and an occasional female wearing a djellabah and a veil, scrupulously covered from head to toe, with only two eyes appearing above the veil.

I went to the Arab bus station for a bus that would take me to the Mount of Olives. It was so strange to me that the Israeli Arabs have their own bus station for buses to take people to the Arab districts of Jerusalem and the Israeli Jews have their bus station downtown for buses to take them to Jewish districts in Jerusalem.

I grabbed my bus at the Arab bus station. The traffic was stopped and then sluggishly moved through the roundabout as the bus wove in amongst the stalled cars. A group of Israeli soldiers had stopped a car ahead.

Upon my return to my room in the Mount of Olives, I sat down on the bed. My pocket burned with the phone number I had deposited there. But a little voice warned me that something strange was afoot.

I called the number. "Mohammad?" "Na'am...."

"Ismi Frank, ana takallama, Engelizi. I met Ala in Bethlehem who gave me your number" (My name is Frank, I speak English)

"Ok, it's alright, where you now?" "I'm in the Mount of Olives."

"We can meet tomorrow at three pm in Al-Aqsa Mosque." "Where in the mosque?"

"Just call...." and he hung up. I tried calling back but it rang and rang and no one answered.

That was strange but I was too tired to worry about it as I slid into the bed and fell immediately into a deep sleep. The voice of Ibrahim calling people to dinner at the rooming house was faint. Even though the acid in my stomach burned as the kitchen smells of rice, potatoes and meat filled the rooming house, I was too tired to eat.

Something spattering unevenly against my window woke me. I looked at the alarm which flashed three am. I had slept about nine straight hours, fortunately without interruption. I looked over and saw rain drops rapidly pelting the glass. I got up and looked out over East Jerusalem. The lights glimmered as if winking, which made me think of my rendezvous that day.

I hadn't visited the Al-Aqsa Mosque yet which was situated next to the Dome of the Rock. It was the third most sacred place in all of Islam. Yet I had heard of great conflicts revolving around that place, including the beginning of the very violent 2nd Intifada triggered by then Israeli opposition leader Ariel Sharon's provocative visit to the Temple Mount.

A voice inside me warned, Stay away, you don't know him, stay away...I mulled over every word we had exchanged during our short conversation, again. Then, I heard a voice in my head saying, It was so weird, that he wanted to meet me inside the mosque. Why not somewhere else? Was something brewing?

I had no clue about what was going on since my visit to Bethlehem; I had closed myself off from the news for a while. Anyway, I desperately needed a break from it as there was so much negative news...killings, conflict, violent Palestinian protests in the West Bank, conflict in Gaza, Israeli soldier attacks...retaliation, reaction to the retaliation and retaliation to retaliation.

The stairs descended to the anteroom and the kitchen. The wind was howling through the curtains and a couple of cats were eating something on the kitchen table. They must have been feral cats because as I entered, they fled through the open window above the sink. I walked to the electric water kettle and pushed the button.

I found fresh mint leaves in a jar and a tea bag, put them in a glass and poured hot water into it. I found some sugar in a bottle and poured some into the glass, stirring the hot water with the tea bag and mint leaves with a spoon. No one had risen yet, but I wasn't ready to see people so I ascended the steps with the hot mint tea to sip in my room.

Much later, I woke up gasping for air; my forehead was pouring sweat and my clammy hands fumbled for my cell phone. It said two pm—I had one hour to get to the Temple Mount. I quickly covered my body with a long, loose shirt, hoping it would flow over me like a robe. Being still half-asleep clouded my thinking so I went to the bathroom and splashed cold water on my face. That enabled me to wake up enough to slide my shirt over me and put on my black pants. I then hurried out the door after picking up my Qur'an.

I bolted down the stairs and ran to the Arab bus. Fortunately, upon arriving at the corner, a bus was waiting to take the passengers to Damascus Gate. I slid into a seat and looked out the window. The bus jolted forward, along with my thoughts. "This is so strange," I whispered to myself. I still hadn't decided if I would go all the way to the Temple Mount and would make a final decision when I got closer. My thoughts were still misty so I let my intuition have more time. For now, nothing seemed to register and I was just moving forward with the bus, dumbly.

The bus stopped near the post office near the Old City and let us all out. I followed the crowd and within a few minutes, was at the entrance to Damascus Gate. Trepidation besieged me as I stood in front of the souk, the crowded market, for the first time. I had breezed in and out of Jerusalem as I rode buses going to and returning from the West Bank a block above the gate; but never had I entered this place, this opening in the Old City wall which would eventually lead to the Wailing Wall, to Al-Asqa Mosque and the Dome of the Rock.

It was a collage of shops, selling everything imaginable: more keffiyehs, tourist pictures of the Al-Aqsa Mosque, mirrors, dried fruit and hijabs. The vendors seemed to hang on me as I meandered through the crowd. I didn't know where the entrance to the Mosque was so I asked one of the vendors who held up a bracelet with the colors of the Palestinian flag; when he realized I was not going to buy, he pointed down the path.

The crowd was a curious mixture of hijabs, keffiyehs, and kamilavkions (Greek Orthodox cylindrical hats), kippahs, shtreimels (fur hats), black fedoras (hats of the 40's and 50's), flat caps, bald heads, short hair, long hair, veiled women wearing black djellabahs. Every color was fanned out like the feathers of a peacock, but I was moving fast, as I imagined the steps ahead were leading me to the Temple Mount.

A man wearing a Muslim skull cap saw me carrying a Qur'an and held out his hand. I took it and he led me down a narrow passage to the left, off the main path. It was teeming with rows of Muslims talking, drinking tea, kids playing with plastic guns.

I looked up and saw a couple of Israeli policemen stopping people from going further; the man pointed to them and then approached them. He seemed to be known by them and was quickly allowed to enter.

The two policemen, wearing the traditional blue uniforms, put out their hands to stop me.

"You can't go in—not Muslim." "I believe in Islam. Let me pass."

A shorter policeman walked over to me; his eyes looked me over from feet to hair, up and down. "I don't believe…."

The man who had led me in had returned. The policeman asked him, "He Muslim?"

"Na'am." My guide tipped his white skull cap towards me. His wiry beard tangled over dark, leathery skin and beady eyes focused on me.

The police officer grabbed my shoulder and led me away from the man with the skull-cap: "Recite el Fatiha."

I couldn't believe that a Jew was requiring me to recite the main prayer of the Islamic faith. But I guess he had orders….

I felt a bit humiliated but there was no way around it; I began to recite. After I had verbalized a couple of the prayers, the policeman turned to the man with the skull-cap, who nodded.

"Ok go!"

I followed the man into a passageway. After walking up steps, The Dome of the Rock was before me. The multicolored Turkish tiles, in blues and whites, greens and golden browns adorned the upper half—inscribed in Arabic—while the lower half was white marble. It fascinated me, held me in awe.

I felt a buzzing in my pocket. It was my cell phone. I took it out and pushed the button.

"Where are you?"

"In front of the Dome of the Rock."

"Meet me inside Al-Aqsa in about 15 minutes." "Ok, but exactly…." He had hung up again.

The voice on the other end had seemed so odd. He spoke as if he knew me, yet he didn't. Then the golden dome was before me, glistening in the afternoon sun. Its high walls soared over me, a protective mantel of vibrant blue and white mosaictiles, braced by columns. Next to the Dome of the Rock, about 100 meters away, was a structure rising like a fortress: the Al-Aqsa Mosque. I walked directly to it. As I drew closer, its huge archway, white and stately, grew larger, until I was directly underneath. Several shelves were at the sides of the entrance and I placed my shoes in one of them. I was about to enter when a man wearing a long beard and a pearl- white djellabah stood in my way.

"Are you Muslim?"

I thought to myself, Here we go again, and then I couldn't stop my words: "I have to do this again! Of course I'm a believer."

"You know a prayer, 'Qul huwal-lahu-Ahad?'"

"Na'am, Qul humal-lahu-Ahad. Allahus-Samad. Lam yalid wa lam yulad wa lam yahun kufwan ahad…." ("He is Allah, the One and Only Allah, the eternal, absolute. He begat none, nor was he begotten, and there is none comparable to Him.")

"Ahlan wa sahlan, my brother," he interrupted my recitation and pointed to the door, welcoming my entry into this house of God.

I entered the Al-Aqsa Mosque which opened into a huge carpeted prayer area. Lines of immense columns alternated with huge archways, a heavenly climate of stately beauty and grandeur. This place, I had heard, held about 5,000 people. As far as I could see either way, this massive space was vacant, except for about three people way up in front.

I walked to the front where a small indentation, a petit alcove was almost hidden in the wall; this was where the Imam led the prayers and was next to the wooden stairs leading up to the pulpit, where the Iman made the sermon on Fridays. A cool breeze, a whisper from God, brought me to my knees, forcing me to sit in the middle of the carpet before the alcove. Three men were praying ahead of me.

The winds of Jehovah, Allah, cradled me, filled me with infinite energy as I sat there. I could not face the alcove as I was trying to figure out what was happening. No words, no thoughts...just being was all I could do.

So when my cell phone shook in my pocket, I was steadfast and clear in my thoughts, unhampered by the fears I had felt during the last phone conversations.

I got up and walked behind a column to separate myself from the worshippers, allowing them to continue in peaceful silence.

"I'm at the entrance of Al-Aqsa—where are you?"

"I'm inside," I replied, my voice trembling, as fear resumed its control of me. I had to shake it loose.

Mohammad's words were muffled, except for the word "coming"...then the phone went dead. I normally cursed myself for not recharging the batteries during the night, but even that had no effect as I was whisked up into the ethereal intensity of this place.

"The bearer of good tidings was upon me, and fortunately I listened to my inner soul and stayed," I faintly mumbled as I silently sat on the cool rug, waiting, waiting...I returned to my place before the alcove and bent my head down. I let my body, mind and soul go into the faith; I let my thoughts freely surge.

The faint music, like soft strums of a harp, rode in with a subtle breeze, which gently fingered and fanned the bangs of my hair. An electric surge of energy entered my body, filling me with absolute "knowing" that my vision of 30 years had led me to the right place. And more importantly, this celestial energy surge pushed out any traces of the ugly demon of fear, allowing my faith—nourished by unconditional love for my brothers and sisters of all origins—to swell.

I felt a tug on my left shoulder and turned my head to face a huge man; my heart stopped...then jump started with his warm handshake. He was wearing a dark mullah skull cap resting on the back of his head—over a short, white stubble—and a dark green, flowing djellabah with a long, green vest hanging down over his belt. A wide grin nestled within a lengthy, flowing white beard, featuring large yellow teeth, no doubt a tribute to many cups of Arabic coffee.

I stood up and walked toward him. His initial massiveness was exaggerated by the cool breeze ballooning his djellabah, as he stood waiting. He reached out his arms and we hugged like old friends. It was surreal....

"Assalym walaykum," I blurted out, barely able to speak, for some reason. The peace and distance during my meditations prevented me from rising quickly to the surface of my thoughts.

"Walaykum assalym," he responded, in a clear, soft voice, and turned toward the distant front door, motioning that I follow him by waving his hand.

I followed and thought I should let whatever happened happen; but somehow it seemed alright, that my original trepidation was a knee-jerk reaction to the unknown, mixed with prejudices based on my knowledge of the history of this sometimes fanatically contested place and its name: Al-Aqsa.

As I walked down the long corridor toward the door, following this man I had no inkling of, the name "Al-Aqsa" returned. This mosque had been the focal point of great spiritual advances—as had the nearby Dome of the Rock—where the prophet Muhammad made his ascent to speak to God with the angel, Gabriel, to pray with Moses, Abraham and Jesus. And, the second Intifada began here. I was also reminded that the Al-Aqsa Martyrs Brigade, which had been involved with planning many of the suicide bombings in Israel, derived its name from this mosque.

As I followed him out the door, I watched him grab his sandals and put them on quickly, but smoothly, like he would do in his own living room. I looked at the lines of shelves and remembered miraculously where I had put my shoes.

He walked out in the courtyard area, still not turning around, as I clumsily bent over, shoved my shoes on and hopped to the cement floor, my feet jamming against the backs of my shoes. I noticed him sitting calmly on one of the benches under a tree nearby—then he looked at me.

I remembered the words of my son, Frankie, who had advised me to take a "chill pill" sometimes, especially when I was stressed, so I took a deep breath, and calmly readjusted my feet in my shoes as I bent over and slowly tied my shoe laces; then I headed out to speak to this strange man.

He was sitting on a cement slab, his pointed Arab shoes drawn up near his torso when I arrived; his smile was wide, and welcoming. I instinctively looked in his eyes for signs of treachery or malice but all I saw were reflections of the Al-Aqsa Mosque in them.

I thanked God that I did not shy away from meeting this man; I was sure this would be a spirit-soaring moment. Thank God I had listened.

I sat down next to him.

"Why do you come here? You're American, you have no reason...."

"I had a vision...."

"What mean, vision?"

"I had an idea that I can help in this fight, this struggle to bring Jews, Muslims and Christians together...."

"You don't know anything...our struggle...."

"I know, I know, but I want to learn. With 'iman' I will understand, I will fight."
(faith)

"Come, learn, then...brother."

This marked the beginning of a strange friendship; he conducted me on a tour of the Temple Mount, notably, the Dome of the Rock.

I followed him to the door of the Dome; he took off his shoes and placed them beside the door—I did the same. Sitting next to the door, a stocky man with a brilliant white shirt, short hair and piercing black eyes leaned forward. His right hand came forward in a chopping motion as he stood up, then walked towards me. "Oh, more questions...." I muttered but the halo of the moment was still upon me and my normal exasperation was replaced by sending those thoughts into extinction, just being without expectations. I'd fortunately risen above all that....

Then Mohammad intercepted the man's approach, saying a few words in Arabic. The man sat back and smiled, his hands at his sides...it was the green light.

I followed Mohammad inside. I didn't need to thank him; if I had, I was sure it would have been perceived as an insult. The marble columns and surrounding stained glass windows shone into my soul, a cradling warmth. It was like coming home to the sparkling tinsel and ornaments on a Christmas tree, visual evidence of the love and welcome of my family.

The love that brings together all beings, a palpable rush of feelings, penetrated me. The hovering building was of marble, stone, colors, glass and multi-colored fibers in the carpet supporting my body bent in prayer, before God. Within, the Prophet Mohammad had begun his nighttime journey, soaring into the clouds; it was a place of symbolic beauty, depicting the connection between the tangible and the intangible, in the form of this opaque structure. It was alive....

As I bent forward, placing my forehead to the ground, in allegiance to Allah, Adonai Eloyahnu, God the Father, Son and Holy Ghost, I voiced, "You, my love, were there intertwined with me, my loving other, and all those I had shared intense love with, my loves, my children, my mother and with faith in love that transcend all experience...the feeling and knowing love, a priori."

It all came to a catharsis of pure spiritual love confirming that although we are essentially a mixture of gases, it's the love forces, the unconditional love spirit that links us, that transforms our physical selves into spiritual beings—beyond the physical incarnation of this love, beyond physical constraints—and links our spiritual essence to the cosmic spirit. So Mohammad's journey was just as much within himself as beyond, to the extent there is no distinction between the spiritual and the physical, the tangible and intangible in this new world order of unconditional love, only oneness with all of creation.

As such, this knowing, this truth makes all wars, all acts of destruction, all acts of violence against plants and animals an act against the self as we're all connected, like the Avatar tree: we are all one, my brothers and sisters.

As I write this, the pure emotion of unconditional love breathes through me, floods me, an irrefutable knowing of absolute truth...the only truth. It is the fulfillment of the cosmic spirit, in this place and beyond. I am one…Mohammad touched my back as I sat before a column, lost in pure, unadulterated meditation.

"Come, my friend."

He led me downstairs into an antechamber, below the main level—the exact place where Mohammad, the Prophet, ascended into Heaven.

"Follow me," he requested, and we proceeded down to the underground cavern. Several men with and without skull caps, one with a white keffiyeh, were praying.

He pointed straight ahead to the edge of a gray substance and said, "This is the rock from which Muhammad—Assalamu alaykum, wa rahmatullah (Blessings and peace of Allah be upon you)—ascended to heaven, with the angel Gabriel."

I stood there transfixed, unable to utter a sound. I fell to my knees then squatted down and began a rakat, a prayer to thank God that I had come to this place, under the tutelage of such a worthy and loving person as Muhammad, a person I had mistrusted and feared.

When I arose, he had vanished. I walked through the small cavern and couldn't find him. I climbed the stairs, looking for the dark-green djellabah, but my eyes scanned this holy, multi-colored haven without seeing him. I walked toward the door. There he was standing near the exit, smiling, smiling.

After leaving the Temple Mount, Muhammad showed me where he earned a living to feed his eleven children and two wives. We passed the Israeli guards and entered the narrow passageway. Almost directly to the left, he stopped and grabbed a black tarp covering two small tables. I approached and saw key chains with the form of the Dome of the Rock engraved on them, bracelets with Palestinian flags on them, Muslim skull caps, and a mixture of costume jewelry and other trinkets.

As he prepared his stand, two ladies in hijabs appeared and began looking at the jewelry. Words were exchanged and they left without buying anything.

I looked at my watch. It was almost five o'clock; I had promised my friend, David, who I had met for the first time in Ramallah, I would meet him at the rooming house on the Mount of Olives to discuss plans with others organizing freedom marches scheduled for Bethlehem and Jenin.

I turned to Muhammad who was busy arranging the jewelry after the women left. "Asalymu walaycum. I have to go, sadiq." (friend) We hugged.

I never saw him again. I passed by that spot many times looking for him, but he was never there and his stand was gone. But there was an enduring imprint in my memory of the exact spot where his stand had been.

After briefly meeting with David and a few others at the rooming house in the Mount of Olives, I had to return to Paris the next day to resume my work…and to prepare with David for my first dialogue/march to take place in Bethlehem.

Chapter 53: Lighting Candles in Bethlehem

The beginning of a new era took place a few months later: the first peace march. I contemplated the first freedom march dialogue that was to take place where Jesus was born, as I nervously boarded the plane for Israel.

I arrived late in Bethlehem where I met David in a Palestinian NGO for peace, "Lighting Candles." He greeted me with a wide grin and a warm hug. He explained that the electricity bill had not been paid so we'd stay there in complete darkness. He gave me a candlelight tour and then led me into the depths of the office space with a flashlight. I thought to myself of all the Palestinians he had helped—helped to survive, find jobs, even with the NGO—but he couldn't pay the electricity bill. He let me roll out my sleeping bag in one of the offices in the building. It was cold as there was no heating, either, so I slid into it without even changing my clothes and was soon deep in sleep.

The next day we visited a cultural center and watched a movie about the plight of Ethiopian Jews in Israel. David and I handed out fliers for our march, which would take place in Bethlehem in three days. At the center, we met Corey Balsam, a Jew from North America, who had written an article entitled "Challenging Zionist Indoctrination: Birthright Israel Unplugged," about the activities of a group by the name of "Birthright Unplugged."[84] Corey told me he had participated in Aliyah[85] a couple of years ago and claimed it was now more a program that furthered aggressive Zionistic views as opposed to objectively informing Jews of their culture and traditions in Israel. He spoke:

"So I really believe that Aliyah is useless and just indoctrinates instead of informs."

I responded, "But I think it's a good experience for Jews to take advantage of

---

84 Birthright Unplugged – Turning Knowledge Into Action. Director: Alwan, Dunya. 2004-2012. <http://www.birthrightunplugged.org/>.

85 Hebrew word meaning spiritual elevation. It is defined as the ingathering of exiles, immigration of Jews, and is a fundamental principle of the State of Israel and Zionism. The Law of Return is the manifestation of that principle. It grants the right of every Jew to come to Israel as an 'Oleh' (Jew immigrating) and become a citizen. Israel. Ministry of Foreign Affairs. Aliyah. 29 October 2002. <http://www.mfa.gov.il/MFA/MFAArchive/2000_2009/2002/10/Aliyah>.

their culture and I have faith they'll remain aloof from the indoctrination; they don't have to buy into it."

"If they're strong...but indoctrination can corrupt thinking and thus defeats the purpose of a Jew seeking to understand the nature of his culture in Israel."

The next day I returned to Ibd'aa, the refugee center I had visited before, while David visited friends in Jerusalem, with the understanding we'd come together in a couple of days to do the interfaith freedom march/dialogue in Bethlehem. I walked up the stairs to the last floor where I would drink coffee and meet with Areej. She had called me and said she would definitely meet me at the refugee camp, this time. As I passed the second floor I heard loud music and clapping. I stopped and opened the door.

I recognized a rap singer and member of DAM that I had seen before in the Jenin Refugee Camp. A man at the door explained that the music session was reserved for the Refugee Camp Youth and DAM was the invited guest that day. I closed the door and continued my trek upstairs until I reached the top floor. I walked through the familiar door and saw an exuberant black-haired girl in her middle twenties wildly gesticulating, almost jumping from her seat.

She was Areej. She smiled as the fingers of her left hand combed through her hair. She was a dark beauty...and I tried to keep my mind on interfaith, unconditional, universal love as opposed to exclusive love; this was going to be a challenge. She was looking at me, her lips around the end of a cigarette.

"Kayfa halak?" (How are you?) she asked, her dark eyes penetrating me. "Alhamdu lil-laah. Wa anta?" (Praise be to God. And you?) "Not so good. I tried to return to the US to lead an interfaith group, and they won't let me back in the country."

Here we go, I thought. "Why?"

She looked at me, as her lips wrinkled in a semi-smirk; her eyes told me the rest. I could only shake my head in solidarity and hold out my hand to her. She held mine, as if it were the last thing she could do or the last thing she would do. All of sudden, the room filled with people from downstairs. Areej stood up and began helping move the chairs. I started to stand up and she quickly came to me and put her hands on my shoulders, pressing them gently downward.

"You're our guest."

I sat down. Her eyes, haggard and wretched as she seemed to force some memory away, reached mine, and then she froze, looking into something familiar. For an instant she seemed to capture my eyes, probably confused, certainly weary, but not judgmental. Through only eye contact, she seemed to connect directly to my pain, my struggles, my passion, not taking them off mine—without fear that what she saw would adversely affect her during this strange moment of silence. Time froze for an instant.

She unveiled her womanly energy and multi-tasking capabilities to the maximum as she arranged the tables into one long line, set them and opened the windows. She, along with a group of Palestinian boys and girls, some wearing hijabs, worked together to serve plates of hummus and round bread, the hors d'oeuvres.

266

The energy synthesized into an example of people giving, living their faith and love, giving rise to thoughts that there is nothing that can defeat faith, love and caring; walls and checkpoints can asphyxiate the people, guns can maim and kill, jails can imprison, but nothing...absolutely nothing...can take their faith, their love, their spirit or their soul away, unless they let it. The soul of these people resonated resilience and someday, I knew they would overcome—with pride and dignity—the ignominious walls and checkpoints...with faith, with 'iman.' (faith)

There was no doubt!

The long tables were soon filled with people who were served rice and chicken. I sat at a table next to theirs and ate with Areej, in silence. Then I saw a member of DAM sit down. I went to him and strangely, he somehow remembered me standing in front of the crowd in Jenin during the performance, even though he had been madly singing and playing. It was a strange reunion, so strange that I asked him if he had been following me, from Jenin to Bethlehem. He smiled,

"Maybe...."

Chapter 54: To Rachel's Tomb

The next day we engaged in a march/dialogue in Bethlehem. David and I were to start at the Church of the Nativity and end at Rachel's Tomb.[86] The idea was that we would start at a place sacred to Christians and Muslims and end at a place sacred to Jews (as well as Muslims and Christians).[87] We were joined by Jeff, a young man and peace activist, who we had met at the rooming house at the Mount of Olives and was now living in the West Bank.

While we were walking, Jeff shared his fears about marching for peace in the West Bank. He told us that the last time he had marched for peace, the leaders were arrested and some were imprisoned. I told him I recently had a meeting with Omar Al Sahaf, who was also previously imprisoned by the Israelis and presently was a high civil servant employed by the Palestinian government. I also told him that Mr. Al Sahaf gave me his phone number and informed me that if anytime I had a problem with the Palestinian police during a peace march, to have them call him. Jeff shrugged, his doubts only partially assuaged; but he stayed with us.

I thought to myself, Well, we'll find out soon enough!

Then David showed me a book written by his Jewish friend, Levi, who would join us later with his wife. He handed it to me asking me to skim it as Levi would ask me about it and I should try to humor him with a basic understanding of it. I skimmed the book which included meditations, prayers and a general discussion of spirituality and tolerance. I was confused as to why David asked me to do that; soon I would discover why!

We grouped together, and started handing out fliers to people coming out of the Church of the Nativity as well as those sitting in the square next to the church.

---

86 Rachel, the wife of Jacob, was traveling with him when she died giving birth to Benjamin (Genesis 35: 19-20). Jacob buried her at the spot called "Rachel's Tomb." It's considered the 3rd holiest site in Judaism. Some Muslims claim that it was the site of a mosque and also claim that it is part of the Palestinian Territories. Under the Oslo accords of 1995, the State of Israel would maintain control over it and in 2005, incorporated it within the West Bank Wall on the Jerusalem side, thus excluding West Bank Palestinian Authority residents. After protests by local Arab residents, UNESCO in 2010 declared that Rachel's Tomb is located within the Palestinian Territories and would be considered a World Heritage Site.

87 "Rachel's Tomb." BibleStudyTools.com. 2012. <http://www.biblestudytools.com/encyclopedias/isbe/rachels-tomb.html>.

Then all of a sudden, the muezzin blared out: "Allahu Akbar, Allllllllllaaaaaaaaaaaaahu Akbar," from the minaret across the square.

After the call to prayer, the church bells rang, calling the faithful to mass. I thought to myself that the sounds were a manifestation of our message: interfaith acceptance, understanding and sharing. Now all we needed was a synagogue nearby.

David and I rolled out our sign which read, "Freedom March", in Arabic, Hebrew and English. We held it high. As soon as we had done that, a lean, mustachioed member of the Palestinian police was on me, as I led the group. He spoke to me first in Arabic; getting no response, he spoke in broken English: "What you?"

"I'm Frank, an American, and we march for peace, for one God, 'La Ilaha Ilanla.'"

He stepped back. I could feel Jeff's warm breath on my neck as he shrank behind me.

"How know my religion?"

"I study Islam—I'm a believer!"

Of course, I didn't lie as I did believe in Islam; he didn't need to know, however, that I believed in Judaism and Christianity as well!

I continued walking with David and the others behind us. "Halt, you no authorized!"

"Yes I am; an important civil servant with the Fatah Government, Omar Al Sahaf, has authorized it!"

He looked at me unbelievingly, furrows wrinkling his forehead.

"Here; call him!" I handed him Omar's card with his cell number on it.

He reached in his pocket and pulled out a cell phone and called the number, his brown spindly, hands moving rapidly over the dials.

I heard one word, "Marhaba...." and the rest I couldn't understand. Then he turned away, speaking a stream of incomprehensible Arabic. I realized that sooner or later I would have to test whether Omar would decide to help me or imprison me; but the suspense was killing me!

"Na'am...." he gulped, then he hung up.

He turned, his face exuding the desire to make up for stopping us.

"You are clear, go...."

It worked! I howled inside.

He smiled, and pointed to the road up a ways, where we had originally been headed. Then he turned and walked up the road toward the Church of the Nativity.

David had since walked ahead and was talking to a blond lady. As I approached, his red cheeks shone and he smiled broadly.

"This is Dominique; she will join us. I met her at the cultural center." He gently placed his hand on her back.

The Nordic-looking lady shook my hands. Her long, blond hair fanned out over her shoulder, in straight strands. On the right side of her head, a black beret held her hair in place. She jumped in line along with Jeff. We walked a block chanting, "Allahu Akbar, La Ilaha Ilanla, Adonai Eloheinu, Adonai Echad and God the Father, Son and Holy Ghost!"

Mainly kids and adolescents surrounded us, some raising their hands, clapping, yelling, singing. Groups of people turned and raised their arms, repeating, "Allahu Akbar." Old men with red and white keffiyehs yelled at the top of their voices, "Hourriyya Palestine." (Freedom for Palestine) I picked up on it and yelled, "Hourriyya Palestine, hourriyya Israel." (Freedom for Palestine, Freedom for Israel)

When I said "Hourriyya Israel", two young men with short-cropped hair on the sides and longer on top, pointed toward me, confusion and perhaps hate on their faces. So I gave the loudspeaker to David walking next to me and joined the group. The dialogue had begun. "Sadiq, the wall makes two prisoners: Yahoudiyy are also in prison: they can't come here, you can't go to Jerusalem." I reached out with two fingers and one nodded. The other shook his head saying, "Jews try make us slaves; they can go anywhere. We no!"

"Sadiq, the Yahoudiyy from Israel cannot easily come here, to Rachel's Tomb nearby, cannot always go to the Hebron synagogue. Walls and checkpoints hurt them too, hurt everybody." While I walked to the front of the group, David yelled in the bullhorn, smiling, "All for one, one for all."[88] That inspired me to raise my hands and abruptly cross them like they were being handcuffed or chained. I got everyone's attention!!

Then I screamed, "Hourriyya koula wahad!" (Freedom for everyone) and forcefully separated my hands, breaking the handcuffs or chains holding them.

I looked over to the group I had spoken with before and they were all waving their hands, even the ones who weren't sure of saying, "Hourriyya Israel." We had gotten over the first hurdle...but there were many more to come.

As I walked ahead with the bullhorn, I heard David say, "Hey, Levi!"

I turned to behold an intense set of blue eyes and brown hair flopping beneath a multi-colored skull cap. A short, dark-haired woman walked by his side. She had a round, light-brown face and Oriental eyes.

David gushed with pure emotion, "This is a friend of mine, Levi, and his wife, Maura." I saluted them with my hand. "Welcome." I took the bullhorn and continuing walking. "Koula wahad, Mouslim, Yahoudiyy, Masihiyy, hourriyya." (Everyone, Muslims, Jews, Christians, freedom) Maura, not taciturn in the least, immediately understood that in a peace march, you need to take initiative immediately or the fleeting moment passes. She grabbed the bull-horn and began chanting peace and love and a Bah'ai song as we shuffled down the street.

We were now six people leading the march with about 30 people around us.

We walked in front of the Holy Land Trust offices, an NGO that was very active in defending the rights of Palestinians in Bethlehem and in other West Bank cities. A member of that organization, a brown-haired woman, joined us along with a young man. She was a secretary with the organization and he was in charge of managing the rebuilding of structures destroyed by Israeli soldiers during confrontations with the Palestinians. The two from the Holy Land Trust grabbed the sign, the man carrying

---

88 Motto by the three heroes, Athos, Porthos and Aramis of the book, The Three Musketeers, by Alexandre Dumas.

one side, the lady the other. They took their places ahead of the contingency and walked quickly.

The wind was cold as we walked, chanting, but our faith warmed us. About half-way down the main stretch of road, there was a bit of a lull; right at that moment, a store owner invited us inside for refreshments. We decided to take a break and drink mint tea inside his souvenir shop. We sat in a circle drinking hot tea and sharing our ideas of interfaith dialogue with the owner. He was tall, dark and wore a long black beard and a moustache, with a white skull cap on his head. He served the scalding hot tea as I watched the steam rising through his moustache, upwards, upwards...I wondered if there was a price attached to this as I drank my tea, waiting....

We said our goodbyes after about a half an hour, then continued our walk. But it turned out that Levi was after something much more selfish than bringing people together under the banner of peace: About half-way through the march/dialogue, Levi drew close and asked, "Did you read my book?"

I nodded, "I skimmed it. Very interesting!"

"You must follow it, embrace its truth. These marches or dialogues you organize... are they doing any good?"

After that question, I looked at Levi, blue eyes blazing: "I'll apply it as long as it conforms with my personal views, teachings." I looked at his eyes, determined that the discussion stop there.

He frowned, as if were expecting me to unconditionally accept his views and perhaps become one of his followers. He then tried another, more friendly approach. He put his arm around my shoulders and explained in detail the system he had created, giving people hope, providing the answer to their dreams.

His aura of self-importance appeared to set him apart from us; to him, we were perhaps merely spiritual plebeians, cowering before his pure transcendental beingness. He seemed intent on trying to convince me of that, to bring me into his hypocritical web. He recounted that some people in India he had met appreciated his spiritual leadership so much, they called him "Baba," which he said means father in Hindi.

Perhaps he was the proclaimed "Baba" of the people in his own mind. It would not take long to confirm that Levi was a vicious charlatan. Because I rejected his philosophy and refused to consider him my "baba" or even a spiritual leader, the "baba" showed his true colors upon his return to Jerusalem after the dialogue/march in Bethlehem. There he engaged in a smear campaign to discredit me, starting with my book, *Storm Over Morocco*. His criticisms of the dialogue/marches I organized also seemed to lift the veil over his ulterior motive: to attract people to his cult any way he could, get them to flock around the Baba...and then pocket their money. He started his movement by first discrediting the work of anyone else trying to bring people together for peace.

I remember our conversations. Face to face, he seemed very kind and supportive of our interfaith dialogues. But when my back was turned, he did not hesitate to stab me by accusing me of being what he was: an insincere and incompetent charlatan, diatribes of hateful words began to flow from this sanctimonious man's mouth.

His true motives were subsequently revealed in an email I received from him, after his return to Cyprus, which was part of a mass mailing seeking help— including money—to create a "spiritual" movement under his tutelage in Cyprus. It seemed that Levi was only interested in creating a cult under the "Baba," as he often designated himself.

Such a travesty was not ignored by the masses he tried to hoodwink into following him as he soon returned to Israel in debt and seeking refuge: he was soon to lose his property in order to pay debts. He borrowed money and passed bad checks among his friends in Jerusalem and then fled Israel, leaving his friends holding the bag, liable for the debts he had no intention of paying back.

He was the epitome of the "false prophets" warned about in the New and Old Testaments and the Qur'an. I acknowledged the irony of traveling all the way to the Holy Land, to the land of the true prophets, to sometimes run across those not aligned with truth. I concluded that since the "Baba's" one main goal was to snag adepts for his cult he wanted to establish in Cypress, the driving force behind him was the familiar "money, greed and power" and had nothing to do with bringing peace to the land through interfaith harmony, understanding and unconditional love.

At the end of the march in Bethlehem, in front of the wall, we were greeted by an army of taxi drivers, who grabbed the loudspeaker, yelling "Hourriyya Palestine." Such courage was demonstrated before the foreboding towers jutting up from the wall, like deadly mushrooms. Inhabited by Israeli soldiers, I imagined they were looking down, scoffing at us and our interfaith march/dialogue.

This event turned out to be a spiritual turning point. I sent messages to people all over the world about the march, including the peacenik Jews. None responded, which confirmed I was now on their permanent black list because I had included the word "occupation" in the fliers sent before the march. One of them, Rabbi Moshe, who in the past had been my friend, was coming to visit me in Paris after his participation in an interfaith event in the south of France.

Was he coming to castigate me for including in my fliers the following words: "The occupation of the West Bank must end as a precursor to peaceful coexistence?"[89]

Or perhaps he came to spy on me and later report back to the peaceniks in Israel? In any case, Moshe was a mainstream Jew who had possibly black-listed me and I had trepidations about his visit.

---

89 Author has printed literature.

Chapter 55: The Spy?

As I sat in my Paris apartment, looking out the window onto a patio lined by flowers and trees, a quiet rapping on the door broke my meditations.

I opened it and there standing before me was my friend, Moshe. He stood in the doorway, his long, reddish beard flowing over his white robe. His eyes glinted as they surveyed me. We hugged in the doorway and I led him into the dining room still cluttered with boxes and lamps, etc., as I had recently moved and had not had time to unpack yet. He laid his backpack in the corner.

He was always trying to be the matchmaker so I wasn't surprised when, over tea, he told me about a French lady who was returning to her Jewish roots and looking for a soul mate. Without waiting for my response, he said I'd meet her during my next visit to Jerusalem as she had moved there to do Aliyah and eventually apply for Israeli citizenship. I opened my mouth but before I could utter anything, Moshe blurted, "It's Shabbat; what's the plan?"

I had planned to introduce Moshe to members of the Sephardic community that I had lived with when my ex-wife Sylvia and our three children were with me in Paris. It was just a couple of blocks away.

When we opened the door to the courtyard of the apartment building, all the memories enveloped me: I remembered the warmth of being surrounded by my kids, my wife and the Jewish families. It all radiated from the corners of the courtyard, cradling me in its mystical welcome. The feelings were exactly like the ones I had felt so many years ago, before all this wandering to help bring interfaith peace. I was still drawn to the hearth of this cozy place, surrounded by multi- colored flowers: pinks, violets, blues and an overhanging grape arbor weaving its way across, forming a ceiling over the outside courtyard.

I looked above to the window of my adoptive family and Leah, my adoptive mother, was looking out the window, sweeping her eyes over the patio, as usual. Our eyes rose to the grape arbor above, gently lifted by some distant force, as if announcing its welcome. But everything drifted into slow motion; we only had two short flights to walk up but it seemed to take us an hour to get there as the memories kept flashing by.

It was the wind on which rode the unconditional love I'd been searching for all these years—and here it was, welcoming me, again. I looked at Moshe who was heading up the stairs, looking back at me barely moving as I ruminated over the same steps I had traveled for three years, on the way to see my happy, smiling kids and receive the warm hugs of my wife and my Jewish family. He didn't know what was going on as he looked back, a tight smile on his face. But I knew: it was the Creator's way of welcoming me home.

We reached the top of the narrow, wooden stairs and I saw where the door had been, the opening to the apartment I shared with my ex-wife and three kids for three years. A bitter emptiness struck me as I noticed the door was plastered over and didn't exist anymore. I surmised that they had joined the first floor apartment with our second floor apartment and had no more use for the second floor door...our door! "Attaches amoureuses" (Bonds of Love)

One more flight of stairs and we headed to the right. Leah's door was open and she was waiting for us inside. "Shalom, Mère," I announced, reaching over and grabbing her around her shoulders, giving her a big hug and a kiss on her plump cheeks.

"Shalom, Fils," she said.

"This is my friend, Moshe, from Israel."

She responded, smiling. Her two or three missing front teeth and her long, reddish-brown hair made her look like an old washer woman. But she was my second mother, having taken my wife, my three kids and me under her wing when we were foreigners in a strange land.

We sat around a table in front of familiar steaming cups of Turkish coffee. It was strange sitting almost in the same spot that I had at one time sat next to my ex-wife as we drank coffee, chatting with the lady of the house we called "Mom."

No matter what time it had been arriving home late, after work, I visited with her and her husband, Yosef; I was always welcome. One time I walked in when Leah and Yosef were both sick, lying in bed. I sat at the foot of the bed to visit with them. Even sick, they would never ask me for anything. I returned with bread and bags of fruit, stuck them on the chair in the dining room and took off. They had both been asleep.

Now I was sitting there with Moshe. He was struggling with his French. Leah proudly showed him the picture of the grand Rabin of Jerusalem. Moshe knew his name.

A cool breeze blew over the arbor, into the window and over our faces, a cool, nostalgic breeze that had fanned my face so many times when I sat here, holding my two daughters and recently-born son on my lap, eating kosher couscous with them.

We descended the steps and walked under the grape arbor before opening the main door; before leaving, we entered the synagogue, Beth Hamidrach, at the entrance of the apartment complex. It was an hour before Shabbat services and the Rabbi was reading to a young boy from the Torah. The boy looked about thirteen years and was practicing for his Bar Mitzvah.

We walked about a half a block down the street where the rue Basfroi met the rue de Roquette. There on the right was a synagogue that looked a bit like a bunker, hidden under a meshing of iron gates and sashes. We had to open a metal gate and then the door of the synagogue. I had never been inside this synagogue, the Adath Israel. I could never understand how an orthodox Ashkenazi synagogue found itself in the middle of the Sephardic Jewish community. We were met by the Rev. Rav, wearing a long black robe and fur hat.

An adolescent boy greeted me with a huge smile, as if he knew me. "Romano, remember me?"

I knew his face from somewhere, but not his name. "My name is Baruch and you lived with us, next door. You remember, the Levi family?"

"Of course, Baruch," I reached out and we hugged. "But I thought you attended the Sephardic synagogue at the entrance of the apartment."

His lips curling up at the ends told it all, like Moshe, who, when I had asked if he was Ashkenazi or Sephardic, responded by saying he had moved beyond that distinction, and made it clear that he was neither Ashkenazi nor Sephardic, just "Jewish." I thought that if Ashkenazi and Sephardic Jews had the same approach as Moshe, perhaps there would be less tension between the two Jewish groups in Israel. Bravo, Moshe!

"You know, Romano, we go back and forth between the two synagogues: Ashkenazi Jews go to our small Sephardic temple, and we come here. We're one big family. Don't you miss living here?"

I had to say "yes" and we hugged again. There were many orthodox Jews wearing black hats and praying here. But the orthodox nature of the place did not siphon any warmth away. It was welcoming and I must admit I felt at home, as many of the Jews I had lived next door to for years were coming up to greet me and meet Moshe. He was then whisked away by the Rabbi and taken to the front of the room where he was asked to lead the Shabbat prayers.

Little did I know that this was the beginning of a closer connection to Judaism. Moshe was already scheming to introduce me to a French girl who had recently finished Aliyah in Israel, and had evolved from a non-practicing Parisian Jew to an orthodox Jew living in Jerusalem. But I suspected that his goal went further than helping me find happiness; it might have been also to entwine my life more closely with practicing Jews and distract my focus away from the West Bank and Palestinians. It seemed he was obsessively worried that if I traveled to the West Bank, I would favor the Palestinian cause over the importance of preserving the State of Israel.

Moshe had to return to Israel and during my next visit to the Holy Land, he was determined to introduce me to Dalia.

Chapter 56: Cupid

The plane set down at Ben Gurion airport at six in the morning. On leaving customs, I went to pick up my garment tote bag; then I headed down the path near the fountain, the reverberation of its surging waters echoing throughout the high- ceiling room. This was the entrance to Israel; at the foot of the fountains masses of people gathered applauding, cheering their friends and loved ones as they entered the Holy Land, even at six in the morning.

The magic of Israel enveloped me, as I watched the multi-colored balloons rising to the top of the dome of the airport while people sang, ushering the new arrivals into the dynamic new world, welcoming especially Jews to their homeland.

I felt the hand of the people, the songs and the prophets embracing me and leading me down the steps and past the fountain. I ordered a blended coffee and sat, watching the show. People in kippahs, those in Muslim skull caps were there to greet people coming off the plane from all over the world.

Orthodox priests wore their tall hats looking like towers rising over the people. All were taken up in the spirit of welcome, as brothers and sisters of the faith. Whether one was wearing a Jewish kippah or a Muslim skull cap, no one seemed to care.

This was Israel, part of the epicenter for world conflict and potential world peace. I just wanted to hang out here in the airport, not go out into the real world, where religious and political interests sometimes overwhelmed me.

I had been invited by Moshe to a Jewish-Sufi prayer gathering and would meet Benjamin and him there so I took a shuttle to Jerusalem. I arrived several hours before the meeting so I walked the streets of Jerusalem, my head down, almost not knowing where I was or where I was going. My entire being had taken a trip, so very far away, to the land of our forefathers, to this sometimes primitive yet vibrant place, to the epicenter.

I found the address on Harraps street and started walking up the stairs to the top. It was slow going as I was dragging my heavy tote bag up the steps. I knocked on the door and almost immediately Benjamin, with his black side curls and multi- colored kippah, greeted me. His large, beefy jaws were tight and his blue eyes moved rapidly from left to right.

"Come in, Frank—we've been expecting you." Benjamin pulled me gently into the room and firmly shook my hand. He was the leader of the interfaith peace NGO headquartered in this apartment.

The room was filled with Jews wearing kippahs, Muslims in Keffiyehs, joined by Christians and Sufis sitting in a circle. They were discussing the Sufi faith and how it blended with all faiths.

Moshe was his omnipresent self, laughing, gesticulating but not too busy to nod as I walked into the room. I walked over to him; his eyes twinkled as he reached my ear.

"The French girl is coming—you'll meet her." Cupid was at it again!

Ibrahim, the owner and manager of the rooming house I stayed at in East Jerusalem, brought in a basket full of fruit, enough to inspire Benjamin to comment, "Our dear friend, Ibrahim, is always feeding us, thank God!"

We all nodded in unison. A man played a sad but feeling song on his guitar as we sat in a circle. Benjamin gave him an envelope after his performance. I heard a door closing and looked to the corner near where Moshe was sitting and saw a tall lady wearing an old-fashioned hat with a flower in it, like the type my grandmother wore to church. Strands of her light-brown hair draped over her cheeks and her small, discreet smile was fresh, innocent and slightly open. Her warm blue eyes were curious, steadfast, like the gaze of the Mona Lisa. She was impervious to the voice raised by the speaker; she glanced over the crowd like she was looking for someone, as she sat next to Moshe.

Moshe saw me and hurried across the room with her hand in his and in a moment, they were before me.

"Frank, I'd like you to meet a French friend, Dalia." "Bon soir. Enchanté."

"Bon soir."

After the songs and more discussions, Benjamin did the closing prayers. Moshe, Dalia and I stayed to help clean up until she announced her departure. Moshe nodded his head in her direction but I didn't get the hint. He scurried over to me and discreetly asked if I would be chivalrous and accompany her to her apartment, as it was midnight and sometimes the streets were not safe.

We wound around the late night streets of a slumbering Jerusalem. The stars illuminated the path obscured by overhanging clouds, their glow pinprick patterns against a black sky.

I took her to the steps of her apartment and bid her good night. But destiny would bring us together soon.

Chapter 57: Black Masks

In the death throes of fighting a hidden foe and grasping for invisible hands, sweat poured down my cheek; the strong taste of brine brought me to half-consciousness, my eyes blurred, still semi-shut. From the minaret nearby, the muezzin wailed the call to morning prayers; my head reverberated with his cries, in unison with echoing calls from the Mount of Olives—it was five am.

My eyes opened. It was still dark outside. I rose to my window overlooking the lights of East Jerusalem. It looked so calm, so lonely, but somehow the bright, warm lights soothed the conflict within me.

I was back in my room at the pension house owned by the great man of peace, Ibrahim, who I had seen the night before at Benjamin's place at the Jewish-Sufi meeting. During one of the myriad protest actions in East Jerusalem, he was known to have intervened in a conflict between groups of rock-bearing youths facing the sights of M-16's held by Israeli soldiers. They were protesting the confiscating of Arab housing for the building of an Israeli apartment complex. He managed to stop the conflict, potentially saving many lives. His kindness and generosity allowed me to sleep and eat in his place, with a small donation. Without him, I could not stay for long periods in the Holy Land. Ibrahim helped a lot of people from all over the world, of all faiths, that way....

I walked down the stairs to the kitchen, filled my cezves with water, put two large spoonfuls of Arabic coffee grounds in it and then set it over the gas flames. When the coffee started to boil, the air bubbles piercing the surface, I took the cezves off the stove and poured its contents into a large cup. As I sipped the strong coffee, I contemplated the day's visit to Hebron; this would be my first to the city where Abraham, Sarah, Isaac, Rebecca, Jacob and Leah were buried beneath a mosque attached to a synagogue. I didn't relish heading to this contested place; I nervously remembered reading about recent battles there between stone-throwing Palestinians and Israeli soldiers.

I was used to being alone this time in the morning. Being prepared to help bring peace to the land was my interest, my cross and my passion. I would learn to love and hate going into the West Bank: I loved it because I felt that I was making my small contribution to a peace movement which would eventually give rise to a durable peace in the area; I hated it because each time I headed there, I had to go through a maze of checkpoints, walls, and I could never anticipate what would happen during the dialogue/marches. I would sometimes be stopped, detained, arrested or harassed by the Palestinian Authority Police or by Israeli soldiers, depending on the jurisdiction. I guess nothing is worthwhile without a struggle because at the end of the day, I was able to organize and participate in interfaith peace dialogues and marches there, mobilizing the people and bringing hope to some who had lost it—Jews, Muslims and Christians alike.

This trip was, however, only an information gathering trip to help me plan future interfaith dialogues and marches in Hebron.

I waited at the top of the Mount of Olives for an Arab bus to whisk me to the Damascus Gate where I would pick up a shuttle that would take me directly to Hebron. My friend, Abdullah, in Ramallah, had given me the name of a friend, Mujeeb, who had spent 17 years in Israeli prisons, and was a former major general in the Fatah government who would help me generate support for the interfaith freedom marches in Hebron. I called him on my cell phone from the shuttle that was on the way to Hebron about 15 minutes outside Jerusalem. The shuttle was full of the traditionally dressed women wearing hijabs, men with or without keffiyehs and some children.

"No, don't come—all the roads are closed; Hebron's been blockaded for about a week," Mujeeb hurriedly warned me.

"I didn't hear about anything in the news; what's going on?"

"The house of a terrorist who was accused of organizing suicide bombers attacking Israel had been surrounded. The members of the family, his wife and children were allowed to leave the house; he remained. The Israeli soldiers opened fire, shooting hundreds of rounds into the building, killing and decapitating the man."

I asked the shuttle driver, who told me he'd be able to at least take us within a few miles of the city due to the Israeli roadblocks set up at all entrances to the city; we'd have to walk the rest of the way. I relayed him the information Mujeeb had just given me, and that he said we were coming at our own risk.

The shuttle, in typical Palestinian style, burned rubber over the road, racing over the rocky, arid terrain, seared and cauterized by the sun's relentless heat. Maybe there would be no tomorrow so I focused all my strength on today and "let the cards fall where they may." I surmised that with all the challenges of living here, a new crisis wouldn't change much of anything. I briefly mulled over the idea that the shuttle may have to turn back, frowning as the driver slammed on his breaks. But it was only because a lone, scrawny camel was aimlessly crossing the road, the end of the leather strap around his neck scraping the ground.

The driver turned and told the passengers that we had arrived at the outskirts of the city and there was a road block with a line of Israeli jeeps to greet us. I stuck my head out the window and saw soldiers were milling about. A line of cars was crawling by the jeeps; in front of each one, a helmeted Israeli soldier looked attentively at the passengers and examined their documents.

It was our turn. An Israeli soldier in front motioned us to stop. He came to the passenger side and requested papers. His khaki green helmet partially covered the top of his eyes, making him look part man, part phantom. Everyone nervously rustled papers. The soldier looked at the passengers sitting next to the driver. One was a short-haired, bearded man with a woman wearing a white hijab. The soldier then glanced in the back seat, in particular at the short-haired, dark Palestinians, both with black moustaches…then at me. He waved for me to leave the vehicle.

Oh no—this is it! Somebody reported my coming; I'll be interrogated then maybe deported I was freaking out.

After examining my photo and comparing it to my face a couple of times, he said, "Go to car," and I was free to return with my passport.

The shuttle rumbled down a narrow road which fed into a wider street until lines of parked cars and buildings growing in size made it appear we were approaching the city. Shops with clothes, fruit and falafel lined the street in the largest city in the West Bank. A few Palestinian police were lingering around on the sidelines, on the fringes of the roundabouts, in parked vehicles or leaning up against them smoking cigarettes, their black and dark green berets atop their close- cropped heads.

I quickly called Mujeeb to tell him that I had gained entrance to the city of Hebron and that apparently the total blockade of the city, preventing all vehicles from entering or leaving had been replaced by a checkpoint.

"Wow— unbelievable! I pick up," he declared, as I handed the cell phone to the driver so Mujeeb could tell him where to drop me off.

The driver drove the shuttle to the side of the busy street in front of a café. He turned and pointed to the sidewalk. I took my cue, paid him thirty shekels and left the vehicle, dragging my luggage from the trunk and placing it on the sidewalk, where I waited.

In ten minutes or so a slick, black car pulled up along the curb next to me. I leaned over and saw a stocky man with a full moustache smiling, motioning me to the door.

The window slid open and I popped my head in.

"Asalyum walaykumm," he muttered through his moustache, with a stiff upper lip. Being an ex-major general with Fatah forces, I expected that.

He motioned me in back of the car, where I slid my luggage into the open trunk. I returned, opened the door and slid in next to the driver who clasped my hand strongly.

He drove me up what seemed an endless road, finally turning into a driveway. In a few minutes, we were sitting under a dense grape arbor with green and dark purple grapes hanging in huge clusters, tantalizing us as we sat under them, sipping Arabic coffee.

It was surrealistic; I was sitting in front of an ex-major general of Fatah, who had been a long-term prisoner in Israel; he told me he was in prison for 17 years. I was even more determined to bring something to this land, hungry for a durable peace. I whispered to myself, as I looked over the cement wall to the blue sky, "God hear my prayers; help me have the strength and persistence to help bring something new and efficient for the peace process."

Then he put down his cup and smashed his cigarette into it. "I want to show you something. Follow me."

I had no idea what he wanted me to see. He led me up a narrow flight of stairs to the 2nd floor, into a den in which were placed several wooden chairs facing in different directions, as if a meeting had just taken place. The ash trays were full of cigarette butts and several empty coffee cups were scattered over the table.

At the back of the room was a long table on which were strewn empty cups and a silver tea kettle from which he poured tea into colored glasses. At the same time, I heard a buzzing in front of me and noticed a TV screen with horizontal and vertical lines; he was going to show me a video or a movie.

Mujeeb handed me a glass of tea and then pointed to the TV as he manipulated a remote control with his left hand. All of a sudden, the image of a car full of people appeared; a man with a mustache sat in the middle, with several young boys and a girl in a hijab.

"Those are my children with me during the parade after my final release…."

"You mean, when you were released from prison…?"

He interrupted and completed my statement, "…after 17 years…."

Silence reigned as we watched and heard the pandemonium in the streets: at least a hundred cars drove by honking, turning; people peppered the air with accolades; a younger Mujeeb with a black mustache nodded, smiled, and pointed to his kids.

The video was often clouded by people walking in front of Mujeeb's party—some wrapped in Palestinian black and white keffiyehs, others wearing black masks—sometimes placing a hand over the camera lens, often blocking the view of Mujeeb.

I looked closer and noticed these shadowy people were leading the parade, and were all carrying a dark stick held out. I looked even closer…and recoiled as I noticed that the dark sticks were AK-47 rifles, the wood stock occasionally showing in the dark, then covered by a cradling arm.

"Mujeeb, who are those masked people leading the march with those guns?" The startling truth became evident to me even before he spoke. Without hesitation, he exclaimed, "Oh, those are members of the Al-Aqsa Martyr's Brigade assigned to protect us, that is, my family and myself."

His insidious smile curled under his dense moustache as his eyes stared at the tube, probably reliving this singular moment.

"What were they protecting you from?" A long silence followed. My question was never answered.

Chapter 58: Under the Grape Arbor

The next day after lunch, we sat under the same grape arbor, under the branches hovering over us—in flowing patterns of intertwined deep blue and green vines, like sensual embracing depicted on Italian porcelain—while hands offered us its succulent gifts. Mujeeb got up and reached in his pocket, pulling out a pocket knife; after opening the small blade, he cut off a bunch of purple grapes and laid them before me.

They were garden sweetened, a delight, as they weren't from the store and had not been processed nor permeated with pesticide.

The juice from the grapes moistened the corners of my mouth and welled up there. When my mouth was full, it streamed down, dropping on the cement patio. I reflected on what he had told me about Al-Aqsa Martyr's Brigade protecting him as shown in the video we had seen last night.

Mujeeb was a mind reader. "As for last night, let me explain to you about Al-Aqsa. I'm a member of Fatah, and members of Al-Aqsa are the militant, armed branch of the party."

He stopped there, providing me time to regroup my thoughts about Al-Aqsa. I had learned that its members were involved in a myriad of suicide bombings during the Intifada and that it sometimes carried out the attacks with the help of Hamas, a militant Islamist group.

But something was seriously nagging at my thoughts. Even though Mujeeb was recommended by my friend Abdullah, I needed to know if Mujeeb was involved with suicide bombings. I had to carefully select the moment to ask that delicate question; I certainly did not want him to think I was questioning him, or worse, spying on him. I was at his mercy.

The whole controversy of the origins of the Intifada came to mind and the reaction of some Palestinians to attacks by Israeli soldiers, excursions into Palestinian territory and the extending of the settlements, leading to their involvement in suicide bombing.

He went into the kitchen to make more coffee and returned in a few minutes with trays with two small cups full of Arabic coffee; just the medicine I needed to give me a jump start.

That would give me enough jolts to have courage to ask him about his views on suicide bombing. I'm very much opposed to suicide attacks and my non-violent peace work would not allow me to be in any way linked to anyone even indirectly involved with them.

We sat in silence sipping coffee. He lit another cigarette and sat back in his chair.

The moment had come. I tried to work up to it: "What do you think about Palestinian involvement in the Intifada?"

"You mean the suicide bombing!"

He could still read my mind.

Before waiting for my quibbling response, he said, "Well, I'm against it. I visited many a house to try to convince our youth to concentrate on bringing peace through hard work, working together, armed resistance, if necessary. When I was a soldier I believed that sometimes you have to pick up an arm...but not suicide." I nodded and blew a quiet sigh of relief out my nose as I put down my coffee cup. That was the end of the conversation. I breathed deeply, deeper than I had before. I had dodged a bullet...it would not be the last.

I decided to return to Hebron for a future dialogue march in the famous no- man's land; the pictures I had seen of it looked like a war zone. But that is precisely where interfaith dialogues had to bring the people together—the lost war zones, no man's land—where the fighting had been the fiercest, where the greatest need for interfaith exists.

As I returned to Jerusalem, I received a message from Moshe on my cell phone, inviting Dalia and me to join him and his family for Shabbat dinner and to stay the night in his Moshav, not far from Jerusalem.

Chapter 59: Moshav Modin

I picked up Dalia in a taxi and we headed for a bus stop, our rendezvous point with Moshe and a friend. They picked us up shortly after the taxi left us somewhere in the hills outside Jerusalem and took us to Moshav Modin.

While dinner was being prepared and before Shabbat Kiddush prayers and supper, Dalia and I took a walk around the Moshav. We returned after fifteen minutes. Moshe was sitting outside and motioned us to sit next to him. His wife and sons surrounded him, along with three students from a local yeshiva, as he began Shabbat evening prayers.

We prayed and supped under an old tree in his garden. The trunk grew out from its jagged, ancient roots, its gnarled branches intertwined overhead, protectively. As we recited prayers and sang, the glow of the evening penetrated us and brought us together under Moshe's sky roof. I looked over to Dalia sitting next to me; I felt a connection between us. We held hands half way through the prayers; her touch melded us together. Our feelings had not yet been consummated in lovemaking, but I was not in a hurry, as her hand in mine felt right—a true, simple sensuality cementing our connection.

As we sat there, even though I only knew a few words of Hebrew, I knew Adonai Elohaynu, (Lord is Our God) and whenever it was spoken, I repeated it. After the initial prayers, Moshe's wife retreated to the kitchen to prepare the food; rice, hummus and different dishes, including eggplant, were brought out by Moshe's kids.

The next day, Dalia and I went to the synagogue for prayers and something unexpected took place: The sermon and many of the prayers were almost completely in English. Moshe explained later that many Jewish immigrants at the Moshav came from the US and some were accomplishing Aliyah.

That night, after an elaborate end of the Shabbat ceremony, Moshe accompanied us to the bus stop. While waiting, we started talking about Palestinians and my upcoming trip to the West Bank. After announcing to Moshe I intended to return there, he released a stream of emotional words accompanied by flailing hands; I had hit a delicate nerve. He warned me not to trust Palestinians, that they were treacherous and could take me hostage or kill me. I was shocked that a peacenik Jew, who was often involved in interfaith peace activities with Muslims and Christians, could paint such a negative picture of the people he was supposed to work with for peace.

I wondered if the true reason he carried on like that was because he did not want me to experience first-hand the suffering of the Palestinians in the West Bank that would give rise to compassion and a true understanding of the conflict.

Dalia was watching for the bus as Moshe continued his diatribe. Because he saw I was not persuaded by his discourse, he felt inclined to relate a story that he believed would remove any doubts.

He told me that his daughter was engaged to a famous Israeli archaeologist and was scheduled to take a bus with him to an archeological site somewhere in Northern Israel. For some reason, she could not make it to the bus stop, but agreed to meet up with her fiancé later that day at a prearranged meeting place in Northern Israel... except that time never arrived.

While waiting for the bus to take them to the site, a group of about 30 young men and women, including her fiancé, were allegedly attacked by two armed Palestinians. Two men dressed as members of the Palestinian Authority Police drove by and stopped; the car backed up and stopped again. The two men got out and pointed machine guns at the adolescents, spraying them with bullets as they waited for the bus. Moshe's daughter's fiancé was killed in the massacre. His daughter, just by a quirk of fate, was not standing next to him and if she had been, would also have perished.

"You see, you can't trust many of them!" His faced reddened with emotion as he discussed the cruel massacre.

I convinced my heart that he trusted many Palestinians and rationalized that he was just overpowered by emotions, which could often overcome reason. But I still tried to understand why he recounted that story and the reason for his impassioned behavior when talking about Palestinians. Heretofore, I hadn't perceived him as being an emotive person. I surmised that he must have loved the son-in-law he was deprived of or was outraged on behalf of his loving daughter. So horrible can things be. "Les attaches amoureuses"....

The bus came and before we boarded, I turned to Moshe, and said, "Can you condemn all Palestinians as being untrustworthy over the foul deeds of a minority of them?"

That sent Moshe into deep concentration as we walked to the door of the bus. When Dalia and I boarded, Moshe, who had regained his senses, waved, yelling out as he smiled through his reddish-brown beard, "Come back!"

"OK—see you in Paris!"

He smiled, his eyes squinting below reddish eyebrows, then relaxed his lips. As the bus began to move, I waved out the window. Moshe didn't see me and just stood there motionless, following the bus with his eyes....

Chapter 60: Dalia

We were in the bus taking us down a main street in Jerusalem, when Dalia pointed out the window at the corner of Jaffa and Sha'are Yisrael streets, telling me that a terrorist had attacked a few days earlier, in that very spot. She explained that an East Jerusalem Arab driving a bulldozer knocked over two buses, killing three people and injuring many others.[90] I think it was later confirmed that the young man was working independently of any terrorist group and committed the acts spontaneously.[91]

In her blue eyes I saw a hopeless, forlorn look. I held her hand and she did not pull it away. It was Shabbat and I looked forward to pronouncing the Kiddush with Dalia, who had invited me for the first time to her apartment. She was renting a house in the Talpiot District overlooking Abu Tor, a mixed Jewish and Arab neighborhood in Jerusalem.

We were happy to have found each other. Being the man of the house, at least for that night, I recited Kiddush, while holding up the wine. Dalia covered the bread, the two loaves of challah, and handed me the phonetic Hebrew that I read over the wine.[92]

That night, our union was consecrated. As she rolled back the sheets, I could not wait for an official invitation as our love had been made sacred under the blessings of Kiddush, of Shabbat. As she returned to where I was sitting, I reached around her back and gave her a gentle tug in the direction of the bed. We both melted into the sheets, clothes and all. We went beyond our Shabbat obligation as the sweet union was made complete that night under the stars of this captivating city. The distant strumming of a harp woke me. I leaned over and a hint of the outline of Dahlia was illuminated by the porch light beaming through the bedroom curtains. I got up and walked to the living room, looking out over the shimmering lights of Abu Tor.

I returned; helping Dahlia to her feet, I held her tightly in my arms as we shuffled to the living room. I gently sat her in the sofa and slipped beside her. The intermittent

90 Jonathan Lis Haaretz Service. "Three Dead Dozen Hurt in Jerusalem terror Attack." Haaretz. 2 July 2008. <http://www.haaretz.com/news/three-dead-dozens-hurt-in-jerusalem-terror-attack-1.248950>.

91 Ibid.

92 Jewish Virtual Library. "Shabbat Evening Home Ritual." Judaism 101. 2000. <http://www.jewishvirtuallibrary.org/jsource/Judaism/Shabbat2.html#Kiddush>.

lights sparkled and glistened in the mother country, where her children were born…and sometimes suffered. From the cradle, I had learned love, tolerance and understanding; looking down on the valley of lights inspired me beyond the parameters of time and space. These were lights of peace that I absolutely had to find a way to shine together, for all time and for all people.

The spirit of the land pleaded with me, bled with me: my heart was bonded to this country. I knew this magical place would be always close to me. I refused to let the trials awaiting me let my heart become jaded and I would train my heart to be always elevated to the truth of cosmic love, never allowing the human condition to blind me to my purpose. Such was my destiny.

Let the love light forever shine into my heart, keeping it forever open, pure, trusting, vital. I hoped to always rally my heart, in the face of adversity, no matter what….

Could I stay this way, always faithful to my ideals, giving and unconditionally loving? I know if I could, I would be healed, purified and overcome the burden of my personal tragedies; then I could turn around and help bring others to the light, heal others, with my loving strength—breathe life into interfaith freedom, free of pessimistic thoughts and beliefs.

This girl and I, even though our union was just a few days in the making, would unite with the cosmic, unconditional spirit of love starting tonight, symbolically on the Shabbat.

We returned to the bedroom. No curves of the bed could subdue our undulant waves; we were united into one, our bodies and hearts welded together. As the shimmering Jerusalem light crept through the tears in the old beige curtains, we finally slept….

The next day, we shared a sumptuous repast, with za'taa, eggs, a homemade jam made from tasty sweet apricots, and kosher feta cheese spread on toast. I busied myself making Arabic coffee, my specialty. Dalia allowed me to prepare it. She had given me a cezves with a long-necked handle to prepare the coffee. As usual, I put in two tablespoons heaped with the Arabic coffee grounds, placed it in the pan and filled it with water. The contents slowly came to a boil, after which I placed it on the drain board to cool a bit before serving.

We munched on toast covered with thick apricot jam, which oozed a bit on the table in between mouthfuls, and washed it down with coffee.

During breakfast, she told me her story. She was normally taciturn but perhaps the closeness of the moment or the vibes of this magical city loosened her tongue. She started talking about her life, her past, mainly in France.

Once she interrupted her story, her eyes shimmering: "This must be because we're in Jerusalem: everything here is so intense, and happens with such great passion."

There I truly believed her. She went on about her life in Paris. She related that she didn't get along with her parents growing up and was constantly fighting with them. In spite of that, she was a stellar student, maintained good marks and after high school was even selected for a very prestigious preparatory school—in the "Grandes Ecoles" school system in France—called "Hypokhagne."

She couldn't put up with constant disputes with her parents and moved away from the family apartment. She was relieved of the daily conflict. Her parents apparently were also relieved and gladly purchased a small studio apartment for her. The pressure was intense at "Hypokhagne"; isolated and depressed, she ended up having a nervous breakdown and refused to eat for days. Her mother visited her and seeing the miserable state Dalia was in, took her to an insane asylum, where she was promptly interned. I cringed as I remember the story of Camille Claudel— the famous sculptor and lover of Rodin—how they had interned her, which ended her creative life and started her life of darkness within the walls of a sanatorium.

Dalia wrote messages to her father and pleaded to be released. He finally came and convinced the resident doctor that Dalia just needed a little loving care and was not "crazy" and he committed to taking care of her. She was released.

She went on and on, telling me more things about her past. Indeed, I thought to myself, this must be Jerusalem; where else would a usually very reserved woman I hardly knew tell me her life story? I heard her life story even before I really knew her. She also shared with me that, in search of meaning, she spent years in Asia in an ashram to learn Buddhist meditation. She had finally returned recently and then traveled to Jerusalem where she had finished "Aliyah," returning to her Jewish roots in Israel. I felt a kind of return to my own Jewish roots that I felt in me so I was happily a part of it.

We began living together, starting with the first Shabbat we had shared. The magic continued…she was learning Hebrew at Hebrew University in Jerusalem and studying the Torah. At the same time, she was experiencing a rebirth of her Jewish faith that neither she nor most members of her family in Paris had really practiced, other than visiting the synagogue during special holidays like Yom Kippur.

To make up for that, she now strictly practiced Judaism, especially with the strict observance of Shabbat. That weekend, it was magical, as she focused on abiding by the orthodox rules of Shabbat, since we hadn't strictly followed them during our first Shabbat a week earlier. That meant she could not touch lights, or computers or telephones.

I had to briefly travel to Paris to teach a course but I returned later for Yom Kippur, the Day of Atonement. We both stayed the entire day in the French- speaking synagogue, Emouna Chelema, in the district Baka, in Rehov Rivka, Jerusalem. She had obtained reservations for us, in advance. We followed the rules and fasted the entire day. Toward the end of the day, I felt light-headed, a bit weak, but my faith blossomed. I recalled feeling the same sensation when I had fasted during Ramadan during a visit to Morocco many years earlier. As I prayed in the synagogue and put the tallit over me, I tried to sneak a look at Dalia who was on the women's side of the synagogue, behind a semi-transparent curtain. Several times I walked to the curtains and slightly drew them back; there she was dutifully praying with the other women, her white head scarf bowed.

But the day after Yom Kippur, during Shabbat, marked our first dispute. What sacrilege! But it was an inevitable fight. She recounted to me on Friday, right before Shabbat commenced, that she was at her favorite market in the old city purchasing fruit and vegetables when she met a mutual friend, Shlomo, a local bookstore owner who we had visited that week. She had invited him Shabbat morning to do Torah readings with us, which was often the custom for Shabbat. However, she forgot that we had already made commitments with other friends, the Baumanns, who were invited to join us for Torah readings/songs the same day.

Upon her return that night, we were preparing the food for Shabbat dinner because in strict observance of the day of rest, we were not supposed to turn on any electricity during Shabbat. She only had an hour to prepare the food, i.e. use the stove. We concentrated our energy on preparing the food and putting it in containers; it would be heated up in electric hotplates and/or pressure cookers at a pre-determined time. When it was time to eat, automatic timers would click on the hotplates and pressure cookers for the designated period and the food would be ready without touching any of the dials or stove buttons.

Afterwards, we poured the wine as part of Kiddush and discussed the Torah readings we were to study with the Baumanns.

"Oh, no! I invited Shlomo to do Torah readings with us tomorrow. I'm sorry—now I don't know what to do because I can't, according to Shabbat rules, call on the telephone. Plus, we can't really integrate Shlomo with the Baumanns since they are orthodox Ashkenazi Jews and Shlomo is a very liberal Sephardic Jew."

I suggested she telephone Shlomo and cancel, but she reminded me that it was Shabbat and she couldn't. Since I did not observe the rules as strictly as she did, Dalia suggested that I call him. I felt bad about canceling Shlomo's visit and insisted that she must rectify her error. That evolved into a full blown argument and lasted into the night. I was disgusted with her having to follow the rules, not being able to make one little exception. I had never been a strict adherer to rules and often had trouble doing so in my youth, which carried over later in life.

We started arguing, and I questioned why she felt obliged to blindly follow the rules without questioning them, and why she did not assume her mistake by calling Shlomo. Instead, she was putting me in the embarrassing situation of having to call up a friend and cancel his visit on Shabbat, of all days, which is supposed to be set aside for Torah studies and not arguments.

That night as I slept on the couch, I wondered why people felt compelled to strictly adhere to rules they had nothing to do with creating. It wasn't until later that I realized that people submitted to rules because they chose to do so and that I shouldn't judge them.

But my evolution in thought did not help our conflict then. Had Jewish leaders interpreted the Torah as prohibiting certain activities on the Sabbath? Anyway, I crept into our bed early in the morning and she turned over and hugged me. I was forgiven...later, I called Shlomo and cancelled his visit.

A few days later was Sukkot. This holiday commemorates when the children of Israel wandered in the desert for 40 years, living in temporary dwellings. Jews are supposed to build temporary shelters, sukkahs, and live in them as much as possible for seven days, as their ancestors did in the wilderness. Dalia hired local students to construct a temporary cabin on the back porch. Inside, we prayed, ate and spent hours talking for the next few days. They were more irresistible moments for us as we grew closer through prayer and talking, probably more than ever.

A week after Sukkot, on Shabbat, I had to prepare to contact people I would soon meet in the West Bank for a freedom dialogue/march. As I sat there outlining my strategy on a piece of paper and improving the flier, Dalia was in the kitchen, making tea. She brought the steaming tea to the table and set it down on a tray. Then she leaned over and gave me a kiss on the top of my head—through my thick salt and pepper hair; I still felt its warmth.

As she was undressing in the bedroom near the kitchen, I bent my head enough to admire her beautifully curved buttocks, glistening like ripe pears. I glided over her way, and touched them before she could put on her under things. Her inviting body opened and enveloped me in her loving embrace; as the caresses continued, we were slowly drawn to the bed.

Light was streaming through the curtains on a Sunday afternoon in Jerusalem. We started the morning with some sensuous stroking; I traced over her curves and waited anxiously for the caresses to continue.

She was whispering something to me between the sheets, but I couldn't understand her. Finally, she just eased out of bed and said, "Come, I've got something to show you, but you need to put your shorts and sandals on!"

I could feel her cool breath on my neck as she gently held me close to her, while lifting me up with the other hand. I eased out of bed and floated to the bathroom, high on a love-lust cloud. I splashed water on my face then reached for my shorts and put my sandals on in one motion.

Still in a semi-stupor and before I realized I had left the bed, I was already hand in hand with Dalia walking out the door that clicked shut behind us. Her flowing white skirt and white scarf were like markers I followed. We walked and walked through Jerusalem. It was the first walk I had taken and, in fact, my first real day off in months, since I had come to Jerusalem to organize interfaith projects and then to spread them to the West Bank. She walked through a gate that looked like it led up to a house. I peeked in front of her as she coolly walked up the steps then down a narrow sidewalk to a group of tables arranged among palm trees, shrubs, fences and stones placed in circles around flowers in bloom.

I watched the tops of the tall palm trees swaying in the soft, soothing breeze. Looking up and down the sidewalk, I couldn't find Dalia; I kept walking. Then a warm arm encircled me around my waist and pulled me gently over to a table; her eyes sparkled as I bent over and watched them. They did not leave mine, for an instant.

We could have sat there forever, without talking, without making any decisions. "Nice, for a change!" I muttered into the breeze.

A young girl, apparently the waitress, came to us speaking a Hebrew Dalia understood. She waggled her index finger like French people do, which means "Please wait a moment." The waitress retraced her steps.

The air on this sultry afternoon blew lightly against our lips, with the promise of a tender kiss. I had no idea what time it was. It didn't matter. I was under a love spell.

We sat and held hands like long-time lovers, listening to the birds lightly fluttering their wings, reveling among the trees on this Sunday afternoon. Jerusalem took on a whole new light; it had become, thanks to Dalia, more of a place of tranquility—at least for that day—hiding in our little love nest. I still couldn't help wondering that if the same place was in the West Bank, would I be so relaxed? Could I be so relaxed?

That evening, I was on a plane back to Paris as I was bound to start the 2nd session exams at the University of Paris; I would soon return for interfaith marches. Dalia was to travel to Paris in about three weeks, where our love and lives were to resume, in the City of Love. We both wanted that but I was worried, since Paris was where I still suffered in the area of intimacy: I worried that Paris would do us in as it had my other relationships.

Upon my arrival, I regretted having to give up my cozy apartment in the 11th district near the Place Voltaire in the Sephardic Jewish district. I had gone into debt from all the traveling to the Middle East and the United States and I was receiving letters and visits from "huissiers" (the Sheriff, debt collectors) and collection agencies threatening to sue me and garnish my bank account and salary.

So I called a few friends to ask if I could squat at their place for a few months to pay off debts. I got a green light from only one person—Amandine, a friend and former lover—who had a small room in her apartment in the outskirts of Paris. She said I could stay for a few months until I got back on my economic feet; I wasn't sure Dalia would accept my moving in with a former lover, but I felt confident I could convince her it was OK, especially upon her return to Paris in a few weeks. Anyway, I had to move or I'd be stuck in Paris for the next year or so, encumbered with lawsuits and other debt collection activities.

A friend was coming with his car to help me move on a Sunday morning. Everything was stored in boxes the night before. I got up early that morning to take one last walk around the district; even though I planned to return to visit my Jewish friends there, living far away wouldn't be the same as I wouldn't be coming over for Shabbat as often. I walked down the Rue de Roquette and my old haunts; phantom memories of marriage, children, bar mitzvahs, Rosh Hashanah, nesting streamed through me as I swung over to stand in front of the building where I had shared an apartment with my ex-wife and our three infants…before she left Paris and me. It was good-bye again, this time at six in the morning, and years later.

No one walked the streets and it was even too early for the roving street people searching for discarded furniture and other things. I pushed the door code and entered into the courtyard; overhead branches and flowers were flourishing, as before. I touched the mezuzah attached to the synagogue on the right and said a prayer, trying to hold back the tears….

Chapter 61: Saved by the Dead

After I had moved, I called Dalia in Jerusalem to tell her the news that I was temporarily moving in with a friend who charged me little rent so I could pay off depts. I told her that after a few months, I'd return to downtown Paris, where I belonged. She wasn't ready to set up housekeeping with me yet, so that was OK. Then she asked,

"Well, my love, who is this…friend?"

I had to tell her. "Well first, it's an older lady who is a friend, a former colleague and…lover, but we've evolved beyond that."

Deep breathing on the other end told me Dalia wasn't taking that last bit of information very well. I quickly continued, "It's just temporary until I can pay off my debts. No big deal." A somber silence on the other end cast me into a panic zone, as I fumbled for more words.

"Listen, you're my real passion and lady…I…."

Click!

I tried calling back but the line was busy. I had to wait to talk with her when she returned to Paris a few weeks later; but something had broken us and I was too naive, too focused on the move and too anxious to see her to figure it out.

She arrived in Paris three weeks later and I finally was able to contact her. We decided to meet one Friday night for Shabbat in her Paris apartment in the Latin Quarter, the Left Bank. Our last telephone conversation was terse and she was distant and spoke petulantly. My trembling, pleading voice didn't help matters. On the way to her apartment, I decided to get off the subway early and walk several blocks along the Seine towards her place.

I followed the quay of the Seine in the Isle de St. Louis, to my favorite little spot near Camille Claudel's former art studio. But this time, instead of it being meditative and relaxing, I recoiled from the plaque mentioning her name since her catastrophic love affair with Rodin, the famous sculptor, reminded me too much of my relationship with Dalia. Was that a bad omen? My body shook as I pondered that our strong love connection nurtured in Urshalim al-Quds (Biblical and current Arabic term for Jerusalem), the dream city, was fast undergoing a metamorphosis, as my life, turning into a dark void….

I looked over to the rock ledge separating me from another quay bordering the

Seine, and I couldn't help imagining my blood running down in place of the River Seine. Then the blood turned to tears. Was it the end?I shook my head in disbelief—after all we had done together, all the promises of being together until the end of time, all driven to a cold, hardened grave. I recalled living in the Talpiot neighborhood in Jerusalem, celebrating the Sukkot with her in Jerusalem, so in love, so spiritual, and feeling in that magical place.

I hadn't wanted to leave the Sukkot cabin as the morning birds chirped to tell us that it was time to move indoors to the sofa. We had moved and sat there looking down over the lights of Abu Tor, glowing as if each one held the mystery of our passion; I imagined each light a reflection of the stars above, there to guide us, watch over us....

In the early morning, nighttime Mediterranean summer heat would still warm us, without the need for blankets; we were lost in the morning light, alone there, cuddling on the couch.

Walking along the Seine, I only thought of Dalia: her tender, loving and wondrous companionship those days in Jerusalem, returning home to her arms after the West Bank ordeals. "But after all we'd lived through," I muttered to myself, "could it be we're still...doomed?"

The pure passion connection was somehow broken. I fixed my eyes onto the swirling waters of the Seine and convinced myself that we would always have Jerusalem, but I had to hold onto those memories tightly. I left the Isle Saint Louis and followed the Seine to her street, rue Guénégaud, Rive Gauche. I pushed the intercom code she had given me and the door opened automatically. After the elevator took me to the 5th floor, I opened the door and went to the end where a door was half-opened. She peered out, the usually large, loving blue eyes glazed over with gray...she looked at me this time, through narrowed eyes.

We perfunctorily kissed on the cheek French style, on each side. The spark was gone; there was nothing that I could tell her—that my love was strong, that I had to move out. Telling her during our last telephone conversation that I was moving in with a former lover was a mistake, but I couldn't lie.

I wore the kippah she had given me during our whirlwind love affair in the streets of Jerusalem and read the prayers in phonetic Hebrew for Kiddush, after she had prepared the food. The Kiddush was recited mechanically, without the same profoundly deep and spiritual feeling generated in Jerusalem, in our love nest away from this big, voracious metropolis...away from the past and the future, perhaps even away from reality. It was the Jerusalem's surrealistic magic that had taken a hold of us....

That night, she prepared the food indifferently and in silence, without the exuberance spilling over from words spoken through cherry-red, enticing lips. I sat on her couch afterwards and we inevitably intertwined our bodies in silence, trying to recapture the magic; but it felt spurious, flat—it wasn't the same. She didn't want to hear about my new living situation nor even try to convince me of moving elsewhere or even show signs of excitement contemplating living together, as we had done countless times in the Holy Land. Something had seriously infected our pure, beauteous, feeling relationship. It was no longer sacred.

I even suggested that we abandon this city, the place that was killing the magic we had shared, and return to Jerusalem. I told her I'd even buy her ticket with my last euro. I was desperate to get back to the way we were because it hurt too much inside and I needed an antidote, medicine to kill the pain. I needed a cure to this suffering. Her eyes lightened at that suggestion so I finally had her attention, allowing me to draw her away from her melancholy thoughts of us. But I told her that I was committed to remaining in Paris to teach at least the first two weeks of classes, the first day starting tomorrow...she closed her eyes, and maybe her heart. I shared with her my dream of returning to Jerusalem for Chanukah in December, but her eyes remained shut, as if she was focusing on memories, our memories, refusing our today. I wondered if we'd ever return...together.

"Crossing over to your love, there's no return...."

I couldn't stay with her that night; it was too depressing and I wanted to get away so I could start living our memories; that was all we had left. As I heard the easy breathing of her sleep, I slipped out the door. I returned to the Seine at four in the morning, the Mother Seine, my last hope and always there to hold me after the raging storm—and there were many. I had nowhere else to go. It was too late for the subway to take me home and I didn't have enough money for a taxi. But it didn't matter, as I meandered down the Seine, the eternal Seine. I was lost, and even the City of Love couldn't help me.

I avoided the Isle Saint Louis as I was afraid I couldn't withstand the emotional tempest shaking my body, especially viewing Camille Claudel's hideaway yet again. I was a walking mess. I even pictured myself as an emotional skeleton, only the bones of the past, as I walked on the upper Seine while the sheen crested on the silently flowing Seine.

Fighting to hold back the tears, I accelerated, walked fast, pounding the cobble stones lining the street, until I could no longer control my emotions; the tears crept down my cheeks and then began flowing in torrents. I lost control for an instant and a strange force within took over, urging me to climb across the railing and jump.

"Take me, Mother Seine—be done with it. I'm tired."

I looked down and imagined the twinkling lights and magnetic draw of Jerusalem reached out and pulled me from the abyss...I leaned the other way and fell back on the cold pavement. As I stood up, I felt the spirit of Camille Claudel: her hand rested on my shoulder as we stood next to the plaque dedicated to her memory on the side of the old, greying building that had stood there for hundreds of years. I realized that even though part of me had wanted to avoid coming back to this spot, my feet had taken me where my mind refused to go, where I feared to go...and in the end, she had saved me.

I stared where she had stood, in the dim early morning light; the lively spirit of the Seine and the slight whistling of the wind through the swaying trees were my reassuring, caring companions.

Chapter 62: Twilight in Hebron

I had to return to the Holy Land, to Hebron, where I continued following my vision by organizing a peace dialogue/march, alone again. I was desperate to fill my emptied, dry cup as well as escape thoughts of the past, choking me with sweet reminders of what had been. I needed to keep moving, or the pain would shroud my heart. How long I could keep this up?

But, no matter what, I would always have a warm place in my heart for her—Dalia—always…For now, what was left of us and my faith, was an effervescence propelling me forward; being with her had been like finding an oasis from the struggles, sometimes from the horrors of the world.

The shuttle was taking me from Ben Gurion airport to the Damascus Gate in Jerusalem, where I would get a bus to the Mount of Olives. As the bus traveled through Jerusalem on the way to the Gate, the long streets and some of the buildings began to look familiar. Then the shock set me straight up as I realized we were traveling through the Talpiot district, where I had stayed with Dalia in an apartment; my heart wept as memories of not so long ago flooded through me, relentlessly invading my mind.

I averted my gaze to the middle of the bus until we arrived at the Damascus Gate. The driver let me out just in front of it. I wobbled when I walked, as if I had just gotten off a carnival ride. I took a local Arab bus directly to the Mount of Olives.

I planned a march in Hebron with my friend, David. Armed with our trusty sign trumpeting the "Freedom March" in Arabic, Hebrew and English, we were ready to lead an interfaith freedom march. It was Ramadan. David and I walked the streets of the city, normally lined with open stores, sandwich shops and cafés. The normal hustle and bustle was tempered by everyone fasting—the pace was subdued. But the face of one of the vendors remained alive with pent up energy, in spite of his fasting; he handed me a battery for my small digital camera. It must have been about five pm. Fasting had started at sun-up and was almost over.

This was the first time the dialogue/march would take place during Ramadan, and I didn't know when or where to start. We had sent two hundred emails to people announcing it would take place in front of the Abraham Mosque, in the infamous no-man's land—H2 sector—at three pm. I had called Mujeeb and asked him when the best time would be and where should we have it. He said that, to assure the greatest turnout, the best time was after evening prayers, when the people were leaving the mosque.

Mujeeb invited David and me to celebrate with his family and him the breaking of the fast that evening. He picked us up in the old city and drove us around the surrounding hills of Hebron. The mist was rising as the car kept grinding along the mountain road. It was almost surrealistic that we were in the mountains overlooking the big city, outlined by the jagged silhouette of trees and shrubs against a moonlit sky. It seemed so far away from the Abraham mosque where we had to be in a few hours to lead the freedom march.

The car drove up a long driveway to a cement platform, built next to a small farm house. Several people were seated at long tables. We got out of the car and walked toward them. Mujeeb began hugging people and shaking hands. He introduced us to his wife, wearing a black hijab, his daughters, sons and a myriad of family members. There must have been about forty people sitting at a few long tables.

There were old and young couples, a man with short hair and a dark face sitting next to his wife, her head covered by a green and white hijab. Several children were seated next to them, munching.

As we neared, I asked Mujeeb if everyone was breaking the fast. He put his finger over his mouth and gently breathed out, "Shhhhhhhhhh," which meant maybe not everyone was fasting. His official response was, however, "Na'am—kula wahad!" (Yes, everyone!)

I was amazed at their faith, their discipline, to be able to make it through the hot summer days without food or drink. David and I were led to a table in the corner. As we ate, I looked over the ledge of the patio at the lights of Hebron melting into the rising mist; a couple of hundred feet down the slope was a modest wooden structure with several goats tied around it.

I asked Mujeeb what it was and he said they were Bedouins who were also breaking the fast with their nighttime meal.

He smiled, "It's a celebration!"

Trays of chicken were passed around with some type of vegetables. Mujeeb served us; the former major general was not arrogant and made sure we had enough to eat. He was a most sensitive and kind host.

His eyes twinkled as he set down a couple of cups full of an orange soda. It was a feast. As David and I were dreamily looking over the slopes and almost into the Bedouins' tents, Mujeeb came by and said it was time to take us to the Mosque as we needed to start the march, picking up people while they were leaving the mosque.

In a few minutes, we were rolling down the same roads we had climbed about an hour earlier. When we arrived downtown, we saw many men with keffiyehs turning left down an obscure road. They seemed to be headed to the same place.

He let us off in a dark alley, as if we were some kind of secret society. Mujeeb pointed to the dark opening of an alley straight ahead saying that would lead us to the Mosque. David and I got out. As we walked, we heard a faint "Good luck and call me when you're ready." I raised my arm and waved without turning my head as we soon were completely enveloped by our ghostly path, following the keffiyehs ahead of us.

We saw a lit alley way ahead that grew bigger as we approached. In a few minutes, we arrived at our destination and stood in front of the Masgid Ibrahim (Abraham Mosque), after passing through a checkpoint of Israeli soldiers.

We stepped toward another checkpoint, with booths inhabited by Israeli soldiers situated at the entrance to the mosque. We never got inside. An Israeli soldier stood in front of me, his M-16 pointed at me.

"Where going?"

"To the mosque...."

"You can't go in."

"Why not? I want to pray," I responded, as I rolled up the sign and pushed it into the plastic sack with the loud speaker.

"Holiday, stay out here...."

"Come on, this is ridiculous; I've a right to pray. You're...."

He just shook his head and pushed me out of the booth toward the front of the mosque.

I started walking out and then saw David's red face. The soldiers were pointing to the cross dangling from his neck.

"You not Muslim!"

David responded, "But I am; I believe. Let me go in. I'm a Christian but that does not exclude my belief in Islam."

I had to admire him as he didn't seem in the least intimidated by the soldiers. That inspired me to think of a new strategy and I went to David and told him to follow me away from the entrance.

He abruptly turned, ignoring the soldier who was talking to him, and followed me to a place far enough away so the soldiers couldn't hear us. We sat on the curb. I reminded David that Mujeeb had advised that we wait for the end of evening prayers before we march.

David and I sat on the curb, with the sign and the loudspeaker concealed inside a plastic bag. Young adolescents began flocking around us, curious, wondering what two westerners were doing there. We started the dialogue.

One tall, skeletal boy, with black eyes closely examining us, blurted out, when the Israeli soldiers crossed the road, "Jews bad: they take our city. They don't believe in God."

"Listen, sadiq, my friends, I swear many Jews believe in God, believe in you."

"No, they all hate us; I hate them."

I took out the sign, in English, Arabic and Hebrew.

The boy read the Arabic. "Hourriyya Palestine." (Free Palestine)

I said, "Hourriyya Palestine, hourriyya Israel."

"No say, 'Hourriyya Israel,'" was the reply.

As in previous marches, this was always the trigger for interfaith dialogue during the march. I welcomed it as the strategy was to especially get the young people to talk, to let out their frustrations, while directing the dialogue towards interfaith understanding and tempering hate.

"Yes, but one wall makes two prisoners, Palestinians and Israeli Jews," I declared looking into his eyes. He eyed me right back, his dark face frowning.

I continued, "La ilaha illallah, Yahoudiyy say, Adonai Elohaynu Adonai Echad." He frowned again and leaned over to the other kids, who smiled, ignoring his frown, and said, "La ilaha illallah."

I looked over to David, who was repeating, "La ilaha." The kids were smiling. I yelled, "Allahu Akbar!" as people poured out of the mosque. Some adolescents and adults came to us. Girls with hijabs hesitated and stayed at first on the fringes in small groups, watching us. I took the sign out of the bag, unraveled and showed it to about 50 adolescents who were surrounding us. The electricity was sparking, the eyes and arms raised, the hope....

I looked to David, who was watching and nodding. We almost said at the same time, "Let's go!!"

I yanked the bullhorn out of the bag and gave it to David while I found a young fervent boy to hold one side of the sign. We headed down the dirt road following the crowd of Muslims leaving the mosque. The road was bordered by half- destroyed buildings.

We arrived at an Israeli soldier guard tower. At this point, there were at least 50 of us. The guards came towards us double time, reaching out for the sign.

"Stop talking, making noise! Give me paper!!"

Exasperated at attempts to stop us from exercising our free speech rights, I addressed the soldiers:

"We are here for unity, peace; one God, Adonai, Eloyahnu, Adonai Ehad, La ilaha illallah, God the Father, Son and Holy Ghost—together, my friends."

They looked at me like I was mad, but were confused as I had recited part of the fundamental prayer in Judaism, the sacred "Shema." They leaned toward us like they were going to insist. But the boys courageously screened them away from us, forming a human wall and raising their arms, "Allahu Akbar," and the soldiers hesitated, then withdrew a few paces, but were still threatening.

I continued to talk, address directly the soldiers: "We have the right to free speech here, or is this a fascist state?"

"Give me," one thickly mustached military police officer insisted, stretching his hands out. "You not authorized...."

"I don't need to be authorized to speak out...."

We continued marching but the soldiers did not dare follow as we were more than 50 strong; the soldiers dared not penetrate the line of Palestinian boys. But they both were frantically calling on their cell phones. I thought we were home free; I was wrong.

Through a loudspeaker came the deafening words, "You must stop and show your papers!"

I looked ahead and this time saw an Israeli military jeep with two Israeli soldiers wedged between the car and the sidewalk, blocking our path; we couldn't walk around them and had to walk almost single file another way. They waved for David and I to join them, standing in front of the jeep.

The boys walked to the side, around the vehicles, but there was a barrier across the road on the other side of the jeep and they were also trapped.

I took the loudspeaker from David and yelled, "It's Ok, brothers—'eluhuyah'—go back but wait for us." (brothers)

We approached the jeep while the adolescent boys stayed back. Two Israeli soldiers, with severe frowns under their helmets and brandishing M-16s, approached.

"Papers, now!"

David paled while replying, "Here we go again—just leave us alone!"

I had to smile inside as David appeared unafraid and didn't cower, even in the face of M-16s and gruff Israeli soldiers. I loved him and thanked God he was with me.

We handed them our passports. They took them and went into the cabin of their vehicle. We waited. The boys began fidgeting as soon as the Israelis withdrew to their jeep, but instead of abandoning us, they kept their distance, about 10 yards away on the opposite sidewalk.

I turned and motioned to them to wait, that we were coming.

I heard a determined, "La ilaha illallah." They had spunk, those kids!

The soldiers returned and handed us back our papers.

"You can't walk here and make noise," one of them said, pointing down the rows of closed shops to the settlement beyond. "You go straight ahead." The other soldier, a youngster no more than 21 years old, with dark eyebrows and strong brown eyes, said in broken English, "Over there."

We joined our friends on the other side of the sidewalk. The eyes of the soldiers never left us. We took the signs out and began walking fast with our friends and managed to quickly clear the jeep. The soldiers then hurried into the jeep, turned the key in the ignition and headed towards us. But there were too many Palestinians and they stopped. Their eyes followed us as they tightly held their M-16s, like a security blanket.

We had won the first round.

It was getting dark now, and the crowd grew in numbers. Even the girls wearing hijabs finally braved joining us.

As we began climbing a steep hill, I saw David fall back and sit down abruptly on a cement slab, his eyes rolling with fatigue. Even with his weak heart he had kept up the pace! I yelled out, he waved me on, his hand circling around, a sign that he would join us.

I kept pushing up the street as many cars had joined the procession. Everyone was honking and yelling, "Allahu Akbar." It was a freedom party. About 80 to 90 people had joined the procession. Two young Arabs wearing Levi jeans and Addidas were carrying the "Freedom March" sign, one on each side. I handed the loud speaker to one of the young boys who had stayed with us from the moment we had left the mosque. His short brown hair was combed forward over his smooth, brown forehead. He smiled upon receiving the bull horn and immediately wailed fearlessly,

"Houriyya Philistine, Allahu Akbar!" he said enthusiastically.

Then he handed the loud speaker back to me, dictating for me to say, "La ilaha illallah, Muhammad rasullulah," which I repeated. (There is no God but Allah, Muhammad is the messenger of Allah)

"We are with you, Palestinian people; freedom for you, freedom for Israelis," I yelled forcefully, so loud I felt something "ping" inside my head.

I fisted my hands and joined my wrists together, crossing them. Then I vehemently freed them while speaking the words, "Hourriyya Palestine."

That triggered clapping, yells of approval. Another adolescent wearing a beard took my hand and led me up the hill. He pointed to a group of people in the windows, smiling and waving.

It was a moment of pure solidarity with a suffering people. I reminded them that both Palestinians and Israelis were suffering behind these walls and were stuck at the checkpoints for hours.

As we continued marching up the hill on the main road, one car stopped next to us; a curly-headed driver stuck his head out the window. "Are you crazy? This is H2!"

I responded, without hesitating, "Yes...join us!" He parked the car and joined us. We were now a hundred people strong and gaining force. People were everywhere, singing, chanting, "Freedom! Freedom!" Everyone was taking turns speaking through the loud speaker as we continued the long walk uphill in the infamous Zone H2. People drove alongside honking wildly and raucously clapping inside their cars.

A youngster with long, black, wild hair grabbed my shoulders and yelled, asking me to point up to the people looking out the windows above. I looked up and pointed to entire families cheering, waving and clapping.

"Houriyya Palestine! Allahu Akbar!"

Everyone was out, and surprised. I guessed that they didn't see too many marches here, in this lonely H2 zone, this land of broken houses, rubble stacked up beside the road like corpses, waiting to be buried. But the spirit was sizzling, and the smiles of the people sincere.

Everyone was praying for a miracle. I could feel it so strongly, even the Israelis soldiers were praying in private—I was sure of it—that this land would be freed, so they could go home to their families! What was the point of lingering in a contested war zone where life was so fragile?

The march crescendoed at the top of the hill where an older man wearing a keffiyeh motioned David and me and the group of boys in front of us to leave the road, move away from the crowd, which was getting out of control, and follow him into a narrow walkway. I looked behind me and saw the old man motioning a few of the boys walking with us to join me. Then he spoke in Arabic to the crowd in back of us and many of the boys turned and disappeared into the night.

We were led into what looked like a stable. A couple of goats were grazing in a building with walls but no roof; the middle ground was covered with yellowish grass. The old man took the lead and shooing the goats away, set up some chairs for us to sit in. David and I happily got off our feet and sat down, while many adolescents lingered, some speaking a little English.

I had collapsed on the metal chair: my legs were like rubber and my head was

300

spinning from the combination of bright lights and being surrounded by beaming young men raising their hands to shake mine, over and over again. There must have been at least 30 young men squeezed into this 10 foot by 10 foot space, the remains of a house or stable. They welcomed us, with varying levels of English, to this war zone and thanked us for an inspiring few moments of solidarity in their struggle.

The old man sat next to us, speaking Arabic and a few English words. He could see we didn't understand, so he tried Hebrew. I said, "English!"

He smiled, "Ameriki?"

"Na'am," then I pointed to David who added, "I'm British." The old man raised his bushy gray eyebrows, then lowered them.

"Ah, Englandia!" David nodded.

Then the man rose and said, "Come."

He led us up an embankment bordered by cement sidewalks dropping off into nowhere. There were metal trestles bordering the walkway we followed. We followed him to a corner of an abandoned worksite, which would have been an eerie place if so many people hadn't gathered to greet us. Several chairs were set up; a crowd of boys, girls, adults and youths wearing hijabs stood around them. Another older man wearing a white keffiyeh with a black band holding it down on top was sitting in the middle of a row of empty chairs, puffing on the end of a coiled hookah tube.

For the next hour, we drank tea, then coffee. The man with the red keffiyeh offered hookah to me. I accepted and took a puff, trying with all my strength not to cough. As we sat, a cool breeze coming off the desert east of Hebron gently fluttered at my face. It had been another successful march/dialogue. We had managed to keep going in spite of the Israeli soldiers, thanks to the welcome of these spirited young fighters, fighting for their families, for dignity, for freedom in the face of a sometimes hopeless situation—in the face of a stifling occupation. As the hookah smoke made its way up and over my head, I mused that this was just another gleaming day for David and I, consisting of a week or two of intense marches and dialogues. I pondered the fact we were privileged since we could return to Europe to regroup, recharge our batteries, whereas it was a daily struggle for these people who were mostly trapped here. They could not escape it, but they seemed to keep the faith. Exceptional!

I felt my cell phone vibrating. I reached down and unzipped the pouch. It was Mujeeb.

"Where are you?" he asked, his voice trailing off. "I've been driving around for an hour and I still can't find you. I walked near the Mosque, but you disappeared. Got worried!"

"I don't know where I am. Here I'll pass the telephone to my friend who will tell you where to pick us up, and thanks Mujeeb!"

I gave the cell phone to the man with the red keffiyeh who spoke a few words in Arabic then handed my phone back. In a few minutes, we were being accompanied by two young men delegated to take us to a spot where Mujeeb could pick us up. Within minutes, Mujeeb joined us. He could not believe how we had arrived at this location, deep within the most sensitive part of Zone H-2, in the heart of the conflict between the Palestinians and Israel, without having been arrested by Israeli police. I didn't either, but we had just let it happen, followed our vision, to encourage dialogue and understanding, and then let the cards fall; it had worked out…that time!

We learned one thing: that nighttime in Hebron during Ramadan was intense and we could mobilize a lot of people, as emotions were running high. That was the exact time that interfaith dialogue was decisive in diffusing possible conflict and helping to bring peace and understanding by showing solidarity with the people. At the same time, it was crucial to encourage people to release their stifled emotions and help them understand that many Israelis were also working for "freedom." We planned on returning soon to the Abraham Mosque/Synagogue for an interfaith march/dialogue.

After that march, I was destined to make an important discovery and possibly find a missing link to the identity of my own family, this time in the settlement sector of H-2, the Jewish district, prohibited to Palestinians. But first, I needed to return to Israel to share this latest march/dialogue with, I thought, the only peacenik Jews that had not blacklisted me…my friends in Tel Aviv. But I wasn't ready for their frigid reception, and their treatment of me…as an outcast.

Chapter 63: Accused

I had a couple of days before I was to take a plane back to Paris. David's flight was also in a couple of days. I headed to Tel Aviv after the event to rest up while David visited friends in Jerusalem. Miriam and Samuel welcomed me with strong Mediterranean hugs before ushering me to my usual abode on the outdoor couch. Miriam brought in a tuft of herbs for herb tea. We were sitting around the kitchen table drinking tea when Samuel turned to me and asked how my trip to Hebron had gone. I explained to him about David and our leading a group of Palestinians on a peace/freedom walk and dialogue at night, during Ramadan. He interrupted: "You... did...what?" The tone of his voice was unusually threatening.

"We...led a freedom march in Hebron during Ramadan." Then Samuel raised his voice, for the first time:

"Could you explain that what you did could be other than 'irresponsible interference?'"

"I'm not sure what you mean, Samuel, by 'irresponsible interference.'"

Samuel, trying to put a lid on his anger for what I had done, took a deep breath. Then he lectured me:

"You picked the wrong time of year to do that, especially the wrong place—Hebron, the focus of a lot of conflicts."

"I originally was not going to do any march/dialogues during Ramadan, but...."

He interrupted me, "Ramadan; you know that's a religious holiday?"

"I understand that!"

"I don't think you do. That's the time of year when emotions are intense. You could have caused a riot."

"But we focus on non-violent, dialogue marches for peace...."

"Your focus or intentions are meaningless in the face of the foolish risks you took with your friends. You should have known that you could have created a riot. Then afterwards, you can return to your peaceful life in Paris. But what about us? You leave us holding the bag. We have to live here and I have to drive the streets to work. Do you know what it means to drive roads where bombs are planted and rocks and Molotov cocktails are thrown?"

"I don't think there was any chance...."

"Let me be clear: by revving up emotions at such a delicate time, you could have

303

triggered a huge riot that could have had broad repercussions on our lives. That was bad timing, a bad place and that's why it was irresponsible for you...." "Again, I never intended to lead a march during Ramadan, but a Palestinian leader suggested the time and the place, the Abraham Mosque, was perfect."

He tried to interrupt. This time I had to insist: "Hold on; that leader who advised we hold a peace march after prayer in front of the Hebron Mosque at night would not want a riot either. Do you think you know more about the situation in the West Bank than him? He lives there every day. You've never been there."

With that, Samuel calmed down a bit. Even though Miriam and Samuel had been very active in participating in interfaith meetings and projects in Israel, this marked a point where I obviously went over the line, at least in his mind. I was extremely disappointed by Samuel's reaction to our peace march because he seemed to be more concerned with the Palestinian reaction and potential violence toward Israeli Jews— toward themselves—than the underlying cause of the violence: his government's asphyxiating occupation of Palestinian lands.

Samuel's reaction to our march in Hebron led me to believe that some Israeli mainstream Jews were angry at me for mobilizing Palestinians to fight their brutal occupation, for selfish reasons. They seemed to be in denial, like many of the peacenik Jews—perhaps like Samuel—of the serious violation of Palestinian human rights. I knew then—just as with my friends at the Hukuk Kibbutz—Moshe, and the other mainstream peacenik Jews—that my close friends, Miriam and Samuel, would no longer welcome me in their home. The appalling reality began sinking in, that because I had dared to protest the occupation and engage in interfaith activities in the West Bank, I had become a "persona non grata," even in the home of my close friends.

Chapter 64: Bombs on the Beach

I slept that night in my usual place on Miriam and Samuel's roof-top couch. The next day, I jogged down a long stretch of the beach, from Jaffa to the other end of Tel Aviv, wearing my typical jogging outfit. It consisted of old, charcoal baggy pants and an oversized sports jacket. I always liked to dress warmly, even in the heat, because I like to sweat all the impurities out of me.

I jogged between the water and the sand, where beach goers flocked to swim, play beach racket ball and just languish in the hot Mediterranean sun.

They were all wearing swimming suits, some ladies a one-piece, others a two-piece. Jogging by, I noticed everyone, including the racket ball players, was giving me a wide girth. As I jogged up ahead, I passed several lifeguards, more people playing, jumping into the water, circling and splashing. The children, women and men seemed to be looking at me strangely. I felt many sets of eyes upon me. I felt extreme terror... coming from somewhere!

I kept jogging all the way down the beach to the place where big buildings had cropped up, as well as fast food restaurants. I turned up and jogged along the road running parallel to the beach.

In about twenty minutes, on the right, I passed several low buildings joined together on the beach. Something was strange about them so I turned around and jogged down a seafront promenade to have a closer look. One building looked like it was boarded up on the outside, with a crooked sign in black letters reading, "Dophinarium." Part of the entrance was stained black like it had been ravaged by fire. The parking lot was empty and the buildings looked abandoned. To the right, placed on a narrow park row between the street and a parking lot, was a cement post with flower bouquets around it.

That was strange so I jogged nearer to have a closer look and what I saw sent shivers down my arms and through my bones as I stood before it. Before me was a short memorial with names on it. I remember reading about a bombing in Tel Aviv a few years back in 2001 and even recently in 2005,[93] which had shocked the world.

---

93 Israel. Ministry of Foreign Affairs. Tel-Aviv suicide bombing at the Dolphin disco-1-June-2001. 2 June 2001. <http://www.mfa.gov.il/MFA/MF AArchive/2000_2009/2001/6/ Tel-Aviv+suicide+bombing+at+the+ Dolphin+disco+-+1-.htm>. I learned later that on Feb. 25, 2005, at another beachfront club, the Stage Club—just 400 yards north of the Dolphnarium—another suicide bomber had claimed the lives of 5 people and wounded at least 30: people had congregated there to celebrate a birthday. Israel. Ministry of Foreign Affairs.

I quaked thinking that this could be the place.

I remember in 2001, a suicide bomber had detonated a bomb while waiting in line outside the Dophinarium disco, killing 21 people—mostly teenagers, whose families had emigrated from the Soviet Union—and wounding 120; they had all planned to attend a dance party at the discotheque. I trembled as I remembered the pandemonium depicted on French TV after the attack: the multitude of sirens and the bodies being transported on stretchers, most of them in plastic body bags.

Tears rolled down my cheeks; I wiped them away with the sleeve of my jacket. How could something so horrible ever happen? Just kids waiting in line to dance, laughing, anticipating a birthday party—not possible! Oh, God....

As I jogged down the seafront promenade, it started making sense why the beachgoers were so skittish, some downright alarmed, when I jogged near them wearing a baggy jogging outfit, especially the oversized sport jacket in the middle of the hot Mediterranean summer. I didn't look like a beachgoer—no bathing suit or sunglasses—and I wasn't barefoot, carrying a racket, a paddle board or a tube of suntan lotion. I didn't even want to look like a beachgoer; I was just jogging to sweat out my stress and impurities and get some exercise so I could focus only on interfaith activities. As I jogged along the beach again, some paddle boarders stopped and gawked at me. Some stepped into the low, curling waves away from the bizarre jogger wearing a sports jacket, jumping over the foaming swells before they hit the sand. I jogged back toward the beach to avoid the bigger waves rolling in and saw a tanned mother, her blond hair stuck to her back from swimming, grab her half-nude child building a sand castle, whisking him away from me towards the chaise lounges farther up toward the beach café.

Now it was clear: I was an intruder. I wasn't dressed like them, frolicking among the waves like them. I didn't want to be like them…but I hadn't yet gotten used to feeling like an outcast.

The charcoal-black former discotheque diminished in size, the ocean breeze flapping the loose boards haphazardly nailed over the gaping windows. I had jogged here about a year ago while staying with Miriam and Samuel in Jaffa; the mixture of paranoid stares I received had told me then there was something wrong.

I returned to the roof of my friend's house, my head full of questions and my heart somber with what I had seen. I was an outcast on the beach and, I feared, in this house, as well. I left a note on the sofa thanking them. I then gathered my belongings and shoved their keys under the door after locking it. As I walked down the stone steps for the last time, I mused that this house and its people, always welcoming, was no longer a refuge. It was no longer the "ultimo refugio" from some of the peacenik Jews who had blacklisted me. I felt so alone, so empty, even though the cool ocean breeze touched my face, as if reaching out to soothe me.

My friendship with Miriam and Samuel ended that day. But something totally unexpected was to happen during my next trip to Hebron.

Suicide Bombing at Tel-Aviv Stage Club. 25 February 2005.<http://www.mfa.gov.il/MFA/MFAArchive/2000_2009/2005/Suicide+bombing+at+Tel+Aviv+Stage+Club+25-Feb-2005.htm?WBCMODE=PrEditorials-30-Dec-2009Hamas+Incitement+Videos>.

Chapter 65: Attacked

Itook a bus to Jerusalem, dejected by what I had just seen and heard in Jaffa, but buoyed by the anticipation of seeing my friend David at Ibrahim's rooming house in East Jerusalem. We had planned another march/dialogue in Hebron with a French girl, Clémence, who I had met a few months earlier in Jerusalem. Both David and Clémence were to meet me in about an hour at the Damascus Gate before taking an Arab bus to the West Bank, together.

I arrived at the Damascus Gate and looked down at the entrance to the Old City. I envisaged someday organizing a freedom march/dialogue there soon, and then entering the labyrinth of shops and checkpoints with Israeli soldiers, on my way to the Wailing Wall, the Al-Aqsa Mosque and the Dome of the Rock.

As I stood there, I felt a tug at the back my jacket. I turned around and Clémence was looking directly into my eyes. Her intense brown eyes scanned mine, scintillating as they communicated with me. Her dark bangs swept across her forehead and her robust body stood erect, covered with a yellow blouse tucked into faded blue jeans, epitomizing her roots in the Western World.

Looking into her almost too ardent eyes, I had no doubts she would play an important role in today's interfaith march/dialogue endeavor to one of the most contested cities in the West Bank…Hebron.

David soon joined us. Clémence, quick to take the initiative, suggested we take an Arab bus to Ramallah, then change buses there. I responded that David and I had found a shuttle in front of the Damascus Gate that would take us directly to Hebron for 20 shekels each. She shook her head in disbelief but before she could say anything, I had crossed the street toward the shuttles I thought would take us to Hebron. I knew that I'd better act fast or we'd be following her. After all, I was the leader; soon, however, in the unstable streets of Hebron, I would welcome her desire to share that role with me. She was an amazing woman!

She reluctantly followed David as they crossed the street, following me to the concession stands in front of which, I thought, would be a shuttle that would take us to our destination. As we walked toward the line of shuttles, we were approached by a tall man with a high forehead and intense eyes. I knew that I just needed to make a quick deal before we piled into the shuttle.

"Shuttle to Hebron?" I quizzed. "No problem. How many people?" "Three people. How much?"

He wrinkled his brow, but not for long. "50 shekels each."

"No way! We can take a bus for cheaper than that!" "35!"

I started to walk away. "Ok, 30 shekels each."

I kept on walking. He followed me as I walked towards David and Clémence. Without saying a word, I walked between them, flinging my arms around both, pretending to walk back to the Damascus Gate.

"Thirty shekels each...."

"No way; then we have to wait 30 minutes for you to fill up the shuttle. Fifteen shekels."

He giggled, yellow teeth materializing in a way that made his canines appear large and lethal.

"You leave me no choice. Final offer: 25 shekels."

David and Clémence were staring at me by now, nodding, trying to get my attention. Since the price was below what the bus would cost, I knew they wanted me to accept it.

I turned to look up at the tall Arab and said firmly as I turned to walk toward the Damascus Gate, "And my last offer is twenty shekels, and we leave in 15 minutes, max. Whether the shuttle is full or not. In a hurry...."

"Alright, alright...."

Almost at the same moment he said the last alright, I had corralled David and Clémence and we were headed to the shuttle. They looked at me as if I were from a different planet. David shrugged and smiled while Clémence blew air out of her mouth, as French people do to show disgust.

"I've had a lot of practice...." I thought I'd mumble, to quell all doubts.

We piled in. In about 15 minutes, the shuttle was full, including three young women wearing different colored hijabs. We were off.

Somewhere between Jerusalem and Hebron, the shuttle driver turned into a drag racer, burning rubber as the bus charged across the arid plains, careening down village streets; then it streaked down the straightaway into the plains lined with hot stones and barren fields. About half-way to our destination, the driver spoke to me. I was sitting in the last seat, so he had turned halfway around, keeping one eye on the road, the other on me.

"You sure? For 20 shekels, that will barely cover gas. You should pay 30 each." David and Clémence looked at me as if they were ready to compromise with the driver, to calm the air.

"No sir, a deal's a deal," I responded perfunctorily, without looking at him.

When he left us off in Hebron, he tried to increase the price again, to no avail. Under my breath as we left the shuttle, while the angry eyes of the driver watched, I whispered, shaking my head,

"How I detest constant fighting, bartering, but if I didn't, I'd go broke here."

My muttering to myself did not escape the attention of David and Clémence and I wondered if they thought I was over the top since I was now starting to talk to myself. I looked at them and noticed their eyeballs protruding from their sockets as they gaped at me with worried looks. That answered that!

After walking about 15 minutes, the familiar desolation of the Old City loomed before us, a lonely, ancient ghoul slowly appearing from times past. We walked down the rows of closed stores. It seemed that each time I visited this area, fewer shops were open, closed in the middle of the afternoon, when they should have been open for business. The blue-green metal sashes were firmly closed and often padlocked.

Clémence shook her black, wavy head. She spoke in French to me as David walked beside us, looking at the stores with a blank look in his eyes: "Many store owners were forced to close their doors by the more and more frequent visits by Israeli soldiers harassing them, alienating customers and causing them to stay away. No use staying open with no customers coming!" She added, "And thousands of soldiers were called here to protect 400 settlers...incredible!"

My stomach felt almost as empty as the emptiness I felt walking those barren streets. Hardly a soul was out and about. We arrived in the middle of the old city, where a group of Israeli soldiers were running, their M-16's strapped to their shoulders, apparently engaged in maneuvers.

It was distressing to see them in action, even if in defense of themselves, preparing to kill—seeing them run, then crouch, grabbing their M-16's and pointing them at invisible targets. Then they'd place their guns in the initial position behind their backs, and regroup. They ran around an abandoned building and were soon out of sight, like rats running into holes created by accumulated rubbish of an abandoned building.

While we were only visitors, we could feel the tension permeating this ghost town exacerbated by the gloomy echo of nothingness, mixed with feelings that scavengers had licked the bones in this place, until they shone like ivory.

We arrived at the checkpoint located just in front of the Abraham Mosque. To get to it, we had to go through a turnstile, governed by a light. When it turned green, we were greeted by another turnstile which would freeze until opened by an Israeli soldier peering at us over his helmet visor. We got through that after a few tense moments, only to find ourselves face to face with Israeli soldiers.

They stood on platforms on each side of a narrow path, glaring down at us as if we were intruders, invaders of this holy place that should be open to all people. One of the soldiers pointed his M-16 at the opening of my sack which revealed one end of the rolled-up Freedom March sign.

"Open it," he commanded.

I had to unravel it before him until he could read, "Freedom March" in Hebrew, Arabic and English.

"NO! No, you can't."

"I will roll it up and keep it with me, then." "No! You take back."

I had to go back through the turnstile while David and Clémence, who had gotten through the maze, waited for me in front of the Abraham Mosque. I had to walk back through to the closed shops until I found one that was open. Then I rolled it up and asked the shop owner to keep it for me. His son, a young boy of no more than seven years, took the sign and handed it to his father standing in back of the stand full of tourist trinkets: the usual Palestinian flags, key chains with the form of the Al-Aqsa or Abraham Mosques engraved on them, etc. The man informed me that he closed at eight pm and he would hold it for me until then.

I got through the turnstiles and after a quick inspection, arrived in front of the Abraham Mosque where Clémence and David were sitting on the curb, patiently waiting for my return. While Clémence stayed behind to watch our belongings, we walked to the front of the mosque, where several Israeli soldiers were stationed.

We had no trouble getting inside the mosque this time and stayed and prayed. The beautiful chandeliers hovered overhead as the prayers of the worshippers— praying above the tombs of Abraham, the father of the Abrahamic faiths, and his wife Sarah—filled my heart with warmth, even if just for a few minutes. I nurtured that feeling, trying not to think about the war zone outside.

As we left the entrance to the mosque, I noticed that only a handful of Palestinians were milling about, compared to the masses of youths that had greeted us in front of the mosque before, when we had visited during Ramadan. Instead of taking out the loud speaker that I had carefully hidden beneath fliers in the plastic sack, we walked past the Israeli guards.

We passed rows and rows of more shops bolted shut. The same weird feeling settled over me, like a thick black cloud. As soon as we turned the corner and were out of sight of the guards, I pulled out the loud speaker and began to yell, "La ilaha illallah...."

At first, one young boy joined us. He was only about eight years old, but his brown eyes reflected a sad wisdom beyond his years; he flashed a smile showing white teeth. He called his friends, who slowly, one by one, crept out of their houses, some seemingly out of the ruins around us. It reminded me of the munchkins in the movie, "The Wizard of OZ," coming out of their hiding places (after the house fell on the Wicked Witch of the East) at the call of the Glinda, the Good Witch of the South.

I handed him the loud speaker and he recoiled. Taking it back, I put it to my lips, "Allahu Akbar."

Then I handed it back to him.

"Allahu Akbar! Allahu Akbar!" he cried, his face radiating enthusiasm.

In about 10 minutes, about 15 boys and one teenager had joined us. I placed the loudspeaker in front of David, who yelled, "All for one! One for all!" As we all walked down the deserted path, the ruins of homes and other structures strewn over the sides of the road, I thought I saw an apparition. It looked like the neck and head of a camel poking out of a window and nibbling on leaves of a scraggily bush.I blinked and did another take, and indeed, it was what I had thought. We walked by a guard post with two helmeted Israeli soldiers whose eyes followed our every move. I turned away and followed the kids who had taken over the march. Two were in the lead, trading off speaking through the loud speaker, with David close behind. Then a dark-haired boy, no older than eight or nine, handed the loud speaker back to me. I noticed Clémence was no longer walking with us. As I called her name through the loud speaker I glimpsed the wave of a hand about two blocks ahead of us, at the foot of an imposing guard tower. She was speaking to the Israeli guards. I approached.

"Shalom." I was surprised that the soldiers smiled.

It was rare that we dialogued with Israeli soldiers, even though our interfaith work was for everyone. Sometimes I had even found the soldiers were more open to dialogue than others as they were anxious for the conflict to end, so they could leave this unstable war zone and return to their families. And some astounding words had come from the mouth of one Israeli soldier who whispered in my ear, telling me he was against the occupation. Here Clémence had taken the initiative and the dialogue was in full swing before I arrived.

Bravo, I thought to myself!

Then a dusty white car, traveling too fast for these dirt roads, bore down on us, spewing rocks and dirt everywhere, just missing a group of boys walking behind us. I chased it as it rose quickly up the embankment and disappeared behind a veil of dust. I looked back to make sure that the passengers hadn't bothered the boys. It was as if they were used to this kind of behavior. How could people be indifferent towards aggressive drivers? But it turned out the drivers were more than that.

As we walked near the guard tower, I handed the loudspeaker to the group and one brown hand took it. This time it was the teenager, who had draped a black and white keffiyeh over his shoulder; throwing his head back, he yelled,

"La ilaha illa Allah, Wa Muhammad rasul Allah!"

Then I reached for the loudspeaker but the boy refused to give it back and began yelling words I didn't understand as the other boys snickered and laughed. I wasn't sure what they were saying was linked to our interfaith march so I held my hand out for the loud speaker. At that moment, a young boy with closely cropped brown hair and wearing sandals, who had been with us from the beginning, followed the boy still hanging onto the loudspeaker—yelling more words, to the joy of the others—and grabbed it. He was chased by the boys as he circled around and returned, shaking off the other boys. He ran up to me, handing over the loudspeaker.

Our faithful friend was looking out after us. "Maa ismak?" (What's your name?)

"Anwar. Wa anta?" (Anwar, and yours?) "Frank, sadiq!" (friend)

We walked towards the top of the hill where I had walked with David on that massive march during Ramadan. But in the daylight, everything looked different.I squinted looking upwards and my eyes focused on something that we didn't confront here last time: an Israeli jeep parked on top with two soldiers leaning up against it. Another soldier was sitting in the back seat. We walked toward the jeep. I mumbled under my breath, "Their infernal monitoring is…everywhere! Couldn't they just leave us alone?"

But something dissonant was in the air and I was sure something was going to happen. As we reached the top, two Israeli soldiers got out and walked towards me. The kids wanted to keep going as if the soldiers weren't there. They were not afraid. Anwar stepped to the side of the road, grabbed a rock and stepped proudly forward.

"No sadiq, it's ok…."

The boy threw the rock down. In spite of trying to look upset, I couldn't help a smile curling the sides of my mouth: the kid had been ready to confront two M- 16s with a rock....

One short soldier with a dark birthmark on his cheek asked to see my papers. I gave him my passport. David and Clémence were seated on a rock by the side of the road. Then the soldiers climbed back into the jeep to study them.

The one with the birthmark opened the door and motioned me to the truck. "You can't continue; you must return."

"What's going on here? I'm here for everyone: for Palestinians, for you, for peace. We have the right."

"Ok, shalom, shalom. You did it, now go back!" An inscrutable smile spread his lips.

"Go now or I will arrest you. Jail?"

I motioned to David, Clémence and the boys waiting on the sides to descend. We hadn't walked 30 feet when the same dusty white car that had almost hit us before sped down the dirt road heading right for us, until the guards diverted it to the other side of the road. With brakes screeching, it came to a full stop next to us. It looked like the occupants of the car that had been stalking us.

Out popped a young boy with side curls and a black kippah and an older man with a full, black beard. They were two angry settlers! The latter immediately pointed to David, then to his chest, with an ugly frown, making it clear he was referring to David's cross.

He started toward David with his hands clenched and an Israeli soldier, who had wisely been stationed nearby, walked in between them. I stood next to David to defend him and the older settler, with the soldier between them, continued talking to David in broken English, saying several incomprehensible words. Then I understood.

"What, Christian...."

While I was watching David and the settler, I didn't notice that the younger one was creeping up on me from the side.

"You Nazi, what do here?" and he walked straight at me, his hands clenched. One yard away from me, I straight-armed him firmly in the chest and he jumped back; another soldier quickly moved in between us.

Instantly, a third soldier walked between the settlers and us, raising his M-16. The young boy with the side curls didn't seem in the least intimidated as he kept walking forward. The soldier finally reached out an arm barring his advance and the boy took a step back.

I looked down the hill and saw Clémence corralling all the boys, tears streaming down her cheeks. My eyes flicked to David who was now angrily castigating the two who had accosted us...while the soldiers looked on.

As the Israeli soldiers stayed between us, I tried backing up to take some pictures. A white hand with slender fingers covered my lens. The young boy had worked his way around the soldier and had placed the palm of his hand over my lens stopping me from taking the picture. The soldier grabbed him from behind and held him with one arm, while with the other he motioned us to move on.

We didn't need another invitation and gladly walked down the hill to join Clémence and the boys. Tears sparkled at the corners of her eyes as she looked away, apparently shocked by the violent confrontation with the settlers. Ten minutes later I looked up the hill and saw the settlers still madly gesticulating as they argued with the soldiers.

Then a car marked with big Hebrew letters headed right for us, this time coming from the opposite direction. It screeched to a halt and a man wearing a khaki uniform and a dark green beret approached with a nervous smile; he looked worried.

"Who is leader?"

"I am!"

"What you do?"

"We are marching for interfaith peace and freedom for all people and talking with the people, with everyone, including Israeli soldiers."

"You cannot march here. This is too sensitive area!"

"We have the right to free speech here. We are saying prayers in Arabic, 'La ilaha ilanla,' and in Hebrew, 'Adonai Elohaynu Adonai Echad.'"

His eyebrows rose slightly, hearing Hebrew.

"You Jewish?"

"I believe in Judaism, if that's what you mean...."

"You can't do it here...." "But we are...."

"I am the commander of this place, and I command you to stop, now."

His dark eyes widened and he looked at another officer sitting in the vehicle, his face sticking out the window, closely watching us. He was not bluffing.

"Ok, we'll not march here...." "OK?"

"Ok!"

He walked over and opened the car door, stopped, and stared at us. Then he got back in his car, revved the motor, and the car lurched forward, heading toward the soldiers and settlers above.

As his car screeched away, a Palestinian boy picked up a rock and threw it at the car. Fortunately, the rock flew over it as it sped down the road. I looked to see who had thrown it. It was our little friend who had been walking with us. He looked up, smiling mischievously.

"No, it's not ok—don't do that. We walk together, in peace."

After walking down the road for about 5 minutes, I took the loudspeaker out of the bag. Clémence galloped towards me, out of breath,

"You better not, we could get arrested...."

"Look, we said we wouldn't march up there, but we didn't say anything about not marching down here. Let's go!" I grabbed the loudspeaker.

"Allahu Akbar, Adonai Elian Adonai Echad...let's go!"

The boys who were walking with us swung behind us, chanting, "Allahu Akbar!"

David yelled, "All for one and one for all!"

I hadn't needed to convince them as we were on our way again, stomping down the road. After a few minutes, Clémence was no longer with us. I looked back while walking and saw her stopped in the middle of the road about twenty yards away, no doubt undecided whether to participate or not.

As we moved forward, I looked back again while we marched down the hill toward the Abraham Mosque, and I saw her slowly walking in our direction. I was relieved as I thought we had lost her.

We got to the half-way point where two Israeli soldiers were guarding the opening to the Abraham Avenue Synagogue, which was connected to the Abraham Mosque. Clémence had joined us and even walked ahead to talk with the Israeli soldiers. They were smiling so I knew that she had explained to them what we were doing.

When we arrived, David and I walked up to them. The Palestinian boys stayed in back. I turned to them. "We must go into the synagogue." The boys looked confused.

"Allahu Akbar means one God for all, Mouslim, Yahoudiyy and Masihiyy."

The reaction seemed mixed. They began to speak amongst themselves. "Look, I'll come back." I waved my hands in a spiral, to indicate my return. They showed me a collective smile; their heads were bowed as I knew they wanted to go with us. I turned to the Israeli soldiers, shared with them what we were doing. They had apparently heard it all from Clémence and nodded.

"Welcome," they both said, almost in unison.

But their welcome was surely not shared by the aggressive settlers, one of whom we were soon to confront at the threshold of the synagogue.

Chapter 66: Ousted!

David and I walked up the steps toward the synagogue, which had been rebuilt in 1981 after many years of being used as an animal pen and trash dump, before the 6-Days War in 1967. We had entered another world. In front of us was a small platoon of about 15 Israeli soldiers doing some kind of exercises at the foot of the synagogue, and next to the checkpoint.

We got through and climbed up more steps. As we were en route, I had a flashback of a previous visit to the Old City of Hebron.

* * *

I was visiting Hebron with Dominik, a friend from Finland. Our guide that time had been a disgruntled Palestinian with closely-cropped dark hair. As we toured the place, he pointed upwards, showing my friend and me nets placed over the market place to protect them from objects thrown from the windows of the settlers living above. Several items, including chairs, bottles and other things, were caught in the net. I thought it ironic that the settler, the one who had confronted me during the second interfaith march, had called me a "Nazi!"

He walked up a flight of stairs in the corner of an obscure, dilapidated building. Stopping above, he waved us on. I started walking up the stairs and looked back to Dominik who returned a frown. We took another look at the netting off to our right, loaded with objects thrown: a tricycle without wheels, several large stones.

At the top of the stairs, the boy knocked on a door. He was still knocking when we both arrived. The latch clicked; I looked into the peephole and saw a dark face peering at us. The door creaked, the bottom scraping the floor as it slowly open. The boy extended a hand to the man inside who appeared from behind the door with a strained smile—we would later learn why. The man shook my hand and pulled me into a high-ceiling room to a table with several tourist trinkets, including armbands with the colors of the Palestinian flag.

The man who had greeted us sat on a sofa and puffed from a hookah pipe. We sat next to him. The boy and the man engaged in a lively conversation, complete with flailing hands and pained expressions. The room was sparsely decorated: only a pair of Palestinian flags adorned the cracked walls.

The boy turned to me. "Come see this."

He led me by the hand to the other side of the room and pulled aside the long, heavy curtains. He drew me closer to the windows which were dirt-streaked and slightly fogged over. On the other side was a small passage between the present building and another facing it.

"Look; you see that passage?"

His bloodshot eyes fixed on a particular spot; it was in the middle of the passage between the two buildings. "There, a settler threw a Molotov cocktail at that apartment, full of kids. A child was killed and the Israeli soldiers did nothing to save the people or stop the fire."

As quickly as he had opened the curtains he closed them. His face contorted with disgust and his head shook from side to side. I'd heard of violence, including killings and other atrocities on both sides; I wasn't sure his story was completely true and I didn't want to take sides…although I was looking at the remains of the burned apartment.

We sat around a coffee table strewn with tourist items; bands with the colors of the Palestinian flag, small Palestinian flags, pins with Palestinian flags painted on them. Not once did they try to push them on us; the boy just asked us to make a small contribution for the house.

The father of the house, his long, black curls spilling out under a white skull cap, sat smoking hookah. In between puffs, he began to recount his harrowing experience. He trembled when he pointed to his wife—waiting attentively across the room, wearing a pale blue hijab—saying they were constantly threatened by settler invasions into their home. He was forced to stay inside the house at all times and could not look for work.

I turned to the boy and asked him how the family could live. He said that his family helped him pay rent and food. He shrugged.

The boy met my eyes which were staring at the boarded up windows, or at least the gaps where windows should have been. He got up and motioned me to follow him. We proceeded to the other side of the room where a couple of window panes should have been placed, only to find metal bars welded over the metal frame. "The settlers came here with soldiers one day to 'fix' our windows; they would normally be overlooking the settlements, but are now sealed."

We returned to our seats where several glasses of tea waited for us on the end table. The steam rising up reminded me of the haze over a battlefield, in the thick of fighting. From my pores oozed compassion for all the victims, especially the Jews, Muslims and Christians directly affected by this senseless struggle.

We were invited to go on the roof and drink our tea. We ascended and I saw the top of a settlement guarded by an Israeli soldier about 20 yards away. He turned and ordered us inside. The Palestinians were prohibited from picnicking or even walking on their own roofs. I descended the stairs, wondering how people could live like this, day in and day out.

Emotional thoughts ran through my mind: It can't be in the name of God and the revving up of hate over the years can't end like this, at each other's throats!

My thoughts started pouring out of me: And somehow my past is tangled up here. It's so strange that I was called here 30 years ago[94] and found Beit Romano in the middle of the Old City, located just in back of this place, just beyond the sealed windows, on the other side. My name and my intuition have told me some of the mysteries of my past are held here. And yet, when I march hand in hand with Palestinians, I know I was sent here for them, as well as Jews and Christians, to help bring them together. We are derived from the same roots and what is so strange is that near us is the father of three worlds: Abraham, the father of humanity, of pure faith. This faith we bring to this troubled world to bring all people together and at the same time, my roots are crying for discovery.

I had already discovered Beit Romano and suspected I had a connection with it; but only later would I confront the staggering possibility that my own roots were buried deep within the ruins of Hebron's Old City.

* * *

Right before the entrance to the synagogue was an Israeli soldier who smiled and bade us welcome. Before David and I could walk through the door, a man with a beard and side curls flapping wildly quickly jumped from inside and blocked our entrance. He pointed to David's cross he always wore around his neck.

For the second time that day, a soldier slid between David and a settler. The soldier and the man immediately engaged in what seemed to be a debate in Hebrew, ending with the departure of the settler, his long hair streaming as he stomped down the stairs. The soldier waved us through and we entered the famous Abraham Avinu Synagogue, a place of worship connected to the Abraham mosque.

We entered a vast prayer area, where chairs were arranged in front of the main sanctuary lined with bookshelves filled with Torahs. I had been there to pray before and I went to the place where the Torahs in English were stored next to the main sanctuary. I took two and handed one to David who was resting on a bench. The same Israeli soldier who had been our savior at the door sat next to David the entire time; he was our guiding angel that day.

It was during these moments—where an Israeli defended a Christian from another Israeli—it occurred to me they were some of the defining moments of the interfaith movement, of interfaith love and understanding.

As I made my way back to the main sanctuary, my emotions were high and the unconditional love spirit soothed me, its force healing the day's wounds incurred during the interfaith march.

After a short visit, we joined Clémence who was patiently waiting for us at the soldier's station, still talking with them and watching our possessions. She had been an exceptional emissary of our goals of interfaith peace. By the time we returned, due

---

94 My original vision and calling is set forth in my book entitled Storm Over Morocco, 4th Edition, supra.

to her work, I was sure that the soldiers, if allowed, would have gladly walked with us and actively participated in our interfaith dialogue.

But this spiritual warmth burning inside would change to molten heat when I made an incredible discovery in the Jewish settlement, in the middle of the H2 sector, occupied by settlers and the omnipresent Israeli soldiers.

Chapter 67: Deep Secret

We arrived back at the bottom of the hill, back among the gloomy, closed green doors of a ghost town that used to be a bustling market area.

This was the crossroads. Either we went to the right and skirted the Abraham Mosque, heading back through the Old City with our Palestinian friends, or we made our way through the Jewish quarters, through the settlement; Clémence made the decision for us. She walked to the left, away from the Abraham Mosque, trailing words behind her—she wanted to show me something.

I started walking in her direction. I noticed Anwar and his friend, who had been with us the whole time except when David and I visited the synagogue, slinking away from us. I waved for them to join us; the boy and his friend shook their heads.

I turned to Clémence, "What about our friend, Anwar; can't he continue with us?"

Clémence explained to me, without breaking her stride, that the Palestinians were not allowed into the settlement, which was the Jewish district. I quickly turned and waved to Anwar. The boy waved back, lowering his head as he did when I had entered the mosque. A forlorn feeling resonated in my heart as I saw those sad brown eyes separate from us. I felt emptiness, as if I were losing a close friend, and wondered if I'd ever see the boy again. I looked back again and he was gone.

It seemed so unfair that there were such brutal divisions between the Israelis and Palestinians, but those divisions amplified my fervent desire to bring them together. In that moment, Clémence had something to show us. As we walked, my heavy sorrow dissipated as something about this place made me feel like I was coming home.

We were now down to the original three, Clémence, David and me, as we trudged on, passing another Israeli military jeep where two soldiers watched us closely. This time they didn't ask for our papers.

We walked along the usual blocks of closed stores, with the same drab green shutters. For at least five minutes, we saw no one until we walked by a woman wearing the head scarf of an orthodox Jew. She was pushing a stroller and holding the hand of a young boy walking at her side, his side curls swaying with every step.

This marked the beginning of the Jewish district of Hebron. We walked past more Jews, two young adolescents, one with a trace of a beard on his smooth chin carrying a Torah under his arm and another wearing a black fedora hat over his flaming red hair, with tassels streaming out from under a green jacket.

Then something totally unexpected and extraordinary happened. As we trudged on, Clémence brought us to an intersection in the road. I looked up and noticed an inscription on a street sign. I had to give it another look.

It read, "Beit Romano," or "Romano's House."

Clémence spoke, "Welcome home." But she said it a way that was more prophetic than sarcastic. I had been here before and had noticed "Beit Romano" written on the side of a building but not on a street sign.

The words of my Jewish adoptive mother, Leah, came back to me again: "Romano is typically a Jewish name: we know Romanos who are linked to Moranos from Tunisia, where we came from. You have Jewish roots with a name like that, I can feel it."

I had always been close to Jews and Judaism but had never thought to check out my own roots, at least to uncover the hidden past of the Romano family. I just assumed it was Italian, 100% catholic on my father's side. But the sign, "Beit Romano" and the atmosphere of Hebron, along with the welcoming feeling, sparked a major awareness that day. And yes, I strongly felt I had, indeed, returned…home.

Chapter 68: Beit Romano

We continued walking down the street named "Beit Romano." Half-way down was a yeshiva, Shavei Hevron, on the right hand side. At the end of the block was an Israeli soldier perched high above in a look-out tower. Emotion welled up in me and I couldn't understand why. After all it was only the name of a street, right? I thought to myself. My name was there, memorialized and there was no way around that. An indescribable feeling of belonging embraced my entire body, my soul, and stayed with me for days after that. It was a flame within that connected me to generations past, to the mysteries of long ago.

Perhaps herein lay the truth of my own being.

I was not only drawn to the Holy Land 30 years ago during a vision as a facilitator of interfaith dialogue, but possibly also to meet up with my own past, my own family. This was a new, bizarre twist. Was this place beckoning me to come, to discover where my ancestors had immigrated many years before...right to the land I was standing on?

Clémence, feeling that something had spirited me away from which I hadn't completely returned, took my hand and led me down narrow steps into the basement of a settlement building. We passed a settler wearing a black kippah and carrying an AK-47 as he watched his children play on a patio above the stairs that lead us to the place—a basement museum. David followed, silently.

Inside, my discoveries would impact me for life.

On the way in, I picked up a brochure and turned the pages. For some reason, it opened directly to Beit Romano and its origins. It contained the story of a Jewish entrepreneur from Turkey named Chaim Avram Romano, who, in 1870, was one of the first to buy a parcel of land here. He built a residence and a guest house for Jewish senior citizens; a synagogue and Yeshiva were later located on the property.[95]

My emotions were surging, maybe with a touch of madness. It struck me that my strange feelings were beyond naming. The possibility that questions about my origins that had been plaguing me for years could be finally answered in this obscure little museum in the middle of a Jewish settlement—in the middle of Hebron—shook me with excitement. We advanced farther into the museum. More vibrations ran through

---

95 Jewish Virtual Library. "Hebron." Israeli Foreign Ministry. 2012. <http://www.jewishvirtu-allibrary.org/jsource/History/hebron.html>.

my veins as I saw stained glass windows in the back rooms. I was irresistibly drawn to these rooms that depicted in the vibrantly hued panes the story of the cruel massacre of Jews living in Hebron in 1929, which had forced the survivors to abandon the city.[96] The story goes that Jews and Arabs enjoyed an outstanding relationship in Hebron until 1929, when the Mufti of Jerusalem, Haj Amin al-Hussein, made false accusations against the Jews in the Holy Land. That provoked riots by local Arabs in Hebron on August 23rd who attacked the Jews living there, devastating the community.[97] Another unfortunate event took place February 25th, 1994. A Jewish settler, Baruch Goldstein, entered the Abraham Mosque during Friday morning prayers and opened fire, attacking Muslim worshipers.[98] There were many victims of those two massacres.

Tears welled up in my eyes that I could not hold back thinking of those events, even as I stood next to the usually collected and terse Clémence. In a few minutes, I looked around; Clémence and David had left me alone. Could some of these Jews be related to me?[99]

I wondered. And then under my breath, I whispered, "Blood doesn't lie, and intuition lies in the blood."

I had no idea where that came from, and why those words had been buried in me until that very moment. It felt as if Avram Romano was cajoling me to pursue the search and not give up—to respect my roots and trust my intuition. Chills run up and down my arms as I write this, as I realize the truth is alive within me. It's possible that the Romano Jews, originally from Turkey, migrated there from Spain and Italy during the inquisition, where many converted to Christianity, although some Jews chose death over conversion. They then migrated to the Middle East, ergo Hebron, some eventually returning to Italy. My trace of part of my family roots led me to Frank Romano and Fatima Romano, my grandfather and grandmother, Catholics living in Naples, who decided to migrate to the United States for a better life, around 1904.

Here in this museum and later on, I studied the history of the Jews living in Hebron. I learned that Hebron, one of the oldest Jewish communities in the world, dated back to Biblical times.[100] Jews had formed a community there long before the State of Israel was created. After the 6-day war of 1967, when the State of Israel began to occupy the West Bank, including Hebron, many Jews returned to Hebron, their homeland. Those Jews returning home after the 6-day war, in my mind, should

---

96 Ibid.

97 Mausenbaum Ruffina Bernadetti Silva. "Jewish History Begins in Hebron Said David Ben-Gurion." Saudades. 1997-2003. <http://www.saudades.org/Jewish%20_history.htm>.

98 "1994: Jewish Settler Kills 30 at Holy Site." BBC- On This Day. 25 February 1994. <http://news.bbc.co.uk/onthisday/hi/dates/stories/february/25/newsid_4167000/4167929. stm>.

99 Upon my return to Paris, I started to trace the roots of the name Frank Romano. The first evidence of the origins of the name "Frank Romano," was traced to a period before the 19th and 20th centuries in Italy. According to the source, the name derives from a Jewish Community originating in Turkey. Confirmation of that is still pending as the trace of my roots continues, using various sources.

100 Jewish Virtual Library. "Hebron," supra.

not be labeled "settlers" today. However, some Palestinians disagree.[101] It appeared to me that on both sides there is so much hate, that each side is subject to gross exaggeration to exacerbate the hate—a vicious cycle. Then I wondered if people have to hate and where it comes from. I thought that maybe hate is a product of socialization or indoctrination that is used to paradoxically unify people by creating an "us versus them" mentality.

The roots of hate must exist in a highly—sometimes overly—competitive world, in business, politics and even sports.[102] Why do competitors sometimes feel they have to hate each other to successfully compete with each other? That to me is bad enough. I believe intense feelings of hate are unnecessary to successfully compete in the business, sports, political or any other arena.

Hate also spills over into our families, cultural and religious identities, even our sexual orientation, and only serves to polarize us. That horribly skews and distorts our feelings for people deriving from different cultures, etc. and, in part, gives rise to much of the conflict we experience today. I concluded that some people use hate to manipulate people, to achieve their selfish ends, often the acquisition of money and power.

As I left the museum, the warm Holy Land air embraced my weary soul and fueled the decision that I must try, as difficult as it would be, to distance myself from negative, biased feelings and deeply know that hate is an unnatural emotion fabricated and promoted to manipulate people.

The pictures had caused my mind and body to feel grief, soon tempered by the knowledge that the Jews were able to return home after the 6 days war of 1967. My return here, was it by chance or was it a part of the divine plan? I was convinced that my call to the Holy Land was, in part, a call to Hebron. I knew that by returning, I was making an irrevocable statement that I had found the missing link of our family. The proof was a strong, intuitive sense and emotions I felt in this place...or was it my imagination? I would find out!

---

101 Later, a Palestinian informed me that most of the Jews living in "Beit Romano" today are not linked or related to Avram Romano or other original Jews who bought the land to establish the yeshiva there. They should thus be labeled "settlers" and are illegally occupying Palestinian lands. That has not been confirmed but I'm continuing my research on "Beit Romano" as well as the origins of my family.

102 Sometimes sports fans of competing teams, convinced they hate each other, even engage in violent behavior to act out that hate.

Chapter 69: Blood Doesn't Lie

It seemed as though I was walking through this shadowy museum alone, even though Clémence and David were around; but the message was powerful. This place had been a focal point for hate, building up like a volcano, erupting in gratuitous violence. The windows were displayed in a way that light would partially illuminate them, which created an eerie effect, enhancing the gloomy outcome of the fighting: the loss of 67 Jewish lives. Of course, it was a one-sided approach, and there are always at least two sides to every issue.

Although despair enveloped my heart at first, it also acted to spur me on in my work. I was convinced that these moments of brutality were the result of ignorance, by the fact communities often violently reacted to rumors without exploring ways to communicate with each other. Or perhaps some people exploited hot emotions to achieve their goals. I was captive in this whirlpool which now included a conflict between my compassion for Arabs and my possible connection to the Jewish community there. You could say I had nothing tangible at that moment to substantiate feelings that I had been there before, that our family's presence there went as far back as the 19th century, when Sephardic Jews forming the Romano family had come from Turkey. So all I could go on was how I felt, and I felt so very close, in particular, to Sephardic Jews, to the Jewish culture, in general. My feelings largely stemmed from my school days with Jewish friends I was very close to.

Those strong feelings were enhanced later on in Paris, while living in the Sephardic community, especially towards my adoptive mother, Leah. Even though I'd spoken to many orthodox Jews who believed that my Jewish origins could almost exclusively be traced through Mother, I did not share that approach. I believed that being Jewish is a state of mind; it was more important to feel Jewish, feel the culture, identify with it in my heart. It went far beyond genetic links with my father and mother. I didn't feel it was even necessary to believe in Judaism to be a Jew. I've met many Jews who consider themselves 100% Jewish but are also atheists, and do not speak a word of Hebrew. Doesn't culturally identifying with Arabness or Jewishness go beyond a religious identity? It's the underpinnings of heart feelings that take precedence over one's identity, I believe, and, "The blood doesn't lie."

But when I refer to blood, I don't just mean how blood is constituted genetically; I mean cultural identity, raw emotions, intellectual and spiritual magnetic attractions, even more important underpinnings of an ethnic identity. Could that be the same about religion? Is cosmic essence more fluid than interpretations of a particular religious book? That we are encouraged for various reasons to focus on one ideology and exclude others, is that conforming to the cosmic essence? It's perhaps unrealistic to ideologically polarize ourselves since many ideologies—including Christianity, Judaism and Islam, among others— overlap in many ways, without discounting there are also fundamental differences. Should we then ask ourselves why we sometimes so desperately, so fervently, attach ourselves to a particular philosophy, lifestyle, drug, tradition, or ideology? As I stood there reading about the yeshiva built on the property purchased by Avram Romano in Hebron, a warm current, like an incoming Mediterranean tide, flowed through me.

The central source was the magnetic field surrounding this magical Holy Land. The voice of Avram Romano echoed off the walls of this short street as I walked with David and Clémence toward the Israeli soldier tower; not a soul was in the streets. Before reaching the tower, where one lone soldier watched us through binoculars, we stepped into a passageway leading to a statuesque white building. A metal plate was imbedded in the stone, on which was inscribed, "Yeshiva." I thought to myself, Such a strange, almost deserted, place gave rise to a Jewish religious school, but where is everybody? As I contemplated the possible connections of my family to such holy soil, I felt purified, standing before this yeshiva. I felt a strong, vibrational link with the earth as I asked myself, How can it be? I feel as if I've been here before.

Nostalgia, waves of yearnings to go home filled my mind as I looked around.[103] We started winding back toward the Abraham Mosque/Synagogue, where we took a Jewish bus back to Jerusalem. Soldiers had informed us that a bus stopped every hour in front of it. The bus traveled through several upscale settlements bordered by trees, sidewalks and modern one-story houses with lawns and long, clean streets as opposed to the route the Arab shuttle took, mainly through old, shabby Arab villages on the way to Hebron.

Traveling through the settlements helped me understand why settlers were so adamant about holding on to them as they consisted of permanent, well-built dwellings, some with swimming pools. During an interview with an Israeli soldier, he related that a disproportionately large number of Israeli soldiers in the West Bank came from settlements compared to those coming from other places. Would that not make them even more adamant supporters of the Israeli occupation, since they were defending the settlements where they were born and raised, where their families presently resided? The bus let us off at the central bus station in downtown Jerusalem; the Arab buses and shuttles would let us off at the Damascus Gate, near the Old City.

Back in the rooming house in East Jerusalem, after all the events and the catharsis I had experienced in Hebron, I needed several days of rest. David returned to Germany and Clémence to her studies of Hebrew and the Jewish culture in central Jerusalem. Something powerful had hit me in Hebron and I was still not sure what it was.

As I contemplated returning to Hebron, I focused my attention on another part

---

103 Later I discovered during my research that I was standing before the original site that became "Beit Romano" in 1870.

of the West Bank where I intended to organize an interfaith march—the land of Joshua...Jericho. That was where the walls he brought down had been replaced by a whole series of Israeli roadblocks and checkpoints, an indirect siege with echoes from Biblical times.

I was called to organize interfaith marches and dialogues in Jericho that I hoped someday would help bring that proverbial siege to an end. I recalled my disappointing phone call to Adesina in Jericho a couple of days earlier, after returning to the Mount of Olives from Hebron. I was hoping to see her again, especially since I was no longer in relationship.

A different person answered the phone:

"This is Hazika—who's this?" I remember Adesina talking about Hazika and how she was interested in peace marches. "I'm Frank, a friend of Adesina's. I visited her a few months ago. I'm coming to Jericho tomorrow for a peace march I'm organizing. Could you and Adesina join me?"

"Yes, Adesina told me all about you. I'll be available tomorrow and I'd like to introduce you to the principal of the school where I work and also to other people, including the mayor of Jericho."

"Fantastic! Will I see Adesina?"

"I'm sorry to tell you that she got married and has moved to Nablus."

My heart jumped and I could feel the dryness in my mouth. Hazika's silence led me to believe that she knew about our long-distance romance and was waiting to hear my reaction.

"Well, ah...ah...um, yes, I'm sorry I won't see her but, I'm...I'm happy she's happy."

My stuttering, stumbling and my words probably didn't fool her.

"I'm really sorry. As your letters showed, you really cared for her, but...."

I knew that our long distance romance wouldn't last but fantasized on how sweet our life together could have been...but too late...too late! I let out a long breath of air, telling myself I had missed a great lady.

Hazika tried to comfort me, "I'm so...."

I didn't want to hear that so I quickly interjected, "Oh, I'm ok, I'm ok. Look, I'll arrive tomorrow around noon. Can I see you then, as planned?"

"Of course! Of course! Just call me on my cell and give your cell to the driver who will take you to me!"

"OK, shukran. Ma'a salama, Hazika." (Thanks, goodbye)

"Ahlan wa-sahlan, ma'a salama."

I organized an interfaith peace march in Adesina's city, Jericho, one year later since it took me that long to accept my fate: that I would never see Adesina again.

Chapter 70 : Walls of Jericho

I was still exhausted from the Hebron trip but I figured that I'd catch up after I returned to Paris in a few weeks. Anyway, as I sat in my room dizzy with sleep, I bolted upright and shouted out, "I came to help spread the word of peace and I must continue. People are counting on me. When I'm dead I'll have plenty of time to sleep. In fact, then I can sleep for an eternity!"

That got me out of bed and buckling my sandals. It was Jericho, or bust!

I descended the stairs and saw the eternal Ibrahim, the father of peace, in the kitchen. That night I spoke to him at the communal table about the interfaith event in Jericho, eating some of the scrumptious dish he had prepared in a metal container that looked like a huge paella pot. It consisted of a stew made with fresh vegetables: squash, tomatoes and potatoes, mixed with rice.

During our visit, we were joined by a young Chinese adolescent who wore his long, silky black hair in a ponytail and had sparkling eyes. He introduced himself as Huang, as he reached for a couple slices of the flat bread. After breaking the bread into small pieces, he dipped one of them in the dish of stew.

As he ate, he looked at me without saying a word, in that subtle Chinese way; but he said a lot, in his way. I explained to Ibrahim that I was meeting with a teacher in Jericho the next morning who was helping me with an interfaith march to take place that afternoon. The Chinese boy had stopped eating as ravenously so I knew he was listening. I also was convinced that his sparkling eyes were saying he wanted to come.

Ibrahim gave me his usual blessings before I stood up to leave. I peered at Huang whose eyes hadn't left mine for the last fifteen minutes.

"Will you join me here tomorrow morning at 8:30 am?" I asked. He nodded.

I'd return to Jericho, this time not for preparation but for the real thing…the "Freedom March." The faith and trust of Joshua coursed through my blood as I contemplated a visit to one of the oldest centers of conflict in the world. The next morning, Huang and I grabbed the usual accoutrements: the loudspeaker, the sign and plenty of fliers written in Arabic and English. We headed for the Damascus Gate via the usual Arab bus.

In an hour or so, the shuttle driver announced our arrival in Jericho, which roused me from a deep slumber. My blurry eyes slowly focused on Huang who was sitting faithfully by the window, his nose pressed against it. Every once in a while he sat back, adjusted his camera, then pointed it out the window.

I knew we were on the last leg of the trip, because the dust arising behind the taxi signaled we were on the dirt roads leading to the center of Jericho. One of the oldest cities in the world still had dirt roads leading to it; there must be a reason.

And other thoughts invaded my mind:

The sweet Adesina won't be there to greet me with her warm, loving smile; she was married!

I tried to calm my pounding heart and push those thoughts aside as I looked through my window at the magical place we were about to enter. Entering the city, I called Hazika, as planned, then handed the phone to the shuttle driver who would take us to Hazika's office.

As it bounced down the streets in Palestinian style, I reflected on the joyous moments spent with Adesina, in spite of the crisis affecting her during my last visit.

The shuttle left us off in front of the school building where Hazika worked.

Huang and I were led into a room where an African lady wearing a dark-brown blouse and slacks was sitting. A lady sitting next to her was wearing a black hijab. The black lady spoke first, as she reached out: "I'm Hazika and you're the famous Frank I heard about!"

"Yeah, right…famous," I uttered sardonically and hugged her.

She took a step back and looked at Huang, inquisitively. "You are all so, so welcome. Who's your friend?"

"This is Huang." As I introduced him, he extended his hand and shook Hazika's.

"Thank you for coming, for joining our cause. This is my colleague, Nida, who works as an administrator of the city schools here in Jericho."

"Pleased to meet you," I responded. Nida nodded.

"Hazika, I sent you a flier about the freedom march/dialogue to take place today at three pm on Hesham Palace Street, downtown Jericho. You, your family and friends are all welcome to join us."

She looked with wide eyes at her colleague.

"Frank, I remember the flier. But you need to know something. It is so hot, that people stay inside until around seven pm."

"You're suggesting that we change the time, after sending out fliers announcing the march starts at three pm?"

She responded firmly, but with a Cheshire smile that creased her face, "No one will be there; no one at three!"

"But Hazika, we have to return to Jerusalem tonight, and experience tells me we won't find a service taxi to take us back after seven pm. We can't afford…."

"No problem; you can find a service taxi until ten pm in the main square here.

Also, your march is scheduled in the former center of the city. The downtown area of the city has recently shifted to "Central Square" and is no longer Hesham Palace Street where you originally intended to march. That is where you must now have your march/dialogue because that's where the people go."

I turned to Huang who displayed his usual poker face beneath the bright eyes.

His eyes, however, mirrored the confusion in mine. Hazika made some calls and then turned to me.

"I've set up a meeting with the mayor of Jericho, now. Please see my driver outside who will take you to his office."

She stood up to indicate the end of our meeting while Nida got up and walked out of the room. We all headed for the main door through which we had entered a short while before.

I opened the door and she stepped out in the hot sun with me. A van was waiting about 10 yards away with the motor running. Hazika's smile wreathed her face as I gave her a parting hug.

"I'm sorry but I won't be at your march because one of my cousin's kids is sick and I have to drive him to the doctor's this afternoon. I wish you good luck and please come back and visit us again someday."

I thanked her and Huang and I turned, heading for the van. We hopped into the back seat before the door closed and were whisked away to another part of the city.

In about 10 minutes, after we had been dropped off in front of a large gray and white building, Huang and I followed a large woman wearing a gray hijab down a long corridor to the Jericho mayor's office. We were led into a long, oval-shaped conference room, with three chairs around a table. The woman left us there.

A few minutes later, she returned carrying a tray with two cups of coffee on it. We drank in silence.

Not long after, a young, spirited Palestinian man almost sprinted into the room. His red cheeks and hint of a beard contrasted with his white shirt, black pants and pointed black shoes. He quickly came to where we were seated and not waiting for us to stand, shook our hands with nervous vigor and walked around the table to sit down.

"What can I do for you?" were his first words.

I placed my elbows on the table and leaned toward the mayor. "My friend and I, we're here for a freedom march/dialogue that we've scheduled for three pm around the Central Square and we'd like your help and hopefully your participation."

He leaned back, his brown eyes darting from Huang to me, then back to Huang; then he smiled.

"Shukran, my friend. I'm an assistant to the mayor of this city who unfortunately can't be with us right now; he just received a call from our mutual friend, Hazika, and is informed of your project and supports you fully."

But I had some burning questions: "Yes, I...I don't know how to put this, but when our shuttle from Jerusalem approached Jericho, we rode on dirt roads for at least 15 minutes. I...."

He cut me off, almost as if he anticipated my question, and responded quickly, looking at Huang, "Many people, especially Asians—like Japanese NGOs—show up with blueprints and plans to build businesses and improve the infrastructure, like the roads. They ultimately need authorization from the State of Israel; after 3-4 weeks of waiting around and no response, they return to Japan or elsewhere and the plans fail. The complications involved in the authorization process by Israel have unfortunately, as other people here will confirm, stopped potential growth in the West Bank, including the paving of the roads."

Huang and I watched as he seemed to madly gesticulate his frustration away, finishing with a nervous smile, "That prayer—salat—and family unity saves us as we stay close, keep praying. By the way, tell me again when you plan to have this march or dialogue?"

"At three...." He cut off my response.

"At three, no one will be there; it's too hot...they're home. You must return at seven pm or later and people will show up. You'll see...."

I didn't let him finish: "Ok, we'll do it at seven pm."

"Fantastic! By the way, I have a journalist friend who I will call right." He bent down to punch a number on his cell phone with his thumb.

"Marhaba!" he said quickly, and a stream of Arabic followed. He pressed another button with his thumb and looked up at the same time.

"He will be there at around 7:30 pm! Anything else I can help you with?"

"OK, shukran, but we also need to return to Jerusalem tonight."

"No problem. A service taxi goes until nine pm and will take you to Ramallah." The end of our meeting fast approaching, as Huang looked on, I gave it a last shot to explain our goals: "Insh'Allah, (God willing), we'll help end this horrible occupation and facilitate peaceful solutions for working with Israel. We're dedicated to bringing Muslims, Jews, Christians together, to talk, to love, to grow together...."

"Cuellos," (good) he whispered, his eyes shifting from left to right as he raised both hands, palms together, in front of us. "Allah be with you and protect you."

I wondered why he added, "Allah...protect you," but I didn't have time to ruminate over it as he rose, signifying the end of our meeting.

"Oh, how do we get to Central Square?"

"As soon as you leave the building, turn left and you will arrive in about 20 minutes."

He accompanied us down the stairs and out the main door. After saying our goodbyes and Huang and I had turned to go, the mayor's assistant yelled, "I'll send the press...."

The display of my cell phone showed one pm. We had a long wait in this city at the lowest elevation in the world: it was a stifling dust bowl. Following the man's instructions, we soon stumbled into Central Square, around which we planned to have our march/dialogue. It was completely abandoned and the stores and cafés surrounding it were almost all closed. I could barely make out an open door as we passed a café on the left. We walked past a closed Turkish sandwich bar at the entrance to the café.

We walked in. A man with a long face and a bushy black moustache greeted us with a forced smile. I was sure he would announce he was closed.

"Open?"

"Ahlan wa sahlan. Yes, yes, of course!"

We were relieved as we slipped into black, wooden chairs surrounding a solid black table. After we had lunched on kabob sandwiches and drank sodas, I glanced at my watch; it was 2:30 pm. We couldn't stay in the café all day so I suggested to

Huang that we walk around and look for a place to rest ourselves. We walked around the square and all the shops, including the sweet shops, were closed. The fruit stands had burlap sacks draped on them to keep the sun off; the restaurants were in darkness.

We walked on a road leading away from the square; the heat was sweltering as we kept walking. We came across a modern-looking mosque and walked in. It was cool inside and the only sound was that of several fans stationed about the room. It must have been in between prayers, because only two men were sitting in front on the carpeted floor, resting. A third was sitting with his back propped up against the wall, straddling a wooden lectern on which a Qur'an was placed. His lips were moving and must have been reciting from the book.

None of the men looked our way as I placed the plastic bag carrying the sign and the loud speaker in a corner. We then sat with our backs to the wall. My cell phone told me it was only three pm. We had another four hours to wait for our freedom march.

I looked around again to see if anyone noticed we were camped in back. No one was looking at us. I reached in my book bag and took out a small inflatable pillow. Huang was already sprawled out on the carpet, his head resting on the palms of his hands, fast asleep. I lay my head down and I was out in a few minutes....

I dreamed I was shuffling down an indoor corridor, stepping over people whose feet were sticking out from chairs as they sat at cafés. Their frightening stares— white eyes with no pupils—made me walk faster. A group of white-eyed people followed. When I slowed down, a group of men, some wearing red and white keffiyehs with long beards, some floating in their robes, would stop; then as soon as I moved, they continued. I turned the corner and walked into a field. I was barefoot; the hot rocks burned the bottoms of my feet and I was sweating profusely. Someone emitted a bizarre banshee wail, strangely echoing across the fields. I walked faster, sweating, ever faster, the drops of perspiration cascading down on the hard clay as I walked....

*　*　*

I awoke with the loud calling to prayer by the muezzin; the mosque began filling with people. As the streets were empty not long ago, I wondered where all the people were coming from. Huang was now sitting and reading with his back to the wall. When the muezzin called again, I got up and walked to the front of the line to join the people in prayer; Huang kept reading. A kindly, balding man wearing a light-blue djellabah saw me coming and shifted to the right to make room for me.

"Assalamu alaykum." "Alaykum Assalamu."

After the prayer session, I returned to the back of the mosque. It was about six pm. It was time to pack up and walk to the Central Square.

Before we left, a couple of older parishioners visited with us while we were organizing our belongings. One had a red face and wore a white keffiyeh with a black band; the other was bald except for gray tufts around his head. They held out their hands and we shook them.

"Ahlan wa-sahlan." (welcome) That gesture gave us strength. "Where you from?"

331

The question came in familiar broken English with a slight infusion of energy, perhaps to overcome the apathy the sun's rays had generated. The ambience of the mosque was deeply spiritual, prayerful; there, we weren't asked whether we were Muslim, or not.

The words were articulated by a paraplegic man who had limped toward us. Without waiting for a response, he placed his hand in my outstretched hand. He closed his eyes and a short prayer seemed to flow from his lips. I nodded and smiled.

In the silence of our handshake and prayer, I engaged simultaneously in a profound meditative healing session, sending love-filled electrons into his body through his hand still holding onto mine. His head tilted back as the waves of love were undulating through him.

He rose and limped out the door, with renewed energy; then he stopped and looked back. He knew. Then he grabbed the hand of an elderly man, perhaps his father, walked across a patio between the mosque and a gate, and out into the street, where he slipped from view. The symbolism of that meeting filled me with the seeds of love, germinating a stronger knowing in my heart of the oneness I had experienced connecting with the man, through our hands.

Huang and I collected our things and headed out the door to Jericho's Central Square.

I glanced at my cell phone and noticed it was about seven pm. We found our shoes at the entrance, slipped them on and headed for the door. As we opened it, the warm dust-bowl wind blew on us; it reminded me of how it felt to get too close to an open oven door. It also reminded me of our challenge, which was to keep our energy high, so we could mobilize the people during the "Freedom March" in spite of the heavy, sizzling air.

As we left the mosque, more activity was churning in the streets than when we had entered the mosque a few hours earlier. Some young men were riding in mule carts, tapping the backs of the working beasts from time to time with a thick whip, while others were hurriedly opening their stores, folding the burlap sacks, opening doors with large metal keys, preparing for the onslaught. The clanking was barely discernible above the drone of a city reawakening from its afternoon slumber in this hot, muggy setting.

We arrived at Central Square. Its present effervescence was a radical change from the somber ghost town it had been, somnolent under the hot blanket of the desert sky. The sweet shop doors were optimistically wide open and the aroma of their sugary delights wafted into the streets; as I walked by, I fantasized dunking delectable sugar cookies in the rich Arabic coffee.

The middle of the Central Square consisted of a short fence enclosing a small park in which several benches were distributed over a path bordered by grass and short shrubs. A sidewalk, the path of our march, bordered all four sides of the square. I cast my eyes over the benches, sweeping over the grass and bushes, to discover that, apart from a bench inhabited by a couple of older men, the entire park was still empty.

I handed about 50 fliers to Huang and I kept about a 100. I walked inside the park through a narrow passageway and headed for the two on the bench. I saw Huang heading to the stores and cafés surrounding the square.

As I got closer, I said, "Marhaba" and handed them a flier about the march; they turned their sunburned heads to me after reading the short blurb in Arabic, their beady eyes embedded in puffy, shiny skin, burned by the relentless rays of the sun.

I then walked outside the circle to shop owners, fruit sellers, butchers, and in the coffee shops and restaurants situated around the Central Square park area.

People took the fliers and said, "Shukran and Insh'Allah," (Thanks and God willing) implying they might show up.

Huang joined me later, after he had handed out the fliers I had given him. It was time for the march. I rolled out the sign on the periphery of the Square and raised it with the help of Huang. We set out walking around the periphery as I raised my lips to the loudspeaker: "La Ilaha Ilanla, Adonai Elohaynu Adonai Echad and God the Father Son and Holy Ghost."

We walked around the circumference of the square three times, and nobody joined us; but we kept our heads up chanting and handing out fliers.

Then something strange happened. We entered the path leading to the center of the circle where I had passed out a flier to the two men, one older with a white keffiyeh sitting next to an adolescent. Wedged within their bloated faces were yellow-streaked teeth. Their hands trembled as they stretched to touch and grab another flier. Several adolescents, some on bicycles, grouped together on the other side of the square, saw us talk to the two men. As we walked toward them, they dispersed and left. Then one of them turned and came to us. He grabbed a part of the sign and shouted, "Allahu Akbar!"

At that moment, all the others turned and joined us and soon we were a raucous group marching around the square, for peace.

We chanted in Arabic, "La ilaha ilanla," and in Hebrew, "Adonai Elohaynu Adonai Echad."

More people joined us as we chanted; the circle was gradually expanding, alive with anticipation. Each time we finished one tour around the square, a new person came into our ranks; along with the group of adolescents, we had a crowd of about 10-15 boys from the ages of 7-16. The faith displayed by them, in the intense heat, was unbelievable.

One boy shouted, "Hourriyya Palestine" and I had to shout "Hourriyya Israel." This time nobody frowned, nobody complained that I was chanting to free Israel as well as Palestine.

It was another cathartic day, this time in Jericho's oven, in the heavy, sweltering heat that deterred no one. As we turned the corner, Huang tugged on my sleeve and pointed me to a booth halfway down the sidewalk. A member of the Palestinian Police was summoning me to him.

The boys followed me until I arrived at the booth, then waited patiently on the sidewalk. They apparently weren't afraid of the Palestinian police as they stayed with me the entire time. The policeman asked one question: "What are you doing here?"

I told him that my friend and I came in solidarity for all people in the region, and we wanted peace. Instead of interrogating further, the young man gave me a toothy grin and said, "Shukran, ahlan wa sahlan!"

That was a relief because sometimes a police interrogation stopped the march, or worse, the police would route me away to a distant interrogation center. We resumed marching around the square, and it seemed that the crowd was even more energetically chanting, taking turns yelling through the loud speaker.

Each time we walked in front of the Palestinian police station, the man waved. I felt my feet gliding off the ground, buoyed by the faith and total support of this place, even by the Palestinian police.

Then in front of me, a journalist ran up and took pictures with a fancy camera. I recalled that the assistant mayor, before we left the mayor's office, had promised to send the press to our event. I didn't think anything of that as I'd heard lots of promises without any follow-up. But this would be different as days later, when organizing an interfaith march in Hebron with friends, they produced a copy of Al-Quds, the most important Jerusalem newspaper, with a picture of the march on the front page. Only then did I realize that the mayor's assistant did carry out the promise to "bring the press" to the event.

We circled around until we had a group of about 20 people, and until a silent click went off and I realized it was time.

I turned to the group and putting away the loudspeaker, I yelled as loud as I could, "We will find peace together, kula wahad, with Mouslim, Yahoudiyy, Masiyiyy!" (Peace for all)

They cheered louder than a group of 100 would, anywhere else; we wailed and chanted, as we were all immersed in the spirit of interfaith peace. I turned and addressed them: "I want to invite all of you to a cold drink at the café. Follow me!"

They cheered again and that marked the end of the march.

I treated everyone to a cold drink in the same café where Huang and I had eaten lunch earlier that day. The boys began loudly chanting and repeating, "Houriyya Palestine, Mouslim, Yahoudiyy, Masiyiyy" inside the restaurant. Our work had sprung something loose inside these boys, who were laughing, shouting and crying for peace. "Freedom, freedom...."

The owner came out from behind the bar to calm the crowd as it was disturbing some of the customers eating in the tables nearby. I quickly spoke to them, asking for silence. Silence reigned.

"Shukran, ok, you must leave this place now. But first, tell me what you want—orange soda, sprite—and I will bring it to you. Then you must go!"

I took everyone's order then relayed it to the owner who was pleased as the crowd had calmed down. After everyone was served, I thanked everyone and suggested that they leave and they did.

Huang and I sat at a table, contemplating the good will we had just seen, in this faraway dustbowl, one of the cradles of humanity. As we sat in the café after the march, I looked into my coffee cup and the mound of coffee grounds at the bottom.

I couldn't help but think that facilitating dialogue, helping to establish peace in the Middle East, would be one coffee ground at a time.

Chapter 71: Sheik Bukhari

The last time I had paid my respects to the "Wailing Wall" was during a two-hour silent prayer session there with my friend, David. I had worn my kippah, a present from my love, Dalia, a love lost in the confusion of my round-trips to the West Bank and life in Paris.

After we had prayed for an hour, we left to meet Sufi Sheikh Abdul Aziz Bukhari, Sheikh of the Naqshbandi Sufi Order and head of the Uzbeki Holy Land Community in the Old City, Jerusalem. He also ran the Uzbek Cultural Center out of his house in Jerusalem. We wound through the Via Dolorosa in the Old City.

It was a narrow alley paved with old, gray/brown stone, occasionally shadowed by overhanging arches. Windows were built into old, imposing stone buildings at eye level, set within the walls about a foot and encased in stone. Stone steps jutted out into the path, leading up to solid wooden doors. That was reputed to be the path Jesus was forced to walk leading to the place of his crucifixion.

We avoided colliding with carts carrying fabrics, vegetables, or coffee by darting in and out of the pathway. Vendors lining the streets vied for our attention, entreating us to taste a sugary desert or feel a handmade woven tapestry.

Our Jewish friend, Benjamin, had helped David arrange the meeting with Sheik Bukhari. We called him as we wound our way up Via Dolorosa; he insisted that we keep a low profile upon our arrival at his door and he'd explain later. We arrived a few minutes late and pressed the doorbell. A young, dark-haired girl opened the door, its bottom grating on the cement as it opened into a courtyard. We followed the girl to the top of a narrow flight of stairs at the edge of the courtyard. She walked regally up a couple more flights of steps to an unmarked door.

Her key turned and we followed her into a lavishly furnished drawing room. She motioned that we sit on high-backed Arab couches as she climbed the stairs in the middle of the room. A few minutes later she descended the stairs, her warm, earthy smile tempering my first impression of a queenly demeanor; she poured the tea.

Sheik Bukhari and Benjamin arrived about 15 minutes later. The door opened and a man with a gray beard and a wide smile was followed by a dark-bearded Benjamin, who walked through the door and headed for us. We had sunk down a foot or two into those cozy sofas.

"Ahlan wa sahlan. I'm Sheik Bukhari; glad to meet you."

I shook his hand. His smile reflected intense warmth and a bit of sadness, causing it to droop and tremble a little, in spite of his attempt to hide it. He opened another door farther down the corridor and motioned us to follow him. David and I grabbed our tea and followed Benjamin into the back room.

Sheik Bukhari sat in a high-backed easy chair, a broad smile beaming out from his full, gray beard. He wore a multi-colored skull cap. I had never met him yet he had opened his home up to us. He waved us into an antechamber filled with exquisite relics and paintings done in the Uzbek tradition and pointed to large, comfortable sofas where we were served another round of warm drinks by his gracious daughter, this time strong Arabic coffee...my medicine!

Around us were multi-colored woven tapestries and rugs[104] hanging on the wall, behind wooden china cabinets lavishly laden with handmade pottery with blue and pearl-white designs, and other relics from the Uzbek community. In addition, antique chairs embroidered with glittering gold and silver thread lined the room, along with a few old musical instruments and clocks with beautiful wooden inlays featuring ornate wood carvings that reminded me of rococo designs on the ceiling of the Sorbonne in Paris.

Majestic silver urns were displayed in the wooden china cabinet above, solid and stately; they were remnants of another time, a world that would perhaps be considered uncultured by some, but which produced works of sublime beauty and passion. On the walls hung portraits of probably several generations of Bukhari family members, notably of an elderly man wearing a creamy white turban. Displayed on these walls was the story of the family which had been living in the Old City since 1616, steeped in the rich culture embodied in these multicolored works of boundless artistic energy. In addition to the vases, tapestries and other relics, I was later informed there were about 200 original handwritten manuscripts in Arabic, Uzbek, and Persian dealing with, but not limited to, religious matters; bookshelves were full of leather and tinted paper-bound books.

During our ensuing discussion about interfaith events in the Middle East, profound warmth pervaded my entire body. In such moments, I had no room in my heart for hate. I always remembered that moment and strived to fill my body and mind with unconditional love and understanding, so I would have no room for the ignorance, greed and lust for power and money that is often a precursor of hate. Maybe that was a key to peace: to help people fill their hearts with love so that there would be no room for anything else! These worthy and profound feelings emanated from this home, were shared by members of the Bukhari family.

Benjamin, sitting across from me, was not wearing his famous multi-colored kippah and his orthodox Jewish side curls were not showing. Instead, he was wearing a large Muslim skull cap with his side curls tucked in. He followed my eyes and proffered an explanation. He was another mind reader: "You know Sheik Bukhari has been threatened by Islamists who do not agree with his interfaith activities, his work with Muslims, Sufis, Jews and Christians."

---

104 Morton, Shafiq. "Sheik Bukhari : The Real Hero." Jerusalem Peacemakers. 7 March 2011.<http://jerusalempeacemakers.org/in-memoriam/sheik- buchari-the-real-hero/>.

"I don't understand."

Benjamin patiently responded as Sheik Bukhari, sitting next to him, nodded: "Even in the Old City, there seems to an evolution not only toward more orthodox, even extremist Judaism, but also orthodox, even extremist Muslims, some advocating that nothing can come of working with non-Muslims for peace."

"As such," he added, "to avoid fanning the flames of hate and misunderstanding and bringing down the wrath of some extremist groups against my friend here and his family, I disguise myself every time I visit here." He smiled, nodding: "I think you understand now why I asked you to keep a low profile when you came to visit today."

As we sipped our tea, silence prevailed after Benjamin's remarks...a contemplative silence. I mused that the profound resonance of the years within these aged walls of the Old City had not completely absorbed the tension still existing here, especially among religions.

Among those who wanted to work for a durable peace in the region was Sheik Bukhari—a true believer, who sincerely believed it was possible—as opposed to the extremists on both sides, who wanted to impose their ideology and didn't seem to want peace. Sheik Bukhari had spent a lifetime engaged in inspiring people to expand their thinking while expanding their hearts—to think beyond the confines of their intellectual "comfort zones" and try to understand other ideas, cultures, ideologies. What he was trying to do was enhance good faith among the members of different religions, thereby helping to facilitate their continued work together, to bring about the spirit of unconditional love and understanding, thus reducing the impact of fanaticism. He was walking a delicate tightrope, especially here in the Old City. He strived to do that in order to, little by little, help bring about a change in attitude through sharing with each other. He endeavored to show by example how people could live their lives in peace, without imposing on others. He was willing to "do the walk and not just the talk." I so admired him.

The next day, in honor of Sheik Bukhari, I was to lead my first ever march/ dialogue at the Damascus Gate, the opening to the most sacred place in all of Judaism, the Wailing Wall, and the third most sacred place in all Islam, the Temple Mount.

We were warned that a strange mixture of Israeli soldiers and possible extremist groups would greet us the next day, but we had to take that chance to keep the flame of peace going.

Chapter 72: Miracle at Damascus Gate

D avid and I had sent about a hundred emails to people mainly this side of the wall—the Jerusalem side of the check-points, barriers to the free circulation of people—that had cropped up everywhere in the West Bank.

But this march at the Damascus Gate, the opening to the Old City, was designed to especially involve Israelis since it was not only difficult for them to travel to the West Bank, it was illegal under IDF laws. We sent invitations especially to members of an NGO mainly run by Israeli Jews and some Palestinians. We had no idea who planned to show up as decisions about participation in marches/dialogues, for some reason, were often made at the last minute.

The next morning, David and I awoke and sat again at the table of Ibrahim, who had prepared for us a complete breakfast. We walked into the breakfast room to find our plates on the table filled with eggs and a pile of za'atar next to them. After eating the hardboiled eggs dipped in salt, we dipped bread in olive oil and then into the za'atar and washed it all down with a cup of strong Arabic coffee.

Arriving before the Damascus Gate, chills ran through me remembering its history, almost overpowering my concentration. Here Jesus had carried the cross to his death, the temple was destroyed, leaving a wall, Abraham had nearly sacrificed his son and Muhammad had ascended to God....

And now we were there to lead a non-violent interfaith march/dialogue with Jews, Muslims, Christians and people of all faiths, traveling through the souk, passing the entrance at the foot of the Wailing Wall and proceeding almost to the doors of the Al-Aqsa Mosque.

We arrived about two hours before the march. It was 100 degrees that afternoon, as we looked down at the entrance of the Damascus Gate; only a few people lingered there. We descended to the entrance of the souk and tied our Freedom March poster to the railing on one side of the entrance, in plain view of all passersby.

Muslims entered wearing their white skull caps and djellabahs; Jews wore kippahs, some also with fedora black hats, their side curls attesting to their faith; Greek Orthodox priests wore their cylindrical hats and were arrayed in a multitude of colors. Most reached out for the fliers we passed out.

Often the Muslims reached out first and smiled. However, one wearing a white skull cap stood in front of me and tore up the flier, throwing it on the ground and

338

spitting on it. Then he yelled at me, in perfect English: "There will never be freedom—you're wasting your time!"

Then I tried handing the flier to orthodox Jews, without much success, as they were perhaps skeptical about anything labeled "Freedom March." Or maybe it was because they deemed we were subverting what the State of Israel was doing in Israel and in the West Bank.

A short man scurried up to us wearing a blue, flat cap Jews often wear, and reached out to shake my hand. I shook it, looking into his eyes, which all but jumped out of their sockets as he greeted me. His high octane enthusiasm rubbed off on all of us as we crowded around him. He spoke to me in English, with a slight accent:

"This is fantastic; bravo! Where you from?"

Not knowing where he was coming from, I responded that I was staying with friends in East Jerusalem.

"But what country, originally?"

"The United States; I live in...."

He cut me off for another handshake. "I'm with you! When you march?"

"In about an hour."

"Ok!"

An hour later, he was still with us. Before grabbing part of the poster to carry, unabashed, right in the middle of the souk, he turned his head and smiled:

"I'm an anti-Zionist Jew and I believe in your freedom march. I love it." I wasn't sure what he meant by anti-Zionist.

"You're so welcome to join us. What's your name?" "I'm Joseph; and yours?"

"My name's Frank and that's David over there, handing out fliers."

I went to the plastic bag and busied myself unrolling the sign when I felt a thumping on my shoulder. I turned. "Hey, friend."

It was Uri, who I had met at an interfaith event about a year ago in the Abu Tor district. I hugged Uri, a liberal Jew, and very much involved in the interfaith movement. He was lean with short brown hair, wearing a trimmed goatee and his head was always covered with a tweed flat cap. Uri stretched another exuberant smile across his face that jacked up our moods so that we energetically marched for peace, for freedom, for cosmic love. I thought to myself that he was another with boiling-over energy, just what we needed! This march/dialogue was off to a great start!

The sign was extended out in front of me and before I knew it, Uri had one side and Joseph had grabbed the other. David turned the loudspeaker on and handed it to me. We were ready to shoot out from the starting blocks!

I put my lips to the loudspeaker and yelled, "Adonai Elohaynu, Adonai Echad, La ilaha ilanla, and God the Father, Son and Holy Ghost."

"Join us brothers and sisters as we march for peace. Hourriyy Israel! Hourriyy Palestine!"

I headed for the Gate followed by my two Jewish friends, one an anti-Zionist, the other a peace worker. David followed them, continuing to hand out fliers, and two Muslim girls wearing hijabs who had joined us just before we started, followed David. As I entered the open door, there were several vendors selling keffiyehs, handkerchiefs, kippahs, Muslims skull caps, and many other items. I felt a soft tap on my left shoulder and turned around to find myself in front of a woman with a round face framed by a black hijab and troubled brown eyes. I bent down to her lips which were moving, but the noise all around prevented me from hearing her. Her mumbled whispers expressed in broken English her deep conviction in freedom for the Holy Land and the need to dialogue with Jews and Christians. Her hands were holding on to two young children looking up at me with tiny, curious brown eyes, staying close to their mother.

She spoke again: "I want march with you but we arrested? Israeli soldiers everywhere in souk…you crazy?"

I answered her as truthfully as possible, "Little crazy; why not? Normally we can speak our minds. After all, we have a right to speak out. Besides, when we get closer to the soldiers I make sure they know we are reciting Jewish prayers as well. It should be ok…but I can't promise…."

We proceeded into the souk. I marveled at the courage of the young Muslim mother, who even though I couldn't guarantee complete safety from arrest or being detained by Israeli soldiers, chose to step forward with us, walking and dialoguing for peace, for love of all brothers and sisters.

Then she did the unthinkable. She reached for the loudspeaker. I almost fell over as I handed it to her. She yelled at the top of her lungs into the loudspeaker, "Hourriyy Palestine, kula wahad!"

My legs almost collapsed with excitement, amazement and admiration for this mother, risking possible arrest or detention with her two children clinging close to her, as she was now leading the procession. The two other girls wearing identical white hijabs quickly caught up to her and yelled along with her, "Hourriyya Palestine! Hourriyy kula wahad!" they repeated, as we walked through the market.

This was truly an interfaith procession, with Jews, Muslims and Christians leading the way. People in the market yelled "Hourriyy!" and "Allahu Akbar!" We had all heads turned and some were following us. Others joined us walking down the path.

She yelled out again, "Hourriyy, kula wahad, Israel, Palestine!" as she held both kids with one hand, demonstrating astounding "hyman" (faith), the key to durable peace here and everywhere.

Incredible! Her courage pushed us forward. She was the magic carpet which carried us down the path; she held us firm and took us on a ride to peace and freedom through her faith and her courage. She walked with the loudspeaker to her lips, overtaking the two Jews carrying the sign. Uri and Joseph shouted with her as they marched, waving their hands, hijabs, flat caps, signaling the V sign.

Then she turned and handed the loudspeaker back to me. I handed the loudspeaker to Uri, who spoke, chanted and shouted for peace, love and understanding, taking turns with Joseph, as they both held the sign. They chanted and used their words to cajole people into loving unconditionally, helping to bring about universal peace.

"Adonai, Eloyaynu Adonai Echad, Allahu Akbar…hourriyya everyone!"

It was a contingency of peace walking through the Old City, up the Via Dolorosa, the steps Jesus had walked.

Joseph handed me the loudspeaker and I repeated, "Hourriyya Palestine!" but added "Hourriyya Israel!"

Suddenly a young Arab walking with us looked puzzled and corrected me: "La'a Hourriyya, freedom for Israel." (No freedom)

I was happy to engage the young man as this was what the march was all about, in my mind: it was about marching and dialogue, at the same time. I responded, looking right at him, while handing the loudspeaker to Uri: "Yes, hourriyy Israel as well as Palestine. Israelis are prisoners behind the wall as well, my friend. And look, two Jews with us are with you and we're all together. Allahu Akbar!"

He nodded, apparently accepting my explanation, or maybe he was riding on the interfaith wave of peace spurred on in particular by the Muslim mother followed by Uri and Joseph carrying the sign, "Freedom March," in three languages.

Then I handed the loudspeaker to him and he grabbed it, yelling, "Allahu Akbar!" and extended it back to me, insisting he had said what he wanted to say.

But then he added, as we turned the corner to walk up a narrow path, "Israelis are free, we are in prison...."

Then he turned away trying to hide his frown.

"It's Ok, sadiq, I understand...we'll talk more."

He nodded again as I grabbed the loudspeaker, excited that we could dialogue and march at the same time, a sine qua non for the march. I cried passionately, "La ilaha ilanla! Allahu Akbar!"

We approached a fork in the market: two paths, one it seemed going toward the Wailing Wall, the other continuing along the Via Dolorosa. Booths were on either side, some selling café, others tourist trinkets, key rings with the Wailing Wall depicted on them or the Al-Aqsa Mosque, more keffiyehs.

I picked the path continuing down the Via Dolorosa as I looked back at the marchers, who nodded and continued following—we were all caught up in the effervescent colors of the market and the bustle. Several Israeli soldiers were placed two-by-two along the path, apparently stationed there anticipating our march. Heads turned as I belted out again, eyeing the soldiers, "Adonai, Eloyaynu, Adonai Ehad," in Hebrew. The Israeli soldiers let us pass, nodding. However, another young man's head turned toward me. I noticed a huge mark in the middle of his forehead, like a charcoal mark, the point where his forehead touches the ground during prayer, no doubt.

His white djellabah flailed in the wind of his anger as his enraged eyes fixed on me, upon hearing my Jewish prayer.

I caught his eyes on mine, embraced them, gazing directly into them, as we walked stride for stride. I put my arms on his shoulders and spoke, "But it means the same thing as La Ilanha Ilanla; one God!"

"Ok, ok," he smiled, since I had put it that way.

But I didn't know for sure whether it was ok out of resignation, acceptance or lack of comprehension. I'll never know for sure, but I was optimistic I had succeeded in communicating an interfaith principle that Muslims, Jews and Christians can embrace and share. The man stayed with us until the end of the march.

The souk vendors turned their eyes to us. A customer bent over a table trying on a bracelet bearing an inscription of a Palestinian flag, turned his head, leaving the bracelet on the table. He screamed, "Allahu Akbar!" I repeated it and gave him the loudspeaker: "Allahu Akbar" he repeated, his tongue rolling the r in the Arabic way.

My eye caught the boy, who had originally frowned, now smiling as he threw back his head during an unbridled surge of emotion and yelled, "Na'am, Allahyu Akbar!"

This was a dialogue, not like the one in Jericho and in Hebron; but they're all different, I mused. It seemed as though my calling for facilitating dialogue is communicating with the people in the streets—at the grass roots level—rather than participating in the more grandiose meetings of others working for peace, with cameras clicking and mouths watering over hummus and other delicacies served in the five-star hotels.

The Daniel Pearl grassroots movement comes to mind, which is truly founded on the enlightened principle of bringing interfaith dialogue to the people, into the synagogues, mosques and churches, as well as the community centers. Those events are not held in five-star hotels, venues that tend to exclude many of the people who want to attend but can't afford to. Also, the grassroots events avoid making broad statements about durable peace that are broadcast worldwide without any follow-up: just empty words spoken by those hungry for the instant limelight and not sincerely trying to make a difference in the peace process. Those grandiose statements and promises made tend to fall into "les oubliettes." (tend to be forgotten)

It was time to hand the loudspeaker to the boy; his brown hand wrapped over it and he grabbed it away from me. I gladly gave it up.

"Bismillah...." (In the name of God, Allah), he eagerly declared at the same time he placed the loud speaker in front of his lips. He then uttered a stream of Arabic words which triggered a roaring applause from the men in the booths who raised their arms in approval.

Then a chorus of "Allahu Akbar!" came from the crowd.

I would scream, "Allahu Akbar!" then wait for the crowd to repeat, "Allahu Akbar!" again and again. The marchers and vendors and some of their customers would retort, "La ilahla ilanla," echoing as we marched toward the end.

As we got back on the Via Doloroso, this time a sharp pain pierced my skull... and I felt the crown of thorns that had gouged the hallowed temple of Jesus, not so long ago, when he had walked down the same path. He was the epitome of a man of peace, of unconditional love....

It was hot: my parched throat ached for refreshment and my legs were beginning to feel like noodles, but I couldn't help but reflect on Jesus' thirst and the awful sour vinegar given to him, yet he did not complain...he asked God to forgive his transgressors.

He shared his message, even through his death, and although the world was deprived of his life, his wisdom, his words have endured.

I'm privileged here to be able to share my spiritual passion, in writing. Jesus was happy to share his words with all who would listen. Somehow, he must have known his teachings would be forever memorialized; that's what was important—to share the word—and his great faith became immortalized, giving people strength for all time.

The same goes for Mohammed: he was also enlightened and dedicated to sharing his words, while entrusting others to write them down.

We walked along, hand in hand, holding on to each other, helping each other hang on until the end. I called out on the loudspeaker, "Shalom, Sal'aam, peace brothers and sisters!"

Our march took a turn to the left, up a flight of stairs, now moving away from the Wailing Wall and out an exit. Some of the marchers had fallen away, taking the various paths winding through the labyrinth of the old city, but they were still in our hearts....

The path took us through an arched entrance leading us outside of the Old City; we looked back at the solid stone wall surrounding it. Our march was almost at its end.

I stood back and made a quick accounting of the marchers who had not been engulfed in the labyrinthine streets of the Old City. One of the Jews, Uri, was there, followed by the faithful, omnipresent David, then two young Arab boys and the two girls in hijabs; the mother with her two kids had disappeared before we got to the Wailing Wall, after passing the two Israeli soldiers.

Uri said he knew of a great café/bookstore nearby and took the lead. During the walk I continued yelling in the loudspeaker for interfaith unity, unconditional love for all brothers and sisters. However, after a few minutes, my mouth's raspy dryness stopped me; I needed to drink.

I could feel my edge slowly ebbing, ebbing as the sun continued beating down on us—we all needed refreshment.

Uri led us down a narrow sidewalk bordering a street lined by the typical mixture of vendors selling anything from home utensils to electronics. By then I was weary and desperately thirsty but I continued to ride the bright wave of the incredible march/dialogue in this Old City.

Finally, we were led into an upscale, western-style bookstore, with wooden bookshelves full of books written in English and French, along with a selection written in Hebrew and Arabic. A café was situated upstairs.

Uri led us up narrow wooden stairs to the café where we sat as a waiter took our order. I looked around the table to see who had made it through the market of the Old City and who had followed Uri all the way to our stopping point. Two Arab boys who had helped hand out hundreds of fliers were contentedly sipping their sodas from tall bottles while Uri, David and I waited for our coffee. We had requested Arabic coffee but the waiter proudly brought espresso, as if to say, "This more chic." Even though drinking Italian "ristretto" espresso was second nature, I had grown accustomed to street Arabic coffee, which rivals any espresso for taste and strength. The caffeine lift was much needed to replenish my energy after the intense march.

I sat there nursing my espresso, still wondering why Moshe and many mainstream Israeli Jews had abandoned us; not one had showed up for the marches/dialogues. Neither Moshe nor any Hukuk interfaith group organizers were responding to my telephone calls or emails, even after I had sent them fliers announcing the next interfaith march/dialogue.

I sat there trying to visualize working with them harmoniously on interfaith events; but Benjamin had warned me that they might abandon me, blacklist me.

Chapter 73: Blacklisted

Benjamin and I were walking near Jaffa Gate in Jerusalem with a group of friends. He was, along with Moshe—who acted sometimes as his assistant—one of the leaders of an internationally renowned interfaith peace NGO. I asked him why Sarah of Hukuk Kibbutz and Moshe wouldn't respond to my phone calls or emails, when they were so prompt in responding before.

Benjamin replied, "Frank, if you insist on using the word 'occupation' in your fliers, and discuss the importance of Israel withdrawing from the occupied territories or Palestine before there can be peace in the land, you will lose the support of the mainstream Jews like Moshe."

I pondered that. As we walked in silence, I couldn't help but think that he was including himself in that group, even though he was the only mainstream peacenik Jew still responding to my emails and inviting me to some events. Then I wondered if he would also terminate our relationship.

It was unbelievable that my continued friendship with all those peaceniks depended on changing the wording of the flier.

"You know my focus is to bring people together for interfaith peace dialogues, during marches. It's a spiritual thing, but I can't deny...."

Benjamin interrupted, "You need to be true to your vision, Frank, of interfaith unity without political interference."

"But...."

"Hear me out, Frank. That is, don't let politics take over the dialogue, marches.

Mainstream Jews think that the word 'occupation' triggers hate against the State of Israel and opens the Pandora's box of emotions preventing a true dialogue, preventing the sharing of ideas in a constructive, unemotional way."

"Here, Benjamin; here's a sample flier with the words that Moshe and all the other peacenik Jews reject."

I pointed out the paragraph that many mainstream Israeli Jews objected to: Moreover, removing most of the West Bank settlements would help in diffusing the tension accelerating since 1967. As such, the occupation of the West Bank must end as a precursor to peaceful coexistence on the condition that adequate security measures are taken by both sides to secure the borders and preserve the peace.

He pushed the flier away.

"I know what it says, Frank, as I read every flier you've sent me for your events."

"Before I sent the flier out to hundreds of people, I remember asking Moshe about that and he said I should not use negative terms. He made an analogy between that paragraph and citing the occupation of Europe by Hitler and the Nazis which would ignite hate against the Germans."

"I don't know where you're going with that."

"Well, for instance, Moshe suggests that I replace the word 'occupation' with a more positive phrase, 'Israeli involvement in the West Bank.' He even suggests I don't talk about Israel's intervention in the West Bank at all as it, again, would inspire negative emotions."

"I agree; why bring politics in to inflame people, driving them to feel irrational emotions that would stifle communication and stop the dialogue in its tracks?"

"I'm a firm believer in keeping positive, Benjamin, for sure, and keeping any negative stuff out. But I asked even the most liberal Palestinians, who have Jewish friends, whether the interfaith peace marches/dialogues would make any sense if I left the term, 'occupation' out of the tract. You know what the response was?"

I looked at Benjamin walking beside me. He looked back at me for the response.

"They said no!"

I continued. "You know, my friend, even though my focus, like yours, is on non-violent interfaith peace, I can't deny what's happening; I can't kick out references to what is happening. Besides, it's a compromise I've made with Palestinians as my work is to mobilize them, as well. I'd lose them if...."

I stopped and Benjamin sighed, compressing his lips. As we approached our destination, I tried to learn more from my friend. "I appreciate you taking the time to explain these things—at least that's more than my other Jewish friends have done lately. But it seems that there is a denial of what is really happening. Aren't we being a little overprotective of the State of Israel? I'm definitely in favor of preserving the State of Israel, but we do have the right to criticize...."

Benjamin interjected, "You do important work; but remember, you'll lose people, lots of Israeli Jews...your friends. Stick to your vision you told me about...your true interfaith non-political calling!"

I returned to the Mount of Olives in deep thought and wondering where I was to go from there after the incredible Old City march. I also thought about the vision Benjamin was referring to and I prayed I was being faithful to it.

But dreams of following my vision were shattered by the murder of a friend and fellow peace activist.

Book IV

Death and Rebirth

"...do not leave me in this abyss, where I cannot find you! Oh, God! it is unutterable! I cannot live without my life! I cannot live without my soul!"[105]

---

105 Emily Brontë, Wuthering Heights (London: Penguin Classics, Penguin Books, 2003), Vol. II, Ch. 2, p.169.

Chapter 74: Lance Wolf

The soothing night air on the Mount of Olives softly fanned my face as I looked out the open window over the glimmering lights of East Jerusalem, in the valley below. The lights illuminated a place suffering from repression, but persevering. The inhabitants are subjected to a network of complicated and often unfair rules, regulations and encroachment on their land; but the Arabs in East Jerusalem fight on, with faith. It's the same struggle as that in the West Bank, with the same results: fighting on, with the help of a myriad of volunteers, including many Jews, Muslims, Christians and members of other faiths. Yet, I've asked the same questions so many times: "Where is everybody?" or when my bus or shuttle arrives from Damascus Gate to Hebron or Jenin, "Where are all the peace workers, or even tourists? People don't come here. Why?"

I walked down the stairs of my rooming house. At the bottom of the stairs I heard the familiar clinking of dishes, glasses being set on the table. Lance, a Jewish American and recently made an Israeli citizen, was sitting in his usual place, doing his usual thing—breaking off pieces of flat bread and popping them into his mouth. It seemed so odd that he was eating bits of bread since his ultra-skinny frame seemed to need something more. His beady eyes were downcast, focusing on his glass of mint tea clasped between his bony fingers, his jaw was set and strands of black and white beard flowed over his wrinkled cheeks.

He had been a resident in the rooming house for over a year and worked with Ibrahim, the owner, to improve his website and help him send emails in English. He was saying to me that I was an oasis for him, as the house was visited by many NGO Protestant do-gooders, there to impose their ideas, their ideology, instead of exploring potential solutions to the conflict.

"Good to see you, Bro." He always greeted me that way before we did our traditional bear hug.

"It's great to see you too, man!"

Then he would start: "Man, I thank God for your visit. I'm constantly surrounded by either some fascist Christians who want to impose their solutions on the world, or by radical Jews, Nazis who blindly support the State of Israel in everything—and I mean everything—including the abuses perpetrated by Israeli soldiers in the West

Bank, the massacres committed after 1948. You name it! When you're here, at least I've some support, from somebody," he chuckled in his raspy, cigarette voice way, "otherwise I'd go insane. Lot of talk about peace, nobody doing anything; at least you're trying to do something. You know the Jerusalem peaceniks are organizing 'The Hug.'[106] Ok, we both think something is better than nothing, right?"

I broke in, "I hear you, but hugging is great! The principle of that event is fabulous, bringing together people of all races, religions for unity, in the name of love, of Jerusalem, but I wonder if there is much follow-up after The Hug?"

Lance nodded as he played with his tea bag. "But we all need to roll up our sleeves and go into Palestinian refugee camps and Jewish settlements, to work with them, do the walk as well as the talk. Everyone's doin' the talk, but the walk...."

I nodded as Lance continued: "I even wonder if The Hug and other activities help bring Moslems, Jews, Christians and others together for a durable peace or do they mainly serve as atonement for guilty Israeli Jews, help them believe they're doing something when they're primarily concerned with overcoming guilt, with no serious intentions to change anything, to free the Palestinians in the West Bank, for instance. What's peace, love, hugs, without freedom?"

"But let's hug." I alluded to "The Hug" a bit facetiously. We hugged again, leaning over the table, knocking a basket of fruit on the floor. Our belly laughs could perhaps be heard all the way to the Wailing Wall and the Dome of the Rock. "You're in the field: us computer buffs are tucked in these sort of secure places doing our job, too, but you're doing the real job."

"Ah, thanks Lance, but you know that's not true. You folks work day and night on the internet to set things straight. You're on the front lines, too." He shrugged. I had to add, "Bro, I still can't understand why more people don't go to the West Bank."

He cut me off, "Come on, Frank; you know." Lance didn't have time for naiveté or anything that was superfluous, for that matter. "Folks are afraid—the Western media has made sure of that, focusing on violence...."

I interrupted, "Well, it's time for the Western media to come to the West Bank and see for themselves! That it's not a violent place, and journalists and other people— Jews, Christians, you name it—will be welcome with open arms, as long as they don't walk down the street yelling, 'I'm a member of Mossad, the CIA, or...I'm a settler!'

Lance started laughing uncontrollably, his smoker's raspy laugh.

Lance was my greatest ally and supporter, along with my friend, David. Every morning before David and I would set out to organize and participate in another freedom march/dialogue, Lance would always be waiting downstairs in the kitchen. We'd drink coffee together, in the partially shaded morning sunshine.

One morning I got up from the chair; he reached out his hand and I shook it. "Be careful," he said. "Be careful. Even though you and I are different, you're the

---

106 The Jerusalem Hug is organized mainly by peacenik Jews and takes place yearly in Jerusalem. Its main objective is to bring together people of all faiths at different points of the Old City and form a human chain through holding hands, hugging, creating one big human circle. The idea is that people unite together paying tribute to Jerusalem as the center of the world for interfaith peace and unity. The Big Hug-Lovers of Jerusalem. "The Big Hug Around the City of Jerusalem." Lovers of Jerusalem.org. <http://www.loversofjerusalem.org/logistics.html>.

man in the field, I'm the computer man working for peace through internet messages, websites—we're on the same page. I still love you, Bro."

"I love you, too."

That was the last time I saw him and those were the last words we exchanged. As I had to return to Paris for my daughter's birthday on July 14th, I left for the airport directly following the last march/dialogue, without seeing Lance.

A month and a half later, while I was visiting the States for an author tour in Houston, Texas, and Manhattan, I received a Facebook message from a Japanese boy, in the name of Ibrahim, who was staying at the rooming house in East Jerusalem. The message read: "Lance in a coma in a Jerusalem hospital."

I was frozen to the screen and couldn't move. I could feel the shock opening my eyes wide—it seemed like a part of me died, right there.

The Japanese boy requested information about members of Lance's family so he could inform them. I quickly responded that I had no information about his family in the States but I wanted more information about Lance, why he was in a coma, etc.

A week went by and the boy had not responded. I wrote directly to Ibrahim and got no response. I assumed he was too busy trying to help Lance—visiting the hospital, informing his family—to answer my emails. I called him but I only got his message center. Another week went by and still no news. I felt so useless, so far away and I couldn't help him.

Out of pure frustration I did an internet search and quickly found out what had happened: Lance never woke up from the coma and was pronounced dead at Hadassah Hospital in Jerusalem on August 28th, 2010, and buried the next day![107]

The thought kept reoccurring—driving the point into my heart—how empty, how meaningless was his death! The underlying story of how he died produced more emptiness: He was apparently hanging out in the Kikar Hahatulot (Cat Square) district, the bar section of Central Jerusalem, when two adolescents approached him asking for a cigarette. They were apparently drunk.

Lance asked them to leave him alone. It eventually evolved into a dispute and one of the adolescents picked up a board and hit Lance on the head and fled. It was all caught on one of the many surveillance cameras throughout the city. He lay bleeding for at least 50 minutes even though the TV footage caught several passersby and cars stopping, but not lending a helping hand. The police stated that his life may have been saved if he had been taken earlier to the hospital.[108]

When I read this, I muttered helplessly, "What was he doing there? In that place where allegedly he was beaten up before? Was he looking for solace, escape?"

After all the time that Lance had spent as a peace activist, to die in such a

---

107 Liddman, Melanie & Lappin, Yaakov. "J'lem Teenager Suspected of Killing Man Over Cigarette." The Jerusalem Post. Jpost.com. 31 August 2010. <http://www.jpost.com/Israel/Article.aspx?id=186570>.

108 Nassen, Nir. "Teens Suspected of Beating U.S. Jew to Death in Jerusalem." Haaretz. Haaretz.com. 31 August 2010. <http://www.haaretz.com/news/national/teens-suspected-of-beating-u-s-jew-to-death-in- jerusalem-1.311266>. Also, here's an article about Lance Wolf and his life in a guesthouse, a magical place where we stayed in East Jerusalem: Littman, Shany. "The Hostel that Doesn't Ask." Haaretz. Haaretz.com. 24 September 2010.

senseless way touched me deeply. And, ironically, the Arab youths, albeit allegedly drunk, didn't know they were killing a peace activist, a friend to them and to all people. He was a bro, a brother...my bro! Oh God...why?

After the initial shock and emotional upheaval calmed a bit, I wrote this down... in pain:

To Lance,

I never thought I'd be doing this,
writing a poem about you.
I assumed you'd always be there ranting and raving your clarion calls.
You'd be waiting, drinking your tea, in the kitchen,
and you'd always say as you hugged me,
as I made my way to the door,

before I plowed on to the West Bank, to Damascus Gate, For peace, for love,

"Be careful!"

I'd respond, half believing it,
"You're in the trenches; you live here, my friend, every day. You're the one."
As I walked to the Arab bus, I mumbled:
"You incredible crackpot, speaking the sometimes ugly truth not fearing even
to yell at the top of your lungs
in the middle of a room
filled with militant peaceniks . . .
with bowed heads."

Didn't make sense, then
Makes sense now.

But you're dead!
And I still hear your words, "Be careful . . ."

Well, for you, I won't be careful!!!
In my comfort zone of illusions/delusions you took my breath away.
But you're not around, Bro, to hug.

As the muezzin cries to prayer early, at first light,
the moon dew shimmering in the trees
the haze, subdued and heavy over the Mt. of Olives steam rises,
curling over your tweed moustache,

your face is there, it's there . . .

Your friend,
Frank

In my shock, I repressed my reaction to the killing of my good friend, for days; I was in denial that it happened. It was in the plane returning to Manhattan from Houston where the brutal truth of his murder showered me with acid rain.

Bright reds, then blues, floated before me as I slunk into my window seat. Nothingness, confusion, meaninglessness…darkness shrouded me. My nerves were frazzled; no feelings effused through me. My tears dried up…I moved through my life but felt no life force within.

Lance had dedicated a lot of time to the peace movement while living in Ibrahim's house, so convinced that the State of Israel was wrong in its occupation of the West Bank, and was surely on the same blacklists as me. Yet to die like that…such a waste. But I guess that meant we needed to be prepared to die at anytime, anywhere, in any manner….

God bless us all and help us be prepared, at least for death….

A strong soul in the peace movement was forever taken from us. The muezzin's evening calls seemed hollow, empty at the thought of my ally, my strongest ally, no longer there to say "Be careful…." and no longer there to share his realistic views on the sincerity of some of the empty-promise peace workers. He was one of the few who saw clearly as he sifted through all the verbiage, spoke from his heart…pure passion, pure intelligent emotions. I missed him sooooo much!

I was saddened that my visits to the Holy Land would no longer include hearing the resonance of Lance's beautiful, but sometimes dissonant, voice. His chidings to keep me on track would be more a memory than a moving engine, but it was a powerful memory and I'm thankful for that. His rebirth would be in the renewed spirit of the movement for peace, for truth…what he believed in. I felt his presence—it was as if he were still alive.

Chapter 75: The Reunion

Before Lance died, during one of my long conversations with David and him in the kitchen, as usual, Ibrahim had entered wearing his white keffiyeh with the agal (black band) around his head: "Don't want to break it up but Frank and David, we're supposed to go to an interfaith meeting, now."

Lance headed upstairs to his computer while David, Ibrahim and I left the building, heading to the town square to take a taxi. In 10 minutes, we arrived at a long, off-white building. We were escorted to a back conference room, where about 30 people were seated around a table.

Most, if not all, the people were Jews, some wearing kippahs, others wearing baseball hats or flat caps. As I sat down, a clamor was heard next to me. The cheery, red cheeks of my friend, Jason, from Paris, flashed in the crowd. There he was sitting a few seats from me.

"Shalom, salaam, Frank," he whispered in that typical interfaith greeting.

I hadn't seen him for a while so I felt an emotional response to his hello, a customary salutation in Jerusalem. I flashed back to our first meeting in Paris....

I had met him at an interfaith group run by a catholic priest in Paris, consisting of Muslims, Jews and Christians. Five or six people sat facing the monstrous wooden desk of the priest, perhaps meant to maintain a certain distance between his audience and himself. Jason and I were present: he wore his kippah over a slightly balding head. His curious eyes were searching, sincere, beaming a message that I immediately understood: he was there to find solutions to the crisis in the Middle East and was ready to do more than just talk about it.

I connected with him. The meeting with the priest was full of exuberant expectations that we were going to do something for peace. A lady wearing a hijab energetically promoted the importance of meeting together in Paris, first, for interfaith understanding. She was probably right to start out in Paris, but Jason and I were mainly interested in visits to the Holy Land, at the epicenter for such activities.

After the meeting, Jason I walked to the subway together. Our conversation there marked the beginning of a glorious friendship that started in the Paris subway and would continue in the refugee camps in the West Bank. In the subway car, we were alone, at least in our minds, free to express ourselves, as desired. Something about the raw freedom of the Parisian streets was riveting, that no other place in the world could provide the same feeling of being totally incognito, stimulating the flow of ideas. That was Paris...Jason spoke first as we hung onto the subway railings.

"It's great we met and it seems that we're on the same page. I want to visit soon Israel and do Aliyah, to understand my roots; but my return to Israel is mainly prompted by my desire to be at the heartthrob of potential world peace through interfaith work."

I couldn't wait to follow up: "I've visited there a couple of times and I've felt the energy from the interfaith works in Israel. I'm organizing events in the Galilee but Palestinians invited to join us can't make it through the checkpoints and the labyrinth of walls. It's only recently that I extended my activities to the West Bank."

He shook his head. "Walls and checkpoints are not the solution. I like the idea that you want to work with both Israelis and Palestinians, on both sides."

We were standing and as we conversed, the car filled with people. Jason reached his subway stop, St. Paul. He said sincerely, with a smile that covered his red face, "Shalom, my friend. Shalom."

We hugged and he opened the subway door, stepping onto the quay. I got off at the Bastille.

I would have fainted in disbelief if someone had told me then that the next time we would meet would be in Israel, and that I would take him to the West Bank with me, even though the IDF makes it illegal for the Israeli Jews to go there.

But that's exactly what happened!

Chapter 76: Facing AK-47s

My eyes half-opened to the moon suspended in the Holy Land sky; my spirit was buoyed by the muezzin calling, "Allaaaaahu Akbar...." Still slightly asleep, I turned on my side, dreaming about my trip to Jenin, the place destroyed by Israeli tanks during the resistance to the occupation, and renowned for being a center for suicide attacks on Israel. My eyes opened and I quivered at the thought of the last time I had gone there, my tense visit to the refugee camp to prepare for this interfaith march. This would be the real thing....

But the last time I had visited Jenin, a member of the Palestinian authority warned me I needed written authorization before marching. I subsequently had traveled to Ramallah to ask my friend, Abdullah, what I should do about getting authorization for my next marches/dialogues. I trusted his advice as he had spent 28 years in Israeli prisons.

I called him and he invited me to his house. As he sat across the table from me, his smile showed missing teeth, but his aura glowed in spite of the years in prison.

His white hair was striking next to his tanned cheeks. Creases in his face deepened as he smiled, creases acquired during the many years of captivity, no doubt. He stood up to take the tray his wife handed him with steaming hot Arabic coffee and cookies.

I then asked his advice about whether I was obliged to seek written authorization for freedom marches and dialogues I organized in the West Bank, under the jurisdiction of the Palestinian police. He answered that it was useless to apply for written authorization which would probably never be officially granted, would arrive too late or would be denied. He remembered that I had told him I had met Omar Al Sahaf, who was also previously imprisoned by the Israelis and presently was a high civil servant employed by the Palestinian government.

His solution was simple: All I had to do was call Omar and inform him of the time and date of each freedom march and request that he vouch for me. Then, if apprehended by the Palestinian police during a peace march, just give them his and Omar's phone number and Omar would have me released immediately. If Omar was unavailable, Abdullah said he would contact him on my behalf. That confirmed what Omar had instructed me to do during our previous meeting in Ramallah.

I recalled that applying that procedure, I was forthwith released by a Palestinian policeman who had detained me during a previous march in Bethlehem.

Standing up after our conversation had ended, Abdullah reminded me he was short in stature, but not short on persistence and tenacity. I asked one more question: "I also organize peace marches in the sectors of the West Bank controlled by Israeli soldiers. What do I do if they detain me or arrest me for marching in their jurisdiction?"

Abdullah didn't answer that question and shook my hand wishing me "good luck" during the upcoming peace marches.

It would not be long before I would test his advice as my next march was scheduled in a couple of days, returning to one of the hottest places in the West Bank, the Jenin Refugee Camp, controlled by the Palestinian police. On the bus back to Jerusalem, my hands trembled contemplating the Palestinian police again.

I would have been a bit more confident if David hadn't called me at that moment to tell me he had to return to Germany for a doctor's visit. I would be on my own! I meditated the rest of the way and gained back some of my lost confidence, as I realized that I would always have God and the prophets with me. I wasn't alone, after all!

To complicate things, a day before the event, I received a call on my cell from Jason who had called me recently to tell me he had finally finished Aliyah since he had seen me during the interfaith conference in Jerusalem, and had become an Israeli citizen. I rejoiced on the phone with him, congratulating him and commending him for following through with his original vision.

The second time he called was for a different reason: he would be ready to join me for the march/dialogue in Jenin. I had sent him an invitation but I didn't think he'd join us because of the IDF law prohibiting Israeli Jews from entering areas under the jurisdiction of the Palestinian police, especially in hotbeds of Palestinian dissidence, like Jenin. I warned him of the law but he said he knew about it and thought it would be ok, that somehow he'd get around it. I had no idea what he meant by that. Anyway, he would meet me at the Damascus Gate at 9:30 am the next day before taking the Arab bus to Jenin. Huang, my Chinese friend, also said he'd go with us. But that's not all!

Early the next day, the morning fog had obscured the moon, making me squint as my eyes looked over the lights of the valley below my window. The responsibility weighed heavily on me as I had to ensure the safety of Jason and all those marching, including all the Palestinians. They trusted me and I was glad for that but I tremulously articulated the fears and frustrations churning inside me: "I can't guarantee anyone's safety in this unstable world where anything can happen. Oh, God, help me; give me strength. I'm losing it...."

I pulled myself from the covers and bent over to snap the Velcro flaps of my sandals. I walked to the computer room and faced a full moon glowing through the window. My eyes fastened on the moon, mesmerized, as if it could solve the mystery of what would happen that day. I splashed water on my face from a basin I had brought in the room with me, while the moon reflected on the wall in back of me. It was still there, staring at me...I got down on my knees and prayed.

Later that morning, I descended the steps to run into a crowd of anxious Japanese tourists and my buddy from China, Huang; everyone was waiting for me in the kitchen to travel to Jenin. Huang had mobilized the whole crowd to participate in the march/dialogue—hallelujah! I returned upstairs to pick up the sign, the hundreds of fliers and the faithful loudspeaker.

Then as I stepped toward my door, the cold hand of fear seized me again, trying to prevent me from leaving my room. At that moment, pulling the covers over my head seemed a lot more appealing than walking through the unstable refugee camps of the West Bank, shouting "Adonai Elohaynu Adonai Echad" in Hebrew, and "Allahu Akbar." I fought with these thoughts, pleading that I was supposed to lead a group of foreigners and Palestinians in an interfaith march destined to mobilize the hearts and minds of people, to help bring about peace. Then my mind shifted to the dreaded checkpoints as well as the usual rigmarole: Israeli soldiers, the Palestinian police, questions, people shouting, being detained, sometimes arrested....

I swallowed, pushing myself and saying, "I've got to go through with it!"

I started for the door and remembered I wasn't alone. I hurried down the stairs saying to myself that if I didn't answer the call to do something about the humanitarian disaster in the West Bank to bring people together, to at least help raise peoples' consciousness about the situation and at the same time find a solution for a durable peace, WHO WOULD? I can't just say that's not my problem!

If I only didn't harbor that wretched thought of being the lone guiding light of that interfaith event. Another voice inside countered, God said you weren't alone and, Bucko, there are a lot of people working in solidarity together, and...people are waiting for you now. SO MOVE IT!

I headed downstairs.

As I descended, the noises of pots and pans clanging, forks hitting the table and cups dropping in the kitchen greeted me. At the foot of the stairs, I turned the corner and faced a group of anxious faces, looking at me. Heat pumped through me, revved me up, but at the same time I sighed. It'd be rough with all these people to worry about, not to mention the scores of Palestinians waiting to march and dialogue with us on the other side of the wall.

I got the group on the Arab bus headed to the Damascus Gate, where we would pick up Jason. The bus driver let us out near a post office and we walked the rest of the way.

Above the entrance, at the top of the stairs leading to the Damascus Gate—the spot where we had marched not long ago—Jason was waiting with his usual enthusiastic smile suffusing his round face. We hugged and with Huang and the Japanese tourists, headed up the hill to the Arab buses that would take us to Ramallah, where we'd change to a shuttle headed to Jenin.

I stepped aside next to the door of the shuttle, number 18 to Ramallah, and let everyone enter. I counted heads. Not counting Huang and Jason, there were eight of them.

I watched Jason stare out the window, his eyes busily examining the terrain. He didn't seem worried even though the IDF had declared Jenin off limits for Israeli

Jews to visit zone H-1, controlled by Palestinians. That meant if he were caught by an Israeli soldier who decided to enforce the law, Jason could go to jail and/or pay a fine.

This was his first visit to the Northern West Bank and I'm sure not without trepidation; I watched him closely out of the corner of my eye, but he didn't show any fear even after I explained the possible consequences of his visit to this prohibited land. He would not have to worry about the checkpoint now as Arab shuttles were rarely stopped at checkpoints leaving Jerusalem. Returning from the West Bank was another matter....

Jason and I both agreed that the reasons for the IDF law, making it illegal for Israelis to enter the Palestinian-controlled parts of the West Bank, were dubious; officially the purpose was to protect Israeli citizens and avoid having to spend time and money to free Israelis taken hostage or worse, recover bodies and retaliate against attacks against Israelis in the West Bank. Unofficially, we were convinced that the law was adopted to prevent Israelis from visiting the West Bank...prevent them from seeing first-hand what Israel was doing to the Palestinians...prevent them from feeling compassion.[109]

Before arriving at the Ramallah bus station, I asked the driver to let us off in front of the entrance to the shuttle buses headed to the North. We walked onto a ramp leading up to a shuttle bus station full of yellow vans parked haphazardly. I took the lead as we wove between shuttle buses driving down the ramp. Then we entered the station amidst horns blaring and people yelling at drivers as they ran to catch shuttles that were moving forward with their doors half open, toward the main street. Smoke from the kabob grills filled the air, transforming the scene into an otherworldly vision.

That was fitting as I expected this day to be like being in hell, even though I was elated by the numbers of people to start the march. Still, the responsibility weighed heavily on me...two Japanese tourists stayed in one shuttle with a group of Palestinians while the rest of us, including Jason, Huang and myself, completely filled another shuttle. I was the last one in and the door closed behind me as the shuttle began to roll forward before I could sit down. The shuttle traversed the arid plains north of Jerusalem, on its way to Jenin. The Japanese tourists gazed attentively, their eyes on every man wearing a keffiyeh and woman in a hijab walking by the window; this was their first trip to the West Bank.

We arrived about two hours before the scheduled march.

I reminded myself that Jenin was a sensitive place, where the most violent confrontations had taken place between the IDF and Palestinians during the Intifadas. It was still unstable and I didn't know if we could return that evening to Jerusalem. I anticipated the possibility of being stuck in Jenin that night as sometimes the shuttle

---

109 The UN Office for the Coordination of Humanitarian Affairs in 2007 stated "The analysis shows that more than 38% of the West Bank is now taken up by Israeli infrastructure. Roads linking settlements and other infrastructure to Israel in conjunction with an extensive system of checkpoints and road blocks have fragmented the West Bank into a series of enclaves separating Palestinian communities from each other. The socio- economic impact has been profound." The United Nations. Office for the Coordination of Humanitarian Affairs. "Occupied Palestinian Territory." 2007. <http://www.ochaopt.org/>.

buses and taxis stop returning to Ramallah in the late afternoon, especially when there are conflicts with settlers.

I thought of visiting my friend, Jabber, to see if he could put some of us up for the night. I had called him the night before to set it up, but he wasn't answering his phone. When I stay the night in Jenin, I usually stay with his family and him on the side of a hill in the outskirts of Jenin.

I led the group to the courtyard looking directly into the picture window in front of Jabber's office; he was a homeopathic doctor, and we could see him through the window talking with two women wearing hijabs. I knocked on the door. He got up from his desk with a wide smile and came to the door with an outstretched hand that I grabbed. His coffee-stained teeth matched his untucked brown, short-sleeved shirt, and sweat stains under his arms reminded me of the hot, sultry day before us.

I asked him in English and Arabic if the entire group could stay at his house that night. He hesitated, looking at the crowd standing before him in the courtyard.

"My friend, I have room for you and one other person...." His head tilted down, in apology. I reached out and grabbing his hand, I backed out toward the group waiting for me. His eyes met mine, surprised as the two in hijabs turned toward us.

"No problem, Jabber. Thank you for helping at least two of us. We'll maybe see you later."

My voice trailed off as my eyes returned to the nine sets of eyes still waiting in the courtyard. I walked passed them and they turned, following me into the street. I needed to find a café where we could recuperate from the long, bumpy ride from Jerusalem and where I could leave them while I tested Abdullah's theory that I should apply for oral authorization for the march before we started. I knew I could chance doing the march without authorization, as I'd done in the past, but if we were halted, the whole group could be arrested. That would be too risky, especially since Jason, an Israeli Jew, was marching with us. I feared that if he were arrested, the Palestinian Authority would turn him over to the IDF and he would be punished.

As we were waiting for lunch in a café next to Jabber's office, I excused myself, after explaining to Jason where I was going. I informed him that if I didn't make it back within an hour, he should lead the group on a visit of the town, especially the "Freedom Theater" in the refugee camp, and then return to Jerusalem.

It was time to test Abdullah's theory, again. I walked down Abu Baker Street; the Palestinian Police headquarters was located at the end; in fact, the downtown headquarters consisted of two or three squad cars parked next to each other. Next to them, a group of officers usually stood, including the commander.

As I walked down the street, I remembered again speaking to a thickly- mustached Palestinian police officer during my last visit there; he had informed me that I needed written authorization for a peace march because it was an especially sensitive place.

I approached the end of the street and saw the usual three police cars parked alongside each other. The usual group of Palestinian Authority policemen were in front. I went right up to them and asked the one next to the tall, lanky policeman carrying the AK 47 if the commander was present. He was short but stout and seemed to be the one in command as he wasn't carrying a weapon.

"Ahlan wa sahlan. No, not here now."

I showed him a flier in Arabic mentioning the location and the reason for the march. He took it and after a minute he looked at me,

"Cuellos, good. Where?"

"Right here, Abu Baker Street...."

He looked at me, from my shoes to the top of my head.

"So can I go?"

"Wait, wait! I have to call the commander!"

He called on his cell phone and two minutes later a small unmarked car drove up and I was escorted into it.

"What's going on? Where are you taking me?"

The driver wouldn't speak to me. He drove off into a mesh of winding streets and then swerved into a carport where he stopped and left me with a guard in full uniform at the entrance to a drab, gray building.

In a few minutes, I was seated in an office with three policemen sitting behind their desks, watching me; one was looking at my passport, another was reading the flier. A young, clean-shaven officer, who was probably delegated the task of interrogating and scolding me announced, "You need paper to do march."

I mumbled to myself, "Oh no, here we go again...."

"What paper?"

"You know—authorizing you."

I replied, "Look, I have a friend who works with the Palestinian authority, who knows me and said...."

"What's name?" "Omar Al Sahaf" "You know Omar?"

"Ana sadiq. Call him! Here's his card."

Before I embarked on this trip, I had called Omar to inform him of the time and place of the peace march in Jenin.

Omar responded, "Bravo!"

"Thanks, but could you please answer your cell phone since the Palestinian police could call you to confirm your authorization of the march?"

"No problem!"

"Shukran, ma'a salama."

Now the crucial moment had come and I prayed Omar would answer his cell. If not, I would try contacting Abdullah. If I could not contact either of them, I feared I would have to cancel the march or if we marched without authorization, I would maybe rot in a Palestinian prison along with the other marchers; and Jason...I didn't want to think about what might happen to him.

The man telephoned Omar's cell phone.

"Marhaba! Omar...."

The conversation lasted about 30 seconds.

"You're free to go!"

It was like magic! One of them adjusted his beret then pointed to me and then dipping his hand, indicated I was to go downstairs, immediately. I entered another unmarked car and was whisked away to the center of the city where I was unceremoniously deposited on the main street before the car sped away.

As I entered the café where the marchers were, I ruminated, Abdullah was right about Omar! I'll never doubt him again!

Then I thanked God as I saw my friends seated around the same table, some eating sandwiches, others drinking coffee. I looked at my watch and it was ten minutes to two o'clock pm, the hour the march was supposed to start. I walked over and took my seat next to Jason who was in the middle of a conversation with Huang. I gave them the "thumbs up" sign and they both clapped.

Then I announced to everyone, "It's time—let's go!"

We walked to Abu Baker Street. It was full of people, shoppers and vendors, selling everything from appliances to radios to groceries. We joined the crowd. I had marked in the fliers that the march would begin at 2 pm at the Main Square which was about a block up the street; we kept walking. I passed out stacks of fliers in Arabic, and some in English, to everyone in the group and they started handing them out.

On arriving at the Main Square, I looked around to see if any of the Palestinians I had sent fliers to were there. I didn't see anyone but it didn't matter. I looked back and there was already a crowd following us. I noticed that Jason and the Japanese youths were talking to people on the sidewalk and handing out fliers. I unraveled the sign and handed it to Huang. Then I took out the loudspeaker and turned it on.

"Assalamu walaykum...." and we were off. "La ilaha ilanhla, Adonai Elohaynu Adonai Echad."

In a few minutes we had about a hundred people following us, chanting...a mass of smiles, people lifting their hands up, waving. A couple of Japanese youths were in a small group with Palestinians, smiling, talking, chanting. We walked en masse down Abu Baker Street; people waved, thanking us for coming together in solidarity for interfaith peace in the Middle Eastern heat.

In front, before I could raise the loudspeaker to my lips once again, Huang had grabbed my arm and was saying something, pointing to a man walking towards us.

"That man police. He told me to stop." Finally the large man stood in front of me.

"Stop—you must stop. You not authorized...here my card."

A Palestinian plainclothes policeman was trying to stop us, one hand waving at us while holding his card—which I refused to look at—while his other hand a cell phone to his ear.

"Yes, we've been authorized. Please get out of my way!"

I pushed him gently aside. I just couldn't let him stop us after all we'd been through, after wasting that time being interrogated. I looked in back and Jason was following, a scowl on his face.

I turned to Jason: "No worries; we've been authorized...let's keep going!" "La ilaha ilanla, we are here for peace. Hourriyy Palestine! Hourriyy Israel!" I yelled with even more force, buoyed by the sight of the Japanese following, chanting.

By the time we arrived at the intersection, there were 10 policemen there to greet us, barring the route. I inwardly smiled since they had finally grouped enough

Palestinian police; but it was too late for them as we had finished our march. I frowned, deepening the furrows on my forehead as much as I could, displaying a theatrical mixture of anger and surprise.

The policeman who had initially stopped us could only repeat, "Stop! Stop!" and then a few unintelligible words. A young man I had met earlier pushed through the line of policemen and asked, "Remember me at the police station?"

I remembered he was one of the policemen who had interrogated me.

Now my anger took over. "Yes! Could you tell these people to leave us alone?"

"The march was authorized. You authorized it!"

"Wait, I'll call...!"

"Call whom? It's been ok'd. You're wasting our time."

I stopped in the middle of the street. He immediately turned and began calling on his cell phone. He lifted one finger which I assumed meant wait a minute and/or stop talking while I call, but by that time, I was tired and frustrated, and kept complaining, "Can't believe you won't let us march!"

He finally put a hand over the speaker of the cell phone, and uttered, "I helped you last time. Give me a couple of minutes to straighten this out—it should be ok!"

"Of course it should be ok. Come on—I'm tired of this harassment!"

He put his finger over his mouth to stop me from talking while he spoke to someone on his cell. Meanwhile, a man with a black beret and in full uniform came up to me with an AK-47 strapped over his shoulder. He leaned toward me, his straight, hard jaw uncomfortably close.

"Let's see your papers. And incidentally, I want to see the papers of everyone who's with you."

Nerves jolted me as that was absolutely the last thing I wanted to happen. Jason and everyone else were at risk of arrest. I had to think fast. I saw Jason and Huang with the Japanese youths on the sidewalk as I faced the policeman standing in the street. Jason would have problems if he handed over his papers to the Palestinian police. At that moment, as I handed him my passport, inspiration hit me. Seeing Jason still lingering on the sidewalk about 10 yards away, I spoke French to him, knowing only he would understand. I had to almost shout at him over the noise and confusion in the streets.

"Jason, Jason!"

I had no problem getting his attention as his eyes were already on me.

"Get out of here and take everyone with you. I'll call you on my cell if they let me go. If you don't hear from me in an hour, go back to Jerusalem as fast as you can."

He looked confused, frowning again as he stood there looking at the police encircling me.

"GO—now! I'll explain later...."

As the policeman on the phone grabbed my arm, I could see Jason grabbing Huang and everyone on the sidewalk and in an instant, I was alone with the police and masses of people around us. Jason, Huang and the others had disappeared into the crowd. Several police agents continued to surround me, one bent over scrutinizing my passport, another one continuing to call. I was relieved that Jason and the others had gotten away…and was feeling the afterglow of that incredibly boisterous march with masses of people. We had made our statement!

Finally the man on the phone turned to me and said, "It's ok—sorry!"

I smiled sardonically and headed for the sidewalk where I quickly hid in the crowd. I looked back and the uniformed policeman who had asked for my papers and for those of all the marchers was flailing his hands in frustration, apparently arguing with the man who had approved the march. I called Jason on his cell and we rendezvoused a couple of blocks from the shuttle station. I met Huang, the Japanese marchers and him with hugs and slaps on the back. I had to cut off the celebration to look for a shuttle that would take all of us, as it would be our only means of transportation back to Jerusalem. I hoped it wasn't too late as I truly needed to get everyone out of Jenin before the Palestinian police changed their minds and started looking for us. Anything was possible in that place!

As we approached, the haze of rising smoke signaled our return to the usual bedlam. It was around five pm so it was still possible to get a shuttle back, but it was never certain. As we approached, I prayed that the Israeli settlers who were purported to have thrown rocks at the shuttles traveling from Jenin to Jerusalem would not lead to cancellations of all traffic headed there. I would find out on arrival. It didn't take us long to travel the last few blocks to the only source of transportation out of that place. Even though today's march blessed me with new and vital energy of hope, at the end of it, I was exhausted and preferred to leave to recharge my batteries as well as shield the activists from a possible police investigation. I passed through the sea of yellow and approached the area where the Ramallah shuttles were parked, waiting to fill up and then charge out of the station before entering the vast, arid plains on the way to the capital city of Palestine. Before I reached the place, several shuttle drivers approached and asked where I was going.

I responded, "Ramallah" and before I could finish articulating the word, they enthusiastically pointed to a corner of the building at a waiting shuttle. I rounded the building with the group following me: first Jason, then the group of Japanese tourists and Huang. A short-haired, gold-toothed man greeted me, shaking my hand with his right hand, and waving us on with the left. The Japanese piled into one, the other was already full with three places left, for Jason, Huang and me. It was not too late.

As the shuttle raced down the highway, I began to relax. The day was like a big blur…our parading through downtown Jenin. A collage of images coursed through my mind as I leaned my head back on the hard seat: the desperate plainclothes policeman shoving one hand into my face while his other hand held his cell phone jammed into one of his ears; the ten Palestinian policemen waiting for us and turning when we arrived; the lit-up eyes of the marchers, confidence turning to fear as they watched my interrogation; my waving them away and their eyes following me, surprised and confused; being surrounded by the Palestinian police proudly carrying their AK-47s. Machine guns against our flyers seemed so ridiculous, as I lay my head back. But at the time, it was unsettling why such numbers of police were dispatched for such a small event. I fell asleep somewhere in the middle of the march…. "La ilaha ilanla" resonated over and over in my dreams while the Japanese tourists walked, their faces forward, dark eyes shining.

They kept walking right through the barrier created by the Palestinian Authority policemen, who turned panic-stricken faces to try to stop them. But they kept on marching....

The shuttle jolted forward, wrenching me away from my dreams. I awoke as it was passing some high ridges of jagged rocks on the right. I was told that between Jenin and Ramallah, there was an alleged Israeli settlement atop high ridges from which settlers sometimes hurled rocks down on the passing Palestinian shuttles. At least that was the reason they gave me for the shuttles suddenly stopping travel from Jenin to Ramallah. That rumor was never confirmed.

On arriving in Ramallah, we grabbed a bus to Jerusalem for the last leg of our journey, but my worries about Jason getting arrested by the IDF at the checkpoint were just beginning. A long line of cars, stretching for at least a mile, was waiting at the Qalandia checkpoint when we arrived. By now, exhaustion had set in and I was nodding off, which made the waiting less tedious; but it still seemed like an eternity. We finally arrived at the gate. The typical Israeli soldier carrying an M-16 walked down the aisle of the bus. Since there were people standing in the way, he was having trouble getting through. Another Israeli soldier stepped up and was telling the driver something as the first soldier looked on. It turned into a heated discussion, the two soldiers left and the driver yelled something out the open door. I soon found out why.

The driver was told that since the bus was too full, it would have to leave a few riders off there and turn around and get in the back of the line. The driver spoke in English that we must leave the bus now and told us we could catch another bus later. It was clear he was addressing all the non-Palestinians, the English-speaking foreigners...us. Several others, including a couple of British citizens left the bus. The bus driver motioned to me and Jason to leave. Jason got up. I placed my hand on his shoulder and told him to stay put. I was afraid that if we got off, we'd have to go inside the building, where we'd have to pass through the metal detectors and show our ID's to the soldiers. The controls on the inside were far more rigorous than staying in the bus and showing our passports to an Israeli soldier quickly walking down the aisle. He sat down. The bus driver got up and addressed us personally. I told him that my friend and I were not getting off, and that was it! He waved his hands vigorously and then returned to his seat. The stalemate persisted until the shuttle driver busied himself making a U-turn and heading back to the end of the line, about a mile down the road.

The waiting started all over again. In the confusion, he forgot about us. It was infernal, the frustration of traveling at a snail's pace over the same ground, approaching the checkpoint gate yet again. I wondered if we'd be turned back again. My frustration turned to satisfaction as I contemplated the impact of the infernal waiting on Jason, an Israeli Jew, who now was subjected to the same kind of treatment endured daily by Palestinians trying to get through the infamously slow checkpoints. I knew Jason would share his compassion for this insufferable treatment of Palestinians with other Israeli Jews and denounce the checkpoints. Nothing like suffering first-hand to nourish compassion…Another 90 minutes later, we were back at the gate. The familiar M-16-holding soldier entered first and was able to walk to the back of the bus as all the people in the aisle had left. He was followed by the other Israeli soldier who this time asked us for our papers, passports. When the soldier got to Jason, I held my breath. He handed the soldier his French passport with Aliyah written on it. The soldier looked at Jason then back to the passport, then returned his passport. He was in!

When we arrived in Jerusalem, I was sound asleep. The dark paths, traveling along the somber wall…I slept soundly until we started riding down lighted streets, waking me in time to see throngs of Arabs with skull caps and orthodox Jews wearing kippahs and fedora hats streaming down the sidewalks. Vendors sold batteries, food, clothes, toys and books. Jerusalem, the City of Lights, seemed to welcome me warmly, cradling me and healing me from the shock of coming into such close contact with guns, soldiers and policemen. My eyes slanted open; the light streamed through them, revitalizing my soul. There is something there that God will help me see. The light from His embrace will sustain me in my work for peace; through cosmic love shall all brothers and sisters come together, in freedom and in peace. I left the bus with Jason half-asleep, but I needed to share with him one more thing—I just couldn't remember what it was. We walked down the road that would take us to the local buses: he would take his Israeli Jew bus to West Jerusalem; I would take an Israeli Arab bus to the Mt. of Olives.

Then I remembered: "Jason, I just wanted to explain why I was a little brusque back there in Jenin when I told you to get out."

He nodded as if he already knew. "They were asking for the papers of all those participating in the march and I didn't know where that would lead—possibly to arrests—especially you with your Israeli papers."

"Pas de probléme; j'ai compris!" (No problem; I understood). And we parted with a hug.

Chapter 77: Soul Food

The echoing calls of dozens of muezzins suddenly filled the morning air as I turned over; the prayer that I had just uttered anchored my very being as I slid into uninterrupted sleep.

I awoke again while the muezzins' calls echoed, entreating me to prayer. I was inspired to bow my head and pay homage to the creator, to profoundly thank God that I was allowed to live to lead more interfaith groups. The conflict in the Holy Land was heating up and I desperately needed to share with others what I had learned to convince them to join the interfaith marches/dialogues in Israel and Palestine.

Upon returning to the Mount of Olives, I took a shuttle to Ben Gurion Airport; next stop, New York City. Time to make a breakthrough there and help bring Americans to the Holy Land!

As the shuttle sped down the incline, past the bushes, trees and houses on the left, I found myself mindlessly drifting with the clouds....

As we approached Tel Aviv, the glow of the rising sun over the Mediterranean pushed back the temperate moon. My thoughts were on my passion, inflamed by the growing light. I pushed away any thoughts meant to cast doubt on or cool my drive. After what I had experienced in Jenin, there was no more room for fear!

I imagined being a part of the waves of peace and freedom across the Holy Land, especially with the last trip to the refugee camp in the North, considered the most dangerous, unstable place in the West Bank. Yet it was an incredible victory for peace as we got through it and we were able to even involve an Israeli Jew and get him through the checkpoints. Jason was the courageous one, there!

Ben Gurion airport emerged ahead and the shuttle left me off in front. My flight was delayed so I wouldn't be boarding for another four hours. I went to the airport coffee shop to sip on some espresso and get my emails.

I was still basking in the success of the Jenin march. It seemed like anything could happen now and the interfaith movement was catapulted into a new dimension. I needed to share it with as many people as possible, and get people involved. Only with mass support could we help bring a lasting peace to the Middle East.

The best way to communicate with people in the United States was to set up another series of author events, conferences and talks concerning my book, *Storm Over Morocco*. But the main goal was neither seeking the limelight, nor even profits

366

from selling books: it was to share with more and more people about the interfaith movement in the Middle East and to solicit their support.

I scheduled a series of author events for my book in New York City, New Jersey and in the Los Angeles area, over a four-week period of time; I was leaving for the States via Paris that night. The events were mainly scheduled in bookstores and some synagogues, churches, libraries and community centers.

I clicked on an email message blinking on my screen. It was from Dedra, my friend in Houston, who had sent me a message suggesting that I could reach more people through a TV talk show interview in her city. She said she had spoken to the host and thought she could get me on the show with at least a week's notice. I quickly went on the travel website and found a cheap round-trip ticket from Los Angeles to Houston. It turned out that after the East Coast events, followed by a trip to Los Angeles, I had one week between author events. I was able to reserve a cheap ticket from Los Angeles to Houston during that week. I sent an email to Dedra, confirming my arrival in three weeks, and she responded saying she'd contact the host to get me on the Houston talk show. In addition, she said she had found me a place to stay during my visit. Bingo!

On arriving in Paris, I just had time to change luggage and clothes and get some sleep before I was on my way back to the airport, destination, New York.

After several author events in bookstores, a library, and at a poetry club meeting on the East Coast, I headed to Los Angeles for more author events, in Barnes & Noble, Borders and some independent bookstores. Each author event would typically start by my showing up and handing out about 200 fliers. Then I'd give a short presentation followed by a discussion on my book, *Storm Over Morocco*, about my experiences in Morocco back in the 70's. After the presentation, I'd sit at the table provided and sign books for customers. The highlight of the discussion, and the purpose of my being there, would be to talk about my recent experiences in Israel and Palestine.

After a week of events in Los Angeles, I went to the LAX airport and took the plane to Houston, as planned. On leaving the plane at the Houston airport, I was jumping with anticipation since Dedra would be waiting for me. There would be no mad dash to a shuttle or a cab; someone would be picking me up. I grabbed my bags from the baggage turnstile and headed to the exit. I rolled my suitcase out the sliding doors and there in front was her sports car and her beaming eyes honing in on me.

There she was, all dressed up, her beautiful black face shining, honking her horn like crazy. She jumped out of her car and came running to hug me. Then she reached over and grabbed my suitcase strap and started pulling it toward her sports car.

We had some catching up to do but first I needed to rest as I was exhausted from all the traveling. She had to work during the day so she let me sleep all night and the next day. She arrived the next night and I was still in bed.

She came in and gave me a kiss on the cheek and I reached out and grabbed her. She managed to get loose and shook her head. "Man, aren't you hungry?"

"Let me take you out dinner, love…soul food."

We ate the best southern ribs I've ever had. There was no sweet potato pie for dessert, but Dedra said she'd ask her sister to make one for me during my stay. It was a deal.

During dinner, she shared her intimate spirituality with me and her dreams of world peace where people of all faiths and races would live in harmony.

We visited her sister who prepared an entire "soul food" dinner the next evening with corn bread, black-eyed peas, smothered pork chops and red soda, a red- colored drink I had never drunk before.

Two days later, we walked into the studio early for the talk show, in the center of Houston. We were greeted by the guard whose warm smile and strong handshake pulled me through the door. He acknowledged Dedra by caressing her cheek. We passed by a large room in front of us with an array of TV cameras and several camera crew members pushing and pulling the machines into place, some at the touch of a button; others had to be wheeled. In the back were several rows of chairs already set up for the audience. Three stools were placed around a table in front of the line of cameras where I assumed the live interview would be.

Dedra stood at the door, her broad, fire-red smile filling her face and the room, and waved to a member of the crew who turned his nappy head, his smile curled around a tight black mustache. She called everyone "honey" in that typically gushing Southern style.

Dedra then turned and without forgetting me, took my hand, gently pulling me into an adjoining room; she then pushed down on my shoulder—a gentle suggestion I was to sit down. She started taking off her gloves, her coat and placed them over the back of a shiny brown sofa. I did the same, turning around and when I turned back towards her, she had flown out the door and was talking with a tall, short-haired black woman at the entrance. She was wearing jeans and a red shirt with a placid, confident smile. Dedra pulled her in and literally placed her hand in mine, as we shook.

"This is Shauna, the producer of the show."

About 45 minutes later, we were sitting in front of the table and a slender black assistant, with a goatee and sallow features, was standing in front of us securing the microphones to the right places on our shirts. It was ten minutes to show time and the host had not shown up yet.

A few minutes later, a brouhaha was whirling about at the main door; several people began pouring into the room followed by a short man with slicked-down hair pulled into a tiny pony tail. He was wearing a shiny priest's cassock and a black sash. He held his head high, walking to the podium directly in front of the cameras. Our table was a bit off to the side, just enough to make us seem like more of a side dish, an afterthought. He must have been the host, or rather star of the show.

All hands, including those of the man who had set our microphones were swarming over him. He seemed to be at ease commanding everyone's attention: one focused on his microphone, another on straightening his tie, and yet someone else was combing his hair while handing him notes. Finally Shauna, the producer, walked up to brief him on the show. He was definitely the star, wearing dark glasses, which he removed only when the camera was on him, and a smile to compete with any sleazy entertainer. He smoothed down the sides of the priest's cassock, making sure there were no creases in it before the camera rolled. But still his eyes hadn't noticed us, the invited guests waiting for an "eentzy weentzy" bit of recognition.

I looked at Dedra who returned my look, her eyebrows raised....

He counted down, 10, 9, 8, 7, 6...and suddenly we were viewing a screen in back, apparently the usual footage of the beginning of each show. It showed the same host, this time sitting in back of a limousine accompanied by two busty women, one on each side, as the limousine inched closer to the main door of a luxury hotel. The car stopped and a doorman immediately opened the door. The three entered a hotel arm-in-arm to attend a conference, led by...who else but the host, Dr. Ceasar. Then the cameras showed him making a speech inside the hotel to several people, a speech about how to become successful, in particular, how to get rich, quick.

Before the screen went blank, a cameraman signaled to the host by raising five, then four fingers, etc. The cameras zoomed in on the host.

"I'm Dr. Ceasar and I welcome you, sisters and brothers of the faith...." As if someone had just pushed his button, he automatically went into his spiel that he was here by the grace of the Lord, to bring people success in God's house, . . and he went on and on. One viewer called in and asked him about his "how to succeed" program, the evidence being the initial part of the talk show, i.e. the limousine, hotel.

He then reached in his pocket and pulled out a $20 bill, wrapped around a wad of dollar bills, before the camera and said he'd give out money to any member of the audience who guessed the answer to a question; he asked a question and someone in the audience, possibly planted by him in advance, approached and he pulled out a couple of $20 bills from the wad of $1 bills and handed them to him.

After 30 minutes—as a distraction or side show—he announced that he had guests on the show, but only 15 minutes were left...then 10.

"Now I've got a real treat for ya'all. I've got a man who came all the way from Paris, France, to be with us...Dr. Frank Romano, author of *Storm Over Morocco*.

The audience clapped, on cue. "And the beautiful Dedra is interviewing him. Kindly listen up...he's got a story to tell."

The interview was over in seven minutes. Dedra was brilliant and I told the story of my pivotal experience in Morocco, and how it had motivated me to organize interfaith dialogues in the Holy Land.

The host hugged Dedra and shook my hand, then clapped; the audience clapped again.

"Thank you audience, guests, and all you people out there; it's time to go." Then the scene shown on the screen at the beginning of the show, but in reverse—with the limousine driving up, the door opening and the host and the two busty ladies sliding in—was shown and they were off. After that footage ended, the producer shouted, "Cut!"

We talked with about 40 people in the audience and after another round of handshakes, hugs, we headed for the back door.

"That was ridiculous! He acted like we weren't there. Then he gave us short shrift, like we were an afterthought, like nothin'...." Dedra was livid and I could even see a glimpse of red in her cheeks.

"But you were great, baby," I said.

"Oh honey, I'm sorry I got you into this...."

"Are you kidding, Dedra? It was succinct, provocative and most importantly, I had another chance to share with people about the book and encourage people to do what they can for world peace, especially in the Middle East."

As we were leaving, she turned to have a few words with the Doctor who was departing through a side door into a crowd—probably his groupies patiently awaiting him—but I managed to slowly pull her arm, then her body, away from him to the back door where we slid out into the night air.

"It's ok, Babe. It'll be broadcasted in a week and that means I'll share my experiences with many people. Give him credit; he's got fans out there and many people watching. Can't knock that!"

She was still fuming, stomping her feet as we walked. Her mood was lightened by our shared laughs over the host's slicked down hair, the slinky black robe that look like a preacher's and the gaudy introductory footage showing Dr. Ceasar accompanied by two beautiful women to a five-star hotel, where he gave a "get rich" speech.

"Man, that was tacky. It seemed so contrived, orchestrated to look like something voluptuous and plentiful to viewers; but turned out empty, meaningless...." I couldn't resist.

"He would have made a great illusionist!" I piped up again, followed by our wild laughing and gasps for air. I thought we were going to fall over right in the parking lot.

Then Dedra got a bit serious: "Here, surrounded with sanctimonious people who, on one hand—at every occasion—utter, 'Praise the Lord' but at the same time, want to exploit us, take all we got, even our hearts, as a tool...disgusting."

I looked over to Dedra, grasping the steering wheel, and her flashing eyes: She was still angry, in spite of our convulsive laughter.

"What's up, hon?"

She just reached out and held my hand with her free hand as she drove on; her thoughts seemed far away.

"Let's go out—let's party. I want to celebrate another opportunity to get the word out, to do God's work." Her grim silence greeted that outburst.

"At least we tried...."

Now her hand found my lips as she placed one of her fingers over them.

"I know just the place...." Thank God she calmed down and I hoped was getting in the party mood. But that would be my challenge....

That evening, she took me to an African-American discotheque. I was the only white in the crowd, but I didn't feel uneasy at all. In fact, it wasn't the first time I'd been in this kind of situation. When I was a student at San Francisco State University, I used to go stag to a discotheque in Chinatown, called the Rickshaw. African-American ladies, not at all bashful, would come up to me at the bar and ask me to dance and we'd twist and turn on the discotheque floor.

We didn't seem to bother anyone as we moved to the beat of The Temptations and James Brown in the hot Houston disco. White and black, black and white...it didn't matter as we blended, twisted and turned. Everyone smiled and seemed to be fused together, heads bobbing and bodies shaking; even with a whisky on the rocks in one hand, nobody missed a beat! The music engulfed me as we swayed and turned to the soul beat—Houston soul, Houston energy. Black rap then replaced ghetto soul music over the loud speakers and our movements were shaking and transforming into an ecstatic blend of brilliant colors, lights and flashy faces.

After that, per my request, she took me to another soul food place in downtown Houston for ribs and cornbread, again. Loved the stuff!

Then I could say I had a much needed African-American fix. But thankfully it wasn't over yet…she invited me to stay with her for the next four days. White and black entwined in rapturous harmony, in a maelstrom of sensations only cooling upon deep, deep sleep.

Cooking was not Dedra's forte; she was more into organic foods. Throwing pieces of fruit and spoonfuls of yogurt into her blender to make a devastating smoothie was the highlight of her culinary prowess. I made peanut butter sandwiches and bought a beef burrito for protein, a time or two. My second night there, we returned to her sister's house for more soul food. In the middle of dinner, I recollected my first taste of soul food years ago in an after-hours soul food restaurant in the middle of the Western Addition, an African-American ghetto in the heart of San Francisco.

I was on semester break in 1970 at San Francisco State University and was living in the dorms until I was asked to leave, along with all the other dormitory students, since the policy was to get everybody out for spring cleaning. Our rooms were so rank, anyway….

Being thrown out on the street, and not ready to leave the city scene or to stay with my parents in Santa Rosa, I went to the Western Addition, the African-American ghetto, because I was told I could get a cheap room there and I didn't have much money. I easily found a room in one of the residence hotels that lined McAllister Street. Every time I'd leave my room, I'd walk by a man's room by the name of Rodney; his door was always open as he lay on a double bed in the corner watching everybody walking by. Both legs had been amputated due to a car accident. When he heard noise in the hall, he'd hoist himself into a wheel chair and frantically wheel himself to the entrance, just in time to catch the passersby in the hallway.

His smile showed a row of crooked teeth on the bottom and perfect teeth on the top, which were the remnants of a set of false teeth. But he smiled just the same and what a smile! I used to joke to myself that it rose in the East and set in the West as it spread across his face.

Every other morning when I walked by his room, he would ask me to buy him a loaf of white bread. I'd buy it and bring it up to him and he'd greet me lying on the bed, putting out his hands like he wanted me to pass it to him and I did. His belly laugh would burst out as he yelled, "Touchdown!"

I'd follow that with, "Have a good breakfast" then I'd take off for my daily visit to Reality House West, a drug treatment center, to participate in a rap session. I had been invited to participate in an encounter group with drug addicts and ex drug addicts, pimps and other street people as a representative of the non-drug user world, or as they put it, "the normal world," or as others put it, the "non up" world. That made me laugh because I wasn't so sure how "normal" I was, or what even "normal" meant. I'm still not sure what that means, now!

As I briskly walked down the sidewalk of a dismal, quiet street that connected my street to the one the center was on, the only thing I noticed was the strong smell of stale urine. It was a somber path, but it was the only direct way to the rap session. I arrived at the front door. It looked like the door to an abandoned department store as I pushed it open. I peeped through the opening and noticed a faint light but no one was moving inside.

I walked to a door opening into a barren hallway. Still no one stirred. I thought that weird because yesterday's rap session was in the front office off to the left which was now in darkness. Then voices bounced off the walls that seemed to be coming from a small lighted room at end of the hall.

I walked through another half-open door and found myself in the middle of a human collage, a mixture of all classes, woman and men: some men had long braided hair, tattoos; a disheveled woman wore a short skirt, her nappy hair sticking out around her headband—all were African-American, except me. A younger man with a black beret on his slightly-frowning face showed years of a hard life. Next to him was a light-skinned black man, his cheeks with a faint sprinkle of freckles. An old man with a trimmed white beard was sitting at the head of the group and appeared to be the moderator for the day.

The white-bearded man waved me to an empty seat next to a lean young man with very dark skin and a dense afro, combed upwards.

The woman started first: she recounted her path of woes leading up to her heroin addiction. She had lost all hope and was miserable, leading her to drug use that quickly escalated into hardcore drugs and prostitution to feed her ugly habit. She admitted that she shouldn't have gotten started. Those words were gold to me as I learned directly from the street woman, from her experiences, what not to do, no matter how down and out I was. They stayed with me the rest of my life, fortunately!

After it was over, the black man next to me, Nate, told us his story. He was a pimp and furnished prostitutes with drugs so they could turn tricks. He drove a big pink Cadillac and everyone knew who he was in the ghetto. After a while, he became a heroin addict, like the prostitutes working for him. Then he got busted and that was the beginning of him breaking the habit "cold turkey," while in jail.

His smile went horizontally across his face, wide and mischievous. He looked around the group, and turned to me, whispering, "Now don't you get strung out like me. Look'y here, these are young folks. That lady over there is only 37 years old, but she looks 60."

Then he quickly put his finger to his lips, "Shhhhhhhh." His stern look told me to keep that to myself. Sixty years old...wheewwwwwwwww...I exhaled slowly.

He continued talking to the group: "I might be a former pimp/drug dealer/drug addict right now, but I beat the habit—I ain't pimpin' no more, but still 'jivin.'" Soft chuckles filled the room.

I found out later from one of the counselors at the center that because Nate had successfully kicked the heroin habit and had valuable life experiences to share, in spite of his youth—he was no more than 30 years old—he had been selected as one of the counselors at the center. In fact, he was a former graduate of "Reality House West."

One day after another rap session, Nate sat beside me again. I was, as usual, in awe of his stories: his life on the streets, shooting up heroin in hotel bathrooms and running prostitutes back and forth all over the city. He leaned over to me and asked me to follow him. I followed him out to the coffee machines and he pulled out two cups of steaming coffee, handing me one. I didn't drink coffee yet, but I took it and thanked him.

"Look, you're young and green, but I think you're cool com'n on down here. I trust you, man!"

He took a cigarette out of his top pocket and offered me one. I shook my head and he lit it.

"I'll just get down to it. I'm a manager of a soul food place and I need a dishwasher and some help with bussing tables this Friday night. I can't pay you but you get a free soul food dinner and the vibes, the vibes, man…you'll see. Can you hep' me out?"

"I'd like that…."

"Not so fast—we open at 12 midnight." He smirked, and flashed his usual crooked smile, scratching his head. "It's an after-hours place…."

I could walk fast to the place in seven or eight minutes from my room but the Western Addition was a mean and hungry place, especially after 11 pm. I was walking briskly, almost running along the abandoned streets on the way to Nate's restaurant when a car screeched its brakes and drove on the sidewalk across my path, cutting me off. Two tough-looking blacks got out, one wearing a flat cap, the other a white hat with a black band around it; both were wearing silver chains around their necks. One walked in back of me while the other approached me from the front. I froze, as I couldn't move forward or backwards. There was nothing I could do.

The one in the flat cap grabbed my arms pinning me to his body while the other checked my pockets. They obviously didn't find what they were looking for as the one behind me released me within seconds while his partner immediately headed back to the driver's side and revved the car instantly, even before his partner had eased into the passenger side. As they spun out, I thought I heard one of them say something like "Italian____." They were definitely looking for somebody and thank God I didn't fit the description.

I walked down a wide street, following Nate's instructions, and came upon a trailer-shaped building, built on the curb and extending partially into the street. It was 11:10 pm, about an hour before I started work.

At the back side of the rectangular building, a door was half open. I knocked but there was no answer so I pushed the door open and spread aside beaded curtains. Nate was standing in back of an oven staring out the window at something in the streets; he was wearing a white apron and a pearl-white chef 's hat clamped over his bulbous afro.

373

Without taking his eyes off the streets, he reached his hand over and I clasped it. "I knew'd you make, it. Take it easy for a while; we ain't open yet."

As much as I tried, I just couldn't picture him being a pimp, riding the streets of San Francisco, his black pimp hat slanted over his eyes and long, colorful scarf blowing in the wind through his window. I tried imagining him picking up a tired, lipstick-smeared woman to collect money, perhaps scold her then drive her to a new location, kiss her roughly and then discharge her back to the streets. I guess seeing him looking out the streaked window with a cute little white apron fixed a different impression in my mind.

With the apron and chef 's hat, he looked more like a short-order cook in a fast food joint. But no, he was an after-hours soul food cook. The aroma drifting out from the kitchen was provoking my salivary glands and causing my eyes to water.

He dried his hands on the apron and this time turned to me and shook my hand again, "Welcome to the joint. People start coming around when the bars close at 2am. Then we be swamped. This is one of the only after hour soul food places in the ghetto."

At two in the morning, all the tables were full and I was washing dishes with a passion, especially after eying and smelling my prize at the end, a barbequed ribs dinner with a sweet potato pie finale.

The kitchen was juxtaposed to the dining area, only separated from it by a beaded curtain. I washed down the huge pans, including a giant saucepan and frying pan, soaping them liberally, rinsing them with hot water and hanging them on the huge hooks overhead. I slightly opened the beaded curtains and spied on a bald black man with two girls, one on either side, who was singing a tune. The two girls were hitting the forks and spoons together for percussion. Next to him were five beautiful African queens, their extensive afros glistening with afro-sheen, dressed in black and violet tights over their slim bodies. They were also chiming in by hooting and hitting the sides of their glasses with forks, knives and spoons. Nate spread the beaded curtains wide and looked directly at the cause of the commotion. His laughter could be heard over the loud jam session.

"Right on!" He spurred them on.

He pulled the beaded curtains shut and headed back to the kitchen. In a few minutes, he returned with steaming chicken still sputtering in the frying pan along with a plate that he handed to me piled high with corn bread. As I set the plate of cornbread in front of the bald man, Nate chimed, "Hey, Romano, would you bring the black-eyed peas? They's on the stove!" While we dished out the food I had to keep myself from salivating on their plates.

It was 5:30am when the last customer, a young man, contentedly wiped his forehead and mouth with a napkin and then stumbled out the door. As I sat in a chair looking out the window at the empty street, hunger pangs caused my stomach to rumble. Then Nate called out, "Got your dinner up and bring'in 'er out!"

Just ruminating over the food I'd been serving that night got the saliva moistening my thirsty mouth. In a few minutes, Nate returned with a plate of cornbread covered by a thick white cloth, fried chicken in a dish, the leg almost totally covered with a layer of black-eyed peas. He looked down with pride as he placed the plates before me.

"Sorry, kind of messed up—no more ribs!"

"Oh, no problem. It looks great. What about you?"

"No, are you kidding? I've been nibbling all night. I'll just straighten up the kitchen. You, ah…." he looked at me with those jaded, mischievous eyes, "jest enjoy—you earned it! And, ah, thanks Frank, you done good!"

"Frank! Oh Frank!" I saw a palm pass across my eyes. "You tired, man. Have some more cornbread." Dedra was hovering over me, like a Jewish mother, making sure I was stuffed.

That same warm feeling spread through my stomach and brought it back to life after all those months of eating on the run: quick meals in Paris, grabbing a plane, hastily purchasing a sandwich, crashing in airports, traveling to Israel, then to the West Bank, Arabic coffee, Palestinian falafel, then back to the airport—then kosher chicken on the Israeli airplane back to Paris.

"This was down home cooking—the best!" I exclaimed, as I pushed onto my fork the last of the black-eyed peas, with a piece of cornbread.

Laughter broke out at the end of the table. I overheard Dedra joking with her sister, Shauna, who was telling her, "How you go'in keep a man without no cook'in, you bad girl?"

Returning to Dedra's place, we took a country road detour. The sultry evening breeze drifted through the crack in the window as I looked at the blinking stars. This was our evening as we listened to music on her tapes: Earth, Wind and Fire, the Temptations and all the oldies that we both loved. She finally had to stop the car so she could move her body to the beat, our bodies flailing out the window as we danced, sitting in the front seat.

That night, we made love until a tinge of morning light shimmered on the tops of the field grass; I slowly glided to the window to wake us from this dream-filled night. I didn't care a lick that she couldn't cook….

At some time during the evening, we started talking marriage. It came up, and shifted a bit the evening's smooth vibes. She was earnest, but I was still a bit hesitant as I had been married and divorced twice and had four kids.

Her shining eyes and enticing words, already calling me "husband," resonated in my ears and sounded like family. But it was too soon after the broken engagement with Dalia, and the shadow of Sylvia was still hanging over me; so I was still a bit skittish about it. That did not prevent me from fantasizing about being caught in her perfume-scented web, walking up the aisle with her. She had me in her woman's power.

The next day, she shared with me the importance for her, as an evangelist preacher, of getting married. She made it clear that for us to move forward, marriage was mandatory, even if it meant being in a long-distance marriage where I lived in Paris and she stayed in Houston, getting together whenever possible…a long, long distance marriage!

So marriage all of a sudden evolved into a condition for our continued relationship and I was definitely not ready for it. I left Houston the next day, headed back to Los Angeles and then to the Silicon Valley for the scheduled author events.

As the plane soared, leaving behind Los Angeles and memories of several author events in shopping malls, it began climbing over the gray arches of the mountains below. Then a strong force yanked my meditations away from the humid valleys of Houston, cutting me off from the loving thoughts of Dedra. I fixed my eyes on the clouds ahead.

As the plane set a course for San Francisco, a distant, persistent humming sounded a warning. In the middle of the Silicon Valley, I would discover the reason: I was to meet a strange man who had shadowed me in Morocco, years ago...during a violent storm.

Chapter 78: The Target

I walked down the line of rail cars of this enormous relic from the past, headed toward the Silicon Valley from San Francisco. As I was more used to the sleek, fast trains of France, this was a strange step into yesteryear, I thought, looking out the window of the old-fashioned chugger.

Earlier, I had frantically picked an entrance and grabbing the rail, pulled myself up onto the platform and opened the door to the train, before the doors locked and it began to reluctantly inch forward. I opened the window to watch the train slowly slide away from the dregs of San Francisco, the lower abandoned side. An old-time train whistle blared as the wheels clanked, jolting me. The last time I'd seen something like this was in a movie showing a train robbery perpetrated by an unruly gang on horseback.

I rested my head on the back of the seat, still swimming in Dedra, her eyes that radiated, her faith…and her words, "Praise the Lord" going through my mind, over and over….

I was tired of all this traveling, but turned my head on the seat and grumbled, "But praise the Lord, who said it wouldn't be hard work? But I'm blessed to be able to do this, to share with people, to live and to learn…and I am still open to learning."

I knew deep down that when I stopped learning, I'd be a dead man, a dead man walking. So why are you complaining? I asked myself.

It was the end of September and the beginning of Indian summer in San Francisco. The cool breezes and ever-present summer clouds were now replaced by a warm, sparkling sun early breaking through the clouds and lingering. This was home, only an hour away from where I'd gone to high school, in Santa Rosa. Here in San Francisco, I had been hauled down Market Street in a paddy wagon after being arrested during an anti-Vietnam rally at San Francisco State, where I was a student.

I remembered again in the holding cell how the police had brutally beaten up the black kid and how I had clanked the bars of my cell in protest. Then they came at me threatening to do the same in San Francisco, the city by the bay, another city of love, like Paris.

Now I was on this train headed south to talk about my book. But in my heart the book, the presentations, the book signings, were really a pretext to do what I really wanted: share with people about the importance of coming to Israel, the West Bank, to participate in the interfaith peace/freedom movement. Hopefully more people would join me, over time.

The train chugged slowly through my past under the Indian summer sun, its whistle breaking the inner silence like a distant memory...the sweet afternoons in Santa Rosa walking in the foothills around the city to arrive at Howarth Park, the cool lake, passing under the moss-laden oak trees....

Then my thoughts switched to my last visit with my kids in San Francisco, Juliana, Frankie and Regina. We had organized our yearly poetry recital and music concert in Café La Bohéme on 24th Street in San Francisco, one of my hangouts when I was a law school student. An eclectic group of about fifteen artists, musicians, foreigners, Americans, Latinos and street people sat around in a circle in the middle of the café and joined in the music, poetry and drinking great coffee. As usual, my goodbyes with my kids were filled with promises to return soon as I turned away, fighting back tears while grabbing my bags and heading for the taxi to take me to the train station.

Until the train reached Palo Alto, new memories invaded my serenity: a new homecoming. I was five years old, growing up with brothers and a sister at Stanford Village, an old Army barracks converted into student housing after World War II, while my father struggled to get through graduate school at Stanford University and my mother dutifully worked to help him.

Both Mom and Dad were very busy and the other kids and I were often left with a network of babysitters that we could easily manipulate. I remembered I was able to sneak away from them frequently and often got into trouble. I had formed a gang (of only two five-year-olds) that was organized to relieve a local stationary warehouse of its supplies. We succeeded somehow in opening a part of the wall from the outside and began extracting paper, pencils and other office supplies. We didn't know it was wrong to do that until a policeman came to the house. Wasn't much he could do before the embarrassed smiles of my parents. The biting strap I felt that night was my father's way of teaching me the difference between right and wrong....

The metal on metal grinding of the wheels uprooted those memories and brought me shrilly to the present. The conductor, as in the old movies, walked the aisles announcing our arrival in Palo Alto.

I left the train. It was about 10:30 am on a Saturday as sleepy suburban downtown Palo Alto was slowly awakening to a new day. I walked down University Avenue towards the Borders store where the event would later take place. My eyes were searching for a café where I could get some strong coffee to help jolt me into the present. Even though I had arrived over a week ago from Los Angeles, before that I was in Houston, then New York City, New Jersey, Paris, the Middle East, then back to Paris, again. I was convinced I had permanent jet lag from all the traveling.

Sometimes I'd even arrive at an airport for a short stop-over at midnight somewhere in East Europe on my way to the Holy Land from Paris, and when it was time to head for the boarding gate, I had forgotten to read my boarding pass and headed for the gate of the plane heading to San Francisco or New York.

But this beautiful sunny day of this strange homecoming, I felt light-headed as I almost skipped down the street, chanting under my breath, "But Praise the lord, I'm still blessed…a strong cup of coffee will bring me back!"

Then I wondered if I was going slightly mad, that is until I saw the overhanging Borders store sign in the distance that changed my focus from questioning my sanity to the job at hand—the author event. I looked at my watch and it was about an hour and a half before it was to start. That was about right as I liked to hand out fliers for about an hour before each event, giving me a chance to meet and talk to people. I looked down at my book bag bulging with fliers.

Passing them out would have to wait until I could medicate myself with my favorite black substance, a nice steaming cup of hot coffee. At that moment, my eyes spotted a place with tables outside. I ducked in and ordered a red eye, a shot of espresso in a cup of their strongest house coffee.

The outdoor part of the coffee shop was already inhabited by people spreading papers, books and opening laptops on tables; some were grouping together for a morning coffee klatch. Others just stared ahead like me, zombies waiting for the effects of their coffee cradled between their hands to help them inch towards awakening, as they listened to slow jazz in the background.

Shortly after I drank my red eye, my eyes popped open and I started going around to the tables handing out fliers to the eclectic customers, from preppy university types to bohemians with long hair and cut-offs.

Then I headed to the bookstore. The entrance, lined with magazines and books, looked more like the entrance to a resort, with tables out front where people sat and sipped their coffee reading, telling stories and looking up into the cloudless sky of a warm Silicon Valley afternoon.

I walked inside. The small coffee shop was to the right and the cashiers on the left; stacks of books materialized before me. After I walked through the entrance, I took a right into another service area with more stacks of books and an information booth. In front of the booth, in a place where customers had to pass on their way to this section of the store, were two stacks of *Storm Over Morocco*, with one in a display case in front of me. That brought me clearly to the present! A few empty chairs were in front of the table. I walked to the information desk and a bearded youth, with eyes deeply set and appearing beyond his years, looked me over and had me identified already.

"So you're the author, Frank Romano?"

He peered at me with sunken cheeks and lips creased in concentration.

"Well, I didn't think I'd be recognized that soon."

I reached out and shook his hand. He muffled his coughing. "I saw your photo in the papers and on your web site." He let my hand go as he voiced a hearty "Welcome," pointing to the stack of my books.

He saw my eyes lighting up as I viewed my books already laid out.

"I'll announce your arrival over the loudspeaker. There were several people looking for you earlier, and two books were sold already. They're probably in the stacks and will be back when I announce the event."

"Good job—thanks! By the way, what's your name?"

"It's unimportant, compared to your name." He looked away as his lips turned lightly downward, touching the edges of his beard.

"Important to me, guy!"

As I extended my hand to him, he turned, his face brightening, the corners of his mouth slightly turning upwards.

"Jeff!"

"Pleasure and thanks for setting this up!"

As I walked to the table and stooped over, arranging the books into smaller piles, a strange buzzing flooded my right ear; I looked to the right and a man with a blue snow cap standing slightly behind a tall bookshelf moved behind a stack of books in the corner.

Then the echo of a voice filled the room: "The author of *Storm Over Morocco*, Frank Romano, is here to share his story with you...."

The rest I did not pay attention to as I walked over to the stacks where the man stood, taking out fliers from my book bag; he had disappeared. I handed out a few fliers to people in the stacks then I returned to the table. Already about seven people were sitting in the chairs set out in front of the table displaying my books.

I walked to the table and nodding to Jeff who nodded back, I started the short presentation as more people shuffled in; soon there was standing room only. I spoke about my travels to Morocco and was getting to the part where I was held captive in the mosque. About in the middle of my talk, the strange man with the snow cap appeared from behind the stacks and started walking toward the group. I looked at him directly and he nodded before sitting in one of the folding chairs hastily set up by Jeff to accommodate more people.

At the end of the presentation, I was signing books and answering questions when I saw the mysterious man still seated, as if he was waiting. Chills fluttered down my back. I handed the signed book to a lady who had brought her daughter to meet an author, in person. I looked down and patted her head and she beamed through her black bangs.

Out of the corner of my eye, I saw a sun-parched face cracked at the edges under the snow cap, towering over the lady. He smiled, his blue-gray eyes bulging. He had me in his space.

Then he stood over me after the lady left with her son. "Remember me?"

A question like that, asked without warning made me recoil. "Don't think I do!" I blurted out, as another lady walked in front of me, squinting inquisitively.

"I'll be back!" he said over his shoulder, after turning away.

The dark-haired lady in front of me had moved closer when the other lady had left with her daughter, turning her head to watch the man slink back behind the stacks again. She was carrying one of my books.

"You're Frank Romano...." "That's me...."

"I'm so happy you haven't left yet as I bought your book earlier today and they said you'd be here to sign it for me."

I felt a mixture of total insecurity, despair and intrigue regarding who the strange man was, at the same time trying to smile at the lady who said she was from Eastern

Europe. Her dark eyes fixed on me as I signed her book. Her multi-colored headscarf was wrapped around her head as if it protected something precious, something delicate inside. Her hand trembled as it leafed through my book. She asked me to sign another copy for her son.

I finished signing the books just as the mysterious man turned the corner of the bookshelves, in front. It looked like he was feigning reading a book on a book table, while his eyes glanced towards me.

The lady noticed and her nervous laugh preceded her standing up and bidding me farewell. As she walked by, looking at the strange man who had turned away, she whispered, "Good luck!"

I thanked her and gave her my card, inviting her to stay in touch through email. The man knew it was his turn and walked towards me, but stopped when he got to one of the empty chairs in a row behind the front.

"Well, can we finally talk?"

I was still standing in front of the table and looked down at him sitting across from me...without responding. Didn't know what to say!

"I guess you don't remember me!" My eyebrows raised.

"You were in Morocco about 30 years ago, right, say about 1977 or 1978?" "I was definitely there!"

"Well, I was there, too!"

This hit me like a sledge hammer, took me totally off kilter so I had to sink down on a chair. But he seemed to want to tell his story, so I remained silent.

"Aren't you wondering why?" "Yes, but...."

Without waiting for me to mumble a few words, he got up and sat in a chair directly in front of me and continued his story.

"Do you remember talking to a man about your stay in Casablanca?"

He sat in silence, giving me time to think. His question had sent me back about thirty years after I had escaped from the fanatic sect in Casablanca. I was going crazy after being shut up in a hiding place in Casablanca and had momentarily left the place where friends were hiding me to get some air. During the walk, I remembered meeting a couple of American servicemen stationed in Casablanca. That surprised me as I wasn't aware of an American military presence in the country, left over from WWII. The two men, stout and wearing short military haircuts, had invited me for a beer at a downtown club. I was so homesick that I didn't want to leave them and I accepted. In a few minutes, we were walking though the wooden swinging doors opening into a bar and pool room.

"I remember entering a club and...."

"But you don't remember sitting down and having a long conversation with one of the patrons...about your Moroccan adventure. Do you remember talking with a man asking you a series of questions about your adventures?"

I looked at him sitting across from me and the abandoned chairs in back of him in the middle of the bookstore, as he talked to me about what had happened 30 years ago. He knew a lot about the details of my visit to the club that were not in any of the editions of *Storm Over Morocco*, nor in any other published writings. Then the reality jolted me, as I thought, That was him; he must have been there...."Were you an American soldier?"

He cut me off. "No, I wasn't one of them."

That confused me as I thought all the people in the club were American G.I.s. More silence passed as his hot blue eyes penetrated mine, seeming to dissect my thoughts...waiting...waiting....

I was now wracking my brain, trying to remember; the pieces started coming together. I remembered sitting on a seat drinking beer and talking for what seemed like hours to a man who seemed exceptionally interested in what had happened to me. It was all coming back. Strangling emotions seized me as I thought, It is totally surrealistic that I am speaking to this man in the Silicon Valley, not far from the protective Stanford campus where I had lived with my family so long ago, about Morocco...Morocco was steeped in my memories; memories of far-away places and faces began appearing, coming into focus and disappearing. Salt and pepper strands of hair had drifted down from the snow cap onto his creased, sun-tanned forehead, which drew nearer to mine.

"I was working for a US special investigations team when I was assigned to investigate a group of American servicemen in Casablanca. I was ordered to find out who among the American G.I.s stationed in Morocco was involved in an illegal export/import ring, perhaps trafficking drugs from Africa into the US."

He looked up but he knew that by now, he had given me enough hints to convince me I was sitting in front of either a member of the CIA or a Pentagon Intelligence Division agent.

He continued his story: "When you arrived at the club, I was in the middle of the investigation. I overheard you telling your story to one of the men who was shifting between playing pool and listening to your story. When he left to focus on the pool game, you remained on the bar stool sipping your beer. I came and sat down next to you and started asking questions about your involvement with the Muslim cult and your escape."

Then a light went on inside me. I remembered having a long conversation in an obscure bar with a man sitting next to me.

"I remember now. That was you?" He nodded.

"Wow, this is unbelievable that after 30 years...I...." I blurted out. I noticed that the Borders employee at the info booth had heard my outburst and was leaning forward, his beard sweeping the counter.

"Believe it, but it's not over." He paused and looked over my shoulder, then to his left, as if at a stalking phantom. "Do you remember me leaving you for about 15 minutes?"

"No, I don't remember that!" I responded abruptly, not knowing where he was going with this conversation. Then an idea struck me...I was unnerved and felt a pain in my chest as I mused, Maybe he is still on a mission, to spy on me...maybe to recruit me...but he wouldn't be telling me this if....

He interrupted my anguished thinking: "Well I left to call my boss in the US on my cell and to inform him about you. He ordered me to investigate you as well as the others. He added that I was to get your address, follow you and continue investigating you if I discovered you were involved with fanatic Islamists, in any way."

I sat there just listening, still wondering if he could possibly be for real—could this conversation be happening? He continued, "I returned and you were still sipping your beer at the bar. In fact, you didn't seem to be in a hurry to leave."

"I wasn't in a hurry to go back into hiding even though I should have stayed where my friends were hiding me. Couldn't stand being cooped up all the time."

"Anyway, I asked you more detailed questions, where the mosque was located, about how you got into the mosque, who were your friends, and how you escaped, what was the name of the group, your present address and where you were headed once you could flee Morocco? You don't remember that?"

"I vaguely remembered that I felt better spilling it all out of me, my frustrations, my fears and there was someone there."

"That would be me...."

I did remember, almost as if it had happened yesterday. Then I shuddered as I realized I had been investigated by US intelligence, as if I were a spy, a member of a fanatic sect or even maybe a terrorist. I was confused and disgruntled, thinking about what I had gone through.

"But why? What risk was I?"

"It was the potential risk. Mind you, I was sent to investigate other people and I ran into you. US intelligence was no dupe to the danger of fanatic religious groups and terrorist cells that were being formed even back then, when most people didn't know anything about them. That's our job, right? Then I ran into you; bingo! It was my boss who ordered me to investigate you on the spot, and I totally agreed with that."

"Right!"

I sighed, a bit resigned to what he did. But I remained skeptical of the necessity to investigate me, especially after telling him I had escaped from that brutal Islamist cult. How could he even think I could be mixed up with a fanatic Islamist group, and possibly terrorists?

"Anyway, after our long discussion, you left. You said you had to get back to the family who was hiding you. I followed you there!"

"What?"

"Come on...doing my job!"

This was amazing—unbelievable!

"But later I faxed a final report to my boss, and guess what it said?"

I was now thinking, Enough of this suspense—this whole story is crazy. I almost wanted this conversation to end and for him to go away. But my curiosity....

"Anyway, I concluded you not a risk and no longer involved with that fanatic Islamist group and there was no evidence you were involved with terrorists. I concluded you had, however, been a victim of a fanatic Muslim cell that should be investigated."

"What happened next?"

"My boss called me and took me definitively off your case and ordered me to focus on the investigation of US servicemen in Casablanca and the illegal export/ import business."

He had me: I was frozen in my chair, speechless, numb...."If you don't believe me, you can probably find a copy of the report. You're a lawyer; you just apply for a copy of it from US intelligence services under the FIA, the 'Freedom of Information Act.'"

He reached out, shook my hand and laid his card in the palm of my hand; then he stood up and quickly disappeared behind a stack of books. On the card was written a name and a phone number, nothing else. After a few seconds, I finally realized what had happened and stood up and chased after him, as I wanted more information, wanted to find out what agency he worked for....

He was long gone. The whole conversation was so weird; and then it hit me that maybe he wasn't supposed to have told me all that!

On the slow chugger back to San Francisco that night, I wondered if I'd see the mystery man again, maybe on one of my trips to Israel and the West Bank. I looked off to the low-hanging clouds on the horizon, curling around the tops of the trees.

As the train wove through the mist settling over the wistful fringes of a cool San Francisco twilight, I fell into deep contemplation of one of the most challenging, enigmatic marches/dialogues following the Hebron twilight event, in the heart of the Jenin refugee camp. That marked one of the only marches/dialogue where I failed to talk my way out of being arrested and detained by the infamous Palestinian Police.

West Bank interfaith activities were revving up there and David had called me, asking me to immediately return to the Holy Land and lead an interfaith march and dialogue in, of all places, the Jenin refugee camp. I hadn't even had time to digest my conversation with the mystery man when my thoughts took me back, back into the fire....

Chapter 79: Back into the Fire

The taxi rocketed down the road, swerving left and right, kicking up dust and dirt as I stared out the window at the arid hills of the West Bank, a hodgepodge of endless rocks and earth.

To keep focused and to overcome acute anxiety, I tried to recall my 30-year vision that had led me to this jagged place formerly known as Judea and Samaria, deep in the Holy Land.

The taxi from Bethlehem—carrying David, my friend and retired doctor from England, Bram, a Dutch student, and me—swerved off the main road and headed up a steep dirt road. The constant thumping and lurching of the car wrenched me from my meditations and forced me to return my attention to the intense conflict between Palestinians and Israeli soldiers. That had inspired this trip to Jenin, in the West Bank, for a freedom march.

I asked the driver, "Why are we doing this, Sayyid (sir)?" The driver responded, "Need to pick people up."

The taxi drove up to a closed iron gate. The inscriptions outside were in Arabic. I asked the driver where we were and he responded that we were in front of the gate of the Palestinian Authority (PA). It was the Palestinian Police Training Center and we were there to pick up a couple of agents headed to Jenin.

My eyes met David's and our eyebrows rose at the same time. I tried to push from my thoughts that these agents were sent to monitor our freedom march, which now may be doomed.

Oh my God, I thought to myself. The worst luck of all! And so the odyssey began...and there was no escape.

The gates opened and the taxi inched through. Two men approached from behind carrying duffle bags, as the driver got out and swung around to the trunk. He lifted it open and the two men from the Palestinian police threw in their bags. A light-haired man, wearing a green beret and a khaki uniform, opened the front passenger-side door and sat down. He slid toward the driver to let in a dark-haired man also wearing a green beret. They both looked about twenty years old.

That began our journey into one of the most contested areas of the West Bank, where the greatest resistance to the IDF, the Israeli Defense Forces, had taken place. Alleged terrorists had been harbored there.

Ironically, we were sharing a taxi with reinforcements for the Palestinian police sent to Jenin, perhaps to observe our march. This event had been promoted publicly and the Palestinian police could have found out about it from Omar, a Minister of the Palestinian government I had called about two weeks earlier to inform of our plans.

The driver proceeded down a spidery tangle of obscure back roads and dirt passageways. I asked him why we were following this route and he responded that since he was transporting the Palestinian police, he must try to avoid the Israeli military checkpoints. What irony, I thought to myself, that even the PA avoided the dreaded Israeli military checkpoints...I thought the Palestinian Police and the Israeli government were working together.

David complained that the driver's erratic path was making him car sick. Turning, I looked over at him; his face was already buried in a plastic bag. As loud retching noises filled the taxi, the light-haired police officer winced.

And then the inevitable happened; the same policeman turned his head and pointing at me, asked, "Why are you going to Jenin?"

I did not know how much he knew already so I assumed the worst: that he had been informed and had been sent to keep us under surveillance. "I'm organizing a freedom march, to bring together people of all religions, to help them come to a peaceful, non-violent understanding."

I knew I had to pick my words carefully as a wrong one could get us all arrested. I also knew that an intense interrogation would follow, having dealt with the Palestinian police before. As predicted, the officer immediately turned around again and asked me the question I had anticipated and dreaded: "Who are you meeting in Jenin?"

The taxi rumbled down the dirt road and David's face remained in his plastic bag. We had an elaborate plan to meet up with our Palestinian contacts after calling them upon our arrival. I knew I could not reveal anything about the people involved to the police; our associates would not appreciate being subjected to an investigation.

"Oh, just some friends."

"Please give me their names and their telephone numbers."

Now I had to engage in serious theatrics to avoid arrest as I could not give them that information. David's vomiting grew louder and louder. I placed my hand on his shoulder and asked him if he was alright. He nodded, raised his head revealing flushed cheeks in place of normally pale ones, and quickly plunged his face back into the sack.

Taking advantage of the distraction David provided and the rattling of the taxi as it climbed over rocky, dirt roads, I responded to the police officer, "I don't understand...."

For a time, we could hardly hear each other's voices and the policeman turned his eyes toward the road—I thought perhaps he had had enough. Five minutes went by before he once again stuck his nose in my face; the interrogation proceeded. But David, the deafening roar of the motor, and my feigned ignorance of the officer's English combined to thwart further interrogation. In frustration, he finally turned around and shoved a cell phone in my hands. "This is boss—talk to him."

"Salem Walekum," I began. "Ana Frank. Wa anta?" (I'm Frank. And you?)

The man on the other end responded, "Walekum Salem" and then followed with a long sentence in Arabic. I started speaking English but it appeared that he did not understand English very well. Then he asked, "Spreche Deutsche?" (Speak German?)

"Ya, aber mein Deutsche ist nicht so gut," (Yes, but my German is not too good) I responded, and the conversation quickly turned to German.

This bizarre experience continued as the taxi sped down back roads, churning up a trail of dust behind us. After the conversation with the head of the PA of Jenin ended, I passed the cell phone back to the officer, who promptly asked me what was discussed.

"He gave me his cell phone number that he wanted me to call once I arrive in Jenin."

He seemed to understand that and turned his head around. I felt relieved, thinking the interrogation had ended. But, no...A few minutes later the policeman turned his head to me again and asked, "You have friends in Jenin; give me their phone numbers."

To protect my friends (I did have their phone numbers written in my little black book), I responded, "In fact, upon my arrival in Jenin, they are to phone me. So I don't have their numbers."

He seemed dissatisfied, but when he proceeded to interrogate me further, David emitted such a wretched sound that the police officer turned his head back in disgust. And that was how it remained until the taxi thundered by the Jenin refugee camps into the downtown taxi station. Yellow cabs were parked haphazardly, honking, inching forward and backwards, barely discernible through the haze of shish kebob smoke rising from the barbeque pits at the center of the station.

A strange mixture of black headbands (aqals), white keffiyehs, hijabs, suits and jeans were visible everywhere, on those running toward or away from cabs or nervously gunning their cars, as if at the start of a race. All that provided the backdrop for the lawyer/theater skills I used to separate us from the policemen, who remained stuck to us like parasites as we left the car— they wanted us to go with them. I pled with them to let us stay at a café until my friend had recuperated. I raised my voice and pointed to my poor sick friend who, even though he felt better, chimed in with his own theatrics, grimacing as he spit in the plastic bag he was carrying. That was too much for the young policeman. After cupping his hand over his ear and dialing the air with his index finger— reminding me to call his boss— he frowned while walking backwards, almost tripping over his colleague. They both turned and were quickly engulfed by the sea of people and taxis. Bram and I accompanied David to a café where he could recuperate from his ordeal. I bought him several cans of soda to soothe his stomach before Bram and I left to hand out fliers for the march, scheduled to take place inabout an hour.

But something wasn't right. The first time I had visited Jenin, not so long ago, there were only a couple groups of police, mainly parked in the center of town. Now Jenin was teaming with Palestinian policemen. On almost every street corner there was a group of them, carrying AK-47s.[110] I explained to Bram that we must avoid the Palestinian police at all costs because the march had not been authorized and we could be arrested. His blue eyes opened wide but before he could think about it, I grabbed him and pulled him into the street. So we played cat and mouse with the police…Bram seemed uneasy as I hid my fliers in my book bag and asked him to do the same as we passed a police patrol. I looked back a few moments later and could not find him. I backtracked and found him sitting in a café drinking tea.

I sat down beside him and explained, "I've been stopped by the police several times during marches. I just give the name and phone number of Omar Al Sahaf, a high civil servant with the Palestinian government, who I have already informed of the peace march. I'm immediately released thereafter. Anyway, that is exactly what happened during the last peace march I organized in Jenin."

He did not seem convinced as he shrugged his shoulders and turned away. But when I got up to leave, Bram also stood up and followed me. I watched him give fliers to a group of children in back of me who crowded around him. He was smiling.

Praise God, I thought to myself. Now he's getting into it.

Each time we passed the police, we hid the fliers. By doing that, we succeeded in handing out from 200 to 250 of them, until the inevitable happened. Someone must have given a flier to a policeman and then pointed us out. As we walked the streets, I felt a tap on my left shoulder. Turning around, a member of the Palestinian police faced me, with his finger on the trigger of his AK-47.

I was escorted to an alley between two buildings and held by two policemen until others showed up. I looked around and noticed that Bram was not with me so I hoped he had walked away and joined David in the café. Minutes later, he was pulled into the alley by two stocky policemen.

Then the questioning began. As I was the leader, they started with me. Bram was standing at the opening of the alley. I shouted out in English to Bram, telling him to just walk away and saw him turn around and walk out; he was soon pulled back by a short, lean youth wearing the typical green beret of the Palestinian police.

A short, stout man with a full moustache beckoned me to follow him, speaking in Arabic. I reached into my business card clip and pulled out the name and phone number of Omar Al Sahaf. Giving the card to him, I spoke: "La arabiyya—engelizi (No Arabic, English). This is the telephone of Omar Al Sahaf, an important member of the Palestinian government. Call him; he knows about the march. There should be no problem!"

---

110 We were told later that police were swarming Jenin in preparation for Eid al-Adha (Festival of Sacrifice), a Muslim holiday that would commence on Friday, November 27th, about four days away. It commemorates the triumphs and trials of Abraham, in particular, the one where he was asked by God to sacrifice his own son to prove his faith. However, the added number of police patrolling the streets was to curb any potential violence or manifestations opposing another event that was to take place in Iraq the first day of Eid, four years after the execution of Saddam Hussein in 2006. Iraqi authorities had recently issued death sentences against 126 prisoners, collaborators of Saddam Hussein's regime, nine of whom would be executed on that same Friday. Saddam Hussein had apparently been revered by many Palestinians because he had paid many millions of dollars to the Palestinian families of those killed fighting Israel since the uprising in 2000.

He combed the business card and taking out his cell phone, called the number on it. After a few words, he led Bram and I to a police car whose tires screeched as it hastily transported us from the downtown area. It didn't work this time!

After a 15-minute ride to the outskirts of the city, we were taken to a drab, three-story building and dropped off in front. We were greeted by two police agents and taken inside. I don't know what had happened—why Omar did not tell the police to let us go—as he had done in the past. I feared this was the day I would see the inside of a Palestinian prison.

We walked up the stairs of an old building surrounded by more men wearing green berets. I was relieved, especially for Bram, that no cells with bars were in sight. I could not see his face but I was sure he was panicking by that time. Guilty thoughts flashed through my mind; I wished I had not involved him. My legs began to buckle slightly as we were led into a long room before a man wearing a green beret and a full uniform.

The unfolding scene reminded me of a gloomy spy picture I once saw, where Russian prisoners were interrogated in old, dilapidated East European dwellings. We were about ten feet from the Palestinian police sergeant who raised his eyes, almost hidden under thick, dark eyebrows. His bushy moustache almost totally concealed his stern lips and his beady red eyes followed us like a laser beam tracking system. I couldn't suppress a shudder as we approached. The walls were barren, other than a photo of possibly the President, with the Palestinian flag as a backdrop, hanging in back of our interrogator.

I anticipated being subjected to an immediate scolding on our illegal activities, maybe a threat to escort us out of the West Bank or worse…jail. Instead, he asked us if we would like to drink coffee. I nodded and so did Bram, whose eyes avoided mine as I turned back to him, silently seeking pardon for getting him arrested. It did not come as he continued to avoid my looks. The telephone rang and the sergeant picked it up, at the same time a cell phone in front of him began vibrating. After answering both calls he faced us, his intransigent eyes coldly looking us over and then scrupulously surveying a copy of one of our fliers.

"What you're doing is illegal; you know that?"

I tried to maintain a calm, confident expression on my face to relax Bram, to make him think I was not worried, even though I was. Because Omar had perhaps refused to have me released this time, I feared anything could happen. Bram, his brown hair swept over a creased forehead, seemed to say in his expression, "You never warned me about this."

I responded by fixing the most unworried look possible on my face, my eyes beaming confidence and the corners of my mouth subtly turned up.

The officer continued: "Even though the idea is good—freedom for us," he continued, alternately staring at Bram, then at me, using his right hand to emphasize his thoughts and grasp the flier. His smile showed yellowing, clenched teeth poking through his wiry moustache. He repeated himself, "You know you do illegal?"

I feigned lack of understanding even though I had heard of the law that said people were required to receive authorization before any marches were held in the

West Bank. I responded, "I've had several marches: in Bethlehem, in Hebron and I've never had to get permission…."

He cut me off, his lips closing in a tight smile, "You must know Jenin is different; it is very sensitive…very dangerous place."

He looked up, his eyes gleaming, almost threatening. I thought to myself that I had never submitted for approval of a peace march in the West Bank for a reason: if I did apply for authorization and was denied, then I could not plead ignorance of the regulation if I were arrested. There would be no defense. His green beret slanted downwards as he tipped his head to look at the flier again.

"I'll take it to the PA myself to get approved; come back in a week."

I considered that an opening and quickly responded, with slight emotion, "I'll be back in Paris by then to teach and I won't be back here for some time. The march will have to be cancelled!"

He raised his hand abruptly calling for silence. I stopped. He sighed, lifted up his cell phone and called. After speaking a few words in Arabic, he put down the phone.

"Do you want to try to get approval now, no guarantee?"

I quickly responded, "Na'am."

He immediately stood up and ushered us out the door and down the stairs to a waiting car. Once inside, I peeked at my watch which showed it was 1:00 pm, the exact time scheduled for the beginning of the march. I turned to Bram, who was watching me.

"They can't start without us, as we're the leaders!" I exclaimed, but was not sure for whose benefit I said that, his or mine.

Perspiration began welling up and flowing down the sides of my face as I imagined the press from Bethlehem, the Palestine News Network (PNN), showing up and then returning to Bethlehem, since there would be no marchers to interview. I pulled out my cell phone and tried calling the journalist named on the PNN business card but I could not get through. I whispered through clenched teeth, "That's typical for the West Bank."

I looked at Bram, who responded with a sympathetic smile. I breathed deeply and shook my head. After weaving between a series of small, white buildings, the car stopped in front of a drab, green office building. We were immediately met at the door by a white-haired man dressed in a suit, followed by a very tall, dark man who spoke perfect English. They took us to an adjoining room where a group of men, all wearing white shirts, were sitting around a table, where a balding man with tufts of black hair and wire-rimmed glasses presided. We sat down in seats provided for us. I sighed as I anticipated more interrogation; all pairs of eyes closely watched us. The balding man in charge motioned that I should stand up.

I stood.

"Are you the leader of this march?" "I am."

"You've requested authorization of a peace march taking place today. You must wait a week and then…."

"Please forgive me for interrupting. Several people from foreign countries are supposed to attend, as well as members of a Palestinian news agency, PNN, who were coming from Bethlehem to report on the march. We should be starting the march now...."

He cut me off, asking "The Press is coming?"

"Yes, and they will show the whole world about Jenin; to bring peace here, the world must see...."

"Ok, ok, give me the telephone number of that news group, ah...."

"PNN."

"Yes."

I gave him the PNN business card and the man turned and walked toward the window. All we could see was the back of his head, short, black hair and a cell phone mashed against his left ear lobe. I crossed my fingers that he had better luck than I had connecting with the journalist. Several minutes of discussion in Arabic took place after which he returned briskly and sat down, having barked orders to a young man and giving him a copy of my flier.

Then he addressed us solemnly: "It appears that journalists from PNN are on their way. You must realize that it normally takes one week for approval but we've sent your request by fax; you have to thank the police chief for that and because the press is coming, we are waiting for a return fax authorizing the march."

Within minutes, the authorization came from Ramallah and we were being led out a back door to the street where a taxi was waiting to take us to the center of Jenin. The driver was friendly and kept saying "Al-Hamdu-lil-laah." (Praise Allah.)

I hoped that was a good sign. Either he had been informed of our mission or the fare was prepaid by the PA because the taxi driver would not accept payment.

After a thrilling run down alley-ways and other shortcuts, he opened the door with a quick "Bismillah" (In the name of God); we shook hands and then left the taxi, which had stopped in the middle of the street. We picked David up at the café, where we had left him. He handed me the big plastic sack carrying the loudspeaker as he held up one side of the "Freedom March" sign (in Arabic and English) and Bram the other. We walked three abreast down busy Abu Baker Street, the main street in Jenin.

I put the loudspeaker to my lips and belted out, "La ilaha illa Allah, Adonai Elohaynu Adonai Echad, God the Father, God the Son, God the Holy Ghost."

I feared speaking the Hebrew name for God and naming the Christian Trinity in English would upset everyone, as many understood Hebrew and English.

However, the people in this ravaged place—devastated by years of conflict—were open to the principle of one God, even if the religions of Judaism and Christianity were invoked.

"One God is one God. Brothers and sisters of the Book; we want peace, freedom for all. We are all in prison with you: Palestinians, the Israelis, as well, Muslims, Jews, Christians...the whole world is in prison. Let's free ourselves through nonviolent interfaith dialogue and understanding. La ilaha illa Allah, Adonai Elohaynu Adonai, Echad."

I gave the loudspeaker to David and lifted up my hands and crossed them at the wrists, as if they were tied together, then violently separated them, as I yelled, "Freeeeeeeeee-dom! Free ourselves from hate—let's work together for peace."

David, clicking on the loudspeaker and raising it to his lips, belted out, "All for one and one for all!" as we continued marching along.

A huge crowd followed us, chanting, "Allahu Akbar."

Those that could not join us looked up from their work, from their fruit wagons, peered out from doorways of businesses and apartments, wearing different colored hijabs, Aqals and keffiyehs, their mouths smiling...smiling their support. We were then joined by two bystanders dressed up as Tweetie Bird and Mickey Mouse, stretching smiles across the faces of even grim-faced onlookers. This incredible journey was not yet over!

I gave Tweetie Bird the loudspeaker; he took off his mask and blurted out in heavily-accented English, "Freedom for all, peace for all, love and one Allah."

All the smiling, chanting citizens totally surprised me. It didn't seem possible that just a few years ago, this same place had been a war zone where horrendous battles took place—where Molotov cocktails had been catapulted at tanks and many homes were destroyed, many lives lost and many, many tears flowed—and in Israel, as well. In spite of all the pain, the children—many left without parents who had been killed in the tragic clashes with the Israeli soldiers—followed us, ignited hope in us; the feeling was strong.

The hope is to build a bridge across this war-ravaged city to Israel, to develop bonds among Muslims, Jews and Christians working together to rebuild schools and other buildings destroyed in the Intifada. The hope is to rebuild, on both sides of the walls—in Israel, the West Bank and eventually in Gaza—to rebuild structures...and hearts.

Back in East Jerusalem, on the Mount of Olives, Ibrahim served us hot, steaming mint tea. No words were spoken as the hot steam from our cups rose to the roof and joined together, emblematic of a new world of unity, freedom and love we were helping to create, here beneath the sweet olive trees, in this Holy Land.

Chapter 80: Lost in your Arms

A month later, after organizing several freedom marches in the West Bank and interfaith dialogues in Israel, I returned to the States; I was exhausted from constant traveling and mentally and physically drained by the Israeli-Palestinian peace gauntlet. But my soul was deeply nourished. I needed to see my kids and my Mom. My ex-wife was hovering…I still hadn't gotten over her, in spite of the ladies that had diverted my path, so I still wanted to soar with her. After all those worlds and all those miles, I was still in love with her….

"Attaches amoureuses" (Bonds of Love)

I decided I'd take a few days off with my kids, Frankie, Regina and Juliana, in San Francisco before taking the usual Greyhound bus to visit my mom in the mountains of Oregon. After hanging out for hours with them in a café and eating enchiladas, burritos and tacos, they went to bed early because they had school in the morning. After leaving the house—and our desperate goodbyes, to prolong my connection with them—I called Sylvia on my cell. She said she was watching me from the window above.

"Sneaky!"

She giggled, as she had in earlier times when we were so in love…and the words of the song sailed back into my mind "Because you and I've been in love too long to worry 'bout tomorrow."[111] But tomorrow was here! I sighed as the silence on the phone made me nervous. I figured all attempts to see her would be in vain but I'd give it a try anyway.

"How about joining me for an Italian dinner, back where we used to live? Remember?"

"Do you remember?" she softly responded.

Silence prevailed as emotion welled up in my heart; the words were muffled in me.

Thankfully she broke the silence, "Ok."

I looked up and saw the curtains moving. I was surprised that she did not hesitate when she said "yes," as she'd been avoiding all contact with me for the last year. After dinner, we found ourselves in my modest room at a local hotel a few steps

---

111 Ambrosia, "You're the Only Woman," One Eighty, Rubicon Music Co., California, 1980.

from the restaurant, together again after all those years, like old times: warm, starved caresses...until the buses stopped running, until the clang of the cable cars was silenced. I was swept away by the bonds incredibly powerful as ever, that I thought had stretched and snapped long ago. The light from a streetlamp barely showed the side of her soft face, as she lay asleep on the pillow next to me. I lay there next to her, running my fingers over the strand of hair stuck to her soft olive skin. I glanced out the window before crossing into an illogical world of pure, tremulous emotions; the vivid San Francisco sky seemed to reflect my tumultuous feelings. I scribbled a poem on the back of a pillow case that I had written years ago:

> I crossed the line—
> passions streamed from my fingertips
> I crossed the line touching your soft face that I had held so dear
> for so many moments
> I crossed over
> life and death no longer have meaning
> endless searching for sanity
> because I crossed over into pure amor—
> to touch you again
> And die
> because I crossed over into my tears of longing
> I crossed over–never more to return to a controlled existence—
>
> it is no longer possible
> in the reflection of your eyes in the puddle
> leading up to a place where we touched—
> our hearts so interweaving
> so out of breath, gasping—
>
> So, I crossed over never to return
> from a correct life socially acceptable
> flirting with emotional, mental disaster
> upon every breath that I shall ever take
> I will————cross over
> To your love.[112]

She awoke as I finished writing. Her dark lips smiled as she quickly climbed over me and dressed, without looking up. I pleaded for her to stay all night but she was in hurry to get home to avoid her parents noticing her late arrival.

"Would you come back to me?" I desperately whispered.

I lay there as she stuck her shoes on her feet; she staggered, slightly off-balance, bracing against my leg still sprawled on the bed. Being in the same room with me as in old times, breathing the same air, laughing, loving....

---

112 Romano, Frank. "Over the Line." Crossing Over, supra.

I shivered with longing. As I lay watching her prepare to leave, the last few hours came back in a whirlwind of déjà vu as I remembered gently having relieved her of her clothes and all those moments in darkness shared—and the sounds of lovemaking. Her scent was uniquely potent, almost too strong, making me so dizzy it almost knocked me over; I had to sit on the bed. It all came back then, churning my unquenchable passion for her, then gushing through me like an uncontrollable tide of red hot flames. After so many nights reaching for her in the dark, I felt dizzy again, my head buzzed, my heart strangely vibrated...could I ever feel the same for anyone else?

Now she was going home, not fighting to stay as she had in Paris, until she couldn't stand it anymore; she had been in a foreign world, with me by her side-but it hadn't been enough. The tears came again and I didn't bother to stop them. What can I do...? I wondered, throwing on my sandals and overcoat, stumbling as I followed her out the door. She's left me alone again...this time I will never be with her again, like this...and I knew it—it had to happen one day; but why today?

Screams reverberated inside...I felt the last twitches of death as I stared at her tail lights slowly disappearing in the blur of lights. My heart stilled and I felt the void...a cold tomb enclosed me. I tried to fight my way out, reaching for the light, straining to breathe. I could hear only our song, "Dreamwalk,"[113] over and over again...throbbing in my soul, resounding in the cool morning breeze of a sleeping San Francisco.

Returning to the hotel room, I was drained and my heart was frozen. I opened the window, looking out into the night, and quickly thawed as my eyes fell on the dark outline of Victoria Pastry, a North Beach bakery below, where we had bought all our birthday cakes, cappuccino cakes, St. Honoré, chocolate, panettone, and Italian candies before Christmas. Then I visualized our kids rampaging with excitement around the apartment.

Those places we had shared with our babies somehow traversed the barrier to repressed memories; I was surprised they were still alive, breathing, festering wounds, deep within me. The special memories of times shared with the family would never leave. But with her, I could no longer be....

On the bed I spotted her beige, frilly panties, crumpled up next to the pillow. I buried my face in them, breathing her in deeply for the last time; traces of her scent were still there. The panties embraced me like a long lost lover as I desperately quivered with erotic ecstasy, to the core of my being. A gentle vibration rippled down my loins as my passion began to slowly rise. I wanted her again...and again. I then laid them gently in the corner of the suitcase I later hid under my bed in Oregon.

I wanted to love, to be loved unconditionally, but I was always testing; I wondered if my tests were too severe, too demanding, if I was looking for perfect love, unrealistic relationship...."Oh God," I pleaded as I crashed to my knees, "help me!"

"Crossing over to your love, there's no return...."

---

113 White, Peter. "Dreamwalk." Excusez-Moi. Sin-Drome Records. Sherman Oaks, CA. 1990. (White is a British jazz guitarist and songwriter.) We had decided this was our song one night in San Francisco—one lost night—reminiscing about the love refusing to release our hearts even years after our divorce.

Who to turn to, who to call? I rose, looking out the hotel window in the Italian district as the sun was coming up, people were stirring and the streets glinted in the morning light. I looked up through a corner of the window to Coit Tower, as the mist of an early San Francisco morning enveloped it, causing it to disappear.

I reached out to my mother, the only one who never gave up, who always believed in me all through the years, even when I was a ghetto dweller and fear had driven most of my friends away, including my Dad. But she was never afraid! Her face appeared in my mind, smiling, encouraging...I couldn't call her, yet—it was too early and I didn't want to awaken her from her reveries, perhaps of my father whom she often dreamed about....

Ashes of love....

The sun's light filtered through the clouds as the rusty brakes of the first bus screeched. I searched the sky overhead, and all I could see was Rosalia's familiar face, while she gently, ever so gently, bit her top lip. I remembered her quick breaths and the shimmer of her moist eyes, like a moonlit Mediterranean night. I closed my eyes and looked again, but she was also gone....

However, my next visit to the "inner womb of the Mediterranean"[114] would lead me to the killing fields.

---

114 Romano, Frank. "Mediterranean." Crossing Over, supra.

Chapter 81: Return to Killing Fields

December 2011

The taxi left me somewhere in the Jenin refugee camp and then burned rubber away from me. That time, for some reason, the driver would not take me all the way to the theater so I walked in its general direction, the place where my friend, Juliano, had been murdered a year ago. The clouds were streaked with gold and red, a turbulent layer of iridescent fluff lying over the brow of the skyline. Night was hanging over the heart of the refugee camp and I walked alone. Every step brought me out of the jet-lag that seemed to have taken over my being after so many flights to the US, Paris, the Middle East and back again. I'd returned to the source of my interfaith marches and dialogues for freedom, riding on the back of endless faith— to face war, evil, unbridled violence, vengeful madness—a voice for solidarity in a sometimes hopeless situation, in the place where Juliano was blasted with five bullets to his gut.[115]

I unintentionally stopped, led by subconscious radar which halted my body and turned my head, like a robot, to stare at the bullet holes slammed in the side of a chalky white building during the last Intifada, the conflict between the Palestinians and Israelis. Someone had showed them to me during my last visit. The holes bored into long cracks, as if a further assault on an already festering sore.

My eyes fixed on the shadows in the holes, dark and foreboding. Then my French friends' words echoed inside my head,

"Stay away from the refugee camp, at least until the storm over Juliano's murder has blown over."

My head shook as if shaking off those words, while I walked along the dirt road leading to the Freedom Theater. I had convinced myself that I could not keep away just because of the ratcheting up of the conflict there. I at least owed it to my friend to return to the "killing field", where his blood had flowed to the cold rubber mat on the floor as he sat next to his one-year-old son, looking up during his last moments, over the head of his wailing son. I desperately needed to be in the exact spot of the grisly scene, where the five steel rockets tore into his chest, where he was face-to-face, almost chest-to-chest with his black-masked assailant. Maybe he was lulled into

---

115 His life and murder are recounted in detail in Ch. 45, "Julian Mer-Khamis," Love and Terror in the Middle East, 4th Edition.

believing that the man was one of the actors in the theater group approaching him with his mask on, at least until he felt the sizzling penetration of the burning steel....

Then I recalled again the moment I had heard of his death while I was in Paris hunched over my desk, at the exact moment I was writing the chapter in this book[116] about how Juliano had helped me in my endeavors to lead dialogues and marches for peace in the Holy Land. Impossible....

The storm hit me hard as I shook with rage, walking—endlessly walking—and visualizing angry waves, frothing and bitter, throwing me over the rocks and onto the shore of restless Middle Eastern beaches. I swayed and began tottering, almost losing myself; I forced myself to stop and sit on a wooden stump at the side of the dirt road. I was frozen in a pathetic pile, all hunkered up, as I imagined myself trying to do something about Juliano's death. Then I shook with disbelief as I realized that, despite Juliano's courageous efforts to bring us together—the East the West and all that lay in between—only a few months after his sudden departure, most people had lost all interest in him...what he had lived and died for.

Then the warnings of my friends came back to me again, telling me to skip this trip. I sat there not knowing what to do. But it was too late to worry about that. I jolted up remembering the one lesson I had learned while organizing freedom/peace marches and dialogues there: When things get hot, you strip off some of your clothes and wade in, and let the waves caress you and pull you. You plant your foot down in the hard sand, holding firmly as it gives way under your sole—if not, the tide drags you away.

I trudged forward in what I assumed was the direction of the Freedom Theater. At that point, I was totally lost and just hoped I would reach my destination, like a homing pigeon lost in a violent tempest. As I walked, I reflected on my many visits there leading dialogues and marches, dedicated to building bridges for peace between Israel and Palestine. I reasoned that in spite of being arrested several times and harassed by the Palestinian police not far from where I plodded along through the dust, these efforts were necessary, perhaps even key to helping bring peace to the area, where politicians and religious leaders had completely failed.

For motivation, I didn't have far to look. All around me were people fighting for peace, for freedom, people who had lost their homes, close family members, relegated to surviving with nothing and very little income. The Bantustans were created by the myriad of crisscrossing walls and checkpoints, often cutting off one Palestinian city from another as well as resulting in the uprooting of a myriad of olive trees that were serving as the sole source of income for many Palestinian families. They were surrounded by hostile forces—Palestinian police and a layer of Israeli soldiers—and were plagued with violent disputes amongst themselves. During the second intifada about 10 years earlier, many people even lost their homes as many were bulldozed by Israeli soldiers; yet they were still surviving, some were even thriving in the rubble and...still fighting.

Their stories of disparate treatment, missing family members and people humiliated at checkpoints enflamed me and I shook with emotion trudging along the narrow paths weaving among primitive white dwellings.

---

116 Ibid.

But something was different. Normally I could reel in my emotions, but they were so fired up that I feared they would draw me into a kind of paroxysm if I didn't let them out. They were nose diving and spiraling wildly out of control. I couldn't stop them; they burned my insides to cinders, propelling me forward while forcefully pushing fear to the sidelines. There would be no more timorous, priggish gestures, hands flailing in the air, then covering my head as if to bury it in the sand. I clenched my fists to face the devil.

Grasping for strength, to pull myself out of the black quagmire of my thoughts, I changed gears as I focused on tender lovemaking with past flames, the primordial caresses from which I imagined the world was created, in my mind, a model for bringing about world peace. If more people made love intensely but tenderly, transcending ones being, the undulating mutual embrace would bring the world to the threshold of peace and wipe away the cold, robotic thrusts passing as lovemaking between those engaged in heartless, lifeless relations. The living dead, many people don't seem to be able to transcend the physical act of love to the realm of ecstatic, unconditional love, going instead for the release...fooling each other with sugary whispers...sugar like gall.

The recalling of unbridled, tender lovemaking suffused me with molten, impassioned memories, giving me a jolt of much needed strength. The thoughts scalded my blood and swept through me, helping me visualize and route out my constant enemy...fear. I stopped abruptly and blurted through clenched teeth,

"But the world better not forget him...can't believe it!" I cried within, wiping the tears with the back of my hand.

I had subconsciously stopped, as if I could smell the closeness of the blood, sweat and dust emanating from Freedom Theater. I envisioned the dust rising from the floors of the partially destroyed theater after the Battle of Jenin, as depicted in Juliano's film, "Arna's Children."[117]

I looked down from the rise in the road, and there it sat, the Freedom Theater. The theater offices were situated about 100 feet down at the bottom of the driveway, wedged between several white houses and a large theater space on the right. That was where Juliano and I, a few years before, had attended a concert. Juliano was the master of ceremonies and organizer of the concert that day which had featured DAM, a famous activist Palestinian rap group. I could remember the words, "Meen Erhabi, Anta Erhabi"[118] that Tamer Nafar, the lead singer, had bellowed out—echoed by everyone in the crowd—boys hanging onto each other with hands stretched out and girls in hijabs singing and dancing to the torrid beat and words, "Hurryah Palestine."[119]

Then I envisioned myself standing in the middle of the crowd while I looked down on Freedom Theater. For some reason, the words of a poem I wrote when I was 17 returned, taunting me:

---

117 Producer: Juliano Mer-Khamis, "Arna's Children," supra.

118 "Who's the terrorist, you're the terrorist"

119 Hurryah, means Freedom in Arabic.

> ...then silence as if nothing happened.
> The wind is quiet, the leaves are still, not a sound.
> But if you concentrate on the air
> love vibrations are faintly felt ...[120]

But love vibrations stopped as I desperately tried to feel spiritual love and even forgiveness, but God forgive me, all I could feel at that moment was...rage. I swung my right arm in front of me; my clenched fist reminded me that I was not clapping as I had done during DAM's spirited performance, with the Palestinians echoing the lyrics and gyrating their bodies to a primal beat, in front of their seats.

No, there would be no more cheering near the place where the life of my young friend had been viciously snuffed out. Then I shifted my eyes to the ground as I realized that somehow I had made it to the theater and was standing like a fool, unable to move in front of it.

"Bouges cretino!"[121] I cried, a mixture of French and Italian flowing from my angry lips.

I was frozen after recollecting events that seemed to have taken place decades earlier as I continued standing like a stone-cold statue, trying to calm myself for fear of losing it—losing it completely. My legs buckled as I hit the ground on my knees, uttering under my breath, "Stop, emotional sop; you're useless. Get up!"

After bending over and pushing myself until I could slide my legs underneath my torso and stand up, I headed down the path toward the Freedom Theater, pulling my dead-weight luggage.

I had called Adnan, the temporary director of the theater, who would be waiting for me inside. I arrived at the bottom of the hill and stood in front of the sliding door which, like me, seemed to hesitate as it grudgingly scraped open after triggering an automatic eye when I got within a foot of it. Then it flashed through my mind that my friend had been murdered a few paces after leaving the building; he could have easily been followed and attacked as he worked inside, thus making this holy place his tomb. I saw an internet picture of Adnan, who was waiting for me inside, while scanning articles about the tragedy before arriving in the Holy Land.

The newspaper photo, taken a few months after the murder, shows him being arrested and dragged out of the theater by Israeli soldiers after they attacked the Freedom Theater, during their "investigation" of, or in retaliation for, Juliano's murder.[122] But the fact Juliano was an Israeli Jew had nothing to do with his death, I thought, as I grimly shook my head.

I stepped in front of the sliding door that continued sliding open like a snake winding through gravel. It finally opened wide then seemed to nervously close a bit then jerk open, finding me lingering in the door stop. I hesitated. The words of my

---

120 Frank Romano, from the poem, "Festival of Life," p.13, Crossing Over, supra.

121 "Bouges", French word, means move. "Cretino", Italian word, means idiot!

122 "Israeli Soldiers Arrest Two Palestinians." PressTV. 27 July 2011. <http://www.presstv.ir/detail/191023.html>

friends bore down on me, making me wonder why I was about to do what I was going to and that maybe I should turn around and high-tail it out of there.

Too late...My memories floating on the sultry night air had pushed me to the threshold of this place as if they were trying to punch me through to help lead this faltering revolution. It was too late to withdraw; the door to the theater opened and Adnan stood in front of me. He looked just like the picture; he was a dark, pensive man with short black hair, a permanently furrowed brow hovering over a tight smile spread across his thin face. His face sprouted a week's growth under a spreading mustache; two flaming brown eyes pierced my entire being, studying me—they passed over me like two bright red crystal scanners. His small, tight lips drooping down at the corners matched the shape of his black, crescent eye brows, which were creased in several places.

His hand extended toward me which I shook. "Adnan?" He nodded as he released my hand and grasped the black handle of my suitcase, pulling it in. "Thanks for having me in spite of hard times, the loss of your leader, Juliano...." His dark eyes closed—he opened them, a smile curling over his white teeth. He then seemed to lose himself as his eyes glazed over; he was somewhere else. I looked away, hoping that my eyes would meet up with his focused out there somewhere, maybe on Juliano dancing with the original actors of the theater; many of whom were killed during the 2nd Intifada.

Reality hit me as I realized they were now followed to their graves by Juliano. "God, why?" I sighed under my breath.

My eyes skimmed the walls around me and then returned to Adnan. But his eyes were still cloudy and distant, glistening, mirroring a lifetime. They reflected so much in the inscrutable silence that enveloped us; then his hand gently pulled mine into a larger room that apparently served as the office. I toted my bags behind me, with the other hand. The stillness of this place, coupled with remembrances of previous vigorous conversations I had here with Juliano, made me feel that there was almost nothing left to talk about.[123]

And if there was, a confused panic rose inside me as I mouthed words that could not escape my lips. He pointed to a green sofa chair planted below the window. I immediately recognized it to be the chair I sat in when I had interviewed Zakaria Zubeidi in 2005 or 2006; he was still hiding from Israeli soldiers due to his involvement as the head of Al-Aqsa Martyrs' Brigade Jenin,[124] an organization marked as a terrorist group by Israeli and US authorities. Adnan shuffled to the middle of the room where he sank down into a chair next to a large table. He sighed—his tired smile matched his eyes, sunken deep into their sockets. I feared he and the theater would languish there, never to rise again to the great heights that it had achieved under the leadership of Juliano. Even his picture hanging on the wall, recently added to the pictures of the young actors who had perished during the conflict, was a grim reminder of a brighter

123 Chapter 45, "Julian Mer-Khamis."

124 A Palestinian group which emerged during the Second Intifada, around 2000. It has carried out attacks against Israeli settlers, Israeli soldiers and has organized suicide bombings in Israel. "Profile: Al-Aqsa Martyr's Brigades." BBC news, supra. Also, see Chapter 43, "Jihad," footnote 68.

yesteryear. I wondered if Juliano's absence would usher in a new era of hysterical confusion.

I looked at Adnan and he nodded as if saying he knew exactly what I wanted. "Our friend and yours, left us...." He shook his head, unable to continue.

"Like you and I, Juliano had many enemies...."

For the first time since I arrived, a faint, sardonic smile flickered at the corners of his mouth. I shrugged to indicate to him that having enemies was our daily bread and that it was no "big deal", my way of coaxing him to get to the point.

Then I realized I was falling into "Juliano's way," a man who was always terse during conversations, especially those about freeing Palestine. He had been decidedly against wasting words and time.

I uttered under my breath, "I soooooooooooo miss you...."

"We all have our theories, but seriously, no one knows; no evidence was found. I was jailed...."

I interrupted, looking away, "I know."

He told me that even Juliano's good friend, Zakaria[125] who was connected by many overlapping branches in this ghetto, had no idea who the murderer was.

Then he stammered, emotions finally overcoming his rigid demeanor. Shuddering, he spit out in a shaking voice, "I warned him after the last firebomb attack on this building in 2009 that he should install cameras around the place. He just looked at me and smiled, brushing it aside. He wasn't even afraid for himself...almost like he felt that if he were to die, it was destiny. Maybe he was just naïve, thinking that the death threats were empty, and that no one really wanted to...." he hesitated and his voice broke slightly then continued, "you know...."

"Yeah, I know...." I reached out and held his arm. I had to bite my lip.

His voice ebbed into a whisper as he withdrew again; not wanting to push further. Knowing we would discuss more in the morning when we were better rested, I tried to change the subject by asking him if I could "crash" in the freedom theater, in the back room, as I had not arranged for sleeping yet. He hesitated, then apologized that he had no way to accommodate me since the guest house was not ready to receive guests yet. He turned away in silence as if to contemplate something that he did not want to share with me. I wondered if he wanted, at least for now, to enshrine the back room where Juliano spent a lot of time, excluding everyone, including me, from the premises.

He turned his gaze back to me and said I could roll out my sleeping bag on the

---

125 Zakaria Zubeidi had been granted amnesty in 2007 by Israel, with other Al-Aqsa Martyrs' Brigade gunmen, on condition he surrender his arms to the Palestinian Authority, promise to stop terrorist attacks against Israel and join the Palestinian Authority police force. However, amnesty granted him was revoked by Israel in December, 2011. "Israël revoque l'amnestie de Zacharia Zubeidi." (Israel revokes amnesty of Zacharia Zubeidi) UJFP. (Union Juive Française pour la Paix- French Jewish Union for Peace). 3 January 2012. <http://www.ujfp.org/spip.php?article2078&lang=fr>. Following an international campaign, amnesty was reestablished in February, 2012. "Zacharia Zubeidi libéré suite à une campagne internationale." (Zacharia Zubeidi Freed after an International Campaign), UJFP. (Union Juive Française pour la Paix- French Jewish Union for Peace). 18 January 2012. <http://www.ujfp.org/spip.php?article2109&lang=fr>.

carpet of the back theater and sleep there. He began to apologize again; I shook my head telling him that I sleep on the floor all the time in a sleeping bag, in airports and even in the streets, and that the floor here would be perfect, praise God!

That night, I turned around several times outside the Freedom Theater, and found myself in the exact spot where Adnan had said Juliano was gunned down while driving his car with his child sitting next to him and the nanny in the back seat. The place where his car was parked on that fatal day was now an empty spot on the pavement, inhabited only by soft murmuring of spirits carried by the cool spring breeze circling the leaves in a whirlpool over my head. When the gust relented, the leaves fell one by one, like parachutes, to the hard, flat ghetto.

When I had lived in a California ghetto about 40 years earlier, a shooting took place there almost every week. I heard of men, women and sometimes children dying but since I didn't know them, even though I felt a deep ghetto solidarity and mourned their loss, I wasn't directly connected to any of them and could ride out the killings without letting them get me down. But this was different. I had known Juliano...the empty space that was once filled with his healing, bolstering energy had become the place where he spent his last few seconds of life.

I tried to visualize his last expression but could only imagine a resigned, empty stare. I imagined the five bullets penetrating his barrel chest, sending a man of strength—of vision—away from us, as he slowly shut his eyes, drifting away, away from the bridges he had created between Palestinians and Israelis...slowly drifting far, far away from his family, his children and his wife. But he knew the danger and the risks, albeit necessary to help bring a desperately needed peace to this land....

Looking over the buildings in the camp, I stood below the frozen night sky as the wind blustered, freezing everything to a standstill while families hovered together inside their houses. It all came back: memories stormed back into my consciousness, in particular, of scenes in the movie made by Juliano about his mother's work. Yousef was always the joker in the acting troop. As a young boy, he played a king in Juliano's theater production, "The Little Oil Lamp."[126] But the joker in him was transformed into silent brooding due to an event that was to mark him forever.

I reflected on a week during the Second Intifada, from April 3rd to April 11th, 2002, the battle between the Palestinians and Israeli soldiers in the depths of the Jenin Refugee Camp. For eight days, the skies swarmed with helicopters and warplanes ejaculating missiles and air-to-surface rockets that pulverized the camp. The shells bursting into unadorned, white buildings, crushing them into powder, reverberated in my imagination. I looked up and remembered reading that Juliano's and his mother Arna's theater had been totally destroyed and was rebuilt into this new theater. My insides drained through this misery and I grew cold as I reflected on Yousef's story:

On October 18, 2001, during the Second Intifada and before that major battle, Israeli tanks shot into Ibrahimiya Elementary School. Yousef, employed as a homicide investigator in a nearby police station, ran to the scene and found a girl hemorrhaging from shrapnel wounds and carried her to the hospital. She didn't make it and Yousef

---

126 "Palestinian Biographies-Zacharia Zubeidi." Lawrence of Cyberia-blog. 9 August 2004. <http://lawrenceofcyberia.blogs.com/palestinian_biographies/zakaria-zubeidi-biography. html>.

laid her lifeless body down.[127] According to his friends, something hardened inside him after that, which later drove him to become a suicide bomber.[128]

After Yousef was killed by Israeli police following his suicide attack, Juliano interviewed a friend of Yousef's who said that Yousef loved freedom but the last two years of his life, he had felt imprisoned.[129] I wondered if he threw himself into death due to intense frustration and despair, or for other reasons. The causes of suicide attacks, like Yousef's, were sometimes understandable but not ever—oh, my God—never justified. I wondered if Juliano had done the same thing, but without taking any victims with him, by sometimes throwing his life into the fray without taking steps to protect himself...and then I wondered if I sometimes did the same thing. If so, God forgive Juliano and God forgive me.

I returned to the Freedom Theater and walked through the sliding doors; Adnan was sitting on the couch smoking a cigarette. He turned to me. His red eyes peered through drooping eyelashes and without saying anything, he handed me a set of keys on a metal clasp. He got up, motioned me to follow him to the main door and inserted one of the keys in the keyhole. Turning to me, he asked me to lock it after him and said he would return later that night or in the early morning.

"Frank, when I leave, close and lock the door behind me. Oh, by the way, if you want Wi-Fi, you need to sit on the bench outside the main door or inside next to it. You may hear noises coming from people in the bordering apartments...." He shrugged and looked at me strangely, as if searching my eyes for the signs of possible betrayal, looking for anything irregular indicating that I had come not as a freedom activist and friend of Juliano's, but as a spy to watch him for terrorist activity or clues to Juliano's murder. I looked back into his eyes that had turned into cold crystals camouflaging his deepest thoughts, but unable to disguise his lingering bereavement and perhaps suspicions. I had to look away.

He nodded after a minute of silence and turning to the door, walked out, shutting it behind him. I locked the door and went to where I had placed my computer; carefully taking it out of the computer bag, I returned to the door and reopened it. After the familiar sliding door scraped open, I stepped out into a patio where I sat on a bench and opened my computer to access emails. While I was reading them, a group of inquisitive children appeared from all directions, flooding the patio. They asked me questions in broken English such as, Do you believe in God? or Are you Muslim? Say something in Arabic.

Soon we were engaged in a full-blown discussion. A young girl wearing a green hijab sat on my lap, her cheeky smile flashing whenever she turned her head. Two young boys, one wearing a Palestinian black and white kheffiyah around his neck, the other with a Muslim skull cap, were slapping each other's hands away as they grasped to shake mine. They would sometimes touch my leg and sometimes I felt a hand surreptitiously slip into a pocket. Coming out empty, someone would say,

---

127 Chapter 45, "Juliano Mer-Khamis."

128 Ibid.

129 Producer: Juliano Mer-Khamis, "Arna's Children," supra.

"Money?" I would smile and say, "Bidoon money".[130] Their smiles did not cease and we continued to have a raucous time reciting a part of "Al Fatiha"[131] added to my recounting of life in Paris, the subways, the people.

After an hour, I noticed the numbers of boys and girls swelling. Even the warmth of their exuberant presence could not divert me for long as I was desperate to read my messages, especially from those helping me with the next interfaith marches I was organizing in Palestine and Israel. I finally grabbed my computer and stood up; walking to the door of the Freedom Theater, I went in, turned just before the door shut and waved. I could see hands flying before the inexorable sliding door slammed shut. I plopped down in a chair next to the main door and for the next half hour; silence engulfed the place as I skimmed my messages. No one insisted on entering the theater so I assumed the theater was off limits for kids at night.

Then the familiar scraping of the sliding door warned me someone was coming. I continued my work with an eye on the door which began to slowly creak open. A boy's head stuck through; his brown eyes widened as they found mine staring at him. Then he withdrew and let the door swing shut. His muffled steps clattered down the patio pavement and soon a total, eerie silence reigned. He was the last child to leave the patio. The sounds of children playing were quickly replaced by night sounds from the surrounding houses: voices, some shrill, then a low chattering while cupboards opened and closed, interrupted from time to time by the low rumbling of cars passing in the night.

I walked to the sofa flanked by two easy chairs and sank down, its arms folding around me. Before my mind descended into darkness, I flashed back on the article I had read about the 2009 fire bomb attack on this place. My thoughts drew me into deep chasms of paranoia as I remembered Juliano telling me during our last meeting he had received death threats, notably by members of the community that did not agree with his unconventional methods in guiding the theater group. In particular, they protested his allowing girls and boys to regularly rehearse and perform publicly together, which according to some people, violated moral codes and promoted other unwelcome liberal values.[132] I cringed as I recalled reading that he was considered an "unwelcome proselytizer for Western values who let their daughters act with boys and even take the leading roles."[133]

He was also severely criticized for allowing actors to play the role of pigs in a theatrical production based on the book, Animal Farm,[134] by George Orwell, because pigs were considered impure animals in the Islam religion.[135]

---

130 Bidoon, Arabic means "without."

131 The prayer "Al Fatiha" is the most important prayer in Islam.

132 Urquhart, Conal. "Israeli peace activist Juliano Mer-Khamis shot dead in Jenin." The Guardian. 4 April 2011.<http://www.guardian.co.uk/world/2011/apr/ 04/israeli-peace - activist-shot-dead>.

133 "Juliano Mer-Khamis, Jew, Arab, Actor and Activist, Died on April 4th, Age 52." The Economist. 14 April 2011. <http://www.economist.com/node/18557289>. 133 Ibid.

134 Ibid.

135 Khoury, Jack, Issacharoff, Avi & Pfeffer, Anshel. "Israeli Actor Juliano Mer-Khamis Shot

My insides churned thinking about an article I had read recounting that he was never really accepted as one of them, as a Palestinian, and that even some of the actors in his theater group, as well as their parents, suspected he was an Israeli agent, a spy for the occupation.[136] A long stream of air escaped from my lips in a loud whisper, "Why? How is it he gave his heart always, and that was not enough?"

I pummeled the heavy air as I wondered how Jewish extremists could ignore his Jewish side by considering him an Arab, even after he was able to show Zakaria Zubeidi a path other than violence.[137]

I stammered in a low voice, "Not enough to show the extremists he was working for peace, for a better world...unbelievable!"

I was desperate and needed a warm embrace, a handshake, something warm, something loving...NOW...to take me away from these cruel, morbid thoughts. I looked up and saw strange shadows that oozed over part of the window on the opposite wall. I looked closer and spied two young children, their black hair spilling over their eyes, faces straining forward as they scrutinized me through the streaked window, their heads sometimes cocked sideways. They were probably wondering who the madman was seated in the shadows of their community center.

I got up and walked to the window as they retreated into the dark passage of the alley outside. I closed the curtains and returned to the sofa where I sat back; tears came like velvet over my eyes as I turned away from the window. Darkness folded over me.

All noise from the surrounding houses suddenly stopped, as if a signal were received sending everyone to bed. Sitting there in the middle of the Freedom Theater at midnight, I admired Juliano even more as I contemplated the daily challenges he faced, holding his head high during the stifling occupation, brushing aside daily death threats and pushing his fear back, mastering it.

Sometime later I slipped into the sofa and my eyes closed. I woke up to a heavy funereal air. Light from a street lamp diffused through the curtains formed a blurred silhouette of a man who appeared to be sitting at the table across from me, with his back turned. I recoiled and desperately looked around, seeking a place where I could run, until I blinked and the shadow disappeared. I assumed it was just an illusion perhaps formed by a surreal crisscrossing of light and shadows.

I fell back to sleep and awoke with a gasp. Panic struck; my shoulders hunched over and my hands shook while seizing the hand rests. I had forgotten where I was! A trickle of sweat oozed down my face as I desperately surveyed the room for anything familiar. The shadows revealed nothing. Was I in heaven or hell?

A warm glow suffused me as I imagined lying in bed in the family home in Ashland, Oregon. No, it couldn't be, and panic struck again as I automatically groped for the alarm clock sitting next to my bed in Paris. Thick, musty air

Dead in Jenin." Haaretz.com. 4 April 2011. <http://www.haaretz.com/news/national/israeli-actor-juliano-mer-khamis-shot-dead-in-jenin-1.354044>.

136 "Juliano Mer-Khamis, Jew, Arab, Actor and Activist, Died on April 4th, Age 52." The Economist, supra.

137 Ibid.

engulfed me as my arm flapped in space, not touching anything. No, I wasn't there, either!

I sobered quickly, finally waking to the reality that I was far away from home, somewhere. I got up and groped the wall until I found a light switch and turned it on. I was in the hallway and the light shone on the faces of the actors and Juliano. I sat in front of the pictures while it all came back to me, where I was, and the realization that these time warp blackouts were happening more often due to my constant travels from Europe to the States and to the Middle East. My reaction had reached proportions that were beyond jetlag...beyond anything I could understand.

I breathed in deeply and blew out, focusing on my surroundings. Slowly standing up, I shuffled to the back door where I felt for the light switch and flipped it on. I walked down the corridor to the back of the theater where Adnan had stashed my luggage. Pulling my sleeping bag out of my suitcase, I laid it on the floor and placed my blow-up pillow on it. I lay down without taking my clothes off and was out....

That night, I dreamed I was walking on the sand in a place shrouded in mist. It was so quiet, I could hear the crunch of each footstep as it settled into the sand. Each foot lifted, raining down grains of sand. . The mist became heavier so that I could only see a few feet in front of me. Then it suddenly lifted and the vastness of infinite sands spread in all directions.

Nothing was visible on the farthest horizon, except a tiny, greyish dot off to the right. I walked toward it and as I approached, the dot looked more like a Djellabah crowned by a pointed hood. Closing in, I noticed the black and white striped patterns on the enormous back of someone sitting in the sand with his legs crossed. I swung to the front and saw the face within the hood...it was Juliano. His dark eyelashes were closed and hovered over a glimpse of his full lips. Ever so subtly, their corners stretched upwards into a faint smile creasing the edges of his smooth, olive skin....

Chapter 82: In the Midst of a Riot

September 2013

The invisible flames of the hot, restless Middle Eastern sun seared the sides of the Arab bus, taking me from Jerusalem to Palestine...another world. Even though I was always anxious to continue my work there, every time I crossed the barrier into the West Bank, my stomach churned as the bus wove between the cars chaotically, honking at those blocking our path.

The dust rose and formed an umbrella of haze over our heads, and then settled on desperate drivers with rolling eyes and harsh words. I couldn't help but think that things would be completely different when borders were drawn between Palestine and Israel, and the roads leading from the checkpoint into Palestine were rebuilt following modern standards, designed to contain the daily masses of cars and trucks. One of the perverse consequences of the Israeli occupation of the West Bank was that Palestine—with limited resources—depended largely on donations for road maintenance. When donations stopped or were delayed, government spending often froze and many, in particular civil servants, were not paid until the money flowed again, and that could take months.

I mused that an organized system of modern roads would replace the unruly stampede of desperate drivers in this sometimes lawless no man's land. I couldn't help but think that the occupiers willed it that way, keeping the Palestinians on edge, unsettled, in constant turmoil, feeling endless frustrations, hoping they would give up fighting and eventually leave the land that they had inhabited for hundreds of years... to Israel. That strategy shared (with me) by some Israelis was confirmed by an Israeli soldier I interviewed in Jerusalem two years hence. Ironically, many Israelis agree with the right of Palestinians to their lands and to a state of their own.

But today, it was a disaster, a modern day, relentless human rights disaster. A cold tremor suffused my already weary body as I looked out the window, without seeing...just a blur. My heart pounded in my chest as the bus jolted to a stop; the dust poured through the open window settling on my face. From an invisible faucet spewed an endless wake of cars and trucks as we left behind the infamous checkpoint at Qalandia, situated between Jerusalem and Ramallah.

Qalandia checkpoint is one of the epicenters of the Middle East conflict. For freedom, understanding and love, I come to this place several times a year, to this very spot, this unbridled 24-hour turmoil. Memories of a recent demonstration invaded my mind. Only a few months ago, I had helped organize the Land Day demonstration.[138]

We, Muslims, Jews, Christians, Palestinians, non-Palestinians, Europeans and Americans set out eighty persons strong from the Qalandia mosque, singing peace mantras. That continued for about 30 minutes until we heard shouts and the angry cries of Palestinians running in the opposite direction as we approached a rising layer of dreaded tear gas. Medics following us ran to the front of our line and handed out cotton laced with alcohol that we stuffed in our noses to temper the hot, choking fumes. The gas cloud lifted to show the brow of a line of Israeli soldiers dressed in riot gear holding plastic shields, their heads completely hidden behind plastic task squad visors.

Now the bus grumbled as it approached the place in the middle of the road where I had lain a few months earlier, gasping, grasping and slowly drifting away.

* * *

Nerves jumped inside me as the shuttle drove over the exact spot where a tear gas canister had been mercilessly shot at me plunging through my flag, burning a hole in it and then clanking on the ground beside me fizzing and sputtering, where I was talking to members of the press and non-violent peace activists. None of us had been throwing rocks but we were tear gassed anyway. It was treacherous! As the canister spit throat-splitting fumes into the heavy air, the group scattered. My anger, for being directly targeted, froze me where I stood, the pounding heat of the tear gas searing my brow. Without thinking, and remembering what some Palestinians activists had done in similar circumstances, I held my breath as I ran to the canister and gave it a huge kick, aiming for the other side of the road.

As it tumbled, end over end, toward the side of the road, I exhaled and then inhaled deeply; while inhaling, the wind suddenly shifted and the fumes returned and vengefully engulfed me, entering my lungs before I could stop inhaling. My throat screamed as I inhaled the fire air; a gasping cough exploded from my lungs. I almost lost consciousness and dropped to my knees as a tidal wave of fluid flowed from my nose and eyes. I froze in the middle of the street—cars screeched to a stop on either side of my drooping body. Not one honked. I was thrust in a time warp, semi-conscious; all my strength was focused on resisting the hulk of my weak body dropping like a lead weight onto the hard asphalt. Suddenly, two strong hands seized my arms and dragged me to the side of the road.

When I came to I was lying on my back, a hard, cold object jammed over my mouth and nose; a cool flow seeped down my throat and into my panting lungs. A gasping cough escaped my lips as I grabbed the object and yanked it from my face. I looked up and through a film of tears, faintly perceived the outlines of two dark faces, two pairs of squinting eyes looking down at me like concerned mother hens.

---

138 Land Day (usually on March 30st) is a protest against the appropriation of land and re-sources in the West Bank perpetrated by the State of Israel. It notably commemorates the first massively organized protest against those actions held in 1976, during which several Palestinians were killed and many were imprisoned.

A hand brushed my shoulder. "Breathe easy, my friend, slow breaths…you'll be ok."

I turned my head and spit a lump of phlegm on the ground as a stream of liquid drained from my nose onto the pavement. In a few minutes, I was amazed at how rapidly I revived. I turned and looked up to thank the medics and all I saw was a board hanging from a dilapidated building. They had gone, probably back to the middle of the demonstration to save someone else, dodging flying tear gas canisters, rubber bullets and those odious water cannons spraying a foul-smelling water to disperse the demonstrators–a rank mixture reeking of vomit and sewer water.

I could have sat there for hours and justified it as I had a good excuse, but couldn't. As one of the organizers, I couldn't let down the other demonstrators who were putting it all on the line that day. I stood up, grabbing my flag with the hole in it still steaming, and headed back to join them.

* * *

I arrived late at the bus station in Ramallah and went straight to where I needed to take a shuttle to Jenin. I had organized a freedom dialogue/march scheduled the next day for the streets of Jenin, one of the most contested cities in the West Bank. It was probably too late to find the van that would take me over the arid plains of the northern West Bank. I walked briskly to the entrance of the shuttle station, where I met a man drinking a cup of coffee and leaning against a post. He shoved his hand, palm up, towards me in which I placed a couple of shekels. I began to walk up the ramp to the shuttle station when the man, in a broken, raspy voice, informed me that the shuttles had stopped running for the night.

My legs then took me like a homing pigeon to the same hotel where I had stayed during my first day in Ramallah, the West Bank, so, so long ago. I rented a familiar room and stood in front of the window on the 3rd floor and looked down on the shadows below.

It was midnight, the hour of suspense in this phantom city; a sordid, dark haze crept over it like death, yet it was not dead. Midnight is the moment in a big city when the street buzz usually crescendos into an intense stampede of shoes clomping the sidewalk on the way to a club, café, bistro, show or restaurant. Now, even years after my first visit, the streets had muffled to a sullen pitch, enclosed by buildings standing on sagging pillars, adorned by a few solitary Shawarma sandwich shops on the ground level. It was misleading as there was an undercurrent of life here, behind closed doors.

The typical crisscrossing of lights I'd seen in many metropolises from signs blinking, entreating the night to enter into the realm of glitter and dazzle, was non-existent here! Almost total calm blanketed one of the largest West Bank cities, except for the clanking of coffee cups and smoke streaming from a hookah bar below; a layer of sweet smoke separated the smokers from the emptiness of the streets below.

My eyes cast across the street to the blackness peering at me from the abandoned windows of the same buildings I had seen before. The eerie bleakness of this place cast me into a somber mood. Desperately needing to cling to a memory of a familiar scene, I saw before me not the gloomy profile of a cement building but instead, an apparition…a shadow rising from a lonely midnight pond blanketed by a thin layer of mist and surrounded by the imposing spread of branches from the pine trees of a rugged Southern Oregon mountain.

My reaction to the phantom buildings was different than when I had first stood here. Instead of a gripping fear, I felt a bitter loneliness, as when I walked the cliffs of the Oregon coast alone, with only the distant foghorns chanting their eerie mantra in the blackness to accompany me.

As soon as my head sank into the pillow, my thoughts shifted to yesterday's dialogue/march I had organized in the streets of Bethlehem. It had begun at the Church of the Nativity and ended at Rachel's Tomb.[139]

I had stayed the night at Dheisheh Refugee Camp at the Ibdaa Cultural Centre Guest House,[140] where I performed volunteer work during the day. It was my usual lodging during my recent visits to Bethlehem.

When I awoke my eyes opened in the hazy darkness; it was so early I could still hear the fading barks of the wild dog pack withdrawing into hiding as the day began, after their night of marauding. I usually arrived several hours before a march to prepare, in particular, to observe where the Palestinian police were stationed in order to bypass them during the march, if possible.

The feeling was different this time because during the past few years, I had benefitted from the ultimate trump card: My friend Abdullah, a Palestinian hero and the man who held the record for the longest stay in Israeli prisons (28 years in jail). He had introduced me to Omar, who worked with a cabinet minister of the Palestinian government. If I ever got into trouble, especially if I were arrested by the Palestinian police, I would inform the arresting officer that Omar and my friend were aware of and approved the march. Then I would give them their phone numbers. After a short conversation with Omar or my friend Abdullah, the police would release me to continue the demonstration.

But that was not to be, this time. A month before the demonstration, one night in Paris, I had an urge to call Abdullah. I called him about an hour before the breaking of the fast during Ramadan, when he answered his phone.

"Sadiki Abdullah…Assalamu alaykum sadiq."

"Alaykum assalamu, my friend. Where are you?"

"In Paris, just calling you to wish you well and your family during Ramadan."

"And you, are you fasting a bit?"

I responded, "Souillah," followed by his raspy laugh. "After we arranged your papers to come to France for a series of lectures, I didn't hear…."

"I was stopped at Allenby gate and refused passage to Jordan where I was to take my plane. . !"

---

139 Chapter 54, "To Rachel's Tomb."

140 Ibdaa Cultural Centre Guest House helps the youth in the camp develop skills, express themselves creatively and provides leadership training. Another objective of the Centre is to educate the international community about the challenges of Palestinian refugees living in an occupied West Bank.

"Ahhhhh, unbelievable, especially since your trip was approved...."

His deep breathing was magnified over the phone.

"Abdullah, don't worry, it's another challenge and a perverse consequence of this wretched occupation."

He breathed out and silence reigned again.

"I'll tell you what. When I arrive in Palestine next, we'll return to the French authorities. After you receive your papers...."

"No that's ok, you don't have...."

"That's the only way, Abdullah. And after receiving your papers and authorization from Mr. Abbas[141] to travel and the ticket from the Palestinian authorities, we'll go together to France."

I could feel his smile over the phone.

"Hah, hah. Ok, inchallah...I have to pray before breaking the fast."

"Ok, my friend. I'll call you when I arrive in Palestine in a month, and with jiddan hyman, we'll do it!" (a lot of faith)

"Right, shukran, ma salaami."

"Alaykum assalamu."

An hour later I received a Facebook message from his cousin, a friend of mine that Abdullah had passed away. I closed the computer and reached over and turned out the light...The heavy darkness of this news seeped into every thought and pore; it felt as if a part of me was dying, shutting down, to dull the shock of my loss. Memories of this former prisoner/hero filled my thoughts, as he had been my inspiration as well as my savior from the bleak and sometimes torturous prisons of Palestine....

As the luminescent fingers of dawn slowly penetrated the tears in the curtain covering my window, my eyes slowly opened an unwilling crack, letting in a tiny light—my escape route—at the end of a collapsed tunnel. But there was no escape. I was abruptly reminded of the demonstration I had planned for the West Bank. I wanted to close my eyes, shoving the thought away. But the more I tried to push it out of my mind, the more unyielding it became.

What to do now in this foreboding, unstable place? Although I could contact Omar if I were arrested, since Abdullah had passed away, I wasn't sure if Omar would still feel obliged to vouch for me.

I was now faced with cancelling or proceeding without my safety valve, without the life-saving back-up of my friend. I decided I had to continue since I had already sent the fliers out and many people had been notified, including the press. Besides, I had come all the way from Paris to do this and couldn't let anything stop the dialogues/ marches as I believed they would prove fundamental in bringing people together... for peace...in this insane, cruel war zone. I contemplated that this place was way "over the top" and needed desperately to return to humanity, to the way it was years ago when Muslims, Jews and Christians lived, more or less, in peaceful harmony. At least they had found an equanimity before the eruption of the Intifadas, the terrible conflicts from which this land had not yet recovered.

---

141 Mr. Mahmoud Abbas, the President of the Palestinian Authority.

The morning mist slowly arose, like ghostly fingers opening its grip and slowly floating upwards, replaced by a wistful sun, its morning glint reflecting on the faceless buildings lining the street winding upward to the Church of Nativity. As the taxi wound around a turn, I cast my eyes over the surrounding hills, on a group of structures that did not show the same tired, faceless look like the ones bordering this road. The taxi driver, following my gaze in the rear view mirror, informed me they were Israeli settlements on Palestinian land. I wondered if they were the solid, newly built, modern buildings typical of Jewish settlements, thus adding to the other settlements near and around Bethlehem. I wondered how many Palestinian families–who owned that land and were pushed into overly populated housing projects in the refugee camps–were still mourning the loss of the lands they had been cultivating for hundreds of years.

The taxi slowed its approach as it passed the Palestinian police who occupied a post at the corner of Manger Street, leading to Manger Square and the Church of Nativity. A strong contraction triggered inside of me as I watched two uniformed men carrying AK-47s patrolling the street, next to the taxi. I knew I would have to confront them during the demonstration and as usual, I never knew if the Police would break up the march and put me in a cell. I took a deep breath as we passed by....

The moment the taxi driver opened my door, the fleeting silence inside flowed out the window, chased by the churning street noises and a myriad of tourists. People with flags or signs for quick identification were followed by long lines of tourists traversing the square; long lines were trailing away down Manger Street.

The march/dialogue was to commence in front of the Church of Nativity which I quickly scanned now for activists. A small group of Palestinian adolescents who, with tight-fitting jeans, hands waving and voices raised, were vigorously discussing something. I assumed they intended to join the march. No other activists were in sight. I turned and walked across the parking lot that separates the Church of Nativity from the Mosque of Omar, its minaret looming above the cars parked in a lot on Manger Square. I approached a group of Muslims leaving the mosque after Zuhr (noon prayer). One with a short, black beard turned toward me as he walked slowly, holding out his hand.

"Ahlan wa sahlan, sadiqa."

"Ahlan bi-k."

I shook his hand with my right hand and held out my left, with palm facing out, a signal for him to wait. I then loosened my grip and reached over to grasp one corner of the sign which said "Freedom March" in English, Hebrew and Arabic. The other corner I held with my left hand. Two young men with short, black hair wearing white djellabahs approached me. A third heavy-set man walked behind them. He was endowed with a full black beard flowing over his collar and wore a pearl-white skull cap, his ample stomach causing the front of the djellabah to protrude. The other two were lean and dark.

The man with an aquiline nose curved over a small, chiseled jaw, smiled and said, "Cuellos" (Good). Where are from?"

"I'm American and live in Paris." I pondered that adding my French residence sometimes tempered the sometimes conditioned reflex of anti-American fervor among some Palestinians.

They began chanting "Hourriyya, hourriyya." One of them took hold of a corner of the poster while another held the other one. I gave the third boy the camera who took our picture with our thumbs pointing to the sky.

As I rolled up the sign, I invited the group to join us for the freedom march that would start in about an hour at the Church of Nativity across the way.

They nodded as I strolled away, across the parking lot to the place where Jesus was born. The group of adolescent boys was standing where I had left them a half hour ago; they were still flailing their arms and rolling their eyes, in the heat of an endless discussion. I figured that the only way to attract their attention was to unroll the sign and parade in front of them. As I walked in front with my sign unraveled, one of them turned and pointed, drawing the other sets of eyes; but they quickly turned back to their conversation. Then I pulled my loud speaker out of the bag and drew closer. I caught the eye of one with short hair, a slender mustache hovering over his upper lip and eyes flashing. That did it! Now five sets of hands reached for it as five mouths, almost in unison, sang out "Masirat al hourriyya" (Freedom march), reading the Arabic on the poster.

For the next hour they took turns speaking into the loud speaker, some shouting peace mantras; one with a long nose projecting out over a bushy mustache grabbed the loud speaker and blurted out several incomprehensible words that provoked snickers from the boys. I was elated the boys were enjoying themselves and hoped they'd join the march, but the clicking of tongues by Arabs walking by, which they do when disgusted, indicated the language might be turning raw.

During a monologue by one of the boys which elicited more laughter and tongue clicking, a man with a blue and black uniform wearing a black beret approached us. He grabbed the loud speaker from the hands of the speaker, who turned his head towards us with mock concern in his dark brown moon eyes, pleading his innocence as he muffled a giggle. Fortunately the policeman didn't hear it or feigned not hearing it.

Then the Palestinian policeman held out his other hand to me and a short stubby finger curled, motioning me to follow. I followed him away from Manger Square as he descended toward the main street below. Before arriving at the corner, he led me up a flight of stairs without railings, winding up the side of the building. My eyes automatically followed the stairs upward, as we ascended to the top step two flights above. Since no door appeared at the top of the stairs, it seemed to launch into the deep blue sky.

Suddenly, a well-built man—muscles bulging out of his blue shirt, his neck stretching the collar—faced me. His jowls were planted solidly on his neck, completely hiding it. They jutted out of his brazen, tanned face over which was stretched a tight smile. He had suddenly swung into my path blocking my climbing higher on this bizarre stairway that led either nowhere or into the clouds.

"Sayyid, who are you?"

"Frank Romano." He nodded as if he expected the name. His dark eyebrows raised over a bristling mustache.

414

"I know who you are and we appreciate what you're doing. But promise me that you won't let the boys speak with loud speaker any more, ok?"

"I promise!"

He reached out his hand and I took it. He returned the loud speaker to me with the other hand. I took it as I released his strong grip, and then turned while he held my arm before releasing it.

"Good luck!"

I nodded and walked down the stairway to the heavens, this time alone. I headed back to the group. Upon returning to the corner with the loud speaker securely placed in a plastic bag, I was greeted with smiles and handshakes. To my surprise, no one reached for the loud speaker; they seemed to have anticipated the instructions of the police and somehow knew the drill: no more loud speaker for them!

Then I finally understood what had just happened.

I reflected on the more than 20 freedom marches in Israel and Palestine that I had organized during the last few years; I had not obtained official pre-authorization for any of them. As such, they were all quasi illegal. But this time, I felt especially vulnerable since my friend Abdullah, the Palestinian hero, was no longer around to use his star power to release me from custody if I were arrested during a freedom demonstration. I had to admit that he was the main reason why I had stayed clear of Palestinian prisons, to date. Now, I was especially worried because a couple of Jewish friends were bringing a group from Israel to join me. If anything happened to them....

A few nights before arriving in the Holy Land, while I was still in Paris I had called Sulaymin, a Palestinian friend living in Jenin, and asked him what I could do to stay out of jail. It turned out I had called the right person...bingo! He just happened to be the cousin of the chief of police in Bethlehem. As I stood in front of the small door opening to the Church of Nativity where another great man, a great hero had been born, I pondered, *The man I just spoke with on the steps was no doubt an agent of the Chief of Police.* It was confirmed later during the demonstration in Bethlehem since, for the first time, I was not detained and interrogated by the Palestinian Police either at the beginning of the march, during or at its end. The Palestinian police kept their hands off us this time!

Then a long, yellow taxi drove up next to me with the familiar crown of metal rising about ten inches above the roof, to which a suitcase was sometimes tied for lack of room inside. The back window was open and familiar eyes were staring at me coupled with a broad smile splashed across a familiar face. It was Jason; as promised, he had brought his friends for the march. He was my courageous friend who had participated in the Jenin march.[142] That day, he had barely avoided arrest and perhaps jail and/or paying a high fine if he were handed over to the Israeli police by their collaborators, the Palestinian police.

He jumped out of the car, his blue eyes beaming under the rim of his baseball hat, as he reached for me. We hugged in the middle of Manger Square. I looked directly at his baseball cap, nodded and couldn't help but smile. His eyes followed mine and he smiled in return, indicating he was thinking the same thing: he had decided to

---

142 Chapter 76, "Facing AK-47s."

follow my advice by wearing his Yarmulke under a baseball hat when travelling to the West Bank. My eyes descended down his shirt to his belt from which dangled two tzitzits,[143] one on each side. I thought to myself that they were discreetly dangling below his shirt and would not be noticed nor would they be a problem. I was wrong!

Jason and I hugged, grasping each other strongly, as only old friends do.

"Shalom, so glad you made it, Jason; it wouldn't be the same without you, my friend. God bless...."

Jason interrupted, "Moi aussi (Me too)! By the way, I brought three friends. You remember Isaac and...."

I stepped toward Isaac with short, energetic steps. He was a bit surprised and started backwards. But I had already grabbed his hands, stopping his backward motion, and pulled him toward me into a hug. After we separated he stumbled backwards, smiling timidly. His blue-grey eyes sparkled above wispy growths on his cheeks and chin. His cheeks were chiseled to a point; the upper teeth clamped shut on the lowers behind semi-closed lips, opening into a tight smile.

"Frank, this is my mother, Sandrine. She's visiting from France and has come in solidarity with us. And my friend...Vincent from Jerusalem."

A tall, bushy-haired man loomed before me as he reached for my hand. His long nose protruded from a dark, sun-tanned face, revealing nostrils like hairy nests. It hung over the giant span of a toothy, anxious smile. Vibrant waves rose in my bosom, meeting his pizzazz. I was immediately energized. I nodded and mumbled to myself, "Wow, won't need to blow my energy fuses trying to motivate this group. If more people could join me with such gleaming vigor...huhhhhhhh," I exhaled smoothly, relieved.

I then turned my attention to a short, feminine version of Isaac. Her cheeks were also chiseled to a point but they were fuller, perhaps better nourished with the rich and voluptuous French food.

"Welcome, welcome Sandrine!" I reached down to shake her hand but she had already lent me her cheek to kiss in the French way. We kissed each other twice, right to left. Her face lit up as her smile raised the corners of her mouth, unlike her son's measured, tight smile. Her velvety chestnut hair smoothed over her oval head and contrasted with the wrinkles imbedded in the sides of her eyes and brow.

I checked my cell phone. It read 1:30 pm, about an hour after the publicized beginning of the march/dialogue. I swept my eyes over Manger Square, up to the small door that leads inside to the sanctuary of the church. No other activists were in sight.

As I unrolled the sign I walked ahead of the group.

"Let's go."

I motioned Jason to join me, expecting his friends would follow. Out of the corner of my eye, images of flailing hands were still visible. I turned toward the brouhaha and noticed a wave of hands flapping in my direction, coming from the group of adolescents. They were still standing or leaning against the walls of the Church of

---

143 Tzitzit – fringes hanging down from the shirts of some Jews, notably orthodox Jews, to remind them of the commandments and not to fall into the trap of sin.

Nativity. I walked towards them at the same time taking the loud speaker from the plastic bag and lifting it to my lips.

"Allahu Akbar, yallah!" (God is great, let's go!)

A newcomer standing with the boys, a black and white keffiyeh spilling over his head, reached for the loudspeaker. I withdrew it to my chest, shaking my head.

"The police!" The boys nodded. They knew. The newcomer looked sheepishly at the group then at me. He begrudged a slight nod.

I pointed to Jason and the others waiting in the middle of Nativity square, next to the church, their eyes glued to me.

"See my friends; they have come from Jerusalem to march for peace, for freedom. Join us...."

I hoped and even expected that they would join the march, riding on a magic carpet fueled by their apparently boundless enthusiasm. I turned and walked toward Jason who was leading his friends to join me. I looked back and the Muslim adolescents didn't budge, ironically remaining attached to walls of the Church of Nativity, although their smiles and incessant waving egged us on.

The ardor of strong hearts in those walking with me renewed my strength and enhanced my passion to meet those waiting for us in the streets, compared to the times I had begun a freedom march in Palestine...alone. But even then, I felt blessed as I tried to concentrate on the radiant energy of the cosmic stream guiding me, telling me, *It's going to be alright, if you keep the faith and your head up and remember... you're never alone!*

I endeavored to follow the vision that had come to me in my room, my "chambre de bonne" (servant's quarters) high above the River Seine in Paris 30 years before[144]— alone or accompanied, to keep singing of unconditional love and sharing the word of peace/freedom until I had no more vocal chords, keep on trucking until my feet moved no more.

I reflected that I would have walked alone today focusing on that vision, knowing that soon I would be surrounded by enthusiastic eyes and hands greeting mine; but having Jason and his friends beside me empowered me even more.

We walked down the hill to Manger Street, where we were immediately joined by many Palestinians waving, laughing, nodding, some waving their hands leaning out of windows overhead, yelling "Allahu Akbar." The group gained momentum as it moved down the street.

Then something strange happened. I was holding one corner of the poster, Jason the other, as we walked along followed by his friends from Israel and a growing number of Palestinians. We were so totally immersed in communicating with the crowd as we flashed peace signs, smiling and reciting mantras, neither of us spied a young boy sneaking up behind Jason holding a bright object in his hand.[145]

---

144 Storm Over Morocco, 4th Edition, Supra.

145 After the march, we retreated to a hookah bar near the former offices of Holy Land Trust (a peace activist NGO headquartered in Bethlehem); while we rested drinking Turkish coffee and mint tea, Isaac recounted the incident. Jason's eyebrows raised and his mouth twisted in a furtive smile as he glanced at me, and smiled again. I smiled back as Isaac berated both of us for being oblivious to the danger. Jason's and my brows matched above our silly grins. I

The boy crouched as he followed Jason. He then flicked his finger and extended his arm so the flame from the cigarette lighter was directly underneath Jason's tzitzit, flapping in the wind. Fortunately Isaac was walking behind Jason. His eyes were drawn to the odd crouching of the boy and the flicking of the flame rising to sear the dangling threads. Isaac leapt forward and rising over him, slapped the hand holding the lighter which tumbled to the ground; the boy dashed forward and was hidden in the crowd.

* * *

My eyes closed and I drifted into a deep sleep. I was floating over the barren dunes of the Sahara when I suddenly crossed the desert and flew into Bethlehem; sinister grey clouds floated over the brow of darkness.

Then a dark arm stretched out, firmly holding a cigarette lighter, its flame curling upwards, its hot tongue finding the end of a string dangling from Jason's belt. The light from the dancing flame was reflected in the angry face behind it. The enflamed red face loomed monstrously over us, replacing our compassion for the suffering here with escalating panic.

After the young man lit the dangling string, flames immediately coiled around Jason, who burst into a fireball. A spine-chilling wail filled the air....

* * *

The muezzin's shrill voice broke the silence and I awoke gasping for breath, sweat pouring down my face.

Later that morning, on the way to the shuttle station, I waded through the hungry street vendors, some pulling at my clothes cajoling me to check out their wares: medjoul dates, a myriad of spices, orange, green and black powders producing titillating sensations, seducing me with other-worldly Middle Eastern aromas, a world in which I was amazed to find I now walked. It was the real thing and not just a fantasy, this time!

I had to smile at the blur of vendors who lined the streets, now a palpable fantasy and not just me dreaming, cooped up in my Parisian apartment. My dark eyes fell on a round-faced vendor, meeting his round, opaque eyes above a wistful, expectant smile. His sincere gesture resonated spontaneous naivety, without a drop of an ulterior motive. He had draped over his arm several black and white, red and white keffiyehs. Stepping back he slowly waved his arm backwards, entreating me to regard the perhaps fake Persian rugs hanging in the back of his store.

I slept for about two hours, during the entire bumpy ride to Jenin. Contrary to what usually happens—each time I felt a bump, my eyes would jolt open with the shock—this time I appeared to go deeper in sleep with each bump. My eyes, caked with road dust, finally squinted and slivered open as the shuttle rumbled to the taxi station near the Jenin refugee camp.

---

considered that a long time ago, we had assumed the risk of "lone wolf crazy attacks" and had decided not to let them get us down and or divert us from our path. I love the guy!

I had left Ramallah early to meet Vincent and Sandrine in Jenin, two of the activists who had participated in the freedom march in Bethlehem a couple of days earlier. Unfortunately, Jason had to work that day so he could not join us. We had all been invited by Governor Dwikat of Jenin for lunch with his assistant, Sulaymin, the same man I had called to help with the authorization of the Bethlehem march. He picked me up from the taxi station and returned me later to the station to pick up the two activists.

I stood in front of utter bedlam, the Jenin taxi/shuttle station, my eyes sweeping over it searching for Vincent and Sandrine. A baggy blue shirt flagged my attention and scraggly chestnut hair that stood out like a mangled flag. That led me to them. They were surrounded by a crowd of taxi drivers simmering, talking and shouting, wedged in between parked yellow taxis. A dense layer of smoke blowing overhead from the kebob stands settled on the crowd and obscured my vision. I lost them. The smoke cleared in time for me to see Vincent and Sandrine walking towards me. We saw each other at the same time and waved. Vincent's hair was even more frazzled than when I had seen him in Bethlehem: wild strands waved over the sides of his full face. I guessed that his enhanced mangy look must be due to the stress of the gauntlet he had just passed through, starting with desperately seeking a shuttle bus from Jerusalem, then climbing the ramp in Ramallah with cars passing on all sides as there was no place pedestrians could walk up to catch the shuttle. Then came the agitated shuttle ride over rough, pot-holed roads to Northern Palestine.

Sandrine's eyes met mine with a nervous smile as she looked around. I hugged them both and led them to Sulaymin who was waiting for us in a taxi across the street. I turned my head toward Sandrine walking next to me; her eyes were apprehensively darting about until they fell on me, wide and glassy. Her lips thinned as her head dipped and nodded toward the Palestinians hurling about in the streets, begging me to take a look.

I thought to myself that it was true, Jenin could quickly turn into fiery pit of emotions and violent retaliation, as in the past, especially during confrontations with Israeli soldiers. But today was just another day!

But I didn't sense danger, so I met Sandrine's gestures with a shrug of my shoulders, slightly lifting my hands as if to say, "Ho hum!" But I sympathized with her first reactions which reminded me of my first visit to Jenin a few years ago. Then, my nerves had erupted into trembling as I walked alone down these same streets, with my teeth gritting as I tried not to show alarm. It wasn't that I was immune to fear now but that I mastered it better and refused to let it control me as it had in the past.

I turned to her. "Sandrine, you'll see—it'll be ok. Yes, this place is unstable but remember: for the first time since I've been leading these events, today the demonstration has been pre-approved, even directly, by the Governor. For once, I can almost promise there will be no arrests or interrogations during the march. But you...."

I was going to complete the phrase with, "but you never know," but stopped short as it would only feed her anxiety even more.

The circumference of her eyes was now smaller and her lips opened slightly, no longer tense. She was relieved.

Since we only had less than an hour before the demonstration, I asked Sulaymin to take us to the Palestinian sandwich shop near his cultural center where I had eaten with him before.

He didn't respond, spoke to the taxi driver and proceeded to completely ignore my suggestion. In a few minutes the taxi pulled up in front of one of the best restaurants in Jenin, where I had dined with Governor Dwikat and Sulaymin about a year ago.

We sat around a massive round table while Sulaymin explained that Governor Dwikat could not join us. As we shared with Sulaymin all the details of the march in Bethlehem, the waiters began adorning the table with a spread like I had never seen before. There were ceramic dishes heaping with lamb kebobs, plates of hummus, a beige pâté of chick peas and spices shaped like a huge donut; the hole in the middle was filled with small ponds of olive oil. A swarthy waiter, slicing the air as gracefully as a swan, smilingly lay wedges of "fatayer fallahi" zataar bread (bread baked with the Palestinian herb zataar, made from wild thyme) on the table. The air was filled with the scent of roasting thyme with olive oil.

Dishes of okra stew (Bamieh) were served with a lentil soup (Shorbat Adas); the taste prickled with a slight taste of lemon. I sprinkled a little cumin into the soup. The room now filled with the odor of onions roasting in a rich olive oil, local no doubt. Then the head waiter, closely followed by two assistants, surrounded us with plates of eggplant dip (Mutabbal). We dipped pita bread into the eggplant then grasped pieces of lamb kebob and popped them into our watering mouths. This wasn't just lunch, it was a feast!

This ambrosial repast ended with mint tea and sugar cookies; I dipped a cookie into the rich liquid, straddling pieces of mint leaves clinging to the sides of the steaming cup. After we drank our tea, the head waiter returned with the bill and placed it in the middle of the table. Then the bubble burst as I contemplated paying, at least for my comrades and myself. I reached into my pocket and felt a heavy hand on my pocket trapping my hand inside.

A short chuckle jiggled Sulaymin's lips. "No! You and your friends are the guests of the governor, today. Besides we were your guests in Paris...."

It was true that I had paid for his and the governor's meal and hookah when they visited Paris a few months earlier; but since my return to Jenin, he refused to let me pay for anything, including Palestinian sandwiches. Anyway, it would have been futile to insist as these Palestinians were exceedingly generous and would be upset, even insulted, if I either insisted on paying or dared refuse their hospitality.

I tried offering to pay the tip, only to be met with the dismayed, incredulous eyes of our benefactor. I obviously did not insist.

Sulaymin dropped us off at the beginning of Abu Bakir Street, the place where the demonstration was scheduled to begin. As we exited the taxi, I looked around to see if any other activists or journalists had showed up. No teams of journalists carrying cameras were in sight nor could I see any activists carrying signs or loud speakers.

"Are you ready?" I asked my companions.

They both looked back, their eyes squinting beneath furrowed brows and the corners of their mouths drooping down; I followed their eyes directed at the shop owners lining the street, going about their businesses as usual; some street venders were selling vegetables or mint bushes, others displayed brightly-colored fabrics draped over their arms. Shoppers were meandering from one vendor to the next, touching, talking, haggling, like bees drifting from one flower to another, collecting pollen. A long stream of people were entering and exiting a nearby bank through revolving doors.

"Here?" Vincent exclaimed.

"Why not? I don't know what happened to the press or the other activists; maybe they got stopped at the checkpoints. That's happened before, especially to those coming from Israel. It's ok—I sometimes start alone and am joined...."

He flashed a tense, half-smile, his lips contorted on one side of his mouth, a couple of teeth protruding. "But...."

I knew I had to act before he could utter another word, and before his anxiety overwhelmed him and Sandrine's. I quickly unraveled my sign and removed the loud speaker from the plastic sack.

Vincent shook his shaggy head, visibly incredulous we could march through a major city with a handful of people. I knew he was comparing this motley group with the Bethlehem march a couple of days ago. There we started out with a few more people and had only taken a few steps before a crowd of Palestinians joined us. Here it wasn't obvious that we could get the attention of the people jostling for deals with the vendors, hustling and bustling as they interwove among the fruit and vegetable carts lining the streets.

Even before the sign was completely unraveled I launched my voice through the loud speaker: "Kula wahad, hourriyya Palestine, hourriyya Israel...."

I looked back. Vincent had disappeared but Sandrine approached dauntless, her lips pursed as she grabbed a corner of the sign. I looked at her and her eyes beamed squarely into mine, telling me she was anxious to begin. I breathed a silent sigh of relief as at least I could count on one person to be at my side....

We slid between honking cars into the middle of the street heading toward the center square. In past events, at the town square about seven blocks away, we had almost always been greeted by a swarm of khaki shirts and uniforms waiting to harass and/or arrest us on the grounds that our demonstration was not officially authorized. In fact, we were detained once and almost arrested even after having received oral authorization, albeit not official authorization, by one of the street police. As we moved along smiling and yelling peace mantras in the loud speaker, I prayed it would be different this time, especially since I had informed Vincent and Sandrine I had obtained authorization from the governor himself. However due to the situation, the truth was there would never be a definitive guarantee that peace marchers would not be harassed and/or arrested by the police.

The shop owners waved and the pedestrians all seemed to chant with us "Allahu Akbar" as we walked. Adolescent boys smiled, some waving Palestinian keffiyehs.

Today the crowd seemed especially hungry for a sign, for a palpable sign that there was still hope for the forgotten masses in this place at the northern tip of the West Bank, far removed from Ramallah, the Palestinian doorstep to Jerusalem.

Sandrine and I walked along, chanting "La ilaha illallah! Adonai Elohaynu Adonai Echad! God the Father, Son and Holy Ghost." At first no one contested my speaking Hebrew or English. A group of adolescent boys raising their hands flashing the "V" sign, chanting, yelling and running to shake our hands, followed us down the street. In a few minutes we had collected 50 or 60 boisterous youths and a couple of smiling adults as we proceeded; one of them came and took the corner of the sign so I could move to the front with the loud speaker.

"Shukran!" I yelled.

After chanting "Adonai, Elohaynu Adonai Echad," one boy with a crew cut and sparkling grey eyes came to me and extended his hand over the hand that held the loud speaker. It was an unambiguous request for me to stop talking into the loudspeaker and turn my attention to him.

"Why speak Hebrew, for Jews...."

I reached out and grabbed the boy's hand and led him to the side of the road, turning the loudspeaker off. I looked back; Sandrine and the boy holding the other corner of the sign had also stopped. Waving my hand in a half circle, I motioned them to proceed without me.

"Ma ismuk?" (What is your name?)

"Ismael."

"Ismael, because it means the same thing as 'La ilaha illallah'."

His head cocked to the side, and his lips mumbled something inaudible. I looked back; Sandrine and the boy had not moved. My eyes quickly shifted to the crowd following them. A man standing in back of them wearing a white djellabah extended his hands toward the sky, as if asking *What is going on?* So I quickly moved to the front while flipping the loudspeaker on and putting my lips to it, wailed:

"Kula wahad, hourriyya Filistine!"

I glanced back to the man in the djellabah who was now smiling, nodding and swaying his arms as he walked with us. After a while, it seemed as if we were floating on the molten heat that suffused our veins, building a relentless momentum gained by marching with these remarkable people. The music revved up with every step; we embodied the rhythm and power of Ravel's "Bolero."

The brouhaha around us had captured my attention, so much that I had forgotten what lay ahead: In spite of the Governor's guarantees, I expected that the Palestinian police awaited us a block away. I shifted to my tiptoes and peered over the crowd to the end of Abu Bakir Street where we typically had confrontations with police and were sometimes harassed and/or arrested. This time I couldn't see their omnipresent vehicles or jeeps, with the unmistakable word painted on the side: POLICE.

I glanced back again and saw that Sandrine was carrying the sign by herself, one end curled and dragging the ground. I quickly reached her and took hold of the other corner and stretched the sign to the maximum as we continued our march. A couple of times, a group of shouting boys joined us. One grabbed the corner of the sign and motioned me onwards. I was thus freed again to focus on speaking through the loudspeaker and waving my free hand, cajoling the Palestinians to join us, some wearing black and white keffiyehs, some pearl white skull caps—all marching, laughing and shouting. I smiled at Sandrine and she returned the smile. We were propelled forward, only by the heat waves generated by the exuberance of the Palestinians. It was enough to melt the resistance of even the most skeptical onlooker.

"Ana amerikiyy, ma'a sadiqati fransiyy, kula wahad hourriyya Palestine, hourriyya Israel." (I'm American, with French friends, everyone wants freedom for Palestine, freedom for Israel)

When we arrived at the square, I—by reflex action, and without reflecting on the governor's word—quailed, motioning the crowd to stop, expecting the immediate intrusion by the relentless police, the abusive seeping of the blue or black capped police into our ranks, slamming the brakes on our non-violent march.

I cynically thought how many times I had been promised safe passage, either by assistants of Palestinian cabinet ministers or by other officials, only to be arrested. My eyes shifted back to the square and to my disbelief, still no police arrogantly brandishing their AK-47s were in sight. There was at least one police vehicle parked in the square, 24/7; but not this time. The wind swirled overhead; dust and papers whirled with it, settling on the vacant street where police vehicles usually parked. The police, for once, had completely abandoned the square. The governor had kept his word! I exhaled a long sigh.

Palestinians, including some girls wearing dark green hijabs, crowded together behind the sign at the end of the march at the intersection of Abu Bakir Street and another street in the middle of town. Then some young boys and girls came forward and clamored to touch us; some reached for the loud speaker which I freely handed to them. They spoke a few words through the loud speaker then returned it, their smiles enhanced by the gleam in their eyes.

At the end of the march they expectantly waited—twisting their necks to seek us out—for us to pronounce the parting words. I passed the loud speaker to Sandrine who shook her head, her lips forming a trembling smile. I drew the loudspeaker to my mouth and spoke in a mixture of English and Arabic. I ended with a short prayer and they nodded and slapped their hands together; the echo filled the town square.

I rolled up the sign and took Sandrine's hand; we walked down a road adjacent to the one taken for the march as the people turned and smiled, making way for us.

As we walked, I felt a light tapping on my shoulder; turning around, I was greeted by a flushed face and a wide, toothy grin. It was Vincent, the wild strands of his hair almost standing on end. I nodded and motioned him to join us. Poufy hair sticking out from behind a camera popping up above the crowd from time to time assured me he was always with us during the demonstration.

I thought to myself, *He probably feared the press taking pictures and publishing them in Israeli newspapers. Being a leftist activist, he had probably already brought the reactionary Israeli government down on him and hence had to keep a low profile.*

Even though the march was over, a true, unconditional spirit of love nurturing peace and understanding, bolstered by their—our—faith held us like a protective giant hand. It was the potency of the Palestinians' never-ending faith that empowered us—their unswerving devotion to their people, their culture and their freedom in spite of the disastrous war with Israel a few years before that had resulted in the destruction of most of the buildings in the refugee camp as well as many in downtown Jenin.

The tide of unconditional love ebbs and flows with each heartbeat and with each one, we grow closer to the cosmic love spirit, the molten source diffusing through our veins and bringing us together on the lighted path. This is the path that leads us away from the dank, shadowy tunnel of evil, away from bones rattling in the howling winds of despair, selfishness and raw fear. This self-inflicted evil can, like the relentless suction of a parasite, drain and condemn us to the black void of emptiness.

We were free....

I sat in front of a computer at Sulaymin's cultural center, contemplating my return to the Freedom Theater,[146] where I usually crash during my visits to Jenin. That night, I planned to sleep at the Freedom Theater, again. It was a place established by my late friend, Juliano Mer-Khamis, in the middle of one of the most contested places in the Middle East, the Jenin Refugee camp. I reflected that every time I crossed the threshold into the sanctuary of the theater, emotions churned through my chest, subsiding somewhere in the recess of my empty stomach. Since Juliano's murder, a morose veil seemed to settle on the theater as my heart was still mourning his loss.

My eyes returned to the computer screen still displaying a blurred light; they refused to focus. Then the screen glowed, enticing my attention; but it remained blurred, mirroring my thoughts. They had taken me back to the arid fields at the foot of the Atlas mountains in Morocco and over the smooth sands of the Sahara, where my search had taken me many years before.[147] Visions of souks and veiled women streamed before me, in Maghreb (land of the setting sun), so completely absorbing me that I didn't notice Sulaymin standing over me, until I felt a hand resting on my shoulder.

"I know you want to stay at the Freedom Theater, like always, but why not stay here tonight? You might think...."

"They're expecting me...."

He walked to his office, wisely leaving me to ponder his invitation. I needed a calm, meditative evening; the emotions were still whirling inside me from the march earlier in the day and from ruminations over my work with Juliano and the void left by his absence. Tonight I needed to assuage my tendency to jump into the fray without letting too much thinking—or fear—psych me out, thus preventing me from doing what I had to do. I had learned to listen to gut feelings, without stifling thought, then act upon them. Going to the Freedom Theater would be like jumping into the middle of it, and I usually don't shrink from that. However, tonight I needed to withdraw and serenely plan my next interfaith dialogue and/or demonstration in Israel and the West Bank.

I walked to the office and accepted Sulaymin's offer to sleep at the cultural center. He was sitting with eyes fixed on his computer screen, the corners of his thin lips creased downwards in a frown, a bright red hue seeping over his olive cheeks.

---

146 Chapter 45, "Julian Mer-Khamis."

147 Storm Over Morocco, 4th Edition, supra.

"Thank you for the invitation; I've decided to sleep here."

He looked into my eyes; his brown eyes shined under his hawkish eyelids, squinting and flattened for battle. He lowered his head and his eyes swept the ground in front of me.

"You're welcome." He raised his head as his lips tightened. "Another Palestinian boy was gunned down by Israeli soldiers in the Jenin Refugee Camp tonight, after your freedom march." He lowered his head again, stood up and bid me a terse "Tisbah alal khair" (Good night) and left.

I walked to the back room where my bed awaited me. The sweltering heat of Northern Palestine, rising from the smoking rocks on the barren hills and crusty dirt surrounding Jenin, swelled in stifling layers in the back room of the guest house where I was to sleep that night. Barely puffing on the heavy air, I lay down, my eyes fixing on the holes in the curtain, through the metal bars and into the darkness. Riding under the halo of the magical day no longer insulated me from my subconscious mind. Something profoundly unsettling invaded my thoughts: the death of the Palestinian boy. I thought I had lost my breath and gasped for a second. I recovered my equanimity by taking deep breaths as I sat at the edge of my bed; then I rose, turned the key and shuffled to the bathroom. I shoved my head into the cold water streaming from the high faucet.

The next morning, Sulaymin and I walked briskly down Abu Bakir Street. Heavy black smoke coming from burning tires was pilfering the dry air, tunneling upwards and dissipating above. The entrance to Abu Bakir Street, where we had marched and dialogued the night before, was now streaming with hordes of mainly adolescent boys spinning around and around the square, fists raised high and chanting angry slogans. Some hollered with shrill voices, creased brows and violently flapping mouths. It was an angry mob and appeared out of control as the boys drifted aimlessly in the street. The massive hordes of people burning tires showed that the killing the night before had given rise to a full-blown riot.

Small groups of four or five adolescents suddenly broke off from the main group to confront store owners who still dared to keep their shop doors open. The boys violently pulled down the shutters, which hit the ground with a jarring clank as the owners cowered inside. The unruly crowd apparently expected the shops to close their doors in solidarity with the protest of the killing of their fallen comrade.

As I stood on the sidewalk watching the rampaging crowd, I spied a pale white pick-up truck inching its way through the mass of honking cars; angry heads popped out of windows as drivers were weaving in and out of the crooked stream of vehicles. Pedestrians desultorily slid in, behind and out of vehicles, their opaque shapes hidden by clouds of pungent bluish exhaust rising all around as the cars gunned their engines in frustration. The bed of the pick-up was filled with young bearded men; one was waving a black and gold flag, an Islamic Jihad[148] flag, which curled and swayed behind the slow-moving vehicle. It was followed by a small blue car proudly displaying a jagged gash on the right fender, reminding me that this place was a simmering war

---

148 Chapter 43, "Jihad," footnote 68.

zone. I fantasized that the car's wound came from a bullet shot by an Israeli machine gun during the last intifada.

As the blue car slowed behind the pick-up truck, a stocky arm grasping the wooden butt of an AK-47 thrust out of a window pushing aside black curtains, followed by a shiny barrel pointing toward the sky. It swiftly discharged a stream of bullets whizzing through the air. Boom-shake, a thousand times in quick reverberations flashing like a haunted storm, masked for a minute the shrill screams and chanting slogans of the rioters. After several rounds were fired, the arm pulled the Kalesnikoff back into the car as an automatic window closed behind it…The gun shooting through the blanket of smoke coupled with the angry wailing and fists raised shook me to the core; my hands began to tremble as I backed up. It seemed like the livid mob was working itself into a rabid frenzy and…we were in the middle of it. But I just stood there paralyzed, wanting to leave but couldn't….

Then something extraordinary happened that would, for days afterwards, shock me to the very roots of my soul. As a couple of hundred adolescents turned the corner, one of the boys pointed at me; a group of about fifty adolescents immediately broke off from the group and began running towards me. I backed a couple of paces to the door of a closed shop behind me but there was no refuge. I was trapped. The boys closed in on me. So I stood there facing them, dumbfounded….

Helplessly stupefied by the approach of the group, I awaited my fate. In a few seconds I was surrounded by a boisterous group of unruly boys with masses of black hair—some wearing skull caps, others white djellabahs—raising their arms in a fist and slapping them down on their thighs. A group of about ten of them raised their hands almost simultaneously and the others followed; they gesticulated "thumbs up" and fifty pairs of hands repeated the gesture. A hand coming out of nowhere grabbed my benumbed hand clasped to my side and pulled it up, closing in on it in a hearty handshake. He was shaking my hand—shaking it, that's all! I thought it was the end and now, they waited their turn to shake my hand…shake my hand. Unbelievable! Then as fast as they had surrounded me, as if answering a silent call, they retreated, first walking backward while facing me and waving, then turning and bolting full speed to catch up with their comrades as they circled the place. Some looked back before joining the others.

I looked at Sulaymin; his eyes were enormous in their sockets, to the limit. I looked back to the town square and it was quickly abandoned. The massive wave of adolescent fury had disappeared as fast as it had assembled. Only the residue of burning tires remained, some melted into a pile of black, sooty fibers covering the ground, from which a hellish vapor carried a putrid stench of burning rubber and urine.

We walked back to the cultural center in unbroken silence to pick up my luggage before I took my shuttle to Jerusalem. I had a plane to catch headed for France the next day.

*   *   *

That night, I lay in bed in Ibrahim's Youth Hostel in East Jerusalem, unable to sleep. I was still under the spell of the catharsis experienced in the middle of Jenin, a center of conflict and ironically, a place of rebirth. Warmth flooded down my sides into the quick of me, permeating my body in the torment of confused emotions. I desperately grabbed a pen from the top pocket of my leather jacket and began to write. My hands trembled, as the following words flowed unedited from my pen:

Did you gun me down?

in the camps tonight
thin shadows bedded under the stars
An explosion shook the wistful timbers
of the overgrown hut
and the helmet shouts wake up---
Bang and a kid went down

Did you gun me down?

The next day, I watched on the sidewalk
a wild, red-eyed mob
circled the town, circling the block,
invading the street, hordes
Some carrying Islamic Jihad flags
some shooting off AK-47s into the sweltering heat
others broke statues, ramming their fists into shop windows.
The Police, overwhelmed, had disappeared,
avoiding clashes I was told
The boys came back, hundreds of them
Tires were ignited,
the air reeked of blazing dirty rubber....
my throat stung

Did you gun me down?

Then...then, something so, so strange happened
The chaotic, frenzied mob turned the corner—
about 50 boys pointed at me
started walking, then running towards me

Will you crush me down?

Too late to pray...too shocked to move,
I knew what unbridled, enraged mobs could do
tight lips then smiles and then....

427

they seemed to lift their thumbs in unison
And, I was surrounded by kids
reaching out to shake my hand.
I shook them dumbfounded.
I was standing next to the governor's assistant
who the boys totally ignored.

I don't get it!
Then as if a horn had called them, they returned,
almost running backwards,
retreating back to the hordes,
then disappeared behind the layers of smoke
settling on the streets covered with debris.

Why didn't you crush me down?

Something had happened
Your eyes told me: love deeply embedded
somehow tempered the vicious bitterness
of flaming red eyes.
When they settled on mine,

Your eyes told me....
They told me

In the middle of dark despair, loathing and tears of profound frustration...in the middle of it, I learned a lesson. The red eyes of bitterness were tempered with love. From then on, I would never again let fear lead me astray or doubt that there would be hope. There is hope.

I would return to the Middle East, as helping to bring peace to the Middle East was a true vision I held deep within, not based upon a Messiah complex or a death wish. I prayed for strength, for courage to keep evolving as I helped unite people with unconditional love in the light of the true, forgiving cosmic spirit.

And sometimes, I'm lost in the search. But with each step I take for peace as I pass through the Damascus Gate and with each freedom march through the refugee camps in the West Bank, the power of my vision is renewed.

The End

Epilogue: How to Get Involved Locally in Interfaith Peace

I wrote this book to share with a wide audience my belief in the possibility of peace through grassroots activities in Israel and Palestine. A lot of the Middle East conflict is due to misunderstandings and lack of communication, notably among religious groups. As such, I strive to encourage people to organize interfaith dialogues in their own communities to help break down those barriers.

These will give rise to breaking down the stereotypes attributed to Jews, Muslims and Christians, as well as learning about other cultures, notably religious cultures.

Here are my suggestions on how to do it:

- Schedule interfaith events in your community centers, schools, churches, synagogues and mosques or just invite members of other religions to speak at those venues.

- At the beginning of an interfaith dialogue, someone should talk for a few minutes about the main elements of Judaism, Islam and Christianity— since many people are unaware of their common aspects—without ignoring their differences.

- During interfaith events/dialogues, lead meditations on peace, love and understanding in a way that people of different faiths would be comfortable. Perhaps avoid leading a communal prayer session as some orthodox Jews, Muslims and Christians prefer not to pray with members of other faiths.

- During interfaith meetings, some groups like to engage in channeling, where a person is selected to channel the words of God in the presence of the interfaith participants. Afterwards, they sometimes break down into groups to discuss God's words. Perhaps one should avoid channeling in an interfaith event as many people, in particular orthodox Muslims and orthodox Jews, do not feel comfortable with a person acting as mediator between God and individuals.

- During the events, try to avoid discussions of a strictly political nature or current events in the Middle East since they often lead to arguments, often curtailing the interfaith event.

- Knowledgeable and compassionate leaders need to take the lead in developing a true discourse of peace and understanding which will result in a true dialogue, and not a debate dominated by religious leaders, politicians or others intent on imposing their ideas. Knowledgeable and compassionate leaders can also help participants understand sensitive terms such as Zionism and Jihad.[149]

- Serve refreshments during events as barriers tend to fall more quickly when participants break bread and/or drink together.

- During the events, it also helps to break down barriers by sharing an international, cross-cultural song or music, whether it be live, CDs or from other sources.

- Avoid organizing events in fancy hotels, as it's essential to bring the dialogue to all people, not just to the privileged few.

- Town-hall styled dialogues, notably between Muslims and Jews—such as those led by Judea Pearl and Dr. Akbar Ahmed of the Daniel Pearl Foundation—are good examples of an effective way of bringing the word to the people…to all people.

- Many people are unable to attend interfaith events. However, they could greatly contribute by forwarding invitations to interfaith events they receive to family and friends. They could also help promote them by sending blurbs to those coordinating the event sections of TV and radio websites. They can also organize and engage in dialogue through email chat groups.

---

149 The term "Zionism" originally revolved around the concept that Jews have a right to a homeland. Jihad, meaning struggle in Arabic, is a term used in a religious sense to mean struggle to maintain one's faith, to defend Islam and/or to improve Muslim society. Definitions of Zionism as well as Jihad have often been misconstrued.

Photos

Sign destroyed during freedom march, Old City, Hebron, West Bank, April 11, 2010.

Friday night Ramadan march, Hebron, West Bank, Sept. 12, 2009.

March with Disney characters, Jenin, West Bank, Nov. 23, 2009.

Palestinian Police waiting for freedom march participants, Jenin, West Bank, July 10, 2010.

432

Together as one, Jenin, West Bank, July 10, 2010.

Peace activists attacked by Israeli settlers, saved by Israeli soldiers,
Hebron, West Bank, April 11, 2010.

About the Author

FRANK ROMANO earned a PhD at University of Paris I, Panthéon Sorbonne, and a JD at Golden Gate University, Faculty of Law, San Francisco. He is a Maître de conférences (assistant tenured professor) at the Université Paris Ouest Nanterre La Défense in the Anglo-American Literature and Civilization Department, an adjunct professor at Golden Gate University, Faculty of Law and a member of the California and Marseille Bars. At present, he teaches law, literature, history and philosophy of law at the Université Paris Ouest Nanterre La Défense and practices law in France and in the United States. The author actively organizes and participates in interfaith events involving Jews, Moslems, Christians and people of other faiths in Israel and Palestine. Dr. Romano has also authored a book entitled *Storm Over Morocco*, published by AB Film Publishing, *Dans l'ombre du muezzin* [In the Shadow of the Muezzin (to be published in French by L'Harmattan in April, 2014)], *Globalization of Antitrust Policies* (Mondialisation des politiques de concurrence), published by L'Harmattan in French and a book of poems entitled *Crossing Over* published by World Audience, Inc. He has written many articles published in Europe and in the United States where he is often invited to speak at conferences. He can be reached at: frankfro@aol.com.

CPSIA information can be obtained at www.ICGtesting.com
Printed in the USA
LVOW11s1736030814

397249LV00001B/4/P